Psychology

APPLIED TO EVERYDAY LIFE

RICK M. GARDNER

University of Colorado at Denver

WADSWORTH
THOMSON LEARNING™

Australia • Canada • Mexico • Singapore • Spain
United Kingdom • United States

WADSWORTH

THOMSON LEARNING

Editor: Edith Beard Brady
Development Editor: Michelle Vardeman
Marketing Manager: Katie Matthews
Project Editor: Rebekah Mercer
Permissions Editor: Charlotte Thomas
Text Designer: Van Mua
Art Editor: Van Mua
Production Manager: Cindy Young
Manufacturing Manager: Lisa Kelley
Photo Researcher: Cheri Throop
Copy Editor: Marne Evans
Illustrator: Precision Graphics
Cover Designer: Van Mua
Cover Image: © Photodisc®
Cover Printer: R. R. Donnelley, Crawfordsville
Compositor: Thompson Type
Printer: R. R. Donnelley, Crawfordsville

Printed in the United States of America
1 2 3 4 5 6 7 05 04 03 02 01

For more information about our products, contact us at:
Thomson Learning Academic Resource Center
1-800-423-0563

For permission to use material from this text, contact us by:
Phone: 1-800-730-2214
Fax: 1-800-730-2215
Web: http://www.thomsonrights.com

Library of Congress Cataloging-in-Publication Data
2001091991
ISBN: 0-15-506794-X

Asia
Thomson Learning
60 Albert Street, #15-01
Albert Complex
Singapore 189969

Australia
Nelson Thomson Learning
102 Dodds Street
South Melbourne, Victoria 3205
Australia

Canada
Nelson Thomson Learning
1120 Birchmount Road
Toronto, Ontario M1K 5G4
Canada

Europe/Middle East/Africa
Thomson Learning
Berkshire House
168-173 High Holborn
London WC1 V7AA
United Kingdom

To Betty Ann,
whose support and encouragement
made this book possible.

PREFACE

As a professor of psychology for many years, I have noticed that a gap exists between possessing knowledge of psychology and applying that same knowledge to one's everyday life. Too often, psychology textbooks and instructors emphasize theory and research, but neglect to assign an equally important role to how one can actually use this information. As a result, while most students find psychology an interesting field to study, they often fail to understand fully how this knowledge can be used to improve their lives.

In addition, surprisingly, many of us—including many psychologists and psychiatrists—often behave in ways that seemingly ignore or contradict many of the well-known principles of psychology. These observations have led me to the conclusion that it is not enough to merely "know" psychology; one must also commit to using that knowledge in everyday life. I have written this text in a manner that I hope will bridge the gap between *knowing* and *doing* psychology, between perception and implementation of psychological theory. Throughout *Psychology Applied to Everyday Life,* I illustrate principles that I use in my own life—in more than thirty years of marriage, in raising two children, in personal, professional, and administrative relationships, and in teaching. And throughout, I encourage the reader to do likewise. In short, *Psychology Applied to Everyday Life* is dedicated to the idea that psychology is a science that begs to be *used,* not merely studied.

This concept of bringing together understanding and action in psychology is exemplified in the structure and approach of *Psychology Applied to Everyday Life.* Within a comprehensive coverage of the traditional topics found in the introductory psychology course, I've worked to create an individualized, interactive environment in order to bring psychology and its practices into the realm of the personal and the immediate. For example, we'll examine many of the widely held misconceptions in society—particularly with respect to those that apply to our common, everyday conduct and experiences—and explore the psychological research findings that shows them to be false. Most college students and lay people, for instance, believe in statements such as the following: "To change people's behavior toward members of ethnic minority groups, we must first change their attitudes," "Personality tests reveal your basic motives, including those you may not be aware of" and "Under hypnosis, people can perform feats of physical strength which they could never do otherwise." I believe that the exposure of inaccurate or unsubstantiated information in psychology, or any scientific disciple, is essential to readers' knowledge of a topic, as well as their ability to use the information personally in an effective and beneficial manner.

MYTHS OF MENTAL ILLNESS

Common Misconceptions

Americans hold several misconceptions about people who are mentally ill. This is probably due, in part, to the distorted information often presented in the news media and in the movies. Some of the most common misconceptions about mental illness include the following (Sue, Sue, & Sue, 1997):

1. *It is easy to spot mentally disturbed people because of their abnormal behavior.* People with mental illness typically do not behave consistently in ways that distinguish them from other individuals. If you were to visit a mental hospital, you would find it difficult to distinguish the patients from the staff based on their behavior alone.
2. *Mental illness is inherited.* It is sometimes believed that if one person in a family has it, other family members will probably suffer a similar fate. Except for a few exceptions, such as certain types of schizophrenia, depression, and mental retardation, heredity does not appear to play a major role in mental illness. As noted in the first chapter, heredity may *predispose* an individual to certain disorders, but the environment is the critical factor in triggering the behavior.
3. *Mental illness can never be fully cured.* Many people believe that once individuals become mentally ill, they can never fully recover. Nearly 75% of those patients who are hospitalized with severe disorders go on to lead full and productive lives with no major recurrence of the disorder.
4. *An inherent emotional weakness is responsible for mental disturbance.* There is a belief that people can avoid mental illness or cure themselves of it if they try hard enough. Many psychological problems are triggered by events over which

Evaluating Psychotherapy

Effectiveness

How effective is psychotherapy? The answer depends on how you ask the question and who makes the judgment. Consumers of psychotherapy are generally satisfied. In 1995, *Consumer Reports* surveyed its 186,000 subscribers about their experiences with psychotherapy (*Consumer Reports*, 1995). Of the 4,000 individuals who reported receiving psychotherapy, 44% who characterized their emotional state as "very poor" prior to treatment reported that they felt good following therapy. An additional 43% who started therapy in a "fairly poor" emotional state also reported significant improvement. The magazine reported that almost everyone who sought help did experience some relief in that therapy helped them feel less troubled and experience more pleasant lives. Not surprisingly, those clients who began therapy with the most severe problems reported the greatest progress. Overall, 62% reported that they were highly satisfied with their mental health provider. By contrast, only about 50% who sought assistance from their family doctor were highly satisfied. Research has shown that family doctors are not very good at diagnosing psychological problems

Psychology Applied to Everyday Life works, therefore, to enforce critical thinking and skeptical analysis of information not only in the field of psychology, but in the vast array of topics in this information age.

Each chapter of *Psychology Applied to Everyday Life* begins with a chapter outline covering primary concepts,

1

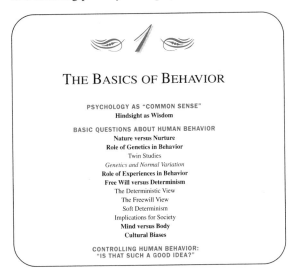

The Basics of Behavior

explores historical and contemporary psychological research and theory,

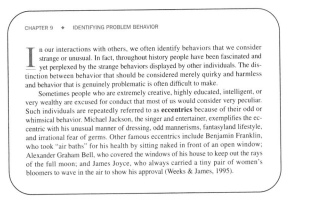

CHAPTER 9 ✦ IDENTIFYING PROBLEM BEHAVIOR

In our interactions with others, we often identify behaviors that we consider strange or unusual. In fact, throughout history people have been fascinated and yet perplexed by the strange behaviors displayed by other individuals. The distinction between behavior that should be considered merely quirky and harmless and behavior that is genuinely problematic is often difficult to make.

Sometimes people who are extremely creative, highly educated, intelligent, or very wealthy are excused for conduct that most of us would consider very peculiar. Such individuals are repeatedly referred to as **eccentrics** because of their odd or whimsical behavior. Michael Jackson, the singer and entertainer, exemplifies the eccentric with his unusual manner of dressing, odd mannerisms, fantasyland lifestyle, and irrational fear of germs. Other famous eccentrics include Benjamin Franklin, who took "air baths" for his health by sitting naked in front of an open window; Alexander Graham Bell, who covered the windows of his house to keep out the rays of the full moon; and James Joyce, who always carried a tiny pair of women's bloomers to wave in the air to show his approval (Weeks & James, 1995).

and applies the theory and research just covered in a variety of ways, including

✦ self-evaluations for better self-understanding, allowing readers to assess their skills and behaviors in areas such as study habits, ability to take tests (test-wiseness), memory, and creativity.

✦ **TABLE 1.3** ✦ **Study Habits and Attitudes Inventory**

Read each question carefully and completely, answering each as honestly as possible. Circle the letter o that best describes you.

1. My goal in school is to:
   A. Pass enough courses to stay in school
   B. Maintain a C average
   C. Maintain a B average
   D. Maintain an A average
2. Realistically, my goal is to receive:
   A. Mostly A's and B's
   B. Mostly B's and C's
   C. Mostly C's and D's
   D. Mostly D's and F's
3. When do you review your notes?
   A. After each class
   B. Frequently or weekly
   C. Seldom
   D. Rarely

D. More than 5 days prior to the exam

8. For a three-hour class, how much time do you spend studying per week?
   A. 0–1 hour
   B. 2–3 hours
   C. 3–4 hours
   D. More than 4 hours
9. Do your parents pay your college expenses?
   A. All
   B. More than half
   C. Less than half
   D. None
10. How do you usually study?
   A. Alone
   B. With others

14. Which courses ar likely to complete assignments from
   A. Courses you a terested in
   B. Courses you a terested in
   C. None of the al
15. When in class, I u
   A. Take as many possible
   B. Take some not
   C. Take few note
   D. Take no notes
16. When given an as I usually begin it
   A. Immediately
   B. After a few da
   C. The day befor

✦ **TABLE 5.2** ✦ **Test of Creativity**

This test is one frequently used by psychologists to measure creativity. The test is called a Remote Associates Test (RAT) because it measures your ability to see relationships between things that are only remotely associated. Read the instructions carefully before beginning the test.

Instructions: Look at the three words and find a fourth word that is related to all three. Write this word in the space provided.

Example: What word is related to these three words?

paint doll cat ______

The answer is "house": house paint, dollhouse, and house cat.

Here is another example:

stool powder ball ______

The answer is "foot": footstool, foot powder, and football.

You have 20 minutes to complete the following items:

1.	call	pay	line	______
2.	end	burning	blue	______
3.	man	hot	sure	______
4.	stick	pal	ball	______
5.	blue	cake	cottage	______
6.	man	wheel	high	______

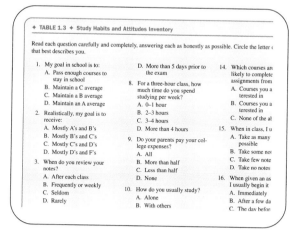

Additional self-tests evaluate characteristics such as power, love style, happiness, hostility, and persuasion

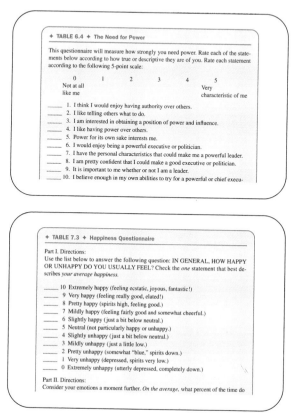

✦ **TABLE 6.4** ✦ **The Need for Power**

This questionnaire will measure how strongly you need power. Rate each of the statements below according to how true or descriptive they are of you. Rate each statement according to the following 5-point scale:

0	1	2	3	4	5
Not at all like me					Very characteristic of me

_____ 1. I think I would enjoy having authority over others.
_____ 2. I like telling others what to do.
_____ 3. I am interested in obtaining a position of power and influence.
_____ 4. I like having power over others.
_____ 5. Power for its own sake interests me.
_____ 6. I would enjoy being a powerful executive or politician.
_____ 7. I have the personal characteristics that could make me a powerful leader.
_____ 8. I am pretty confident that I could make a good executive or politician.
_____ 9. It is important to me whether or not I am a leader.
_____ 10. I believe enough in my own abilities to try for a powerful or chief execu-

✦ **TABLE 7.3** ✦ **Happiness Questionnaire**

Part I. Directions:
Use the list below to answer the following question: IN GENERAL, HOW HAPPY OR UNHAPPY DO YOU USUALLY FEEL? Check the *one* statement that best describes *your average happiness.*

_____ 10 Extremely happy (feeling ecstatic, joyous, fantastic!)
_____ 9 Very happy (feeling really good, elated!)
_____ 8 Pretty happy (spirits high, feeling good.)
_____ 7 Mildly happy (feeling fairly good and somewhat cheerful.)
_____ 6 Slightly happy (just a bit below neutral.)
_____ 5 Neutral (not particularly happy or unhappy.)
_____ 4 Slightly unhappy (just a bit below neutral.)
_____ 3 Mildly unhappy (just a little low.)
_____ 2 Pretty unhappy (somewhat "blue," spirits down.)
_____ 1 Very unhappy (depressed, spirits very low.)
_____ 0 Extremely unhappy (utterly depressed, completely down.)

Part II. Directions:
Consider your emotions a moment further. *On the average,* what percent of the time do

✦ **TABLE 7.1** ✦ **Driving Anger**

This test describes common situations that occur during driving that may make you angry. Imagine th situations described is actually happening to you while driving. Then, rate the amount of anger that v voked in each situation, using the following rating scale:

1 Not at all
2 A little
3 Some
4 Much
5 Very much

_____ 1. Someone makes an obscene gesture toward you about your driving.
_____ 2. You pass a radar speed trap.
_____ 3. Someone runs a red light or stop sign.
_____ 4. Someone honks at you about your driving.
_____ 5. Someone is weaving in and out of traffic.
_____ 6. A police officer pulls you over.
_____ 7. You are driving behind a large truck and cannot see around it.
_____ 8. A bicyclist is riding in the middle of the lane and slowing traffic.
_____ 9. Someone is slow in parking and holding up traffic.
_____ 10. A truck kicks up sand or gravel on the car you are riding in.
_____ 11. Someone speeds up when you try to pass them.
_____ 12. A slow vehicle on a mountain road will not pull over and let people by.
_____ 13. Someone backs right out in front of you without looking.
_____ 14. You are stuck in a traffic jam.

Scoring:
Add up all the scores listed below. The higher the score, the more likely it is that you are easily provoke while driving. You may compare your driving anger with that of other college students by using the char

Score	Percentile	Score	Percentile
21	0	47	50
26	1	49	60
30	3	50	64
32	5	52	72
35	10	54	79
38	17	56	86
40	22	57	89
41	25	59	93
42	28	60	95
43	32	64+	99
45	40		

Interpretation: The percentile tells the percentage of people who score at or below your score. For ins of 40 falls at the 22nd percentile, which means that 22% of drivers have a driving anger score at or lov and 78% have a higher score.

SOURCE: Reproduced with permission of authors and publisher from: Deffenbacher, J. L., Oetting, E. R., & Lynch, R. S. Develop anger scale. *Psychological Reports,* 74, 1994, 83–91. © Psychological Reports 1994.

✦ Specific suggestions for changing one's own behavior, particularly those that are a threat to a person's health or safety

APPLICATIONS: Controlling Noise in Your Environment

In your search for some peace and quiet, you have three choices: escape the source of the sound (often impossible), block the sound with earplugs, or mask the sound. **Masking** refers to the use of one kind of sound to block another. Perhaps you have played music to block out the sound of street traffic while you study. One of the most effective masking noises is **white noise.** White noise consists of a broad spectrum of sound frequencies or pitches that together sound like the noise of a waterfall or a running fan. You may have noticed how difficult it is to understand someone's speech while an air conditioner fan is running. You can still hear the person speaking, but it is difficult to make out what is being said. Several companies market electronic devices to mask sounds, often sold as "sound conditioners." They all produce either white noise or some close derivative of it, such as the sound of rain or a waterfall, to mask sounds. Many people find these devices particularly helpful for sleeping in a noisy environment and for studying. More recently an electronic device has been invented that cancels out noise. Unfortunately,

our evolutionary history, as happiness led to behaviors that obtained food and shelter, and encouraged social interactions and sexual behavior, all important for the survival of the species. It was primarily happy people who came up with new inventions, explored new lands, and engaged in creative endeavors. Furthermore, when we are feeling happy we are much more likely to help others, what psychologists call the "feel good–do good" phenomenon.

APPLICATIONS: Fourteen Fundamentals for Being Happy

Perhaps you were not fortunate enough to inherit a happy disposition. Is there anything you can do to be happier? Michael Fordyce (1977, 1983) developed a program to help people live happier lives. He outlines 14 basic principles for increasing happiness, even if you weren't born happy. The following is an extremely abbreviated description of his 14 fundamentals for a happier life:

APPLICATIONS: Changing Behaviors That Cause Illness

Let's examine some of the unhealthy lifestyle behaviors that contribute to poor health and/or premature death and see how you can change them.

Smoking

The latest data from the U.S. Centers for Disease Control and Prevention (CDC) show that 24.1% of all adults are smokers. The rate has dropped only .6% since 1997, despite all the publicity about the negative health effects of smoking. Surprisingly, recent surveys indicate there is an *increasing* rate of smoking among college students. Smoking is most common among persons aged 18 to 44 years (27.7%) and least common among persons aged 65 years or older (10.9%). Sadly, the low percentage of elderly smokers may be accounted for by the fact that many of them have already died from smoking-related illnesses. Each day, 3,000 more teenagers become regular smokers (Novello, 1990). Smoking is directly related to nearly a half million deaths annually in the United States (Raloff, 1994). Smoking incidence is inversely related to education level and socioeconomic status, with people living below poverty level being much more likely to smoke. Only 11.3% of people with a college education are smokers.

One must wonder why people continue to smoke when the deleterious health effects are widely known. One reason, which is now widely accepted even by tobacco companies, is that smoking is addictive. Nicotine has been found to be as addictive as both cocaine and heroin. It should not be too surprising that people are positively reinforced for smoking. Nicotine causes certain pleasant effects. For instance, it increases the release of certain neurotransmitter substances in the brain that improve mental alertness, sharpen memory, and reduce tension and anxiety (Pomerleau & Pomerleau, 1989). People also use smoking as a coping mechanism

APPLICATIONS

Detecting Suicidal Intentions in Others

At some time in your life you will probably have personal contact with an individual who is planning to commit suicide. I related to you earlier several such instances that I have encountered personally among my professional colleagues. I have also dealt with several instances of suicidal planning among my students. Is it possible to detect suicidal intentions in others? No set pattern indicates suicidal intentions and, in each of the cases that I experienced, I was caught off guard by the act. Nevertheless, there are some warning signs that should alert you that someone intends personal harm.

1. Talk of suicidal plans or making vague references such as "After I'm gone. . . ." or "If I wasn't around any more. . . ." It is a common myth that people who are serious about committing suicide never talk about it beforehand. In actuality, the opposite is true. Be alert to suicidal comments from your friends, however vague or incidental. Any direct threats to commit suicide should be taken very seriously.
2. A sudden increase in giving away personal items, especially items that are very meaningful to the individual.
3. Sudden and inexplicable withdrawal from contact with others.
4. Indications of feelings of helplessness or depression.
5. Sudden changes in mood states.
6. Increase in aggression or risk taking.
7. Experiencing a sudden life crisis that results in emotional shock, such as the

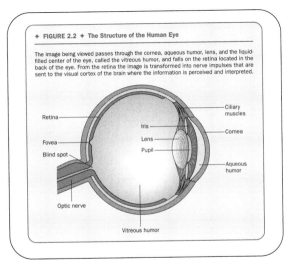

✦ FIGURE 2.2 ✦ The Structure of the Human Eye

The image being viewed passes through the cornea, aqueous humor, lens, and the liquid-filled center of the eye, called the vitreous humor, and falls on the retina located in the back of the eye. From the retina the image is transformed into nerve impulses that are sent to the visual cortex of the brain where the information is perceived and interpreted.

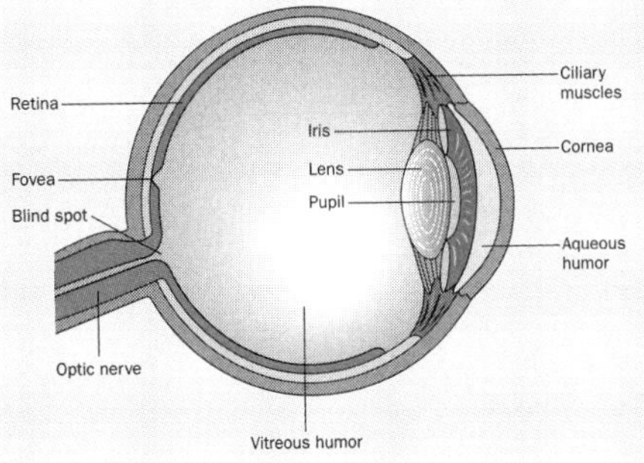

Each chapter ends with a bulleted summary of key concepts for quick memory drilling, and a list of key terms and their definitions.

Finally, a significant part of any good college textbook in this modern, visual age is a supportive, dynamic, and explanatory art program. Throughout *Psychology Applied to Everyday Life,* drawings,

photographs, cartoons and quotations are used to illustrate key points, encapsulate detailed and often lengthy theories, and further clarify some of the most difficult concepts.

Supplements

Psychology Applied to Everyday Life offers a variety of supplementary resources for both instructors and students. The Instructor's Manual/Test Bank, prepared by Tia Cavender, contains a variety of examination questions, including multiple choice, short-answer, true-false, and essay. In addition, the manual provides a set of classroom activities for each chapter. Many chapters contain exercises that can be copied and distributed directly for use in the classroom, which should prove interesting to students, and help illustrate how one can apply the material presented in the main text. For example, students can conduct a simple word association test in class that will allow them to see how emotional indicators can reveal an individual's guilt. A related exercise demonstrates how manipulating facial expressions can affect one's emotions. Other exercises allow students to make predictions about success in therapy and to study how group processes occur in decision making. Relevant web sites where the instructor and students may find related information are also included.

The book's web site, at *http://www.harcourtcollege.com/psych/gardner,* features student and instructor resources including web links, web activities, quizzing, audio glossary, course management tools, and more! Also visit the Wadsworth psychology home page at *http://www.wadsworth.com/psychology* for additional information and resources.

Acknowledgments

A psychology textbook, or any similar academic endeavor, relies on the information gathered over the years by many earlier scientists, philosophers and educators, all of whom prevailed because of their love of knowledge and quest to learn. To those many, many individuals I am grateful. To those individuals who personally contributed to the completion of this book, I want to acknowledge and express my appreciation. Several individuals at Harcourt College Publishing were very helpful in the development and production of this text, particularly Lisa Hensley, the psychology acquisitions editor, for her initial support in moving this project from an idea to a manuscript and both Michelle Vardeman and Rebekah Mercer for their support, encouragement, invaluable editorial input, and their contributions to the subsequent development of this text.

I am particularly indebted to Tia Cavendar who served as my graduate assistant throughout the development of the text and gave unsparingly of her time and dedication. In addition, she assumed the primary responsibility for the development of the instructor's manual. Her unflagging encouragement and dedication to this project served me in countless ways. I would also like to thank my wife, Betty-Ann, for her expertise in editing the original drafts of the text and her constant encouragement. I would never have undertaken or completed the text without her support and assistance. My thanks also to the reviewers of the text, including Nancy Armbruster, Mott Community College; Mike Chase, Quincy University; Sue Frantz, New Mexico State University at Alamogordo; Lenore Frigo, College of Southern Idaho; Guadalupe King, Milwaukee Area Technical College; Andrea Markowitz, University of Baltimore; Gerold Robbins, University of Colorado at Denver; Lee Wertzler,

Mount Royal College, and Tod Wiebers, Henderson State University, who provided many helpful suggestions. In addition, Chris Mendosa and Krystina Ann Finlay made helpful suggestions on specific chapters within their domain of expertise. And finally, my thanks to all the people I have mentioned in the text who have provided me with the numerous personal anecdotes and illustrations of behaviors. Even though I have omitted most of their names, they often enriched my life and, at the very least, served to fill the invaluable role of illustrating just how important it is to apply psychology to one's everyday life.

Of final and significant note, I am indebted to the University of Colorado at Denver for its continuous support and its generosity in granting me a sabbatical leave to complete this project.

Contents in Brief

CONTENTS

CHAPTER 3: LEARNING 71

CHAPTER 4: MEMORY 111

1

The Basics of Behavior

Human behavior is endlessly fascinating to observe. If you are like many people, you enjoy watching people and observing their behavior. Sitting in a busy airport or at a crowded mall, watching people go by offers fascinating snapshots into a variety of human behaviors. Sometimes we feel we can "get to know" things about people, even from these brief observations. A young couple who walks by has a verbal argument. That allows us to draw conclusions about the state of their relationship. An ill-behaved child acts out in the presence of a seemingly uncaring mother. We then conclude things about how good a parent she is.

Psychology has been one of the most popular college majors in the United States for the past 2 decades. Over the years, many psychology majors have told me that they decided to major in the subject because, in middle school and high school, their friends always talked to them about their problems. These students almost invariably believe that they have special abilities to help other people with their problems. Female college students are more likely to express these sentiments even though many males share similar feelings. Often college students who major in psychology are quite surprised to learn that the study of psychology involves a lot of "hard" science, including biology, physics, physiology, biochemistry, and mathematics.

Psychology as "Common Sense"

Many people who are skeptical about the field of psychology have expressed the belief that psychology is really nothing more than "common sense." These people often believe that most human behavior is easily explained, especially if one just thinks carefully about it. As a professor of psychology, I have often been surprised at the very strong opinions most people maintain about various aspects of human behavior despite having received no formal training in the field. In fact, many people do not believe that one needs any formal education to understand human behavior.

In the English language, there are many proverbs or sayings about human behavior, many of which are contradictory. For instance, consider the pairs of sayings below:

> Absence makes the heart grow fonder—Out of sight out of mind.
>
> You can't teach an old dog new tricks—You're never too old to learn.
>
> Opposites attract—Birds of a feather flock together.
>
> Look before you leap—He who hesitates is lost.
>
> Spare the rod and spoil the child—You catch more flies with honey than with vinegar.

We often use these axioms to explain behavior. If psychologists discover that inconsistent parental discipline results in unruly children, we proclaim no surprise. Everyone knows, of course, that if you spare the rod you spoil the child. When other psychologists reveal that most criminals were raised by caretakers who regularly used physical punishment, we also express no surprise. As our Aunt Minnie told us many times, you catch more flies with honey than with vinegar.

We frequently use these sayings to affirm a belief that we have about behavior or to explain why some behavior occurred. We encourage our children to select their friends on the basis of factors other than appearance alone because, we believe,

✦ TABLE 1.1 ✦ Conceptions About Psychology Test

Rate each of the following statements as "true" or "false."

T	F	1. Wisdom increases as people become older.
T	F	2. We feel pain when the amount of damage occurring to tissue exceeds the rate of repair.
T	F	3. Mental health professionals who have many years of experience are generally more effective than therapists who are just starting out.
T	F	4. People who abuse their children were frequently abused themselves as children.
T	F	5. Most mothers suffer from the "empty-nest syndrome" when their youngest child leaves home.
T	F	6. In our dreams, we frequently act out our forbidden fantasies.
T	F	7. A skilled hypnotist can hypnotize people against their will.
T	F	8. It is necessary to make mistakes if we are to learn.
T	F	9. Learning must be meaningful for us to remember it.
T	F	10. With the assistance of others, it is possible to remember events that took place in the first 2 years of your life.
T	F	11. Males and females show equal abilities on most psychological tasks.
T	F	12. Mental health professionals who have advanced graduate degrees (master's or doctorate) are generally more effective therapists than those with only a bachelor's degree.
T	F	13. Lie detectors (polygraphs), when used by a skilled professional, are usually accurate.
T	F	14. In order to change a person's behavior, we must first change the person's attitude.
T	F	15. Hypnosis has proven to be effective in helping people to diet or stop smoking.

"You can't tell a book by its cover." Our children are advised to try especially hard to be friends with others who are particularly quiet or shy because, we also believe, "Still waters run deep." Interestingly, in my travels in foreign countries, I have found that almost all of the popular expressions that we use in the United States have close correlates in other languages and cultures. For instance, while we say that we know something "like the back of our hand," a German knows it "like the inside of my pocket." The fact that so many of these colloquial expressions give contradictory advice demonstrates the lack of consensus that often exists about explanations for human behavior. You should know, however, that professionals in psychology often disagree about various aspects of human behavior.

In Table 1.1 you will find a list of 20 statements about human behavior. Read each statement and mark whether you believe the statement is true or false on the basis of what you currently know about human behavior. Do not worry if you seem to be marking more items true than false or vice versa, but instead consider each item on its own merits and according to how you feel about it. If you are not sure of the answer, make your best guess.

Earlier we spoke about how many aspects of human behavior are very controversial, even among some professionals in the field. The 15 questions in Table 1.1 reflect statements about which many people often disagree. All statements in Table 1.1 *are false* because none is supported by current research findings. To find your score, count the number of questions that you indicated were false. If you are like the typical freshman or sophomore, you will have marked about 40% of these questions, or 6 of the 15, as "true" (Gardner & Dalsing, 1986). If you marked fewer than this number as true, you should be congratulated. You hold fewer misconceptions about human behavior than the average college student does. However, do not be discouraged if you marked more than average. Research has shown that with further training in psychology the number of misconceptions drops dramatically (Gardner & Dalsing, 1986).

The purpose of this test of misconceptions is to impress upon you that making conclusions about human behavior involves much more than the simple application of "common sense" or the acceptance of what is commonly held to be true. Many things about behavior that most people believe are true have been shown to be false when exposed to the harsh light of scientific verification. Psychology is a science, and it draws conclusions about behavior based on the application of scientific methods. There is little room in science for conjecture and intuition, unless they lead to research that verifies or refutes such opinions with empirical findings. Theories and concepts that psychologists used to believe were true now have been shown to be false, after further scientific experimentation. An example of this was the widespread belief that "only children," or those without siblings, are spoiled, have more adjustment problems, and are less likely to achieve than children with siblings. Subsequent research has shown that "only children" perform slightly better in school and on intelligence tests and are more likely to achieve admission to prestigious colleges than children with siblings (Falbo & Polit, 1986).

Hindsight as Wisdom

One difficulty found in the field of psychology that escapes many other scientific disciplines is that psychology sometimes documents the obvious. Human behavior is often so variable that almost any research findings seem obvious and easily explained. I once conducted a research project on body image in which I examined what body region women (and men) look at when judging their own body size (Gardner & Morrell, 1991). We used eye-tracking equipment to measure where people's eyes fixated while looking at photographic images of themselves. We found that women spent more time looking at their stomachs than at any other body region when attempting to judge their body size. Almost invariably, when I told women about this finding, they replied with some variant of "So what else is new?" or "You get grant money to find out these kinds of things?" Psychologists refer to this as the *I-knew-it-all-along phenomenon* or, more commonly, **hindsight bias.** Once people know the outcome of an experiment, the results suddenly seem less unexpected or surprising than if you asked them to predict the outcome. I quickly discovered this phenomenon by first asking women what body region they thought they looked at most when judging their body size. Many women told me that they focused on the size of their thighs. These women were always far more surprised at my findings than the women who only heard the final results of my study.

Pseudoscientific writings are always more popular among the populace than are writings reflecting more rigorous science. Unfortunately, pseudoscience abounds in the field of psychology.

We are all guilty of hindsight bias at one time or another. After we know the outcome of some event it always seems more obvious, less surprising, and more explainable than if we were asked to predict the results. People who do this regularly are often called "Monday-morning quarterbacks" ("It was third down and long, he should'a thrown the football instead of trying to run it up the middle!"). This hindsight bias is just as applicable to historical events as to sports. Few people predicted the recent fall of communism in Eastern Europe, but there have been no shortages of pundits who now claim that such an event was easily predictable and explainable. Explanations of the causes after an event are referred to as **post-hoc** or after-the-fact explanations. The next time that the stock market takes a large drop, watch for the "expert" analysts to come forward to explain the reasons why it happened. If you are like me, you will wonder where these experts and their wisdom were hiding immediately *before* the market dropped. A similar phenomenon occurs during election years. Immediately after the elections are over, a host of people will claim they knew how the election was going to turn out all along and the reasons for the results as well. According to Richard Thaler, a University of Chicago economics professor who has studied the behavior of stock investors, events that actually happen will be thought of as having been predictable. Events that do not happen will be thought of as having been unlikely. So you won that drawing at the supermarket for a free vacation? Of course, you had a lucky feeling that you were going to win all along. You didn't win the drawing? Of course not, the odds are nearly impossible!

Post-hoc explanations do little to advance the science of psychology, and they often impede its progress. Everyone needs to be aware of the limitations of post-hoc explanations and should avoid using them to explain events or the behavior of others.

Although the terms hindsight bias and post-hoc explanation are similar, they are not synonymous. Hindsight bias is when the *explanation seems clear* after the outcome, while post hoc is when you *try to derive an explanation* after the outcome. In other words, with hindsight bias you *claim to have predicted* the outcome, and with post hoc, you *attempt to explain* the outcome.

Understanding human behavior is a complicated business. Common sense can serve us well in our everyday lives, and it should not be totally discredited. Nevertheless, we cannot reliably count on common sense to help us understand or predict human behavior. In this book you will see how research often contradicts popular conceptions in many different areas of psychology. Hopefully, the knowledge that you gain will help you question and analyze the commonly held assumptions about why behavior occurs as it does. Psychology is a dynamic and exciting field of study with constantly changing vistas about the causes of human behavior.

Basic Questions about Human Behavior

For many years psychologists have debated certain fundamental questions about human nature and behavior. Generally, psychologists have agreed that there are no "right" or "wrong" answers in this debate. However, arguments on both sides warrant attention and discussion because these issues affect the assumptions we make about human behavior. Your beliefs about these issues will color the way you view behavior.

Nature versus Nurture

Consider the tremendous diversity that is present in human behavior. Looking only within your own circle of acquaintances, you will see a great deal of variability. Some are shy while others are outgoing. Some have talents in art and music, while others may possess mechanical skills. Some may be struggling with alcohol and drugs while others are seemingly immune to these problems. Psychologists have questioned what is responsible for this great diversity that we see in behavior. Behavior is a result of two factors: genetics (heredity) and experience. The relative importance that each of these factors contributes to behavior constitutes the **nature–nurture issue.** It is important to note that all of behavior depends upon both heredity *and* environment. Behavior could not develop without both of these factors being present. The primary issue facing psychologists, then, is the determination of the relative contribution of each factor on the behavioral differences between individuals. Where do you stand on this issue? Is behavior influenced more by genetic factors or more by the experiences a person has had with environmental factors? The short self-test in Table 1.2 will help you clarify your personal beliefs in this debate. You should complete this test before continuing with your reading.

Role of Genetics in Behavior

One of the biggest changes in the field of psychology in the past 2 decades has been the increasing appreciation and acceptance of the role of heredity on human behavior. There now exists a subfield of psychology called **behavioral genetics** that focuses on this very topic. When I was an undergraduate in the 1960s, there was a widespread belief among most psychologists that an individual's experiences (nurture) were by far the most important determinants in behavior. Abnormal psychology textbooks reported that the mental disorders labeled schizophrenia and autism were caused by bad parenting. Alcoholism and drug abuse were identified as learned behaviors, without any suggestion that heredity might be a significant contributor.

Several breakthroughs in behavioral genetics, beginning in the 1970s, have led to major changes in how psychologists view the role of heredity on behavior. Today, it is

✦ TABLE 1.2 ✦ Nature versus Nurture Attitudes Test

Answer each of the questions according to whether you believe the statement is mostly true or mostly false. There are no "right" or "wrong" answers—answer the questions according to what you believe.

T	F	1. If you work hard enough, you can accomplish almost anything you set out to do.
T	F	2. Some people are just born dumb, and there is not much that can be done about it.
T	F	3. The best predictor of how smart you will be is to look at how smart your parents are.
T	F	4. To be a really great artist or musician, you have to be born with some natural talent in those areas.
T	F	5. Hard work will get you further in life than inborn intelligence.
T	F	6. Personality traits are largely inherited and not likely to change very much after early childhood.
T	F	7. Most criminal behavior is due to the unhealthy environment that criminals usually grow up in.
T	F	8. Males and females are the same at birth; it is only the different way that society treats them that causes the differences we later see.
T	F	9. People can inherit a strong predisposition for alcoholism.
T	F	10. Both genetics and the environment play a role in the development of human behaviors, but a person's experiences with the environment are probably more important.

Scoring:

Score one point for each of your answers that match those below:

1. F 2. T 3. T 4. T 5. F 6. T 7. F 8. F 9. T 10. F

Interpretation of Your Score:

Points	Interpretation
9–10	You fall clearly on the "nature" side; that is, you believe that behavior is strongly influenced by hereditary factors as opposed to the effects of experience.
7–8	You believe that, in most cases, hereditary factors (nature) are more important than the experiences that a person has had.
4–6	You believe that genetics (nature) and experiences (nurture) are about equally important in influencing behavior.
2–3	You believe that, in most cases, the experiences a person has had (nurture) are more important than hereditary factors.
0–1	You fall clearly on the nurture side; that is, you believe that behavior is strongly influenced by the experiences a person has had as opposed to hereditary influences.

generally accepted that genetic factors contribute importantly to most areas of psychology (American Psychological Society, 1998). According to a summary report issued by the American Psychological Society (APS 1998 report), genetic research has convincingly demonstrated that genetic factors contribute importantly to most mental illness.

Twin Studies

Much of the research examining the role of genetics has studied the similarities and differences in twins. Studies with identical twins have been particularly helpful

"This is your side of the family, you realize."

Psychologists have increasingly realized the importance of inherited behaviors during the past 20 years.

because the twins develop from one fertilized egg and therefore share identical genetic makeup. Comparisons of identical twins are often made to fraternal twins, who develop from two fertilized eggs. On average, fraternal twins share 50% of the genes that can vary among humans. Research has revealed that if one identical twin is schizophrenic, the chances are 45% that the other twin will also be schizophrenic. Fraternal twins, on the other hand, have only a 15% risk of schizophrenia occurring in both members. Similarly, autism, which is one of the most heritable disorders, presents a 60% risk of occurrence for identical twins compared to a 10% risk for fraternal twins.

Genetics and Normal Variation. Genetics is also important in normal variation. Although widely accepted that variations in height are genetically determined, it is only now recognized that differences in weight are almost as heritable. Despite our best attempts at dieting and exercise, differences in weight are much more a matter of nature (genetics) than nurture (environment). According to the APS report, genetics has also been found to be important for differences in cognitive abilities, intelligence, personality, school achievement, self-esteem, and substance abuse. According to this report, genetic factors are often as important *as all other factors combined.* For instance, it is now generally accepted that 50 to 60% of the variation in intelligence within a group of people is due to genetic factors. For example, if two individuals have IQs of 110 and 130, about half the difference between these two scores is due to genetic factors, while the remainder is due to environmental factors.

There is no question that the environment (nurture) plays an important role in the development of behavior. However, recent genetic research has shown that it is important to take genetics into account even when studying the environment. For example, parenting is considered to be one of the most powerful variables in the family environment. Nevertheless, research during the past decade has convincingly shown the role of genetics on parenting styles. You have probably heard it said that people raise their children the way they were raised. Parenting styles were thought to be the result of environmental factors and influences. Today we are increasingly convinced that we may inherit such parenting styles. Other important environmental factors such as childhood accidents, life experiences, and social support have also been shown to have a strong genetic involvement. In fact, there is increasing evidence that people create their own environmental experiences for genetic reasons. For instance, a person who is genetically gifted in mathematics will likely seek out an environment that will complement those abilities. Such a person would likely select math courses in high school and college and would probably score high on math aptitude tests, thanks both to a natural math aptitude and previous experiences with mathematics. It is in this manner that genes form the experiences that subsequently mold who we are.

There seems to be no end to the surprising findings about genetic involvement in behavior. For example, there appears to be a genetic role in the number of hours that we watch television (Plomin, Corley, DeFries, & Fulker, 1990). Identical twins reared apart have very similar religious convictions (Waller, Kojetin, Bouchard, Lykken, & Tellegen, 1990). Studies on identical twins have also shown a substantial genetic effect on how optimistic people are (Schulman, Keith, & Seligman, 1993). The idea that genes might play any role in television watching, religious devotion, or optimism certainly would have been ridiculed 2 decades ago.

A recent book by Judith Rich Harris (1998) entitled *The Nurture Assumption: Why Children Turn Out the Way They Do,* has ignited a heated discussion over the importance of parenting on children's development. Harris's thesis is that parents' importance in shaping their children's development has been greatly exaggerated. She argues that children's behavior is shaped far more by peers, friends, and schools than it is by parents. According to the author, the main contribution that parents make is through the genes that they supply their children. As evidence of her view, Harris notes that children often behave in one way at home and in a completely different manner when out in the world at large. One example she cites is birth order. The eldest child typically bosses the younger children around at home, and the younger children submit to the tyranny. When in other environments, however, the younger children are not submissive, and the oldest child is not particularly bossy. Harris does not dismiss the influential role of environment, but, instead, minimizes the importance of parents in the child's environment.

You might think that most psychologists would dismiss such a controversial view of parenting, particularly since the author has no doctorate in psychology or an academic affiliation. In fact, her views were originally published in *Psychological Review,* one of the most prestigious journals in psychology. The American Psychological Association awarded Harris the prestigious George A. Miller Award for the best journal article in general psychology for 1997.

Joseph LeDoux, a behavioral neuroscientist, has argued that both nature and nurture contribute to who we are, although the proportion that each contributes is in dispute (LeDoux, 1998). He argues that both genetics and environmental factors

Many behaviors that were previously thought to have been entirely learned have more recently been shown to have a genetic basis. This includes behavior such as religious devotion.

achieve their effects by altering the synaptic organization of the brain. **Synapses** are what connect brain cells and allow the cells to communicate amongst themselves. LeDoux notes that the particular patterns of synapses in a person's brain, and the information that those connections encode, are the keys to what a person is.

Many of the synaptic links already exist at birth, hence the influence of nature. Experience then alters synapses as well, by either creating new ones or changing the strength of existing ones. This is a process known as **synaptic plasticity.** Much of this alteration in synapses occurs in early childhood as the brain develops. However, we know that plasticity in the form of learning and memory continues to shape the synapses throughout our lifetime. LeDoux argues that given the enormous capacity of the brain for synaptic plasticity throughout life, it is difficult to imagine that children are shaped by their experiences with their peers but are not affected by what occurs with their parents. As he notes, most of a child's early years are spent primarily with parents rather than peers.

Role of Experiences in Behavior

This discussion of the relative importance of genetics (nature) is not intended to downplay the importance of experiences (nurture) in shaping our lives. For most aspects of our behavior, experience plays at least as important a role, if not a more important one, than does genetics. Limitations are placed on us by our genetics but, within those limitations, experience shapes our lives. Furthermore, the kinds of experiences that we have can completely nullify our genetic potential. No matter how mathematically gifted you might be, you would never realize your potential if your environmental situation conspired to prevent an exposure to mathematics. In addition, at least at this point in time, there is not much we can do to alter our genetic makeup. We do, however, control many of our environmental experiences, and it is that realm to which we devote most of our attention in this text. Nevertheless, it is important to recognize that both nature and nurture play important roles in human behavior.

Finally, your personal views on the relative importance of nature and nurture on behavior can make a big difference in many aspects of your life, including how well you do in school. Children who believe people are "born smart" (nature) have a tendency to give up in school if they do not get good grades. On the other hand, children who believe that hard work is responsible for success (nurture) focus on what they need to do to learn. These children view failure as part of the learning process. By middle school and high school, the children with the "nurture perspective" show the most progress in their schooling, with some earning the top grades in their class (Dweck, Hong, & Chiu, 1993). These findings illustrate that your beliefs about nature versus nurture can affect you in many ways, including how hard you work and whether you believe that other people's abilities are fixed or capable of change. Equally important is society's collective view on this controversy because that view will determine the amount of money and effort that will be devoted to improving the living conditions and educational opportunities of its citizenry.

Free Will versus Determinism

As you read this chapter, keep in mind the following questions. If you so desired, could you at any time stop reading this chapter and go do something else? Could you rip out the page of this book right now, if you really wanted to? If you are like most people, you would respond, "Yes, of course, I could do anything I wanted to." This brings up the issue of free will versus determinism, which is an issue that has been hotly debated for centuries by scientists and philosophers.

The Deterministic View

Science has always been interested in the causes of events. Beginning as early as the Renaissance in Europe, scientists began to look for scientific explanations for events they saw happening. Their careful observations led them to believe that everything observable that happens in nature has a cause. This assumption of causality is called **determinism.** For example, consider a rock rolling down a mountainside. As the rock rolls downhill, it strikes the ground and the objects in its path which, in turn, causes its speed and direction to change in a seemingly unpredictable fashion. However, if we carefully examined the path of this rock, we would see that its changes in speed and direction were actually all determined. In fact, the rock blindly followed the laws of nature as it progressed down the hill, striking the ground and the objects in its path and reacting precisely as the laws of physics would predict.

As psychology evolved into a science, people began to question whether the same paradigm was true for human behavior. Since humans are part of nature, perhaps all human behavior might be similarly driven by some determining factors. According to the determinist view, this is precisely what happens. The determinist believes that everything we do is caused by something, even though we might be unaware of what the determining factors really are. Taken to its extreme, this belief implies that any choices or decisions we make are not made freely, but rather are made in reaction to these external factors. Such a view would state, for instance, that you have no choice of whether you stop reading this chapter or whether you rip out one of its pages. Your behavior is being controlled by a set of complex external factors of which you are likely unaware.

The human will has no more freedom than that of the higher animals, from which it differs only in degree, not in kind.

ERNEST HAECKEL
The Riddle of the Universe VII

Most psychologists do not subscribe to such an extreme deterministic view. They believe that our behavior is driven by a combination of internal and external factors. One example of an internal factor might be your goals. Presumably, you want to keep this textbook after the course is over. Or perhaps you wish to sell it as a used book to the bookstore (something that causes those of us who are authors of textbooks to shudder!). This internal goal might dissuade you from ripping a page out of the book. Psychologists know internal motives and goals are important influences on our behavior; therefore, a strict deterministic viewpoint is seldom heeded. Other internal factors that influence behavior are your genetic makeup, all of your past experiences, and your environment.

The Freewill View

The alternative to determinism is **free will.** In its extreme form, freewill proponents maintain that our behavior is not controlled by the environment, by past experiences, or by genetics. According to this viewpoint, we are essentially able to ignore the effects of such factors and are free to behave how and when we want. In its extreme form, the concept of free will is difficult to defend. Psychological research has provided conclusive scientific evidence that the environment, genetics, and our past history do influence our behavior, at least to some extent. Even human behavior that seems random and free of external factors rarely is. If you ask someone to pick a number randomly between 1 and 10, that person is more likely to select a number in the middle of the range rather than at the extremes. Someone asked to select a book randomly from a shelf surely would be influenced by the titles, colors, and sizes of the choices. Similarly, you are technically free to select any empty seat in a classroom, but studies show that both personality variables and past experiences influence where you choose to sit and that you are likely to sit in the same area each time.

Although it seems plausible to believe that we can behave in any way we like, this extreme view flies in the face of what we know about the factors that affect behavior. Our strong beliefs in free will are an illusion, albeit a believable one, because our behavior is being influenced by so many determinants that we are incapable of recognizing most of them. To a certain extent, we are indeed held hostage by our genetics, our previous experiences, and our environment.

All theory is against the freedom of the will; all experience for it.

SAMUEL JOHNSON

Soft Determinism

Most psychologists have adopted a view called **soft determinism** that incorporates a less extreme view of determinism than the one already described. Imagine a continuum with free will on one end and determinism on the other: Soft determinism lies in between. According to this view, our behavior is affected by the combined influence of our current environment, past experiences, and genetics. Nevertheless, we do make choices and set goals even though they are undoubtedly influenced by these factors. If complete free will truly existed, the science of psychology would be unnecessary. If behavior were totally free from external and internal influences, psychological research would be unnecessary because all such research is conducted in order to discover how these various factors influence or "determine" our behavior.

But to return to our original questions, could you "choose" to stop reading right now or to tear a page out of this text? Yes, you could, but whatever your choices, they would be influenced by several factors from your genetic makeup as well as your past experiences and present environment.

Implications for Society

The debate over free will versus determinism goes beyond being merely an interesting philosophical discussion. A belief in one or the other viewpoint has implications for how one views many aspects of our society. Let's take law for example. Our system of laws is predicated on the belief that people have control over their own behavior. If behavior falls outside of the boundaries of acceptability that society dictates, our legal system invokes consequences to punish the behavior and decrease the probability that it will reoccur. As the saying goes, "Don't do the crime if you can't do the time." Our legal system accepts the notion that our behavior is free to a certain extent while still acknowledging that external factors also play an important role. These external factors, such as past environment and family history, are often taken into consideration in deciding a just punishment. Thus, law, like psychology, adopts the middle position between the views of extreme determinism and free will.

Even though most psychologists take an intermediate view on this issue, their consensus should not imply that they are always in agreement. Some psychologists maintain that genetics have a large influence on our behavior, while others claim that it is only a minor influence. A strong belief in the effect of genetics on behavior tilts a psychologist more to the determinism end of the scale. Other psychologists, known as **humanistic psychologists,** emphasize the capacity of people to make conscious decisions about their own lives. This branch of psychology leans more toward the freewill end of the continuum. Your personal views on this topic often will influence how you view other people's behavior. If you are a strong believer in free will, you are likely to hold people accountable for their behavior because you believe that they are free to behave as they wish. If, on the other hand, you subscribe to a strong determinism view, you are more likely to explain an individual's criminal behavior as, for example, a product of genetics and past criminal history. In other words, you would attribute the criminal acts to factors beyond the individual's personal control. Like most psychologists, you probably hold an intermediate view between these two extreme positions. The debate over free will versus determinism has raged for centuries and likely will continue for several more.

Mind versus Body

Another important issue in psychology involves the question of whether the mind and the body are one and the same. Like the free will–determinism issue, this philosophical discussion has been going on for centuries. In the 17th century a French philosopher by the name of René Descartes championed the view that a person's soul (mind) was separate from the brain. More recently, psychologists have argued that mind and brain are one and the same. They argue that the complex interactions among the brain's nerve cells are what is responsible for consciousness.

Psychologists even disagree on how much of human behavior can be explained by conscious and unconscious processes. Although we do not have a complete understanding of how the brain works, we do know that it is the entity responsible for consciousness. Furthermore, consciousness is not dependent on stimulation from external sources. Studies of people who have been almost completely paralyzed due to strokes or accidents reveal that they fully retain the ability to remember and to think.

Many psychologists believe that all behavior can (and should) be explained in terms of how our brain and central nervous system function. A series of seminal experiments by Wilder Penfield and his colleagues offers some supporting evidence for this view. Patients who were undergoing brain surgery had areas of their exposed brain electrically stimulated. Patients were under local anesthesia and fully conscious during the operation, which allowed them to report the sensations they felt during their brain's stimulation. When certain brain areas were gently stimulated with electrical current, some patients reported vivid memories, often of events that occurred years earlier and that had, heretofore, been long forgotten. In one case, an elderly man reported memories of a band concert that he had attended as a child. Other stimulations resulted in the sound of clicks, the sensations of color or movement, and sensations in various regions of the body (Penfield, 1975). This research has shown that different mental tasks, such as language, memory, hearing, and vision, activate different areas of the brain (Phelps & Mazziotta, 1985).

> The mind grows and decays with the body.
>
> **LUCRETIUS**
> *De Rerum Natura III*

Contemporary studies are suggestive of a link between mind and body. Psychologists have even debated whether we need a concept such as *mind.* For a while many psychologists avoided using the word "mind," but the term has more recently regained its respectability. You might say that psychology lost its mind temporarily but now appears to have regained it.

The debate about the relationship between the mind and the brain will not be resolved in the near future. Nevertheless, continuing research on the connection between the two offers exciting prospects of better understanding the interrelationships between the two entities. As with the issues of nature versus nurture and free will versus determinism, your views on this controversy will affect the way you examine behavior. If you believe that the mind is something separate from the body (and the brain) then you probably believe that science will never be able to study it objectively despite the technical sophistication available. If you believe that the mind is an outgrowth of our biology and that it is a complex function of the nervous system, then you share the beliefs of many psychologists and other scientists. They hold the common belief that the mind is capable of being investigated objectively and that the future holds great promise for a clearer understanding of precisely how it works.

Cultural Biases

Each of us lives in a culture with rules and customs specific to that culture. A culture defines the habits, skills, morals, laws, customs, sports, arts, and any other learned behavior practiced by members of a society. It defines the way of life for a group of people. As such, culture has a powerful influence on how we perceive the world and the behavior of others.

There are large cultural differences in almost any aspect of human behavior. Cultural differences exist with what societies consider to be abnormal behavior, correct emotional expressions, personality traits, treatment of the elderly, language and thought processes, interpretation of facial expressions, spousal abuse, and sexual behavior, to name only a few. It is well known that behavior is shaped and molded by the cultural context within which a person lives. It is nearly impossible for us to observe and study behavior without these cultural factors affecting our views. Your awareness of the impact of cultural differences is necessary as you read about the applications of psychological principles in this text. Otherwise, you may tend to believe that others should think and act as we do.

Much of the research on human behavior that you will read about in this book, or in any other American psychology textbook for that matter, was conducted on people of northern European/North American descent. This occurs because introductory psychology classes in American colleges and universities constitute one of the largest pools of research subjects. Since these college students are predominantly white, nonimmigrants, and from the middle- and upper-socioeconomic class, a legitimate question might be whether we can generalize from the behavior of this specific group to human behavior in general. It has been said that in many respects we are like all others, like some others, and like no others. By studying people of other cultures we are able to determine exactly how we are similar and how we differ. Unfortunately, there has not been a strong emphasis on cross-cultural research in American psychology, which is both surprising and disappointing given the cultural diversity that exists within the United States. Only with a reversal of this trend will we gain a better understanding of how the cultural context affects behavior.

Fortunately, many of the basic processes that we study in human behavior appear to follow the same rules, irrespective of the cultural context. For example, memories are stored through processes that are, for the most part, independent of the specific language being used. Similarly, how we perceive our world through our sense organs is also largely independent of the cultural context. Nevertheless, you need to keep in mind that research findings about human behavior and the conclusions from those findings are potentially colored by the "cultural lens" through which the behavior is being observed.

Controlling Human Behavior: "Is That Such a Good Idea?"

One major goal of this text is to teach you how to apply psychological principles to influence behavior. You may wonder if controlling behavior is such a good idea or if knowledge of this kind is potentially dangerous. You might question whether people would use this knowledge to manipulate others or whether some unscrupulous leader would use this knowledge to create a totalitarian state, such as that described in Aldous Huxley's *Brave New World.*

There is never a shortage of self-help books on how to control not only your own behavior but the behavior of others, as well. A trip to any bookstore will reveal whole sections of books with this objective, but this is not a new phenomenon. People have been writing such books for centuries. Perhaps one of the earliest books in this regard was *The Prince* by Niccolò Machiavelli published in 1532. In this book Machiavelli instructs the reader on how to acquire and keep political power. His advice is couched in cold practicality and includes the recommendation that it is better to be feared than loved. If cruelty is necessary, he recommends that it be committed all at once and not over an extended period. Machiavelli recommends that one should never listen to advice, presumably his own included, unless it is requested. Tyrants throughout history have found the advice contained in this book very helpful. Fidel

Castro was reportedly one of Machiavelli's most ardent fans. In fact, Castro included the book on his recommended reading list for revolutionaries following his overthrow of the Cuban government in 1959. One of Machiavelli's legacies has been psychology's adoption of the term **Machiavellian** to refer to individuals who are manipulative and obsessed with acquiring power.

Should writings on how to control human behavior be banned? Knowledge has the potential for good or evil. Atomic energy science has killed hundreds of thousands of people and yet saved countless more through peaceful applications. Psychology has discovered powerful tools about how behavior is acquired and how it can be controlled. The potential for misuse of this knowledge certainly exists, as does the potential for its use to improve people's lives. In actuality, everyone attempts to influence the behavior of others in almost any social interaction. Whether we are dating, interacting with our spouse, or dealing with fellow employees or the boss at work, we are usually attempting to influence others. Most of the time, however, people's attempts to influence or persuade others are unsystematic and haphazard. It is my hope that the skills you learn from this textbook will help you improve the quality of your life and assist you in your everyday dealings with others.

The field of psychology deals with "real world" problems and offers solutions for many of the problems facing society, such as: how children can be taught more effectively; how prejudice can be reduced or prevented; how aggression can be prevented and controlled; how the treatment of people suffering from mental disorders can be effectively improved; how the effects of stressors on health can be diminished. In addition, psychology offers the potential for enhancing our lives. Through psychological research we better understand the causes that increase happiness and those that do not. Advances have been made in understanding the process of love, how learning and memory can be facilitated, how the brain works, and numerous other areas, many of which will be discussed in the following chapters. Psychology is an exciting and dynamic field. Little wonder that it is one of the most popular college majors in the United States today.

APPLICATIONS: How to Study This Material

Numerous studies have been conducted examining college students' study habits and attitudes as they relate to academic success. Some of the findings have been surprising. Before we review those findings, you can take the brief test in Table 1.3 that will measure your own study habits and attitudes.

Predictors of Academic Success

A great deal of research has been done to find predictors of academic success. Most colleges and universities admit students based on their grades and their scores on aptitude tests, such as the SAT and ACT, which are specifically designed to predict success in college. Several studies have suggested that students' study skills and self-concepts are also important predictors of academic success (Gadzella & Williamson, 1984). Even though much of the research in this area remains somewhat controversial, certain facts do emerge. Students who use their teachers as resources tend to have better academic success (Tollefson, Cox, & Barke, 1979).

✦ TABLE 1.3 ✦ Study Habits and Attitudes Inventory

Read each question carefully and completely, answering each as honestly as possible. Circle the letter of the answer that best describes you.

1. My goal in school is to:
   A. Pass enough courses to stay in school
   B. Maintain a C average
   C. Maintain a B average
   D. Maintain an A average
2. Realistically, my goal is to receive:
   A. Mostly A's and B's
   B. Mostly B's and C's
   C. Mostly C's and D's
   D. Mostly D's and F's
3. When do you review your notes?
   A. After each class
   B. Frequently or weekly
   C. Seldom
   D. Rarely
4. How often do you skip classes?
   A. Almost never
   B. Seldom (once a month)
   C. Occasionally (once a week)
   D. Almost always
5. Do you complete class assignments?
   A. Almost always
   B. Most of the time
   C. Some of the time
   D. Almost never
6. How many clubs or organizations are you a member of?
   A. 5 or more
   B. 3 or 4
   C. 1 to 3
   D. None
7. When do you begin preparing for an exam?
   A. The day before the exam
   B. 2–3 days prior to the exam
   C. 4–5 days prior to the exam
   D. More than 5 days prior to the exam
8. For a three-hour class, how much time do you spend studying per week?
   A. 0–1 hour
   B. 2–3 hours
   C. 3–4 hours
   D. More than 4 hours
9. Do your parents pay your college expenses?
   A. All
   B. More than half
   C. Less than half
   D. None
10. How do you usually study?
   A. Alone
   B. With others
   C. Alone and with others
   D. I don't study
11. What percentage of your classes is of personal interest?
   A. Under 25%
   B. 25%–50%
   C. 50%–75%
   D. 75% or more
12. I study in a room where:
   A. The radio and TV are off and I am alone
   B. The radio and TV are usually off
   C. The radio or TV is usually on
13. How many times a week do you eat breakfast?
   A. Every day
   B. Three to four days
   C. One to two days
   D. Rarely
14. Which courses are you most likely to complete assignments from first?
   A. Courses you are *least* interested in
   B. Courses you are *most* interested in
   C. None of the above
15. When in class, I usually
   A. Take as many notes as possible
   B. Take some notes
   C. Take few notes
   D. Take no notes at all
16. When given an assignment, I usually begin it
   A. Immediately
   B. After a few days
   C. The day before it is due
   D. The day it is due
17. During an average weekday, how many hours do you spend watching television?
   A. 0–2 hours
   B. 3–5 hours
   C. 6–8 hours
   D. More than 8 hours
18. Why are you attending college?
   A. I want to attend
   B. My parents want me to attend
   C. I have a scholarship
   D. None of the above
19. When I have a difficult homework assignment
   A. I seek assistance
   B. I don't seek assistance
   C. I don't do it at all

(continued)

✦ TABLE 1.3 ✦ Continued

Scoring: Match up your answers with the scores below and compute your total score.

Answer	Score	Answer	Score	Answer	Score
1. A or B	0	7. A	0	13. A	2
C	1	B or C	1	B	0
D	2	D	2	C or D	1
2. A	2	8. A	0	14. A	2
B, C, or D	0	B	1	B or C	0
3. A	2	C	2	15. A	2
B	1	D	1	B	1
C or D	0	9. A, B, or C	0	C or D	0
4. A	2	D	2	16. A	2
B	1	10. A	2	B or C	1
C or D	0	B or C	1	D	0
5. A	2	D	0	17. A	2
B	1	11. A	0	B, C, or D	0
C or D	0	B or C	1	18. A	2
6. A	2	D	2	B, C, or D	0
B or C	1	12. A	2	19. A	2
D	0	B or C	0	B or C	0

Interpreting Your Score:

Nixon and Frost (1990) reported an average score of around 20 points. If you scored near this value, then your study habits and attitudes are probably about average. A score well above or below this average indicates study skills, habits, and attitudes that are likely above or below the average of that for most college students. If your score is low, you may wish to adopt some of the study suggestions contained in this chapter.

In the interpretation of your results, you should be aware that scores on tests such as this are only moderately correlated with college students' grade point averages. A low score on this test does not necessarily doom you to failure, and a high score, unfortunately, is not a guarantee of good grades. Predicting academic success with precision is very difficult as many college and university admissions officers can attest.

Reproduced with permission of authors and publisher from: Nixon, C.T., & Frost, A.G. The study habits and attitudes inventory and its implications for students' success. *Psychological Reports,* 1990, *66,* 1075–1085. © Psychological Reports 1990.

Group study, as opposed to studying alone, has been shown to result in *less* overall academic success (Tollefson, et al., 1979). Studying alone has also been associated with better grades (Schuman, Walsh, Olson, & Etheridge, 1985). Some of the findings might appear to most college students to be counterintuitive. As one example, students who spend either a small or a large amount of time studying earn poorer grades than students who spend an intermediate amount of time in the endeavor. This is likely due to the fact that students who earn poor grades do so either from a lack of motivation that results in spending little time studying or from an inability to learn the material that results in spending large amounts of time studying. Thus, the motivated student with good abilities spends an intermediate amount of time studying and receives better grades.

Studies show that college students tend to stay with whatever study methods they have been using previously, even when those methods have proven ineffective and have resulted in poor grades. However, several useful study techniques have been developed. One of the most effective and best known is a method called the **SQ3R method.** The abbreviation SQ3R stands for *survey, question, read, recite, and review.*

1. Survey. Before beginning to read the chapter, you should get an overview of what the chapter contains. You can do this by skimming through the pages and looking to see what general topics will be covered in the chapter. In particular, you should look at chapter titles and headings as well as any underlined or highlighted terms. This part of the SQ3R method takes only a few minutes but is an important component of the study method.
2. Question. As you skim the chapter and after you have finished, ask yourself questions about the material. For example, ask yourself to identify the main points of the chapter as well as its most important points. Look at the chapter title and subheadings and try to generate a question. These questions will serve to get you actively involved with the material, which, as we will see in a later chapter, is a very important tool for learning.
3. Read. Read the chapter carefully and, as you do so, see answers to the questions that you generated previously. Reread the sections, if necessary, until you can generate the answers to these questions. Underlining is helpful for many students because it identifies important points for later review. Some students overdo this technique by underlining or highlighting almost all of the text. This defeats the purpose of underlining and should be avoided. Also, avoid using texts that other students have highlighted or underlined. The previous user probably has marked different things than you will find important. If you must use a book that has already been marked up, use different color highlighting to distinguish your markings. Finally, write notes and/or questions to yourself in the margins of the book. These can be helpful later when you review the material. I have known students who refuse to make any marks in their textbooks, either because they want to keep them in pristine condition or because they intend to resell them to the bookstore. For most students, a textbook that has been well learned is one that is dog eared, ink smeared, coffee stained, and marked up.
4. Recite. Recitation involves putting the material that you have read *into your own words.* Do not repeat the words or phrases used by the textbook but rather formulate your own. Pretend that you are explaining the material to someone else. Did you ever wonder how professors seem to have such a fluid command of the material they teach? Part of the reason is that their lectures require them to recite the material repeatedly. Perhaps you have heard it said that if you really want to learn a topic, then you should teach it. You can emulate this process through recitation techniques and thereby further increase your active involvement in the material. Recitations can be either written, verbal, or both. When

you finish reading the chapter, see if you can summarize the material in your own words. Through the use of the recitation process, you will be practicing the same process that likely will be required on an essay test.

5. Review. Finally, go back and review the key points. Look at the parts of the text that you have underlined and the notes that you have taken during your reading. Review the chapter headings again, and review the answers to the questions that you generated earlier.

Although not formally part of the SQ3R method, I would add a fourth "R," namely, rest. If you have followed the above procedure carefully, you deserve a break. We will learn in a later chapter that learning is retained better if it is spread out over time as opposed to "cramming." Reward yourself with an activity that you like during your rest period.

As was noted earlier, most college students are reluctant to abandon their old study habits even when they have not been successful using them. If you have trouble preparing for exams, I hope you will try the SQ3R method. Many research studies have examined the effectiveness of this approach, and they are unanimous in showing how useful it is. Try it—it works! In addition, in later chapters of this text, we will be discussing many other techniques that you can use to accelerate learning and facilitate memory.

SUMMARY

- Although human behavior is very interesting to observe, using common sense is often of little help in understanding why behavior occurs.
- Many individuals hold misconceptions about behavior that are not supported by research findings.
- People often possess a hindsight bias in which the outcome of some event is deemed obvious after it becomes known.
- Post-hoc or after-the-fact explanations are offered for why such events occurred. Such biases and explanations impede the scientific study of psychology.
- An important issue in psychology revolves around the relative contributions of genetics and environmental factors as explanations for human behavior. The subfield of behavioral genetics examines the role of genetics on behavior. Research on twins has shown that many psychological disorders have a genetic component.
- Other diverse behaviors that have been shown to be genetically influenced include television-watching behavior, optimism, and religious devotion. Some have argued that the role of the environment through parenting has relatively little effect on children's subsequent psychological development and behavior. Others have argued that both genetics and the environment influence behavior by causing physiological changes in the brain. Most psychologists today believe that both genetics and environmental factors exert powerful influences on human behavior.
- In some circumstances, environmental factors can nullify genetic potentials.
- Another important issue in psychology involves the question of free will versus determinism. The belief that all behavior is controlled by a set of complex internal and external factors is called determinism. The alternative view of free will maintains that our behavior is not controlled by the environment, by past experiences, or by genetics. Most psychologists take an intermediate view and believe that behavior is affected by the combined influence of our current environment, past experiences, and genetics. The choices we make and the goals we set are influenced by these factors.
- Whether one believes in free will or determinism can have important implications for society.
- Another issue in psychology is whether the mind and the body are one and the same. Contemporary research in psychology has shown that there is a very strong link between the two.

- It is important to understand that research findings and conclusions about human behavior are greatly affected by cultural biases.
- Some people question whether it is a good idea to study how to control human behavior. The potential for both good and evil arises from such study. The field of psychology has uncovered many tools to help humankind and to help enhance our everyday lives. While the potential for misuse of these tools exists, the positive potential outweighs the negative aspects.
- Several factors have been shown to predict academic success, including study skills. The SQ3R study method has been shown to be a powerful way to improve study skills. In this method, a person initially surveys the material, generates questions about the material, reads the material carefully, recites the material in his or her own words, and then reviews the material, looking for key points.

KEY TERMS

behavioral genetics: involves the study of the role of heredity on human behavior.

determinism: an assumption of causality; the belief that everything we do is caused by something.

free will: the belief that human behavior is not controlled by the environment, by past experiences, or by genetics, and that humans are free to behave as they want.

hindsight bias: the tendency to believe the results were foreseeable, once the outcome of an event is given; aka, the "I-knew-it-all-along phenomenon."

humanistic psychologists: psychologists who emphasize the capacity of people to make conscious decisions about their own lives; adhere more to a freewill view.

Machiavellian: a term for individuals who are manipulative and obsessed with acquiring power.

nature–nurture issue: the controversy over the relative importance of genetics and environment on human behavior.

post-hoc explanation: explanation of the cause after an event has occurred.

soft determinism: a less extreme view of determinism; the belief that human behavior is affected by the combined influence of environment, past experiences, and genetics.

SQ3R method: A study technique that includes surveying the material, asking questions about the material, reading the material, reciting the material in your own words, and reviewing the key points.

synapses: gaps between brain cells; allow the cells to communicate among themselves.

synaptic plasticity: a process in which synapses in the brain are altered by experiences; alterations occur by creating new synapses or strengthening existing ones.

2

Sensation and Perception

At any given moment our body is being bombarded with millions of sensory stimuli of which we are not aware. Stop and think about how your left foot feels right now. When you suddenly shift your attention to your foot, you can become aware of those sensations. Perhaps your shoe is too small and you feel the pressure on your foot or your new socks feel particularly smooth against your skin. Sensations of which you were totally unaware a few moments ago are now being perceived in a vivid fashion.

Sensation versus Perception

Psychologists draw an important distinction between the terms *sensation* and *perception.* **Sensation** refers to the process of converting the physical stimuli that are striking our sense receptors into neural (i.e., electrical) impulses that our brain can understand. The conversion of physical stimuli into electrical impulses is called **transduction. Perception** is a more complicated process whereby our brain interprets the sensations and gives them meaning. Sensation *and* perception are both critical for us to make sense of our environment.

Imagine that you overhear two Turkish students having a conversation in the library. The amplitude of the conversation that strikes your ears is sufficient to allow sensation to occur. Assuming you do not understand Turkish, the sensation of the conversation would have no meaning. You have sensation without perception. If, however, the Turkish students were so far away that you could not hear their conversation, then you would not have sensation or perception. Thus, you can have sensation without perception but cannot have perception without sensation.

It is the mind which creates the world about us, and even though we stand side by side in the same meadow, my eyes will never see what is beheld by yours, my heart will never stir to the emotions with which yours is touched.

GEORGE GISSING
The Private Papers of Henry Ryecroft

The Five Senses

We perceive our external environment through five senses: vision, hearing, smell, taste, and touch. Through these five senses we interpret the multitude of sensory images that assail our sense receptors at any given time. Often we use information from a combination of senses to interpret the meaning of a stimulus. For instance, the sense of taste often depends on information from the sense of smell.

Two Other Senses

Kinesthetic Sense

We use our senses to communicate with both the external world and the internal environment of our bodies. We constantly receive sensory messages from our internal sense receptors that give us information from our muscles, tendons, and joints. Information from these receptors is known as **kinesthesis.** It tells us the position of our limbs as we move and allows us to perform simple movements, such as standing and walking. Imagine trying to walk in total darkness without any information about the location of your legs and feet. The temporary loss of kinesthetic information explains why you have so much difficulty walking when your foot "falls asleep."

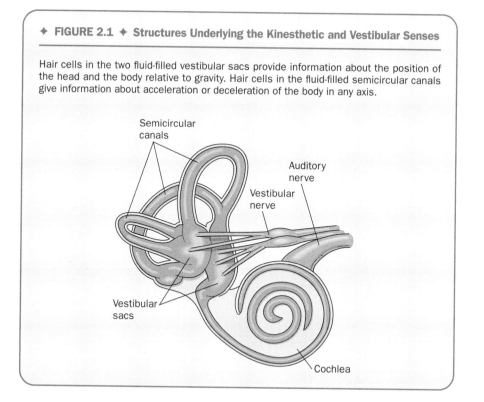

✦ **FIGURE 2.1** ✦ **Structures Underlying the Kinesthetic and Vestibular Senses**

Hair cells in the two fluid-filled vestibular sacs provide information about the position of the head and the body relative to gravity. Hair cells in the fluid-filled semicircular canals give information about acceleration or deceleration of the body in any axis.

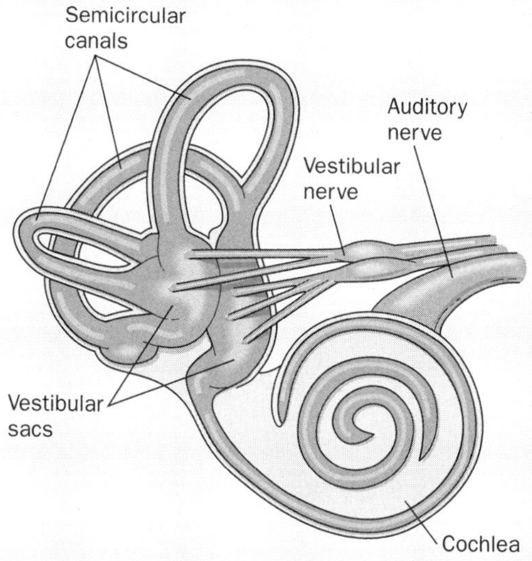

Vestibular Sense

The **vestibular sense** provides us with information about our body position, movement, and acceleration, all critical factors for maintaining a sense of balance. Two fluid-filled **vestibular sacs** in our inner ear provide this information (see Figure 2.1). As our body or head moves, hair cells inside these sacs bend in proportion to the rate of movement. The bending of these hair cells sends electrical signals to the brain. In addition, three **semicircular canals,** also located in the inner ear, provide information about whether the body or head is accelerating. Whenever we move or rotate our head, the fluid in these canals moves and bends hair cells that also send electrical signals to the brain. Because the semicircular canals are located on three different axes, they can respond to movement in any direction. The vestibular system responds to *changes in motion,* not constant motion. For example, we receive feedback when we are accelerating in our car but not when we are moving at a constant speed.

Motion sickness occurs when we receive discrepant information from the vestibular sense and vision. If you are in an enclosed space, such as an airplane or a boat cabin, when a rocking motion begins, only the vestibular sense detects the motion. The visual system does not because all the surrounding visual cues are rocking right along with your body. The result of this discrepant information is a feeling of nausea. If you focus your view on something stationary, such as the horizon or a

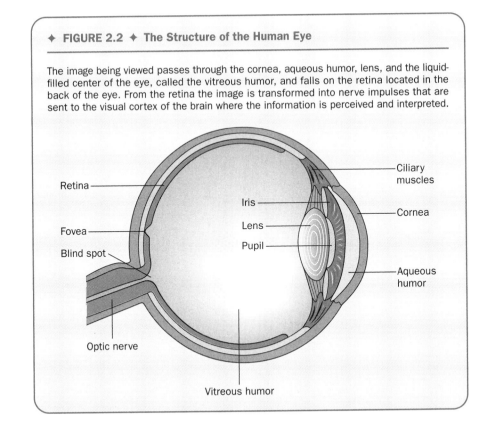

✦ FIGURE 2.2 ✦ The Structure of the Human Eye

The image being viewed passes through the cornea, aqueous humor, lens, and the liquid-filled center of the eye, called the vitreous humor, and falls on the retina located in the back of the eye. From the retina the image is transformed into nerve impulses that are sent to the visual cortex of the brain where the information is perceived and interpreted.

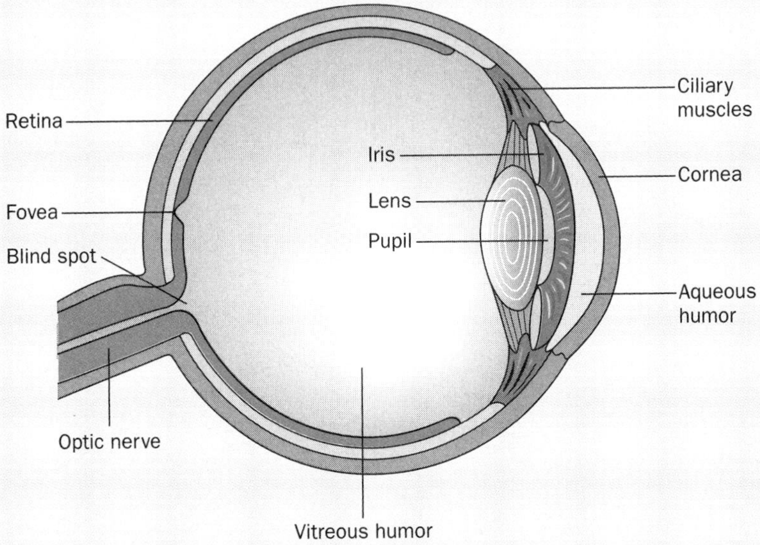

large object on land, your visual system will recognize that your body is rocking, and the information sent to the brain by your visual and vestibular systems will agree. This agreement helps avoid motion sickness.

I will give a brief overview of how each of these sensory systems works and discuss how our knowledge of these systems applies to our daily lives.

How Our Sense Organs Work

Vision

Basic Structures of the Eye

> The eye of a human being is a microscope, which makes the world seem bigger than it really is.
>
> **KAHLIL GIBRAN**
> *A Handful of Sand on the Shore*

Because most people consider vision to be the most important sense, we will consider it first. The eyeball works in ways similar to a camera. Just as a lens focuses an inverted image on the film in the back of a camera, the eye is designed to focus an inverted image on the **retina** located on the back of the eye (see Figure 2.2). The image first passes through the **cornea** that partially focuses and bends the light rays. Behind the cornea lies the **iris** or colored part of your eye. Muscles in the iris expand or contract to make the opening in the center either larger or smaller. This opening is called the **pupil.** The primary function of the iris and pupil is to let in more or less light, depending upon how dark the viewing environment is. Behind the pupil lies the **lens,** a clear membrane with tiny muscles attached. These muscles pull on the lens and change its shape, making it more or less convex or bulging. This changing of the lens shape is called **accommodation** and allows the lens to focus the inverted image on the retina that lies on the back surface of the eyeball. Thus, the visual image is projected onto the back of your eye very much like a movie projector casts an image on a movie screen. Movie projectors, like the human eye, also have lenses that adjust to sharpen the picture's focus on the screen.

Visual Receptors

Two kinds of receptors on the retina allow for the transduction of the light energy of the image into electrical nerve impulses that the brain can interpret. These two receptors, called **rods** and **cones,** contain photosensitive chemicals that undergo complex chemical changes when light strikes them. During these chemical changes, a tiny electrical impulse is transmitted through the **optic nerve** to the visual cortex area of the brain.

Each eye contains about 6 million cones located mainly in the center of the retina. By contrast, approximately 120 million rods lie primarily on the periphery of each retina. Rods and cones, which contain different chemicals, respond differentially to light. The rods are much more sensitive to light but are not sensitive to color. When you enter a darkened room, your eyes automatically compensate for the reduced illumination. This occurs because the pupil expands or dilates to allow more light to the periphery of the retina. In addition, the sensitivity of the cones is decreased while the rods slowly become more sensitive. While pupil dilation occurs almost instantaneously, the shift in sensitivity from cones to rods gradually occurs over a period of about 20 to 30 minutes. This process of switching sensitivity from high illumination levels to low illumination levels is called **dark adaptation.** You probably have experienced walking into a darkened movie theater after being outside on a bright sunny day. For the first few minutes, you can see practically nothing as the shift from cones to rods occurs. After about 20 minutes you find that you can see amazingly well in the darkened room. When dark adaptation occurs completely, your eye becomes 10,000 times more sensitive to light than when you first entered the darkened room. When you walk back into bright sunlight, you may find it momentarily painful until your pupils have a chance to reduce the amount of light entering your eyes. If you have ever had an eye exam where the doctor used drops to dilate your pupils, you probably experienced this sensitivity to light and needed sunglasses to reduce the amount of light entering your eye until your pupil regained its normal function.

Only cones allow you to see color. They are concentrated in the center of the retina where the image we are viewing is usually focused. The cones are connected to the optic nerve in such a way that allows the perception of finer detail. Therefore, when you want to see something in great detail, use a high level of illumination and center the visual image in the middle of the retina. However, other images in the periphery that fall on the rods will appear blurred. You can demonstrate this to yourself by concentrating on a word in this text and then noticing how focused adjacent words are.

The nerves from the rods and cones connect to other cells that help process the visual information. They eventually converge and exit through a hole in the retina. The resulting bundle of nerve fibers makes up the optic nerve that carries the neural

✦ FIGURE 2.3 ✦

To demonstrate your blind spot, close your left eye and look at the circular dot. Slowly move the page closer to your face. When the page gets about 9 inches from your face, the cross will disappear.

impulses to the brain. The optic nerve exits through the retina at the **blind spot** where there are no visual receptors and images are not sensed. You can experience your own blind spot by following the instructions in Figure 2.3.

Even with a blind spot, you do not have a corresponding blind area in your field of vision because the "missing" information is present on the retina of your other eye where the blind spot is in a different location. If you close one eye, a blind area still does not occur in your field of vision because your eye is constantly making small, rapid movements called **saccades.** These throw the image on a swath of receptors that prevent the image from falling exclusively on the part of the retina with the missing receptors.

Visual Disorders

Our eyes are remarkable organs, but they are not infallible. Some people are **farsighted;** that is, they can clearly see objects that are far away but those things that are close up are blurry. Individuals who are **nearsighted** can see only close objects with clarity. These conditions are most frequently the result of an irregular eye shape: The distance between lens and retina is too large or too small for the lens to focus the image on the retina. Wearing glasses or contact lenses often compensates for these problems. Nearsighted individuals can benefit from a surgical procedure called refractive eye surgery, where a doctor uses a computer guided laser to alter the shape of the cornea. Nearsightedness is more common than farsightedness.

Aging also affects our ability to see clearly. As we age, the muscles that pull on the lenses weaken and the elasticity of the lens itself decreases. People with perfect vision when they are younger almost always find that they need to wear reading glasses for magnification by the time they reach age 50. Another condition common in aging is **cataracts,** a disorder in which the lens becomes cloudy and occludes fine details. People with severe cataracts can have the lens replaced with a contact lens in a surgical procedure that is commonly done in outpatient clinics in less than an hour.

APPLICATIONS

Knowledge about vision can be frequently used in our everyday lives. For example, the muscles in your eyes need to rest, just as the rest of the muscles in your body do. If you spend a lot of time doing detail work or reading small print, you should rest these muscles by occasionally looking away from your work and looking at objects that are at varying distances from you. Focusing on objects that are close to you requires that you put tension on the small muscles in your eyes that control the shape of the lens. Give these muscles an occasional break by looking away.

Seeing in the Dark

We can see better under dim-light conditions when the image is projected on to our peripheral vision where the rods are located. While training for a pilot's license, I was taught to view objects by looking to the side of whatever I was trying to see when flying at night. You can demonstrate to yourself how peripheral vision is better than central vision for seeing dim lights. Watch a television set for about 10 minutes in a darkened room. Turn off the set. The glow of the screen will fade and eventually you will not be able to see the screen at all when looking directly at it. However, if you direct your gaze a short distance from the screen in any direction you will see that the screen still appears quite bright (Worchel & Shebilske, 1995). This information can be helpful when you are driving a car at night. Signs are most easily read when looking slightly away from the sign itself so that the image falls in the periphery of your retina. You can also detect movement more easily in the periphery of your vision (seeing out of the corner of your eye), a helpful fact when driving your car, engaging in sports, or walking in a bad part of town.

Driving at night often exposes us to changing levels of light. When first learning to drive, you were probably taught not to look into the headlights of oncoming cars at night. It takes the pupils in your eyes about 20 seconds to recover from the glare, and your vision is seriously impaired during that time. A lot of bad things can happen in 20 seconds on a crowded highway, particularly if you have consumed alcohol, which significantly increases the recovery period.

A deficiency of vitamin A can cause you to have poorer night vision. Remember when your mother told you to eat your carrots, so that you could see better? She was right—carrots contain vitamin A, which helps produce a chemical that is important for the rods in your eye to function properly. Taking massive doses of vitamin A, however, will not help if you already have normal levels of the vitamin in your system.

Motion Detection

The ability to detect movement is one of the most primitive, yet critical, capabilities of our visual system. It is vitally important to know whether we are moving relative to a stationary object, an object is moving through our field of vision, or some combination of the two is occurring.

Size matters in motion detection. Size influences our judgment of how fast things are moving. In general, large objects are seen as moving more slowly than small objects. A large animal that is moving at the same speed as a small animal will be judged to be moving more slowly, as will a train compared to a small car.

An object that falls on the periphery of your retina, where the rods are located, will appear to move more slowly than an object that falls in the center, where your cones are located. In most situations, we are receiving information about the speed of motion from both of these sources. However, under levels of low illumination the information is coming primarily from the periphery, which will cause us to underestimate the speed of an object.

Driving a car even a short distance requires thousands of judgments regarding how fast objects are moving. Faulty judgments about the speed that an object is moving are the cause of many automobile accidents. Driving at night is particularly hazardous as the reduced level of light will cause us to rely on receptors in the periphery of the retina and, as we have discussed, will cause us to underestimate the speed we are driving. Speed kills, at least in part because at night it deludes us into believing we are moving slower than we actually are. Driving at night or in foggy or hazy conditions requires more frequent monitoring of the speedometer to counteract this tendency.

Have you ever misjudged the speed of a large oncoming truck when merging onto a freeway? We learned that large objects are incorrectly perceived as moving more slowly than small objects. We need to be particularly aware of this phenomenon when driving. Many car–train accidents occur when drivers misjudge the speed of a train as it approaches a crossing. We are deluded into believing that the train is moving slowly, and thus overestimate the amount of time we have to cross in front of it. It is a good idea to remind yourself, when driving, that size alone is no determinant of how fast an object is moving. This simple reminder could very well end up saving your life.

Hearing

Most people consider the hearing sense to be second in importance to vision. In actuality, a loss of hearing can be more debilitating than a loss of vision. Blind people can still communicate effectively with others through the sense of hearing. Deaf individuals, on the other hand, are much more likely to feel a sense of social isolation. As older people begin to lose their hearing and develop difficulties in communication, they are more likely to withdraw and to become suspicious of others. We often underestimate the critical role that hearing plays in our everyday lives and neglect this sense in ways that may cause permanent damage.

Physical Basis of Sound

All sound consists of changes in air pressure brought about by the disturbance of air molecules. Without air molecules there would be no sound despite the many loud explosions that you have witnessed in the vacuum of outer space in *Star Trek* and other science fiction movies. When an object moves through the air, it produces a disruption in the normal movement of the air molecules. If a physical object were to suddenly move toward you, it would cause the molecules in front of it to pile up or be compressed. This, in turn, would cause high air pressure to develop in front of the object. If the object now were suddenly to move away from you, it would leave a partial vacuum or low air pressure area in its wake. An object that is vibrating rapidly back and forth, such as a guitar string, creates a series of alternating high and low air pressure waves. These pressure waves travel through the air much as a wave is transmitted through water. Sound waves travel through air at a speed of 760 miles per hour, the speed of sound. When the traveling wave of high pressure strikes the eardrum, it causes the flexible membrane to bend inward. Conversely, when the wave of low pressure strikes the eardrum, the membrane flexes outward. Thus, the eardrum is made to vibrate at the same frequency as the vibrating physical object that produced the alterations in air pressure.

Characteristics of Sound

Sound waves are defined by the number of cycles in high and low air pressure that occur in a given time span. The number of cycles or vibrations that occur per second is called **hertz (Hz).** The human ear can perceive a range of vibrations between approximately 30 Hz and 20,000 Hz. The frequency of Hz determines the **pitch** of the sound that we hear. High-pitched sounds have higher frequencies whereas we perceive lower frequencies as low-pitched sounds.

The loudness of a sound depends on the amplitude of the air pressure waves. If you were to lightly strum the guitar string, only small changes between the high and low pressure waves would be created. Sound amplitude is measured in **decibels (dB).** Under ideal conditions, humans are able to hear a sound near 0 decibels. At a decibel level of about 125 dB, sound creates pain and hearing damage may occur. Normal conversational speech occurs in the range of 35 to 60 decibels. Figure 2.4 illustrates the decibel level associated with commonly heard sounds.

In addition to pitch and loudness, sounds also have a quality or **timbre.** Two people singing the exact same musical note at the same amplitude will create two very different sounds. Timbre is created when a number of waves of differing frequency and amplitude are mixed together. We can break down any sound into all of its component frequencies in order to examine what goes into the timbre of a sound. Police use this method to create "voice prints" from telephone voice recordings. Most police and fire stations and 911 call centers routinely record all incoming calls, a fact that many people do not consider when calling in a false alarm, making a crank call, or filing a false report. You should remember that your voice can identify you just as accurately as your fingerprints.

Basic Structures of the Ear

Figure 2.5 illustrates the major structures of the human ear. Sounds enter the outer ear and set the **eardrum** vibrating in the same fashion as the sound itself. When the eardrum begins vibrating, the vibration is transmitted through and amplified by the three tiny bones connected in the middle ear called **ossicles.** These are the smallest bones in the human body that together approximate the size of a grain of rice. The first bone touches the eardrum and the last one rests against the window of a fluid-filled, coiled, inch-long tube called the **cochlea.** The cochlea has a flexible membrane called the **basilar membrane** that runs down its length. As the ossicle vibrates against the window of the cochlea, it generates waves in the fluid-filled tube that cause the basilar membrane to flex. Different pitch sounds cause the basilar membrane to flex in different locations. Low-pitch sounds stimulate the basilar membrane at its wider end while high-pitch sounds stimulate it at its smaller end. The brain interprets the pitch of a sound by monitoring where on the basilar membrane the stimulation occurs.

> Tones that sound, and roar and storm about me until I have set them down in notes.
>
> **LUDWIG VAN BEETHOVEN**

The basilar membrane contains **hair cells** that are set in motion by the flexing of the basilar membrane. As the hair cells move, they generate neural impulses that are eventually collected and transmitted to the brain via the **auditory nerve.**

Sound Localization

If you are walking along a busy street and a friend unexpectedly calls your name, you automatically turn your head in the direction from which the sound came.

✦ FIGURE 2.4 ✦ Decibel Levels of Everyday Sounds

At about 130 dB the sensation of sound becomes painful and can damage the ear. Dangerous time exposures are shown for each sound intensity level.

Decibel Level	Examples	Time Exposure Until Hearing Damage
180	Nearby rocket launch	
170		
160	Shotgun blast	Hearing loss certain
150	Jet plane taking off	
140	Emergency siren nearby Stereo headset—high volume	All exposures dangerous
130	Pain threshold	Immediate danger
120	Loud rock concert, thunder	
110	Walkman style stereo headphones at full volume	
100	Subway, lawnmower	
90	Bus, motorcycle, snowmobile Food blender	Less than 8 hours
80	Noisy automobile, heavy traffic	More than 8 hours
70	Typical automobile	
60	Normal conversation	
50	Business office	
40	Rainfall	
30	Quiet room Whisper	
20		
10		
0	Quietest sound that can be heard	Safe exposure

On the other hand, while driving home you discover a squeaking noise inside your car but are unable to determine its origin. How does our auditory system localize the source of a sound, and what can we do to improve that ability?

It appears that we are born with an ability to localize sound since even newborn babies are able to do so (Castillo & Butterworth, 1981). We use two aspects of sound

✦ FIGURE 2.5 ✦ The Major Parts of the Human Ear

The coiled cochlea is enlarged to show details.

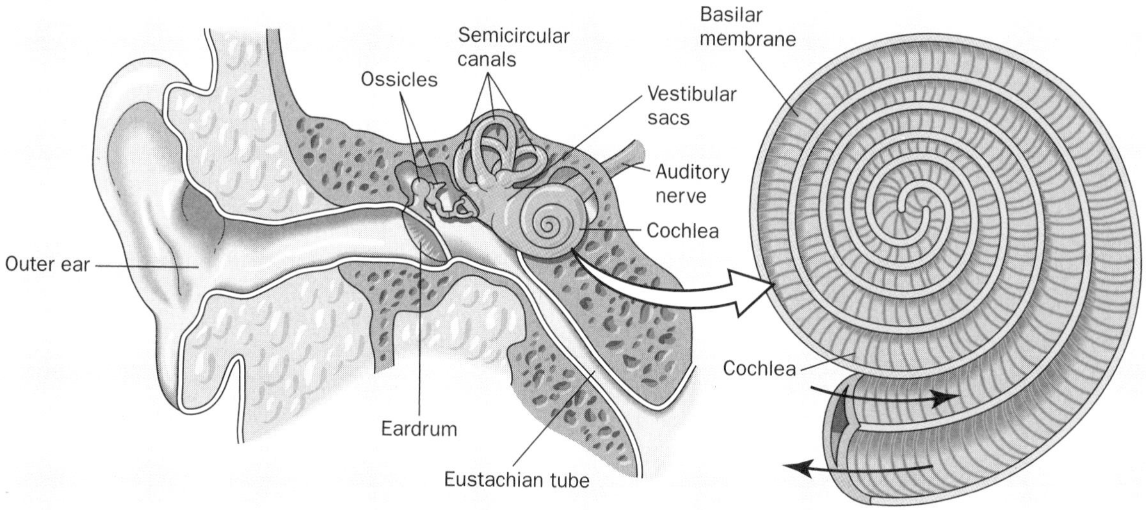

to localize direction: **relative loudness** and **arrival time.** Relative loudness is the most effective way to localize sound. When a sound occurs off to our right, the sound reaching our right ear will be slightly louder than the sound reaching our left ear. Our brain monitors this difference and calculates the direction of the sound source. Relative loudness is particularly effective when locating the source of high-pitched sounds. Arrival time, the second method, works best for lower pitched sounds. A sound occurring off to our right is detected by our right ear slightly before it arrives at our left ear. Since sound travels through air at 1,100 feet per second, you can see that the arrival differential between your two ears would be extremely small. Scientists have found that we can reliably detect the source of a sound when the time of arrival is only 5 millionths of a second different at our two ears. A sound source directly in front, back, or on top of you will result in sounds that reach both ears at the same time and with identical amplitude. As you might expect, sounds coming from these sources are the most difficult to localize.

APPLICATIONS: Localizing Sounds

The ability to locate quickly and accurately the source of a sound can be of life-saving importance, especially when driving a car or when walking or biking along a busy highway. Needless to say, these activities are best engaged in without the benefit of Walkman-style stereo headphones blasting your favorite music. Recently, a student at our university was killed instantly while wearing such headphones when struck by a car at a campus intersection.

The easiest sounds to localize are those that produce brief clicks. It appears that the brain has an easier time comparing the input from the two ears when the sound is a brief burst of noise as compared to a steady sound. When driving, a series of short, sharp horn blasts better signals the other driver of your location when compared to "laying on" the horn. If you are lost in the woods and people are looking for you, loudly striking two sticks or rocks together is preferable to yelling a long drawn out "Heeeeelp!!!" although a combination of the two would probably be more helpful, as well as cathartic. The old strategy of firing a gun to reveal your location would also qualify. Remember that low-pitch tones travel greater distances than high-pitch tones, which explains why fog horns sound as they do.

Have you ever wondered why people cock their heads slightly when they are trying to localize a sound? We learned earlier that a sound striking both ears at the same time is difficult to localize. By cocking your head you are slightly altering the position of your ears to obtain better arrival time and relative loudness discrepancies. Notice that dogs also do this when trying to identify unknown sounds. Localizing a sound inside an enclosed space in a noisy environment, such as a car, can be a devilishly tricky matter. That squeak you are looking for is probably ricocheting off of several hard surfaces and giving you conflicting messages about its origin. Auto mechanics and frustrated car owners often use a device similar to a stethoscope to help isolate the sound source.

Finally, a sound's loudness is a good signal of an object's distance. In general, the louder the sound the closer the source. Moving sounds also provide an additional source of information. If a sound grows louder, you interpret it as coming closer to you. You may have noticed that as a train or car approaches you the sounds become increasingly high pitched. After the object passes you the sound drops sharply to a lower pitch. This phenomenon, called the **Doppler shift,** occurs because the sound waves bunch up and have a higher frequency as the object approaches and then spread out and have a lower frequency as the object speeds away. This explains why you will assume that, of two competing sounds, the sound with the higher pitch is closer to you. Military personnel who are on the receiving end of an artillery barrage quickly learn to use all these cues to determine the location and proximity of incoming shells and to discriminate between incoming and outgoing fire.

Hearing Loss

Most of us live in noisy environments. Incessant city noises, noise in our workplace, and even the noises that we are exposed to during leisure activities—all have the potential to injure our hearing. There are two major kinds of deafness: **conduction deafness** and **nerve deafness.** Conduction deafness occurs when there is blockage of the outer ear canal by earwax or some foreign object. It is also caused by damage to either the eardrum or the small bones (ossicles) in the middle ear. Several diseases, as well as injuries, can cause conduction deafness. It can, however, be helped with the use of a hearing aid, which makes sounds both louder and clearer. In recent years surgical procedures have been developed to replace the ossicles with synthetic devices. Torn or perforated eardrums can often be repaired with little permanent damage to hearing.

Hearing loss from nerve deafness is more difficult to treat. In this case, deafness results from damage either to the auditory nerve or to the hair cells on the basilar membrane. As with conduction deafness, various diseases can be the culprits. Hearing aids cannot help because auditory messages are actually blocked from reaching the brain. Recently, electronic cochlear implants have been developed that bypass the hair cells and stimulate the auditory nerves directly. Cochlear implants do not transmit sounds that approach the quality experienced with normal cochlea function. For some people, implants allow them to hear a telephone conversation. In others, implants might enhance their ability to distinguish words when lip reading. Most importantly, though, cochlear implants allow individuals to hear warning signals, such as doorbells, telephones, and alarms.

APPLICATIONS: Avoiding Hearing Loss

Figure 2.4 illustrates the amount of potential hearing damage associated with prolonged exposure to a variety of sounds. Prolonged exposure to sounds greater than 80 to 85 decibels can damage the hair cells on the basilar membrane. Rock concerts often generate noises at 120 dB or higher. College students who regularly attend loud concerts suffer greater hearing loss when compared to those students who do not (Hanson & Fearn, 1975). Many musicians in rock bands have suffered permanent damage to their hearing, and audiences at such concerts share similar risks. A sound of 130 dB, not unheard of at a rock concert, poses an immediate risk to hearing. You should never sit in front of the speakers at concerts where the music is highly amplified. Any vigorous activity such as dancing or other exercise increases the risk because blood flow is diverted from the inner ear during such activities. Walkman-type stereos with headphones can present sounds at 115 dB or more and produce hearing damage if exposure occurs over prolonged periods. If you can hear the sounds from the headphones of people wearing such a device, there is a very good chance that their hearing is being damaged. A similar danger exists with the powerful stereos that are now in fashion in some cars. Many municipalities have laws penalizing users if the music from such cars can be heard at a given distance. As with headphone devices, if you can hear the stereo in an adjacent car, it is likely that the user's hearing is being damaged. While the sound may be merely annoying to you, it is gradually destroying the hearing of the listener.

Have you ever experienced a ringing sound in your ears following a very loud noise, particularly a noise such as a blast from a gun or an explosion? This ringing sensation, known as **tinnitus,** indicates that hair cells have suffered damage. In addition to a ringing sound, the noise may be a buzzing, roaring, whistling, or hissing in the ears. Hair cells do not have the ability to repair themselves and, once damaged, are lost forever. People who are regularly exposed to sharp noises, such as hunters, should always wear ear protection. As a general rule, anytime that you are exposed to a noise that is painful or causes a ringing sensation, you should take immediate steps to avoid damage to your hearing.

Common sources of dangerous levels of noise in the environment include woodworking equipment, chain saws, gasoline engines, heavy machinery, and airplanes. People who engage in activities that can damage their hearing are often unaware of the damage being done because the onset of hearing loss from prolonged noise exposure usually occurs very slowly. Noise-induced hearing loss is usually, but not always, helped by the use of a hearing aid.

As with vision, normal deterioration in hearing occurs with age with the loss beginning after age 20. It affects the highest sound pitches first and gradually affects the lower pitches as well. Generally, men are affected more than women. There is no treatment to prevent or reverse age-associated hearing loss although hearing aids are usually beneficial.

How Noise Affects Behavior

Not only can loud noises affect our hearing but our behavior as well. Constant exposure to noise can be very stressful. People who are continuously exposed to a high level of noise, such as in factories or near airplanes or highway traffic, suffer more from anxiety, high blood pressure, and feelings of helplessness. Studies have shown that noise is most stressful when it is either unanticipated or uncontrollable (Glass & Singer, 1972). This is precisely why it is so much more stressful to hear your neighbor's stereo blasting than it is your own or to tolerate your children's "horseplay," which presumably you are able to control. It is also why the sudden, repeated loud bursts of laughter from the adjoining table in a restaurant can be so annoying. Stimuli that we can anticipate and control are always less stressful.

Sometimes it seems impossible to escape the cacophony of noises that greet us at every turn. Many of these noises are beyond our control. "Piped-in" music or blaring televisions are omnipresent in our society—We are exposed to them in elevators, inside (and even outside) restaurants, in hospital waiting rooms and department stores, and even when kept "on hold" while using the telephone. In some cities certain styles of music, such as Frank Sinatra and Barry Manilow, are played loudly to prevent teenagers from loitering around specific areas.

APPLICATIONS: Controlling Noise in Your Environment

In your search for some peace and quiet, you have three choices: escape the source of the sound (often impossible), block the sound with earplugs, or mask the sound. **Masking** refers to the use of one kind of sound to block another. Perhaps you have played music to block out the sound of street traffic while you study. One of the most effective masking noises is **white noise.** White noise consists of a broad spectrum of sound frequencies or pitches that together sound like the noise of a waterfall or a running fan. You may have noticed how difficult it is to understand someone's speech while an air conditioner fan is running. You can still hear the person speaking, but it is difficult to make out what is being said. Several companies market electronic devices to mask sounds, often sold as "sound conditioners." They all produce either white noise or some close derivative of it, such as the sound of rain or a waterfall, to mask sounds. Many people find these devices particularly helpful for sleeping in a noisy environment and for studying. More recently an electronic device has been invented that cancels out noise. Unfortunately, it only works for repetitive sounds such as the noise from a lawnmower or the drone of a jet engine.

TASTE

Basic Sensations

We are able to taste four basic sensations—sweet, sour, salty, and bitter. Any other taste sensation represents some combination of these four. Sensitivity to the four sensations varies with bitter being most sensitive, followed in order by sour, salty, and sweet. Most poisonous foods are bitter, which probably explains why we have evolved a greater sensitivity to that particular taste. Similarly, food that has undergone bacterial decomposition usually tastes sour, which accounts for our sensitivity to this sensation.

The discovery of a new dish does more for human happiness than the discovery of a new star.

ANTHELME BRILLAT-SAVARIN
The Physiology of Taste

Taste and Aging

The aging process affects taste, as it does both vision and hearing. Taste buds only live a few days and then are replaced. This comes in handy when you burn your mouth with a very hot substance and kill off a few thousand receptors. As you become older some of these taste buds are not replaced, resulting in a diminished sense of taste. Heavy smoking or alcohol consumption accelerates these aging effects. You may have noticed that older people use more salt and spices on their food to enhance taste and compensate for these aging effects. Young children can taste substances much more intensely and, therefore, often avoid strong tastes that appeal to older people, such as the taste of liver. For this very reason, most commercially prepared baby foods have a very bland taste. Children's enhanced taste sensitivity also explains why adults often label them "picky eaters."

APPLICATIONS: Factors Affecting Taste

Eating is a big source of pleasure in our lives. By better understanding how the taste sense works we can enhance our enjoyment of foods.

Smell and Taste

Earlier in this chapter I mentioned the important role that smell plays in taste. **Flavor** is different from taste because it depends on both odor and taste. You have probably noticed that when you have a bad head cold everything you eat tastes like cardboard. If your eyes are closed, the taste of many common food substances cannot be identified when the sense of smell is absent. Under these circumstances, fewer than 5% of people could identify tastes of coffee, cherry, molasses, garlic, apricot, pineapple, root beer, chocolate, cranberry juice, or dill pickle juice (Mozel, Smith, Smith, Sullivan, & Swender, 1969). Try eating something with your eyes shut and your nostrils tightly pinched. You will find that all foods taste blander under these circumstances. Young children often employ this tactic when their parents insist they eat something they do not like. Great chefs greatly appreciate the importance of smell when preparing dishes and often rely heavily on this sense in the course of preparing a meal. Some researchers even maintain that smell is more important than taste in identifying and differentiating among foods.

Temperature and Taste

You may have noticed that the temperature of foods can greatly affect how they taste. When the taste receptors are cooled, they become much less sensitive to the taste of sweet substances. Temperature has only a slight effect on bitter substances and does not affect the tastes of sour or salty. If you like the sweet taste of soda pop, drinking it warm will enhance the taste. And how about the warm beer that the English enjoy? The bitter taste is only slightly enhanced by the warmer temperatures, perhaps accounting for the failure of that custom to catch on in America.

Taste Preferences

Why do individuals have such strong taste preferences? We know that taste preferences change with age and most people have less preference for sweet tastes as they get older. These changes are due, in part, to physical changes in the taste receptors as well as learned preferences. Often people have a negative reaction to their first taste of a substance but eventually "acquire" a taste for it. Few people enjoy their first taste experiences with coffee, beer, or cigarettes, but later in life many feel they cannot function without them. Many parents struggle with children who they perceive to be finicky eaters. Most children develop an aversion to new foods around the age of two. Moreover, getting children to taste a new food only once will not change their inclination to eat it again. Instead, children who are encouraged to eat a new food about 10 times, even if in very small quantities, are more likely to acquire a preference for it (Birch & Marlin, 1982; Birch, 1990).

You have to ask children and birds how cherries and strawberries taste.

JOHANN WOLFGANG VON GOETHE

SMELL

The sense of smell is known as the **olfactory sense.** Many people would rank the sense of smell as among the least important of our senses. At those times when we are faced with a foul odor, we may actually wish that this sense did not exist at all. Nevertheless, our sense of smell often warns us of danger and, even more frequently, adds significantly to the pleasure in our lives.

It has been observed that one's nose is never so happy as when it is thrust into the affairs of another, from which some physiologists have drawn the inference that the nose is devoid of the sense of smell.

AMBROSE (GWINNETT) BIERCE
The Devil's Dictionary

Smell Receptors

The sense of smell in humans is not well understood. Smells occur when gaseous molecules in the air dissolve in the mucous lining high in the nasal passages of the nose. Scientists disagree about exactly how these molecules activate the smell receptors in the nose. The most dominant theory today asserts that receptors in the nose are configured to match the physical shapes of the molecules suspended in the air. This theory is often referred to as **lock and key** because the physical structure of the air molecules must match a compatible opening in the nasal receptors. When the "key" of an air molecule containing an odor is inserted into the correctly fitting "lock" receptacle of the nose, an electrical impulse is generated. These impulses are sent directly to the **olfactory bulb** located below and toward the front of the brain and directly above the upper nasal passages. Each nostril contains about 30 million **olfactory receptor cells** that give us the remarkably good ability to detect smells. In fact, we can detect a single drop of perfume in an empty three-room apartment (Galanter, 1962). The reason we sniff the air when identifying a smell is to increase the air circulation over our smell receptors.

Smell Sensitivity

Some individuals believe that the sense of smell is poorly developed in humans, particularly when compared to dogs and other mammals. The fact is that dogs, when compared to humans, have smell receptors with the same level of sensitivity for detecting odors but also have 100 times *more* olfactory receptors. Another advantage for dogs and most other mammals is that their noses are close to the ground where odors are concentrated. Smells are mainly absent in the rarefied air 5 feet above the ground where most human noses are located.

As with the other senses, we rapidly detect a new odor but quickly adapt to it after only a few minutes. This is because the olfactory receptors in our nose fatigue very quickly and quit signaling the brain. We also keep our sense of smell sharp by breathing through one nostril more easily than the other. To keep the smell receptors working in top form, your nose alternates the nostril that is processing most of the air and changes the "open" nostril every few hours. During a brief transition between nostrils the air flows equally well into both.

Loss of Smell

Just as some people cannot hear certain sounds or see certain colors, some individuals cannot smell certain odors. This condition, called **anosmia,** supports the idea that there are certain receptors for certain odors. In fact, 1.2% of the population suffers from permanent anosmia and cannot smell anything (Gilbert & Wysocki, 1987). These people suffer many ramifications of this disorder, including an inability to cook, loss of interest in food, depression, loss of interest in sex, as well as life-threatening risks from their inability to smell smoke or natural gas. Some individuals suffering from anosmia have even committed suicide (Douek, 1988).

APPLICATIONS

Odors, Memory, and Feelings

Odors have a powerful ability to evoke long distant memories and feelings. Even when we are unable to recognize what an odor is, we are often able to recognize episodes that were associated with it. When I was very young, my elderly aunt was living in our home. She used to save the household cooking grease and convert it to soap by boiling it with lye. This produced a very distinctive and pungent odor that I did not have the opportunity to experience again for over 4 decades. Recently, while visiting a museum where they were demonstrating the art of making soap, I immediately identified the once familiar smell and a flood of pleasant memories came over me. I distinctly remembered the old metal pot and large wooden spoon my aunt used and the warm feelings I had when she would allow me to help her in the

What is the most precious, the most exciting smell waiting for you in the house when you return to it after a dozen years or so? The smell of roses, you think? No, mouldering books.

ANDREI SINYAVSKY

kitchen. Many of you have probably had similar experiences with odors that you have not encountered in years.

For all sense modalities except smell, sensory information is first sent to a central area of the brain, called the thalamus, where it is then relayed to specialized areas of the cerebral cortex. For the olfactory sense, information is sent directly to an area of the brain called the limbic system that is involved in emotion, motivation, and memory. For this reason smells have their unique ability to recall memories and feelings. Perhaps you can think of ways that you could put this knowledge to use. Wearing a distinctive smelling perfume or cologne around special individuals in your life can stimulate vivid memories and feelings associated with you whenever they encounter the smell, even if you are absent. Of course, a distinctive and unpleasant body odor could work in a similar fashion although with less desirable effects. One study found that college students who completed a word memorization task while smelling the aroma of chocolate remembered the words better the next day when the smell of chocolate was again present (Schab, 1991). If you are studying for a test in the presence of a particular odor, you might want to bring that same smell with you when you take the test.

How Odors Affect Behavior

In the United States, sales of scented products exceed $19 billion annually (Foderaro, 1988). Since pleasant odors elicit pleasant memories and feelings, department stores have experimented with various smells in an attempt to influence their customers' purchasing habits. Real estate salespeople often recommend that homeowners have the smell of freshly baked bread wafting through their home when it is being shown to prospective buyers. Practitioners of a new field called **aromatherapy** have used various fragrances to treat a wide variety of both psychological problems and physical ailments. Even though strong scientific evidence for the effectiveness of aromatherapy is still lacking, other research indicates that odors can affect our behavior. For instance, an ever-growing number of companies have introduced various fragrances into the heating and air-conditioning systems of their buildings with the belief it will affect employee conduct. Supposedly, the smell of lemon, peppermint, and basil increases alertness and energy while lavender and cedar promote relaxation and reduce tension (Iwahashi, 1992).

Wearing perfume or cologne to a job interview can strongly affect the rating that the job applicants receive (Baron, 1983, 1986). Male and female applicants who only wore a fragrance were judged more positively, but those who wore a fragrance and gave the interviewer many positive nonverbal cues were judged as manipulative. In addition, introducing pleasant fragrances into work settings increased workers' confidence in their ability to perform various tasks, raised the goals they set for themselves on a clerical task, improved the workers' mood, and increased workers' willingness to compromise with opponents during negotiations.

Smells That Make Us Sick

Some people have severe allergic reactions to certain smells, including many of the perfumes used in personal hygiene products. Magazines that used to contain "scratch and sniff" samples of perfume generally have discontinued this marketing strategy because of the ill effects on some readers. Many products today, including detergents and other common household products, are being sold in unscented formats.

People who know that they will be in close contact with others, as for example in a crowded airplane, should exercise restraint in using perfumes and colognes.

I hope you have come to appreciate just how important your sense of smell is to your everyday life. While people take precautions to protect their vision and hearing, the olfactory sense is often neglected. Exposure to chemicals including ammonia, photo-developing chemicals, and hairdressing mixtures can affect the ability to smell. Allergies, infections, and blows to the head also cause loss of smell. Take the same precautions to protect your sense of smell as you would any of your other sense organs.

PAIN

Our understanding of the phenomenon of pain is incomplete. Until 20 years ago, we believed that pain was experienced when the amount of damage that occurred to tissue exceeded the rate of repair. We now know that this theory is incorrect. Pain typically results when the sensations of pressure, heat, and cold reach a certain level. Pain receptors are found throughout the body although they are more concentrated in certain regions, such as your fingers, neck, and the back of your knee. Almost any sensation can cause pain if it is applied in a sufficient amount. We learned earlier that both light and sound can be painful under certain circumstances. In other cases, pain can occur in the complete absence of sensation. Amputees often feel intense pain in arms or legs that are missing, a phenomenon often referred to as **phantom limb pain.** Also, people suffering from psychiatric illnesses frequently report pain when there is no organic basis for it.

The Purpose of Pain

Although the perception of pain is unpleasant, it plays an important role in our well-being and survival. Some individuals are born without the ability to detect pain, while in other cases, diseases can bring about this condition. Individuals with this incapacity have lives fraught with hazards. Without the ability to detect pain, we are unaware when our body is too hot or too cold or when a serious injury has taken place. All animals, including humans, have evolved efficient ways to detect the sensation of pain because it has a biological value for survival. Even very simple organisms have ways of detecting and avoiding aversive stimulation. Often we make automatic responses to pain that remove us from a dangerous situation. If you place your hand on a very hot object, you will automatically withdraw it without having to think about what to do. In many cases, reflex actions, which require no learning, allow us to respond appropriately to painful stimuli. For humans, the fear of pain is also a powerful motivator that encourages us to make appropriate responses to avoid its adverse consequences.

> The least pain in our little finger gives us more concern and uneasiness than the destruction of millions of our fellow-beings.
>
> **WILLIAM HAZLITT**
> *American Literature,* "Dr Channing"

Types of Pain

There appear to be two different types of pain: (1) the sharp, immediate, bright pain such as what we experience when we prick our finger with a pin and (2) the deep, dull, aching pain that occurs from a blunt blow to our body. Sometimes we experience both of these sensations with pain. The first kind of pain is transmitted through large sensory nerve fibers to the brain while the second kind is carried by smaller nerve fibers. The large fibers allow the message to be transmitted faster to the brain so that immediate action can be taken. When your finger is pricked, you need to withdraw it right away. The smaller fibers that send the information more slowly are appropriate for the dull, aching variety of pain that does not require an immediate reaction. The slow fibers also carry most other information about both touch and temperature sensations. In all cases, the nerve fibers first transmit the pain information to the spinal cord that then carries the information to the brain. This is why spinal cord injuries can often leave individuals with no sensation of pain or touch in parts of their body.

APPLICATIONS

Distraction and Pain Perception

Pleasure is oft a visitant; but pain / Clings cruelly to us.

JOHN KEATS
Endymion, Bk. I. 906

Pain is no evil unless it conquers us.

GEORGE ELIOT

We feel less pain when we are distracted. You have probably experienced a cut or injury to yourself but not realized it until later because you were engaged in activities that distracted you at the time. Many dentists have used music successfully to distract their patients and help control their pain. The Lamaze method for childbirth emphasizes concentration on special breathing techniques while looking at an attractive picture to reduce pain. Dwelling on pain makes it worse. Injured athletes often are not affected by pain once they become focused on their performance. How many times have you seen a football player limp back to the huddle only to perform brilliantly on the next play? Anything that focuses your attention on something else will reduce the sensation of pain and offer relief, such as becoming absorbed in a good book or movie, reading aloud, or meditating. These techniques are most effective for mild pain or pain that lasts for a brief duration.

Being in Control of Pain

Control is an important factor in the sensation of pain. People who believe that they are in control of pain suffer much less from it. For instance, the pain from pinching yourself is much less intense than if someone else pinches you because you can stop the self-inflicted pain at any moment. Taking a fake pill or injection, otherwise known as a **placebo,** often controls pain as effectively as pain-killing medications. Hospitals often help patients control their pain by allowing them to press a button to dispense morphine whenever they feel the need. Under these conditions, patients will use less morphine than when they have little or no control over their medication. Patients in nursing homes often complain about feeling too hot or too cold. In facilities that have installed dummy thermostats that the patients can adjust, the patients report much higher levels of comfort even though the thermostats have no effect on the actual temperature. Whenever possible, you should arrange painful circumstances to be under your control. For example, you can lower the pain of a visit to the doctor or dentist by arranging some signal with the practitioner that will stop any procedure that you feel is too painful.

The Interpretation of Pain

The manner in which we interpret pain also affects its perceived intensity. If a friend gives you a "friendly" punch in the arm, it will be interpreted as less painful than if someone did it in anger. Football players often butt heads or punch and slap each other to celebrate a good play. Any such action by an opposing player would probably result in a brawl.

Distinguishing Chronic versus Acute Pain

It is important to distinguish between acute and chronic pain. Acute pain comes and goes and is generally controlled by either over-the-counter or prescription medicines. Chronic pain is more persistent and more likely to torment us. Patients suffering back injuries, cancer, arthritis, and other illnesses often suffer from persistent, chronic levels of pain. In any given year, there is a very good chance that you will suffer from pain sufficiently intense to interrupt your daily life. Twenty million Americans suffer from arthritis and another seven million from low-back pain. The National Center for Health Statistics estimated that in 1988 one quarter of the American population experienced moderate to excruciating pain that required major therapy such as narcotics. Also in 1988, 19% of the population were partially disabled by pain for periods ranging from weeks to months. Medical treatment that is effective for acute pain is generally unsuitable for chronic pain, particularly when it is from an unknown cause. Pain clinics, which exist to help these chronic sufferers, use a smorgasbord of therapies, including drugs, acupuncture, hypnosis, relaxation training, and thought distraction. In some cases, portable electrical stimulators are worn to provide mild stimulation next to a painful area. A vibration sensation is then perceived rather than pain. Pain control can range from surgical intervention in severe cases to over-the-counter analgesic remedies such as aspirin in more mild situations. How popular is aspirin as a pain reliever? Ten years ago the annual world output was 30,000 tons.

Sensory Deprivation

Given the sensory overload that we often suffer on a daily basis, wouldn't it be great to immerse ourselves occasionally in an environment devoid of external sensory stimulation? This is what psychologists call being in a state of **sensory deprivation.** Sensory deprivation can be applied to different situations, such as when captors brainwash prisoners of war with prolonged isolation, prison staff punish and control the prisoners through isolation from other inmates and staff, and parents use "time-out" to discipline young children who are misbehaving.

> If we had a keen vision of all that is ordinary in human life, it would be like hearing the grass grow or the squirrel's heart beat, and we should die of that roar which is the other side of silence.
>
> GEORGE ELIOT
> *Middlemarch*

Whenever we are deprived of the sensory information from one channel of information, we attend more carefully to other available sources. To prove this to yourself, simply close your eyes for a few moments and notice how much more cognizant you are of the senses of touch and smell. While it is a fallacy that blind people have more sensitivity to the sensations from their other senses, they do learn to attend more carefully to other sensory sources. Blind people are very aware of sounds when they are walking. Helen Keller, who was both deaf and blind, wrote about how alert she was to smells, touches, and tastes. In some ways, we are always in a state of sensory deprivation because our hearing is restricted to only a certain range of pitches, our vision is limited to a tiny part of the entire electromagnetic spectrum, and many smells and tastes elude us. Our sense organs have evolved so that we can only detect those stimuli that are important for our survival. We are essentially "blind" to all the others.

✦ **FIGURE 2.6** ✦ **Sensory Deprivation Chamber**

Sensory stimuli are eliminated by goggles, earphones, and cuffs covering the hands.

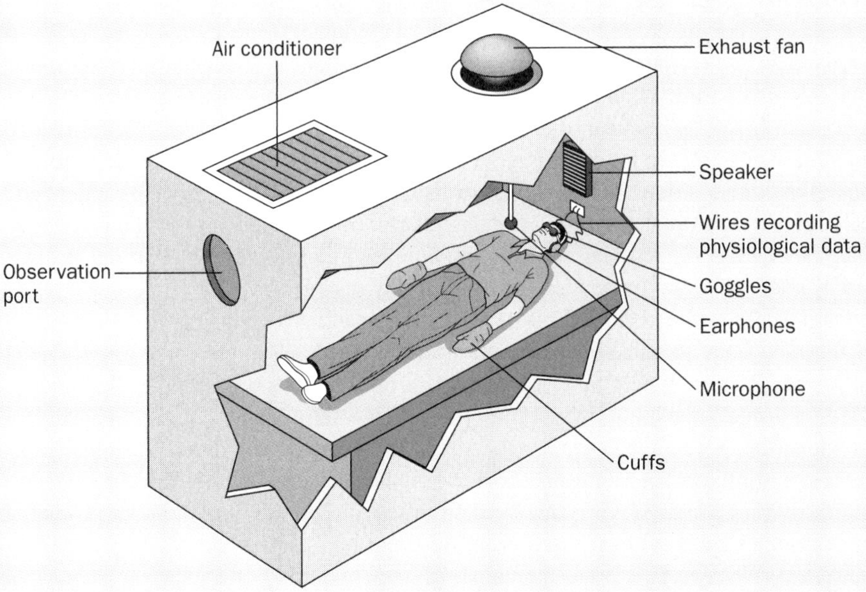

Beneficial Effects of Sensory Deprivation

More recent research on sensory deprivation, also referred to as sensory restriction, indicates that it can have beneficial effects. Psychologists often use small isolation tanks in which subjects float in complete darkness and silence (see Figure 2.6). The water is maintained at body temperature and contains Epsom salts to allow subjects to float near the surface. Unlike the earlier studies, subjects spend only a few hours in these sensory deprived states. Under these deprivation conditions, sensory sensitivity is temporarily increased for vision, hearing, touch, and taste (Suedfeld, 1975) and creative thinking is improved (Hutchison, 1984). Physiological changes include large decreases in blood pressure, muscle tension, and other indications of stress.

A technique called **REST—Restricted Environmental Stimulation Therapy** uses the possible benefits of sensory deprivation on changing personal habits. Studies have shown that only 24 hours of sensory deprivation in a flotation tank can aid people in quitting smoking and losing weight. For example, sensory deprivation combined with tape recorded antismoking messages resulted in a 40% decrease in smoking, maintained for at least 3 months, for people who used REST compared to those who had not experienced sensory deprivation (Suedfeld, 1980). Similar benefits have been found for people attempting to lose weight (Borrie & Suedfeld, 1980). Even brief periods of REST can have beneficial effects. College students, who were heavy drinkers, had a 55% reduction in alcohol consumption during the ensuing 6 months after one exposure to 12 hours in REST and a 5-minute recording on the negative effects of alcohol abuse (Cooper, 1988). It is believed that sensory deprivation results in a state of relaxation that makes people more open to suggestions. Furthermore, patients probably suffer some mental confusion during sensory deprivation that helps them alter their belief systems sufficiently to support changes in their bad personal habits.

APPLICATIONS: Using Sensory Deprivation

We all need a certain amount of sensory stimulation but there are times when we also need to take a break from it. Countless artistic and scientific accomplishments have occurred with the aid of solitude and sensory restriction. Such conditions have played an important role in the history of religion. Both Moses and Buddha reported experiencing religious visions during such times, and Muhammad, while meditating alone in a dark cave outside of Mecca, had a religious experience that led to the founding of the Muslim religion (Payne, 1959). Even the most hectic personal schedule can allow for periods of quiet contemplation. Meditation training teaches people to isolate themselves by focusing on a single word or process in order to block out other sensory stimulation. A hiking trip to the mountains, bicycling by yourself, or just finding a quiet spot in the library can have surprising and long-lasting beneficial effects, both psychologically and physically.

Several companies manufacture expensive sensory deprivation tanks for home use. You might try the poor man's alternative: Close the door to your bathroom, pull down the shades, turn off the lights, run a fan to mask out extraneous noises, fill the bathtub with warm water, immerse yourself, and enjoy some restricted sensory stimulation.

And silence, like a poultice, comes / To heal the blows of sound.

OLIVER WENDELL HOLMES
The Music Grinders

SUBLIMINAL PERCEPTION

Do you believe that stimuli that fall below your level of consciousness can affect your behavior? In 1957 James Vicary, the owner of an advertising and marketing agency, claimed that he flashed messages such as "Eat popcorn" at rates too rapid to be seen during the showing of the movie *Picnic*. Although moviegoers did not report seeing the messages, he claimed that popcorn sales increased 58% during intermission. Seemingly, messages presented below the level of consciousness had the power to affect people's behavior. As a result, people became very concerned that their behavior could be controlled by messages of which they were not even aware. Even a congressional hearing looked into the matter. The following year the Canadian Broadcasting Corporation sponsored a research project to test the efficacy of these types of messages. At the beginning of a popular television show, viewers were told that an unspecified subliminal message would be presented to them sometime during the show. Afterwards, many viewers wrote into the program to report that they had felt a strange compulsion to eat or drink something. However, the actual message, "Phone now," did not result in any increase in the number of telephone calls made during and after the show (Druckman & Bjork, 1991). In 1962, Vicary admitted that he had fabricated the whole story to promote his failing business.

The phenomenon of a message being presented below the level of awareness is known as **subliminal perception.** The word subliminal comes from the words *sub* (below) and *limen,* another word for **threshold.** Thus, the term *subliminal* means "below threshold." Psychologists used to think of thresholds as the *beginning point of sensation,* that is, the minimal amount of energy necessary for a stimulus to be detected. In a home, the threshold is the wooden or metal plate at the bottom of the door of the entrance. It is what you step over when you enter a house—the beginning point of your entry. Think of a stereo system playing music. If the volume is turned all the way down, you cannot hear the music. If the volume is slowly increased, there will be some point where you will begin to hear the music. This amount of volume would be your threshold for hearing.

You have probably seen store displays or advertisements for self-help tapes, CDs, or videos that promise to make you lose weight, stop smoking, gain self-confidence, reduce stress, enhance your memory, improve study habits, become fit, find romance, as well as a myriad of other accomplishments. Reportedly, all of this is accomplished effortlessly and painlessly through exposure to visual or auditory messages that are so weak they cannot be consciously detected. There are presently over 2,000 vendors of such tapes with sales in excess of $50 million per year (Oldenburg, 1990). Many of these tapes sell for $150 or more. And if you do not have time to listen to the tapes while awake, several companies sell tapes to be played while you are asleep. One such subliminal sleep learning tape promises to speed your recovery from illnesses, including colds, flu, surgery, and chronic, even degenerative, diseases. This is accomplished by presenting subliminal auditory suggestions such as "Total wellness is your reality, embrace it now," "Your mind is all powerful; you will heal quickly and painlessly," and "Your whole body radiates health and stamina." Surveys have shown that most Americans have not only heard of subliminal advertising but also believe that it is effective (Zanot, Pincus, & Lamp, 1983). Let's look at the evidence, pro and con, on this issue.

What Subliminal Perception Does

Subliminal perception can affect our behavior, but in ways far more subtle and different from that claimed by the purveyors of self-help tapes. If a word such as *FRUIT* is flashed very briefly, it is easier for a person to recognize a related word such as *APPLE* as compared to an unrelated word such as *SHOE.* This phenomenon is known as **semantic priming** and occurs even when the first word is presented so rapidly that the person is unaware of having seen it. Similarly, if subjects are subliminally exposed to a picture and then are asked to pick between two clearly visible pictures, approximately two-thirds will pick the picture that was seen subliminally. These effects last for about 1 week and then dissipate (Bornstein, 1989).

A more controversial finding is that subliminal exposures might create an emotional response. A subliminal message such as *people hate me* has been shown by some researchers to elicit a slight emotional response in subjects (Masling, Bornstein, Poynton, Reid, & Katkin, 1991). Even though it is unclear how long lasting the effects are, psychologists generally believe that any such effects are very weak and relatively short lived.

What Subliminal Perception Cannot Do

The effects of subliminal audiotapes have been scientifically tested dozens of times. The consensus from these studies is that the subliminal messages have no permanent effects on behaviors such as dieting, smoking, memory enhancement, or any of the other claims made by sellers of the tapes. Why then do some people swear by these tapes and sales continue unabated? Examine the evidence that purports to document the effectiveness of these tapes, and you will see that it usually consists of testimonials by satisfied customers. "Your tapes have changed my life" or "I've gotten a promotion at work and met the love of my life." No doubt these people are unquestionably convinced that these tapes helped them in their daily lives. Recall the placebo effect where people who think they are receiving a medication experience results similar to those who actually take a medication. Similarly, individuals who show commitment to self-improvement by purchasing and using an expensive tape will probably be convinced that it really did help. The United States Armed Forces commissioned one of the most comprehensive evaluations of subliminal tapes and, after an extensive series of well-controlled experiments, concluded that these tapes were of no use for training of military personnel. If you are thinking of purchasing such self-help tapes, you would be well advised to save your money unless you are willing to be satisfied with any placebo effect you might obtain.

Contrary to earlier beliefs, there is no need to fear that subliminal messages sent during movies or television will cause viewers to go on a sudden buying spree. In fact, television and movie producers know the futility of this approach. Instead, they have adopted the more effective approach of presenting product messages well above threshold values. You may have noticed that products, such as specific brands of beer, cigarettes, or soda pop, are prominently displayed on television and in the movies even though extraordinary measures were taken to hide product identity until recently. Of course, these products are more likely to be shown being used by the film's hero and not by a serial killer. Today, manufacturers pay huge sums of money to have their products clearly displayed in *above*-threshold messages in order to influence our purchasing preferences.

APPLICATIONS: Using Subliminal Perception

Few applications can be made from subliminal perceptions. The documented effects are so weak and transient that they could not be easily applied to improve your life. Do not waste your time or money on audio or visual tapes that make promises that the sellers cannot deliver. A careful analysis of some of the current auditory tapes on the market show that no subliminal message is contained on the tapes. In fact, the newest sales ploy has the sellers admit that the previous technology was ineffective but that new "pioneering technological advances" effectively introduce messages during sleep when certain brain-wave activity is present. Do not believe it. Often these tapes are sold by people who purport to have doctoral degrees and who have written books with fancy-sounding titles. Do not fall for their grandiose claims, which are based on pseudoscientific (i.e., faulty) research or, more likely, no research whatsoever.

Extrasensory Perception and Paranormal Phenomena

We have learned about how we perceive sensations in our five primary senses. Are we limited in our perceptions to the information gathered by our sense receptors? People who believe in **extrasensory perception** or **ESP** believe that we are capable of gathering information beyond these traditional channels. The "extra" in extrasensory means *something additional or beyond,* thus implying that perceptions can occur in the complete absence of any sensation. These phenomena are also referred to as **paranormal** because they function outside of the normal sensory channels. Have you ever had a "mystical experience"? The majority of Americans report that they have. One of the most common experiences is **déjà vu,** which in French means "already seen." This experience often takes the form of a compelling and sudden feeling of remembering scenes or events that you are actually and knowingly encountering for the first time. Over two thirds of Americans report having had such an experience.

Beliefs in ESP are widespread in the United States. A 1991 Gallup poll indicated that about half of Americans believe in ESP (Gallup & Newport, 1991). Other Gallup polls show that 69% of Americans believe in angels, 50% believe they have their own personal guardian angel, and about 50% believe in the existence of unidentified flying objects from outer space. A British newspaper survey revealed that 59% of the respondents believed in ESP, that females were more likely to be believers (70%) than males (48%), and that the percentage of believers increased slightly with age (Blackmore, 1997). Furthermore, these beliefs are becoming increasingly common with successive generations. Interestingly, individuals who actively participate in organized religion tend to report fewer mystical experiences than do those who practice religion privately (Levin, 1993).

Varieties of ESP

There are four main kinds of ESP that have been investigated: (1) **telepathy** or the ability of one person to send thoughts to another person or for a person to perceive another's thoughts; (2) **precognition** or the ability to perceive future events, such as political and historical events, catastrophes, and (presumably) stock market changes and future lottery numbers; (3) **clairvoyance** or the perception of an event that occurs far away, such as knowing that a relative who lives in another state has suddenly died; and (4) **psychokinesis** or the ability to use only one's mind to control physical matter, such as levitating an object, bending a key, or making an object move. Although technically not a type of perception, psychokinesis is frequently studied by investigators interested in psychic phenomena.

Scientific Studies

He who could foresee affairs three days in advance would be rich for thousands of years.

CHINESE PROVERB

Some psychologists have attempted to study various paranormal phenomena using accepted scientific procedures. The most famous psychologist to do so was J. B. Rhine who founded the Duke University Parapsychology Laboratory in 1927. Scientific studies are also being carried out in laboratories in Russia, Britain, Japan, Scotland, Brazil, and the Netherlands. Several journals in the United States are dedicated to publishing studies in this area. Active research in this area has continued for over 130 years.

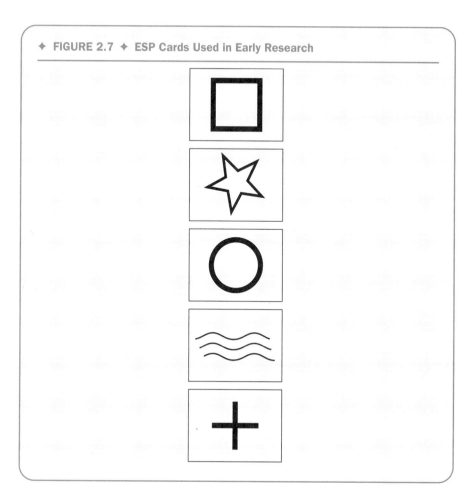

✦ FIGURE 2.7 ✦ ESP Cards Used in Early Research

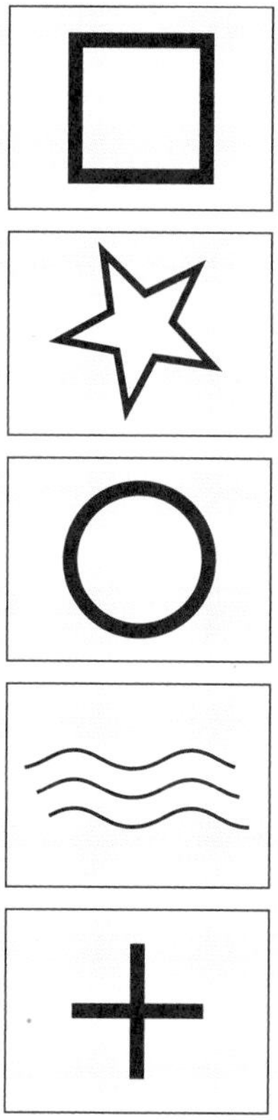

Attempts to Use Paranormal Phenomena

Police departments have hired psychics in attempts to locate missing persons, bodies, or crime evidence. American businesses sponsor precognition research to gain the obvious advantages that foreseeing the future would provide. Even the United States military has attempted to use ESP. Many Americans were shocked to learn in 1995 that the Central Intelligence Agency (CIA) had spent $20 million over 2 decades to study clairvoyance. For example, they trained people to try to locate the bunker where Saddam Hussein was hiding during the 1991 Persian Gulf war. The CIA also spent months training individuals in a practice known as "remote viewing," where they were taught to transcend space and time in order to find people, places, and things remote from them, to go both forward and backward in time, and to use the five primary senses to "see" details of military targets (Morehouse, 1996). How effective was this? As of this writing, Saddam Hussein is still alive and well. The CIA discontinued the program after concluding that it was totally ineffective.

Testing for ESP

You can test your abilities in clairvoyance by using a method identical to that used by J. B. Rhine in his early research. Using the stimulus cards illustrated in Figure 2.7, a person, called the sender, sits in a room and concentrates on one of the five symbols. At the same time, the receiver tries to determine which of the five symbols the sender is transmitting. One would expect to get 20% correct guesses by chance alone since there are five stimulus cards. Any ability to consistently guess over 20% would be evidence of clairvoyance. But do not get too excited if you are able to guess even 40% correctly on a few trials because such deviations from chance are expected. You will need to test yourself on several hundred trials to control adequately for chance deviations.

You must also be careful to control for any procedural flaw that might give a subject unintended information about which symbol is being transmitted. For example, there is now good evidence that early researchers using this procedure sometimes allowed the senders to give cues about the cards being "transmitted" through facial gestures, lip movements, or subtle auditory cues. Therefore, the sender and receiver should sit back to back or, even better, be placed in separate rooms with no visual or auditory communication with each other.

Results of Scientific Studies on ESP

After 130 years of experimentation, most psychologists remain highly skeptical about the existence of any paranormal phenomena. For every experiment claiming positive results, there are many others that have failed. Much of the experimentation that has supported the existence of such phenomena subsequently proved to be methodologically flawed. Paranormal phenomena that were reported in one laboratory setting could not be replicated in other laboratories. In addition, people who demonstrated these phenomena on occasion were unable to exhibit their abilities consistently when called upon to do so. Reports in the popular press of amazing feats of telepathy, psychokinesis, and precognition by stage performers such as Uri Geller (who was a trained magician) were subsequently found to be based on sleight of hand and other forms of deception. In fact, fraud has been the hallmark of many of the individuals attempting to demonstrate the existence of paranormal phenomena. Experiments using rigorous scientific techniques have consistently failed to reveal the occurrence of any paranormal phenomena (see, for example, Druckman & Swets, 1988).

But what about those highly publicized psychics who make such astounding predictions about the future, particularly around the beginning of each calendar year? An examination of hundreds of New Year forecasts of leading psychics between 1978 and 1985 that were published in the *National Enquirer* revealed that out of 486 predictions, only 2 were shown to be accurate (Strentz, 1986). I challenge you to make 100 predictions about events that will occur in the next 12 months. Write down your predictions and check on their accuracy 12 months from now. I believe that you will do at least as well as the most highly acclaimed "psychics" by chance alone. And what about those psychics who help the police when every other method has failed? These people usually generate hundreds of predictions, such as "the body will be found near a lake, close to some trees, on a small mound overlooking a populated area. . . ." Sure enough, out of these hundreds of guesses, some prove to be accurate. However, on the whole, such psychic guesses are no more accurate than those made by others (Reiser, 1982). It is the media attention given to the occasionally correct guess that leads many to believe in their psychic abilities.

Yes, but what about dreams? Who has not had a dream that subsequently forecast an actual event? Everyone dreams several times a night, often about events that are causing us some emotional turmoil. If you had a dream that correctly predicted the death of your elderly grandmother, you should not be too surprised. Her elderly condition and your concerns about her well-being probably had been in your thoughts recently. We tend to attach a great deal of importance to the occasional dream that accurately forecasts an event while forgetting about the hundreds or thousands of dreams that foretell nothing. When is the last time you remarked to a friend that you dreamed about an event that subsequently did not happen? There is no solid scientific evidence to suggest that dreams forecast future events.

The Persistence of Beliefs in the Paranormal

Over 100 years of research indicates that there is no reliable scientific evidence to support any ESP phenomena and yet such beliefs persist in a large proportion of people. Psychologists have struggled to find an explanation for this phenomenon. In my experiences as a university professor, I have found that beliefs in ESP are strongly held and defended by well-educated and otherwise clear-thinking college students. Even my own daughter, who holds a graduate degree, has heard me explain the evidence against ESP on numerous occasions but continues to believe firmly in its existence. If anything, beliefs in things outside the mainstream of science, such as astrology, the Loch Ness monster, Bigfoot, UFOs, near-death experiences, out-of-body experiences, and the Bermuda Triangle, are increasing in popularity. What can account for the popularity of these beliefs?

The flowering of beliefs in things mystical can be traced, in part, to the increasing media attention paid to such events. The popularity of television and movie themes related to mysticism increases annually. The New-Age movement has attracted many adherents, particularly younger people, who want and need to believe in something more than that which can be explained by science. The most common reason cited by people holding these beliefs is personal experiences (Blackmore, 1984), and the more personal experiences people have, the stronger their beliefs (Glicksohn, 1990). Most of us have experienced the déjà vu phenomenon and occasionally dreams that seemed to predict the future. For many people the power of these subjective experiences nullifies any skepticism advanced by science. One "mystical experience" is more powerful than 100 scientific studies that show the failure to confirm its existence.

People also hold an increasing skepticism in the ability of science to explain things. Indeed, there are many things that science cannot readily explain, and with no scientific explanation readily available, many people quickly default to a more mystical explanation. For instance, if circular patterns suddenly appear in wheat fields, it must be the work of UFOs. If eviscerated cattle are mysteriously found in ranchers' fields, it is only further evidence of the work of visitors from another planet. Paranormal phenomena are always handy interpretations for what science cannot readily explain.

Finally, it should be noted that justified skepticism does not imply that we should close the door on the possibility of paranormal phenomena. There is much that we do not yet understand about how the senses work. The history of science is replete with ideas that were originally dismissed as foolish but later proved to be true. There have been studies that suggest some ESP effects may exist although the research has not been replicated in other laboratories by other investigators. Certainly further investigation is warranted. Only through rigorous scientific investigation with the best investigative tools available will we eventually discover whether any such phenomena exist.

APPLICATIONS: Beliefs in the Paranormal

Beliefs in the paranormal are relatively harmless unless they begin to affect the way we live our lives. Many people enjoy reading their horoscope in the morning just for the fun of seeing what is predicted for their day. I enjoy reading the fortune in my cookie at Chinese restaurants, but I do not live my life according to its dictates.

Even highly educated individuals fall under the spell of alleged paranormal phenomena. A former colleague at another university who had a Ph.D. in industrial psychology firmly believed in the phenomenon of out-of-body experiences. He assured me that he could leave his body at will and transport his spirit to any place he wanted, although his body and spirit always appeared firmly connected. Another former colleague and clinical psychologist firmly believed in the power of pyramids. There was a belief among many people during the 1970s that pyramids had magical powers and that objects placed under the point of a pyramid could be affected in many different ways. For example, many people believed that a dull razor blade could be sharpened by pyramid power. My clinical acquaintance believed that sexual experiences could be enhanced if they occurred under a pyramid. In fact, his belief was so strong that he hired a contractor, at great expense, to remove the roof over the bedroom of his home and erect a large, ornate, copper-sided pyramid.

For those of you who believe that you have paranormal abilities, some easy money can be made. More than 20 years ago James Randi, a famous magician and skeptic of paranormal phenomena, offered $10,000 to anyone who could demonstrate *any* paranormal ability before a group of experts qualified to judge its authenticity. The money went unclaimed and has now increased to $1,000,000. Details on claiming this money can be obtained at www.randi.org/research/index.html. If people had the ability for precognition, they should be able to predict accurately what lottery numbers will be drawn. Based on the number of lotteries that are functioning successfully and according to the laws of chance, it does not appear that such abilities exist. And anyone with psychokinesis should be able to control the numbers that appear on a dice table in Las Vegas. If people truly possessed such ability, every casino in the world would go bankrupt.

Enjoy your "mystical" experiences, your déjà vu occurrences, and be surprised when a dream forecasts an event in your life. Just keep in mind that research to date suggests that all such phenomena fall well within the principles of what we know governs our daily behavior and that no recourse to paranormal phenomena is necessary. Like many people, though, I hope that these phenomena someday are proven true because it would open entirely new vistas about human potential.

Visual Illusions

You may believe in the old saying that "I've got to see it to believe it." If you do, you are in for a lot of deception. In fact, quite often seeing is deceiving. An illusion occurs whenever there is a discrepancy between the actual physical characteristics of a stimulus and our cognitive interpretation of that stimulus. As we interact with our environment, we are continuously inundated with many visual illusions of which we are totally unaware. Fortunately, most of these illusions are such that they allow us to function quite normally in our environment. We do not stumble around, walk into walls, or fall off cliffs. Yet very often our interpretation of visual information is inaccurate. Illusions are not limited to the visual sense but can occur in each of the senses. In this section we will confine ourselves solely to visual illusions since that is where we experience most of the illusions we encounter daily.

Reality is merely an illusion, albeit a very persistent one.

ALBERT EINSTEIN

Illusions in Nature

You have probably noticed that illusions often occur in nature, and many animals and plants have developed illusions that serve a survival function. Some butterflies have evolved markings on their wings that mimic large eyes that are designed to scare off predators. Living creatures often evolve markings and coloration to make themselves look either larger or smaller or to blend into the environment. In Brazil, several species of bugs have evolved into shapes that resemble an alligator to scare off predators. Plants also have evolved similar kinds of deceptions with the purposes of attracting other animals and avoiding detection. Nature is replete with illusions, and humankind is no exception. As we will discuss later, we often use illusions ourselves to try to attract or repel others.

Don't part with your illusions. When they are gone you may still exist but you have ceased to live.

MARK TWAIN
Pudd'nhead Wilson,
Pudd'nhead Wilson's Calendar

Illusions Caused by the Sense Receptors

Some illusions arise out of processes that occur in the sense receptors themselves long before the information is sent to the brain. An example in vision is the Hermann's grid that is illustrated in Figure 2.8. If you stare at this grid, you will see faint gray spots at the intersections of the white bars. These spots are illusory and, if you try to focus on any particular one, it will disappear. The physiological explanation for this illusion is complicated and beyond the scope of this book. Suffice it to say that it is caused by the receptor cells on the retina of your eye.

Illusions Caused by Cognitive Interpretation

Although the sense organs themselves are sometimes responsible for illusions, more frequently it is the brain's interpretation of the information being sent by the sense organs that is responsible. Perhaps the most famous visual illusion in psychology is the Müller-Lyer illusion illustrated in Figure 2.9. The two horizontal lines appear to be unequal in length but actually are exactly the same. (You may want to measure them to convince yourself!) We know that this illusion occurs in the brain rather than on the retina of the eye. If the horizontal lines are presented to one eye and the "fins" to the other eye, the illusion still occurs, telling us that the misinterpretation of line length is occurring in the brain somewhere.

You may think "so what?" How often am I exposed to two "arrows" like this out in the real world? Actually, more often than you might think. Look at the two

✦ FIGURE 2.8 ✦ Hermann's Grid

Gray spots appear at each intersection but disappear when you try to look at one.

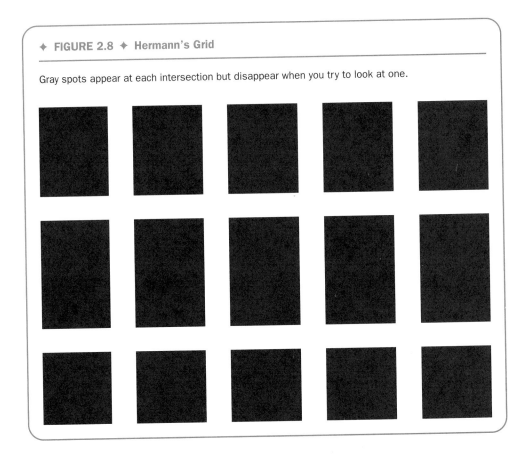

drawings illustrated in Figure 2.10. The receding corner of the room in Figure 2.10 contains the illusion, as does the protruding corner of the building. Both corners are the same height. Since the corner in the first figure is receding away from, and thus more distant from, the observer, the brain concludes that the line is longer than the line that juts out from the corner and adjusts your perception accordingly (Gregory, 1977). This is an example of how previously learned spatial relations affect the way we perceive the world.

Further evidence of learning's role on perception can be demonstrated if we showed this illusion to a group of South African people called the Zulus. The Zulus live in a "round" world with rounded huts that are arranged in a circle. They have little experience with rectangular shapes since even the tools they use and the toys their children play with are curved. When shown the Müller-Lyer illusion, the typical Zulu does not see the distortion in lengths that we do (Gregory, 1977). It appears that our past learned experiences with rectangular shapes cause this illusion.

Another illusion that we encounter frequently in our environment is the vertical–horizontal illusion illustrated in Figure 2.11. A line that is vertical will be perceived as longer than an equivalent horizontal line. In nature, a tree that is standing appears taller than a tree lying on the ground. In addition, a bisected line will appear shorter than an undivided line. Both of these factors are at work in the vertical–horizontal illusion and cause the horizontal line to appear about 30% shorter. Imagine

✦ **FIGURE 2.9** ✦ **The Müller-Lyer Illusion**

Are the two horizontal lines the same length? Measure them and see.

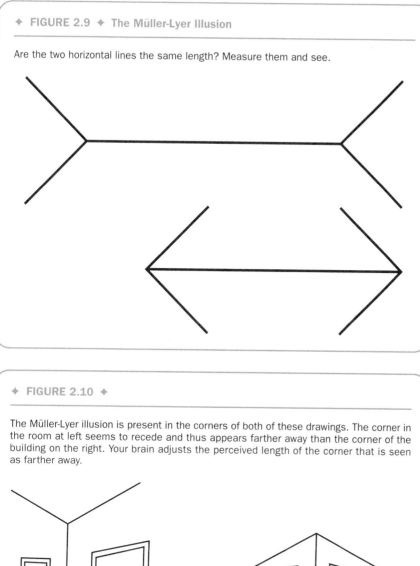

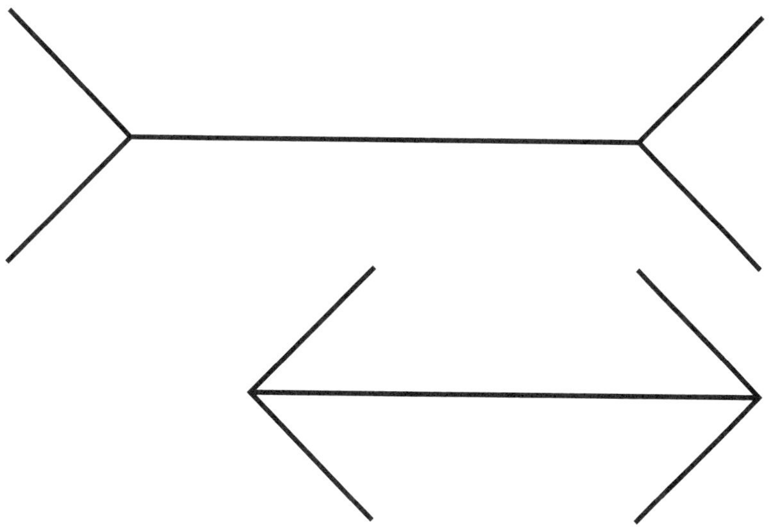

✦ **FIGURE 2.10** ✦

The Müller-Lyer illusion is present in the corners of both of these drawings. The corner in the room at left seems to recede and thus appears farther away than the corner of the building on the right. Your brain adjusts the perceived length of the corner that is seen as farther away.

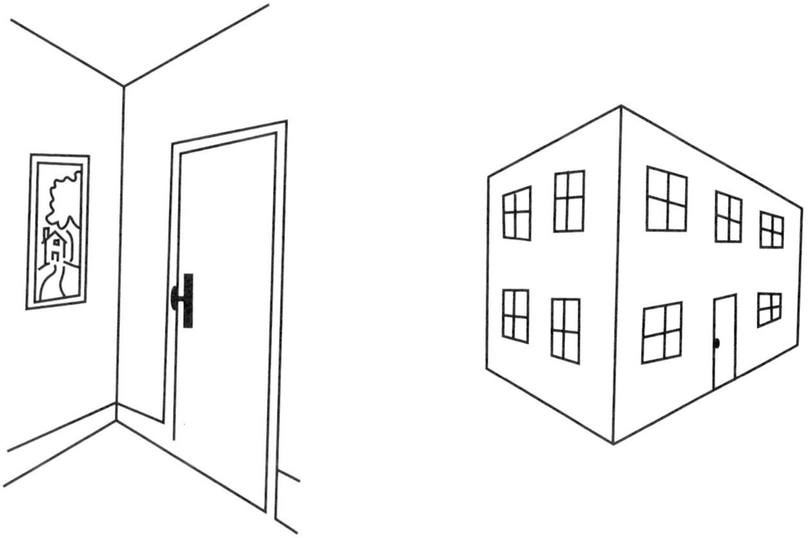

✦ FIGURE 2.11 ✦ The Horizontal–Vertical Illusion

The vertical line appears to be longer than the horizontal line. In general, vertical lines appear longer than horizontal lines. Contributing to this illusion is the fact that a line that is bisected by another will also appear shorter.

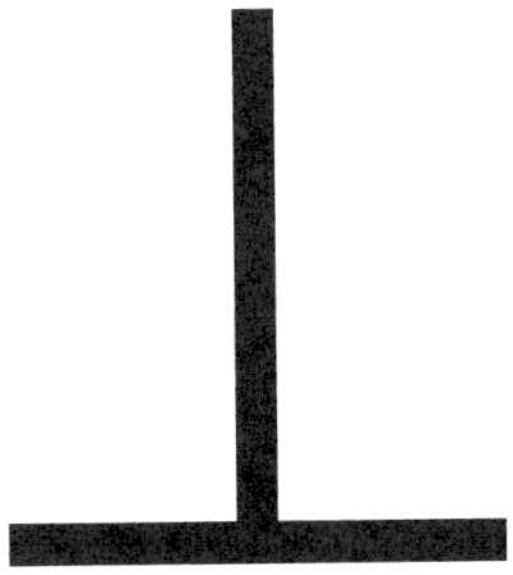

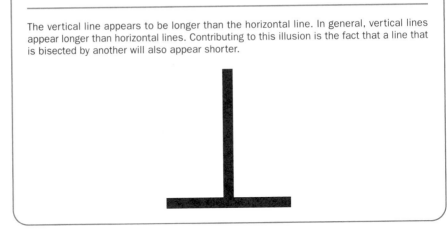

how many thousands of times a day you are exposed to this illusion in your usual activities.

Figure 2.12 further illustrates how the angles at which lines cross each other can greatly influence how we perceive them. The long thin lines are actually parallel to one another but do not appear so. This particular illusion, known as the Zollner illusion, was accidentally discovered in the 1800s by a man who saw the pattern on cloth he was purchasing for his wife. It is one of many illusions in which distortions are introduced when lines cross other lines at certain angles. These illusions have created problems for architects for thousands of years. The ancient Greeks found that vertical columns caused the floors and roofs of their temples to appear to sag in the middle. They compensated for this effect by constructing the buildings with slight curves to compensate for the illusion. In addition, the Greeks discovered that vertical columns appear to be thinner in the middle than at the ends and to spread apart slightly at the top. In turn, they compensated for this illusion by building the columns with a slight bulge in the center and by having the columns lean together slightly. The Acropolis in Athens is perhaps the most famous example of where all these techniques were used. The ancient Greeks were very knowledgeable about optical illusions and often used them to give the appearance of symmetry and perfection to their architectural creations.

Illusions of Size Distortion

A common perceptual illusion is size distortion. Have you ever noticed how much larger the moon appears when it is on the horizon as compared to when it is high in the night sky? This moon illusion, as it is called, occurs partly because a horizon moon is seen from behind reference objects such as trees, houses, telephone poles, and mountains. These reference objects give the brain additional cues about how far away the horizon is, thus making the horizon seem more distant than the sky overhead, which provides no such reference cues. Thus the moon on the horizon appears more distant and therefore larger. Quickly prove this to yourself by taking a piece of

✦ **FIGURE 2.12** ✦ **The Zollner Illusion**

Are the long thin lines parallel to one another? They are in actuality. The distortion is caused by the angles of the short lines crossing the longer lines. This is an example of a category of illusions called crosshatched illusions.

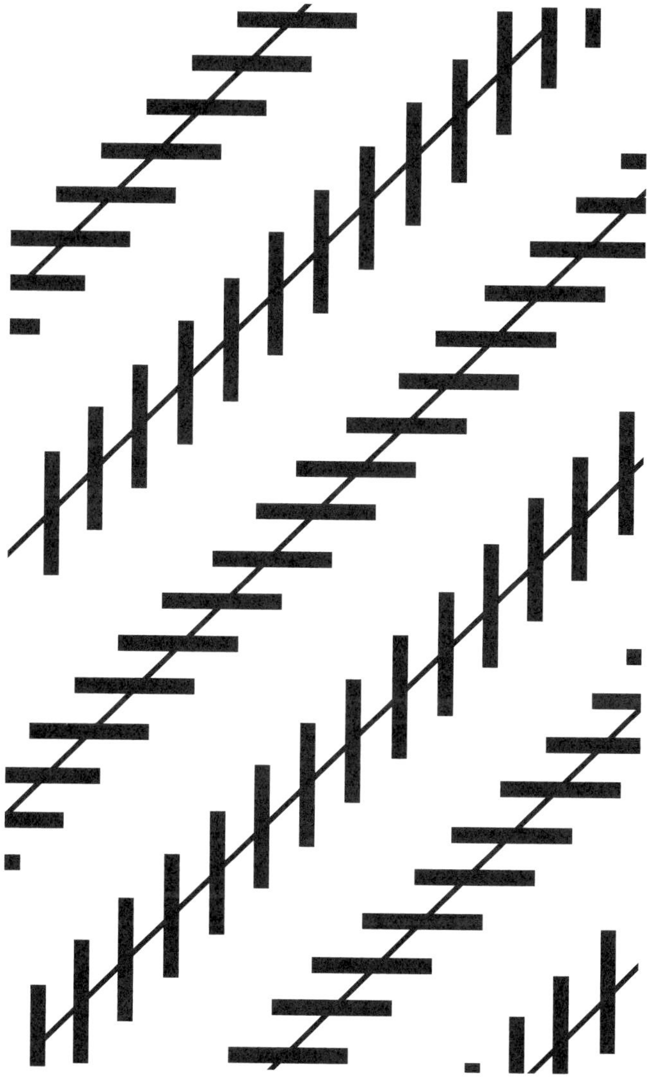

paper and punching a hole in it so that you can view the horizon moon without the reference objects being present. The size will be instantly reduced.

We often judge the size of an object by comparing it with objects around it. Look at the center circles in the two drawings illustrated in Figure 2.13. The inner circle on the left appears smaller in comparison to the larger circles surrounding it.

The Greek Acropolis in Athens

The ancient Greek architects realized that the vertical columns used in the design would result in several vertical illusions that would make the floor and roof appear to sag in the middle. The floor and roof of the building actually curve slightly to compensate for this illusion. The columns also bulge slightly in the center and lean toward each other to compensate for another illusion that occurs when vertical columns are used in building design.

A short individual standing in the midst of a group of basketball players will appear even shorter than he actually is.

Another size distortion occurs when a bright object is surrounded by a dark object. Under these conditions, the bright object will appear larger at the expense of the adjacent darker objects, a phenomenon referred to as **irradiation.** Using the

The moon appears to be much larger when it is viewed just above the horizon. Viewing the moon behind reference objects such as trees, buildings, or mountains leads our brain to conclude that the moon is closer to us and hence larger as compared to when it is in the overhead sky with no reference points.

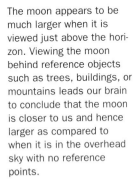

moon again as an illustration, have you noticed that during a crescent moon the lighted part appears larger in radius than the faint outline of the darker portion, as demonstrated in the irradiation illusion illustrated in Figure 2.14? When bright light falls on the retina where the nerve cells are located, more nerve fibers react than were actually struck by the light. This causes what is called a "spreading

✦ FIGURE 2.13 ✦

Are the two center balls the same size? We often make judgments of size based on comparison objects that are nearby. The two center balls are equal in size.

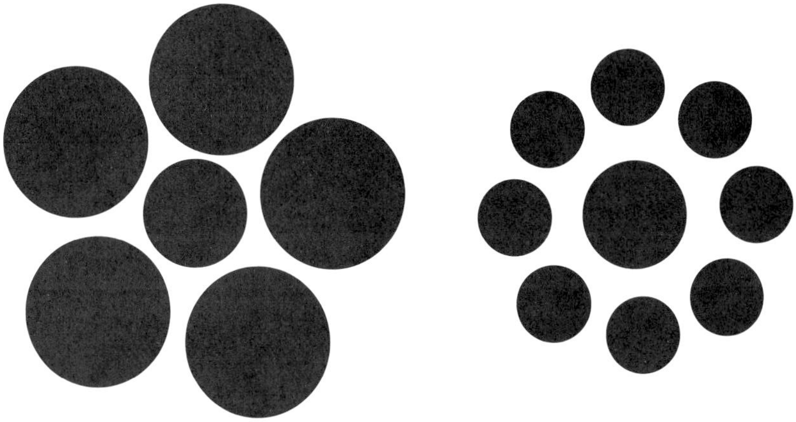

✦ FIGURE 2.14 ✦ The Irradiation Illusion

Note that the white circle on the left appears larger than the dark circle on the right. A bright object surrounded by a dark object will appear larger than a dark object surrounded by a white background.

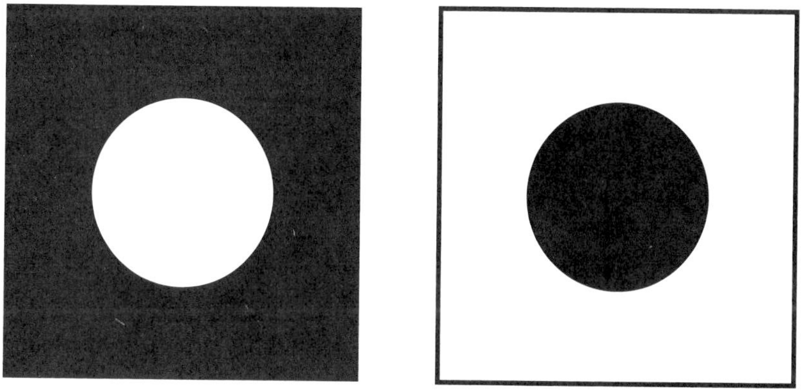

✦ **FIGURE 2.15** ✦ **The Necker Cube**

An example of an ambiguous figure. Is the shaded wall closest to you or farthest away? It depends on how you interpret the figure. Stare at the figure for a few minutes and see if you can make the shaded wall move to either the front or the back.

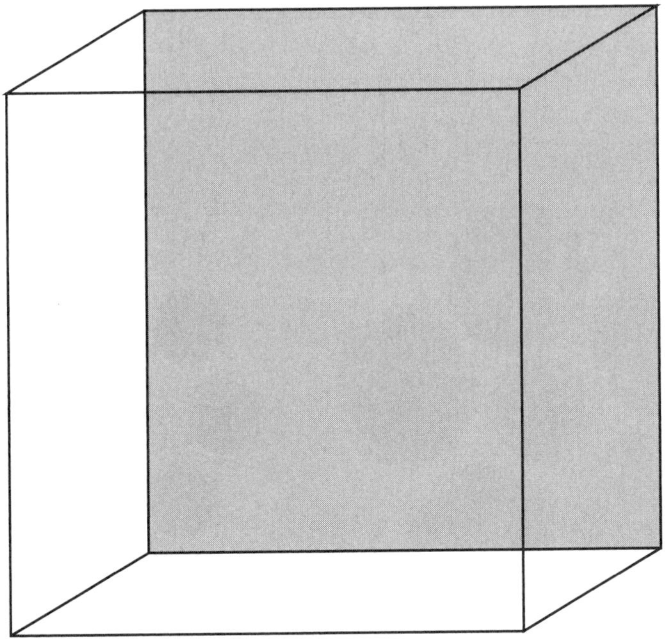

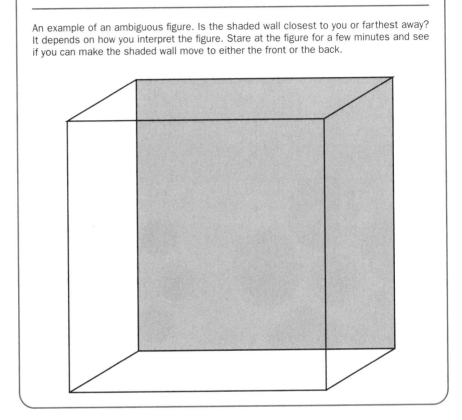

effect" (hence the name irradiation) that makes the bright object seem larger than it actually is.

Ambiguous Figures

Sometimes we are presented with visual information that can be interpreted in more than one way. Psychologists refer to these as **ambiguous figures,** the most famous of which is the Necker cube presented in Figure 2.15. If you continue to stare at this cube, you will see that there are two interpretations. The shaded side may be seen as either the front side or the back side of the cube. If you look steadily at the cube, you may see these two interpretations alternate back and forth. Another example, known as Schroeder's staircase, is shown in Figure 2.16. At first glance, this appears to be a staircase that could be climbed from the lower left to the upper right. If you try, however, the figure can also be seen as an upside-down staircase. This alternative interpretation may take some effort on your part to see. The upper-left wall now becomes the wall closest to you. You might have to stare at the figure for a few moments in order to see both interpretations. A final example of an ambiguous figure is shown in Figure 2.17 where the figure can be interpreted as either a beach ball or a view from looking down a large pipe.

What if everything is an illusion and nothing exists? In that case, I definitely overpaid for my carpet.

WOODY ALLEN

✦ FIGURE 2.16 ✦ Schroeder's Staircase

Another example of an ambiguous figure. At first glance it is a normal-looking staircase that you could climb going from lower left to upper right. If you stare at the figure for a few moments, you can make the figure reverse and become an upside-down staircase. Concentrate on making the upper left-hand wall appear closest to you to see this effect.

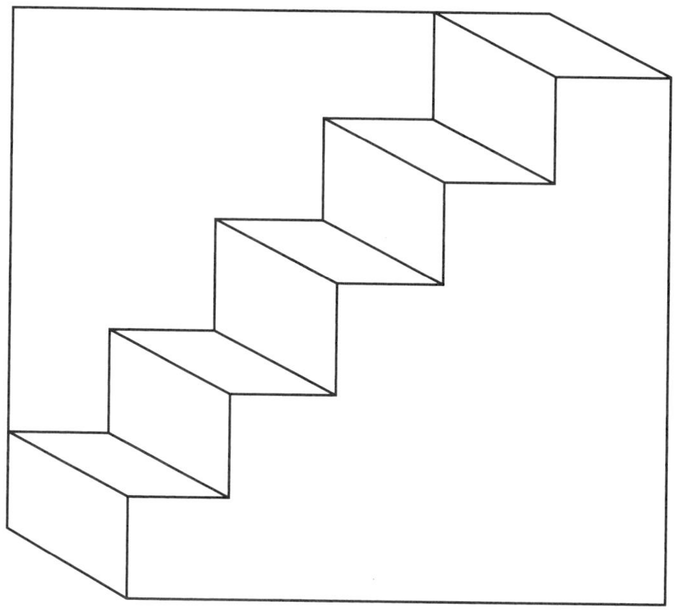

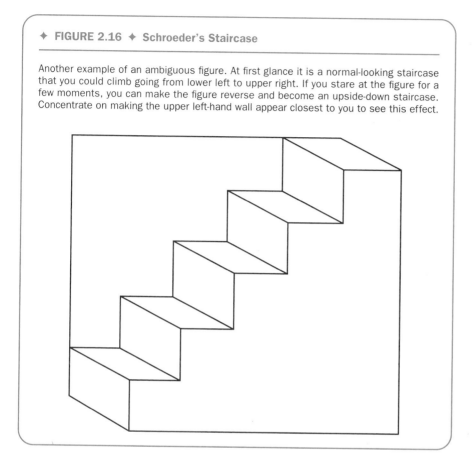

Psychologists are not clear about how we interpret ambiguous figures. In many cases, ambiguity exists about the depth of a part of the stimulus. The brain interprets the depth in one of two ways, and the meaning of the figure changes depending on which interpretation is made. In Figure 2.17 for instance, if the small inner circle is seen as being closest to you, then the interpretation is clearly that of a beach ball. However, if the small circle is seen as being more distant than the outer circle, then the interpretation is clearly that of looking down a pipe. The context in which the stimulus appears is one critical factor. If we saw this figure lying on a beach, we would interpret it as a ball whereas, if it were part of a construction site, we would interpret it differently.

Ambiguous figures emphasize the importance of the meaning that we attach to a sensation. Often the meaning is not an integral part of the sensation itself but instead must be determined by us. The context of the stimulus, as well as our past learning experiences with similar stimuli, all play a role in what meaning we give to it. In the real world, we often face ambiguous stimuli from each of our sensory systems and impart certain meaning to the sensations we experience. We must remember that perception and sensation are not always synonymous and saying that "I saw it all very clearly" actually means only that "I *interpreted* what I saw."

✦ **FIGURE 2.17** ✦

Is it a beach ball or the inside of a long pipe? Our interpretation can switch back and forth, but we cannot have both interpretations at the same time. The context in which the figure is seen would be a big factor in how we interpret its meaning.

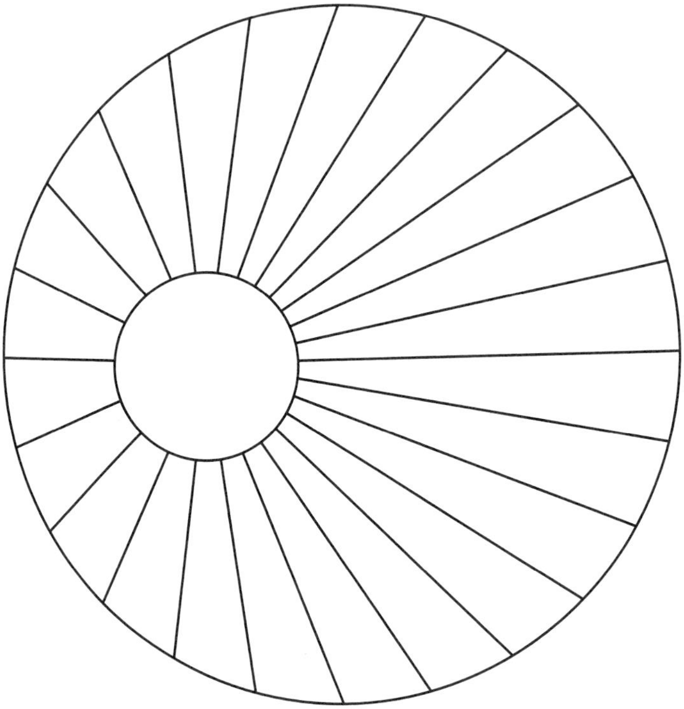

Illusions of Movement

We discussed earlier how, under some circumstances, we could perceive movement where none existed. Psychologists refer to this as **illusory movement,** a phenomenon that can be easily demonstrated. For example, the **autokinetic effect** occurs when a stationary light is viewed against total darkness. Under these circumstances, the light will appear to be moving in unpredictable ways. Most observers will report that it jerks, swoops, and glides. You can demonstrate this effect by setting a small penlight on a table in a darkened room. (The demonstration is most effective if you block off all but a pinpoint of light by using electrical tape with a small hole in it.) Make certain the room is sufficiently dark so that only the light, and not any stationary reference objects, is visible. Observe the light in silence with several of your friends and later report what you saw. Invariably, each of you will have seen the light move differently. You can also demonstrate the powerful effects of suggestion on the movement by telling people that the light is moving first up and down and later back and forth. Many people can even be convinced that the light is tracing out

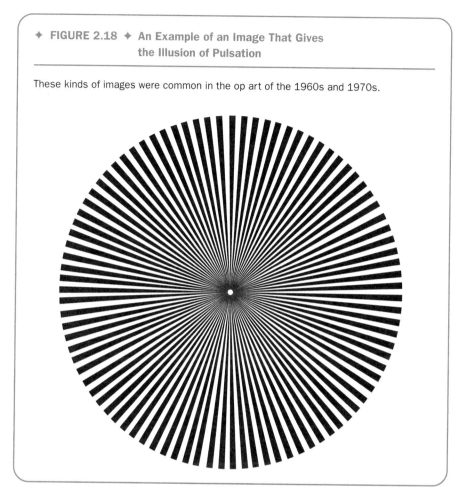

✦ **FIGURE 2.18** ✦ **An Example of an Image That Gives the Illusion of Pulsation**

These kinds of images were common in the op art of the 1960s and 1970s.

their name in the dark! Although there is some debate about exactly what causes this effect, psychologists now believe that it is caused in part by the small movements (saccades) that our eyes constantly make.

A related phenomenon, called the **phi phenomenon,** occurs when two lights situated next to one another turn on and off in an alternating fashion. If the lights are located close enough to each other, the perception will be of one light moving back and forth. This illusion is used to good effect on advertising signs, particularly in Las Vegas, to give the appearance of movement. A motion picture is also an example where individual still pictures shown in rapid sequence give the illusion of movement.

The design in Figure 2.18 illustrates another form of illusory motion. If you stare at the design for a few seconds, it will appear to pulsate. These kinds of pulsating drawings were popular in the 1960s and 1970s in a genre of art called "op art." The pulsating movement occurs because your eye is unable to bring the entire stimulus into focus at one time, partly because constant eye movements shift the image onto different parts of your retina. If you view this illusion through a tiny hole

✦ **FIGURE 2.19** ✦

By spinning this disk clockwise the spirals appear to be spreading outward. Look at the spinning disk for about 1 minute and then stop the disk suddenly. The spirals will suddenly appear to be moving in the opposite direction. The opposite effect can be obtained by spinning the disk counterclockwise.

punched in a piece of paper held close to your eye, you will see that most of the movement stops.

Sometimes objects that are moving in one direction will suddenly reverse direction. You may have noticed that when your car stops abruptly after driving fast, the car may feel like it is moving in reverse. The next time you are by a waterfall, stare directly at it for a minute or so and then quickly shift your gaze to something stationary. The stationary object will appear to be moving upward. You can also illustrate this illusion by using the disk shown in Figure 2.19. Cut out a photocopy of the disk and paste it on cardboard. Punch a small hole in the center and insert a pencil underneath so that you can spin the disk. Spin the disk clockwise for a few seconds until the spiral expands. Then stop the disk and observe what happens. The spirals will now appear to contract. You can get the opposite effect by spinning the disk in the reverse direction. These illusory movements are apparently caused by the fatigue of certain physiological mechanisms designed to detect motion in the visual system. Presenting a repetitive motion to these mechanisms causes them to fatigue and results in a perception of movement in the opposite direction when the motion suddenly stops.

APPLICATIONS

You probably think of visual illusions as something fun to look at, and indeed, magicians make effective use of many of them in their performances. Illusions have a darker side, however. In fact, they can kill you. Approximately 8,000 collisions occur between cars and trains each year because, in large part, the illusion that large objects move slower causes drivers to overestimate the amount of time they have before the train reaches a crossing. One sixth of all airline accidents are estimated to occur because of visual illusions (Kraft & Elworth, 1969). Recently a U.S. Marine pilot flying at 300 feet accidentally sheared the cable supporting a ski gondola, killing 20 people. During the pilot's trial, his defense attorney presented evidence that a visual illusion partly caused the pilot to misjudge the height at which he was flying. A military jury subsequently found the pilot innocent of negligence. More recently, investigators determined that John F. Kennedy, Jr.'s fatal airplane crash resulted in part from his spatial disorientation due to an obscured horizon.

A disproportionate number of automobile and airline accidents occur at night or during obscured viewing conditions, such as haze or fog. You may have noticed that these are precisely the ideal conditions for demonstrating many perceptual illusions, including the autokinetic effect and the phi phenomenon.

UFO Sightings Possibly Explained

Visual illusions are likely the explanation for at least some unidentified flying object (UFO) sightings as well. Again, you may have noticed that these sightings usually take place at night or in some remote spot where viewing conditions are less than ideal. Films of UFOs are invariably so poor that it is difficult to make out exactly what object is being viewed. If UFOs do exist, one would believe that, occasionally, they would appear at a time and location that permitted ideal viewing conditions by many people simultaneously. The autokinetic effect would explain why a small spot of light in a night sky would appear to jerk and dive erratically at seemingly high speeds. Add the power of suggestion to the autokinetic effect to explain the confirmation of these movements by other observers. However, it would be overstating the case to assert unequivocally that all UFO sightings can be explained by visual illusions. Many well-documented instances cannot be discounted as visual illusions, and there may well be intelligent life in outer space. Given that there are trillions and trillions of planets in the universe, the odds favor the existence of life elsewhere. These beings may even be advanced enough to travel to other planets, as we ourselves have. The existing evidence, however, does not support the contention of many well-intentioned witnesses that such objects have visited our planet.

Creating Illusions about Our Appearance

Most fashion-conscious men and women have learned to use illusions to their benefit. Vertical stripes make you look taller while horizontal stripes make you look fatter.

Half the work that is done in this world is to make things appear what they are not.

ELIAS ROOT BEADLE

✦ **FIGURE 2.20** ✦ **How the Color of Clothing Can Affect One's Perceived Size**

The two figures are identical except for the color of their clothing. This is an example of the irradiation illusion in which a dark object on a bright background will appear smaller than a white object on a dark background.

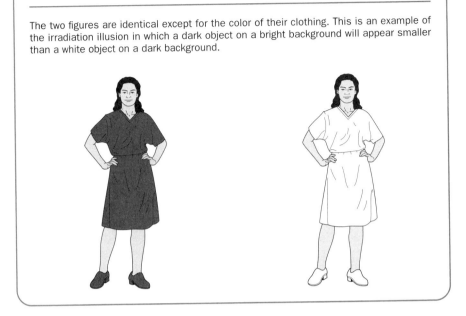

Dressing in different colors can also make you appear larger or smaller. Wearing black, a "slimming" color, rather than white applies the irradiation illusion to favorably distort one's perceived size. Figure 2.20 illustrates the apparent size difference when the same woman is dressed in black as compared to white. Magazines often contain articles on techniques to alter one's appearance that employ the use of visual illusions. Table 2.1 illustrates some of the more common suggestions on how to hide figure deficiencies. These rules apply equally to men and women. It is commonly said that wearing a tie reduces a man's weight by 10 pounds.

Illusions in Art and Architecture

The application of visual illusions in art and architecture is particularly important. All paintings are essentially illusions because they attempt to reproduce a three-dimensional view on a two-dimensional surface. Past masters such as Leonardo da Vinci, Rembrandt, Velasquez, and Monet used many of the principles underlying illusions to great effect. Art gallery collections reveal that as the centuries passed artists made increasingly effective use of illusions in their paintings. Our earlier discussion of the Parthenon showed that if the ancient Greeks had not employed these many illusions in their design, they would not have achieved the aesthetic perfection for which this building is renowned. Architects have learned that the level and the square will not guarantee perfection in the finished design. In addition to size and shape considerations, architects must judiciously apply the use of color and lighting to the design to guarantee a pleasing effect. Any successful artist or architect will have learned a great deal about visual illusions although usually through trial and error rather than formal study (Luckiesh, 1965).

✦ TABLE 2.1 ✦ Frequently Used Fashion Tips to Alter One's Appearance

These fashion guides typically use two perceptual principles: (1) Draw attention away from problem areas and toward more attractive features, and (2) Use visual illusions to alter size or shape.

General Rules:

- Dark colors slim and elongate your body. Light and bright colors tend to enlarge your shape, and draw attention to your body.
- To appear taller, wear solid colors rather than patterns or prints.
- Use only one color or tone to make your figure look tall and slim.
- Vertical stripes make you appear taller, horizontal make you appear shorter and heavier.

Lengthening a Short Figure

- Wear clothes that provide an unbroken vertical line.
- Match the color of tops to bottoms.
- Wear pants without cuffs.
- Wear heels.

Making a Short Neck Appear Longer

- Wear open collars on shirts and sweaters.
- Wear V-necks, oval necks, or slit-necks that show skin.
- Avoid turtlenecks and collars that close high up.
- Do not wear scarves, bulky furs, or ruffles that are close to the neck.
- Tie scarves under the collar.
- Keep hair well off of shoulders.

Making a Large Stomach Appear Smaller

- Avoid wearing anything that cinches in the middle.
- Wear tops and bottoms of same color to emphasize the vertical line.
- Wear pants with pleats.
- Avoid big pockets and pants or skirts that button in the front.
- Wear narrow belts in same color as skirt or pants.

Making Short or Heavy Legs Look Long and Slim

- Wear darker shades on bottom, lighter on top.
- Avoid hosiery with heavy, defined patterns. Socks or stockings with fine vertical ribbing narrow the leg.
- Match colors of hosiery and shoes.
- Wear shoes of skin tone. Avoid white shoes.
- Wear shoes with 2- or 3-inch heels. Avoid flats.

Summary

- The distinction between sensation and perception is important. Sensation involves stimuli striking our sense receptors while perception involves the brain's interpretation of that information. Perception involves the five basic senses, namely, vision, hearing, smell, taste, and touch, all of which decline with age.
- Kinesthesis provides information about the internal environment of our bodies while the vestibular sense supplies information about body position, movement, and acceleration.
- The eye contains structures that include the cornea, iris, pupil, and lens and functions in ways similar to a camera.
- Receptors called rods and cones lie on the retina, which is located on the back of the eye. These receptors respond to light. Rods are sensitive to lower levels of light while cones allow us to see colors.
- Our eyes become maximally sensitive to lower levels of light after about 20 to 30 minutes. Night vision is facilitated by looking slightly to the side of an object and by not looking directly at objects that are brightly illuminated.
- The most common visual disorders are nearsightedness, farsightedness, and cloudy lenses called cataracts.
- Motion is detected by interpreting information from the retina and the movement of eye muscles, as well as the movement of objects relative to one another. Objects are perceived as moving faster when they are small or when the image falls in the center of the retina. Determining an object's speed is more difficult at night or when vision is partially obscured.
- The ear consists of structures that translate changes in air pressure into the perception of sound.
- Sounds vary according to pitch, loudness, and the quality or timbre of the sound.
- Sound is localized by using the cues of relative loudness and arrival time. Brief sounds, such as clicks, are easier to localize than sounds of longer duration. Changes in intensity and pitch also allow for judgments about the distance of a sound.
- Hearing impairment involves (1) conduction deafness that occurs when something blocks the sound from entering the inner part of the ear and (2) nerve deafness that occurs when there is damage to the hair cells or nerve fibers inside the cochlea. Hearing aids only help with conduction deafness.
- Hearing loss, which normally begins after age 20, can be reduced by avoiding prolonged exposure to loud sounds.
- Noises that are unanticipated or uncontrollable are stressful and can affect behavior, but noises that cannot be avoided can sometimes be hidden by masking them.
- The four basic taste sensations are sweet, sour, salty, and bitter. Taste preferences are primarily learned. Factors that affect taste include smell and temperature.
- The sense of smell is called the olfactory sense. The precise way in which smell receptors work is unknown. Our adaptation to smells occurs fairly rapidly. Humans have fewer smell receptors than some animals and thus less sensitivity to smells.
- Odors are often associated with distant memories and have the ability to affect behavior both positively and negatively.
- Pain plays an important role in our lives by signaling when something is a threat to our well-being. It is also a powerful motivator for behavior.
- There are two types of pain, including the sharp, bright pain and the dull, aching variety. Anxiety increases the perception of pain while distraction lessens it. Feeling in control of pain also makes it more tolerable. It is important to distinguish between intermittent acute pain and more persistent chronic pain.
- Sensory deprivation refers to the absence of most external sensory stimulation and causes people to attend more carefully to available stimuli. It can have beneficial effects such as increased sensitivity in vision, hearing, touch, and taste, improved creativity, and successful modification of bad habits.
- Subliminal perception refers to messages presented below the level of awareness. It affects our behavior in very subtle ways but, despite popular belief, cannot be used to make us purchase things, improve our memories, or eliminate bad habits.
- Paranormal phenomena, or ESP, implies perception that occurs beyond the known sensory channels. Varieties include telepathy, precognition, clairvoyance, and psychokinesis, none of which have been proven to exist by scientific examination. Even though these phenomena have no practical applications in our lives, many people hold strong beliefs in their existence despite scientific evidence to the contrary.
- Visual illusions are commonly experienced in nature and in our everyday life. They are caused either by physiological functions in the sense receptors or by our cognitive interpretation of sensory information. Commonly experienced illusions include size distortion, illusions of movement, and ambiguous figures that can be interpreted in more than one way.
- Illusions affect our lives beneficially through art, architecture, and personal enhancement and negatively through distortions that cause accidents and personal harm.

Key Terms

accommodation: changing the shape of the lens, which allows the lens to focus the inverted image on the retina.

ambiguous figures: visual information that can be interpreted in more than one way.

anosmia: a condition in which an individual cannot smell certain odors; supports the idea that there are certain receptors for certain foods.

aromatherapy: the use of fragrances to treat a wide variety of psychological and physical problems.

arrival time: method of sound localization that detects the source of a sound by when it arrives at each ear; most effective for lower pitched sounds.

auditory nerve: responsible for transmission of neural impulses to the brain.

autokinetic effect: a perceptual illusion that occurs when a stationary light is viewed against total darkness; the light will appear to be moving in unpredictable ways.

basilar membrane: a flexible membrane located in the cochlea; flexes when vibrations from the ossicles send waves throughout the fluid in the cochlea.

blind spot: the place where the optic nerve exits through the retina and where no visual receptors exist.

cataracts: a visual disorder in which the lens becomes cloudy causing difficulty with seeing fine detail.

clairvoyance: the ability to correctly forecast a future event.

cochlea: a fluid-filled and coiled tube that the ossicles rest against.

conduction deafness: caused by blockage of the outer ear canal, or damage to the eardrum or ossicles; can be helped with the use of a hearing aid.

cones: receptors on the retina, mostly located in the center of the brain, which are color sensitive and allow for the perception of finer detail.

cornea: the part of the eye that images first pass through, which bends the light rays, partially focusing the image.

dark adaptation: the process of switching sensitivity from high illumination levels to low illumination levels.

decibels (dB): measurement of sound amplitude.

déjà vu: "already seen"; the strong feeling of remembering scenes or events that are being experienced for the first time.

Doppler shift: change in sound that occurs when an object approaches and then passes you.

eardrum: flexible membrane that vibrates where sound strikes.

extrasensory perception (ESP): the ability to gather information beyond the five primary senses; implies that perceptions can occur in the complete absence of any sensation.

farsighted: can clearly see far away, but things up close are blurry.

flavor: sensation that depends on both odor and taste.

hair cells: activated by the flexing of the basilar membrane; generates neural impulses that are collected and transmitted to the brain.

hertz (Hz): the number of cycles between high and low air pressure that occur in one second; related to a sound's pitch.

illusory movement: a perception of movement where there is none.

iris: contains colored muscles that expand and contract; controls the amount of light entering the eye.

irradiation: a perceptual illusion in size distortion that occurs when a bright object is surrounded by a dark object.

kinesthesis: information from muscles, tendons, and joints sent to sense receptors; the information tells the position of limbs, allowing for movement.

lens: a clear membrane that focuses the inverted image on the retina.

lock-and-key theory: a theory maintaining that an electrical impulse is generated when the "key" of an air molecule containing an odor is inserted into the correctly fitting "lock" receptacle of the nose.

masking: the use of one kind of sound to block another kind of sound

moon illusion: an illusion in nature whereby the size of the moon appears larger when it is on the horizon as compared to when it is high overhead.

nearsighted: can clearly see up close, but things far away are blurry.

nerve deafness: caused by damage to either the auditory nerve or the hair cells on the basilar membrane; cannot be helped by a hearing aid because the auditory messages are blocked from reaching the brain.

olfactory bulb: where electrical impulses are sent to detect smells; located below and toward the front of the brain, directly above the upper nasal passage.

olfactory receptor cells: receptors responsible for detection of smells; approximately 30 million cells in each nostril.

olfactory sense: the sense of smell.

optic nerve: a bundle of nerve fibers that transmit electrical impulses to the visual cortex of the brain.

ossicles: three tiny bones in the middle ear; transmits and amplifies vibrations from the eardrum.

paranormal: phenomena that function outside of the normal sensory channels.

perception: the complicated process whereby our brain interprets sensations and gives them meaning.

phantom limb pain: a phenomenon where amputees feel intense pain in arms or legs that are missing.

phi phenomenon: a perceptual illusion of movement that occurs when two lights situated next to one another turn on and off in an alternating fashion.

pitch: the high or low tones of a sound due to vibration of sound waves.
placebo: a fake pill or injection.
precognition: the ability to correctly perceive future events, such as political and historical events, or catastrophes.
psychokinesis: the act of using the mind to control physical matter (i.e., levitation, bending an object).
pupil: the opening in the middle of the iris; regulated by the iris.
relative loudness: method of sound localization whereby the brain detects differences in sound intensity in each ear, and calculates the direction of the source of the sound; most effective when locating the source of high-pitched sounds; the most effective way to localize sound.
Restricted Environmental Stimulation Therapy (REST): a therapeutic technique in which sensory deprivation tanks are used to help change habits (such as smoking, dieting, and alcohol consumption).
retina: the surface at the back of the eye where rods and cones are located.
rods: receptors on the retina that are sensitive to black and white but not to color.
saccades: small, rapid eye movements.
semantic priming: the phenomenon in which a word is easier to recognize after a related word has been flashed previously.
semicircular canals: three fluid-filled canals located in the inner ear that provide information about directional changes of the body or head.
sensation: the process of converting physical stimuli into neural impulses that our brain can understand.
sensory deprivation: a state of being with reduced external sensory stimulation.
subliminal perception: the phenomenon of a message being presented below the level of awareness or "below threshold."
telepathy: the ability of one person to send thoughts to another person, or for a person to perceive another's thoughts.
threshold: the point at which sensation awareness begins.
timbre: created when a number of different waves of differing frequency and amplitude are combined and mixed together.
tinnitus: a ringing sensation that indicates that hair cells have suffered damage.
transduction: the conversion of physical stimuli to electrical impulses.
vestibular sacs: two fluid-filled structures located in the inner ear that provide information about body position, movement, and acceleration.
vestibular sense: gives information about the position, movement, and acceleration of the body, allowing for a sense of balance.
white noise: a broad spectrum of sound frequencies or pitches; sounds such as the noise of a waterfall or a running fan; one of the most effective methods of masking sound.

3

LEARNING

Our ability to learn new things is one of the most important and basic capabilities that we possess. While we often take this capability for granted, our lives would be very different if we were unable to learn. As humans evolved into more and more sophisticated and intelligent organisms, the role of learning became increasingly significant. Biologists have discovered that the more complex the organism, the greater the importance of learning. One-cell organisms have little, if any, ability to learn. Their simple behaviors are guided by a repertoire that is largely intact from the moment they come into existence. As we move up the phylogenetic scale into more complex and highly developed organisms, the role of learning generally becomes more critical while the role of innate or inborn behaviors decreases in significance.

The Mind as "Blank Slate"

Human beings, who are almost unique in having the ability to learn from the experience of others, are also remarkable for their apparent disinclination to do so.

DOUGLAS ADAMS
Last Chance to See

Humans, unlike less complex organisms, are born with a limited set of innate skills. The 17th-century philosopher John Locke (1632–1704) coined the term **tabula rasa** or "blank slate" to describe this condition. During the 17th century, children carried a piece of black slate with them to school and wrote on it with chalk, much as we use paper and pencil today. Locke believed that when humans were born their mind consisted of such a blank slate and that their experiences with their environment resulted in writings on this mental slate. He maintained that heredity provides us with no knowledge of the world, only learning does. As we discovered in Chapter 1, the field of behavioral genetics has demonstrated that this view is too simplistic. It now appears certain that we are born with certain genetic predispositions or behaviors that we are genetically inclined to display under the right environmental circumstances. Nevertheless, Locke was mainly correct that such behaviors do not exist at birth and require some interaction with the environment before they reveal themselves.

Think for a moment about how completely helpless a newborn baby is. A newborn child would only survive on its own for a few hours without assistance from others. Outside of a few reflexive responses, such as the leg jerking in response to being tickled on the foot or the pupillary reflex to bright light, the infant is relatively insensitive to most stimulation from its environment. Very quickly, however, children learn to recognize their mother's voice and are comforted by its sound. The "blank slate" of the human mind quickly begins to fill with the writings of our interaction with our environment. Without this ability to learn and adapt, humans would never have evolved into the complex organism that we see today. Understanding how learning occurs is critical for all areas of psychology. The act of falling in love, socializing with others, becoming fearful, preferring certain experiences and not others, and nearly every other aspect of human behavior is closely governed by the laws of learning.

The Components of Learning

Learning is not compulsory . . . neither is survival.

W. EDWARDS DEMING

The definition of **learning** is *a relatively permanent change in mental state or behavior due to experience.* At first glance this definition seems deceptively simple, but it is quite specific about what does and does not constitute learning. Consider the following:

- Learning refers to a *relatively permanent* change and not some temporary change that might be due to factors such as fatigue, motivational state, injury, drugs, or disease. Our behavior may change under the influence of marijuana, but we do not consider this change to be learned. We may *learn* to use illegal drugs, but the behavioral changes caused by those drugs are considered outside the realm of learned behavior. Similarly, extreme fatigue will alter our behavior but not in a learned fashion.

- Learned behavior is not behavior that occurs automatically to a stimulus such as a reflexive response. We pull our hand away from a hot stove reflexively because of the pain rather than learning. Reflex responses occur automatically to a stimulus and require no learning.
- Certain behaviors occur as a result of physical development and maturation. When we are very young, we have no voluntary control over certain muscles. These muscles can only be controlled and used after a certain level of physiological maturation occurs. Changes in behavior due to development and maturation are not considered learned.
- Learning does not have to occur as a result of direct experience. We can learn *vicariously* by observing the actions of others. For instance, you can learn to solve a mathematical problem strictly by observing how someone else does it. This is called observational learning and will be discussed in more detail later in this chapter.
- Learning does not always result in positive changes in behavior. We can learn bad habits as easily as we do good ones, perhaps more easily. Racial prejudice is a good example of a learned behavior that has negative consequences.
- Learning is adaptive. Through this process, we learn which behaviors are appropriate and useful and which ones are not.

Learning versus Performance

Psychologists draw an important distinction between learning and **performance.** Learning means that we have acquired the capability to behave in a certain way while performance is reflected in the actual behavior itself. The fact that we have learned a behavior does not mean that we will actually perform it. Usually performance only occurs in the right situation and when there is motivation to do so. You may have learned to play the trumpet but probably would not do so in the middle of a college lecture unless it was the right situation (a music-performance class) and you were motivated to do so (the professor asked you to perform). Furthermore, we can find ourselves in situations where we have learned to do something but cannot perform the behaviors to demonstrate the knowledge. College students are very familiar with this phenomenon. They sometimes study material until they know it very well but then cannot perform on an examination. This leads to the familiar claim that "I knew the material but couldn't answer the questions on the test!" This indeed can be the case and is not always a lame excuse for doing poorly. Professors develop tests of performance, such as college exams, to reflect how much has been learned. Therefore, test grades actually are based on your performance and not on learning.

Finally, note that you can have learning without performance but cannot have performance without learning. You might challenge this statement by responding that you could guess the correct answers on 10 true/false questions and that would show mastery of the material (performance) without any learning. However, such chance occurrences are not considered to be examples of learning. You were just lucky, and there was no permanent change in behavior that would allow you to do the same on subsequent tests.

Overview of the Major Types of Learning

Psychologists believe that learning can take several forms, including classical conditioning, operant (also called instrumental) conditioning, and observational learning. (Note that psychologists treat the word *conditioning* as synonymous with learning.) Let's look at an overview of these three forms of learning before we examine each in detail. Classical conditioning allows us to form associations between events in our environment. Among other things, it allows us to learn to expect and prepare for events to occur. Operant conditioning allows us to repeat behaviors that bring about positive consequences and to avoid behaviors that result in unpleasant consequences. Observational learning allows us to learn by watching the behaviors of others.

As you read this chapter, notice that much of the research on principles of learning was done with animals. For example, the seminal research by B. F. Skinner was conducted with rats and pigeons while Ivan Pavlov worked with dogs. Sometimes people are skeptical about how relevant the research findings conducted with animals are for humans. The reason psychologists use animals is that animals allow us to better control for variables that affect learning. For instance, with animals we can control for previous experience, motivational level, and genetic background, whereas it is nearly impossible to control for these factors in humans. Furthermore, decades of experimentation with both humans and nonhumans have shown that the two learn in basically the same fashion. Variables that affect learning in animals have very similar effects on humans. Obviously, certain aspects of learning, such as the learning of language, can best be studied in humans even though some psychologists have demonstrated similarities between chimpanzees and humans (Gardner & Gardner, 1969). For both animals and humans, learning serves to allow adaptation to the environment and to affect species survival and proliferation.

In this and following chapters, I will frequently refer to research that has been conducted on animals. Some individuals believe that it is wrong to use animals in any way, regardless of the potential benefits to humans. Most psychologists disagree strongly with such a view. Unfortunately, in earlier times there were instances where animals were mistreated during research. In recent years, steps have been taken to ensure that this will not happen. Today, all animal experimentation must be approved by a board of experts that includes a veterinarian. Animal researchers must document, prior to beginning their research, that animals will be adequately housed, that they have enough space to exercise properly, and that their diets are appropriate. Furthermore, animals must be treated humanely at all times. There are rigorous local, state, and federal laws and regulations that govern all aspects of animal care and use with serious penalties for those who violate them. Although some individuals may disagree, most scientists today believe that the benefits from animal research fully justify their use in experimentation, but only if the animal's rights are carefully protected.

Learning Not to Respond

You probably think of learning as acquiring an appropriate response to some stimulus. Sometimes, however, we must learn *not* to respond to a stimulus. The process by which a repeated presentation of a stimulus does *not* cause a response is called **habituation.** Almost all organisms, both human and animal, will react automatically to a sudden and unexpected stimulus. If you are driving in your car and you suddenly hear a loud bang, you will automatically look for the source of the sound. Recall that even newborn infants will turn their heads to locate the source of a sound. This automatic response to an unexpected stimulus is called an **orienting response.** It is nature's way of making certain that we pay attention to stimuli that might be important for our survival.

Classical Conditioning

Very shortly after the birth of my first child, my wife came home to find me at the dining table holding my son in my arms and a soda straw in my mouth. I also held a spoon in my hand while an empty water glass sat nearby. Not surprisingly, my wife wanted to know what the heck I was doing to our child. I explained that I was curious to find out whether an infant only a few days old could be classically conditioned. Under her very watchful eye, I demonstrated how the tink of a spoon against the glass would cause my son to blink. I would tink the glass and immediately afterward blow a soft puff of air on his eye. A puff of air on the eyeball makes humans automatically blink in response. After a few pairings of a tink followed by a puff of air, I demonstrated to my increasingly suspicious wife that the sound of the spoon against the glass alone, without a puff of air, would now regularly elicit an eye blink in my son.

Early Research in Classical Conditioning

My rather crude experiment followed the pioneering research done by the Russian medical doctor and physiologist Ivan P. Pavlov (1849–1936). Pavlov spent 2 decades investigating digestive processes in dogs. The dogs were held in a harness that constrained their movements. When food powder was placed on a hungry dog's tongue, it caused the secretion of digestive juices into the stomach. The food powder also caused the dog to begin salivating. Pavlov measured the more accessible salivary response by connecting a tube to the salivary ducts in the dog's mouth so that the amount of salivation could be calculated precisely. The dogs were regularly fed in metal pans that were stored in a cabinet. In the process of preparing the dogs' food, Pavlov noticed that this noise from clanking the pans caused the dogs to begin salivating in anticipation of their meal. Since these particular stimuli did directly produce salivation in dogs, Pavlov concluded that the dogs had been conditioned (i.e., had learned) to salivate to these sounds. He became so intrigued by these findings that he largely dropped his research on digestion and spent the remainder of his scientific career exploring how this conditioning process worked.

Stimuli and Responses in Classical Conditioning

Pavlov began a series of experiments to explore this phenomenon that today we refer to as **classical conditioning.** He discovered that a previously neutral stimulus can acquire the ability to elicit a response if it is paired with a stimulus that already elicits the response. In some of his early research, he conditioned his dogs to salivate to the sound of a tone that he produced with a tuning fork. When presented with a tone, dogs will initially make an orienting response to the sound, including increased alertness, and turn their heads toward the sound. After several trials, habituation will set in and no response occurs to further presentations of the sound. Pavlov then presented the tone and, shortly thereafter, dropped food powder on the animals' tongues to stimulate reflexive salivation. After several trials, the animals would salivate at the sound of the tone alone. The food powder is known as the **unconditioned stimulus** or **UCS.** It is a stimulus that causes an automatic response (salivation, in this instance) without any need for prior conditioning, hence the term *un*conditioned stimulus. The automatic response to the UCS is called the **unconditioned response** or **UCR.** It is an *un*conditioned response because no conditioning or learning was necessary; the response is a reflexive response to the UCS. The originally neutral stimulus, the tone in Pavlov's experiment, which comes to elicit the conditioned response, is called the **conditioned stimulus** or **CS.** And finally, the response that has been conditioned to the previously neutral stimulus is called the **conditioned response** or **CR.** Importantly, the CR is always an adaptive response that in some way serves the organism's need. It prepares the organism for some event, good or bad, that is about to occur. In Pavlov's dogs, the salivation prepared the dogs to eat the food that would be forthcoming shortly after the CS.

Extinction and Spontaneous Recovery

Pavlov investigated several other phenomena related to classical conditioning. After conditioning had taken place and the tone caused the dog to salivate, the UCS (food) could be omitted and the dog continued to salivate to the sound of the tone alone. However, if the tone was repeatedly presented without again being paired with food, the salivation response gradually weakened and eventually ceased altogether. Pavlov called this weakening of the CS–CR association **extinction.** The previously neutral stimulus (tone) that has acquired the ability to elicit the conditioned response (salivation) will have that ability extinguished (hence the term *extinction*) unless food powder is occasionally paired with it. Once extinction has occurred, further presentations of the tone will produce no salivation. The tone is once again a neutral stimulus, just as it was before the conditioning took place.

One day, so the story goes, after Pavlov completely extinguished one of his dogs to salivating to a tone, he put the dog back in its cage. After about an hour, he returned the dog to the harness, intending to again condition the salivary response. He sounded the tone but inadvertently omitted dropping food powder on the dog's tongue. To Pavlov's surprise, the dog again salivated to the tone even though the salivation response had been completely extinguished an hour earlier. Pavlov called this **spontaneous recovery** because the salivation response had "recovered spontaneously" without any further introduction of food powder. He also noticed that the dog salivated less than it did at the end of the original conditioning trials. In fact, a CR that occurs during spontaneous recovery is always weaker than the CR that existed before the extinction process began. Pavlov found that he could again extinguish the CR by presenting the tone several times without any food powder. This time the process of extinction took place faster and with fewer presentations of the tone alone than it did initially. However, if the dog were allowed to rest following this second extinction, another spontaneous recovery of the CR would again occur in an even weaker form. In order to completely extinguish the response, Pavlov found that he had to repeat the extinction process several times and allow for spontaneous recovery to occur between each session. Interestingly, he found that it took longer to extinguish the response than it had to originally acquire it. Furthermore, relearning the CR following extinction occurs very rapidly. Only a very few pairings of the food with the tone bring the CR back to its original strength. We will see later that these findings are very important when we talk about the applications of classical conditioning to our own behavior.

To make this material more relevant, you might want to try to classically condition a friend. You can easily replicate the experiment that I did with my newborn son and use all the new knowledge that you have just acquired about the classical conditioning process. Use a straw to blow a puff of air into the subject's eye. Immediately before the puff of air, make some kind of distinctive sound, such as snapping your fingers, tapping on a table, or some other similar sound. After several conditioning trials (sound stimulus followed immediately by the puff of air), present the sound alone and see if the person blinks. Once the blinking response has been acquired, present the sound alone and carefully monitor the eye blinks. Continue to present the sound alone until the response has been completely extinguished. Then let the person rest for several minutes. Check for spontaneous recovery by presenting the sound alone and see if the subject blinks. Reextinguish the blink by again presenting the tone without the puff of air. Another good UCS is a sharp loud noise. To demonstrate this, use inflated balloons as a UCS to produce a startle response. Present some neutral stimulus, such as a sound or even a tap on your friend's arm, followed shortly by popping the balloon. Observe how, after only a few trials, the neutral stimulus will produce an anticipatory startle response.

Stimulus Generalization

Pavlov also noticed that dogs salivated when he used a tone different from the one he used originally to condition the dogs. The more similar the new sound was to the original CS, the greater the amount of salivation. Conversely, the more dissimilar the sound from the original, the less the salivation—although Pavlov found that even a very dissimilar stimulus (a buzzer, rather than a tone) would cause some salivation. This tendency to respond to similar stimuli is called **stimulus generalization** because the response "generalizes" to other similar stimuli.

Discrimination Learning

Pavlov's dogs also learned to respond to certain tones but not to others. This ability to distinguish between conditioned stimuli is known as **discrimination.** In some respects, discrimination is the opposite of stimulus generalization because it requires that the organism respond to certain stimuli and not others even if the other stimuli are similar. In order to accomplish this, Pavlov would classically condition the dogs to one tone with food powder and then present a different tone without food powder. Training would continue until the dog salivated only to the tone associated with the food powder. This discrimination process could be quite lengthy, particularly if the two tones were similar to one another.

Relevance of Classical Conditioning to Everyday Behavior

When students first learn about classical conditioning, many naturally wonder what possible relevance the topic of a dog learning to slobber at the sound of a tone has to their everyday life. Learning to blink to a particular sound also does not seem germane to our daily experiences. In fact, though, we know that classical conditioning is an important part of our everyday learning. It serves two functions. The first is the ability to recognize stimuli that *predict* the occurrence of an important and relevant subsequent event. For example, we learn to associate the sound of a snake's rattle with the potential pain it can inflict, which allows us to take appropriate evasive action. The second function is the capacity for a neutral stimulus to acquire the properties of a stimulus with which it has been paired. If the neutral stimulus is paired with something pleasurable, it will take on pleasurable properties itself. If it is paired with something unpleasant, it takes on unpleasant properties. A doctor's white lab coat is a neutral stimulus that children often find paired with unpleasant medical procedures such as shots. The sound of a dentist's drill, once a neutral stimulus, has probably come to have powerful properties associated with it whenever it's heard.

Conditioned Emotional Responses

When a previously neutral stimulus acquires the ability to arouse an emotional response, such as feelings of fear, anger, disgust, tenderness, contempt, or longing, then we say that the response is a **conditioned emotional response.** *Almost any neutral stimulus, by being paired with some pleasant or unpleasant stimulus, can acquire an emotional response.* Just as Pavlov's dogs learned to salivate to a previously neutral stimulus, we learn to respond emotionally to previously neutral stimuli.

Think about stimuli that regularly evoke an emotional response in yourself. Perhaps you have an intense fear of snakes or spiders. Do you have a dislike for certain colors? How about the sight of a dentist's chair? If a police car pulls up behind your car while you are driving, do you find that you are uncomfortable? These are all things that were neutral stimuli at one time but, through the process of classical conditioning, have come to elicit an emotional response. Let's look at how this process occurs.

Learning to Fear. Many people are nearly incapacitated by fears, thoughts, or behaviors that they feel powerless to control. A **phobia** is an unreasonable fear of a specific object or situation.

When I was an undergraduate, a friend of mine fell asleep while driving and suffered severe injuries when he crashed. After physically recovering from the accident, he found that he had such an intense fear of automobiles that he could no longer drive or even ride as a passenger in a car. This reaction is not uncommon for people involved in serious automobile accidents. Based on what we have learned about classical conditioning, we can trace how this fear developed. The automobile, which was initially neutral or probably even elicited a positive emotional response for my friend, became paired with the trauma and pain associated with the crash (the unconditioned stimulus, in this example). That UCS led to an unconditioned response of fear and strong emotional arousal, a normal reflexive reaction to an automobile crash. Just this one pairing of CS (car) and UCS (trauma) and the resulting UCR (fear) caused an association to be formed. Now the previously benign stimulus, the car, took on the ability to elicit an emotional response, namely fearfulness. My friend not only avoided cars exactly like the one he crashed but all cars and trucks, evidence of stimulus generalization to other similar objects. Even several months after the accident he still avoided driving. Apparently extinction had not yet set in.

A fear response can be classically conditioned even though a person has not directly experienced the fear-inducing stimulus. If a parent has a deathly fear of heights, the child may develop a similar fear just by observing the parent's fearful responses. Fear responses to an object can occur just by reading about it or observing a vivid account in a movie. Immediately after the movie *Jaws* was released, the percentage of people swimming in the ocean dropped significantly, an example of observational learning.

Phobias are a very common psychological disorder with which many people learn to live. The most common phobia in the United States is a fear of snakes, followed by a fear of high, exposed places, mice, flying on an airplane, and closed-in, small spaces such as elevators. Sometimes these phobias can be debilitating to an individual's everyday life. Fortunately, this disorder is easily treatable.

A conditioned emotional response can occur to almost anything. If you have been mugged in a dark alley, you will probably find yourself fearful if again faced with having to walk down another alley. People whose homes have been burglarized often report feelings of discomfort being in their home afterwards. Many times we are unaware of the circumstances behind these emotional responses. When my wife and I were deciding on a name for our firstborn son, we went through the usual process of systematically listing different possibilities and often rejecting a possibility by claiming, "I never liked that name!" In fact, the conditioned emotional response that we had to various names probably occurred through classical conditioning. For instance, the name William is a perfectly good name, in fact a family name, but one that I associate with a bully who used to terrorize me in elementary school. The previously neutral stimulus of the name "William" paired with the boy who bullied me fits into the classical conditioning paradigm thus:

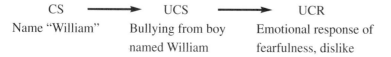

CS	→	UCS	→	UCR
Name "William"		Bullying from boy named William		Emotional response of fearfulness, dislike

Almost every time I saw this boy, he bullied me so that I received repeated pairings of the CS–UCS, resulting in the conditioned emotional response to his name "William." Of course, I also had a conditioned emotional response to the boy in question as well as to his name. However, I have learned through the process of discrimination not to have an emotional response to every person with that name.

Often we react negatively to people or things without any awareness of why we do. Frequently there is a classically conditioned response that accounts for our dislike although we have no memory of the particular circumstances. For example, many people express a preference for or against people with certain traits or appearance, such as hair color, stature, dress, and so forth. Can you imagine circumstances whereby you would be conditioned to react negatively to people based on these or similar identifiable traits?

Many human behaviors contain a component that is learned through classical conditioning, including some that you probably would not suspect. Let's examine some of these.

Examples of Classically Conditioned Behavior

Falling in Love

The person with whom you fall in love starts off as a neutral conditioned stimulus. However, through mutually shared activities, this neutral stimulus acquires the ability to elicit a positive emotional response. Walking together holding hands, kissing, telling each other how much they like one another; all are activities that cause lovers to associate warm, loving emotions with their partner's face, actions, personality, and voice. When they are apart, looking at a picture of their lover will evoke the conditioned emotional responses, as will recalling a memory of the individual.

Of course, love can take some interesting twists and turns that parallel classical conditioning phenomena. People fall in love (acquisition) and they fall out of love (extinction). Sometimes after breaking up (extinction), the couple will regain the old feelings they had for one another (spontaneous recovery) and reunite. Not infrequently, one or the other of the partners will become attracted to another individual, often one who has similar qualities to the original partner (stimulus generalization). "Love at first sight" can often be explained as a case of generalizing feelings to another person who possesses stimulus attributes (hair, voice, personality, style of dressing, mannerisms, etc.) similar to a person with whom we previously had strong feelings. You have probably noticed that many people repeatedly fall in love with the same kind of person, even when the relationships never seem to work out. Love is a very complicated emotion and one that cannot be explained strictly in terms of classical conditioning. Other facets of the emotion of love will be explored in Chapter 7.

Sexual Attraction to Objects

One of the more curious aspects of human behavior is the tendency for some people, usually males, to form a strong sexual attachment to an object. These sexual attachments to objects, typically articles of clothing, are known as **fetishes.** A common fetish among men is sexual arousal by women's shoes. Psychologists believe that classical conditioning is likely involved in this sexual attachment. A man who is sexually aroused by a woman wearing high-heel shoes, for example, may find that the shoes alone are sufficient to elicit arousal. For reasons that are unclear, some people are more susceptible to developing fetishes than others. Hence, there are probably processes at work besides classical conditioning to account for the formation of such sexual attachments. Nevertheless, when a sexual attachment to an object does occur, it is likely through the process of classical conditioning.

The word *fetish* is commonly misunderstood to mean a "fixation" or "preoccupation." Although these alternate meanings are appropriate in some situations, it is important to know that in the context of psychology, a fetish is a *sexual attachment.* For instance, you may hear a classmate admit to having a "belt fetish," meaning a preoccupation with looking at people's styles of belts. However, it could be understood to mean a sexual attachment to belts. So the next time you are tempted to confess an unknown "fetish," you may want to choose your words carefully!

Food and Taste Likes and Dislikes

All of us have certain foods that we like and dislike. As discussed in Chapter 2, many different sensory components influence the preferences, but classical conditioning also plays a role. One Thanksgiving many years ago, my young son happened to become very ill with a fever and rash only a few hours after having our traditional turkey dinner. The emergency room physician diagnosed scarlet fever, which developed from a strep infection. It was several years before he would eat turkey or stuffing during the holidays, vividly recalling and firmly stating that the turkey had caused his illness. He had experienced what is known as **conditioned taste aversion,** the phenomenon of avoiding to eat something that has previously been associated with illness. The CR in this case was the emotional component of the illness that was associated with the turkey dinner. As is always the case, the CR was only fractionally as strong as the UCR; that is, he did not become ill when he was subsequently exposed to turkey at Christmas. Nevertheless, the CR was strong enough that it caused him to avoid eating a once favorite meal. Furthermore, we also noticed that chicken lost some of its appeal to him, the result of stimulus generalization.

APPLICATIONS

Health Applications

Unfortunately, taste aversion sometimes works to our disadvantage. Cancer patients often become violently ill with nausea and vomiting after undergoing chemotherapy treatment. Patients frequently associate this reaction with the last meal they consumed before treatment. Consequently, they are unable to eat the same food substances that preceded their treatment. After numerous treatments, patients can find that they have developed taste aversions to many different foods, which results in their refusal to eat and the severe loss of weight. To combat this effect, physicians often recommend that only one specific food item always be eaten prior to chemotherapy so that the taste aversion will be restricted to that particular food item only. Unfortunately, this technique is not always effective because some cancers themselves cause nausea that can generalize to whatever food substance has been consumed. Other things that cancer patients can do are (1) keep the interval between eating and chemotherapy as long as possible, (2) eat only foods that already have familiar and positive associations, and (3) eat only bland foods to minimize the greater potency of strong tastes to become a conditioned stimulus. These strategies illustrate how classical conditioning principles discovered by Pavlov can be beneficially applied in a medical setting.

In some instances, conditioned taste aversions can be therapeutic. Giving individuals a substance that induces severe nausea whenever alcohol is consumed has been effective in treating alcoholics. Similarly, people have been assisted in quitting smoking by placing substances in the tobacco that give off an unpleasant taste. Such techniques are more effective than other therapies, such as treatment that pairs alcohol consumption with shock, because of our biological predisposition to associate illness with substances that are consumed.

Stimuli that are paired with a medication may eventually come to elicit the same response as the medication. As an example, Spencer, Yaden, and Lal (1988) paired a distinctive odor (CS) with a drug that reduces blood pressure (UCS). After repeated pairing, the odor alone was able to reduce the patient's blood pressure. Similar findings have been obtained with painkillers. For example, if a distinctive sound or odor is consistently paired with the administration of morphine, the sound or odor will eventually offer some pain relief by itself.

There is even some tentative evidence that the body's disease-fighting immune system can be classically conditioned. If a person takes a drug that elicits the immune response and the drug has a certain smell or taste, the smell or taste by itself may later come to elicit the immune response without the drug.

The principals of classical conditioning have been used successfully to treat bed-wetting. A bed pad has been developed that causes a loud sound to occur the moment it detects moisture from urine. The sound serves as a UCS that elicits the UCR of waking up as soon as bed-wetting begins. After several such pairings the child begins to associate the sensation of a full bladder (CS) with waking up. Several commercial products are available for this purpose and have proven to be effective.

Classically Conditioned Attitudes

Can our attitudes toward others be shaped by classical conditioning? All the evidence suggests that this is the case. Robert Baron and Donn Byrne (1997) discuss how classical conditioning may cause us to form attitudes about other people. They describe a situation in which a young child sees her mother frown and show other signs of disapproval each time the mother encounters members of an ethnic group. The child is initially neutral toward members of this group. Ethnic minorities often have visible and identifiable features that can include skin color, accent, and style of dress. Each of these features is paired with the mother's negative emotional reactions. Through the process of classical conditioning the child comes to also react negatively to these ethnic features as well as to members of the group. This process is illustrated in Figure 3.1.

The mass media have been accused of contributing to the formation of these attitudes by infrequently portraying ethnic minorities in movies or on television. Furthermore, when ethnic minorities are portrayed, it is often in low-status, comic, or criminal roles. The ". . . news media often portray Blacks engaging in activities that are defined as threats, unreasonable demands, militancy, failure, or burdens on the mainstream American culture" (Pan & Kosicki, 1996; p. 149). Such media exposure furthers the attitude-formation process previously described.

Of course, such attitude formation is not limited to ethnic minorities. If women are consistently portrayed in certain roles by the mass media and in other aspects of our culture, we should expect that it will affect our attitudes of what the proper role of women should be. Overweight people are frequently portrayed as the butt of jokes and as buffoons on television and in the movies. Such pairings have undoubtedly contributed to the negative attitudes and stereotypes many people hold about overweight individuals. Prejudice and stereotyping are very complicated topics, and the explanations for it go far beyond simple classical conditioning. I will explore this topic in greater detail in Chapter 12.

Advertising

Can you be influenced in your decisions about what product to purchase by advertisers using a classical conditioning paradigm? Absolutely. Furthermore, chances are that you will be totally unaware of being influenced. If you think about it, advertising presents an excellent opportunity to bring about a classically conditioned response in an unsuspecting consumer. For classical conditioning to occur, advertisers need to present a neutral stimulus (CS), which is the product they are attempting to

✦ FIGURE 3.1 ✦

Classical conditioning of attitudes takes place when a young child sees her mother indicate signs of emotional discomfort when she encounters members of a certain ethnic group. The child initially has no emotional reaction to the characteristics of this group of people. After repeated pairing of the mother's emotional discomfort with these characteristics, the child acquires negative emotional reactions to the characteristics as well.

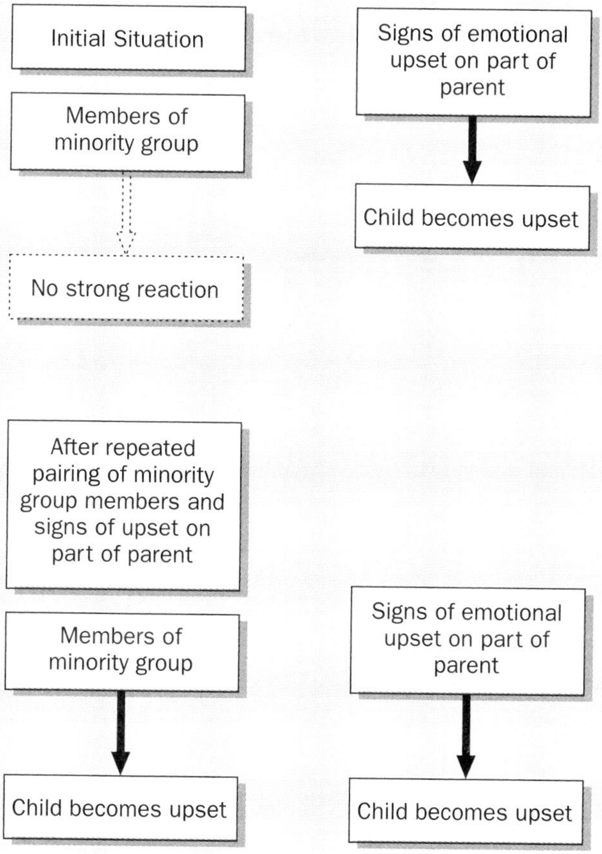

SOURCE: From Baron, Robert A., & Byrne, Donn, *Social Psychology* (8th ed.). © 1997 by Allyn & Bacon. Reprinted by permission.

sell. This needs to be followed with a UCS that elicits some kind of reflexive response. There are a wide variety of visual stimuli that have these properties for us. For example, a picture of an attractive male or female will cause some sexual arousal in most members of the opposite sex. Now, let's see how advertisers can put this all together to sell some beer. It actually is quite simple. The advertiser shows a visual image of the beer paired with some very attractive males and females cavorting in skimpy bathing suits on a beautiful, pristine ocean beach. As consumers, we view

Advertisers often attempt to enhance the desirability of their product by displaying their product with attractive males or females. The intent is that viewers will be sexually aroused by the picture and will then associate the arousal with the product. This is an example of the way that advertisers attempt to exploit classical conditioning in their advertisements.

the CS (beer) paired with the UCS (attractive, sexually arousing male and female models) and it elicits a pleasurable response in us. The classically conditioned message is that the beer product alone will elicit the CR of enjoying ourselves on a beach with sexually arousing members of the opposite sex.

You might be saying to yourself that you would never fall for anything so simplistic. Experimental research and sales figures suggest otherwise. One study tested the hypothesis that the presence of an attractive woman would help sell new cars. Researchers showed adult males a picture of a car either with or without a sexually arousing, provocatively dressed woman standing next to it. The researchers then asked the subjects which cars cost more, were better designed, would go faster, and were more dangerous. Overwhelmingly, the males chose the car paired with the woman. When asked if the presence of the woman influenced their judgment, only 1 out of 23 thought it had (Smith & Engel, 1968).

We all worry about accidents or other catastrophes that might occur to us. Frequently, advertisers will pair their product with some fear-reducing stimulus. One prominent tire company ran ads of an infant sitting safely inside a tire that was traveling down a road and presented the message that you should buy their product ". . . because so much is riding on your tires." A recent advertising campaign on television for an insurance company showed images of a house bursting into flames and an automobile rolling unattended down a hill, violently crashing into various objects. The CS, consisting of the logo for the company and a soothing message about how their insurance can "put things right," is paired with reverse footage of the house bursting into flames, the flames disappearing, and the house returning to normal. Likewise, the rolling car reverses direction, undoing all the damage it caused rolling down the hill. The hoped-for CR to these scenes is a reduction of the anxiety introduced by the scenes of disaster, and the goal is that the insurance company's name will become conditioned to elicit such feelings of reassurance.

Think about the myriad products advertised on television to solve health problems. Almost invariably, there is an image of an individual suffering from the problem (anything from dandruff to hemorrhoids), accompanied by distressing sounds or visual images. Shortly thereafter, the product is shown, usually accompanied by pleasing visual images and music, followed by another vision of the person completely cured of the offending health problem.

The beauty of using classical conditioning in advertising is that it is effective, yet the recipient is ordinarily unaware of the influence. Remember, in classical conditioning the CS serves as a signal that some other event is about to happen. This, of course, is exactly the message that advertisers seek to deliver. As you watch television or look through magazines, see if you can identify the UCS that the advertiser is using and the CR it is hoping to produce.

In summary, classical conditioning plays an important role in our behavior. It is particularly important in the role it plays in our emotional reactions to stimuli, in our motivations, and in our attitudes. If a given stimulus is a reliable predictor of what is to happen, then we learn to respond to that stimulus. If it is not a reliable predictor, then we learn to ignore it. Classical conditioning allows us efficiently to learn to fear certain things and not others. It enables us to make appropriate preparations for eating and to learn what foods make us ill. It does not, however, control our body movements. Golfers have learned through classical conditioning to be fearful when a nearby golfer shouts "Fore!", but it has not taught us to cover our heads or seek shelter from the potential danger. It has taught us to salivate at the mere thought of a juicy steak but not how to locate a steak house to satisfy our hunger. It may have even taught us that a certain sports car is "sexy" but without another kind of learning, you would still be driving your old unsexy clunker. To learn appropriate responses toward or away from various stimuli requires another kind of learning.

Operant Conditioning

Behavior and Its Consequences

Behavior has consequences. Sometimes the consequences are favorable and sometimes unfavorable. The feedback that we receive from our behavior teaches us which responses are appropriate and which are not. The feedback we get after responding guides our future decisions about how to behave. A child who has tantrums when not allowed to get his way may be reinforced by the parents "giving in" to stop the child's misbehavior. If the child is then allowed to do whatever he wants, he will quickly learn to throw a tantrum the next time he wants to have his own way. If you inadvertently put too much salt on your food, the food will taste bad and you will

✦ **FIGURE 3.2** ✦ **Thorndike's Puzzle Box Used in His Early Research on Operant Conditioning in Cats**

The animal could escape from the box by making a certain response. In this example, tilting the black pole would allow the door to open, permitting the animal to escape.

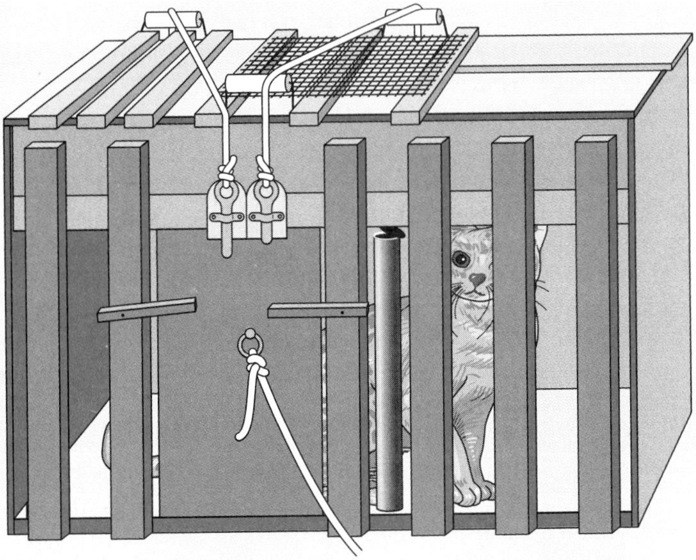

exercise more caution the next time you use salt. In both cases, the probability that individuals will respond in a certain way has been altered by the consequences of their behavior.

In nature there are neither rewards nor punishments—there are consequences.

R. G. INGERSOLL
Lectures and Essays, Third Series, "Some Reasons Why"

Edward Thorndike, a Harvard graduate student in the early 1900s, conducted some of the earliest research on how the consequences of behavior affect learning. His pioneering research was done with cats that he placed into puzzle boxes from which they could escape if they made a certain response, such as pulling a string or tilting a pole (Figure 3.2). Thorndike would place a small food reward just outside the door to the box as an added incentive for the cat to escape. When the cat was required to tilt a pole to escape, Thorndike found that the cat would initially engage in a variety of behaviors such as pawing at the door, biting the door, and so forth. Eventually the cat would strike the pole with his body, often by accident, and escape. Thorndike found that the next time the cat was placed in the box, it again made pawing and biting responses but would again bump against the pole to escape. After several repetitions, the amount of time it took the cat to tilt the pole to escape became shorter and shorter. At some point, the cat learned to immediately tilt the pole without hesitation.

Thorndike reasoned that certain of the cat's responses had been strengthened while others had not. Pawing at the door and scratching the walls did not produce the desired escape, and the responses were weakened. Bumping the pole led to the desired escape and reward, and was strengthened. This led Thorndike to formulate his views in the **law of effect.** To paraphrase Thorndike, the law of effect states that *an organism is more likely to repeat a response that leads to favorable consequences.* In the terminology of psychology, we would say that the cat's behavior was reinforced for tilting the pole. A **reinforcement** is some event that increases the probability that the response that preceded it will be repeated in the future. Changing behavior by following it with a reinforcement is known as **operant conditioning,** so called because the organism must operate on the environment in some way to get the reinforcement. It is also called **instrumental conditioning** because the behavior of the organism is instrumental in getting the reinforcement.

You should note an importance difference between operant conditioning and classical conditioning. In operant conditioning the organism's behavior is critical in determining whether or not the reinforcement will be given as well as when it will be given. In classical conditioning, the organism's voluntary behavior plays no role in the outcome of either the UCS or the CS.

Acquisition of an Operant Response

The pioneering work in operant conditioning was conducted by B. F. Skinner (1904–1990), who elaborated upon the principles originally formulated by Thorndike. Skinner created a device he called an **operant chamber** but that has been more frequently referred to as a **Skinner box,** a term Skinner himself disliked. This device, illustrated in Figure 3.3, allowed Skinner to carefully control both the stimuli that were presented as well as the rewards that were given to the organism during the operant learning process. Much of the early research in Skinner boxes was conducted with rats, although similar devices were designed for pigeons and other animals.

A hungry rat is placed inside the box that contains a bar and an empty food tray. The animal is permitted to explore the box freely, which it naturally does, since rats are very curious creatures. The goal is to get the hungry rat to press down on the bar after which a small food pellet automatically drops down into the food tray. In this case the response to be learned, known as the **operant response,** is pressing the bar and the food pellet, called a **reinforcer,** is the reward. The food pellet is called a *reinforcer* because it strengthens (i.e., reinforces) the behavior that led to it: Every time the rat presses the lever it is rewarded with a food pellet. The food pellets used are typically quite small, so that the rat can consume several of them and still remain hungry. It is important that the rat remain hungry so that there will be continuing motivation to obtain the food pellet.

Shaping a Response

Rats placed in a Skinner box do not march right over to the bar and begin pressing it to obtain food pellets. Pressing a bar to get something to eat is not normally how a rat goes about feeding. It is necessary to teach the rat to make this fairly complicated response, and it is done in a series of small steps known as **shaping.** To "shape" any organism, you want to build upon existing behaviors by selectively rewarding some and not others. When the rat is first placed in the Skinner box, it will begin to explore the various nooks and crannies of the apparatus. The rat must initially be taught that food pellets can be obtained in the food tray. The experimenter waits until the rat's explorations take it to the food tray, at which time a food pellet

✦ FIGURE 3.3 ✦ A Skinner Box, Designed to Study Operant Conditioning

Note that the box contains a bar that the rat can press, after which a food dispenser will automatically drop a food pellet into the food tray. The box also contains a speaker and a signal light that are used for other kinds of operant conditioning, such as discrimination learning and stimulus generalization. The bottom of the box contains an electric grid that can be used to deliver a mild electric shock to the animal.

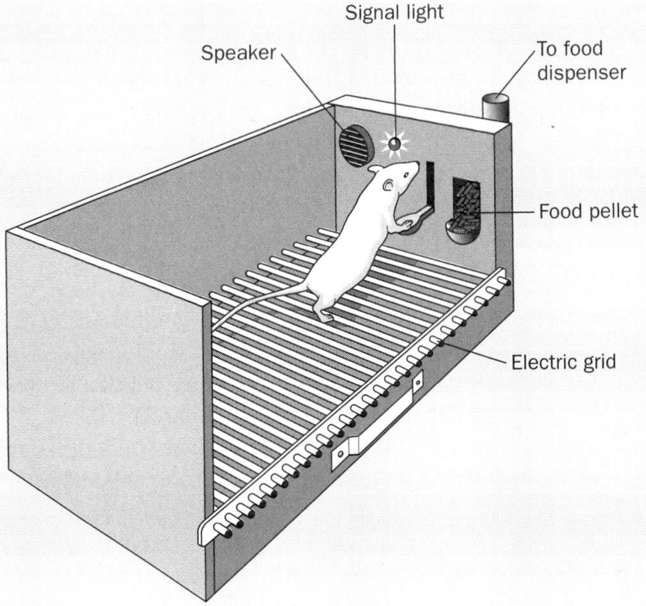

is immediately dropped into the tray. After eating the food, several more pellets are given so that the rat associates the food tray with the food pellets. Nevertheless, the experimenter wants the rat eventually to back away from the food tray, approach the bar, and then press it to obtain a reward. To accomplish this series of behaviors, the experimenter will begin rewarding each small step as it occurs. Each small step toward the final desired response is known as a **successive approximation.** The first part of this sequence involves the rat backing away from the food tray. When no additional food pellets are forthcoming, the rat will eventually back away from the tray. As soon as this occurs, the experimenter drops a pellet to the rat, which leads the rat to return to the tray to feed. Repeated several times, the rat learns that it must back away from the food tray to obtain a reward. Next the rat will be required not only to back away from the tray but also to turn toward the bar. If the rat turns away from the bar, no reward is given. Eventually the rat will make the desired response, and a food pellet will be delivered. It is important that the reward follow *immediately* after the desired response because the last response that occurred will be the one that is strengthened. Next the rat is required both to turn toward the bar and approach it before a reward is given. Then the rat is also required to touch the bar with its paw before earning a reward. By reinforcing each small step in the chain of behavior, the rat learns to make the desired response. Although this probably sounds quite complicated, a person experienced in this procedure can usually teach a rat to press the bar in less than 10 minutes. The key is to reward each successive approximation to the desired response immediately and not to reward any behaviors that are outside the desired response.

Extinction and Spontaneous Recovery

If the experimenter discontinues giving the animal rewards for pressing the bar, the learned behavior will slow down and eventually stop, a phenomenon called extinction. If the rat is removed from the Skinner box and returned sometime later, the bar pressing will begin again even though no reward is provided. This phenomenon is called spontaneous recovery. You will recall that similar behavior occurred in classical conditioning following extinction of the conditioned response. In operant conditioning the recovered response is not as strong as it was before extinction and fewer unreinforced trials are necessary for extinction to reoccur. In order for complete extinction to transpire, this process may need to be repeated several times until no further spontaneous recovery occurs.

APPLICATIONS

If you think about it, shaping is the very procedure that we use when we try to teach a child to learn a task. To teach children to tie their shoes, you first teach them how to figure out which shoe goes on which foot and give them verbal rewards after they are successful. Then you teach them how to snug up the laces, again followed by verbal rewards. Following successful completion of this, you teach them how to begin the knot, and so forth, until the final sequence of behaviors has been learned, one small step at a time.

When we want people to change their behavior, we sometimes tell them to "shape up!" If we want to change someone's behavior, we are well advised to follow a shaping procedure similar to the way the rat was conditioned to press the bar. To illustrate the power of this technique, you may wish to try and shape up one of your professors.

Shaping a Professor

You should select some fairly simple behavior that your professor does not regularly do that you want him or her to do consistently. Perhaps you have a male professor who rarely makes eye contact with you during his class, and you wish to shape the response of looking at you more frequently as he lectures. As with the hungry rat, so too do you need to find some way to reward your professor when he makes a successive approximation to the desired response. Throwing food to the professor when he looks at you would be rather disruptive, but there are other rewards that are even more effective. Think about what a professor finds rewarding while giving a lecture. One of the most powerful rewards a professor can get is feedback that the audience finds what he says to be important or interesting. Now think about how you as an individual can dispense such a reward. It is actually quite simple: Whenever your professor looks up and in your general direction, you should be

Students in the classroom can shape their professor's behavior by selectively reinforcing certain behaviors, while not reinforcing other behaviors. Nodding the head in agreement is one powerful reinforcer that can be used to shape behavior.

very attentive, smile, and even nod your head slightly, indicating that you agree with whatever he has just said.

These rewards should be delivered in a subtle manner—do not suddenly sit upright in your seat, grin like the Cheshire Cat from *Alice in Wonderland,* or vigorously nod your head in agreement. Merely indicate your interest and agreement in the subtlest manner possible. It may help if you sit in the front row where your presence may be more noticeable. First reward him for merely looking in your general direction, next require him to look at you for a short interval before dispensing the rewards, and finally require that he look at you for several seconds before rewarding him. Keep track of how frequently your professor glances your way. I have suggested this assignment to many students and rarely does it fail to work. You might think that the professor will quickly catch on to what you are doing, but there is virtually no chance that this will happen. Professors are only too happy to find students who are interested in and agree with what they say. They never question the motives of an interested student.

If you can learn from hard knocks, you can also learn from soft touches.

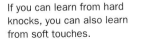

CAROLYN KENMORE
Mannequin: My Life as a Model

Many years ago some fellow graduate students and I decided to shape one of our professors into giving his lecture at the side of the classroom by the window. We all conspired to reinforce any successive approximation the professor made toward the window, using the reinforcers I described previously. Whenever the professor made a successive approximation to the desired response, we all smiled, asked questions, and generally looked interested in what he was saying. When he failed to perform the desired response, we looked bored by displaying behaviors such as looking away, yawning, and so on. First we reinforced him for merely looking toward the window wall, then we required him to take a step in that direction, then a few steps in that direction, and so forth until by the end of the hour he was indeed standing by the window lecturing! We never had any indication that he was aware of what we were doing and, at the next class meeting, we noticed that he started his lecture from near the window. If you decide to try this, enlist at least half the class members to assist you because a single person dispensing reinforcements will be insufficient to shape a complex response such as this. Too many uncontrolled reinforcements being given by others in the class will prevent the desired response from being shaped.

If you decide to shape up one of your professors, you can also test for extinction and spontaneous recovery. After the behavior is well formed, stop all reinforcements and notice how long it takes for the response to extinguish. Finally, check for spontaneous recovery the next time the class meets.

Shaping as a Means of Persuasion

Shaping is also a powerful tool in persuading individuals to do something they do not want to do or something they have not considered doing. For example, a student who is interested in becoming acquainted with another student wisely will try and shape the other person's behavior in a series of carefully designed steps. The hopeful suitor may start by choosing to sit next to the other student in the belief that such proximity would help in becoming noticed. At first, the student would merely greet the prospective date by saying "hello" or "good morning" at the beginning of class. The next steps might be to engage in short but rewarding conversations before or after class, request to borrow lecture notes, offer to study together, and so forth until the prospective date has been shaped to respond positively to the suitor. Of course, this is exactly the sequence that most people go through as part of the dating game although they often violate some of the rules of shaping. It is important that the successive steps be small and that each step be reinforced positively.

Shaping can even be used to change people's opinions as any good salesperson soon discovers. If you want to get people to agree with a political point of view, start by getting them to agree on some noncontroversial generality and verbally reinforce any agreement. By selectively reinforcing their agreement in successive small steps, you would hope to eventually convince them of your point of view.

Reinforcements in Operant Conditioning

Positive Reinforcement

There are two types of reinforcement: positive reinforcement and negative reinforcement. **Positive reinforcement** involves stimulus events or behavioral consequences that *strengthen* the responses that immediately precede them. In other words, if something happens after a certain behavior that increases the probability of that behavior occurring again, we can say that the behavior was positively reinforced by whatever happened. If you find a five-dollar bill lying at a certain location on the street, you will likely look in that same spot again the next time you pass that way. Finding the money will have positively reinforced your behavior of looking at that location.

Some reinforcers, called **primary reinforcers,** strengthen behavior because they satisfy some basic biological need that we have. If you are hungry, food would serve as a primary reinforcer. Other primary reinforcers include water, air, and sexual pleasure. Of course, there are many other reinforcers that shape our behavior. In fact, only a relatively small percentage of our behavior is rewarded by such primary reinforcers. You probably receive many reinforcements for attending college, but how often is that reinforcement delivered in the form of a primary reinforcer? Another category of reinforcers, called **secondary reinforcers,** has acquired its reinforcing properties by being paired with primary reinforcers. Money is an extremely powerful reinforcer for most people but, in and by itself, does not satisfy any biological need. You cannot eat, drink, or have sex with it. However, money can be used to obtain food, drink, or even sexual pleasure. Because of this association with primary reinforcement, secondary reinforcers acquire the ability to reinforce or strengthen behavior. For instance, a college diploma is just a piece of paper that does not meet any of our biological needs. We work hard to attain it because we know that it will permit us to get a better job and earn more money which, in turn, allows us to satisfy our biological needs. In addition, the diploma brings us increased status, praise, and approval from others, all of which are also secondary reinforcers. You will recall that it was secondary reinforcers that we used to shape our professor to lecture by the window.

Are primary reinforcers more powerful than secondary reinforcers? It all depends on the situation. If you are not hungry, the power of food to reinforce a response will be quite low or even aversive. On the other hand, a stimulus object that has yet to be paired with a primary reinforcer also will not have powerful reinforcing properties. Let me illustrate this with a story about my son that occurred when he was very young. I used to regularly give him a penny so that he could obtain a gumball out of a gum machine (back in the days when gumballs only cost a penny!). He quickly learned the value of a penny and would become quite excited if he found one on the street, knowing that he could cash it in for a gumball. One day at the bank, where there was a gumball machine, I was getting some money for a vacation. I sat my son up on the bank counter, held up both a shiny new penny and a one hundred–dollar bill, and asked him which one he would rather have. Without any hesitation he chose the penny. The penny had acquired secondary reinforcing properties through being paired with the gum. He had never experienced a hundred-dollar bill and, therefore, it had acquired no reinforcing properties for him. That would change soon enough, however!

Can behavior reinforce behavior? It can, according to what is known as the **Premack principle.** According to this principle, *a behavior that has a high probability of occurring can reinforce another behavior that has a lower probability of occurring.* Let's assume that children come home from school with homework to do. With most children, watching television is a behavior with a higher probability of occurring than doing homework. Stated another way, television viewing is a preferred activity compared to doing homework. The mother might tell the children that they can watch 2 hours of television but they first must do 2 hours of homework. She is using the higher probability, preferred behavior to reinforce the lower probability, least preferred behavior. People often use this tool to reinforce their own behavior. An example of this would be if you tell yourself "I will allow myself to go to the movies after I clean my room." The Premack principle is a very powerful tool for changing behavior.

Negative Reinforcement

Sometimes we perform an act that allows us to avoid or escape something negative. For example, we take an aspirin to escape the pain of a headache. In this case, the removal of the pain is reinforcing the act of taking aspirin. This is an example of a **negative reinforcer** or *an aversive stimulus that strengthens responses that permit an organism to avoid or escape from it.* Notice that it is the *reduction* of the headache pain that is the negative reinforcer, not the headache itself. Examples of negative reinforcement are putting on a coat when it is cold, turning down a stereo that is too loud, or paying your bills on time to avoid the consequences of not doing so. I remember a joke from my childhood about one person asking another why he was banging his head against the wall. The other person replied, "Because it feels so good when I stop." This individual was being negatively reinforced for the behavior of *stopping* the head banging. Negative reinforcers are similar to positive reinforcers in that they *strengthen* the response that preceded them.

Punishment

Students often confuse negative reinforcement with the application of an aversive stimulus. The application of an aversive stimulus *after* a behavior has occurred constitutes **punishment.** *Any consequence to a behavior that decreases the probability of the undesired behavior from being repeated constitutes punishment.* Spanking a child for misbehaving represents punishment. If you slap someone for saying something inappropriate to you, then you have punished that behavior but *not* negatively reinforced it. You have negatively reinforced the person if they stop saying inappropriate things to you and you *stop* slapping them. The distinction between punishment and negative reinforcement is an important one. Punishment has the effect of stopping a behavior, while both positive and negative reinforcement have the effect of strengthening behavior.

Distrust all in whom the impulse to punish is powerful.

FRIEDRICH WILHELM NIETZSCHE

Just as there are two kinds of reinforcement, there are also two kinds of punishment. **Positive punishment** (which sounds like an oxymoron) involves the use of an aversive stimulus to stop or weaken a behavior. The aversive stimulus can be physical, such as pain or electric shock, or psychological, such as verbal threats, physical posturing, or giving someone a "dirty look." The above example of spanking a child for misbehaving is an illustration of positive punishment. In **negative punishment** the undesired behavior is weakened by the *removal* of a rewarding or pleasurable stimulus when the undesired behavior is exhibited. Different examples of negative punishment include (1) taking away teenagers' driving privileges when their grades fall below a certain level, (2) using the procedure called "time out" when misbehaving children are removed from a situation and made to sit by themselves for a specified period of time, and (3) imposing a fine or jail sentence on an individual who has violated some law.

In some cases, the same behavior can result in both positive and negative reinforcement simultaneously. Cigarette smoking is positively reinforcing for the pleasant taste that smokers claim it evokes but it is also negatively reinforcing in that it reduces the craving for nicotine. Similarly, drugs such as crack cocaine give a pleasant feeling of euphoria while at the same time reducing the craving for the drug. Breaking substance abuse habits is very difficult because of the double reinforcement inherent in the behavior.

In other instances, negative reinforcement and punishment can be applied simultaneously. Take the example of a parent yelling at a child to pick up toys. Assume the parent continues to yell until the child finally complies. Has the child been punished or negatively reinforced? The child has been punished because the act of leaving the toys out resulted in an aversive stimulus. The child has also been negatively reinforced because the act of picking up the toys resulted in the cessation of the aversive stimulation: yelling. In this instance, the act of leaving the toys out was punished and the act of picking up the toys was negatively reinforced.

Men are not hanged for stealing horses, but that horses may not be stolen.

MARQUIS OF HALIFAX
Political Thoughts and Reflections, "Of Punishment"

APPLICATIONS: Using Punishment Effectively

If you want to change behavior, which is more effective, reinforcement or punishment? As a general rule, reinforcement works best. However, there are certain circumstances where punishment is the only practical alternative. If a child is engaged in a behavior that is likely to lead to injury, an immediate judicious application of punishment to stop the behavior is appropriate. Similarly, if individuals are harming themselves, such as those who engage in self-injurious behaviors because of psychiatric problems, immediate punishment may be warranted.

As a general rule, the more strongly ingrained the behavior, the more resistant it will be to the effects of punishment. A child who repeatedly leaves clothes lying on the floor without consequence will resist the effects of punishment that the parent suddenly applies. Parents who ignore their child's propensity to lie, thinking such behavior is "normal" for young children, will find the behavior very resistant to change when they finally decide to punish it.

Behavior that is strongly motivated will also be more resistant to punishment. Punishing a very hungry child for snitching a cookie before dinner will be less effective than for a child sneaking a cookie after eating a meal. Inappropriate sexual behaviors in adults are resistant to the effects of punishment because of the strong motivational drives that initiate such behaviors.

In recent years psychologists have significantly changed their views about the effectiveness of punishment. Originally it was believed that punishment only suppressed behavior temporarily and did not eliminate behaviors permanently. Recent research, however, suggests that punishment can be effective if applied in certain ways. The following four variables are critical in making punishment maximally effective:

1. Timing. For punishment to be effective it should occur as quickly as possible following the undesirable behavior. Immediacy is critical. Even very brief delays will greatly reduce its effectiveness. In several states police use unmarked vans to photograph speeding cars as they pass. The drivers then receive a citation about 10 to 14 days after the offense. This lengthy delay in punishment probably will dilute the effectiveness of this kind of enforcement. A child who starts to run out into a busy street should be punished immediately in order to ensure that the behavior stops at once and does not reappear in the future. Telling a misbehaving child "just wait until your father (or mother) gets home" is never a good idea, although one frequently implemented by frustrated parents. By the time the parent arrives home, the child has probably forgotten what behavior initiated the punishment, making the effectiveness of any punishment at that point negligible.

   Unfortunately, some inappropriate behaviors are rewarding in the short term but punishing in the long term. Drinking too much alcohol at a party, for example, is reinforcing during the act and not punishing until the next day. People with severe hangovers swear they will never drink too much again, but the delayed effects of the punishment permit the behavior to be repeated. Other examples of immediate reward with delayed punishment include incurring large credit-card charges, overeating, and engaging in unprotected sex. In fact, crimes against the person, such as assault, theft, rape, and murder, may also fit this pattern (Dinsmoor, 1998). As criminologists have found, such behaviors are resistant to the effects of punishment.

2. Severity. The more severe the punishment, the better the suppression of the undesired behavior. Behavior that is severely punished will also stay suppressed for a longer period of time. Some parents adopt the strategy of beginning with a mild punishment and subsequently introducing more severe forms if the

behavior continues. Such a strategy may seem humane but, in the long run, will require more severe punishment to finally suppress the behavior. I witnessed this at a restaurant recently. A couple came in with two young children and sat at a booth nearby. The children quickly became bored and began to horseplay. The father politely asked them to "settle down." As the children continued their misbehavior, the father issued the second warning in a louder voice, accompanied by some finger pointing, and the third warning in an even louder voice, accompanied by grabbing the children by their arms. The level of punishment that this father eventually had to use was far more severe than if he had used a moderately strong punishment at the first occurrence of misbehavior. Let me state that I am not advocating the use of punishment in these circumstances because better alternatives exist, which I will be describing later in this section.

Obviously, the severity of punishment must never be such that injury results. In most states, criminal child abuse is defined as any act in which a child exhibits evidence of skin bruising, bleeding, or soft tissue swelling, as well as the more serious consequences often associated with corporal punishment. In most cases, the level of severity necessary to suppress behavior completely and permanently must be very extreme (Dinsmoor, 1998). When using punishment, a parent who resorts to the degree of severity necessary to produce such a result may very well be physically injuring a child.

3. Feedback. Whenever possible, feedback should be given so that the individual knows specifically what behavior is being punished. Imagine a police officer pulling you over, issuing a ticket, but failing to tell you which law you violated. Under these circumstances, the punishment would be ineffectual. In most circumstances, especially with children, the linkage between the "crime" and the punishment needs to be made explicit. If a parent arrives home several hours after the misbehavior and administers a spanking, little benefit will come of it. Both the delay of punishment and the lack of feedback will negate any desirable effects. The need for feedback is especially critical when punishment is delayed. It is helpful to take a child to where the misbehavior occurred and explain the specific behavior that is being punished. Also importantly, parents should emphasize that it is the bad *behavior* that is being punished, not the bad child.

   Of course adults use punishment in their relationships with other adults as well. Frequently they fail to specify to the other individual what particular behavior is being punished. In marriages, this often takes the form of one spouse giving the other spouse "the cold shoulder" or "silent treatment" while the offender is left to wonder exactly what offense he or she committed. Upon making inquiry, the snubbed spouse may only hear that "you *know* what you did!"

4. Positively reinforced alternatives. In many circumstances, punished behavior continues to occur because no alternative or substitute behavior is obvious. Children who are whining often are told to stop, or are even spanked, but are not informed of acceptable alternative behaviors. A child who is whining for attention should be told that this behavior will be ignored and only nonwhining requests will be recognized. The parent then must be careful to positively reinforce nonwhining requests when they occur. Criminals often continue to commit crimes because they fail to see positive alternatives to their criminal behavior. A drug

dealer who is earning several thousand dollars a week illicitly may not see a minimum-wage job as a viable alternative with adequate rewards.

In summary, punishment will be effective only when four conditions are met: (1) the level of punishment is relatively intense, (2) it is delivered immediately and consistently after the undesired behavior, (3) feedback is provided about what specific behavior is being punished, and (4) positively reinforced alternatives are given. These ideal conditions are often impossible to arrange outside of a controlled laboratory situation. For this reason, many psychologists have advocated alternatives to its use. In addition, punishment can have adverse effects associated with its use.

Adverse Consequences of the Use of Punishment

All punishment is mischief: All punishment in itself is evil.

JEREMY BENTHAM
Principles of Morals and Legislation

Although potentially effective in the elimination of undesirable behavior, the use of punishment also has likely side effects. A person who is punished repeatedly by others might reasonably conclude that the best way to get compliant behavior from others is to threaten or use punishment. A substantial proportion of children who are abused by their parents or caretakers will subsequently abuse their own children (Widom, 1989). Prisons are full of violent criminals who received corporal punishment in their youth. Parents who consistently use corporal punishment with their children are unwittingly communicating to them that this is the way to control other people's behavior.

Punishment is also likely to elicit aggression. Children will imitate aggressive behaviors. Seminal research in this area has demonstrated repeatedly that children who witness someone punching an object become more aggressive in their subsequent behavior toward other children (Bandura, 1973). The more parents rely on corporal punishment, the greater the chance of a child's hitting back (Straus, Gelles, & Steinmetz, 1980). By fighting back, individuals who are being punished will have their feelings of anger reduced and, therefore, their aggressive behavior will be negatively reinforced. Research indicates that punishment may lead to depression, spousal abuse, and increased violence in subsequent generations (Straus, 1994).

Another thing to consider is that less severe levels of punishment may lead to suppression but not elimination of undesired behaviors. Children quickly learn to suppress a behavior when parents are present but resume the behavior when they believe they can do it undetected.

Punishment without Control: Learning to Be Helpless

What happens when we are placed in a situation where punishment is being dispensed and we have no control over escaping from it? Research has shown that effects can be devastating (Seligman, 1975, 1991). Martin Seligman and his colleagues trained dogs in shuttle boxes containing two compartments with a short barrier between them. One side had an electrified grid beneath the dogs' feet. The dogs heard a tone and 5 seconds later received a 5-second shock to their feet. Dogs quickly learned to jump across the barrier as soon as they heard the warning tone, and thus were easily able to avoid the shock after only a few trials.

In one variation of this procedure, the experimenters placed dogs that had not previously been in the apparatus into a harness, repeatedly sounded the tone, and then produced a shock. The dogs quickly learned that the tone predicted that the shock was coming, but, because they were restrained in the harness, they could not escape from it no matter how much they struggled. The next day the experimenters again placed the dogs in the shuttle box without any kind of restraint. Surprisingly, they discovered that when the tone sounded, the dogs could not learn to avoid the shock. The dogs obviously realized that when the tone sounded the shock would follow. They displayed fear responses and often cowered on the side of the box with the electric grid. However, they seemed incapable of learning the simple response of jumping over the short barrier to avoid or even escape from the shock. On the previous day, the dogs had learned that they could not escape the shock and, once this behavior was learned, it was nearly impossible to reverse. Seligman coined the term **learned helplessness** to describe this behavior. The experimenters attempted to reverse the effects by forcing the dogs to cross the barrier when the tone sounded. They used a leash to pull the dogs across the barrier to show how to avoid or escape the shock. Nonetheless, this procedure proved ineffective and the dogs remained incapable of learning the new response.

These findings are directly applicable to humans who find themselves in situations where they are receiving punishment and are helpless to escape or avoid it. These situations can exist in prisons, factories, nursing homes, or even colleges. I frequently teach a course in statistics, which is a very difficult topic for many students to master. No matter how hard some students work, inevitably some fail. Like the dogs in the shuttle box, their efforts to avoid the shock of a failing grade are unsuccessful. After experiencing this on one or two examinations, some students adopt a helpless attitude. Like Seligman's dogs, they have learned that no matter what they do they cannot avoid the failing grade. At that point, efforts by the instructor or other students to show them what is necessary to succeed prove ineffectual.

Women in abusive relationships can find themselves in a similar situation. As the man delivers punishment, the woman is unable to escape or avoid it. After repeated episodes, women often develop a helpless attitude and seem incapable of escape from the situation. Like Seligman's dogs, they cower and wait for the next "shock." People who meet consistently with defeat and loss, despite their best efforts, can come to feel "helpless" and often display signs of depression. Learned helplessness, although extremely important in explaining seemingly passive behavior, is just one of many factors that provoke and sustain domestic violence.

Learned helplessness is one of many adverse consequences that occur when punishment is used to control behavior. The real world often lacks the conditions for the effective use of punishment. The use of negative punishment, such as the time-out procedure mentioned earlier, and the positive reinforcement of alternative behaviors are better choices and do not run the many risks inherent with punishment.

Reinforcement Schedules

In the examples of operant conditioning that we have discussed to this point, we have reinforced each response that occurs. In psychology this is referred to as **continuous reinforcement,** and it is an important condition when trying to shape a new behavior.

Continuous reinforcement is unusual in our everyday lives. You would probably have a difficult time thinking of any particular behavior for which you receive reinforcement every time it occurs. Rather, most behaviors are only occasionally reinforced. As a college student, you engage in many behaviors with the goal of obtaining good grades. None of these behaviors is continuously rewarded, however. Sometimes studying hard is rewarded—but not always. Engaging in any sporting activity results in only sporadic reinforcements. When reinforcement is not continuous, it is said to be **partial** or **intermittent reinforcement.** Importantly, *a response that has been partially reinforced is more resistant to extinction than one that has been reinforced continuously.* Skinner observed early in his research that a response that had been shaped with continuous reinforcement extinguished quickly once the reinforcement was discontinued. Imagine a rat in a Skinner box that has been receiving a pellet every time it presses the bar. When the pellets suddenly stop being dispensed, the rat notices. Even though the animal continues to respond for a while, extinction of bar pressing soon sets in. Compare this to a rat that has been receiving a food pellet *on average* every 10 times it presses the bar. The animal would not immediately recognize when the pellets were no longer being dispensed because it had become used to having periods of responses where no reinforcement was given. Under these circumstances, the animal proceeds to press the bar much longer than the animal that previously had been on continuous reinforcement. The finding that responses are much more resistant to extinction following partial reinforcement is known as the **partial-reinforcement effect.** The timing and spacing of reinforcements have a very large influence on behavior.

Partial reinforcement typically occurs in certain patterns known as **schedules of reinforcement.** *These schedules have very powerful effects on behavior and are always present in our lives.* There are four major schedules of partial reinforcement. In some cases, time is the critical factor before a reinforcement is obtained. For example, you may work at a job where you only receive your paycheck every two weeks. These are called **interval schedules.** In other cases, the number of responses is critical for receiving a reinforcement. For example, you may work in a factory where you are paid a set amount of money for every fixed quantity of items that you assemble. These are called **ratio schedules.** There are two types of interval and two types of ratio schedules that cover most partial reinforcement contingencies. Each partial reinforcement schedule affects the rate and pattern of responding as well as the resistance to extinction differently.

FIXED-INTERVAL SCHEDULE. In a **fixed-interval schedule,** a set amount of time must elapse between successive reinforcements. The interval of time can be anywhere from a fraction of a second to years. It does not matter how many responses are made between reinforcements because there are no reinforcers available during this time. It is the behavior at the end of the interval that is reinforced. For the rat in the Skinner box, a set amount of time must elapse before a bar press will result in a reinforcement. As an example, on a fixed-interval–1-minute schedule, 1 minute must elapse and then the next bar press will be reinforced. The number of bar presses during the 1-minute interval is irrelevant since none of them are reinforced. Humans sometimes find themselves on a fixed-interval schedule of reinforcement. Your favorite TV show comes on the same time each week, and you are only reinforced if you turn on your TV at that time. I get paid once a month regardless of how hard I worked during that month. A bus may run on an hourly schedule despite the number of times one looks down the street for it.

This schedule produces a typical pattern of responding. The rat in the Skinner box on a 1-minute fixed-interval schedule should wait 1 minute and then press the bar once, as no other bar press will count. Since rats do not wear watches, instead they make more bar presses than necessary. After being on this schedule for awhile, a distinctive pattern of responding will result. Immediately after receiving a reinforcement, the animal pauses in its responding for a brief while. Then, as the end of the interval approaches, the response rate increases. Humans do wear watches, but their pattern of responding on this schedule is similar. If you are waiting for a bus and know that a bus has just left, your response of looking down the street for the next bus will be infrequent. However, as the scheduled time for the next bus approaches, your frequency of looking will increase. As the interval length between reinforcements grows longer, the total number of responses grows smaller and clusters around the time the reinforcement is expected. If you have only a midterm and a final exam in a course, your studying behavior probably increases as test time nears.

VARIABLE-INTERVAL SCHEDULE. On a **variable-interval schedule,** the first response that occurs after a variable interval of time has elapsed is reinforced. In our everyday lives, we receive reinforcements more typically after varying intervals of time as opposed to fixed intervals. Continuing to call a telephone number that is busy until you get through is a frequently cited example of this schedule. As I am writing this section, I am waiting for the trash company to pick up my trash. It is a windy day and I want to retrieve my garbage cans before they blow down the street. The trash service comes on the same day each week, but since the exact time varies, I have been reinforced for watching for them any time from early morning to late afternoon. As a result I find myself looking out for the trash truck fairly frequently until my looking response is finally reinforced.

When intervals are short, variable-interval schedules produce a fairly high and steady rate of responding. If a bus is scheduled to run about every 10 minutes, then a variable-interval schedule exists since the time probably varies between runs. Under these circumstances, people will look regularly for the bus; in other words, they will display a high rate of responding. When intervals are longer, little or no responding occurs immediately after the last reinforcement but responding increases as the interval increases. If the bus only runs once every 1 to 2 hours, people will begin looking more frequently as time has passed.

Some professors use pop quizzes in their courses. Students never know how much time is going to elapse before they will be tested. The professor is hoping that this will result in a steady and frequent response of studying. As a general rule, a variable-interval schedule of reinforcement produces a steadier rate of responding than a fixed-interval schedule.

FIXED-RATIO SCHEDULE. In a **fixed-ratio schedule,** a response is reinforced after a fixed number of repetitions. A rat in a Skinner box who receives a reinforcement for every bar press is on a fixed-ratio schedule that is a continuous-reinforcement schedule. As noted earlier, a continuous-reinforcement schedule is best when shaping a new response because learning occurs most rapidly under these circumstances. Parents who want their children to learn to be polite should reinforce the behavior every time it happens. Similarly, coaches often reinforce each good play immediately after it occurs. Learning skilled responses will develop much quicker under continuous reinforcement.

In our everyday lives we encounter fixed-ratio schedules of reinforcement on a regular basis. The reinforcements not only come from others but also from our environment. Each time we turn on the faucet, we are reinforced with water. Each time we pick up the telephone, we hear a dial tone.

Often, fixed-ratio schedules require more than one response for a reinforcement. For example, the rat might be required to press the bar 10 times before the response is reinforced with a food pellet. On this schedule the interval of time that elapses is irrelevant. The faster the rat presses the bar, the more frequently will it receive a reinforcement. Working at a job where you are paid by "piecework" is an example of a fixed-ratio schedule. Jogging 2 miles before relaxing in a hot tub or reading 50 pages for an exam before taking a snack break are also examples.

> I had always been fascinated by the bizarre world of cards. It was a world of pure power politics where rewards and punishments were meted out immediately.
>
> **ELY CULBERTSON**
> *Total Peace*

Responding on a fixed-ratio schedule is usually rapid until the reinforcement is obtained, after which there is typically a pause called a **post-reinforcement pause.** The higher the ratio of responses, the longer the post-reinforcement pause. After the pause, responding begins slowly but speeds up as the end of the required number of responses draws near. If a factory worker has to turn out 50 items before being paid, the worker would typically pause after the 50th item is completed and follow with a slowly increasing rate of responding. Students who study very hard for an examination usually take a break from studying immediately afterwards. The more they have studied, the longer the post-exam pause tends to be. With higher ratios of responses, the response rate also tends to decrease. Many employers prefer a fixed-ratio schedule as it produces employees who work rapidly and steadily. However, because employees report that fixed-ratio schedules are exhausting, labor unions have opposed their use. In summary, fixed-ratio schedules produce rapid responding interspersed with post-reinforcement pauses, with the length of pauses directly related to the ratio of responses. After the pause, the rate of responding becomes increasingly rapid (Baldwin & Baldwin, 1998).

VARIABLE-RATIO SCHEDULE. On a **variable-ratio schedule,** reinforcement comes after a varying number of responses are made. As with the fixed-ratio schedule, time taken in responding is not relevant. The faster the response rate, the more rapidly the reinforcement will be obtained. Our long-suffering rat may now be required to push the bar 10 times to get the reinforcement, then 25 times, then only 3 times, and so forth. We all experience variable-ratio schedules in our everyday lives. Examples include chopping down trees where 20 swings may fell the first tree but 60 swings are required for the next; and, similarly, using a manual can opener where the number of handle turns depends on the size of the can. The life of a college student is replete with variable-ratio schedules, such as sometimes working hard to obtain an A and other times hardly working at all yet achieving the same grade. We tend to receive reinforcements from others on a variable-ratio schedule as well, such as displaying varying numbers of courteous acts before receiving any acknowledgment of your kindness. Other examples of a variable-ratio schedule include many activities such as golf, hunting, fishing, and, in particular, gambling and all games of chance.

Variable-ratio schedules result in very high rates of responding and, as will be discussed in the next section, great resistance to extinction. The post-reinforcement pauses are also brief and tend to be interspersed throughout the responses. If the ratios become too large, responding may slow down or stop altogether. Sometimes the ratios start out small and are slowly increased. Using this technique, Skinner was able to get pigeons to peck a key 100,000 times between reinforcements. The pigeons were literally working themselves to death as they expended more energy to obtain the reinforcement than was provided by the food reward itself. In summary, the variable-ratio schedule produces rapid responding, with only brief pauses, and results in great persistence.

Resistance to Extinction

It is often desirable to reinforce a behavior in such a way that the behavior will persist; that is, there will be great resistance to extinction. If we teach our child to pick up his toys, we hope that the behavior will persist without the necessity for constant reminders. It is usually best to use continuous reinforcement during the acquisition of a response and follow that with a schedule of partial reinforcement to resist extinction. When you expect a reward every time, you tend to give up quickly when the rewards suddenly stop coming. On the other hand, if you are accustomed to varying amounts of time or effort being required to obtain a reinforcement, your responses will be more persistent. *Variable schedules, including variable ratio and variable interval, are more resistant to extinction than are the two fixed schedules.* In most instances, a variable-ratio schedule will provide more resistance to extinction than will a variable-interval schedule. Las Vegas is a city built by variable-ratio schedules of reinforcement. As noted earlier, all games of chance involve such a schedule, and gambling behavior is notorious for its resistance to extinction. No matter how much a person wins on a slot machine, there is an almost irresistible urge to continue pulling the handle. Casino owners have learned to keep the ratio of required responses small, allowing the gamblers to win small amounts periodically.

Among the fixed schedules, the fixed-ratio usually results in more persistence than does the fixed-interval. A person who knows that a certain number of responses have to be made to obtain a reinforcement will work more steadily and with greater resistance to quitting than someone who is waiting for a fixed interval of time to elapse.

The highest reward for a person's toil is not what they get for it, but what they become by it.

JOHN RUSKIN

APPLICATIONS: Using Operant Conditioning Principles

We often find ourselves in situations where we try to get someone else to behave in certain ways and stop behaving in other ways. Influencing how others behave is an important part of our everyday activities and something that everyone does, whether they are aware of it or not. Nevertheless, most people do not go about altering the behavior of others in a systematic fashion by using the principles of operant conditioning presented in this section. Over the years I have observed many psychologists both in a work environment and in social settings and have concluded that knowing these principles is "necessary but not sufficient." In other words, many psychologists who are knowledgeable about operant conditioning, including the power of reinforcement and shaping, disregard this knowledge when they attempt to influence the behavior of others. For example, I have observed many psychologists who break every known rule concerning the effective use of punishment when it comes to applying these principles to their relationships with their spouse, children, and colleagues. These individuals lecture in a class about these very principles and then behave in a manner that contradicts what they have just taught their students. My point is that knowledge of these principles and others that you learn throughout this book can be very effective in managing behavior, but only if you commit to using them.

The power of positive reinforcement is one important concept that I hope you have learned from this chapter. In most circumstances, the use of positive reinforcement to shape and strengthen a desired response is better than using punishment to try to extinguish an undesired response. You will have better success reinforcing your messy housemates for any successive approximations they make toward neatness than you will have by yelling and screaming at them for their messiness. Wait for or encourage behavior that approximates the desired response and then reinforce it immediately after it occurs. Continue to shape more complicated neatness responses and eventually use a partial reinforcement schedule to reduce resistance to extinction.

As the psychology department chair, I was the "go to" guy when students had complaints about any of the department's professors. Common complaints that students have about professors include allegations that they are boring, disorganized, and unfair in their testing. These are all behaviors that students can alter effectively by applying the principles of operant conditioning. Earlier I described how a group of graduate students and I shaped a professor to lecture standing next to a window. The same principles will work to encourage and strengthen other behaviors. Students underestimate the power they have in the classroom. Every professor I have ever known was motivated to be a good teacher. Sometimes the right behaviors just need to be shaped by the students.

Perhaps you have a professor whom you perceive to be boring when lecturing. Although you may think that professors are clueless, most are actually quite aware when they are boring their class. The distinctive feedback given by students includes glazed-over eyes, yawning, lack of eye contact, talking during the lecture, reading, and a myriad of other student-perfected cues. Because it is unpleasant for professors to receive this kind of feedback, they may exacerbate the problem further by avoiding eye contact and other interaction with the class while lecturing. This vicious cycle can end up with the professor reading exclusively from prepared lecture notes.

If you find yourself in this situation, try to shape the professor using positive reinforcements. It helps to enlist other students in the class to assist you in this task. First, do not positively reinforce the behavior you want to extinguish. If the professor is reading from notes, do not do anything to reinforce it. If the professor looks away from the lecture notes, even momentarily, reinforce the behavior with smiles, head nodding, sitting forward in your seat, asking questions, and other indicators of interest. Raise your hand and ask the professor to illustrate a point from a personal experience. This will force a response that does not rely on the lecture notes. Reinforce this behavior by showing interest and asking a follow-up question. Talk to the professor after class or during office hours and suggest specific things that would help the students learn. Suggest the use of visual aids and reinforce the professor for doing so. Avoid criticism of existing behaviors. If the lectures are disorganized, suggest handouts that outline the course material. Make sure you verbally reinforce all use of your suggestions. Remember that you will probably have to reinforce successive approximations initially. Do not expect a boring professor to become a captivating lecturer overnight. Keep reinforcing successive approximations until the behavior changes.

How about shaping up the types of exams a professor gives? Let's take the case of a professor whom you believe includes unfair questions on an exam. Undoubtedly, you believe some questions on the exam were better than others. Remember that Skinner reinforced the rat for some responses and not for others in shaping a bar-press response. Similarly, you need to specifically reinforce some of your professor's test-writing behaviors and not others. Perhaps the multiple-choice questions are clear, but the essay questions are poorly worded. After an exam, tell the professor how the multiple-choice questions were really good items in that they accurately measured what you knew about the material. Avoid the temptation to criticize the bad questions. Enlist other students in the class to assist you in this.

Even a few students taking this approach can have a powerful positive effect on a professor's behavior. I can personally attest that students using this procedure on me have found it to be effective. The alternatives that students often pursue include enduring in silence or punishing the undesired behaviors by verbal criticism. Rarely do these produce the desired outcome.

What works with professors also works with friends, spouses, and your children. Never underestimate the power of positive reinforcement. Avoid punishment whenever possible unless self-injurious behavior is involved. If you must use punishment, do so effectively by using the principles discussed earlier in this chapter.

You also need to be careful when using positive reinforcements. Sometimes it can be a case of too much of a good thing. Unnecessary rewards can backfire. Several studies have shown that promising people a reward for a task that they already enjoy doing can lead to losing interest in the task. This is called the **overjustification effect** because a behavior that is already justified becomes *overjustified* by the promise of an added incentive. In some studies, children who were promised money for playing with an interesting puzzle or toy later showed less interest in the objects when compared to children who were not paid to play. If a husband enjoys woodworking, a spouse should not promise to prepare his favorite dish for making her a new table. Surprising a husband with such a favor *after* he completes the table will reinforce the behavior whereas bribing him beforehand may cause him to lose interest in completing the project. People bribed into doing something they already enjoy doing may conclude that the activity must not be very enjoyable if they have to be induced to do it.

Reinforcement is most effective when it is given *after* the desired behavior occurs. For instance, one study compared the performance of baseball pitchers before and after they signed short-term or long-term guaranteed contracts. Pitchers receiving long-term contracts had a guaranteed salary that was not contingent on good performance. Their performance, in terms of innings pitched and wins recorded, decreased after signing the guaranteed contract while the performance of pitchers on short-term contracts remained steady from year to year (O'Brien, Figlerski, Howard, & Caggiano, 1981; as cited in Coon, 1992).

Remember that the desired behavior initially should be shaped using continuous reinforcement. After the behavior is well established, you should switch to a partial-reinforcement schedule. Whenever feasible, you should use a variable-ratio schedule as this will give the most steady rate of responding and maximal resistance to extinction. Well-intentioned parents sometimes make the mistake of trying to reinforce a child for every desired behavior. A child who is always reinforced for being polite will likely extinguish the behavior quickly when such reinforcements are not forthcoming in later interactions with others.

Extinguishing undesirable behaviors can sometimes be problematic. A behavior that has been learned and reinforced for many years will be difficult to extinguish. If your prospective partner has a history of messiness during all of his or her growing-up years, do not anticipate that it will extinguish easily, particularly if the behavior has been previously reinforced. Furthermore, behaviors that have been learned in a variety of settings are also more difficult to extinguish. Messiness that occurs at home, in the car, and at work will be more difficult to extinguish than if it occurred in only one setting. Finally, the more complex the behavior the more difficult the extinction process. For example, a child's misbehavior often consists of several different behaviors, such as crying, fighting, inattention, and disregarding directions. Yelling at a child to "Stop it!" will not be effective when several behaviors are occurring simultaneously. You may need to extinguish each of these behaviors individually. Whether using rewards or punishment, identifying the specific behavior is always best. Promising a reward for "being good" lacks sufficient specificity for children.

Finally, there are some other important principles that should be remembered when using the principles of operant conditioning. Be careful that you are not accidentally reinforcing undesirable behaviors. Children may misbehave just to get their parents' attention. Even though the attention may consist of being yelled at, it is more reinforcing than receiving no attention at all. Children who throw tantrums are often reinforced by parents who give in just to end the tantrum. Many children learn that tantrums in public are more likely to get a favorable response from parents seeking to avoid embarrassment. Consistently ignoring the behavior or using punishment to stop it will result in faster and more permanent changes in the child's behavior. Remember, rewarding alternative behaviors is often a better alternative than punishment. Avoid situations where you are punishing and rewarding a behavior simultaneously. Do not follow a spanking with hugs and kisses. When positively reinforcing behaviors, do so immediately after the desired behavior occurs. I have illustrated these principles with examples of dealing with children, but the same principles apply in our dealings with other adults, as well.

The principles of operant conditioning also work on our own behavior. Just as when conditioning others, we need to extinguish or reinforce certain of our own behaviors. Follow these recommended steps:

1. Describe your behavioral goal in measurable terms. For instance, set a goal of exercising 30 minutes three times a week as opposed to just "exercising more." Make your commitment public by telling your parents or friends about your goal.

2. Keep a record of your progress. Write down exactly what you accomplish and put it in a conspicuous place. For exercising, you might jot down your accomplishments on a calendar. Just knowing that the calendar will have several blank entries where there should not be any helps serve as an incentive.

3. Reinforce the desired behavior after it occurs. I sometimes allow myself to eat a favorite snack after I finish running.

4. Do not reinforce undesired behaviors. If I skip a day of exercising, I do not allow myself any snacks that day.
5. Track your progress in writing. I keep a written record of the number of miles I jog each week as well as a cumulative record of how many total miles I have run. Seeing this number grow larger further reinforces my jogging.
6. Gradually reduce reinforcements. Use a partial reinforcement schedule to reduce the likelihood of extinction. For instance, you might allow yourself a snack after every three exercise periods (a fixed-ratio schedule) or once a week (fixed-interval schedule).

Animal trainers have successfully used operant conditioning techniques to teach a wide variety of highly complex behaviors to animals. To accomplish this, the trainer always utilizes some natural behavior that the animal is likely to exhibit. After reinforcing some simple behavior, the trainer shapes the animal in successive stages to make progressively more complicated responses. Most trainers have found that positive reinforcement is a more powerful tool for training than is punishment. If you have a pet, I would highly recommend that you investigate these techniques further. Most people attempt to train their pets in very inefficient and often ineffective ways.

B. F. Skinner demonstrated some remarkable skills in animals by using these techniques. In one instance, he successfully taught pigeons to play Ping-Pong. During World War II, Skinner demonstrated to the military that pigeons could be trained to direct the flight of a missile. The pigeon was placed in the nose cone of the missile and pecked at the image of a target on a miniature radar screen (Skinner, 1960). He even demonstrated that the pigeons would be more reliable and more accurate than the relatively crude apparatus then being used by the military, although the military remained unconvinced. More recently the U.S. Navy has used operant conditioning to train sea lions and dolphins to locate explosive mines. The Coast Guard has even trained pigeons to locate people lost at sea. The pigeons, who are strapped underneath a search helicopter, have been conditioned to peck at a key whenever they spot something orange floating in the water. Orange is the color universally used by all nations for life jackets. By pecking the key the pilot is notified that an orange object has been spotted.

A version of operant conditioning is frequently used for clinical purposes to treat maladaptive behavior. Through a process called **behavior modification,** reinforcements are used to change inappropriate behaviors, thoughts, and even feelings. Finally, the techniques have also been applied to help people control autonomic physiological functions, such as heart rate, blood pressure, and even brain waves. A procedure called **biofeedback** is used whereby sensors are attached to the body and give feedback to the individual about various physiological functions. For instance, a tone with variable pitches can signal a person about the level of his or her blood pressure. The person concentrates on lowering the tone by using various relaxation techniques. Similarly, biofeedback devices can signal individuals when their brain activity reflects a relaxed state so that people can train themselves to enter this state whenever they wish. Such relaxation training has proven very effective in treating a number of disorders, including headaches, back pain, and high blood pressure.

Learning Involving Both Classical and Operant Conditioning

Behavior is not always learned just through classical *or* operant conditioning. Many learned behaviors involve both processes. Often the reinforcers used in operant conditioning also come to serve as the UCS that classically conditions the organism. The rat that presses the bar in a Skinner box to obtain a food pellet has learned the response through operant conditioning. However, it is likely that learning through classical conditioning has occurred simultaneously. For example, the mechanism that drops the food pellet to the rat makes a clicking noise when it is activated. The rat associates this click, which serves as a CS, with receiving food (UCS) and learns to make a CR to salivate at the sound of the click alone, even if no food is present.

Learning to Be Superstitious

Sometimes new behaviors are learned even though reinforcement is not dependent on the response being made. For example, if we receive a reinforcement strictly by accident, the reinforcer may strengthen whatever behavior immediately precedes it even though the behavior had nothing to do with receiving the reinforcement. Our tendency to attribute receiving the reinforcement to the irrelevant behavior is called **superstitious behavior.** I have witnessed many college students who believe they have a lucky item of clothing that must be worn whenever they take an examination. Athletes who have won an important contest often continue to wear some item of clothing associated with the game or to follow some pregame ritual that preceded the contest. Golfers often have rituals that they go through before hitting the ball—these rituals can be readily observed during televised golf matches.

Superstition is the religion of feeble minds.

EDMUND BURKE
Reflections on the Revolution in France

One of the many odd jobs I had as a student was working as a craps dealer in a gambling casino. As with other games of chance, reinforcements are delivered on a variable-ratio schedule of reinforcement, and it is irrelevant what the gambler did immediately prior to throwing the winning number on the dice. However, I often observed that a person who engaged in some distinctive behavior immediately prior to throwing the dice often continued that superstitious behavior on future throws, such as blowing on the dice, spitting on the dice (the dealers hated this!), saying various things, or tapping the dice on the table. We had one customer who always mumbled something to himself, and turned in a complete circle before throwing the dice. These behaviors were shaped through accidental reinforcements at some point and resisted extinction because they had been partially reinforced ever since. Even animals will engage in superstitious behaviors. Skinner trained pigeons to peck at a lighted key to receive a reinforcement. He noted that a pigeon that accidentally turned in a circle immediately before receiving a reinforcement would often persist in that behavior on future trials, just as our gambler did. Nobody is totally immune from superstitious behavior. The tendency to form causal explanations for events that occur together where no causal relationship exists is one that we all do on occasion. So go ahead and wear your "lucky hat" to the next exam; just do not forget to study hard as well.

Observational Learning

While classical and operant conditioning account for many important aspects of learned behavior, they do not by any means account for all of it. **Observational learning,** in which we learn through observing and imitating the behavior of others, also occurs. It is unlike operant conditioning where we learn a behavior based on the consequences it has for us, either positive or negative. In observational learning we learn by observing what *others* do and noting the consequences it has for them. When a *specific behavior* is observed and imitated, we call it **modeling.** This important kind of learning may be an innate tendency and is observed in a variety of animals as well as humans. Several species of birds learn to sing their characteristic song by listening to other birds sing. If they are deprived of this experience, they will sing a very different song that only remotely resembles the original.

Further evidence of the innate tendency of modeling is seen in infants who are only a few hours old. These newborns will successfully imitate adults who stick out their tongue at them (Meltzoff & Moore, 1992). Modeling can lead to both productive as well as destructive behaviors. We described earlier research by Bandura that showed children would imitate the aggressive behavior of adults. It is perhaps not surprising that children who are raised by parents who smoke or drink are more likely to engage in these destructive behaviors themselves. On the other hand, children raised by parents who are consistently courteous to others will be courteous themselves. Parents play the most important role in early modeling since young children observe parental behavior daily. Unfortunately, many parents tell their children to behave in one way but then model an entirely different behavior. As research has shown, under these circumstances children tend to model what the parents do and not what they say to do.

APPLICATIONS

As parents, we need to be aware of the many ways that behavior is modeled to our children. Not only do we model behavior ourselves, but other family members, friends, and neighbors do so as well. People are most likely to imitate those individuals who they respect and admire. We also model the behavior of those who are similar to ourselves and those whom we perceive as successful. The huge influence that peers can have on children's behavior is evidence of the power of these factors. Teachers also serve as very important role models for their students. Nor are adults immune to modeling. Employees who witness dishonesty or aggression in their superiors may well feel justified in modeling similar behaviors.

> If I am walking with two other men, each of them will serve as my teacher. I will pick out the good points of the one and imitate them, and the bad points of the other and correct them in myself.
>
> **CONFUCIUS**

The mass media, particularly television and the movies, can also be influential in modeling behavior. A child who watches the average amount of television will witness thousands of acts of violence, including murders, in a year's time. Often these acts of aggression are shown to be successful ways to resolve disputes, with little or no unfortunate consequences to the aggressor. Similarly, the pleasures derived from acts of sexual promiscuity are routinely displayed but only rarely associated with the consequences of an unwanted pregnancy or disease.

In sum, as parents and adults we must be aware of the behaviors that we are modeling to children, wittingly or unwittingly. Children are keen observers of all aspects of adult behavior. It is little wonder that children who witness their fathers battering family members often become batterers themselves. As a society, we need to be aware of the influence of the mass media on people's behavior. Sex and violence sell on television and in the movies but also model inappropriate and destructive behavior in vast numbers of people who watch it.

SUMMARY

- Learning is relevant to nearly all human behavior. It constitutes, by definition, a relatively permanent change in behavior due to experience. A learned response reflects the capability for behavior while performance reflects the actual behavior itself.
- Habituation, or not responding to certain stimuli, is also an important part of learning.
- Classical conditioning results when a stimulus that automatically elicits a response is paired with a previously neutral stimulus and the latter stimulus then acquires the ability to elicit the same response.
- A classically conditioned response will extinguish if it is repeatedly presented without occasional pairings with the stimulus that automatically elicits the response.
- Following extinction, spontaneous recovery of the conditioned response will occur after a rest interval.
- A response that has been conditioned to a specific stimulus will also occur to similar stimuli although the response will not be as strong.
- With repeated presentations, individuals will learn to respond only to certain stimuli and not others, a process known as discrimination learning.
- Classically conditioned responses are important because they signal the occurrence of important and relevant events in our lives. Classical conditioning allows a neutral stimulus to acquire the properties of the stimulus with which it has been paired. Many of our emotional responses, including fears, likes and dislikes, and even love are acquired in this way.
- Forming a strong sexual attachment to an object, known as a fetish, also involves classical conditioning, as are preferences and dislikes of certain foods and tastes.
- Health professionals have utilized classical conditioning principles to help cancer chemotherapy patients avoid developing numerous taste aversions. These principles can also be used to condition healthy responses, such as lowering blood pressure, to previously neutral stimuli.
- Evidence suggests that even our attitudes toward others are shaped by classical conditioning. Advertisements often use these principles to condition a positive emotional response to a commercial product. Some products are advertised in a fashion to condition a fear-reducing response.
- Operant conditioning involves changing behavior by following it with a reinforcement. A reinforcement is an event that increases the probability that a response that preceded it will occur in the future. Much of the early research on operant conditioning was conducted on rats and pigeons in a chamber called a Skinner box.
- In operant conditioning, rewarding each small step in the learning process as it occurs shapes a response.
- Extinction and spontaneous recovery of learned responses occur in operant conditioning just as they do in classical conditioning.
- Shaping principles can be used in persuasion, altering the behavior of others, and changing opinions.
- A positive reinforcer involves events or behavioral consequences that strengthen the responses that immediately precede them. Primary reinforcers satisfy some biological need while secondary reinforcers acquire reinforcing properties by being paired with primary reinforcers.
- The Premack principle states that a behavior that has a high probability of occurring will reinforce another behavior that has a lower probability of occurring.
- A negative reinforcer is a stimulus that strengthens responses by permitting an avoidance or escape from aversive stimuli.
- The application of an aversive stimulus after a behavior occurs is called punishment. Punishment can either be positive or negative, depending on whether it involves the application of an aversive stimulus or the removal of a pleasurable stimulus.
- To be effective, punishments must occur quickly, be relatively severe, give appropriate feedback, and be paired with positively reinforced alternatives.

- The use of punishment produces several undesirable side effects. Learned helplessness can occur when punishment is used and an individual cannot control it or escape from it. This sometimes occurs with students who are failing a course and with individuals in abusive relationships.
- Reinforcements in operant conditioning occur either continuously or intermittently. Intermittent reinforcements occur on partial schedules of reinforcement. In a fixed-interval schedule, reinforcements are given after a certain period of time, while in a variable-interval they are given after differing amounts of time. In a fixed-ratio schedule, a response is rewarded after a fixed number of responses, while with a variable-ratio schedule a varying number of responses must be made before reinforcement.
- Responses are more resistant to extinction following intermittent reinforcement. Variable-ratio reinforcement results in the fastest rate of responding with the greatest resistance to extinction.
- The principles of operant conditioning can be effectively used to shape the behavior of others, including the lecturing and test-giving behaviors of professors. These principles can also be used to extinguish undesirable responses.
- Promising a reward for a task a person already enjoys can result in a loss of interest in the task, a phenomenon known as the overjustification effect.
- Operant conditioning principles can also be used to change one's own behavior. These principles have also been used effectively in training animals and in helping people control autonomic physiological functions such as heart rate and blood pressure.
- Many learned responses involve both classical and operant conditioning. These include superstitious behaviors. Other learned responses occur in the absence of classical or operant conditioning. Observational learning, which occurs through observing and imitating others, is an important example.

Key Terms

behavior modification: a process by which reinforcements are used to change inappropriate behaviors, thoughts, and feelings.

biofeedback: a procedure that uses sensors attached to the body, which give feedback to the individual about various physiological functions.

classical conditioning: learning that allows us to form associations between events in our environment.

conditioned emotional response: the process wherein a previously neutral stimulus acquires the ability to arouse an emotional response.

conditioned response (CR): a response that has been conditioned to a previously neutral conditioned stimulus.

conditioned stimulus (CS): an originally neutral stimulus that is paired with an unconditioned stimulus, and elicits a conditioned response.

conditioned taste aversion: learning to avoid eating something that has previously been associated with illness.

continuous reinforcement: when a desired response is reinforced each time it occurs; important when shaping behavior.

discrimination: the ability to distinguish between stimuli.

extinction: the weakening of a response due to lack of reinforcement; occurs in both classical and operant conditioning.

fetish: sexual arousal caused by an object.

fixed-interval schedule: a reinforcement schedule in which a set amount of time must elapse between successive reinforcements.

fixed-ratio schedule: a reinforcement schedule in which a response is reinforced after a fixed number of responses.

habituation: the process by which repeated presentations of a stimulus do *not* cause a response.

interval schedules: a schedule of reinforcement in which a reinforcement occurs after a certain period of time has elapsed.

law of effect: a law that states that an organism is more likely to repeat a response that leads to favorable consequences.

learned helplessness: the inability to learn to avoid aversive stimuli.

learning: a relatively permanent change in mental state or behavior due to experience.

modeling: the act of imitating a specific behavior that was observed.

negative punishment: a behavior that is undesired is weakened by the removal of a rewarding or pleasurable stimulus when the undesired behavior is exhibited.

negative reinforcer: an aversive stimulus that strengthens responses that permit an organism to avoid or escape from it.

observational learning: learning that occurs by observing and imitating the actions of others.

operant chamber (Skinner box): a device used to research the operant learning process; allows control of the stimuli and rewards given to an organism.

operant (instrumental) conditioning: learning that allows us to repeat behaviors that bring about positive consequences and to avoid behaviors that result in unpleasant consequences.

operant response: a term used in operant conditioning that indicates a response to be learned.
orienting response: an automatic response to a novel or unexpected stimulus.
overjustification effect: adding an incentive for a task that an individual already enjoys may result in a loss of interest in the task.
partial (intermittent) reinforcement: reinforcing a desired response periodically, rather than continuously.
partial-reinforcement effect: the finding that responses are much more resistant to extinction following partial reinforcement as compared to continuous reinforcement.
performance: the demonstration of a learned behavior.
phobia: an unreasonable fear of a specific object or situation.
positive punishment: involves the application of an aversive stimulus to stop or weaken an ongoing behavior.
positive reinforcement: those stimulus events or behavioral consequences that strengthen the responses that immediately precede them.
post-reinforcement pause: a pause in behavior occurring after a reinforcement is obtained; the higher the ratio of responses, the longer the post-reinforcement pause.
Premack principle: a behavior that has a high probability of occurring can reinforce another behavior that has a lower probability of occurring.
primary reinforcer: a reinforcer that strengthens behavior because it satisfies a basic biological need.
punishment: any consequence to a behavior that decreases the probability of the undesired behavior being repeated; the application of an aversive stimulus *after* a behavior has occurred.
ratio schedule: a reinforcement schedule in which a reinforcement will occur after a certain number of responses has occurred.
reinforcement: an event that increases the probability that the response that preceded it will be repeated in the future.
reinforcer: a term used in conditioning that identifies something that strengthens a behavior that led to it.
schedules of reinforcement: patterns of partial reinforcements.
secondary reinforcer: a reinforcer that strengthens behavior because it is paired with a primary reinforcer.
shaping: a small series of steps that teaches an organism to build upon existing behaviors by selectively rewarding some behaviors and not others.
Skinner box: see *operant chamber.*
spontaneous recovery: the reappearance of a learned response that had previously been extinguished.
stimulus generalization: the tendency to respond to similar stimuli once a response has been conditioned.
successive approximation: small intermediate steps toward the final desired response.
superstitious behavior: the tendency to attribute receiving a reinforcement to an irrelevant behavior.
tabula rasa: the belief that when a human is born, the mind is a "blank slate."
unconditioned response (UCR): an automatic response to an unconditioned stimulus.
unconditioned stimulus (UCS): a stimulus that causes an automatic response.
variable-interval schedule: a schedule of reinforcement in which a variable amount of time elapses between successive reinforcements; the first response *after* a variable interval of time has elapsed is reinforced; the shorter the interval, the better the rate of responding.
variable-ratio schedule: a schedule of reinforcement in which reinforcement comes after a varying number of responses made—the faster the response rate, the more rapidly will the reinforcement be obtained. These schedules result in very high rates of responding and great resistance to extinction.

4

MEMORY

O memory, thou bitter sweet
—Both a joy and a
scourge!

MME. DE STAËL

Memories. The collective record of our past experiences. They constitute a critical part of our consciousness. Imagine for a moment your life without memories. No doubt there are some memories that you wish you could forget permanently, but for the most part, memories are an essential part of our very being. Without them we would be unable to walk, communicate, or engage in even the simplest of behaviors. Without memory, all of our previously learned skills would suddenly be impossible. We would have no recollection of any of our past experiences. In this respect, an 80-year-old person would be like a newborn infant.

Testing Your Memory

At times, all of us question how good our memories are. As we age, those questions become more frequent. One difficulty in evaluating our memories is that we do not have anything by which to compare them. The short test contained in Table 4.1 will give you a rough idea of how your memory compares to the norm.

Types of Memories

Psychologists categorize memories into three different types: (1) memories of personal experiences, called **episodic memories,** that represent episodes in our lives; (2) knowledge of factual information about our world, called **semantic memory;** and (3) memories of how to accomplish certain tasks, such as typing or driving a car, known as **procedural memory.**

Myths about Memories

There are many misconceptions or myths about memories that are commonly held to be true. Robert Higbee, in his book *Your Memory: How It Works and How to Improve It,* describes several of the most commonly held misconceptions (Higbee, 1988). First of all, a memory is an activity, not a thing. It is a complex process by which we store information in the brain. However, precisely how this happens remains unknown. Secondly, there is no single secret to a good memory. This chapter will set forth several techniques to improve your memory, but keep in mind, no single technique will work in all situations and for all kinds of memories.

Many people believe that some individuals are born with poor memories and that little can be done to correct them. While some small individual differences in memory ability may exist, most people's inability to remember is caused by ineffective memorization techniques. Research has shown that students who earn good grades have discovered and used these techniques whereas students who achieve at lower levels have failed to do so. Do more intelligent people have better memories? To a certain extent they do, but only because highly intelligent individuals discover effective techniques for memorization. Good memory is not inherent in high intelligence.

Some people also believe that there are fortunate people who are endowed with a photographic memory. Allegedly, such people can recall any scene or event in minute detail, as if they had photographed it with a camera. Most psychologists reject this notion. Interestingly, a pharmaceutical research laboratory in New York

✦ TABLE 4.1 ✦ Test Your Memory

Answer each of these questions using the following point scale:

1 point	Not within the last 6 months
2 points	Once or twice in the last 6 months
3 points	About once a month
4 points	About once a week
5 points	Daily
6 points	More than once a day

____ 1. How often do you fail to recognize places you've been before?

____ 2. How often do you forget whether you did something, such as lock the door or turn off the lights or the oven?

____ 3. How often do you forget when something happened—wondering whether it was yesterday or last week?

____ 4. How often do you forget where you put items like house keys or wallet?

____ 5. How often do you forget something you were told recently and had to be reminded of it?

____ 6. How often are you unable to remember a word or a name, even though it's "on the tip of your tongue"?

____ 7. In conversation, how often do you forget what you were just talking about?

Add up your total score. If you scored 7–14, you have a better-than-average memory; 15–25, an average memory; and 26 or higher, a below-average memory.

SOURCE: *Newsweek,* Cowley, G. & Underwood, A.

reported in 1995 that it had created a fruit fly with a photographic memory. This laboratory is currently collaborating with a major U.S. pharmaceutical firm to develop a memory drug for humans.

Many people mistakenly believe that old age dooms us to poor memories. While some memory declines with aging, it is not as extensive as most people believe. Another belief is that memory is like a muscle—the more you exercise it, the better it becomes. Unfortunately, this analogy does not hold true for memory. For instance, you could practice rote memorization of numbers indefinitely and never get any better at recalling them. Memory improves when we use more efficient memorization techniques and don't simply practice.

Another commonly held belief is that if we remember too much useless information, the clutter in our minds will interfere with our ability to recall important things. There is no evidence to suggest that our brains have a finite capacity for memory storage. You should feel free to keep cramming in more and more information without any fear of overloading the system. Finally, there is the widespread belief that humans use only a small part of their mental potential—amounting to approximately 10% of the brain's potential capability. This statistic is often quoted by some "expert" who is intent on selling you a technique to "unlock" the other

90% of your brainpower. As Higbee notes in his book, there is no scientific evidence to support this "10% notion" or any other set percentage of potential. It is impossible to identify what our "mental potential" is or to quantify what percentage of such potential that we are using. However, we do have the ability to learn and memorize more efficiently, and I will discuss several methods for doing so later in this chapter.

Stages of Memory

Psychologists believe that remembering consists of three stages: encoding, storage, and retrieval. Information first must be put into some usable form so that encoding can occur. If you are listening to a lecture given in English, the material is in a form that you are able to encode. Listening to the same lecture in Chinese, for instance, would likely prevent encoding. Next, the information must be *stored* appropriately in the brain so that memories can be later *retrieved.* These three stages occur sequentially. Long-term remembering will not be possible if a disruption occurs at any of the stages. For example, if encoding does not occur, then storage or retrieval will not be possible. Likewise, if we encode material successfully but storage is disrupted, then **retrieval** will be impossible.

An interesting phenomenon sometimes occurs when material has been successfully encoded into long-term memory but we find that we are incapable of retrieving it. This happens when you have the feeling that you know the answer but it is just out of reach. Psychologists refer to this as the **tip-of-the-tongue phenomenon** because you feel that the information is "right there" ready to be retrieved but you cannot immediately recall it. This can be a frustrating feeling, especially when it occurs on an exam. Often we can retrieve a part of the information, such as remembering that the missing word starts with the letter "T," or knowing that the word contains a certain number of letters. We just cannot "spit it out," which seems an appropriate expression since it is "on the tip of our tongue." As you have likely noticed, the best solution is often to stop consciously trying to recall it. Your brain will continue the search and often the answer will suddenly pop into your head.

An analogy exists between how the human brain and a computer memory actually store information. Information must be entered into the computer's memory by putting it in a form that the computer understands. To accomplish this, we type the information on a keyboard. Next the computer must have a way to store this material, which typically takes place on the system's hard drive. Finally, the computer must have a software program that allows it to search the hard drive in order to retrieve information. As we shall see later, though, this analogy breaks down when we compare the accuracy of our mind's retrieval ability with that of a computers.

Three Memory Systems

In addition to the three stages necessary for remembering, there are also three kinds of memories. Information also must pass sequentially through each of these three systems in order to be remembered for the long term.

Sensory Memory

Imagine that someone tells you a telephone number so that you can dial the local pizza parlor. As your friend calls out the number, your **sensory memory** will hold the information very briefly. For auditory information such as this, the information is held somewhat like a brief echo for about 2 seconds. For visual information, such as a picture flashed before you, a momentary image will be maintained for about one-half second. You can see your sensory memory at work by rapidly waving a finger in front of your eyes. You do not see a single finger moving, but rather multiple images of your finger trailing behind. Your sensory memory is holding the images even after the finger moves to a new position. Sensory memory serves as an extremely short-term buffer that allows information to be transferred to the next memory system. All sensory memories fade away (i.e., decay) very rapidly.

Short-Term Memory

Most information that reaches the sensory receptors is not maintained in memory. Even though our senses are bombarded with information, we need to remember only a small fraction of the material. The mechanism of *attention* determines what information is received for processing into memory. If a television is playing in the background, the sounds and possibly the sights are registered by our sense organs, but because we are not paying attention to them, the information does not enter into memory. When your friend calls out the telephone number for the pizza parlor, we attend to that information. It briefly enters our sensory memory and then passes into **short-term memory.** The short-term memory system is only capable of holding the information for a brief period of time, rarely longer than 20 to 30 seconds. This system also limits the *amount* of information that we can hold in short-term memory to about seven items, give or take two. It is no coincidence that telephone numbers contain seven digits.

Short-term memory serves the important function of maintaining unimportant information in a temporary buffer that can be dumped when the information is no longer needed. If you think about all the information that enters your brain, the overwhelming majority of it needs to be remembered only for a few seconds before being forgotten. The time restrictions prevent our brains from becoming cluttered with useless information.

Short-term memory can be easily disrupted if anything interferes or interrupts it during the process. For example, if your friend calls out the phone number but another friend talks to you immediately afterwards, the memory will be disrupted. In fact, I used to experience this type of memory disruption every Christmas when it came time to assemble my children's new toys. First, I would read the instruction sheet that would state to insert part D into part C, using the fastener labeled part H. Then, as I reached for the parts, one of my children inevitably would ask, "How long 'til it's put together, Dad?" At that point, I would have to go back and read the instructions again.

Short-term memory is sometimes referred to as our *working memory* because it is what we use when we do much of our thinking. It is accessed when we make plans and set goals for ourselves. For example, you use your working memory when you are getting ready to go to class and remind yourself to take your textbook, notebook, and lunch with you. You also primarily use your working memory when you engage in conversations with others. It allows you to follow the ebb and flow of a conversation and to respond appropriately. A computer also has a working memory that is known as random access memory or RAM. It is the memory chip utilized when the computer does intermediate calculations and operations before transferring the results to the hard drive for storage.

Long-Term Memory

We evaluate information in short-term memory and then select the material that is important or particularly meaningful to us. This information is transferred to a third memory system called **long-term memory,** a system that allows for the more permanent storage of information. The method by which we store memories in long-term memory is called **encoding.** Think of the three memory systems as a filter or a funnel. Most information that enters the sensory memory is filtered out and discarded. Likewise, those memories that do get through and are transferred to short-term memory also are largely filtered out before reaching long-term memory. Only the information that we deem *meaningful and important* gets funneled or "encoded" into long-term memory. This is where we store everything that we know about the world and ourselves, including all of our educational knowledge, our artistic and athletic skills, and our remembrances of our past. Unlike short-term memory, its capacity is limitless. In fact, the more information you have in long-term memory, the easier it is to add to it. A familiar example of this occurs in the study of mathematics where the knowledge that you have already acquired makes it easier to learn new math skills.

Also unlike short-term memory, long-term memories can be retained for indefinite periods of time, sometimes for a lifetime. This retention of encoded information is called **storage.** Think back to your earliest memory from childhood. For me, it is sitting on my father's lap at the kitchen table when I was 4 years old as he bounced me on his knee. Although some people report memories from their infancy (and some even report memories from when they were in the womb!), most psychologists believe that it is unlikely we can remember events that occurred before the age of about 3 years.

The long-term storage of memories is demonstrated by what happens when we electrically stimulate areas of the brain. As you will recall, in Chapter 1 I discussed Penfield's research in which subjects undergoing brain surgery had areas of their brain electrically stimulated (Penfield, 1957). Under these conditions, patients often recalled vivid memories, including sights and sounds, from their early childhood. Is every experience stored as a memory somewhere in the brain? Penfield suggested this might be the case, but more recent research indicates that relatively few memories are permanently stored in this manner (Loftus & Loftus, 1980).

Continuing with our computer analogy, the long-term memory in a computer is located on the hard drive. Information enters through the keyboard, is processed in RAM (short-term or working memory), and is then transferred for storage (long-term memory) to the hard drive.

We have gained insights into the distinct nature of short-term and long-term memories from elderly patients and individuals who have suffered from brain damage. Documented cases have described individuals who have suffered from brain trauma and, as a result, have no ability to transfer information from short-term to long-term memory. While old long-term memories remain intact, the individuals are now unable to form new long-term memories. I witnessed this occurrence in one of my own relatives who, at age 92, fell and struck her head. Following this trauma, she completely lost the ability to form new long-term memories. She had good recall of events that had occurred before the fall, including events from her childhood, but had virtually no recollection of any of the events subsequent to the trauma. She was consistently unable to remember events that occurred only minutes earlier. For instance, if I left the room briefly during our visits, she greeted me warmly upon my return as if it were a new visit, and had no recollection of my presence only moments earlier. People who suffer from this type of memory dysfunction find it extremely debilitating. They are forced to live exclusively in the immediacy of the present time or in the memories of the distant past.

APPLICATIONS: Basic Tools to Aid Memorization

Getting Things into Sensory Memory

Regardless of whether you want to store information in short-term or long-term memory, the information must first pass through the sensory memory. It is *lack of attention* that prevents this from occurring. People who complain that they cannot remember someone's name, even a few moments after being introduced, usually were not paying attention when the person's name was spoken. As your mother always said, *pay attention!*

Improving Short-Term Memory

One of the best tools for maintaining information in short-term memory is repetition, or what psychologists call **rehearsal.** You probably have found yourself repeating a phone number over and over to yourself after hearing someone give it to you. This simple rehearsal strategy will effectively maintain the information in short-term memory until it is no longer needed. As adults we frequently use rehearsal strategies even though children under the age of 5 do not.

Earlier, I noted that memory capacity in short-term memory is about seven items, give or take two items. One way to increase the capacity to remember is to group or organize information into separate and meaningful sequences known as **chunks.** A single chunk may contain many individual components but is remembered as a single item. For example, words are composed of several individual letters, but it is the entire word that is remembered. The word constitutes one chunk. In some cases, as in recalling a poem, several words may constitute one chunk. When remembering phone numbers, we usually organize the numbers into three chunks, such as 709-698-1735. The chunks are much easier to memorize than the string of numbers 7-0-9-6-9-8-1-7-3-5. The same organization applies to remembering your social security number as three chunks of information rather than as nine separate numbers. When giving these kinds of numbers to others to memorize, you should present the chunks separately, with a brief pause between each.

Most people can hold about seven chunks of information in short-term memory. There is nothing that you can do to increase this capacity. However, the more meaningful the chunks, the easier they are to store. Remembering seven obscure chemical terms is more difficult than remembering seven common words. Whenever possible, try to discover ways to break information into meaningful chunks. Look at the number 149210661776. At 12 digits, this number will be impossible to hold in short-term memory. Can you see three meaningful chunks that would allow this number to be easily memorized? (*Hint:* Think about important historical dates.) How about the chemical 2-dimethylaminoethanol? (No hint here.)

Improving Long-Term Memory

I spoke earlier about how information is selectively filtered out as it passes from sensory memory to short-term memory to long-term memory. Assume that you have been paying attention so that the information actually entered your sensory memory. Further assume that you used rehearsal and/or chunking to maintain it in short-term memory effectively. Now your brain comes to the critical juncture of making the decision of whether or not to encode the material for storage into long-term memory. Because most of the information that enters into short-term memory is only needed momentarily, it can be dumped from our memory as soon as we have completed using it.

Recent evidence suggests that the decision to store or discard information is seldom a conscious decision. Rather, it is handled automatically by a small structure deep in the center of the brain called the **hippocampus.** This structure serves as a filter or gatekeeper and permits only a small portion of the information in short-term memory to enter into long-term memory. How does the hippocampus decide which information should get through? Two factors are important. If the information has *emotional significance,* it is allowed to pass. (You probably remember the name of your first love, but how about your first teacher?) The hippocampus also takes into account whether the information is *meaningful* to you and whether it *relates to other information* that you have already learned. This activity explains why two different people who hear the same information will have very different long-term memories of it. A lecture on constitutional law will be encoded very differently by a chemist as compared to an attorney.

Knowing how the hippocampus functions, do you now wish that your hippocampus would allow more information into your long-term memory? (Be careful what you wish for.) Researchers have occasionally encountered people like this, who can quickly encode huge quantities of words, numbers, or even facts. The downside is that these people are almost incapable of abstract reasoning. They have huge amounts of information in their long-term memories but cannot make any sense of it (Cowley & Underwood, 1998).

Often we need to encourage our hippocampus to allow information to pass into long-term memory. For the information needing more permanent storage, there are several effective tools we can use.

DEEP PROCESSING. For short-term memory the simple act of repeating or rehearsing the item over and over is effective. For long-term memory you can use a rehearsal technique called **elaborative rehearsal.** With this technique you try to link the item to be remembered to other information already contained in long-term memory. Essentially, you are elaborating on what you already know, hence the term *elaborative* rehearsal. This results in what Fergus Craik and Robert Lockhart (1972) called *deep processing* of memories. Simply repeating material over and over is an example of the shallow processing of memories. In deep processing we think about the material from several different angles and relate it to other material that we learned previously. For instance, assume that you are trying to memorize what the term *rehearsal* means within the context of memory. Examples of shallow processing of the word would be noting that the word contains nine letters, consists only of lower-case letters, and contains black letters on a white background. Deeper processing would involve thinking about how rehearsing an item in memory is similar to learning to play a musical instrument or master a sport. Or you might think about how the dress rehearsal for a play differs from regular rehearsals and how these two kinds of rehearsals would affect your ability to remember your lines. Elaborative rehearsal techniques such as these, which link new knowledge to existing previous knowledge, greatly assist in the storage and retrieval of information from long-term memory.

ORGANIZATION. As you know, if your room is organized, it is much easier to find things. Similarly, if memories are organized, they are easier to retrieve. For example, if you were asked to name all the countries in Europe, how would you go about it? It is unlikely that you would begin by naming countries randomly. Instead, you might imagine a map of Europe and start by naming the countries in northern Europe and work your way south. Or perhaps you would start with countries in which you had traveled extensively and work your way outward to less familiar countries. Or you might name all of the former Communist countries of Eastern Europe first. In any event, you are retrieving the information based on some organization of the material.

Material that is organized during the time it is being learned will be retrieved more easily than material that must be organized after it is learned. As you are learning new material in college, you should always strive to put it into some organizational schema. When you take lecture notes, you should organize them around themes or major points. One common technique relies on outlines with different levels of headings. Different topics require different organizations. Memorizing historical material might require an ordering based on the time sequence in which events occurred. On the other hand, learning concepts in physics might require groupings based on categories. Textbooks and (I hope) lectures are organized in a manner that made sense to the writer or the lecturer. However, you may need to recast the organization into a form that is different but more meaningful to you.

Imagine that you are going to the hardware store to buy items that would allow you to repair a light fixture and to touch up some paint. When you arrive at the store, you would probably head to either the electrical or the paint department to begin your shopping. Fortunately, the store shelves are organized to make your shopping easier with all the painting supplies in one area and the electrical supplies in another. Furthermore, the supplies are suborganized by category with all the stains grouped in one place, the paints in another, sandpaper in another, and so forth. As you begin to recall what you need, you might imagine the project to be completed and select items in the sequence that you would use them. After selecting the painting supplies, you would then move to the next category (electrical supplies) and complete a similar sequence. This same approach applies to learning new material. During the learning process, you also need to organize material in some meaningful way so that later you can go "shopping" for it in an efficient and successful manner. The method of chunking, that I discussed earlier, is one type of organizational technique.

Imagery. The ability to conjure up a visual image can greatly help the learning of verbal material. Humans have particularly good memories for pictures. We can take advantage of this asset by creating a picture of the material that we are trying to remember. Words that are tangible, such as "table," "book," and "car," are more easily visualized than abstract words, such as "fairness" and "honesty." However, even these abstract words can evoke images, such as the word "fairness" eliciting an image of the scales of justice.

We are often called upon to learn pairs of words or things together. Learning a foreign language, associating a name with a face, and memorizing the capitals of states are all examples. Imagery can be particularly helpful in these instances. If you are trying to memorize the capital of California, you might visualize a map of the state with a "sack" hanging in the middle of it. When called upon later to recall the capital, the image of the sack would trigger the name "Sacramento." People who are good at learning foreign languages often have the ability to conjure up a visual image that links a foreign word to its English equivalent.

Distribution of Practice. If you plan to study for an exam for 3 hours, should you do it in one 3-hour block or space it out over several study periods? Studying all in one block of time is called **massed practice** or, as it is more frequently known by students, "cramming." Several shorter periods of studying are known as **distributed practice** because the time spent studying is *distributed* over several different study intervals. The amount of time to learn material is about the same with both massed and distributed practice. However, distributed practice results in a significantly greater long-term memory for the material when compared to massed practice. Despite the repeated entreaties of educators, many college students continue to postpone studying and end up pulling an "all nighter" out of necessity.

Why is distributed practice superior to massed practice? It is easier to maintain a high level of attention to the material when the study interval is shorter. You are also more likely to study while you are in different settings and in different mood states, both important factors in memory. And finally, the physiological changes that occur in the brain during learning will occur more efficiently if the studying is distributed.

How should study periods be spaced? There are no hard-and-fast rules. Higbee (1988) concluded that shorter study intervals are usually better for more complicated subjects. Also, distributed practice helps more in the early stages of learning. Nevertheless, study periods can be too distributed. Higbee noted, for instance, that studying for only 10-minute periods 18 times would result in worse performance than cramming for 3 hours straight. As a general rule, study periods should be about 30 minutes or longer. Taking even a brief break between study periods has been shown to be very beneficial for memorization.

Unfortunately, the deleterious effects of cramming on memorization are not always immediately apparent after learning. This then reinforces the behavior of students who study right up until test time. The biggest negative effects are seen when you must recall the material at a later time, such as when you take the final exam at the end of the semester. For long-term recall, distributed practice is always superior. The goal of education is, after all, a relatively permanent infusion of knowledge. Students sometimes mistakenly think they do not care if they remember the material permanently; they just want to get through the examination.

CONTEXT. Learning always takes place within some context. For example, when you study in a given room, the contextual cues include all the sights, sounds, and smells of that environment. Research has clearly demonstrated that recall of material is better when it is done within the same contextual setting as the learning. This phenomenon is called **state-dependent learning.** Psychologists believe that the contextual cues help serve as retrieval cues when the material is to be remembered. I experience this phenomenon when I try to remember students' names. I can easily recall their names when I see them sitting at their usual place in the classroom, but if I run into them at the grocery store, I find it much more difficult.

Whenever possible, you should try to learn the material in a setting similar to the one you will be in when later recalling the material. Several research studies have shown that students who were tested in the same room in which they studied performed better than students who changed rooms. If you cannot study in exactly the same environment, try to find an environment similar to the test environment. For instance, using another empty classroom for studying is better than studying at the beach (or at a bar!). Also, if you are accustomed to sitting in the front of the room during lectures, do not move to the back of the room for your test. If the examination requires you to recall material covered during the lecture, looking at the professor may provide cues that will help retrieval. If you are trying to remember material that you learned in another setting, imagine yourself in that setting. For example, visualize yourself in your own room, sitting at your desk, reading your text, while the stereo plays in the background.

Even the physiological or mood state that you are in while studying can serve as a contextual cue. Students who learned material while in a happy or sad state performed better on a memory task when they recalled the material in the same mood state (Eich, 1995). Depression and drug states greatly interfere with the encoding process and memorization. Therefore, absention from alcohol and drug use during study periods is extremely important.

A particularly interesting finding by Ellis and Ashbrook (1989) showed that our mood will affect emotionally charged memories. When we feel in a good mood, we can more easily remember the good things that have happened to us. We also judge life more favorably and see others as more compassionate and considerate. On the other hand, when in a bad mood, we judge life more harshly and appraise others more negatively.

Figure 4.1 presents, in simplified form, an overview of the three types of memories and the role that attention, rehearsal, and encoding play in the storage of memories. In reality, memory is a very complicated process. In fact, psychologists have only a partial understanding of exactly how memories are stored and recalled.

APPLICATIONS: Mnemonic Systems to Aid Memory

A **mnemonic** system or technique is defined as any technique that aids in memory recall. These techniques have been used for centuries. Mnemonics are what stage performers use when they perform their "amazing" feats of recall, such as memorizing the names of hundreds of individuals or the order of a 52-card deck after seeing it only briefly.

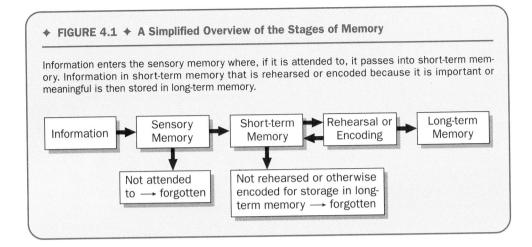

✦ FIGURE 4.1 ✦ A Simplified Overview of the Stages of Memory

Information enters the sensory memory where, if it is attended to, it passes into short-term memory. Information in short-term memory that is rehearsed or encoded because it is important or meaningful is then stored in long-term memory.

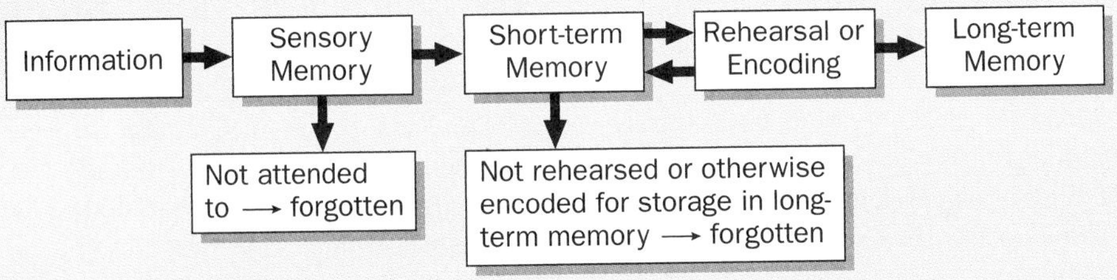

Mnemonic systems work by making material, that is inherently not very meaningful, more meaningful by adding some structure or organization to the material. As you will see, this sometimes is done visually and sometimes verbally. There are dozens of mnemonic systems available, depending on the memory task. I will review only a few of the major systems in this chapter.

Peg-Word System

Have you ever gone to the store to pick up a few items and discovered that, once you are there, you can only remember part of the list? People often think that because they only need to pick up a few items, they do not need to write a list. The **peg-word system** is particularly helpful when memorizing such a list. After only a brief period of memorization, you will find that you can remember the list even several days later (just in case you forget to go shopping when you planned!).

This system involves memorizing a set of "memory pegs" or hooks in advance. You then attach your shopping items to these pegs. Convenient and easily memorized sets of pegs are the first 10 numbers along with words that rhyme with those numbers. For example:

One–bun	Six–sticks
Two–shoe	Seven–heaven
Three–tree	Eight–gate
Four–door	Nine–line
Five–hive	Ten–hen

Take a moment to commit these pairs of words to memory. For most students this will only take a few moments.

Now pretend that you are going to purchase the following 10 items at the grocery store: (1) coffee, (2) milk, (3) sugar, (4) carrots, (5) ice, (6) butter, (7) steak, (8) potato chips, (9) Coke, and (10) pickles. In the peg-word system, we "hook" each shopping item to the number peg, using visual imagery to do so. For instance, our first shopping item is coffee. Use your imagination to hook coffee to the first pair of peg words, 1–bun. For example, you might visualize a can of coffee lying between the two halves of a hamburger bun. Now associate the second item, milk, with 2–shoe. In this case you might imagine a person pouring milk from a shoe. Next is sugar and 3–tree. I visualize a tree with bags of sugar hanging from the limbs. Try and form similar visualizations with the remaining 7 items. Now when you go to the store, you merely have to say to yourself, item 1–bun and the image of the coffee can in the hamburger bun will emerge. I have often had students complete this exercise in class with some arbitrary list of items and then unexpectedly tested their recall several days later. Almost invariably, recall is at or near 100%.

There are some rules that will help when you use the peg-word system. Make the visual images as *vivid* as possible. Imagine the colors of the coffee can, the hamburger bun, and perhaps the colorful table cloth on which it is sitting. Whenever possible, you should have the item to be memorized *interacting* with the peg word. For example, having a coffee can placed inside the hamburger bun would be better than imagining a can of coffee sitting passively beside a hamburger bun. And finally, do not be afraid to use *bizarre* images. Perhaps you imagine your coffee can located in another type of "buns." Bizarre images, even those "R-rated" ones, can help you in your later memory recall. Another advantage of this system is that you can simultaneously recall instantly where an item is located in a list. For instance, if you want to know the *third* item on your shopping list, you merely have to visualize the 3–tree with the bags of sugar growing on the tree.

Method of Loci

In 500 B.C. the poet Simonides was speaking indoors at a banquet to a group of acquaintances when he was called outside to meet someone. While he was outside, the roof of the banquet hall collapsed, crushing all the occupants beyond recognition. When Simonides was asked to help identify the bodies, he found that he was able to do so by remembering the places where they had been sitting. This led Simonides to conclude that one good way to remember things is to associate mental images of those things with a familiar location. This led to the development of the **method of loci.** The word *loci* is the plural form of the Latin word *locus,* which means "location." Greek and Roman speakers used this system to memorize long speeches. They would visualize objects that represented the topics they were going to cover and then mentally would place these objects in different locations of some very familiar place. During the speech, they would mentally "walk" through this place and retrieve the images of the objects as they came to them. The objects then triggered the memories of the topics to be covered.

You can use this system yourself quite easily. First you must be able to visualize some location that is very familiar to you. This might be the inside of your car, the inside of your bedroom, or the areas that you pass as you go to school. I will illustrate how you could use the locations in a room to memorize the grocery list that we mentioned earlier. Using my own home as an example, I will visualize what happens when I arrive home from work. When I pull up the driveway, I see that the garage door is closed. At that location, I visualize hot *coffee* pouring out from beneath the garage door. When I open the door, I can see several cartons of *milk* lying on the floor, which I smash as I drive over them. Next, I come to the door of the laundry room, which I find is *sugar* coated. As I open the door, *sugar* falls from the door at my feet. I then enter the laundry room and there, sitting inside the washing machine, is a bunch of *carrots* being laundered. I would continue this pattern of visualization for all the items on the shopping list. Then, later at the store, I would remember the items on the list by visualizing what happens when I arrive home. I again visualize pulling up my driveway with hot *coffee* still spilling out from under the garage door, approaching the laundry room door still coated with *sugar,* and so forth for each location. As with the orators of old, you could follow a similar procedure if you wished to remember the main topics that you wanted to include in a speech. First you would create an outline of the main topics to be covered and then associate some object with each of those topics. Next you would "deposit" these items in familiar locations. During the speech, you would walk through each of the locations, and the visualized objects would trigger your memory of the topics to be covered.

As with the peg-word method, there are certain rules that you should follow. The objects that you place at the locations should be *concrete,* not abstract. A coffee can or a cup of coffee works better than the fuzzy concept of a coffee aroma. Whenever possible, the object and the location should be *interacting* with one another. Note that I had hot coffee streaming under the garage door, not a can of coffee sitting in front of the garage door. As before, bizarre imagery helps, so let your imagination run wild. Like the peg-word system, the method of loci allows you to remember things in sequential order, which is particularly important when you are recalling topics for a speech. Imagine that you are giving a talk about raising funds for your library. The points that you want to cover are the need for replacing dated books, replacing the worn carpet, repainting the walls, purchasing additional computers, and increasing the staff. First think of a concrete word to represent each point in your speech: a very old book, with its cover in tatters; a roll of threadbare carpet; a paint can, and so forth. Next, place these items in familiar locations and then, as you mentally tour the locations while you give your speech, allow the visualized object to trigger the next topic to be covered. Many accomplished speakers have used this technique very effectively.

The Link System

In the **link system,** we first form a visual image for each item to be remembered. We then link or associate each item with the visual image for the next item. Again, using my grocery list as an example, I visualize a hot cup of *coffee* being poured into a glass of *milk.* I then visualize a cup of *sugar* being added to the concoction, which is then stirred with a large *carrot.* The whole thing is then poured over a block of *ice,* which is placed atop a large mound of *butter.* To recall your list, begin with the first item and proceed as each item leads to the next. You only need to remember the first item to get the process started. As before, the images should be vivid and interacting. Bizarre images may again aid in recall. Like the method of loci, this method also can aid in remembering topics to cover during a speech.

Keyword Technique

In foreign languages, as well as in all of the sciences, we are often called upon to learn the meaning of a word with which we are initially unfamiliar. The **keyword technique** has been shown to be particularly effective for this task. The technique consists of two steps: (1) one or more concrete *keywords* are constructed to represent the foreign language word or the scientific term, and (2) a visual image connects the keyword to the original term. Let's look at how this might work in learning a foreign language vocabulary. During a driving vacation in Germany I had to learn the meaning of common words on highway signs. The German word *langsam* means slow. When I saw this word, I thought of a very "lanky" man that I knew named Sam who moved very slowly. The word *rollsplit* means loose stones. I associated rollsplit with the visual image of a large boulder rolling down a hill and breaking up into smaller rocks. Because *gefahr* means danger, I visualized a person "getting far" away from a burning car by running away. In psychology, many instructors teach students to remember the olfactory sense (the sense of smell) by visualizing an "oily factory" that smells bad. With a little practice, you can become very adept at using this technique. Many research studies show it is far superior to rote memorization.

Remembering People's Names and Faces

The most common memory complaint I hear is the inability to remember people's names. In some occupations, such as politics, this inability can have severe consequences. Imagine how disappointed you would be if a professor could never remember your name in a small class of 20 students. In fact, we all are positively impressed when someone we just met can recall our name after only a brief encounter. I once served under a university president who had the amazing ability to remember a person's name once they had been introduced. In fact, whenever I heard faculty members speak about this president, they often mentioned this ability. Your ability to remember people's names will always serve you well, regardless of what profession you choose to enter. Fortunately, there are mnemonic techniques that can assist you with this.

There are several important steps for remembering a person's name.

1. Get the name. This may sound self-evident but, in many cases, people forget the name because they really never "got it" in the first place. Pay attention when the name is first given. If you don't hear the name, ask the person for it again. Repeat the name out loud, by saying something like "Nice to meet you, *Bob*." Repeat the name while you are looking at the person's face. Ask the person questions about his or her name, such as "Is your legal name Robert or Bob?" If the name is unusual, ask the person to spell it, and then repeat the spelling back to the person. Work the name into the conversation as frequently as you can. When departing, say the name again. All these techniques involve the rehearsal of the person's name in his or her presence and will help strengthen an association between the person's face and name.
2. Make the name meaningful. This is particularly important in remembering last names. When you hear a last name, think of something concrete and meaningful that you can associate with the name. Many American names represent occupations, colors, famous people, metals, or other things that are already meaningful to you. My last name, Gardner, would probably make you think of a gardener. There was a famous psychologist with the last name of Wickelgren, which you might think of as a green wick. Other examples came to mind while I looked at faculty members' last names listed in my campus phone directory: Uszacki makes me think of a used jacket; Synhorst makes me think of a sinning whore; Tornblom elicits an image of a torn bloom on a flower, and so forth. Remember, concrete and less abstract associations will help in later recall.

3. Select a distinctive facial feature. Find some distinctive feature about the person. It is usually best to select a facial feature because it is the most obvious and often most distinctive. Focusing on an item of clothing is not recommended because the person probably will not be dressed the same the next time you meet. When meeting people for the first time, carefully study the physical features of their face. Is there something distinctive about their eyes, their nose, their ears, or their chin? Any unusual dental characteristics (braces, crooked teeth, etc.) or facial hair? No two faces are alike, but you need to practice being vigilant in picking out distinctive features. Several research studies have suggested that it is helpful to make personal judgments about people based on their facial features. Do they look honest, intelligent, moody, or suspicious? While it may seem inappropriate to make such snap judgments about people, it is something that we usually do anyway and, in that case, we can use it to help us remember their name.
4. Form a visual association between the name and the face. Upon meeting Mrs. Underwood, who has a hook nose, you visualize a stack of wood underneath her nose. Mr. Rose has very curly hair, from which you visualize red roses sprouting. Mr. Kochenberger has a coke and a burger sitting in his very large ears. These kinds of visual associations do not come easily at first but, with repeated practice, you will find that you can associate any name with some facial or physical feature of the individual.
5. Rehearse the association. Forming the association and doing the visualization only once usually will not be sufficient. As opportunities arise, practice the association immediately after meeting the person and periodically thereafter, as circumstances permit. This works particularly well when you are at a party or in a classroom where you repeatedly have the opportunity to come into contact with the person.

These techniques for learning a person's name will not come easily at first. You may want to practice your techniques using the pictures and names of people in newspapers and magazines. Do not underestimate the social importance of becoming skilled in this task. It can make a big difference in your future successes, not only in your personal relationships with others but also in other aspects of your life.

There are many other mnemonic techniques available that can be very helpful in learning almost any task. I have covered only a few of the more popular techniques in this chapter. I strongly encourage you to explore this topic further. Research has shown that students who achieve at high academic levels make extensive use of such techniques. In many cases the students discovered and taught themselves these techniques. However, an easier and more systematic method would be to examine one of the many excellent books that have been written on mnemonic techniques.

Remembering and Gesturing

As the tongue speaketh to the ear, so the gesture speaketh to the eye.

SIR FRANCIS BACON

One of the most embarrassing and troublesome times for our memories to fail is when we are speaking. Be it a formal presentation or just an informal conversation between friends, a sudden memory lapse can bring a discourse to an abrupt halt, even if only temporarily. You may have noticed that, during such times, you are more likely to use hand movements or gestures in an attempt to help retrieve the elusive forgotten information.

Recent research by Robert Krauss (1998) has shown that gestures help speakers formulate coherent speech by aiding them in the retrieval of elusive words from memory. He also showed that preventing speakers from gesturing during speeches slowed the fluency of the presentation. Krauss found this to be particularly disruptive to people who were describing spatial relationships, such as defining the words *under* or *adjacent*. So go ahead and gesture when you talk; the evidence suggests it can be a powerful memory aid.

Anxiety and Memory

Most college students can testify to the effects of anxiety on memory. Students often tell me that after an exam, they were so nervous they could hardly remember anything. I am sympathetic to this dilemma since I have witnessed the effects of anxiety on my own memory. In particular, I notice this most vividly when I have to introduce someone. For example, if I am standing with my wife at a party and I see a colleague and his wife approaching, I sometimes become anxious because I know that I will need to recall the names of both in order to introduce them to my wife. The more anxious I become about recalling the names, the less likely I will be able to do so.

Anxiety does not destroy memories; it interferes with your ability to retrieve them. You probably have noticed that after the anxiety passes, you can suddenly remember things just fine. Holmes (1974) has theorized that anxiety causes us to have extraneous thoughts, and it is these thoughts that interfere with our ability to retrieve memories. During an exam you may find yourself thinking about how failing the test will cause your GPA to drop and how you will not be eligible for financial aid next semester. Such extraneous thoughts interfere as you attempt to recall material for the exam. Controlling anxiety is very important. I will talk about anxiety control techniques in Chapter 9.

Other Memory Wreckers

Research has indicated several factors that can influence brain efficiency. High blood pressure has been shown to disrupt memorization, especially if it persists over a long period of time. Insufficient sleep also disrupts the formation of new memories. People who are depressed also have been shown to have poorer memories. Sometimes exposure to excessive information has a negative effect, which is a condition often referred to as *information overload*. I'm sure that you have sat in lectures where so much information was coming at such a fast pace that you wanted to scream, "Stop already! My brain can't handle any more!" This sense of overload occurs because our brain needs a certain amount of time to absorb the information that it is taking in.

Researchers are increasingly coming to understand the important role that stress plays in memory. In the short term, stress can energize us and actually help us in the memorization process. If the stress lasts longer than about 30 minutes, its dark side appears. Persistent stress causes hormones to be released that affect the brain's ability to transport glucose to the hippocampus. Glucose is a simple sugar that our brain uses for energy. Stress causes our brain to "run out of gas." If the stress persists over a period of months or years, it can even kill the brain cells in the hippocampus. I will be discussing the other effects of stress on our lives in later chapters, along with techniques that we can use to control it.

And finally, for you party animals, the effects of alcohol on memory are well documented. The consumption of alcohol alters brain chemistry in a way that prevents the hippocampus from transferring memories into long-term storage. Even short-term use of alcohol will affect memory, as anyone who has binged on alcohol can testify ("Where was I last night, and who was I with, anyway?"). Long-term and excessive use of alcohol can result in permanent damage to the brain. Despite conflicting evidence about whether alcohol actually kills brain cells, there is no question that excessive and prolonged abuse has devastating effects on brain functioning, particularly with respect to memory.

FORGETTING

Americans are increasingly concerned about how well their memory functions. A 1997 study of 178 doctors by Bruskin/Goldring Research reported that 80% of their patients over 30 years of age complained of memory loss. How much do we forget, and how quickly? There is no easy answer to this question. Material that is not meaningful or important to us will be quickly dropped from our memories, even if we have made a concerted effort to memorize it. On the other hand, meaningful and important material can be stored for an indefinite period of time, sometimes with little or no effort at memorization. As an example, most college students can recall precisely where they were when they first heard of the *Challenger* space shuttle tragedy. People over 40 similarly have vivid memories of where they were, and who they were with, when they heard that President Kennedy had been assassinated. I heard the news on my car radio and can clearly recall the specific intersection I was at when I heard the announcement. Memories of unexpected and emotionally arousing events such as these are called **flashbulb memories.** They illustrate that memory encoding can occur with little effort and that the memories so formed are nearly exempt from forgetting. Nevertheless, most of what we try to memorize does require considerable mental effort in order for encoding to occur. Unfortunately, you cannot count on flashbulb memories to remember facts for your world history class.

Most forgetting occurs shortly after learning, with the amount forgotten tapering off after that. For most material, the major part of forgetting takes place in the first few hours, with only smaller decrements after that. When the material is more meaningful and important, the rate of forgetting is slower. In addition, the more thoroughly the material is learned, the more resistant it is to forgetting. Bahrick (1984) examined how well people remembered the Spanish vocabulary that they learned in high school and college. People who had completed five semesters of Spanish were able to recognize about 80% of vocabulary words after a 25-year interval. This occurred even though most former students reported that they rarely used their Spanish skills. Former students who had completed only one semester remembered only about half as much material. Most of the forgetting that occurred did so in the first 3 years, after which retention was remarkably stable, even after 50 years.

Factors Causing Forgetting

Decay of Trace

Memories result in physiological changes in nerve cells in the brain. Research evidence suggests that memories not only leave physiological traces in the brain but also create brain activity. These traces and activity can fade or weaken over time. Such fading can occur in sensory memory, short-term memory, and long-term memory although it is most critical in sensory and short-term memory.

Could you remember a five-letter sequence such as N–T–H–D–K for 20 seconds? You could do so easily by simply rehearsing the five letters over and over during the 20-second retention interval. Lloyd and Margaret Peterson (1959) demonstrated how quickly memories decay in short-term memory when this rehearsal process is disrupted. They gave subjects a sequence to memorize consisting of either 3 consonants, or a 3-digit number. The sequence was followed immediately thereafter by a 3-digit number from which the subjects had to count backwards by 3s. For example, the subjects heard D–S–J, followed by 380, at which point they had to say 377, 374, 371, 368, and so on. When the subjects were asked to repeat the 3 consonants that they had been presented, the Petersons found that the backwards counting effectively prevented the subjects from rehearsing the 3-letter sequence. Figure 4.2 illustrates how rapidly the memory trace decayed under these conditions. Correct recall occurred less than half the time after only 6 seconds, and there was practically no recall after 18 seconds.

You may want to try this experiment with a friend, particularly if you know someone who thinks that she has a very good memory. Most people will be surprised to learn that they cannot remember something for as little as 20 seconds. This experiment only works with very low meaning information. If you give people a highly meaningful word that consists of three letters, such as CAT, they would be able to remember it, even if prevented from rehearsal by counting backwards. You will recall that highly meaningful information quickly enters long-term memory and is not subject to rapid decay. While decay of trace can account for some forgetting in sensory and short-term memory, it is not one of the major causes of forgetting that we experience in our everyday lives.

Consolidation Failure

One theoretical view of memory states that a certain amount of time must elapse for a memory trace to become fully formed and permanently stored in memory. D. O. Hebb conceptualized a memory trace as a neural circuit that was formed and strengthened over time in the brain (Hebb, 1949). He believed that these neural circuits must be activated several times in order for the memory to experience **neural consolidation,** which is the process by which a memory trace becomes permanently fixed by repeated activation of neural circuits. If anything disrupts this neural consolidation, memory will be impaired.

What kinds of things can disrupt this consolidation process? Hebb believed that encoding additional memories could prevent the consolidation of previous memories. It would be as if your brain can only work on one consolidation at a time, and too much additional input can negatively affect memory consolidation.

Supporting evidence for this perspective comes from research with amnesiacs. People who suffer a blow to the head are often unable to remember events that occurred

✦ **FIGURE 4.2** ✦

Percentage of correct recalls of 3-letter consonant syllables (i.e., Q–J–N) and 3-digit numbers at intervals of 3, 6, 9, 12, 15, and 18 seconds when rehearsal of the items was prevented.

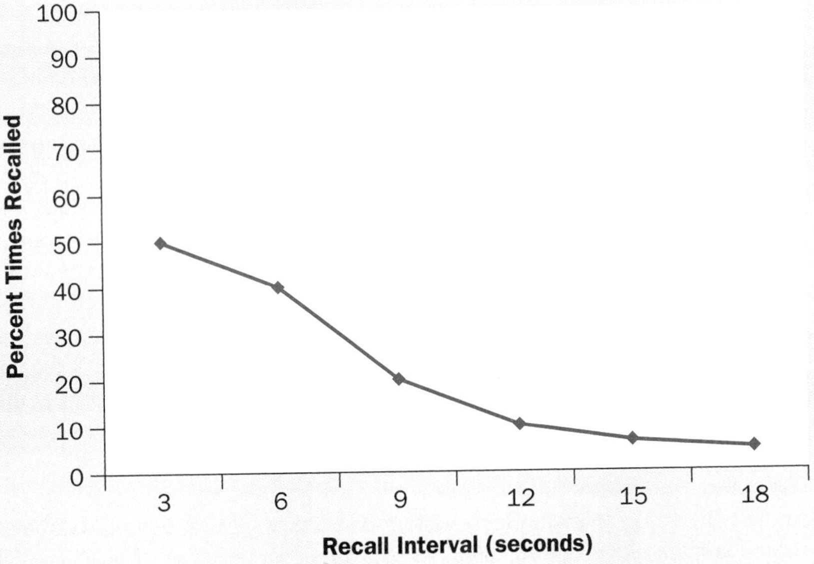

SOURCE: Adapted from Peterson and Peterson (1959).

immediately prior to or after the trauma. The blow to the head appears to disrupt the normal consolidation process. Further supportive evidence comes from preliminary studies with certain drugs that appear to facilitate the consolidation process.

Interference

The most important factor in forgetting is **interference** from other memories. This is particularly true when memories are similar to one another. People who have studied two foreign languages often report that they have trouble remembering a word in one language because of interference from the other language. This is particularly true if the two languages are similar, such as two Romance languages.

Psychologists distinguish between two kinds of interference.

Retroactive Interference. When a newer memory causes us to forget an older memory, it is said that **retroactive interference** caused the forgetting. This can be illustrated by the following:

Group 1	Learn A	Learn B	Recall A
Group 2	Learn A	Rest	Recall A

Subjects in Group 1 learn a list of words called List A, next learn another list of words called List B, and are then tested for recall on List A. Group 2 learns List A, followed by a rest period, and then is tested for recall on List A. If Group 1 remembers fewer items in List A than Group 2, we can conclude that the forgetting by Group 1 was due to retroactive interference. In other words, the learning of List B retroactively interfered with the recall of List A. "Retro" means "going backwards" and, in this case, means that the learning of List B "went backwards" and interfered with the recall of the previously learned List A. Referring back to our previous example, if you learn Spanish first and then learn French, you may find that your recall of Spanish is interfered with by your newly acquired knowledge of French. Similarly, learning to roller skate first, and then learning to ice skate, may result in a decrease in your roller skating skills. Can you remember your previous address or telephone number? It is likely that your present address or telephone number will interfere with their recall.

Proactive Interference. Sometimes an older memory will interfere with our ability to learn and remember new things. Using an illustration similar to the one used previously:

Group 1	Learn A	Learn B	Recall B
Group 2	Rest	Learn B	Recall B

Group 1 learns a list of words called List A, and then learns a second list of words called List B. Group 2 only learns List B. If Group 1 has a poorer performance than Group 2 when recalling List B, then we can assume that List A interfered with the recall of List B. In this case, what was learned previously caused **proactive interference.** *Pro*active, in this context, means "going forward," and the memories of List A "went forward" to interfere with recall of List B.

If you are studying hard for a sociology exam and immediately afterwards study hard for a psychology exam, the knowledge about sociology will interfere with your ability to learn psychology. The knowledge about sociology proactively interferes with your learning psychology. When it is necessary to study two subjects consecutively, it is usually better to study subjects that are dissimilar in order to prevent this kind of interference. For instance, studying algebra first would produce little interference with the subsequent learning of psychology.

Is retroactive or proactive interference more influential in forgetting? While they both play an important role in forgetting, retroactive interference is more frequently the culprit when our memories fail us.

Motivated Forgetting

Sometimes memories that are painful, embarrassing, or threatening to us are seemingly forgotten, a phenomenon called motivated forgetting or **repression.** Sigmund Freud believed that these memories are not actually forgotten but rather are relegated to our unconscious so that we are unaware of them. Freud also believed that even though we are unaware of these memories, they could continue to affect our behavior, and often in maladaptive ways.

Better by far that you
should forget and smile
Than that you
should remember
and be sad.

CHRISTINA GEORGINA ROSSETTI
Remember

Are there memories that you have repressed? One area of our lives where this may regularly occur is in dreams. More than likely you have experienced a vivid

✦ **TABLE 4.2** ✦ **Capacity, Memory Duration, and Primary Factors Responsible for Forgetting in Each of the Three Main Memory Systems**

Memory System	Capacity	Memory Duration	Factors in Forgetting
Sensory Memory	All that is seen/heard	Less than 1 second	Decay of trace
Short-term Memory	5–9 items	20–30 seconds	Decay of trace, consolidation failure, interference, motivated forgetting
Long-term Memory	Unlimited	Unlimited	

dream about something upsetting but then find that you can no longer remember the content of the dream shortly after awakening.

There is an ongoing debate in psychology today about the existence of the phenomenon of repression. There is very little scientific evidence to support its existence (Holmes, 1990). Elizabeth Loftus has questioned its existence, particularly in light of recent court cases where individuals have been convicted of criminal sexual abuse on the basis of suddenly recalled repressed memories (Loftus, 1993). Even if repression proves to be a valid phenomenon, it is not a major cause of forgetting. If you fail your calculus test, it won't be because of repressed memories.

Sometimes we intentionally put something out of our mind, especially if thinking about it is painful or embarrassing. This is called **suppression** and is distinguished from repression by its willful nature. Each of us has had things happen that we would just as soon forget about, and suppression is the mechanism by which we accomplish this.

Table 4.2 summarizes the three memory systems: sensory memory, short-term memory, and long-term memory. The capacity and duration of memories in each system are shown along with the primary factors responsible for forgetting.

APPLICATIONS: Fighting Forgetting

What can we do to offset the effects of forgetting due to decay of trace, consolidation failure, and interference? For decay of trace, which is mainly a problem in short-term memory, we can use a rehearsal strategy to keep it fresh in our memory. Repeating a phone number over and over will usually keep it securely in your short-term memory. Things are more complicated for consolidation failure and interference. Fortunately, many of the strategies to reduce interference will also aid in the consolidation of memories.

Unfortunately, we cannot eliminate the effects of interference in forgetting. The following strategies will help keep interference to a minimum.

1. Learn it well. The more completely material is learned, the less it is subject to the effects of interference. Material cannot be learned too thoroughly, despite the plaintive remarks from students about "flunking the test because I knew the material too well." Even if you think you have completely mastered the learning of some material, there is evidence that further study, called **overlearning,** will aid in retention. Imagine that you were asked to commit a list of 15 words to memory. You diligently study the list until you are able to recall the 15 words with 100% accuracy. Is there any benefit to continuing to study the list? Research has shown that additional study of material that can be recalled will result in greater resistance to forgetting. You have probably experienced this in your own life. Students in my statistics course often practice a statistical technique until they can do one problem correctly and then assume they have mastered the technique. They then seem surprised when they can't do a similar problem on the examination. I always recommend that students continue practicing until they can do 10 or even 20 problems correctly. Material can never be learned well enough. Even after you think you have mastered it, additional study will reap benefits for your ability to recall the material in the long term.
2. Make it meaningful. In order for information to be transferred from short-term to long-term memory, it must be meaningful to us. Interference is a much more powerful factor with material that has low meaning to us. The mnemonic devices I discussed earlier all work on the principle of imparting meaningfulness to material.
3. Sleep on it. You can reduce interference by reducing the number of mental activities that you engage in after studying material. A seminal study by Jenkins and Dallenbach (1924) had students learn lists of nonsense syllables. After studying, one group slept for 8 hours while another group stayed awake for 8 hours, carrying on their normal activities. After 8 hours, the group that slept could remember almost 60% of the items while the group that stayed awake recalled only about 5%. By staying awake, the students were engaging in mental activities that interfered with the recall of the items. This finding also supports the consolidation theory, as sleep allows the neural circuits to be better formed.

   As a graduate student I took a speed-reading course to train myself to read very rapidly. We were required to read several dozen books for our comprehensive exams, which are given near the end of doctoral training. I got to the point where I could read fast enough to complete a book in one hour or less. I often would read one or two books immediately before I went to bed. I noticed that my ability to remember the material was better the next morning than it was immediately after I finished my reading. Apparently it took a night's sleep for the memories to become consolidated in my brain. The old adage to "sleep on it" seems to hold true for memory as well as for making decisions. By the way, subsequent research has shown that speed-reading techniques are not an effective way to learn complex material, so I don't recommend this as a panacea for spending less time studying.

   Avoid the temptation to watch television or read a novel after you complete your studying, as this will introduce interference and prevent consolidation. Go to sleep as quickly as possible after studying the material.

4. Space it out. To reduce interference, avoid studying several different subjects back to back. If possible, you should study each subject in a separate study session with an interval of time between study sessions. Even a brief break between study sessions has been shown to reduce interference and aid in recall (Strand, 1970). Also remember to avoid "cramming" for exams, as this inhibits encoding material into long-term memory.
5. Do something different. Activities between learning and recall should be as dissimilar to the learning task as possible. If it isn't possible to sleep after the study session, you should be careful to do something completely different from the original learning task during the intervening interval before recall. If you must study another subject during this interval, try to study a subject as different from the first topic as possible.
6. Learning contexts. Remember that recall is best if it occurs in a similar environment or context as the original learning. You can also reduce interference between subjects by as much as one-half by studying different subjects in different rooms (Higbee, 1988). If you have two different but similar subjects in the same classroom (two child psychology classes, for example), sit in different locations for each. All of these techniques will help to reduce the interference from one subject to another.

Aging and Forgetfulness

One of the biggest concerns people have as they age is a perceived decline in their mental abilities. You have probably heard your grandparents or other elderly relatives claim they can't remember a thing anymore. When we can't remember something at age 20, we dismiss it as inconsequential. When it happens at age 65, people think it is a sign of a deteriorating mental state. There are a number of misconceptions about the effects of aging on memory. What are the facts?

With short-term memory, older people seem to have the same capabilities as young people (Poon & Fozard, 1980). Deficits appear, however, if information in short-term memory must be processed. For instance, older people are not as good as younger people at doing mathematical calculations to a set of numbers in their heads, although they do fine on paper.

With long-term memory, younger people are better at recalling less meaningful information. However, older people are better at correctly recognizing information (Hultsch & Dixon, 1990), especially if it is meaningful. For example, older people might be poorer at recalling when the Battle of Hastings occurred, but if given 10 different dates, they are better at recognizing the correct one. It is also important to note that these differences largely disappear when people are experts in their field (Charness, 1989). Thus an aged historian would be just as good as his younger colleague at recalling the correct date.

For everyday memory tasks, the differences between young and old are much smaller. Under conditions where subjects intentionally tried to remember factual information, older and younger persons perform about the same. The ability to remember to do things in the future does show some decline with aging (Hultsch & Dixon, 1990). Examples of this would include remembering to take out the garbage or wash the car. Another deficit for the aged is the ability to remember in what context and time something happened. For example, they may forget where they parked their car, or may not recognize that they have told the same story to the same person on several previous occasions. Older persons also have more difficulty remembering names of people they have recently met (Crook & West, 1990).

When can you expect these effects of aging to start affecting your memory? Barring some kind of injury or disease, you should note no detectable effects before age 60. For most individuals, significant changes in long-term memory don't appear until their mid-70s (Schaie, 1989).

APPLICATIONS: Countering the Effects of Aging on Memory

Much of the perceived effects of aging on memory and other cognitive functions is due to the stereotypes we have of older persons. This often leads older people to have expectations that such declines will occur. This can turn out to be a "self-fulfilling prophesy" in which older people expect declines to occur and therefore don't take steps to prevent them. There is increasing evidence that much of the decline in mental abilities can be circumvented by remaining active in intellectual pursuits. Today there is an increasing trend for older Americans to return to college. Badenhoop and Johansen (1980) found that older college students actually get better grades than does the typical 18-year-old. So much for the old saying "you can't teach an old dog new tricks." Older people can remain intellectually active in a number of ways, including returning to school, learning a new language, playing chess, traveling, and reading. If they do, available evidence suggests they should keep their mental abilities well into their 80s (Schaie, 1987). An environment that promotes loneliness and lack of stimulation will accentuate any declines in mental abilities. Unfortunately, these are the very conditions that many older Americans find themselves in, particularly if they are in nursing facilities.

As for the mental deficits that occur with aging, they can usually be easily compensated for by using the strategies to combat forgetting that were discussed earlier in this chapter. Older persons can then fully enjoy the benefits that come with aging, including greater wisdom and a more highly developed intellectual maturity.

MEMORY DISTORTION

Think back to the last time that you ate out at a restaurant. Was the server a male or a female? How old was he or she? Did you sit in a booth or at a table? What exactly did you order? What did you have to drink? How accurate do you think your answers are to these questions? Assuming that you've eaten out fairly recently, you probably believe you can recall this information with almost perfect accuracy. Research suggests otherwise.

Several years ago three other psychologists and I were attending a psychology convention in Albuquerque. We decided to eat at an Italian restaurant several miles outside of the city. While driving to the restaurant we witnessed an automobile accident that occurred immediately in front of us. A car suddenly pulled out from the side of the road and struck another car head on, injuring several of the occupants. When the police arrived they asked to interview eyewitnesses to the accident. During questioning, I discovered that each of the four of us had very different memories of the circumstances involving the accident. In the face of this, the perplexed police officer decided to take no testimony from any of us, and walked off muttering something about psychologists and their memories. We drove back to Albuquerque, arguing vehemently about which of us had the "correct" memories of the accident.

Recent research, particularly that conducted by Elizabeth Loftus at the University of Washington, has demonstrated just how susceptible our memories are to distortion.

Our memories have an almost unlimited capacity to store incidents from our lives. However, the storage process from short-term to long-term memory involves a great deal of organization and transformation. Plus, we have seen that usually only information we deem important or meaningful makes it into our long-term memories. As a consequence, there are a number of changes that take place between an actual incident occurring in our lives and the way we store that information for later retrieval. Psychologists view this as a constructive process because we are literally constructing memories that are meaningful to us. When it is time to remember, we reconstruct those memories. Oftentimes, factual information is the loser in this process.

Elizabeth Loftus has conducted numerous research studies demonstrating how eyewitness reports often distort events that occurred. In one study, subjects were shown a film of a traffic accident. They were then asked about what they saw (Loftus & Palmer, 1974). Witnesses who were asked "How fast were the cars going when they *smashed* into each other?" reported that the cars were traveling much faster than those asked, "How fast were the cars going when they *hit* each other?" The mere way in which the question was asked led witnesses to recall the accident differently. In another experiment, Loftus and Zanni (1975) showed subjects a short film of an automobile accident. Afterwards, some of the subjects were asked "Did you see a broken headlight?" while other subjects were asked "Did you see *the* broken headlight?" Twice as many people who were asked about *the* headlight reported remembering they saw it, although it was not in the film.

Loftus has demonstrated how children's memories are particularly prone to distortions (Loftus & Ketcham, 1994). She has also demonstrated how easily entirely false childhood memories can be created in adult subjects. She enlisted family members to suggest to subjects that their relatives had witnessed events that, in fact, never occurred. By so doing, subjects became firmly convinced that they had actually experienced a variety of events, including being lost in a shopping mall for an extended time, being hospitalized overnight, or spilling punch at a family wedding (Loftus, 1998). Other studies have shown that as children are asked repeatedly about a fictitious event ("Was there ever a time your finger was caught in a mousetrap and you had to be taken to the hospital?"), and as they think about and imagine it, the fictitious incident will seem increasingly real to them. Several studies have shown young children often having difficulty remembering whether they saw or imagined an event, particularly a traumatic event. The tragic consequences are that individuals have been jailed and families torn apart on the basis of children's recollection of traumatic events, such as sexual abuse, that may have never occurred.

Even flashbulb memories are subject to distortion. If you ask people where they were when they heard the news of the space shuttle *Challenger* explosion, they will report their memory in vivid and detailed terms. Neisser and Harsch (1993) collected handwritten accounts from people about the *Challenger* explosion shortly after the event occurred. When asked to recollect their memories 3 years later, many subjects recalled incorrectly where they were when the explosion occurred.

APPLICATIONS

It is impossible to tell how accurate our own memories are. The fact that we are confident of a memory has little relationship to it being an accurate account of the remembered event. False or distorted memories seem very real to us, as real as if no distortions were present. The next time you tell someone that you remember exactly what happened or exactly what you said, be aware that there is a good chance that your reconstructed memories are distorted.

You should also be aware that there are people out there who may wish to intentionally distort your memory. Police detectives often question witnesses or suspected criminals in ways that reflect their own understanding of the events that occurred. There have been numerous documented cases where suspects have come to believe through such questioning that they committed a crime when they didn't. Several have confessed to such crimes, including murder. Lawyers are also adept at asking questions in ways that will give them a desired answer, which is a technique called **leading the witness.** For example, an attorney might ask a witness "You were scared, weren't you?" rather than "How did you feel?" (Mauet, 1992). This is permissible during cross-examination and may influence the judgment of both the witness and the jurors.

It is important to remember that learning and memory recall are not passive processes. We sometimes think of our memory as working like a computer, where information is stored and later accurately retrieved "from the hard drive." In reality, we store and retrieve information based on our personalities, including our belief systems, and on what our previous life experiences have been. Subsequent recall of memories is likely to contain distortions biased by these factors.

MEMORY PANACEAS

There is none among us who wouldn't like to have a better memory. We may not care much about being rich or better looking, but the desire for a more efficient memory is universal. Subsequently, some have claimed to develop purported remedies for all our memory problems. Let's examine some of these.

Hypnosis

Can people who are hypnotized remember events that they could not otherwise? Some police departments believe this is so, and frequently use this technique in obtaining information from eyewitnesses. The Los Angeles Police Department established an investigative hypnosis program in 1975. They claim that hypnosis has been helpful in resolving about two-thirds of the cases in which it has been used (Reiser, 1986). The Federal Bureau of Investigation (FBI) has also used hypnosis extensively and regards it as a valuable investigative tool, while also recognizing its shortcomings (Council on Scientific Affairs, 1986). You have likely read newspaper accounts of people who witnessed a crime but were unable to recall details, such as a license plate number, until they were hypnotized.

Many studies have been conducted on hypnosis and memory. Overall, the evidence suggests it is an unreliable tool for memory enhancement. The greatest difficulty with using hypnosis to enhance memory is that it makes people highly prone to suggestion. In fact, some people are unable to be hypnotized because they are not highly suggestible people. Those who can be readily hypnotized are frequently the kinds of people who will readily respond to nearly any suggestion. This can cause serious problems when they are tested for memory recall.

Several studies have shown that people are more likely to report "hidden" memories during hypnosis, but often those memories are false (Dwyman & Bowers, 1983). Hypnotized persons often respond to what the hypnotist's questions *suggest* they *should* remember. Hypnosis lowers our threshold for accepting distorted memories as correct. As a result, more memories are reported but with considerably less accuracy.

This has led to some tragic consequences. In one case a father was convicted and sentenced to life in prison for the murder of his wife. The conviction was made on the basis of testimony from his son who, while under a state of hypnosis, testified about having seen his father murder his mother and chop up her body and dispose of the pieces. It was later discovered the woman was alive and well, and had merely deserted her family (Kalat, 1993, p. 200). A hypnotized eyewitness being questioned by a skilled police detective who has a preexisting view of the circumstances of a crime may well end up telling the detective what he wants to hear.

Because of these findings, the American Medical Association (1986) has concluded that testimony elicited through hypnosis should not be permitted in courts of law. The only time that hypnosis should be employed is when all other investigative techniques have reached a dead end. Even in these circumstances, investigators need to be aware of the increased tendency for hypnotized individuals to report distorted or completely false memories.

Some hypnotists claim that they can help individuals recall early childhood events that have been forgotten. Through a process called age regression, hypnotized subjects are convinced they are getting younger and younger. Sure enough, subjects participating in this begin to talk and act like a young child. But have they really been "regressed" back to their early childhood? All the available evidence suggests they have not. Specific details of their early childhood, such as dates that events occurred or names of friends and teachers, have been found to be generally inaccurate (Nash, 1987). Furthermore, experts in child psychology have observed that the regressed individuals are not acting or talking like a young child actually would, but rather are behaving in ways they *think* a youngster would act.

Some hypnotists have taken this a step further and claim they have regressed individuals back to a previous life. The actress Shirley MacLain claims memories of a dozen previous lives. A famous account was reported in the book *The Search for Bridey Murphy* by Morey Bernstein (1965) in which a young woman named Ruth Simmons was placed in a hypnotic trance in 1956 and reported the existence of a previous life in 19th-century Ireland. Under hypnosis, she spoke in a thick Irish brogue while describing her previous life in persuasive detail. Subsequent investigations in

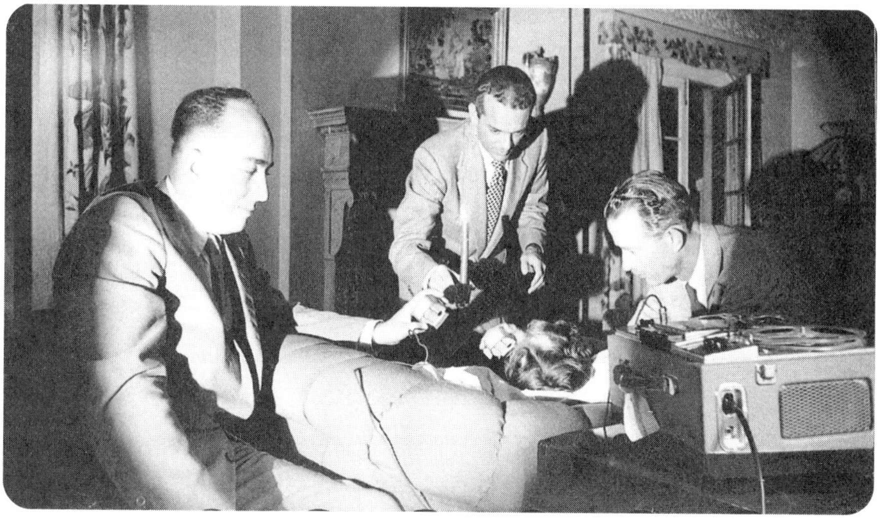

Hypnotist Morey Bernstein, holding candle, conducts the first questioning of Ruth Simmons, a Colorado homemaker who is under hypnosis, in 1952. While in a hypnotic trance, she reported vivid details about a previous life as Bridey Murphy, who lived in 19th-century Ireland. Subsequent investigations failed to confirm any of the details of her claimed "previous life."

Ireland failed to find any record of a Bridey Murphy and could not confirm any of the details she reported. Chicago newspaper investigators also found many parallels between the incidents in her "real life" childhood and those she cited while in the trances.

People who report the existence of a previous life while in a hypnotic trance often give vivid recollections and great detail about their previous lives. However, if asked factual information, such as what was happening historically, what currency was in use, or how people dressed, they are seldom accurate. Under hypnosis, they are in a suggestible state and are giving answers they think the hypnotist wants to hear or that are suggested by the hypnotist. As disappointing as it may seem to some, there is absolutely no evidence whatsoever to support the claim of memories from a past life.

Sleep-Learning

Wouldn't it be wonderful if we could turn on a tape recorder and teach ourselves things while we were asleep? Think how helpful this would be when you fell asleep during a lecture. This is precisely what several commercial products promise. Among the more popular skills that can be purportedly learned in this manner are foreign languages. Having studied foreign languages the old fashioned way, I would be the first in line to purchase such tapes, if they were proven effective. Are they?

The first research project I conducted as an undergraduate student examined this topic. I had subjects sleep in the lab while they were hooked to an electroencephalograph that monitored their brain activity. As we fall asleep, we pass through several stages, from light sleep to deep sleep. I waited until the subjects were in deep sleep and then played a tape recording that taught them Morse code. I then held classroom training sessions where these people were taught Morse code. I compared their learning rate to a control group who had only the classroom training. I reasoned that if sleep-learning took place, the group receiving both sleep and classroom training would learn faster than the group who only had the training while they were awake. My findings indicated that the sleep-learning group learned Morse code slightly *slower.*

Numerous studies have been conducted on sleep-learning, especially in the United States and in Russia (see review in Aarons, 1976). The findings consistently indicate that material learned while in the deeper stages of sleep is not remembered. These findings have led some states to ban the sale of tapes or machines that promise to teach you while you are asleep. There are some findings from Russian research that suggest limited learning might take place if material is presented during the very lightest stages of sleep, those that occur when we are just dozing off. However, this stage of sleep doesn't last very long, so little opportunity exists during sleep for this type of learning. Furthermore, only material that involves no complicated reasoning or understanding can be learned in this manner. If you need to memorize a list of dates or nonsense syllables, this technique might be of limited effectiveness. Overall, sleep-learning is not effective for the kinds of learning and memorization tasks that confront us on a daily basis. Sorry, but it's best if you stay awake during the lectures.

Drugs and Dietary Supplements

Pharmaceutical companies have responded to Americans' increasing concerns about memory loss with a vigorous program of research. Huge amounts of money are being spent, and at least a dozen drugs that may aid memory are currently under investigation. These drugs work on the chemicals in the brain, called **neurotransmitters,** that allow brain cells to communicate with one another.

Many years ago, as an undergraduate student, I worked as a research assistant on a project to evaluate the effectiveness of one of these drugs. A drug had been developed that increased the amount of acetylcholine, a neurotransmitter, in the brain. By increasing the amount of acetylcholine, it was believed that brain cells would communicate more efficiently, resulting in faster learning and better memory. We injected rats with the drug and compared how fast they learned a complex maze with a group of rats that didn't receive the drug. We found the drug did significantly increase how quickly the rats learned the maze. We also discovered, to our chagrin, that it had an unpleasant side effect; it made the rats extremely aggressive. By the time we had completed the study we each had the scars of numerous rat bites and scratches on our hands from the group receiving the drug. Sometime later there was a report in the newspapers about a physician who had obtained some of this experimental drug, and had given it to his son to make him smarter. The son apparently also experienced some side effects, as he subsequently killed his father. Because of these side effects, the drug was never approved for human use. At last report it was being sold commercially as a solvent to clean grease off of industrial equipment.

Despite the surge of recent interest in developing a "smart pill," none yet exists. Every drug under development remains to be proven in clinical trials. There has been some limited success with medications to treat the impaired memory of Alzheimer's patients, but these do not improve the memory of healthy subjects. There is also evidence that estrogen, given to postmenopausal women, not only lowers the risk of Alzheimer's disease, but helps maintain both verbal and visual memory.

Recently, a wide variety of herbs and vitamins have been marketed as memory aids. You have probably seen advertisements for them on television, usually promoted by a well-known actor who testifies to their restorative powers. The most popular of these is *Ginkgo biloba,* an herb that may help increase oxygen flow to the brain. No clinical trials have validated its effectiveness. Vitamin E is an antioxidant that some studies suggest may slow the progression of Alzheimer's, although it doesn't improve memory in healthy individuals. DHEA is a popular hormone substance produced by the adrenal glands. DHEA supplements have been shown to help mice learn faster, but no corresponding evidence exists for humans. Still, if you have a stupid mouse. . . .

DHA is a fatty acid that is present in breast milk and is critical for a baby's brain development. DHA supplements are popular with many people, but no evidence exists that it helps brain function in older children or adults. And for you gum chewers, there is a product called *Brain Gum,* which contains a nutrient called phosphatidyl serine, more easily remembered as PS. According to Brain Gum's developer, PS is a naturally occurring fat that contains phosphorous, which affects the function of brain cells. Thomas Crook, in his book *The Memory Cure* (1998), discusses the value of this nutritional supplement that he claims can reverse age-related memory loss.

All of the supplements promoted on television and in print ads have one caveat accompanying them. That caveat states that the U.S. Food and Drug Administration (FDA) has not approved these substances for use in the treatment of any disorder. The evidence presented on behalf of these supplements is almost exclusively testimonial, based on the purported personal experiences of individuals. It is likely that a placebo effect accounts for many of these reported benefits. Most medical experts recommend against their use, because solid evidence of their effectiveness is still absent and potential side effects are possible. Recently, several controlled clinical trials have begun to scientifically investigate the effectiveness of these supplements. These studies are important because they can evaluate the true benefit, if any, of these supplements compared with a group of individuals receiving a placebo. The prospects of a "smart pill" or "memory pill" eventually emerging from one of the ongoing pharmaceutical research projects seems promising, although a breakthrough in the near future appears unlikely.

APPLICATIONS: An Overview of How to Improve Memory

In this chapter I have discussed a number of factors that can affect your memory. Let's take an overview of these factors, as well as some others that weren't previously discussed. All of the following will help you encode and retrieve information from memory.

1. Pay attention. You will recall that lack of attention is one of the primary reasons things do not enter sensory memory, which means the information also has no chance to enter into either short-term or long-term memory. A recommendation to pay attention may appear to be advice of the "no-brainer" kind, but it is the factor often responsible for failure to encode information. You can't process information that you haven't attended to, which is why sleep-learning is so ineffectual. Be particularly attentive when you know you are going to hear information only one time, such as when you are introduced to someone whose name you wish to remember.

2. Avoid rote memorization. Mindlessly repeating information to yourself is ineffective. I discussed how information that is meaningful to us is what gets passed on to long-term memory. Try and make information meaningful by relating it to other things you already know or have experienced. The more associations you can form the better, as retrieval from memory will be aided by multiple links to other knowledge.
3. Use memory aids. There are mnemonic techniques to help you remember almost anything. Discover and practice these techniques. Strive to develop your own mnemonic techniques. There are several excellent books that can familiarize you with different mnemonic techniques, all of which have proven to be highly effective.
4. Overlearn material. Don't stop learning after initial mastery has been reached. Continue studying the material, as this will greatly aid recall from memory. This will also greatly increase your confidence in knowing the material, which will help if you get anxious during exams.
5. Reduce interference. Remember that interference is one of the biggest factors in forgetting. Reduce its effects by studying immediately prior to sleep, and by not studying similar topics in close proximity to one another.
6. Use contextual cues. Try to learn information in the same contextual situation as you will be in when trying to remember the information. This includes both the physical context, such as the room, lighting, and smells, as well as your emotional state. When recalling, recreate mentally the context you were in during learning.
7. Don't cram. Distribute learning sessions over spaced intervals of time. Remember, two 30-minute study sessions with a break in between will probably result in more learning and better recall than one 60-minute session.
8. Rehearse. Rehearse information as you are learning it. This doesn't mean just reading the material over and over, a technique that has been shown to be of limited effectiveness. Rather, paraphrase the material as you read it, putting it in your own words. Write the material down, or recite your understanding of the material to someone (or even to the wall). Associate the material to other things that you already know.
9. Organize material. Organize the material to be remembered in a fashion that makes sense to you. This is what you do when you develop a good outline of a textbook or lecture material. A good technique for lectures is to rewrite your lecture notes, in outline form, shortly after the end of the lecture while the information is still fresh in your mind.
10. Get feedback. It is best to periodically check to see how much you have learned. Try to outline the material you have read from memory, or recite the material out loud. Use old exams, or practice tests that are in your texts. Remember that it is easy to be lulled into a false sense of believing you understand material better than you actually do. The fact that you clearly understood a lecture or textbook material upon initial presentation doesn't mean you will be able to reproduce that information at a later time.
11. Exercise. There is a growing body of evidence that vigorous exercise helps memory, both in animals (Samorajski, Delaney, Durham, Ordy, Johnson, & Dunlap, 1985) and in humans. It is not clear exactly how exercise helps memory, but

many researchers believe that it increases oxygen and nutrient supplies to the brain. There is some evidence that it boosts natural compounds in the brain that promote cell growth. Exercise also helps control depression, which is known to affect memory. Furthermore, exercising will make you sleep better, which will make it easier for consolidation to occur.

12. Avoid distractions. You may enjoy studying with the stereo or television on, but you are exposing yourself to irrelevant information that can interfere with learning and subsequent memory recall. Focus intently on learning the task at hand, and enjoy the stereo or television during breaks in study.
13. Write it down. Write down important information. Make up a reminder list of things to do, and appointments to keep. This is the most frequently used memory aid, even among memory researchers themselves. Don't be fooled into thinking that you can't possibly forget something that seems important to you at the moment. There is an old Chinese proverb that states "The weakest ink lasts longer than the strongest memory."

SUMMARY

- Memories are categorized into three different types: episodic memories, semantic memories, and procedural memories.
- Common myths about memory include the belief that some people are born with a poor memory, that some individuals possess a photographic memory, and that the brain has a finite capacity to remember. Other myths include the belief that aging causes extensive declines in memory, and that only a set percentage of our brain capacity is ever utilized.
- Remembering consists of the three stages of encoding, storage, and retrieval. Memorization is disrupted unless each stage is completed successfully.
- The three kinds of memories include sensory memory, which holds information very briefly, short-term memory, which holds information for a few seconds, and long-term memory, which permanently holds material that is important or meaningful to us.
- To improve sensory memory, it is important that we pay attention. Repeating or rehearsing information several times helps short-term memory. Long-term memory is aided by elaborative rehearsal, which involves thinking about the material from several different angles and relating it to previously learned material. Long-term memory is also helped by carefully organizing material as it is learned, and by using visual imagery during learning.
- Material that is learned over several shorter periods is retained better than material that is learned during one massed study period.
- Recall of material is best when it is done within the same contextual setting as the original learning.
- A mnemonic system is any technique that aids memory recall by making material more meaningful. The peg-word system uses a set of memory "pegs" or "hooks" to which items to be remembered are associated. In the method of loci, familiar locations are visualized and items to be memorized are associated with these locations. In the link system, a visual image is formed for each item to be remembered. Each item is then linked with the visual image for the next item to be remembered. The keyword technique involves constructing one or more concrete keywords with a visual image. A visual image then connects the keyword to the original term.
- There are several techniques to help associate people's names with their faces. Pay careful attention when you first hear the name. Make the name meaningful to you. Select a distinctive facial feature and use it to form a visual association to the name. Finally, you should rehearse the name-face association several times.
- Gesturing during speaking has been shown to facilitate memory. On the other hand, high levels of anxiety interfere with memory. Other factors that disrupt or prevent memorization include high blood pressure, lack of sleep, depression, excessive amounts of information, high stress levels, and use of alcohol.
- Most forgetting occurs shortly after learning. Forgetting is partially caused by decay in the physiological memory trace in the brain. Forgetting also occurs when a memory trace does not become fully formed or consolidated in the brain.
- The most important factor in forgetting is interference from other memories. Retroactive interference occurs

when a newer memory causes us to forget an older memory. Proactive interference occurs when an older memory interferes with a newer memory. Retroactive interference causes more forgetting than does proactive interference.

- Memories that are painful, embarrassing, or threatening to us may be forgotten through a process called repression. Memories can be intentionally forgotten through a process called suppression.
- Techniques for preventing forgetting include overlearning material, making material meaningful, sleeping immediately after learning, and learning material in spaced study sessions. In addition, activities between learning and recall should be dissimilar to the learning task. Finally, you should recall the material in the same context in which it was learned.
- Aging has only moderate effects on memory. For most everyday memory tasks, the differences in memory between young and old are very small. Significant changes in long-term memory usually don't appear until one is in the mid-70s. Using the mnemonic strategies previously discussed can largely compensate for any such deficit.
- Memories are very susceptible to distortion over time. Children's memories are particularly prone to such distortion.
- Several purported memory panaceas have been shown to be invalid. Memory recall is not enhanced by hypnosis. Learning and memorization during sleep is not effective. So far, there is no drug or health supplement that is known to improve the memory of healthy subjects.

Key Terms

chunks: organizing information into separate and meaningful parts to increase the ability to remember.

distributed practice: intervals of studying distributed over a period of time.

elaborative rehearsal: linking an item to be remembered to other information already contained in long-term memory.

encoding: the method by which memories are stored in long-term memory.

episodic memory: memory of personal experiences that represent episodes in our lives.

flashbulb memories: memories of unexpected and emotionally arousing events.

hippocampus: a brain structure that serves as a filter or gatekeeper and permits a portion of the information in short-term memory to enter into long-term memory.

interference: forgetting that occurs when other learned material disrupts recall.

keyword technique: a mnemonic system that constructs one or more concrete keywords with a visual image.

leading the witness: a method of questioning to get a desired answer.

link system: a mnemonic system in which a visual image is formed for each item to be remembered. Each item is then associated with the visual image for the next item to be remembered.

long-term memory: the memory system that allows for the relatively permanent storage of information.

massed practice: studying in one block of time; aka "cramming."

method of loci: a mnemonic system which aids in memory. Familiar locations are visualized and items are then associated with these locations.

mnemonic: any system or technique that aids in memory recall.

neural consolidation: the process by which memory traces become fully formed and permanently stored in memory.

neurotransmitters: chemicals in the brain that allow brain cells to communicate with one another.

overlearning: continuing to study information that has already been learned. Aids in retention and recall of information.

peg-word system: a mnemonic system to aid memory recall. Uses a set of memory "pegs" or "hooks."

proactive interference: the disruption of a newer memory caused by an older memory.

procedural memory: memory of how to accomplish certain tasks.

rehearsal: repetition to maintain information in short-term memory.

repression: forgetting about painful, embarrassing, or threatening memories; aka motivated forgetting.

retrieval: the process of accessing information from long-term memory storage.

retroactive interference: the disruption of an older memory caused by a newer memory.

semantic memory: knowledge of factual information about our world.

sensory memory: a short-term buffer that briefly holds information and allows information to be transferred to the short-term memory system.

short-term memory: the memory system that holds information for 20 to 30 seconds; limited to seven items plus or minus two. Also referred to as working memory.

state-dependent learning: the phenomenon that recall of material is better when it is done within the same contextual setting as the learning.

storage: retention of encoded information in long-term memory.

suppression: the willful intention of putting something out of our mind.

tip-of-the-tongue phenomenon: the sensation of knowing an answer, but not being able to retrieve it.

5

PROBLEM SOLVING AND REASONING

Our daily lives are filled with instances wherein we need to solve a problem. Psychologists view problem solving as any behavior that directs us toward achieving some goal that is blocked. Sometimes the goal is short term, such as figuring out how to get into your car when you've locked the key inside. Other goals focus on less immediate but still relatively short-term goals, such as how to get your friend to pay back that $20.00 he owes you. At other times we face problems that last throughout our lives, such as overcoming a physical or mental disability. On occasion, we are even faced with problems where our very lives are at stake. For instance, if you found yourself lost in the wilderness, your ability to problem solve successfully could be a matter of life or death.

You probably would be surprised if you kept track of the number of problems that you are called upon to solve in a typical day. A great deal of research has examined exactly how we go about solving problems, and under what circumstances we are or are not able to do so. You are probably aware that humans are generally very good at solving problems. However, you might be surprised to find how we can become almost incapable of solving even a relatively simple problem under certain circumstances. In this chapter I will discuss the general skills of problem solving. To some extent, these skills can prove helpful in solving almost any task, even if your knowledge and experiences in a particular area are limited.

Steps in Problem Solving

Regardless of the nature of the problem, we pass through four stages in the process of problem solving.

1. Understand the problem. First we must understand exactly what the problem is before we can set out to solve it.
2. Create a hypothesis. A hypothesis is sometimes defined as an "educated guess." In problem solving, we generate one or more hypotheses or tentative strategies about how the problem might be solved.
3. Test the hypothesis. In this stage, we test the strategy or hypothesis that we developed by applying it to the problem.
4. Check results. Finally, we check the results to see if our strategy worked. If it did not, we return to Stage 2 and try again.

Problem-Solving Strategies

Frequently we are called upon to solve a problem with which we have had no previous experience. In fact, it is probably rare that we face exactly the same problem on repeated occasions. Fortunately, human behavior is very adaptable, and it allows us to try a variety of strategies until one is found that proves successful. Different types of problems require different kinds of solutions.

Trial and Error

Some problems are solved by simply trying a variety of responses until we hit upon a solution. This approach is called **trial and error.** We commonly use this strategy when we do not have enough information about feasible solutions to try another more systematic approach. This approach is not very efficient and may never result in a successful solution to the problem. When Thomas Edison invented the light bulb, he could not find a substance for the filament that would last more than just a short time before burning out. Eventually he discovered the solution, but only by testing thousands of different substances before finding one that would last.

Algorithms

For some problems we try a more systematic approach, called an **algorithm,** which attempts every possible solution. If you have forgotten the combination to a safe, you might approach the problem by trying every possible combination of numbers. How about if you were asked to solve the anagram B–E–P–R–M–O–L by rearranging the letters to spell a common word? You could systematically rearrange the seven letters into every possible combination until the solution was reached. Since there are 5,040 combinations of seven letters, this solution would take a long time even though the answer eventually would be guaranteed. Computers are quite adept at solving problems such as this because they can perform the necessary operations very quickly. The computer's ability to solve this type of problem has become a problem in itself. Hackers now have the ability to find a person's password or account number by using a computer to try every possible combination of numbers and letters until access is found. Sometimes, though, even computers are not up to the task. Software designed to teach computers to play chess cannot use this strategy because comparison of the trillions of possible chess moves and their consequences are beyond the capability of even the fastest computer.

Heuristics

Because algorithms can be so laborious, frequently it is best to solve a problem by using a rule-of-thumb strategy called a **heuristic.** We learn that certain strategies work in certain situations and not in others. Heuristics only provide us with general guidelines about possible solutions. Unlike algorithms, heuristics do not always lead us to the correct solution. In fact, as I shall discuss later in this chapter, they sometimes lead us astray in our judgments and problem-solving behavior. Still, they serve as useful rules and often save us a great deal of time and effort by reducing the number of alternatives that we must consider.

We use many such heuristics in our everyday judgments. As I discussed in Chapter 2, we make judgments (sometimes erroneously) about how fast an object is moving based, in part, on its size. Similarly, we make judgments about how distant an object is, in part, by the clarity of the object. Blurred objects are judged as further away. We have adopted similar heuristics in solving problems. We bring our own set of heuristics to almost every problem we need to solve. When assembling a jigsaw puzzle, most people begin by finding and assembling the pieces with a straight edge because they know those pieces define the border. After constructing the border, they may find a part of the picture that has a distinctive pattern or coloring and assemble those pieces separately, and so forth. People with a great deal of expertise in a specific area have developed many useful heuristics. When my computer hardware malfunctions, I am usually clueless about the cause. I have noticed that an experienced technician will quickly isolate and diagnose the difficulty by asking a

✦ FIGURE 5.1 ✦ The Best Problem-Solving Solutions Are Often the Simplest

Rube Goldberg was a popular cartoonist in the 1920s and 1930s who concocted very complicated solutions for simple, everyday problems. Illustrated here is his "Simple Way of Hiding a Gravy Spot on Your Vest," drawn in 1916.

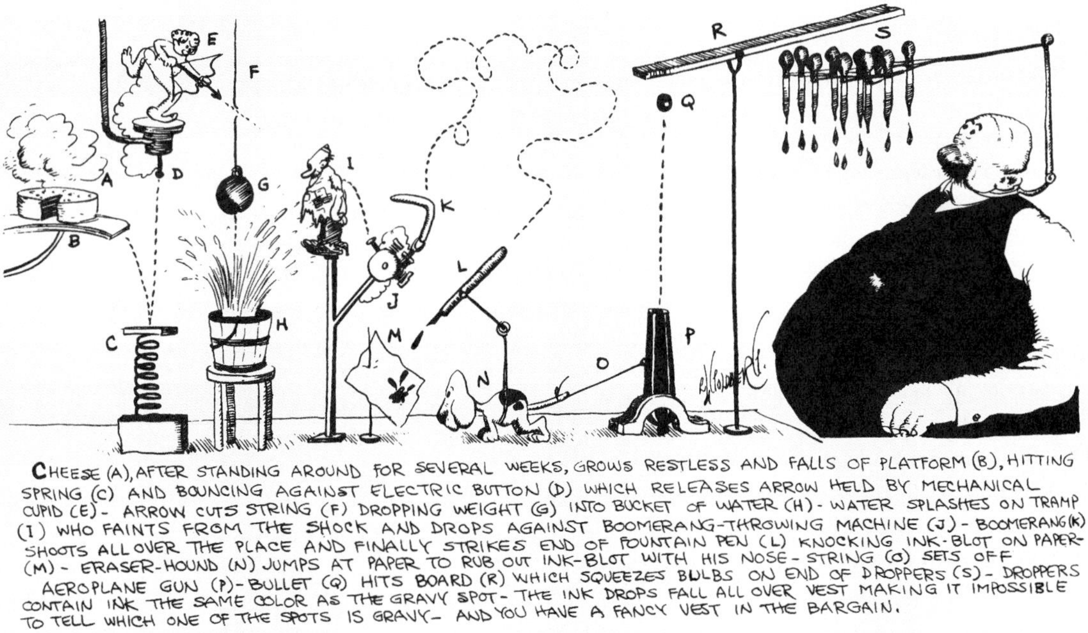

CHEESE (A), AFTER STANDING AROUND FOR SEVERAL WEEKS, GROWS RESTLESS AND FALLS OF PLATFORM (B), HITTING
SPRING (C) AND BOUNCING AGAINST ELECTRIC BUTTON (D) WHICH RELEASES ARROW HELD BY MECHANICAL
CUPID (E) - ARROW CUTS STRING (F) DROPPING WEIGHT (G) INTO BUCKET OF WATER (H) - WATER SPLASHES ON TRAMP
(I) WHO FAINTS FROM THE SHOCK AND DROPS AGAINST BOOMERANG-THROWING MACHINE (J) - BOOMERANG (K)
SHOOTS ALL OVER THE PLACE AND FINALLY STRIKES END OF FOUNTAIN PEN (L) KNOCKING INK-BLOT ON PAPER-
(M) - ERASER-HOUND (N) JUMPS AT PAPER TO RUB OUT INK-BLOT WITH HIS NOSE - STRING (O) SETS OFF
AEROPLANE GUN (P) - BULLET (Q) HITS BOARD (R) WHICH SQUEEZES BULBS ON END OF DROPPERS (S) - DROPPERS
CONTAIN INK THE SAME COLOR AS THE GRAVY SPOT - THE INK DROPS FALL ALL OVER VEST MAKING IT IMPOSSIBLE
TO TELL WHICH ONE OF THE SPOTS IS GRAVY - AND YOU HAVE A FANCY VEST IN THE BARGAIN.

SOURCE: From *Rube Goldberg: His Life and Work* by Peter Marzio, 1973, Harper & Row Publishers, Inc.

series of questions and by trying different operations on the computer. The technician is using rules that he has developed from solving previous, perhaps similar, problems.

One heuristic that most people employ is to look first for simple solutions, before considering more complex possibilities. Often in science the simplest approach is the most productive, and many famous scientific discoveries have used this approach. I am sure that you have seen innovative, yet simple, inventions that elicited the reaction "Why didn't I think of that!" Good advice for many problem-solving solutions is the oft quoted acronym K–I–S–S, which stands for "Keep it simple, stupid!" The opposite of this approach is illustrated in Figure 5.1 by Rube Goldberg, a famous cartoonist known for drawing vastly complicated machines that performed very simple tasks.

Insight

Sometimes the answer to a problem appears quite suddenly to us, a phenomenon called **insight.** This frequently occurs following a period of time during which no solution was envisioned. Insight is sometimes called the "Aha!" phenomenon because this word represents the response we often emit when we suddenly see the solution.

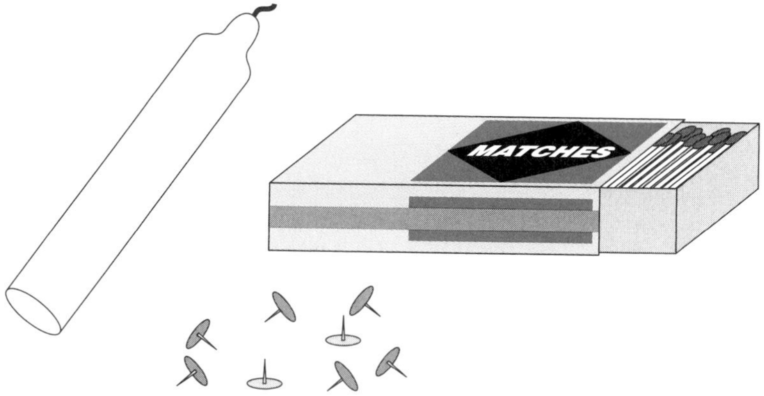

✦ FIGURE 5.2 ✦ A Problem-Solving Task

Using only these materials, show how you would mount the candle to a wall.

SOURCE: From K. Duncker (1945), "On Problem-Solving," *Psychological Monographs* 58, no. 270.

Insightful solutions often occur quite suddenly, with little indication that the solution is impending. I am sure that you have experienced this phenomenon and can attest to what a wonderful feeling of relief and satisfaction it provides. The more knowledge and experience that we have, the more likely an insightful solution will occur.

A classic problem-solving task was presented to subjects by Karl Duncker (1945). He provided subjects with a candle, some tacks, and a box of matches. They were required to attach the candle upright to the wall so that the wax would not drip on the floor. See if you can solve this problem and notice whether the solution comes to you suddenly, as through insight, or more gradually. (The solution is on the following page.)

APPLICATIONS: The IDEAL Problem-Solving System

John Bransford and Barry Stein (1984) developed a five-step general-thinking strategy that they believe leads to effective problem solving. The system is known as IDEAL because each of the letters represents one of the steps:

I = *Identify* the problem.

D= *Define* and represent the problem. Define the problem clearly, keeping it as simple as possible. Do not introduce unnecessary complications.

E = *Explore* possible strategies. Often we fail to solve a problem because we restrict ourselves to a limited number of possible strategies. At other times, we limit ourselves to strategies that have worked in the past. Effective problem solving often involves exploring unconventional solutions.

A= *Act* on the strategies. Develop a solution and try it out. Look ahead to anticipate what the consequences of your solution might be. People who are good problem solvers often anticipate the results of their strategy without actually trying it.

L = *Look* at the results and learn from them. Evaluate how effective they were.

Solution to Problem

The matchbox is attached to the wall with the thumbtacks while the candle is mounted to the top of the matchbox.

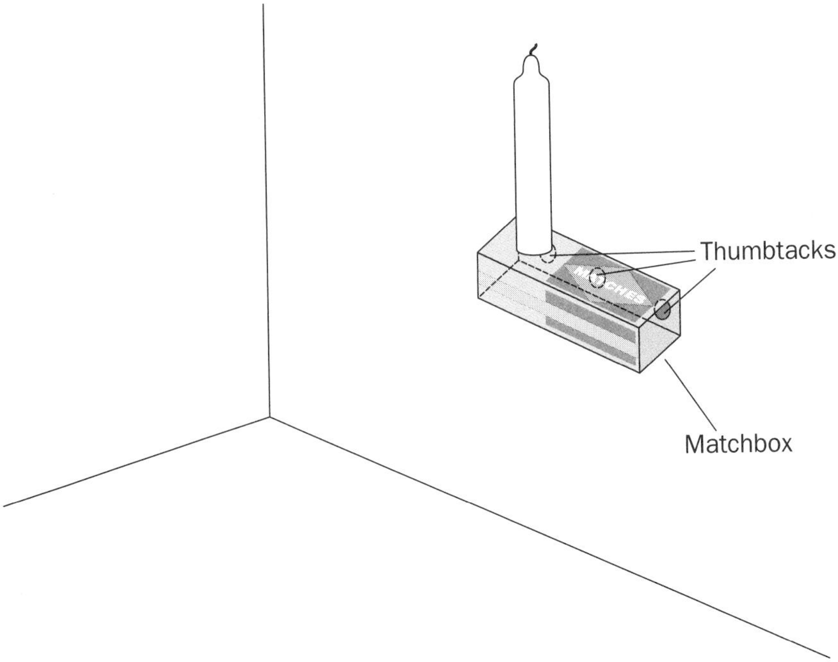

Obstacles to Problem Solving and Decision Making

Lack of Ability

Why are some people so much better than others at solving problems? Innate ability is part of the answer since more-intelligent people are usually better at solving problems. Some people, though, may lack overall intelligence but have specific abilities in one area. An extreme example of this is people called **savants.** These people have extraordinary abilities in one highly defined area but are so mentally subnormal in most other areas that they are often classified as mentally retarded. The most common special abilities that these people display are (1) musical abilities, (2) the ability to perform complicated mathematical calculations, (3) the ability to remember long lists of information verbatim, and (4) the ability to determine what specific day of the week a given date fell on, such as July 10, 1087. Shafer (1996) told of a man who had limited abilities in his native language, English, but could imitate songs in perfect Italian or German. Also, he could flawlessly reproduce a musical piece on the piano after hearing it only once. Another documented case described a young girl with an IQ of only 73 and very limited mental abilities in most areas. Nevertheless, by age 4, she had learned to play the piano, violin, trumpet, clarinet, and French horn. She taught herself to read music and could memorize long pieces just by hearing the music.

Lack of Knowledge

More important than overall intelligence, however, is wide experience or practice on tasks similar to the problem at hand. No matter how intelligent people are, they will not be good at problem solving in an area with which they are unfamiliar. I have known many very intelligent people who could not solve a simple mechanical problem to save their lives. Once I rented a house to two surgeons who needed help in replacing a washer in a sink faucet. They could expertly remove your appendix but had no idea how to "operate" on a faucet.

Expertise and Persistence

In recent years, psychologists have become increasingly interested in studying the behaviors of experts and how they solve problems. These psychologists have concluded that experts are made, not born. As a general rule, it takes about 10 years of hard work and practice in any task domain to achieve expertise. Often the expertise is specific to one area and does not transfer to anything else. To become an expert in any area, you should be prepared to devote at least a decade of hard work and dedication to the task. Persistence is an important characteristic of expertise. There is truth in the saying by Thomas Edison that "Genius is one percent inspiration and ninety-nine percent perspiration."

Confirmation Bias

Once we have formed an idea about how a problem should be solved, we often seek out information that *confirms* our ideas. This phenomenon, known as **confirmation bias,** indicates that we are far more likely to seek evidence that verifies our ideas as opposed to evidence that refutes them. If sales managers believe that men are more effective in sales, they will seek out confirmation of that bias by looking for examples of successful male salespersons while ignoring conflicting evidence. Furthermore, once this confirmation bias is established, people are extremely reluctant to change their minds. Unfortunately, we all seek confirmation of our existing beliefs and this behavior can have detrimental effects when it comes to solving a problem effectively.

Press on; nothing in the world can take the place of persistence.
Talent will not; nothing is more common than unsuccessful men with talent.
Genius will not; unrewarded genius is almost a proverb.
Education will not; the world is full of educated derelicts.
Persistence and determination alone are omnipotent.

RAY KROC, FOUNDER OF MCDONALD'S

Fixations

Another major obstacle in problem solving is the inability to view a problem from a fresh perspective, a phenomenon known as **fixation.** Once we fix our mind as to how a problem should be solved, it is usually difficult to "change gears" and try a different approach. Frequently we will try to solve a problem with a solution that has worked in the past. This results in a **mental set** about how the problem should be solved and sometimes interferes with finding the correct solution. The Luchins water jar problem (Luchins, 1946) illustrates this type of situation. In this problem, you must decide how you would measure out the volumes indicated in the right-hand column by using jugs A, B, and C with the capacities shown in the table. Work each of these problems as quickly as you can.

	With jugs of these sizes			Measure this amount of water
Problem	**A**	**B**	**C**	
1	10	75	3	58
2	9	80	5	67
3	6	47	14	49
4	5	68	7	59

Did you find that the solution to problem 4 took longer? Each of the first three problems could be solved by taking jug B less two times the quantity in jug A and adding the quantity in jug C (i.e., B – 2A + C). The solution to problem 4 was B + A – 2C. If you are like most people, you probably spent some time on problem 4 trying the solution that had succeeded for the previous three problems. It is only natural that we should first try solutions that have previously proven successful. That approach often helps us solve problems. At other times, though, the mental set established by previous solutions hinders our ability to see a problem from a new perspective.

Another kind of fixation is called **functional fixedness.** Sometimes we become fixated on the primary function of a device and fail to see how it could be used for some other purpose. If necessary, a credit card can serve as an ice scraper, and a dime can be used as a screwdriver. Duct tape owes its popularity to the thousands of unusual ways it has been used in solving everyday problems.

There are other mental blocks and fixations that can interfere with problem solving, such as emotional barriers and cultural barriers (Coon, 1992). **Emotional barriers** include inhibitions and the fear of appearing foolish in the eyes of others. Some individuals have an inordinate fear of failure that prevents them from trying risky solutions. **Cultural barriers** arise when it is dictated that problems should only be solved in certain ways. For example, some cultures may discourage fantasies or daydreaming or may discourage the use of intuition in problem solving. Other cultures put a heavy emphasis on using the wisdom and solutions of previous generations in solving everyday problems. In other words, cultural taboos can limit the way we think or act. To a certain extent we are held captive by the values of the culture in which we were raised, and this can impede many aspects of our abilities, including effective problem solving.

Reliance on Authority

We often place an overreliance on things that come from so-called authorities. Advertisers frequently use actors dressed as doctors or pharmacists to sell over-the-counter medications or herbal remedies. Actual physicians tout their credentials when selling their latest cure-all diet book or miracle cure for whatever ailment is the "illness du jour." Our reliance on authority can often lead us down the wrong path for solving a problem. There is no miracle cure for obesity, despite what the latest best-selling diet book by Dr. Whoever claims (see chapter 8 for a further discussion on this topic). History is replete with instances where respected authorities were wrong. Thomas Edison thought the radio was just a passing craze, and religious authorities during the medieval times professed the earth to be the center of the universe. Perhaps nowhere do "authorities" tout their wisdom more than in the management of stock funds. Mutual-fund managers like to extol their ability to pick the best stocks, but the facts indicate otherwise.

Modern scientific methods permit us to be skeptical of authoritative pronouncements and instead use verifiable scientific procedures to seek out the truth. This does not mean that you should reject everything that comes from an authoritative source, as such cynicism would be unwarranted. However, you should question any pronouncement where a person's authority or credentials are the sole or primary basis of the assertion. A few years ago I first noticed a bumper sticker that said simply "Question authority," which may sometimes be good advice!

We often allow our decision making to be influenced by sources of authority. The latest fad health remedy is often advertised with an accompanying picture of an authority. Note the prominent display of diplomas, the stethoscope around the neck, and white doctor's lab coat, all designed to add credibility to this "authority figure."

Overestimation of Control

If you were to flip a coin, what is the probability that you could correctly predict whether it would be heads or tails? Of course, the probability is 1 in 2 or 50%. Despite the mathematical logic of this argument, many people make decisions or try to solve problems inappropriately because of errors of **overestimation of control.** The odds of winning the jackpot in the Colorado lottery are 1 in 5.25 million. However, people continue to buy lottery tickets in spite of these indomitable odds because they believe that the special numbers they select are "lucky" and improve the odds. (In Colorado, you are more likely to be struck by lightning than to win the lottery.) Oftentimes, when people are in a situation where chance determines success, they overestimate their ability to control chance. Sometimes, the events that have preceded an event lead people to believe that the probability of a future event will be affected. If you have been playing the lottery for 10 years and have never won, you might believe that you are "overdue" and that the odds are now more in your favor. Roulette players who have seen black come up five times in row are more certain that red will appear on the next spin, despite the fact that each spin of the wheel is an independent event. These false beliefs are known as the **gambler's fallacy,** which is a type of overestimation of control.

Overconfidence

Even when chance is not involved, many people are **overconfident** about the accuracy of their own judgments. One study involved asking people the meaning of obscure words and then asked them to estimate the probability that they were correct

(Lichtenstein, Fischhoff, & Phillips, 1982). The researchers found that people consistently overestimated their accuracy. In another study, students were asked to predict their own future behavior. They were asked to predict whether they would vote in November, call their parents more than twice a month, and so forth. Students were consistently overconfident in making self-predictions about their behavior (Vallone, Griffin, Lin, & Ross, 1990). As a professor, I have noted that many students overestimate how well they will do on an examination and what final grade they will receive in a course. Similarly, only 2% of American college students believe that there is a good chance they will *not* graduate from college, while in reality nearly half do not. This overconfidence and resulting inaccuracy of judgment often lead students to misjudge the amount of time and effort they need to expend to be academically successful.

Many people feel overly confident in predicting the behavior of others. Quite frequently they are wrong. As part of his doctoral dissertation, David Dunning asked university students to predict how their roommates would answer 2-choice questions such as "Are your lecture notes neat or messy?" and "Do you study alone or in groups?" Students were 78% confident that they could predict how their roommates would answer these questions but, in actuality, were accurate only 68% of the time (Dunning, 1987). Overconfidence in our ability to predict the behavior of others or ourselves can have profound consequences. In a later chapter I will discuss how even experts in human behavior, such as psychologists and psychiatrists, are equally overconfident of their predictive abilities. Confidence in ourselves and in others can be a good thing, as long as it is realistic. After all, what athletic team would welcome team members who were not confident of their ability to win a game?

Heuristics

Earlier I described heuristics as rule-of-thumb strategies that we often use to solve problems. Daniel Kahneman and Amos Tversky spent over 25 years examining how people use these heuristics to make intuitive decisions and predictions when faced with uncertainty (Kahneman & Tversky, 1973). Their seminal research has demonstrated that intuitive judgments are often wrong. You can improve your own thinking ability by becoming aware of these common errors in judgment.

Representativeness

If something is *similar* to items of a particular category, we often assume it is a member of that category itself. This assumption is a result of a **representativeness heuristic.** Consider the following example: A man is described as very shy and withdrawn, invariably helpful, but with little interest in people or the world of reality. He is also a meek and tidy soul with a need for order and structure and a passion for detail. If you were to assess the probability that this man was a farmer, salesman, airline pilot, librarian, or physician, what would your guess be? Most people think that the highest probability is that he is a librarian because he represents the stereotypes most people have of librarians (Tversky & Kahneman, 1982). Judging probabilities in this manner often leads to serious error. If you see a poorly dressed man staggering down the street, you may conclude that he is most likely an alcoholic derelict when, in fact, he may suffer from any number of physical ailments. People often mistakenly think that individuals who suffer from cerebral palsy are mentally retarded because of deficits in their speech and motor coordination. In reality, they are of normal intelligence.

Base rates of the frequency of events are important in making decisions. We often ignore this information in making important decisions.

Categorizing things or individuals by their representative characteristics is something that we all do on a regular basis, and it is frequently a reasonable strategy. However, you should be aware that it could also lead you to incorrect judgments.

Underlying Probabilities

Critical for categorizing is knowing information about the frequency or probability for a given thing to occur, or what is called **base-rate information.** Assume you know that about 25% of Americans smoke cigarettes. If a person were selected at random, what would be the probability that he was a smoker? You would probably guess about 25%, or one in four. If I now described this individual to you as an African-American man who seemed nervous, what would you guess the odds are that he was a smoker? Many people will increase the probability of their estimation given this information, which is irrelevant to the probability that he is a smoker. In fact, a smaller proportion of African Americans smoke as compared to whites.

We often ignore base rates in making judgments. We know that 50% of marriages end in divorce but are surprised when someone we know gets a divorce. We know that smokers have a 50% chance of dying from a disease related to that habit, but we continue to "light up." Furthermore, parents are much more concerned about their children using heroin, morphine, or cocaine, which combined cause less than 8,500 deaths a year, than their use of tobacco, which kills 430,000, or alcohol, which kills 100,000. By ignoring the underlying probabilities, we often engage in or encourage risky behaviors that can have life-threatening consequences.

How good are you at determining the base-rate probability of things? You can find out by taking the test in Table 5.1.

✦ TABLE 5.1 ✦ Determining Base-Rate Frequency

How good are you at determining the underlying frequency of things happening? Below are some questions related to events. Select the frequency that you think represents the likelihood of the event occurring. The correct answers are based on data collected in 1980 and, for some statements, may be slightly different today (Fix & Daughton, 1980).

1. What are the chances of an American chosen at random being murdered in any given year?
   a. 1 in 5,050   b. 1 in 10,230   c. 1 in 14,200   d. 1 in 20,340
2. What percentage of Americans convicted of a crime plead guilty without going through a full trial?
   a. 25%   b. 45%   c. 67%   d. 90%
3. What are the odds that you could flip a coin and have it come up heads 10 straight times?
   a. 1 in 256   b. 1 in 512   c. 1 in 1,024   d. 1 in 2,048
4. In 1950 in Las Vegas a person once rolled the dice in a craps game and won 27 consecutive games. What are the odds that you could repeat this feat?
   a. 1 in 5,458,237   b. 1 in 12,467,890   c. 1 in 18,572,109   d. 1 in 21,362,890
5. Multiple sclerosis is an incurable, progressive disease of the nervous system. What are your chances of developing this disease sometime in your life?
   a. 75 in 100,000   b. 100 in 100,000   c. 150 in 100,000   d. 300 in 100,000
6. You forgot to get a tetanus shot and now you have contracted the illness after receiving a puncture wound. Assuming you receive the best medical treatment possible, what are the odds you will die?
   a. 1 in 2   b. 1 in 10   c. 1 in 100   d. 1 in 500
7. For a man who smokes, what are the chances he will develop a chronic lung disease sometime during his lifetime?
   a. 5 in 100   b. 8 in 100   c. 15 in 100   d. 19 in 100
8. You select an American physician at random. What are the odds that he or she has a psychiatric disorder severe enough to interfere with your treatment?
   a. 1 in 10   b. 1 in 20   c. 1 in 50   d. 1 in 100

(continued)

Framing

Asking a question in a certain way is called **framing,** and it has a big effect on how we answer the question. Consider the following alternatives that Tversky and Kahneman (1981) posed to subjects: Which would you rather have?

a. A certain gain of $250

OR

b. A 25% chance to win $1,000

Before going on, select one of the above.

Now, imagine that someone has just given you $1,000. You must choose one of these two unpleasant alternatives:

c. A certain loss of $750

OR

d. A 75% chance of losing the whole $1,000 (with a 25% chance of losing nothing).

Select one of these alternatives before reading further.

✦ TABLE 5.1 ✦ Continued

9. What are the odds this physician is a drug addict?
   a. 1 in 1,000 b. 1 in 500 c. 1 in 200 d. 3 in 200
10. What are the odds that any given female American will ultimately become an alcoholic?
    a. 1 in 20 b. 1 in 50 c. 1 in 100 d. 1 in 150
11. What are any one individual's chances of someday experiencing emotional depression severe enough to require medical treatment?
    a. 15 in 100 b. 20 in 100 c. 25 in 100 d. 30 in 100
12. Out of 100,000 Americans, how many will commit suicide?
    a. 25 b. 45 c. 88 d. 110
13. One member of a set of identical twins commits suicide. What are the chances that the other identical twin will also commit suicide?
    a. 10 in 100 b. 17.7 in 100 c. 24.3 in 100 d. 32 in 100
14. On any visit to a doctor's office, what are the odds that the patient's problems have an emotional basis rather than a physical basis?
    a. 1 in 10 b. 2 in 10 c. 4 in 10 d. 6 in 10
15. A student is accepted into a Ph.D. program in psychology in the United States. What are the odds the student will successfully complete the Ph.D. degree?
    a. 1 in 10 b. 1 in 4 c. 1 in 2 d. 3 in 4

Scoring:
Compare your answers to the correct ones below:

1. c 2. d 3. c 4. b 5. a 6. a 7. d 8. b 9. d 10. c 11. a 12. c 13. b 14. d 15. b

You should have gotten about 4 answers correct by chance. If you got 8 or more correct, you have a good sense of the base rate of occurrences. If you got 12 or more correct, you have an exceptionally good sense of how frequently things occur. By the way, the odds that you would guess all 15 correct by chance alone are less than 1 in 1 billion.

Most people avoid taking a risk when a question is framed in terms of gain but are willing to assume a risk when the question is framed in terms of a loss (Tversky & Kahneman, 1981). Thus, for the first pair of questions above, 84% of the people asked would take the certain $250 rather than take a 1-in-4 chance of winning $1,000. When faced with two possible gains, they chose the alternative that avoided any risk.

For the second pair of alternatives, 87% chose the risky alternative of a 75% chance of losing everything. When framed in terms of a loss, the people were willing to assume the more risky alternative. Note that alternatives (b) and (d) above are exactly the same. In both cases, you have a 25% chance of coming out ahead by $1,000, yet only 16% chose alternative (b) whereas 87% chose alternative (d). In a series of experiments such as this, Tversky and Kahneman found that people make decisions that will allow the possibility of avoiding losses but will avoid risks when possible gains are involved.

The framing effect also extends to the amount of information available and the type of choice to be made (Shafir, 1993). Imagine that you are a personnel manager and two equally qualified people have applied for a job. However, Person A's application contains more information, both positive and negative, than does Person B's. If you are asked to *select* one of these two applicants, you will focus on the greater amount of positive information in A's application and hire him or her. If you are asked to *reject* one of the applicants, you will focus on the greater amount of negative information in A's application and reject him or her. These are the same people and the same applications, but you make a different decision based on whether you are selecting or rejecting an applicant. This finding should be of more than passing interest to you. Often there are dozens, if not hundreds, of job applicants for a single position, and selection committees will start out the selection process by eliminating the "unqualified" candidates in order to reduce the size of the applicant pool. Under these circumstances, you want to limit the amount of negative information in your application, such as frequent job changes, periods of unemployment, and so on.

Availability Heuristic

Often we are called upon to make a judgment about how common something is or how frequently something occurs. The **availability heuristic** states that we will make these judgments based on how many memories of the event are immediately available to us. In other words, the more available memories that we have of an event occurring, the more common or frequently occurring we judge that event to be. In many cases, this rule leads us to make correct judgments, but sometimes it can lead us astray.

People who evaluate the risk of climbing on their roofs in order to make repairs have more salient and immediately available memories of the one time they fell off the roof compared to the numerous times that nothing eventful occurred. Similarly, events that are given wide coverage in the mass media may lead us to overestimate our chances of being a victim of a violent crime or being killed in an airplane crash. Airlines have documented that air travel drops dramatically in the days following a widely publicized air crash. In actuality, people are much more likely to be killed in an automobile accident driving to the airport than they are once they are on a commercial flight. We also miscalculate the probability of something good happening to us based on the availability heuristic. The likelihood of winning the lottery seems much higher after seeing a previous winner receive wide media exposure.

Mass-media reports also influence risk-related judgments made by a society as a whole (Tyler & Cook, 1984). Recently, there have been many reports on television and in the newspapers about food safety in the United States. These reports have led to a widespread belief that the American food supply is unsafe. As a result, many legislators have proposed laws to correct this perceived problem. Although the American food supply is actually the safest of any country in the world, our collective judgment of risk is influenced by the available memories that we have of reports to the contrary. These effects are greater on societal-level judgments than they are on an individual's personal judgments (Tyler & Cook, 1984). In making judgments about personal risks to yourself, you need to remember that just because an event is more memorable, it does not mean that it is more likely to occur.

Anchoring-and-Adjustment Heuristic

Often we reach decisions by making adjustments in information that is already available, a process called the **anchoring-and-adjustment heuristic.** An example of this is when you purchase a new car, you begin negotiations based on the sticker price; or when you purchase a used car, you begin negotiations based on the advertised/asking price. Similarly, students who contest the grade they received on an exam invariably begin by discussing their grade in reference to the grade they have already received. Research has shown that these initial reference points (also called anchors) have a powerful influence on the final outcome. Often the adjustments that are made are insufficient to offset the influence of the original reference point. If the used car for which you are negotiating is overpriced by $1,000, it is unlikely that any negotiated adjustments in the price will bring it down to what would be considered a good buy. New- and used-car salespeople make frequent use of this fact by asking prospective buyers, "What would you be willing to pay for this car?" The answer allows the salesperson to know what the buyer's reference point is and to negotiate from that point. Retail stores frequently advertise 50%-off sales when, in fact, the sale items either were never sold or were offered only briefly at that inflated price. By shifting our reference point upward, retailers influence us to buy things that we might not otherwise consider if the original reference price was not shown.

I hope this discussion on how we make decisions and solve problems has illustrated how frequently people rely on intuition rather than logic. Intuition often allows us to arrive at a quick answer but, not infrequently, an incorrect one as well. Kahneman and Tversky's important research in this area can enlighten us about the shortcomings of intuition and suggest ways to improve our thinking about problems.

APPLICATIONS: Improving Problem Solving

Incubation

Have you ever been stuck trying to solve a problem and discover that, after you stop trying to solve it, the answer suddenly pops into your head? This commonly occurring phenomenon is called the **incubation effect.** If you find yourself stuck on a problem, try thinking about something entirely different. There is evidence that the brain continues to work actively on problems even after we stop working on them directly. Often, we are stuck on a problem because we keep trying the same solutions over and over. (Remember the discussion of functional fixedness or mental set?) By putting the problem aside, we allow our brain to process the task in different and more effective ways.

Several studies have also documented superior problem-solving ability for those who return to a problem after a delay, rather than working on it continuously. This approach has been shown to facilitate the solution to a variety of problems, including geometric insight problems (Browne & Cruse, 1989) and picture-word problems (Smith & Blankenship, 1989). An example of the picture-word problems used by Smith and Blankenship is illustrated below. The words presented illustrate a common idiom or saying:

timing   tim   ing

Can you figure out what it represents? The solution is "split-second timing" because the second "timing" is split into two parts.

See if you can solve this one:

you   just   me

Can you think of what common saying this represents? If you can't, leave it alone and come back to it later after a period of incubation.

Brainstorming

The term **brainstorming** was coined in 1963 to describe techniques by which groups can engage more effectively in problem-solving activities (Osborn, 1963). Brainstorming techniques have been widely adopted and shown to be effective for both groups and individuals.

The single most important factor in brainstorming is the *suspension of critical judgment by group members.* If you have been in a group problem-solving discussion, you know that there is nothing that will kill the introduction of new ideas faster than having someone in the group say "That is a really stupid idea!" or "That idea couldn't possibly work." In brainstorming, all ideas are initially welcomed, regardless of how extreme they may seem. Only after a list of possible solutions has been developed can a critical evaluation of merit begin. Furthermore, having more ideas available creates better solutions. You are more likely to hit upon a solution if you have 50 ideas than if you have only 5. Because proposed solutions often serve to spin off other possible solutions, freewheeling discussion of ideas should be encouraged. Participants in brainstorming sessions should propose how 2 or more ideas can be integrated into a new idea. In the initial stages, there are no "bad" ideas. When it comes time to throw out ideas, do not spend time trying to justify or defend them. An elaborate justification of your idea will severely inhibit further discussion. Finally, do not worry about whether your idea has already been stated. Criticizing someone by saying "We already discussed that idea" will inhibit that person and the entire group from generating freewheeling proposals.

While brainstorming techniques are often used in group discussion, there is research that suggests the techniques are even more effective when done by individuals. In one experiment, individuals brainstormed problems in advertising either individually or in groups of 4. The combined output of the 4 individuals was greater than the 4 working together, both in quantity and quality of ideas (Dunnette, Campbell, & Jaastad, 1963). When brainstorming individually, it is important to remember not to be critical of your own ideas. Save your self-criticism until you have generated all possible ideas and then objectively evaluate the merits of each one.

Computer-Aided Decision Making and Problem Solving

With the advent of more powerful computers and advanced software, several companies and governmental agencies are turning to technology to help them make decisions and solve problems. In one procedure called **analytic hierarchy process,** a computer program reaches a solution by weighing the various alternatives and then by making comparisons between all possible alternatives (Palmer, 1999). For example, imagine that you must choose between two job offers. Job A has a higher salary but requires you to move to another city. Job B offers better fringe benefits but at a more costly rate than those for Job A. Job B offers flexible work schedules, but Job A allows you to work from your home. Job A allows you better promotional possibilities while Job B allows you to enter at a higher level. Given these and doubtless other considerations, you might find it difficult to make a decision about which job to choose. The decision software works by having you compare each pair of characteristics and assign numbers regarding how important each one is. As an example, is salary more important than job location? If so, by how much? With a large number of factors, the possible number of comparisons rises exponentially. Even though the software essentially does what we try to do in reaching a decision, it also keeps track of every factor as well as the relative importance of each factor.

The U.S. State Department successfully used this approach to select an e-mail system for its foreign embassies. Similarly, Toronto Hydro Corporation used it in conjunction with a large set of hiring criteria in order to select employees from among 800 job candidates. As decision making becomes more and more complex, companies are increasingly turning to computers to aid them in making the best decision about how to solve corporate problems.

Reasoning

Reasoning is the process of drawing conclusions about something, given the available evidence. It is a special type of problem solving used to evaluate the truth or falsity of a statement. When we talk about someone being a "reasonable" person, we are implying that this person draws conclusions based on evidence rather than on personal whims. Reasoning describes the logical rules that people use to guide their thinking. There are two main kinds of reasoning that are used: deductive reasoning and inductive reasoning.

Deductive Reasoning

In **deductive reasoning** we draw conclusions from general statements about what we know to be true to specific and logically consistent conclusions. This is the process that we use when we reach a new conclusion based on what we already know. It often takes the form of the argument, "If A is true, then B is true. Since A is true, therefore B is also true." Sometimes this kind of reasoning leads us to the correct conclusion—and sometimes not. Consider the following example (Galotti, 1999):

All psychology majors are curious.
No tennis players are curious.
No tennis players are psychology majors.

Most people believe that if A and B are both true, then the final conclusion is correct. People use their personal experiences, knowledge, and expectations to evaluate whether A and B are true. Such reasoning can lead us to an incorrect conclusion. Consider the following example (Roediger, Capaldi, Paris, Polivy, & Herman, 1996):

If it is night, then the streets will be dark.
The streets are dark.
Therefore, it is night.

Is this conclusion correct? On first consideration, you might conclude so because it fits correctly with what we know to be true. Indeed, the conclusion might even be plausible. Nevertheless, we cannot make this conclusion because there might be some other explanation for the streets being dark (a solar eclipse, for example). When engaging in deductive reasoning, it is important not only that the conclusions follow logically but also that there are no alternative explanations available.

Inductive Reasoning

When we reach a general conclusion from specific facts or observations, we are engaging in **inductive reasoning.** This kind of reasoning is very helpful to us because it adds new information. Each of us uses this kind of reasoning every day, and it often leads us to correct conclusions, particularly if the conclusion is based on several observations. However, inductive reasoning only allows us to make probabilistic statements because any one exception invalidates the reasoning. For example, if you are in an engineering class where all 30 students are males, you might conclude that *all* engineering majors are males. However, if there is but 1 single female engineering major, your conclusion is false. You might correctly conclude that if a person is an engineering major, that person is *probably* male. Weather forecasters use inductive reasoning to state that there is an 80% chance of rain tomorrow. They arrive at this conclusion by comparing the present weather conditions to previous conditions that have resulted in rain. Many weather forecasters have learned that there are enough exceptions to the rules to make any precise forecast very hazardous.

Science uses inductive reasoning by trying to infer general truths from several observations. However, scientists are rarely in the situation to say that A causes B with 100% certainty. You may notice that most scientific conclusions are stated in probabilistic terms. Scientists do not say that if you smoke, you *will* get lung cancer. Rather, they conclude that the probability of getting lung cancer is *X* times more likely if you smoke *Y* packs of cigarettes per day for a given number of years. Fortunately, scientists often have enough data to make predictions with a very high degree of assurance, but almost never with 100% certainty.

Creative Thinking

The ability to produce innovative and valuable ideas and to solve problems in unique and useful ways is called **creativity.** There are very few topics in psychology about which there is more disagreement than this one. In general, we know that intelligence and creativity are related, but only to a certain extent. The rule seems to be that you must have an above-average amount of intelligence to be highly creative, but beyond that point (an IQ score of about 120), it does not seem to make much difference. That is, you would expect to find creativity differences between 2 individuals with IQ's of 100 and 120 but little or no difference between 2 individuals with scores of 120 and 150. In fact, highly creative professionals have been found to have the same average intelligence scores as their less-creative colleagues (MacKinnon & Hall, 1972).

Creativity involves two different thinking styles (Guilford, 1967). One style, called **convergent thinking,** involves putting together a group of often disparate facts to find a solution to a question or problem. For instance, a car mechanic might pull together information about the sound of the engine, the look and smell of the exhaust, the vibration of the engine at varying speeds, how the car rides, total mileage, and the owner's driving habits in diagnosing a mechanical problem. **Divergent thinking** is the ability to produce a variety of different responses to the same problem. For example, individuals are asked to think of all the different ways one could use a common object, such as a paperclip or a brick. Highly creative individuals are able to think up numerous, appropriate responses while less-creative people only see the objects used for the usual purposes. One theory states that creativity involves *both* convergent and divergent thinking styles. Initially, divergent thinking is needed to generate many different ideas or concepts about the solution. Convergent thinking is then employed to evaluate each of these ideas to determine which is the best solution.

Measuring Creativity

One of the difficulties in studying creativity is finding a way to measure it. Two main approaches have been used. The Remote Associates Test measures the cognitive skill of finding relationships between things that are only remotely associated (Mednick, 1968). In this test, you are given three words and you must think of a fourth word that is related to all three. You can test your own level of creativity using this methodology by completing the test shown in Table 5.2.

Another approach to measuring creativity is the Drawing-Completion Test, illustrated in Figure 5.2. Subjects are asked to elaborate on a series of simple figures and are then judged on the basis of how original and creative their responses were. Figure 5.3 illustrates sample responses that would be judged as creative or noncreative.

Characteristics of Creative People

Are some people born creative or does our environment shape us in that direction? The answer is both. As I mentioned earlier, highly creative individuals are also usually highly intelligent, and we know that part of intelligence is based on heredity. Hence, if you are born with a below-average IQ, it is unlikely that you will be highly creative, irrespective of your environment. Psychologists have also noted several personality characteristics that seem inherent in highly creative individuals. Our personality is also a result of both inherited and environmental factors.

Creative people are able to engage in divergent thinking, producing a large and diverse number of responses to a problem or question. They also may have developed expertise in the area in which they are creative (Brown, 1989). Typically, an individual's creativity is often restricted to a limited number of domains. However, there have been notable exceptions to this rule, such as Leonardo de Vinci (1452–1519), who was proficient in art, science, and engineering. Contrary to popular belief, creativity does not occur in a blinding flash, nor does it result from little effort on the part of the individual. Creative individuals work hard, typically study what has been done previously by others, and then use this prior knowledge in their creative endeavors. They are described as individuals who are open to new ways of

✦ TABLE 5.2 ✦ Test of Creativity

This test is one frequently used by psychologists to measure creativity. The test is called a Remote Associates Test (RAT) because it measures your ability to see relationships between things that are only remotely associated. Read the instructions carefully before beginning the test.

Instructions: Look at the three words and find a fourth word that is related to all three. Write this word in the space provided.

Example: What word is related to these three words?

paint doll cat _______

The answer is "house": house paint, dollhouse, and house cat.

Here is another example:

stool powder ball _______

The answer is "foot": footstool, foot powder, and football.

You have 20 minutes to complete the following items:

1. call	pay	line	_______
2. end	burning	blue	_______
3. man	hot	sure	_______
4. stick	pal	ball	_______
5. blue	cake	cottage	_______
6. man	wheel	high	_______
7. motion	poke	down	_______
8. eye	water	ceiling	_______
9. line	birthday	surprise	_______
10. wood	liquor	luck	_______
11. house	village	golf	_______
12. plan	show	walker	_______
13. key	wall	previous	_______
14. bell	iron	tender	_______
15. water	youth	soda	_______
16. base	snow	dance	_______
17. stop	kart	slow	_______
18. up	book	charge	_______
19. tin	writer	my	_______
20. leg	arm	person	_______
21. weight	out	pencil	_______

(continued)

doing things, alert to opportunities when they present themselves, and able to enjoy solving complex problems (Barron, 1988). Furthermore, creative individuals question prior assumptions and authority, take more risks than usual, reject dogmatic beliefs, and accept other cultures, races, and religions. They also enjoy being creative for the sake of creativity itself and are not driven by extrinsic rewards such as money

✦ TABLE 5.2 ✦ Continued

22. spin	tip	shape	________
23. sharp	tick	tie	________
24. out	band	night	________
25. cool	house	fat	________
26. back	go	light	________
27. man	order	air	________
28. bath	up	burst	________
29. ball	out	blue	________
30. up	around	rear	________

Check your answers with the following suggested answers. There may be other appropriate answers, as well.

1. phone	11. green	21. lead
2. book	12. floor	22. top
3. fire	13. stone	23. tack
4. pin	14. bar	24. watch
5. cheese	15. fountain	25. cat
6. chair	16. ball	26. stop
7. slow	17. go	27. mail
8. glass	18. cover	28. bubble
9. party	19. type	29. black
10. hard	20. chair	30. end

Normative Data

The following normative data were collected on university undergraduates. Calculate the number you got correct and look up your percentile ranking.

Number Correct	Percentile
24–28	95%
21–23	80%
19–20	65%
16–18	50%
13–15	35%
10–13	20%
7–9	8%
1–5	1%

SOURCE: *Exercise for General Psychology,* Rick Gardner. Burgess Publishing, 1980. Reprinted with permission.

or fame. Creative individuals have been found to be social nonconformists who are also ambitious, confident, and perseverant (Martindale, 1989). Unfortunately, they also seem predisposed to mood disorders such as depression. Several highly creative individuals who suffered from various psychological disorders are Chopin, Newton, van Gogh, and Hemingway (Prentky, 1989).

✦ FIGURE 5.2 ✦ The Drawing-Completion Test of Creativity

Elaborate on the figures below in whatever manner seems creative and appealing to you. After finishing, compare your results to those in Figure 5.3.

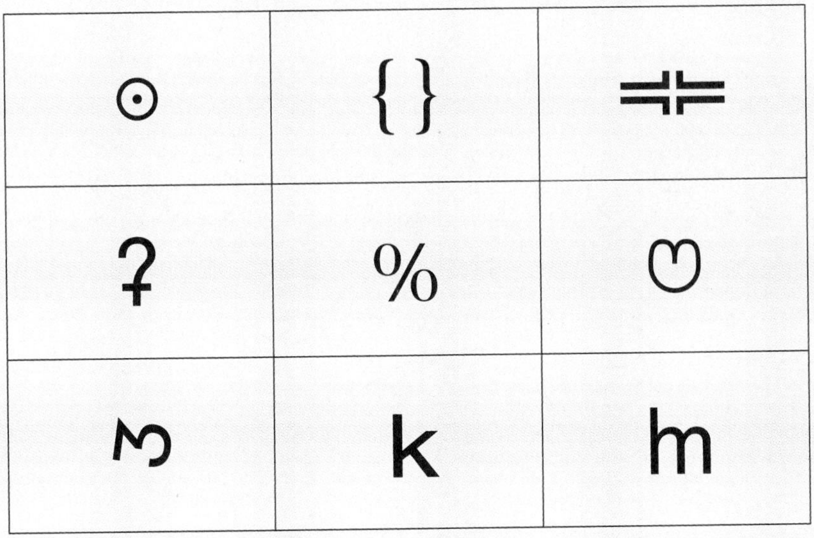

Factors Influencing Creativity

Researchers have found that both age and cultural factors greatly influence creativity.

Age

Different kinds of creativity appear to flourish at different ages. For example, younger people excel at creating poetry, especially when it deals with idealism, romanticism, or passionate love. The writing of novels and creative works of literature appear most frequently in older individuals (Simonton, 1975).

Culture

An individual's cultural setting also can have a great impact on creative accomplishments. Some cultures promote freethinking and risk taking more than others. Cultural views of the role of women have historically played a large role in their creative endeavors. In the past 50 years there has been an increasing emphasis on women being productive outside of the home and family that has allowed more women to make outstanding creative contributions in both the arts and the sciences.

APPLICATIONS: Becoming More Creative

Robert Sternberg and Todd Lubart (1991a, 1991b) are among some of the most influential researchers in the area of creativity. They believe that both individual and environmental factors are important for creativity to occur. Their theory emphasizes

✦ FIGURE 5.3 ✦ Sample Responses to the Drawing-Completion Test

The drawings on the top reflect a relatively low level of creativity while those on the bottom are representative of a much more creative individual. Note the complexity and asymmetry of the more creative drawings.

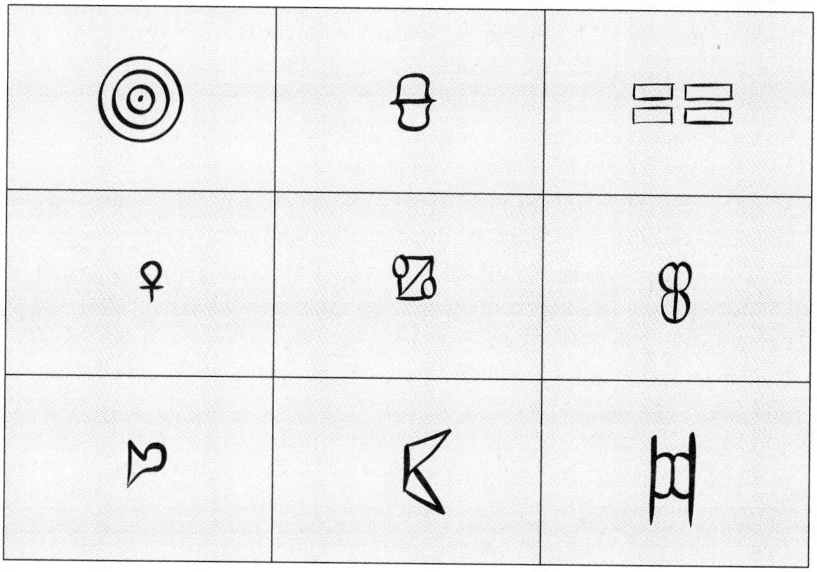

Low Creativity

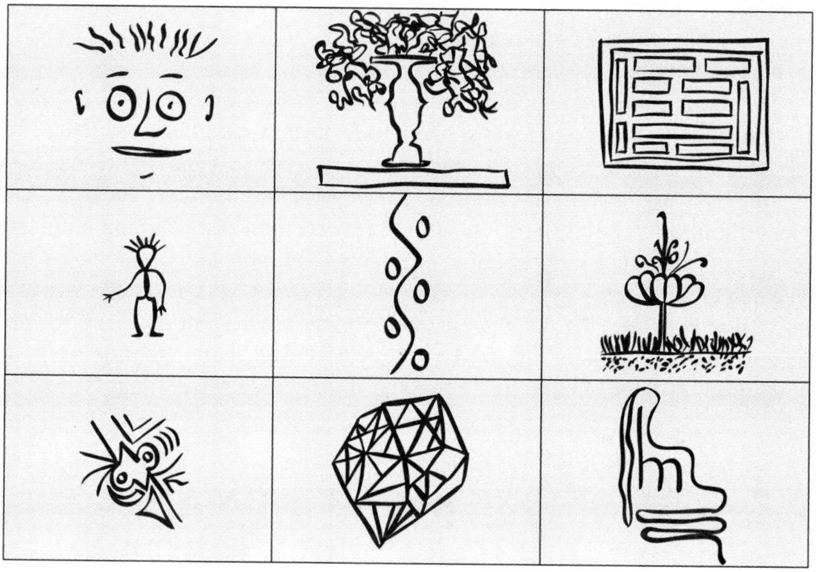

High Creativity

the importance of knowledge, intellectual ability, personality variables, and motivation in creativity. They also emphasize the importance of intellectual style and note that creative individuals tend to look at the "big picture" rather than focus on details and to prefer novelty to tradition or convention.

These views have led Robert Sternberg to recommend ways that individuals can increase their own creativity (Sternberg, 1995, pp. 363–366).

1. Become motivated. The higher your motivation, the more likely that you will be creative. Remember that creativity flourishes best when driven by intrinsic rewards as opposed to extrinsic motivators such as money, status, or fame.
2. Be a nonconformist. Question authority and the commonly accepted ways of doing things. Do not be afraid to violate existing rules.
3. Maintain high standards of excellence. Creativity requires diligence and perseverance. Develop good work habits and self-discipline.
4. Believe in what you are doing. Do not let others discourage you. Be open to criticism but do not allow it to prevent you from pursuing your creative activities. Be your own best critic.
5. Use analogies. Find new relationships by using analogies. Think about the relationship of one thing to another. Scientists who analogized the principles of echolocation used by bats and porpoises invented radar in World War II.
6. Affiliate with those who will encourage your creativity. Avoid friends and work environments where new ideas or risk taking are discouraged.
7. Develop expertise. Remember that the more knowledge and skills that you have in an area, the more likely you are to make a creative contribution. Sternberg suggests looking for gaps in existing knowledge in order to avoid reinventing the wheel.
8. Be committed. Very few accomplishments in life, creative or noncreative, come about with a lack of commitment.

Chance favors only the prepared mind.

LOUIS PASTEUR

Many organizations are coming to appreciate that creative problem solving is a critical attribute in their employees. Numerous businesses, industries, and schools are conducting training courses for this purpose. In our fast-moving technological age, problem-solving skills are becoming increasingly important. These days, employees are finding themselves less able to rely on their past training and instead must depend on their ability to solve problems in unique ways. A person who received a doctoral degree in computer science as recently as 2 years ago would find almost all of that prior knowledge obsolete today. Training in law school emphasizes teaching students to "think like a lawyer" rather than teaching mere facts. Laws constantly change, but critical thinking skills are always current.

Thinking and Reasoning Clearly about Human Behavior

Early in chapter 1 I addressed the fact that people hold many misconceptions about human behavior. These misconceptions often result from fuzzy thinking when it comes to evaluating facts. These misconceptions are not limited to those individuals who have never received formal training in psychology. Eva Vaughan (1977) found that these erroneous beliefs did not significantly change even after students had completed an introductory course in psychology.

Keith Stanovich (1996) has written an excellent book entitled *How to Think Straight about Psychology.* In my judgment, this book should be required reading for all psychology majors. It is essential reading for anyone who wishes to evaluate critically the multitude of misleading information about psychology to which the media and popular press regularly expose us. As Stanovich notes, "Psychology, probably more than any other science, requires critical thinking skills that enable students to separate the wheat from the chaff that accumulates around all sciences" (p. xiii). In this section, I will review some of the information that Stanovich presents to help you achieve critical-evaluative skills.

The Falsifiability Criterion

Theory plays an essential role in the advancement of science. Theories are an interrelated set of concepts that explain known facts and, equally important, make *predictions* about what will happen in the future.

Several ancient cultures, including the Aztecs, believed that human sacrifices were necessary to appease various gods, including the gods that they held responsible for the weather. Their "theory" predicted that a failure to appease the gods would result in catastrophic weather occurrences. As a result, they dutifully offered up a number of human sacrifices to the gods and, undoubtedly, were pleased when good weather followed. If a drought followed, they reasoned that their offering was insufficient to appease the gods or perhaps that the appeasement ritual was not performed correctly.

For theories to be useful, they must not only specify what will happen but also what will *not* happen. The more specific predictions that a theory makes about both what will and will not happen, the more useful the theory becomes. The human sacrifice theory fails critical scrutiny because it explains any possible outcome, good or bad. A theory that accounts for everything is a theory completely devoid of value. Because this reasoning seems straightforward enough, you probably wonder what audacious individual would try to formulate a theory that would explain everything. You only need look to psychology to find the answer.

Karl Popper, an influential philosopher of science, was curious why some theories led to large advances in knowledge while others remained stagnant (Stanovich, 1996). Popper cited Einstein's general relativity theory as one that led to many exciting new discoveries. Einstein's theory, which was very controversial when first presented, made many very *specific* predictions about what would and would not happen under certain conditions. In sum, his theory was structured such that it could be both verified and contradicted. In the years immediately following publication of this theory, the technology was not available to test many of Einstein's predictions. In fact, verification of the truth and possible falsity of the theory is still ongoing today.

Popper noted that Sigmund Freud's theory of psychoanalysis is an example of a theory that cannot be falsified. Freud's theory is very complex, and a detailed description is beyond the scope of this book. Suffice it to say that Freud looked at behavior that had already occurred and then attempted to offer explanations for that behavior. You will recall in chapter 1 that we described these kinds of explanations as "post hoc" or "after the fact." I noted then that such explanations are of little value in explaining what has happened or in establishing a structure to explain future events. Freud and his later followers took precisely this approach. In capsule form, Freud believed that subconscious thoughts (thoughts of which we are not consciously aware) are responsible for much of our behavior. He believed, for example, that in the normal course of development each of us desires to have sexual relations with our parent of the opposite sex. Of course, most people deny ever having such feelings.

Freud explained that people denied experiencing these feelings because the emotions are repressed. In other words, these thoughts and feelings have been driven into the subconscious where we are not aware of them. This is a classic post-hoc explanation and cannot be proven false (or true). By analyzing people's dreams, Freud theorized that dreams represent some form of sexual wish fulfillment. Again, the analysis is made *after* the dream has occurred. Freud never predicted what type of dream he would expect a patient to have. The predictability of certain dreams would have strengthened his theory significantly. Freud's theories were structured such that any behavior could be explained in psychoanalytic terms *after* the behavior had occurred. Stanovich has argued that explanations that explain everything, after the fact, provide an illusion of understanding. In fact, such theories explain *nothing.*

People who believe in extrasensory perception (ESP) often claim that failures to confirm this phenomenon occur because the people who do the testing are skeptics. These skeptics allegedly give off "bad vibrations" that disrupt the fragile ESP phenomenon and prevent it from occurring. Their belief explains why ESP does occur and why it does not occur; in other words, it explains everything and nothing. Imagine a theory in physics about gravitation or magnetism that states the predicted phenomenon will occur only when observed by someone who believes in it. Such a theory would be dismissed out of hand.

Testimonials

Our thinking is often influenced by testimonials from individuals. As you watch television, notice how often this technique is used to support a claim. These testimonials often appear to be candid, extemporaneous reports by individuals as to the effectiveness of some homeopathic medication, weight-loss diet, or get-rich-quick scheme. Late-night television, with its numerous infomercials, is a particularly rich source of these kinds of testimonials. How much should we let testimonials influence our thinking? The answer can be summed up in three words: *Not at all.*

Recently there has been an advertisement on television featuring a well-known actor engaged in physical exercise. The actor states that he exercises regularly to keep his body sharp and takes an herb that has recently been touted to enhance memory to keep his mind sharp. Conveniently, the actor appears to be in his mid- to late 50s or about the time when many people feel their memory is beginning to slip. Convincing as this kind of pitch may seem, the audience is well advised to disregard the data when the effectiveness of something is based strictly on testimonials.

Every therapy ever devised, whether in medicine or psychology, has its individual supporters who are willing to testify to its efficacy (Stanovich, 1996). No matter how extreme or ill conceived the treatment, it will doubtless benefit someone. Much of this benefit can be attributed to what is called the **placebo effect.** The placebo effect refers to the tendency for people to report that *any* treatment has helped them, regardless of whether it has any actual therapeutic effect. In chapter 2, I discussed how a fake pill or injection often serves as a very effective painkiller. Until 1950, physicians relied heavily on placebo effects because there were no effective medications to treat most illnesses. Physicians prescribed sugar pills that came in various shapes and colors in a deliberate attempt to induce a placebo response. Quite frequently it worked.

In order to evaluate the effectiveness of a treatment, there needs to be a comparison group who receives nothing. Today, all pharmaceutical research includes such comparison groups, and the findings are quite often surprising. For instance, a recent study of a popular baldness remedy found that 86% of the men taking it either maintained or increased the amount of hair on their heads. Very impressive results. However, 42% of those taking a placebo reported exactly the same results. A recent review of placebo-controlled studies of antidepressant drugs revealed that placebos and genuine drugs worked with about the same effectiveness (Kirsch, 1997). For pain control, placebos are typically about 55 to 60% as effective as medications such as aspirin or codeine (Kirsch, 1997).

Placebo effects have equally powerful results in psychological therapy. Several controlled studies have shown that many people with psychological problems, particularly those of mild-to-moderate severity, report significant improvement over time regardless of whether or not they received therapy. When therapy works, it is often because of some combination of the placebo effect, the passage of time, and the therapy itself.

Reports from testimonials should not be dismissed entirely, however. Insights gained from such sources can be useful in the *early* investigation of phenomena (Stanovich, 1996). For instance, many medications used today, including aspirin, were discovered by primitive tribes who consumed plant products and discovered their medicinal values quite by accident. Such testimonial evidence can be suggestive, but it is only the follow-up and controlled scientific studies that can verify the effects. The next time that you are tempted to try a product, service, or therapy based exclusively on testimonial data, remember that such evidence *by itself* has no value.

Vividness Effect

When faced with a decision or a problem to be solved, individuals naturally retrieve seemingly relevant information from memory. The more accessible or easily retrieved that this information is, the more likely the person will use it. This leads to what is called the **vividness effect,** which means that the more "vivid" a piece of information is in memory, the more likely we will use it to influence our decision-making or problem-solving behavior.

> No testimony is sufficient to establish a miracle, unless the testimony be of such a kind, that its falsehood would be more miraculous than the fact which it endeavors to establish.
>
> **DAVID HUME (1711–1776)**
> *On Miracles*

Do you find yourself being influenced by vivid accounts of events in the mass media? Most people do. I mentioned earlier that airline bookings always drop precipitously after media accounts of a particularly horrific airline disaster. People suddenly decide that driving might be a safer alternative despite the previously cited statistics that indicate you are more likely to die in an automobile accident driving to the airport than during a commercial airline flight. Reports of a terrorist incident on tourists in a foreign country result in dramatic drops of tourism to that country for months afterwards, even though chances of being murdered are higher when staying in the United States than when visiting most foreign sites.

When purchasing a car, would you be most influenced by the frequency of repair data found in magazines such as *Consumer Reports* or by the vivid testimony of a friend who recently had a bad experience with one particular brand of automobile? All too frequently, we base our decisions and opinions on the information most vivid in our memories rather than on impersonal statistical facts. Such influences are not restricted to individuals. Public opinion is often influenced in a similar manner. Most Americans believe that the crime rate in the United States is on the increase despite statistics that indicate the exact opposite. The Columbine High School incident in Littleton, Colorado, in 1999 took place when two high-school students shot and killed 12 fellow students and a teacher. Subsequent public opinion polls showed that parents had serious concerns that school environments are dangerous places for their children. I suspect that the number of children being home-schooled has subsequently increased even though statistical data indicate that a child is many, many times more at risk of being murdered when outside of the school environment than while attending school.

When it comes to decision making and problem solving, we are all susceptible to the vividness effect. This is because the vivid memories are more accessible and clear to us than the statistical facts that might refute them. The cold facts of objective reason will quickly give way to the vivid memories of recent events. Remember the power of this phenomenon when making important decisions in your life.

Correlation and Causation

We try to understand what causes things to happen in our lives. In our search to understand and explain behavior, we sometimes make the mistake of believing that things that occur together do so because one is causing the other. Sometimes this is true, but often it is not.

When two things reliably occur together we say they are **correlated.** If high rates of poverty are associated with high crime levels, we can say the two are *positively* correlated. Sometimes high values in one variable are correlated with low values in another, which constitutes a *negative* correlation. For instance, the higher the income levels of individuals, the lower the incidence of certain diseases. Usually correlations only suggest a trend, not a perfect rule. Many people living in poverty never commit a crime, and plenty of wealthy individuals develop all kinds of diseases. Nevertheless, a relationship or correlation between two variables is important because it often allows us to predict one thing as a result of knowing another, even though the predictions are often not perfect.

Knowing that two variables are correlated does *not* tell us *why* they are related. Even if variables *X* and *Y* are very highly correlated, we cannot conclude whether *X* caused *Y*, whether *Y* caused *X*, or whether some third variable caused both *X* and *Y*.

To illustrate, consider the correlation that exists between exposure to violence in the media, movies, and video games and the higher incidence of aggressiveness in children. As an example, the two high-school students in Colorado who shot and killed several of their classmates had a history of playing violent video games. Can we conclude from this correlation that such exposure *causes* violent behavior? Simply put:

no, you cannot infer a causal relationship. Other studies have indicated that children with aggressive personalities seek out video games, movies, and television programs that include acts of violence.

Smoking and lung cancer are positively correlated in that the more you smoke, the higher the incidence of lung cancer. For years the tobacco industry argued that this correlation was not proof that smoking *caused* lung cancer. They argued that perhaps some third variable that was not measured, such as stress, was related to both smoking and cancer and was the causal agent in developing cancer. How could we prove that smoking caused lung cancer? By experimentally manipulating the variable of smoking and measuring the incidence of cancer, we would have the proof needed. For example, we could take a group of young people who had never smoked, force half of them to smoke, prevent the other half from smoking, and then measure the incidence of cancer in both groups. Of course, ethical principles would prevent us from actually conducting this experiment. However, animal research that was conducted in this manner conclusively demonstrated the causal link between smoking and lung cancer.

Remember that just because two things occur together, that alone is not proof that one is *causing* the other. The field of psychology has made many erroneous conclusions about behavior because of this concept. For instance, in the 1960s, students in an abnormal psychology class were routinely taught that childhood schizophrenia was caused by certain parenting techniques. Later research showed conclusively that although these two variables were correlated, there was no causal link between the two conditions.

Several public school districts in the United States are facing funding cutbacks because of budget shortfalls. One measure that has been proposed to save money is to eliminate music instruction. A local newspaper recently published an article about a research project that showed scores in math and science were highly correlated with the amount of music training someone received. The implication was that musical training *helps* students in math and science. Perhaps you can think of some other reasons that these two might be correlated. For instance, children from higher socioeconomic families are more likely to be exposed to musical training. It is well known that children from economically advantaged families perform better in school, including math and science courses. Another explanation might be that students who stick with musical training probably have the kinds of personality characteristics that also make them stick with certain academic pursuits, including math and science. Whatever the reason, the only conclusion that can be drawn is that the two are correlated, not that one causes the other.

A final warning about correlations is in order. Sometimes we think that we see a relationship between two variables where, in fact, none exists. These false perceptions are called an **illusory correlation.** Often times, if we *believe* that there is a relationship between two variables, we will be more likely to *notice* and *remember* those instances that reaffirm those beliefs. For example, if you believe that obese individuals are overweight because they eat larger quantities than normal weight people, you will probably take notice of those overweight individuals you see at a buffet loading up their plates with large quantities of food. The obese person who only takes a salad likely will not be noticed or will be quickly forgotten because that image does not confirm your previous beliefs. We all are guilty of this kind of thinking at one time or another. It is important to remember that incidents that confirm

An Example of an Illusory Correlation

When things seem to occur regularly together, we sometimes incorrectly assume they are correlated and that one thing causes the other. Frequent news accounts of how tornadoes have destroyed several mobile homes may lead us to believe that tornadoes have an ability to seek out and destroy such structures.

our beliefs can be just random coincidences and only seem correlated because they reaffirm what we already believe to be true. Also note the similarity between this phenomenon and the confirmation bias described earlier.

Sample Selection

Research with human beings, whether in the social sciences or in medicine, is usually conducted on a limited number of individuals. It is almost always impossible to conduct a study on the entire population of individuals that scientists are interested in studying. Instead, scientists draw a subset or **sample** of individuals and attempt to generalize the findings from the sample to the population as a whole.

In order to make this generalization, it is important that it be a representative sample of the population as a whole. For example, a sample should contain about the same number of females and ethnic minorities that are representative of what is found in the population. If this is not done, then generalizations to the population are highly questionable. Until fairly recently, this was a serious problem in much medical research. Medical research was notorious for primarily studying the effects of medical treatments on white males. As a consequence, the effectiveness of medical treatments for women and minorities was often unknown. Only recently has the

National Institutes of Health (NIH) required that all research projects use samples that are representative of the population as a whole.

To create a sample that is representative of the population, it is usually necessary to take what is called a **random sample.** This is a sample in which every individual in the population has an equal chance of being included. A random sample of 100 students from a university could be selected by putting everyone's name in a container and randomly drawing out 100 names. If this were done, the sample should contain about the same proportion of various kinds of individuals as the population.

It is frequently very tempting to generalize from samples that are not representative of the population. For example, you may hear on a television commercial that 4 out of 5 individuals responding to a survey preferred Brand A over Brand B. The first question you should ask yourself is how was the sample selected? If the respondents were solicited at their homes by phone, the sample is not random because people who are most likely to be at home to receive calls differ in many ways from the population as a whole. Furthermore, the respondents only represent those willing to answer the survey, which also sets them apart from the population as a whole. Very busy people would probably hang up when receiving this type of call (as I do).

Another important factor is the size of the sample. When it comes to samples, *size matters.* As a general rule, the larger the sample the more representative it will be of the population. You would not have much confidence in a survey that only asked 5 people about their brand preferences. Remember, small samples are highly unlikely to be representative of the population, and the results may vary greatly from sample to sample.

We frequently make generalizations about behavior based on nonrandom samples that we have observed. Someone may observe 3 foreign students from the same country who talked very loudly and were obnoxious. It might be tempting to generalize those behaviors to all students from that same country, but such a generalization would be inappropriate because the sample is not large, random, or representative. Sometimes we generalize from extreme or particularly vivid cases, as well. If you meet a particularly attractive female super model that seems decidedly unfriendly, there may be an almost irresistible urge to generalize that all females who are super models are unfriendly. When generalizing about behavior, remember that doing so from small and nonrandom samples is rarely valid.

APPLICATIONS: Problem Solving Applied to Test Taking

I have been discussing how problem solving and thinking skills can be applied to our everyday lives. One of the demands that college students face regularly is drawing on the problem-solving and thinking skills that are required when taking examinations. A frequent student complaint is that students often do poorly on examinations even when well prepared. Other students seemingly are able to perform well on tests despite being poorly prepared. Psychologists have recognized that some students possess cognitive abilities or a set of skills that they can use to improve a test score no matter what the content area of the test (Sarnacki, 1979). This skill has been variously referred to as **testwiseness,** testmanship, or test sophistication. As a college student, you know that at times you are not adequately prepared to answer a specific test question due to a lack of information concerning the content of the question. In these cases, a strategy for guessing is needed. Numerous studies have shown that there are guessing strategies that can be used effectively to increase the likelihood of selecting the correct answer, particularly on multiple-choice tests. Furthermore, students who have developed these skills perform consistently better on tests than students deficient in those skills (Hammerton, 1965; Bauer, 1973). These cognitive skills can be taught to students, and the skills have been shown to generalize to a variety of topic areas typically covered in college classes (Dolly & Williams, 1986). Furthermore, it is not just the most intelligent students who are testwise. There is only a low to moderate correlation between intelligence and testwiseness. Verbal achievement has been shown to be a better predictor of who will be testwise (Diamond & Evans, 1972).

Being testwise involves more than just an ability to guess wisely. Testwise individuals also have been shown to have the following characteristics:

- They use time during an examination more effectively.
- They use strategies to avoid errors.
- They use a deductive reasoning strategy; that is, they reason from the general to the specific.
- They use cues often inherent in tests to correctly answer test questions.

Measuring Testwiseness

How testwise are you? The sample test in Table 5.3 will help you determine how skilled you are in guessing the correct answer when dealing with an unfamiliar content area. Take this test and score it before continuing on with this section.

Becoming Testwise

MULTIPLE CHOICE QUESTIONS. Professors who write multiple-choice or true-false questions often include eight common flaws in their questions that you can use to guess the correct answer. Please note that I am not advocating that you come unprepared to take examinations. These testwise skills will never replace adequate test preparation and are mainly useful for that (I hope) occasional question where you are forced to make your best guess.

Listed below are the eight most common item-writing flaws. The examples come from an actual world history examination covering the period A.D. 1500 to the present.

1. *The incorrect options are highly implausible.* Sometimes one or more of the options will seem highly unlikely given the subject matter being tested. The correct answer likely will not be a flippant remark or contain highly emotive words, such as *stupid, nonsensical, foolish, harebrained,* and so forth.

Example: Roop Kumar

a. developed a ludicrous philosophy about the meaning of life.

b. was a famous stage actor.

c. tried to circumvent "Muslim law."

d. was a leading Italian thinker during the 17th century.

✦ TABLE 5.3 ✦ Testwiseness Scale

Below are 15 history questions. It is not expected that you will know the answers to these questions. There are flaws in each question, however, which should allow you to make a good guess about the correct answer. Circle the one answer that you think is correct for each question.

1. Abd al-Wahlab's religious message was distinguished by the fact that it was:
   a. difficult to understand.
   b. never spelled out in detail.
   c. traditionalist in nature.
   d. never revealed to the masses.
2. The period when the most rapid world economic growth took place was:
   a. 1900–1925.
   b. 1925–1945.
   c. 1945–1975.
   d. 1975–1995.
3. Lenin differed from the Mensheviks in:
   a. his desire to overthrow the tsar.
   b. favoring industrialization.
   c. working diligently with working people toward the implementation of an immediate Socialist revolution.
   d. cooperating with the liberals.
4. During the Industrial Revolution, nationalism:
   a. accentuated class differences.
   b. increased provincial feeling.
   c. declined, especially during the 19th century.
   d. increased international tensions.
5. Robespierre was:
   a. an member of the Estates-General.
   b. a leader of the committee of Public Safety.
   c. a author of the "Declaration of the Rights of Man and the Citizen."
   d. all of the above.
6. In India, the Mughal mansabdari system:
   a. enforced social equality.
   b. provided the emperor with cavalrymen.
   c. provided revenue to the emperor.
   d. permitted politicians to live in one area for life.
   e. none of the above.
7. In 1939 Turkey, women:
   a. were forced to wear veils at all times.
   b. had no rights of child custody.
   c. were allowed to vote in national elections.
   d. could never speak to men in public.
   e. all of the above.

(continued)

✦ TABLE 5.3 ✦ Continued

8. Some historians believe al-Ghazali's synthesis of Shariah- and Sufi-based Islam may have:
   a. led to war with Turkey.
   b. led directly to the development of an extremely closed system of Islamic thought and behavior.
   c. subverted religious belief.
   d. encouraged innovation.
9. The Renaissance represented:
   a. increasing political unity in Italy.
   b. a breakdown in agreements among various Italian political units.
   c. an artistic expression of religious revival.
   d. all of the above.
10. The British occupied Egypt in 1882 in order to
    a. encourage foreign tourism.
    b. prevent the spread of Communism.
    c. establish a Jewish settlement there.
    d. put down a nationalist insurrection.
11. Colonial "tribalism" in Africa was a product of:
    a. uneven development and political competition among tribes.
    b. well-defined religious differences among societies.
    c. the slave trade.
    d. hostilities dating back to the precolonial period.
12. In 1833, the Factory Act made new arrangements for inspection of the mills. This Act was important because:
    a. the inspectors were local factory workers.
    b. the inspectors recommended new legislation.
    c. it gave employment to more people in the educated middle class.
    d. the inspectors had no local ties that might prevent them from carrying out their job; they were accountable to the national government rather than to local authorities, and they were encouraged to develop professional skills.
13. In India, Sati refers to:
    a. the seclusion of all women.
    b. unequivocal prohibition of the remarriage of widows.
    c. the rule requiring that children must marry at a young age.
    d. the suicide of widows.

(continued)

Presuming that you have never heard of Roop Kumar, what kind of person would be most likely discussed in a world history class? Probably not someone who came up with a *ludicrous* philosophy nor someone who was a stage actor. Furthermore, the name does not sound very Italian. That leaves the correct alternative—(c).

✦ **TABLE 5.3** ✦ **Continued**

14. Which system in India allowed the emperor to amass an army of cavalrymen:
    a. mansabdari.
    b. zamindar.
    c. Muharram.
    d. Aurangzeb.
15. Kwame Nkrumah led an African nationalist movement that attained independence:
    a. through a war of national liberation.
    b. by waging a peaceful struggle along with a negotiated settlement.
    c. by inciting a civil uprising among his countrymen.
    d. all of the above.

Scoring:
Count your correct answers using the key below:

1. c	2. c	3. c	4. d	5. b	6. b	7. c	8. b
9. c	10. d	11. a	12. d	13. d	14. a	15. b	

Interpreting Your Score:

Testwiseness	
High	11–15
Intermediate	6–10
Low	0–5

Flaws that are present in testwiseness scale questions. See the text for description of the flaws.

Question #	Test-Writing Flaw	Question #	Test-Writing Flaw
1	1	9	2
2	8	10	1
3	4	11	7
4	7	12	4
5	5	13	6
6	3	14	3
7	6	15	2
8	4		

2. *Either equivalence and/or contradiction among answers.* Sometimes there are 2 answers that are essentially the same. Assuming that there is only 1 correct answer, this can eliminate 2 of the alternatives. Conversely, if two items are exactly the opposite, 1 of them is most likely correct.

Example: The Proclamation of 1763

a. prevented colonists from settling in lands that were procured during the French and Indian wars.

b. provided financial incentives for settling in territory acquired in the French and Indian wars.

c. offered tax incentives to settlers for building a home in territory gained during the French and Indian wars.

d. all of the above.

Both alternatives (b) and (c) are similar and are the opposites of alternative (a). Alternative (d) is not possible as (b) and (c) contradict (a). Only alternative (a) remains as the possible correct answer. Remember that this strategy will work when there is *only 1* correct answer.

3. *Information in other questions provides the correct answer.* As you read through the test, you may notice that a later question contains information that will answer a previous question or vice versa.

Example:

Question 1. Voltaire was a notable Frenchman who made popular ideas that were innovative in science and society. These people were called

a. mercantilists.

b. Jacobians.

c. neo-Marxists.

d. philosophes.

Question 2. Philosophes were French thinkers who

a. made popular new ways of thinking about science and society.

b. started the French Revolution.

c. founded a famous university.

d. all of the above.

Overlapping information in the two questions, both of which discuss philosophes, leads to the correct answers in both question 1 (d) and question 2 (a).

4. *The correct answer is more likely to be very detailed and/or specific than the other alternatives. Correct answers also tend to be longer than incorrect alternatives.*

Example: Condorcet

a. believed in natural selection.

b. believed that developments in medical science would result in sweeping improvement in the length and quality of people's lives.

c. was an economist.

d. authored several books.

Answer (b) is not only longer but also more specific.

5. *A grammatical inconsistency exists between the question and the incorrect options, but not the correct option.*

Example: The Marshall Plan was

a. an American plan to invade France.

b. an British plan for the landings in North Africa.

c. an American plan to help European economies after the war.

d. a French plan for economic recovery.

Alternative (b) can be ruled out because the "an" should be "a."

6. *Inclusion of key words.* Incorrect answers are more likely to include all-inclusive words that appear more frequently in incorrect answers. Examples include terms such as *all, always, must, never, necessarily, invariably, no/none, every,* and *without exception.*

Example: Hong Rengan proposed that China should

a. expel all foreigners.

b. become a modern industrial nation.

c. never engage in foreign trade with Japan.

d. forever maintain a large army in Korea.

Note the inclusive terms in answers (a), (c), and (d).

7. *Similar words in question and correct answer.* Sometimes there is a resemblance between the terminology used in the question and that found in the answer.

Example: African nationalists in Nigeria

a. believed in Socialism.

b. were members of national parties, each of whom were identified with a particular ethnic group.

c. were generally anti-American in their orientation.

d. all of the above.

Note the use of similar terminology in the question and in answer (b).

8. *Logical position.* The correct answer will most likely *not* be one of the extremes of a set of options that can be placed in some natural order. For example, dates or numbers are often listed in this type of order.

Example: By the year ______, American women had acquired the right to vote.

a. 1900

b. 1910

c. 1920

d. 1930

In this example, avoid the first and last answer, and select from among the middle 2. The correct answer for this question is (c), 1920.

Note that sometimes you can use more than one of these rules to help you select the correct answer. For instance, example question 7 has both inclusive terms in the wrong answers *and* the correct answer is both longer and more specific than the alternatives. If all of the above strategies fail and you are faced with a complete guess, select alternative (c). Examination writers are *slightly* more likely to put the correct answer in this position than in any other.

After you have taken the testwiseness scale in Table 5.3, go back and see if you can identify which of the eight flaws listed above were present in each question. The actual flaws are listed at the end of the scale.

Lucinda McClain (1987) examined the behavior of 523 college students during objective test examinations in an introductory psychology course. She compared the behaviors of "A," "C," and "F" students. She found that the best students gave more thorough consideration to the alternatives on multiple-choice questions. The "A" students more often tried to anticipate the correct answer before reading the alternatives. They also were more adept at eliminating the incorrect alternatives. (See testwise suggestions just covered about ways to do this.) McClain reports that she has taught these strategies to students, who subsequently reported that they improved their exam scores.

TRUE-FALSE QUESTIONS. When answering true-false questions, make certain that you mark an answer true only if the statement is *always,* 100% true. Millman & Pauk (1969) give an example of the statement:

Families with more children are poorer than families with fewer children.

At first glance this statement may appear to be true because it is *generally* the case. However, the statement is *false* because it is not *always* true. Be certain that a qualifier such as *usually, generally,* or *on average* is present when judging that a statement such as this is indeed true.

CHANGING ANSWERS. There is a common myth among college students that you should always stick with your first answer on an objective test. Several studies have consistently found that wrong-to-right changes are more frequent than right-to-wrong changes (see review in Benjamin, Cavell, & Shallenberger, 1987). You should review your answers carefully and then feel no hesitation about changing them. Another issue revolves around whether you should skip difficult questions and return to them later. Research findings are inconsistent but suggest that skipping questions may benefit high-ability students while reducing the performance of average- or low-ability students.

Some Words of Caution

Finally, several words of caution are in order. First, a guessing strategy should *only* be used when there is *no* penalty for guessing. Make certain that this is the case before using any guessing strategy. Second, I wish to reiterate that guessing based on flaws in test construction should only be used as a last resort. Nothing will help you on an examination as much as adequate preparation. Your time on an exam is almost always better spent using your knowledge about the content of the material rather than trying to find a flaw in the test construction. Guessing based on content will usually improve your score more than guessing based on test flaws. Furthermore, these guessing strategies will not prove effective on major tests developed by nationally known testing companies. This includes tests such as the Scholastic Aptitude Test (SAT) and Graduate Record Exam (GRE). Companies that devise these types of tests are very aware of test construction flaws and avoid them in their test construction. In summary, testwiseness skills are *not* a panacea for lack of adequate test preparation.

SUMMARY

- Problem solving is an essential and sometimes critical aspect of our everyday lives.
- Problem solving involves understanding the problem, creating a hypothesis, testing the hypothesis, and checking results.
- Problem-solving strategies include trial and error, attempting every possible solution (algorithms), and rule-of-thumb strategies called heuristics. Simple solutions are usually best.
- Insight involves finding a solution to a problem quite suddenly.
- One problem-solving system called IDEAL involves identifying and defining the problem, exploring strategies, acting on those strategies, and examining and learning from the results.
- Obstacles to problem solving include lack of ability and knowledge. Confirmation bias, mental fixations about how a problem should be solved, functional fixedness, and emotional and cultural barriers also inhibit problem solving. In addition, an inappropriate reliance on authority may serve as an obstacle to problem solving.
- People frequently overestimate the degree of control they have over events that occur randomly. Individuals are also overly confident about the accuracy of their own judgments regarding both their own behavior and the behavior of others.
- The representativeness heuristic results in errors in judgment when we categorize things or individuals by their representative characteristics only, without taking other relevant information into account.
- Knowing the base rate at which a given thing or event occurs is important when making judgments about the probability of an event.
- The way we ask or frame a question has a powerful effect on how we answer the question. Most people avoid risk when a question is framed in terms of gain but are willing to assume a risk when the question is framed in terms of a loss.
- The availability and salience of memories of things can affect one's judgment of how commonly those things occur.
- We sometimes arrive at decisions inappropriately by making adjustments in information that is already available.
- Solutions to problems sometimes occur after we stop consciously thinking about them.
- Brainstorming involves solving problems by engaging in freewheeling discussions of ideas, being open to new ideas, and initially suspending judgments about the merits or demerits of alternative ideas.
- Computers can be used to aid in decision making and problem solving by weighing various solution alternatives and then making comparisons between all possible alternatives.
- Reasoning describes the logical rules people use to guide their thinking. The two major kinds of reasoning are deductive and inductive. In deductive reasoning, we draw conclusions based on what we already know, while in inductive reasoning we reach conclusions from specific facts or observations.
- Creativity involves the use of innovative ideas to solve problems in unique ways, and includes both convergent and divergent thinking. Creativity is measured by tests that measure an ability to find relationships between things that are remotely associated and by drawing-completion tests.
- Creative people are intelligent, produce numerous responses to a problem or question, and have usually developed expertise in the area in which they are creative.
- Age and cultural factors also affect one's creativity.
- Tips to becoming more creative include becoming motivated, maintaining high standards, believing in yourself, using analogies, affiliating with encouraging individuals, developing expertise, and being committed.

- It is particularly important to think clearly when reasoning about human behavior.
- To be useful, scientific theories must be able to be proven false. Personal testimonials are of very little value in advancing science.
- A placebo effect occurs when a treatment has no therapeutic value but is nevertheless perceived to be valuable.
- The more vivid or available a piece of information is in memory, the more likely we will use it to influence our decision-making or problem-solving behavior.
- When two events reliably occur together we say they are correlated. Correlation does not imply causality between the two events, nor does it tell us why the events are related. Sometimes we perceive an illusory relationship between two things when in fact no relationship exists.
- Large, random samples are best for making generalizations about a population.
- Testwiseness refers to cognitive abilities or skills that individuals can use to improve test scores. Tips for becoming testwise on multiple-choice questions include ignoring implausible answers, looking for equivalence and/or contradiction among answers, seeking the correct answer from other questions, and looking for detailed or specific answers. In addition, one should observe grammatical inconsistencies, inclusion of key words, and similarities between words in the question and the correct answer. The correct answer is likely not at the extremes of a set of options. For true-false questions, one should mark the answer true only if the statement is always true. Changing initial answers can improve one's test score.

KEY TERMS

algorithm: a problem-solving strategy that involves attempting every possible solution until a solution is reached.

analytic hierarchy process: a computer program that reaches a solution by weighing the various alternatives and then by making comparisons between all possible alternatives.

anchoring-and-adjustment heuristic: the tendency to reach decisions by making adjustments in information that is already available.

availability heuristic: the tendency to make judgments about an event based on how many memories of an event are immediately available in memory.

base-rate information: the frequency or probability for a given thing to occur.

brainstorming: techniques by which individuals and groups can effectively engage in problem-solving activities.

confirmation bias: the propensity to seek evidence that verifies our ideas as opposed to evidence that refutes them.

convergent thinking: the act of putting together a group of often disparate facts to find a solution to a question or problem.

correlated: the relationship that exists when two things reliably occur together.

creativity: the ability to produce innovative and valuable ideas and to solve problems in unique and useful ways.

cultural barriers: obstacles that arise due to cultural constraints that only allow problems to be solved in a certain way.

deductive reasoning: drawing conclusions from general statements about what is known to be true to specific and logically consistent conclusions.

divergent thinking: the ability to produce a variety of different responses to the same problem.

emotional barriers: inhibitions and the fear of appearing foolish in the eyes of others.

fixation: an inability to view a problem from a fresh perspective.

framing: asking a question in a certain way.

functional fixedness: a type of fixation in which we become preoccupied with the primary function of a device and fail to see how it could be used for some other purpose.

gambler's fallacy: the incorrect belief that the odds are in favor of some event because of the outcome of previous events.

heuristic: a "rule-of-thumb" problem-solving approach that involves using a strategy that previously worked in a similar situation.

illusory correlation: false perception in which it is thought that a relationship between two variables exists.

incubation effect: the phenomenon in which the answer to a problem suddenly appears after one stops thinking about the problem.

inductive reasoning: drawing conclusions from specific facts or observations.

insight: a sudden and unexpected realization of an answer to a problem; aka the "Aha!" phenomenon.

mental set: a type of fixation by which we try to solve a problem using only a solution that worked in the past.

overconfidence: the tendency to overestimate the accuracy of self-predictions of success or behavior.

overestimation of control: the act of overestimating the ability to control chance in situations where chance determines the outcome.

placebo effect: the tendency for people to report that any treatment has helped them, regardless of whether it has any actual therapeutic effect.

random sample: a sample in which every individual in the population has an equal chance of being included.

representative heuristic: the tendency to assume that something is a member of a category because it is similar to another item in that category.

representative sample: a group of individuals that have the same characteristics as the population from which they are drawn.

sample: a subset of individuals used to generalize findings to the population as a whole.

savant: an individual who has extraordinary abilities in one highly defined area, but is severely deficient in most other areas.

testwiseness: a set of skills that individuals can use to improve a test score no matter what the content area of the test; aka test sophistication or testmanship.

trial and error: the problem-solving approach that involves trying a variety of different responses until discovering a solution.

vividness effect: the tendency to use the information that is most accessible or easily retrieved to make decisions or solve problems.

6

MOTIVATION

We often use the word **motivation** to explain a person's behavior. We say that a student was highly *motivated* to earn an A in a particular class. Often a person's failure to succeed is attributed to a *lack of* motivation. When we are not motivated, our behavior can be greatly affected despite any abilities or potential that might exist. I have often heard professors describe a student by saying, "He was really smart, but he didn't do well in my class because he just wasn't motivated." What exactly is this phenomenon that we so often use to describe and explain behavior?

Psychologists do not always agree on a precise definition of motivation. Generally speaking, it is defined as the process that *initiates, sustains,* and *directs* behavior. Psychologists use their knowledge of motivation to try and explain why behavior occurs as opposed to how it occurs. To illustrate how motivation works, imagine that you develop a sudden hunger for a snack as you are reading this chapter. You set down the book and head to the kitchen to find something to eat. Assuming that you are successful in this search, you satisfy your hunger and resume your reading.

We would often be ashamed of our finest actions if the world understood all the motives which produced them.

LA ROCHEFOUCAULD
Maxims

Four Components of Motivation

This simple example illustrates the four basic components of motivation. Individuals first have a **need,** which is best defined as a condition that exists when we are deprived of something that we want or require. Needs can be quite diverse and include those that are (1) *biological,* consisting of primarily air, water, food, and sex; (2) *social,* comprised of love, affiliation, approval, power, and the like; and (3) *cognitive* or mental stimulation. Biological needs are of particular importance because, unlike social and cognitive needs, they are necessary for survival. Biological needs are also innate. In the preceding example, you developed a biological *need* for food as you were reading.

Biological needs often take precedence in initiating our behavior. If you are starving, a biological need will likely displace any social or cognitive needs. However, if you are only slightly hungry, a social need for affiliation or a cognitive need for intellectual stimulation may take precedence over the biological need. For instance, perhaps you find this book so intellectually stimulating that you cannot tear yourself away from it, even to eat!

The second component of motivation is **drive.** When a need exists, it creates a drive that impels or "pushes" our behavior. Drives are what activate behavior that is directed toward satisfying the need. Note the distinction between needs and drives. We have a *need* for food, which results in a hunger drive that activates the food-seeking behavior. The two are often thought of as representing the same thing, but it is important to note that one does not necessarily imply the other. Psychologists often use an example of food to illustrate the difference between need and drive. If you went without food for one day, you would have both a high need and drive for food. However, if you went without food for several days you would discover that your drive for food, or hunger level, diminishes even though your biological need for food continues to increase. Furthermore, we can have a drive in the absence of a need. An example might be our drive to satisfy our curiosity about something ("I wonder what's around the next bend in the road"), despite any clearly identified need. Returning to our previous example, your hunger drive activates your behavior to seek food.

The third component in motivation is a **goal,** that is, the objective of the behavior directed toward satisfying an existing need. For humans, goals can be quite diverse, ranging from a hamburger (biological) to a new friend (social) to new knowledge (cognitive). As you can see, the nature of the goal is generally linked to the nature of the need that is to be satisfied.

Some goals are more important to us than others. Psychologists refer to the value of a specific goal as its *incentive value.* Earlier I described drives as "pushing" our behavior. Incentives are things that exert a motivational "pull" on our behavior. Sometimes the incentive value goes well beyond the requirement to satisfy any need. A shiny new sports car may have a strong incentive value even though the car that we presently drive satisfies our need for transportation just fine. The incentive value of new knowledge can be particularly powerful. Many students find an irresistible urge to return to college after being out of school for awhile. By the time my son reached his final college semester, he informed me that he was completely "burned out" and never wanted to take another test. Sure enough, after a year of working, he missed the intellectual stimulation so much that he returned to take additional graduate courses. I have personally witnessed this phenomenon in students hundreds of times during my teaching career. Activities that are aversive to us today can sometimes acquire powerful incentive value a short time later.

In some circumstances, a goal has such low incentive value that it will not motivate us even if there is a strong need. You may be very hungry, but if the only food available is one you strongly dislike, then the goal (food) will have little incentive value and you will not be motivated to eat. Returning to our earlier example, the goal of your behavior would be some food substance that would satisfy or reduce your need for food.

The fourth and final component of motivation is the behavioral **response** that attains the goal and satisfies our need. Under some circumstances, responses are significantly impacted by the level of the incentive value. Avoiding or escaping from pain, or some other form of punishment for that matter, would represent such a situation. In our initial example, your responses to avoiding or escaping from hunger would be putting down the book and searching through the kitchen for a snack.

To summarize this four-step process, we initially have a *need* that results in some *drive.* Our behavior is then directed by a series of *responses* that allows us to attain a *goal* that satisfies or reduces our *need.* The strength of the drive is a reflection of both the incentive value of the goal and the strength of the need.

HOMEOSTASIS

The human body constantly strives to maintain biological conditions at an optimal and stable level, which is a process called **homeostasis.** For example, optimal body temperature is 98.6 °F. As body temperature rises above this level, blood flow to the body surface increases and perspiration begins, lowering the body temperature. If body temperature falls below this level, we begin shivering, which helps to raise our temperature. In addition to these involuntary responses, we also engage in voluntary

The swimmer is highly motivated to make a response in this situation. Although incentives are usually something positive, the incentives in this situation are illustrative of a circumstance where a person is strongly motivated to avoid them.

behaviors that help maintain body temperature, such as putting on or taking off clothing or moving to a different setting.

The human body is constantly monitoring a number of biological conditions, including blood pressure, various chemicals in the blood, water level in the body, and so forth. In addition, our body attempts to maintain an optimal level of sensory stimulation while we are awake. You have undoubtedly experienced times in noisy restaurants or other environments where there was too much sensory stimulation, either from noise, smells, tastes, or even some combination of these sensations. For almost all sensations, our body has some optimal value, called a **set point,** which it attempts to maintain. The concept of set point has assumed increasing importance in psychology in recent years and will be discussed further in this and other chapters.

AROUSAL

Whenever we have a drive motivating us, there is a level of physiological **arousal** that accompanies it. This physiological arousal can vary from moment to moment. When hungry, the sight or smell of food will initiate a complicated set of physiological reactions, including stomach contractions and salivation that prepare us to eat.

As with most sensations, people seek an *optimal level* of arousal. However, the optimal level of arousal varies depending on the individual. Humans learn to seek out activities that will bring an ideal arousal level. If you are feeling bored, you may go to an action or horror movie to bring some excitement and the corresponding physiological arousal into your life. Although people like to be aroused, they do not want to be *too* aroused. A thrilling action movie may arouse you to your optimum level while a horror movie might arouse you to an uncomfortable level. Conversely, a slow-moving drama may not be arousing enough. As with homeostasis, you will vary your choice of movies to bring about your personal optimal level of arousal. In Chapter 2, I discussed the effects of sensory deprivation on people's behavior. In conditions of extreme sensory deprivation, the arousal level is so low that it causes severe discomfort. When you study, you undoubtedly seek out an environment where the amount of sensory stimulation and subsequent arousal is optimal for you.

Marvin Zuckerman believed that people's bodies respond to new, unusual, surprising, or intense stimulation in different ways. He suggests that being at a high arousal level releases a drug called norepinephrine into our systems that makes us feel good. People who are considered to be high **sensation seekers** have nervous systems that operate best at high levels of arousal (Zuckerman, 1990).

High sensation seekers have been found to differ in several ways from low sensation seekers. They have more sexual partners; prefer spicy, sour, and crunchy foods to more bland foods; are more likely to smoke and abuse drugs; enjoy fast driving; and are more likely to get into legal trouble as teenagers. They enjoy more dangerous activities such as skydiving, surfing, and motorcycle riding. Low sensation seekers, on the other hand, are more nurturing, orderly, giving, and prone to activities such as stamp collecting. They enjoy the company of others, even when they are not around very exciting people. Males seek higher levels of sensation than do females. Finally, sensation seeking drops steadily as we get older.

Zuckerman has developed a test called the Sensation-Seeking Scale that measures the optimal amount of sensation that an individual seeks (Zuckerman, Eysenck, & Eysenck, 1978). An abbreviated form of this test is illustrated in Table 6.1. You can take this test and see whether you are an individual who seeks an above average or below average amount of sensation in your life.

Arousal and Task Performance

Arousal also affects how well we perform on a task. Task difficulty and arousal level interact in important ways. On an easy task, a relatively high level of arousal will result in maximum performance. However, while working on a very difficult or complex task, a lower level of arousal is optimum. In either case, moving below or above the optimum level will cause a decrease in performance. When students say that they are trying to get "up" for an examination, they are referring to this very phenomenon. As you can probably attest, if you know that a test is going to be extremely easy, it is harder to get "up" or sufficiently aroused for it. On the other hand, if you know that a test is going to be extremely difficult, arousal occurs more easily. In this circumstance, you want to keep the level of arousal lower in order to maximize performance.

APPLICATIONS

Students often complain that they were so "psyched out" or aroused for an examination that they could not perform well. How will you know when your arousal level is too high? A racing heart and accelerated breathing rate are good indicators. Your blood pressure likely will be high and your pupils will be dilated, although these reactions are not so easily detected.

There are things that you can do to keep your arousal at near optimum levels during task performance. If you have participated in athletics, you know that coaches often teach techniques to raise or lower your arousal level. Similarly, your ability to manipulate your arousal level as a college student may be important for optimal performance on examinations.

✦ TABLE 6.1 ✦ The Sensation-Seeking Scale

This is an abbreviated form of the scale developed by Zuckerman, Eysenck, and Eysenck (1978). Read the following statements and mark those that apply to you.

1. I sometimes like to do things that are a little frightening.
2. I like to try new foods that I have never tasted before.
3. I like wild, "uninhibited" parties.
4. I usually don't enjoy a movie or play where I can predict what will happen in advance.
5. I would like to try parachute jumping.
6. I like to explore a strange city or section of town by myself, even if it means getting lost.
7. I often like to get high (drinking liquor or smoking marijuana).
8. I have no patience with dull or boring persons.
9. I would like to learn to fly an airplane.
10. I would like to take off on a trip with no preplanned or definite routes or timetables.
11. I get very restless if I have to stay around home for any length of time.
12. I think I would enjoy the sensations of skiing very fast down a high mountain slope.
13. I would like to try some of the new drugs that produce hallucinations.
14. I like people who are sharp and witty even if they do sometimes insult others.
15. I often wish I could be a mountain climber.

Scoring: These are average values for males and females at different ages. If you fall well above these average values, you are probably a high sensation seeker.

Age	Males	Females
16–19	4–5	3–4
20–29	4	3
30–39	4	3
40–49	3	2

There are behaviors that will help you reach that optimum level of arousal. Here are some suggestions:

1. Test preparation. First and foremost, be well-prepared for the examination. This will lower your arousal level closer to optimal levels and maximize performance. Begin test preparation early and use distributed practice as opposed to cramming. Starting to study the night before the exam will almost guarantee that your physiological arousal will go through the stratosphere, impairing your ability to learn the material while studying and thus your subsequent performance on the exam.

2. Get enough sleep. Sleep deprivation may make your arousal level higher and will affect your performance on tests involving thought and analysis. Taking stimulants, including caffeine, will raise your arousal level and may also adversely affect your ability to think analytically.
3. Plan ahead. Collect all the materials that you will need early so you can avoid rushing around and gathering them right before the exam. Give yourself plenty of time to arrive at the testing location early and to collect your thoughts before beginning the test. Rushing in late or at the last minute will increase your arousal level even further.
4. Breathe deeply. Before beginning the test, take several deep breaths to relax. The common advice to "take a deep breath and count to ten" is more helpful than you might imagine.
5. Seek help. Most colleges and universities have counseling centers or other facilities where you can learn relaxation techniques and other methods to reduce your test anxiety.
6. Medications. There are several prescription medications available that will effectively control the physiological symptoms associated with arousal. These should only be considered when other techniques fail. You should speak with your physician about the potential side effects associated with these medications.

You might think that physiological arousal during tests and test anxiety are one and the same. Although they are not totally unrelated, psychologists do make an important distinction between the two. Test anxiety is comprised of two major dimensions: (1) worrying, or the negative thoughts and expectations about the possibility of failure and its consequences; and (2) emotionality. Only the emotionality component overlaps with physiological arousal. I will discuss test anxiety in greater detail in the next chapter.

Circadian Rhythms

I have described how momentary changes in arousal can affect performance. Our bodies also undergo more stable physiological changes called **circadian rhythms.** These changes occur in 24-hour cycles and affect a multitude of parameters, including body temperature, blood pressure, urine volume, and adrenaline output. Adrenaline output is particularly important because it affects our level of arousal. Our bodies are at their lowest arousal point about 2 or 3 hours before the time we normally awake and typically peak out in midafternoon. We are our most alert and best able to handle challenging and demanding tasks during the higher levels of arousal.

APPLICATIONS

You can throw your normal circadian rhythm off track by altering your regular sleep cycle. Students who pull an "all nighter" to get ready for an examination will disturb their normal body rhythm. Your body will be less alert, and you will need to spend more time to accomplish less. Psychologists recommend that if you have to deviate from your normal schedule, you should do it very gradually so that your body rhythm can adjust.

Another major disruption of body rhythm occurs during shift work. People who continually shift their work schedules make more errors and perform their jobs less effectively. You are better off working the same shift continuously because your body eventually adjusts to the new cycle.

Jet lag occurs from flying great distances and also disrupts your body rhythm. The effect is most noticeable when flying east as compared to flying west. Most individuals need 4 to 5 days to adjust when flying from the United States to Europe because there is a 7- to 10-hour time difference. Research on circadian rhythms suggests that it is best to fly late in the day when going west and early in the morning when traveling east. Many transcontinental airlines schedule their flights to accommodate these times.

Biorhythms

People sometimes confuse circadian rhythms with biorhythms. The theory of biorhythm states that the human body goes through three cycles: a 23-day physical cycle, a 28-day emotional cycle, and a 33-day intellectual cycle. These cycles allegedly begin at birth and persist throughout one's life. According to this theory, if your cycles line up on a given "critical day," your ability to perform certain tasks is affected. Reportedly, both good and bad effects are more likely to be experienced on these critical days.

This theory has been studied extensively. A thorough Canadian study examined 13,000 occupational accidents to see if the accidents corresponded to biorhythm critical days (Nelson, 1976). This study, as well as several others, has failed to offer any evidence to support the biorhythm theory.

INTRINSIC AND EXTRINSIC MOTIVATIONS

Sometimes people engage in a certain behavior strictly because they find the behavior pleasurable and reinforcing for its own sake. In these circumstances, it is **intrinsic motivation** that is driving the behavior. At other times, a person's behavior is based on the rewards and punishments the behavior may bring. These rewards and punishments represent **extrinsic motivations.** For example, if you are reading a book strictly for pleasure, you are doing so because of intrinsic motivation. If you are reading it because it was a homework assignment and you want a good grade on the examination, then your behavior is being driven by extrinsic motivation.

Usually our behavior is motivated by a combination of intrinsic and extrinsic motivations. For example, the book you are reading may be for a class that you voluntarily enrolled in because you found the topic interesting. Therefore, your reading of the book is partly for enjoyment and partly to earn a good grade on an examination.

Both animals and humans sometimes do things to help others without receiving any direct benefit to themselves. Such actions are called **altruistic behaviors** and are examples of the power of intrinsic motivations. Stopping and helping a homeless person lying on the sidewalk is an example because the behavior is performed without any expectation of extrinsic reward. There have been numerous documented cases where people have sacrificed their lives to save others, perhaps the ultimate example of a lack of extrinsic reward.

APPLICATIONS

If you want to motivate others, should you use extrinsic motivations or rely on the influence of intrinsic motivation? It depends. If you are employing people to work for you, they probably will not work for intrinsic motivation alone. On the other hand, if people are given more extrinsic motivation than necessary to perform a task, their intrinsic motivation to perform will decline. I referred to this as the *over-justification effect* in Chapter 3. As a child, I studied piano for many years. Occasionally, family friends or relatives would come to the house and ask me to play. In particular, I remember an elderly aunt who would bribe me to play by offering me a dollar (I distinctly remember that she always kept the money in her bra!). Others merely praised me after playing. I actually enjoyed playing more when I felt that I was not being bribed. To reiterate, do not reward people for activities they already enjoy doing; the reward may change their perception of the task, causing them to view the activity as work rather than pleasure. If your friend enjoys working on computers, rely on that interest to serve as sufficient motivation to help you out when you have a hardware problem. Offering advance payment for your friend's services may be counterproductive. Offering a reward *after* the service is provided, especially when it is unexpected, may be more rewarding both for the giver and the recipient.

BIOLOGICAL MOTIVES

Biologically based motives influence some important behaviors that are involved in our survival. These behaviors include eating, drinking, and sexual behavior, among other things. However, these behaviors are controlled by more than mere biological drives. There are multitudes of reasons why we engage in eating or sex, for example, which go beyond mere biological factors. In this section, I will concentrate on the two biological motives that drive eating and sexual behavior.

Eating

Eating is one of the most important behaviors that we do to ensure our survival. It is also one of the most pleasurable activities in which we regularly engage. This biological motivation to eat can, when not satisfied, take precedence over just about every motivation. If you have ever gone without eating for even a single day, you know how powerful this motive can be. A starving person is not thinking about the need for social approval, affiliation, or even sex.

A hungry people listens not to reason, nor cares for justice, nor is bent by any prayers.

SENECA
De Brevitate Vitae XVIII

Why do we eat? You might think that the simple answer to this query is "because we are hungry." However, if you think about your own behavior, I am sure that you will be able to recognize many instances where you engaged in eating when you were not hungry. We eat for a lot of reasons: boredom, to reduce anxiety, to fulfill social needs, and so forth. Hunger is only one cue, albeit an important one, that starts the eating response. Let us begin by looking at the role of hunger in eating.

Hunger

Hunger is a state that we experience nearly every day and yet researchers have found it a very complicated topic. Let's examine some of the factors that affect hunger.

Physiological Factors. When your body signals that it is hungry, what is the source of those signals? Most people would probably say hunger originates in the stomach. There is considerable research evidence to suggest that this is not the case. Does your stomach "rumble" when you are hungry? Some of the earlier researchers in eating believed that stomach contractions signaled the hunger sensation. To test this idea, researchers trained subjects to swallow a rubber tube with a balloon attached to the end. By inflating the balloon while it was in the stomach, contractions could be measured. While some of the early research indicated a correlation between stomach contractions and feelings of hunger, later research has not supported this finding. Therefore, psychologists have ruled out stomach contractions as a significant factor in feeling hungry.

In fact, there is increasing evidence that the stomach plays little, if any, role in the sensation of hunger. Researchers have cut the sensory nerves from the stomachs of animals so that stomach sensations are completely blocked. These animals continue to eat normally. Some people have had their stomachs removed surgically because of cancer or large ulcers. Such individuals continue to report normal feelings of hunger (Inglefinger, 1944).

Recent evidence suggests that the body's monitoring of nutrient levels accounts for both the feeling of hunger and **satiety** (the feeling of fullness). After we eat, enzymes in our saliva, stomach, and small intestine convert food into glucose (a simple sugar), fats, and amino acids. The sugars and amino acids are carried in the bloodstream to the liver and eventually to the brain. A small structure located in the base of the brain called the **hypothalamus** monitors the levels of glucose and other substances in the blood. The hypothalamus also receives signals from the liver, which sends signals when nutritional levels are low, and from the upper part of the small intestine. The hypothalamus apparently collates information from these three sources and signals us that we are hungry (Hoyenga & Hoyenga, 1984).

Some early research suggested that the hypothalamus played a critical role in both the starting and stopping of the eating response. There is an area located on the side of the hypothalamus that, when electrically stimulated, will cause an animal to immediately begin eating even if it has just completed a large meal. Another area located on the bottom-middle part of the hypothalamus signals the body to stop eating. If this area is destroyed, animals will eat voraciously even when their stomachs are full. Rats that have undergone this procedure will continue to eat until they become so large that they can barely move (see Figure 6.1). To put this in perspective, these rats gain weight that would be the equivalent of a 150-pound person gaining 700 pounds. Although the hypothalamus is recognized as an important player in both hunger and satiety, the exact manner in which it functions remains largely unknown. The physiological basis of hunger has turned out to be an extremely complex matter and continues to be actively researched. Many researchers feel that the eventual solution to the problem of overeating and obesity will come from research breakthroughs in this area.

Figure 6.1

Damage to one area of the hypothalamus causes rats to eat uncontrollably until they become grossly obese. This rat weighs the equivalent of a 1,000-pound person.

Set Point. One theory of weight regulation that is gaining popularity among scientists is the notion that we have a biological set point, a weight that the body steadfastly maintains (Nisbett, 1972; Powley & Keesey, 1970). It is believed that the brain establishes this set point by monitoring sugar and fat levels in the body as well as other chemicals in the brain. Any attempt to alter body weight above or below this set point is counteracted by altering metabolic rate and hunger. Obesity researchers talk about these countermeasures in terms of how the body *defends* its set point. When weight drops below this biologically determined level, metabolism is slowed down to conserve energy. One study with obese subjects reported a 17% decline in resting metabolic rate with only a 3% reduction in weight during a weight reduction program (Bray, 1969). This is why people who lose weight often feel less energetic and are less likely to engage in vigorous physical activity. The body apparently has an amazing ability to become more efficient in utilizing food under these circumstances. In addition to slowing down metabolism, the body also increases the hunger level to ensure that more food will be ingested in order to raise the weight back to the set point. Not only does hunger increase, but foods that were previously unappealing suddenly become much more desirable. To make matters even worse, when food intake is normalized after weight loss, the body is able to preferentially redeposit any nutrients as body fat (Dulloo & Girardier, 1990; Ozelci, Romsos, & Leveille, 1978).

When weight rises above the set point, the opposite happens. Hunger level decreases, metabolic efficiency decreases, and the urge to engage in physical activity increases. You may have noticed this in yourself. When we put on a few extra pounds, the urge to get out and exercise begins to increase.

The greater the deviation about the set point, the more powerful these compensatory mechanisms become. You can think of this by visualizing a rubber band. When the rubber band is in a resting state or set point, there is no tension on it. However, the more the rubber band is stretched and the farther it deviates from its set point, the greater the tension to bring it back to its natural resting state. The effect of sustained dieting is ". . . to pit the individual's 'will' against an untiring opponent, the set point mechanism" (Bennett, 1984, p. 331).

In evolutionary terms, the biological set point makes perfect sense. Historically, the greatest threat to organisms' survival and their ability to reproduce has been food shortages. It should be no surprise that organisms have evolved mechanisms to replenish and enlarge fat stores efficiently when food becomes available following periods of famine. Organisms that most efficiently increase their fat stores will survive future famines, live to reproduce, and preferentially contribute to the gene pool.

How can you determine what your personal set point is? It's easy. Simply make no concerted effort to gain or lose weight and observe the weight level at which you stabilize. This is your personal set point. Love it or hate it, it is yours.

APPLICATIONS

What can we do to alter our set point? This is a matter of considerable debate by researchers in weight regulation. Unfortunately, there is no "magic bullet" for resetting our set point. Genetic factors appear to play an important role in our metabolic rate, which is critical in the establishment of the set point (Price, 1987). Some people inherit a faster metabolic rate than others. These are the people who can seemingly eat unlimited amounts of food and never gain a pound. The genetic predispositions are very powerful and probably account for the high correlation between the weight levels of children and their parents. Unfortunately, there is nothing you can do to change these genetic factors.

It also appears that our set point increases as we age. Hormonal disruptions, such as those that occur during pregnancy or menopause, may also raise the set point. Living in a cold climate or smoking also may result in small changes to our set point. The health risks attendant with smoking, however, greatly outweigh any minor benefits that might accrue in lowering one's set point. There is some evidence to suggest that adopting an active, sustained exercise regime may help lower the set point and maintain it at a reduced point. Very slow, sustained weight loss may also have some effect although this has not been proven definitively. Finally, some physical illnesses may be accompanied by changes in one's set point. My wife developed severe food allergies when she was 30 years old. This required a drastic change in her eating habits and eventually led to a significant change in her taste preferences. The foods that she was able to eat were lower in calories, which led to a stable weight loss that has persisted over time.

Sociocultural Factors

More than just blood glucose levels are at work when we decide to start or stop eating. We often eat in the absence of hunger. Eating oftentimes plays an important social function in human interactions. For example, we eat more if other people are also eating (Redd & de Castro, 1992). Preferences for certain foods and tastes are heavily influenced by our culture. Within the American culture, there are tremendous variations in food preferences, as evidenced by the immense variety of ethnic cuisines available. Our culture also dictates that we eat three meals a day whether we are hungry or not. These factors often override the physiological signals for hunger or satiety. Most employers give a specific time for lunch during which employees eat regardless of their levels of hunger. Our culture also dictates that the largest meal be eaten at dinnertime compared to European cultures where the largest meal occurs at lunch and a smaller meal at dinnertime. Coincidentally, the rate of obesity in European countries is much lower than in America.

Learning

The role of learning also influences our eating habits. By frequently eating in certain circumstances, such as while watching TV, habits are classically conditioned and difficult to extinguish (see Chapter 2). When I was much younger (and much thinner!), I used to enjoy a snack every night while watching the late news. When I began to gain weight, I discontinued this practice but, for years afterwards, experienced the urge to eat whenever the evening news came on.

We also acquire preferences for certain tastes, such as hot or spicy foods. America's preference for high-caloric, high-fat dishes that are easily available in fast-food establishments undoubtedly has contributed to our country's rapidly increasing rate of obesity.

Psychological Factors

Several psychological states have been shown to lead to overeating, such as boredom (Crisp, 1970), as well as anxiety and depression (Greeno & Wing, 1994). When these psychological states are present, the eating response frequently occurs, even in the absence of hunger.

Do people become obese because of some emotional disturbance? Freudian psychoanalysts have hypothesized, for instance, that some women intentionally become obese as a defense against unwanted sexual advances from men. These psychoanalytic views notwithstanding, there is little evidence that people become overweight because of emotional disturbance. On average, obese people exhibit the same incidences of emotional problems as nonobese individuals (Wadden & Stunkard, 1987). Severely obese people do report higher incidences of loneliness and depression, but this is likely to be a consequence of obesity and not a cause.

Taste, Smell, and Texture

Food preferences for most Americans are hamburgers, cheese, bacon, butter, ice cream, and mayonnaise. The taste of whole milk is greatly preferred to that of 2% or skim milk. What accounts for American's preferences for these types of foods? The answer can be summed up in a single word: *fat.* Americans love fatty foods. Specifically, they like the sensations of taste, smell, and texture that accompany eating fatty foods (Schiffman, Graham, Sattely-Miller, & Warwick, 1998). There have been repeated warnings by leading health organizations about the dangers of high dietary fat. They recommend that only 20% to 25% of calories should come from fat. Despite this, most Americans continue to get over 33% of their calories from fat (Drewnowski, 1990). Several fast-food restaurants tried offering low-fat alternatives but found little demand for these foods. Consequently, they have dropped that low-fat food line. These restaurants returned to offering high-fat beef and cheese dishes. One example is Taco Bell, which began offering an item called "gordita," which means "little fatty" in Spanish.

Is dietary fat a major determinant of body fat? Not according to research by W. C. Willett at the Harvard School of Public Health (1998). He reports that fat consumption within the range of 18 to 40% of energy appears to have little, if any, effect on body fatness. Willett also notes that while Americans have significantly decreased the amount of fat in their diet during the last 2 decades, there has been a correspondingly large increase in obesity. People who go on a low-fat diet show a short-term drop in weight, but compensatory mechanisms appear to counteract this weight loss after about 1 year. Willett concluded that diets high in fat are not the primary cause of excess body fat and that reductions in fat will not be a solution for obesity. A recent Harvard-sponsored conference with 50 worldwide experts on dietary fat concluded it does not matter how much fat individuals eat as long as they eat an otherwise healthy diet. The experts did, however, recommend the restriction of animal fats and partially hydrogenated oils, such as are found in solid shortening.

Why do we love dietary fat so much? At one time in our evolutionary past, fatty foods were probably preferred because they allowed for the rapid storage of fat. This offered greater survival value during the inevitable periods of famine. Famines in the United States are no longer a problem, and this formerly adaptive behavior is now less adaptive. Research into the human preference for fatty foods has concluded

Many fast-food chains and more traditional restaurants have tried offering low-fat alternatives on their menus. Americans have shunned these offerings, and many restaurants have dropped these items from their menus.

that our preference for fat is due to both learned as well as genetic factors (Warwick & Schiffman, 1992). The preference for fat-rich foods is influenced mainly by the sensory appeal related to taste, smell, and texture as opposed to the body's energy needs (Drewnowski, 1995). Whatever the reason, America's love affair with fatty foods continues.

Recently, a wide variety of fat replacements have been developed that mimic the texture and taste of fats. These are now included in many snack foods, including potato chips and ice cream. Contrary to the expectations of many, Olestra, the widely promoted fat substitute from the Procter & Gamble Corporation, has only boosted potato chip and snack sales slightly. Whether these fat substitutes will successfully trick the human body into believing the demand for fat has been satisfied remains to be seen.

Internal versus External Cues

The **externality theory** states that the eating response in obese individuals is more easily triggered by external cues, such as the sights, smells, or sounds of food (Schachter, 1971). Even an external cue such as a clock can trigger the eating response in an obese person by signaling that it is mealtime. This theory also proposed that obese subjects would not work hard to obtain food and would eat greater quantities when the food appeared attractive. According to this theory, eating in normal weight individuals is primarily governed by internal cues, such as the hunger

Externality theory postulates that external cues are the most important cues in eliciting the eating response in obese individuals.

cues that come from inside our bodies. Several ingenious experiments support the externality theory (Schachter & Rodin, 1974). In one experiment, subjects were placed in a room with a clock that was altered to speed up. Obese subjects ate when the clock said it was time to eat while normal weight subjects ate when they felt hungry (Schachter & Gross, 1968). In another experiment, obese subjects were found to eat more sandwiches when they were wrapped in a clear plastic wrap rather than an opaque wrapping. The wrapping had no effect on normal weight subjects.

The externality theory has generated a great deal of interest in psychology, but subsequent research has suggested that it is of limited value. One difficulty with the theory is in the determination of whether obesity leads to increased external cue sensitivity or whether external sensitivity leads to obesity.

After reading about all of these weight-regulation mechanisms, you may conclude that the body does not do a very good job in keeping body weight stable. Actually, just the opposite is true. Most of us keep our weight relatively stable from year to year even though it is often higher than we would like. Your body does a very good job of regulating the calorie input to bring this about. If your exercise levels stayed constant and you consumed, on average, only 20 calories more per day, you would gain an additional 2 pounds a year.

Despite advances in our knowledge about the eating response, much information remains unknown. In fact, as more scientists continue to study this matter, the more complex their explanations appear to be.

Weight and Obesity

Obesity has traditionally been defined as a weight that is 20% (or more) greater than the recommended weight for an individual's height. More recently, a measure called the body-mass index (BMI) has been used. The body-mass index, which measures the ratio of body weight to height, is calculated by dividing weight (Wgt) in kilograms (kg) by height (Hgt) in meters squared (m^2) or [$BMI = Wgt\ (kg)/Hgt\ (m)^2$]. The chart in Table 6.2 will allow you to quickly calculate your personal BMI. The United States federal government has issued guidelines that recommend people keep their BMI under 25. BMI values exceeding 30 are considered obese. Using these guidelines, over one-third of Americans are obese, an increase from one-fourth only a few years ago.

C. Everett Koop, the former U.S. surgeon general, has recommended a low-calorie diet and increased physical activity for individuals with a BMI between 27 and 29. For BMIs from 30 to 39, he recommends these measures plus drug therapy and a very low calorie diet. Individuals with BMIs of 40 and over are considered to be at extremely high risk for health problems. You should be aware that not everyone agrees with these guidelines or with the advisability of dieting when an individual is only moderately overweight.

More die in the United States of too much food than of too little.

JOHN KENNETH GALBRAITH
The Affluent Society

Obesity and Dieting

David Garner and Susan Wooley are two of the world's leading authorities on weight regulation and eating disorders. They have reviewed the findings of over 300 studies on both behavioral and dietary treatments for obesity (Garner & Wooley, 1991). Their conclusions may surprise you.

The majority of adolescent and young adult women today report that they feel fat, even when their weight falls within the normal range. This has led Judith Rodin and her colleagues to characterize the dissatisfaction with body size and shape that is endemic to young women as "normative discontent" (Rodin, Silberstein, & Striegel-Moore, 1985). Two-thirds of high school girls are trying to lose weight, and recent findings suggest that girls as young as 7 years old are dissatisfied with their body size (Gardner, Friedman, Stark, & Jackson, 1999).

There are hundreds of diets and dietary programs for treating the overweight at any given time. Many of the more popular ones have been developed by physicians or others with credentials in the health sciences. There are 2 indisputable facts about these various diet schemas: (1) virtually *all* the programs demonstrate moderate success in short-term weight loss, and (2) virtually *no* evidence exists that significant weight loss can be maintained over the long term by the vast majority of people (Garner & Wooley, 1991, p. 733). Several studies indicate that the weight is gradually regained over time and that many dieting individuals end up eventually weighing more than when they started. Many treatments for obesity report successful weight loss over short periods of time, but very few have conducted follow-up studies for periods covering several years. The follow-up studies that are available typically report that all the weight lost is regained by up to 90 to 95% of the individuals after a period of 4 to 5 years. Recall earlier, I discussed that the increased metabolic efficiency of people who are below their set-point weight resulted in the body's effective propensity to translate nutrients into body fat. The few studies that showed a sustained body weight loss for periods of 4 to 6 years concerned individuals who

I'm fat, but I'm thin inside. Has it ever struck you that there's a thin man inside every fat man, just as they say there's a statue inside every block of stone?

GEORGE ORWELL
Coming Up for Air

✦ TABLE 6.2 ✦ Measuring Your Body-Mass Index (BMI)

Body-mass index is the ratio of body weight to height [BMI = Wgt (kg)/ Hgt (m)^2], and is commonly used to determine whether an individual is overweight. To measure your BMI, lay a straightedge across the lines corresponding to your height and weight. Where the straightedge crosses the middle line is your personal BMI. Individuals with a BMI at or above 30 are considered obese. Individuals with BMIs of 40 and over are considered by many medical professionals to be at high risk for a variety of medical problems.

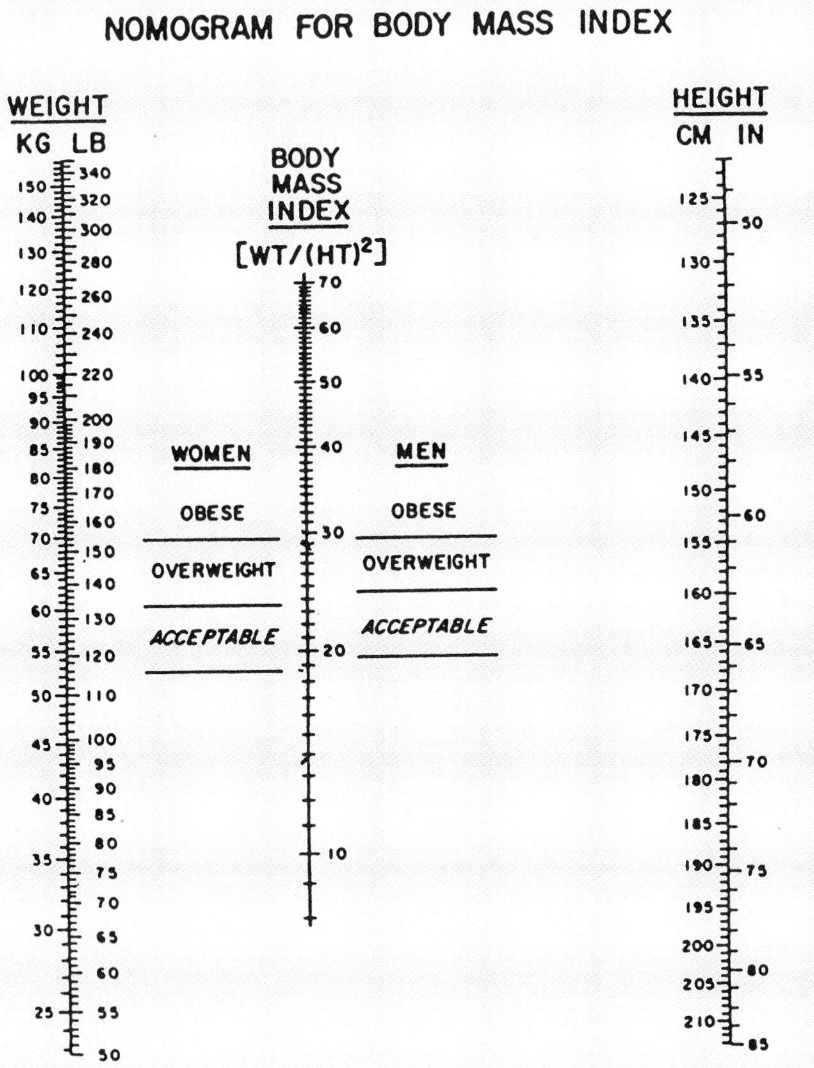

continuously endured low-calorie diets. Garner and Wooley characterize their eating patterns as ". . . much more like those of individuals who would earn a diagnosis of anorexia nervosa than like those with truly 'normal' eating patterns" (Garner & Wooley, 1991, p. 745).

Long-term dieters usually undergo many cycles of weight loss and subsequent weight gain over a period of many years, a phenomenon often referred to as "yo-yo" dieting. There is convincing evidence that efficiency of the body to store fat is enhanced by such repeated cycles of weight loss and gain. The consequence is that the person weighs more after each dieting cycle. Yo-yo dieting also leads to greater accumulations of body fat (Dulloo & Girardier, 1990) and increased cardiovascular risks (Reed, Contreras, Maggio, Greenwood, & Rodin, 1988).

Perhaps the most compelling reasons for dieting are the alleged health risks that accompany obesity. Despite this widespread belief, no reliable pattern of association has been found between premature death and relative weight (Ernsberger & Haskew, 1987). Recent research suggests that it is the *body build* and *distribution of body fat* that are more important in predicting mortality. More health problems develop when there is a large concentration of fat around the abdomen, resulting in an "apple shape," rather than when body fat distributes more evenly *below* the waist, resulting in a "pear shape." In some cases, obesity is associated with a lower incidence of disease, including respiratory disease, infectious disease, osteoporosis, and several other ailments (Ernsberger & Haskew, 1987). Furthermore, there are very few studies in the medical literature that indicate mortality risk is reduced by weight loss. On the contrary, some studies suggest that weight loss increases the risk of death (Garner & Wooley, 1991, p. 754). The few studies that have demonstrated a relationship between obesity and mortality have found this relationship only with individuals who are extremely obese, usually defined as at least 50% over their ideal body weight. Interestingly, a study of Harvard alumni found that thinness, not obesity, was associated with an increased risk of mortality (Paffenbarger, Hyde, Wing, & Hsieh, 1986). The Duchess of Windsor once claimed, "You can never be too rich or too thin." Unfortunately, many American females, from young girls to adults, have adopted this as their mantra. Mortality data suggest that, indeed, you can be too thin.

Dieting may also be damaging psychologically. One famous study involved 36 young men who volunteered to reduce their usual caloric intake by one-half (Keys, Brozek, Henschel, Micklson, & Taylor, 1950). They volunteered for this semistarvation study as an alternative to military service. After 6 months, the men had lost about 25% of their former body weight. Most participants experienced periods of depression, anxiety, irritability, anger, and mood swings (Keys et al., 1950). Nearly 20% experienced extreme emotional deterioration, and some even required hospitalization for psychological distress. Even after regaining the lost weight, several men became more depressed, irritable, argumentative, and negativistic than they had been during their semistarvation period. Several more recent studies further documented the psychological deterioration that accompanies dieting in the nonobese (Garner & Wooley, 1991). They observe that weight loss may make us feel better about ourselves temporarily, but it also sets the stage for another failure experience in the 90 to 95% of the individuals who cannot sustain the weight loss. These deleterious psychological effects probably can be confirmed by the observations of nearly anyone who has watched a spouse or friend undertake long-term dieting. I remember from my childhood the trepidation our family felt when we learned that my mother was about to go on yet another diet. We knew that she would be in a foul mood for the duration.

APPLICATIONS

If dieting is indeed ineffectual, and likely dangerous to your physical and mental health, what alternatives exist for the one-third of Americans who are overweight? After reviewing the research findings on treatment alternatives, Garner and Wooley (1991) make the following suggestions:

1. Increase exercise. Although exercise alone will not result in permanent weight loss, coupling it with reduced caloric intake offers some hope. Even moderate exercise will increase longevity and has numerous other medical benefits, such as lowering blood pressure and cholesterol levels. Exercise also provides benefits to one's self-concept and mood, especially those of depressed individuals.
2. Normalize food intake. Recognize that dieting is self-defeating. Eat and enjoy *every* type of food *in moderation.* Avoid categorizing certain foods as "good" or "bad." Eat three meals a day (obese individuals often skip breakfast).
3. Modify negative body image. Many people, especially those who are overweight and dieting, dislike their bodies. This negative body image is often accompanied by poor self-esteem, social anxiety, vulnerability to depression, and general psychological distress. It is increasingly common in our society to judge one's self-worth almost exclusively on one's weight or shape. You may need to seek professional assistance to modify a negative body image. A cognitive-behavioral intervention has been shown to be particularly beneficial in this regard (Garner & Wooley, 1991). I will describe this therapeutic approach in greater detail in chapter 10.

Finally, is there a safe and effective weight-loss pill in our future? There are currently about a dozen weight-loss and weight-management drugs in development. Pharmaceutical companies are spending millions of dollars in developing these new drugs and in testing their effectiveness. Some work to block the absorption of body fat, others suppress the appetite, and yet others speed up metabolism. Many have unpleasant side effects. It will be at least several years before a safe and effective answer is found. Some researchers believe that drugs alone will never manage appetite and weight control.

Sexual Motivation

The importance of sexual motivation, in both humans and animals, cannot be overstated. Without the urge to engage in sexual behavior, a species would quickly disappear. The drive to have sex differs from other drives that influence our behavior. Unlike other drives, sex does not result in homeostasis. After we eat a large meal, food stimuli, no matter how enticing, will not elicit an eating response. However, the

"You're serious about no snacking between meals, then?"

Just about every solution possible to reducing food intake has been tried at one time or another, all with very limited effectiveness.

sex drive can be aroused almost immediately after the sexual act. Men require a brief recovery period to perform sexually, but the sex drive can be aroused almost immediately. Also, unlike hunger, the amount of the drive is not directly related to the amount of time that has elapsed since the drive was last satisfied. While there may be some increase in sexual desire as time elapses, it does not continue to steadily increase in the manner that hunger does. The sex drive is also unique in that humans seek both its arousal as well as its reduction. Compare this to other drives. We do not typically engage in behaviors to intentionally make us hungrier or thirstier.

When it comes to sexual motivation, important differences appear that differentiate humans from other animal species. In most mammalian species, the sexual act occurs only when the female is fertile. This is clearly not the case in humans who regularly engage in sex at times of the month when the woman is unable to conceive and after menopause when conception is no longer possible.

There is no greater nor keener pleasure than that of bodily love—and none which is more irrational.

PLATO
The Republic III.403

Biological Factors

In most mammals, sex hormones activate sexual behavior. For females this hormone is **estrogen** and for males it is **testosterone.** These hormones fluctuate in normal cycles with female mammals becoming most interested in sex during the peak of hormonal production. Male hormone levels remain more constant and do not correlate as closely with interest in sex. However, male mammals that have been castrated and cannot produce testosterone gradually lose their interest in sexual behavior.

Although short-term cycles of hormones do not affect human sexual desire, longer-term shifts apparently do. Interest in sexual behavior increases with puberty when there is a rapid increase in sex hormones. Anything that prevents or delays pubertal development also delays or retards sexual desire. For humans it can be concluded that sex hormones are a *necessary, but not sufficient,* precursor for sexual behavior. There are many other cues that must be present, in addition to the hormonal factors, for us to become sexually aroused.

External Cues

One sure-fire sexual arousal cue, for both animals and humans, is physical contact. Touching the genitals is a widespread form of sexual foreplay in every culture. The role of smell is less clear. It is known that smells, called **pheromones,** often play an important role in animal sexual arousal. If you have had a dog or cat in heat, you have probably observed the powerful ability of these smells to attract neighboring animals to your yard. The role that pheromones play in human sexual arousal is not as clearly demonstrated. Recently, some perfume and cologne manufacturers have added synthetic human pheromones to their products with claims that they will make the wearer instantly more attractive to the opposite sex. At present, there is no scientific evidence to substantiate such claims. If smell does play any role in human sexual arousal, it is a much less important cue than it is for animals.

One cue that differentiates humans from other animals is the role of erotic material. Humans have the unique ability to be sexually aroused by either looking at or hearing about descriptions of sexual behavior. Contrary to popular belief, both men and women find such erotic material sexually arousing, although women's stated preference for such material is weaker than men's. Erotic material does not have to be an external cue. Humans have the ability to become aroused merely by thinking about such sexual images. In fact, many people use such erotic thoughts to enhance their sexual pleasure during intercourse or masturbation.

The introduction of a new sexual partner is also arousing. This has been demonstrated in several different animals as well as in humans. Animals that are allowed to engage in sexual behavior until they show no further interest will resume engaging in sex if a new partner is introduced. This has come to be called the **Coolidge effect** because of a story told about former U.S. president Calvin Coolidge. The president and his wife were touring an experimental farm where chickens were bred. Mrs. Coolidge asked if a single rooster mated only one time a day. The farmer leading the tour replied that, to the contrary, a rooster mates dozens of times each day. Mrs. Coolidge is reported to have replied, "Tell that to the president." When the president reached this part of the tour, his wife's message was delivered to him. He asked the farmer whether the rooster mated dozens of times with the same hen or with several different hens. He was told that many different hens were involved. "Tell *that* to Mrs. Coolidge," the president reportedly replied. The Coolidge effect illustrates that the sexual urge can be reinvigorated by an appropriate external cue even if the sexual drive appears to have been satisfied by recent sexual activity. Put another way, variety is the spice of life.

Cultural Factors

The stimuli or circumstances that result in sexual arousal are strongly rooted in our culture. Anthropologists who have examined sexual practices in various cultures have discovered an amazing variety of what is considered desirable or acceptable. While heterosexual behavior is universal in all cultures, many cultures embrace homosexual behaviors as well. Culture influences many aspects of sexual activity, including the time of day in which sex is engaged, the appropriate age at which sexual behavior begins, sexual positions, and the frequency of intercourse. Some cultures even find sex with animals acceptable, which is an act called **bestiality.** What is arousing in one culture may be offensive in another. Perhaps the best example of this is body size. Americans are enamored with thinness and find this characteristic to be sexually arousing. Many other cultures find thinness to be completely aversive for sexual arousal. Cultural dictates can change rapidly over time, though. Thinness in a female partner was not considered sexually arousing in the United States until the 1920s.

Learning and Sex

Both classical and operant conditioning play an important role in sexual behavior. In Chapter 3 I described how classical conditioning can result in sexual fetishes. In this process, a previously neutral stimulus, such as shoes or underwear, becomes paired with sexual arousal and subsequently acquires the ability to elicit sexual arousal. Sometimes feelings of sexual arousal are paired with shame or disgust that can lead to later sexual dysfunction (Kaplan, 1974).

Operant conditioning shapes our sexual behavior by pairing pleasurable sensations with certain responses. We learn to repeat behaviors that lead to pleasant sexual consequences and to avoid those that lead to unpleasant consequences. Observational learning also plays an important role. Numerous opportunities exist to model the sexual behavior of others. Increasingly, we are exposed to sexual behavior in the movies and on television, in magazines and books, and even on the Internet. Through observational learning, we learn what behaviors get rewarded and imitate those behaviors. Unfortunately, the sexual behavior modeled in the mass media and movies is often unrealistic and may lead to unreasonable expectations and dissatisfaction in many individuals. The sexual experience is rarely like it is portrayed in the movies.

Sexual Orientation

Sexual orientation comes in four varieties. Those who seek out and engage in sexual relations with members of the opposite sex are considered **heterosexuals.** In all cultures, heterosexuality is the primary sexual orientation. Those who engage in sexual relations *only* with members of the same sex are **homosexuals.** Because of the social stigma attached to homosexuality, it is difficult to estimate precisely how frequently this orientation exists. Although estimates vary, the consensus is that between 2 and 3% of all adults are exclusively homosexual. Homosexuality is almost twice as common in males as in females. Homosexual behavior is frequently observed in the animal kingdom although humans are the only species where individuals adopt an *exclusive* homosexual orientation.

Bisexuals enjoy sexual relations with members of both sexes. It is estimated that around 2 to 3% of adults fall in this category. The fourth category is individuals who have *no* sexual interest in either sex. These individuals are referred to as **asexual** and constitute a very small proportion of the adult population. Asexual individuals should not be confused with individuals who have voluntarily chosen to abstain from sex, which is referred to as **celibacy.** Most celibate individuals have normal sexual interests but have chosen sexual abstention for moral or religious reasons.

It is also important to distinguish between an individual who is a homosexual and someone who has occasionally engaged in homosexual behaviors. Homosexual activities are not unusual in adolescent boys, and one study has estimated that at least 20% of American adult men have had a homosexual experience (Fay, Turner, Klassen, & Gagnon, 1989). Most studies indicate a lower incidence for women.

There are many commonly held misconceptions about homosexuality. There is no indication that homosexuality is related to child-rearing practices or to problems that a child had with his or her parents. One common misconception is that male homosexuality results from parenting by a domineering mother and a passive father. Homosexuality is not associated with the levels of sex hormones present in the blood, and giving individuals additional sex hormones does not change their sexual orientation. Nor does sexual abuse or a forced homosexual experience when the person is young cause homosexuality. The only behavior that has been shown to be related strongly to homosexuality is gender nonconformity in childhood (Bell, Weinberg, & Hammersmith, 1981).

Contrary to the beliefs of some, homosexuality is *not* a disorder. The American Psychiatric Association removed homosexuality from its official list of mental disorders in 1973 and stated explicitly that homosexuality by itself does not constitute a psychiatric disorder. Various psychological and psychiatric treatments for homosexual behavior have failed to be effective, and most therapists today do not attempt to alter sexual orientation. Several studies consistently have demonstrated that homosexuals are no more or less well adjusted than are heterosexuals. The problems that they face are often related to the attitudes of others toward homosexuality. Homosexuals frequently face rejection by their family and encounter discrimination in employment and housing. Despite views to the contrary, homosexuals do not try to seduce others into their sexual orientation and are no more of a threat to young children than are heterosexuals.

There has been considerable disagreement about what causes homosexuality. Sigmund Freud was of two minds on the subject. He believed that homosexuality was a constitutional predisposition and that early childhood experiences were responsible. In his view, the absence of a same-sex parent and the frequency of male adolescent homosexual experiences accounted for this behavior. These views have been subsequently disproved by recent research findings.

Contemporary views of homosexuality suggest that there are probably two factors responsible: heredity and prenatal hormonal exposure. The hereditary factor is indicated by the fact that homosexuality is seen in twins who are genetically related. In identical twins, homosexuality appears in both pairs 52% of the time but in both pairs of fraternal twins only 22% of the time (Bailey & Pillard, 1991). This indicates a genetic role because identical twins share a more similar genetic makeup than do fraternal twins. The role of prenatal hormone exposure is supported by studies that indicate homosexual males have brains that show size differences in two subregions of the hypothalamus (Swaab & Hofmann, 1990; LeVay, 1991). It has been suggested that these size differences might be accounted for by exposure to differential patterns of hormones before the child was born.

Both of these findings suggest that homosexual orientation may be at least partly biological in nature and is not made by choice. Most psychologists believe that experiences also play an important role, but what experiences are most crucial remains unclear.

Whatever the causes, homosexuals continue to receive condemnation and discrimination in their daily lives. Many countries continue to outlaw homosexual behavior, and those who practice homosexuality often face lengthy jail sentences. Condemnation of male homosexual behavior dates back to the Old Testament where sex between men was labeled "an abomination" and persons guilty of it should be put to death (see Lev. 18:22, 20:13). This biblical denunciation undoubtedly had, and continues to have, a significant influence on contemporary Judeo-Christian attitudes toward homosexuality.

Social Motives

Many of the needs that we face on an everyday basis go beyond the biological needs that I have discussed. Most of us have lives where our biological needs are usually satisfied. Under these circumstances, we often focus on our *social needs and motives.* Humans have many such needs. Twenty-seven social needs that motivate human behavior have been identified (Murray, 1938). I will concentrate on just three of these needs in this chapter: the need for affiliation, achievement, and power. These are the three needs that have been most closely examined by psychologists.

Affiliation

Most of us have a need to establish and maintain social relationships with others. This need likely developed in humans because it served to increase the probability of our survival in prehistoric times.

Psychologists distinguish between characteristics that exist as a trait and those that arise as a result of a state. A **trait** is a relatively stable characteristic or disposition that we possess as part of our personality. Some of us have an ongoing need to be with others while others prefer the solitude of being alone. Sometimes the need for affiliation can be satisfied by having a very close relationship with only a few individuals and sometimes by having many relatively impersonal contacts with a variety of people.

Different people have different reasons for wanting to affiliate with others. Four different types of affiliation needs have been proposed (Hill, 1987):

1. Positive stimulation. The need to receive enjoyable emotional and intellectual stimulation from others.
2. Emotional support. The need to receive emotional support or sympathy from others.
3. Social comparison. The need to reduce uncomfortable feelings of uncertainty that exist when we are around others.
4. Attention. The potential for increased feelings of self-worth and importance from the praise and attention of others.

How strong is your need for affiliation? You can take the self-test in Table 6.3 to find out.

The need for affiliation can also exist as a *state.* Psychologists define a **state** as a temporary condition that exists due to a specific situation. For instance, there are

✦ TABLE 6.3 ✦ Test of the Need for Affiliation

This questionnaire will measure how strong your need for affiliation is. Rate each of the statements below according to how true or descriptive they are of you, using the following scale:

1—Not at all true
2—Slightly true
3—Somewhat true
4—Mostly true
5—Completely true

____ 1. One of my greatest sources of comfort when things get rough is being with other people.
____ 2. I prefer to participate in activities alongside other people rather than by myself because I like to see how I am doing on the activity.
____ 3. The main thing I like about being around other people is the warm glow I get from contact with them.
____ 4. It seems like whenever something bad or disturbing happens to me I often just want to be with a close, reliable friend.
____ 5. I mainly like people who seem strongly drawn to me and who seem infatuated with me.
____ 6. I think I get satisfaction out of contact with others more than most people realize.
____ 7. When I am not certain about how well I am doing at something, I usually like to be around others so I can compare myself to them.
____ 8. I like to be around people when I can be the center of attention.
____ 9. When I have not done very well on something that is very important to me, I can get to feeling better simply by being around other people.
____ 10. Just being around others and finding out about them is one of the most interesting things I can think of doing.
____ 11. I seem to get satisfaction from being with others more than a lot of other people do.
____ 12. If I am uncertain about what is expected of me, such as on a task or in a social situation, I usually like to be able to look to certain others for cues.
____ 13. I often have a strong need to be around people who are impressed with what I am like and what I do.

Scoring

Add up your total score based on how you rated each of the 13 statements. Compare your score with the values below.

Affiliation Need	Males	Females
Very high	49+	51+
High	47–48	49–50
Above average	44–46	46–48
Average	41–43	43–45
Below average	38–40	41–43
Low	36–37	39–40
Very low	< 35	< 38

probably certain times and circumstances when you like to be alone, irrespective of any *trait* that you have for affiliation. There are other situations where we need to be around others to share our feelings and concerns. Oftentimes an external event, such as a natural disaster or a public celebration, brings about the need to affiliate. During New Year's Eve celebrations, I have observed total strangers embracing and interacting with each other in a manner that they would probably find unthinkable under other circumstances.

Fear and uncertainty often fuel the need for affiliation. After the 1999 high school shootings at Columbine High School in Littleton, Colorado, students who were interviewed on television often expressed the strong need to return to school so that they could "be with their friends." These students expressed a strong need to share their feelings about the tragedy with others as part of the healing process.

Need for Achievement

Do you have a strong desire to do well in any situation in which you are evaluated? Do you find that you take pleasure in accomplishing something even if there is no external reward for doing so? If you can truthfully answer yes to these questions, then you possess some of the characteristics common to those people who have a high **need for achievement.** People high in this characteristic are often the successful "achievers" in the world. They show great persistence and usually acquire highly developed skills in whatever tasks they pursue. They are very disciplined and enjoy mastering ideas. They also strive to overcome obstacles and to accomplish things that are difficult in as proficient and rapid a manner as possible. Those high in the need to achieve are driven primarily by the intrinsic reward of doing well rather than extrinsic motivators, such as money, fame, or power. Nevertheless, people who are high achievers often reap the benefits of the extrinsic rewards that accompany success.

Measurement of the need to achieve is difficult. Simply looking at how much a person has achieved is not a good measure. High achievement is sometimes the result of good luck or of being born into the right family or situation. Asking people if they are motivated to be successful will not define achievement levels either. You will not find many people motivated to fail, and simply saying that you are motivated to achieve does not mean that you necessarily are. If wanting success were all that was required, there would be far more successful people in the world. There is an old saying—"If wishes were horses, beggars would ride."

Psychologists measure need achievement indirectly by not telling the subject what they are actually examining. They collect the relevant information by showing the individual a series of pictures depicting people in various situations. For instance, they might show a picture of a college student working at a computer such as that illustrated in Figure 6.2. The subject is instructed to make up a story about each picture. The psychologist then counts the number of times the subject mentions striving to achieve a goal in the stories. People with high need achievement will make many references in their stories to attaining goals and success.

> Success is counted sweetest
> By those who ne'er succeed.
>
> **EMILY DICKINSON**
> *Success*

You can study need achievement in individuals by observing the difficulty of the tasks that they attempt to accomplish. You are probably familiar with an arcade game called skee ball, which is illustrated in Figure 6.3. Skee ball is similar

Psychologists often measure need achievement by showing a subject a series of pictures with people in various situations and asking them to make up a story about the picture. What story would you make up about this picture? Individuals with high need achievement generate stories that have themes of success or attaining goals.

to bean bag games and ring-toss, which research psychologists have also used to measure need achievement in both children and adults. In skee ball, you roll a wooden ball along a slightly inclined wooden alley that has its far end curved upward in order to project the ball up into one of several concentric circular troughs. The circular troughs have score values that increase as the circles decrease in size. As illustrated in Figure 6.3, the target worth 50 points is small, barely larger than the ball, and is at the top of the target area. If the ball misses this target, it usually falls into a compartment worth only 0 or 10 points. Aiming for this small target is an all or nothing proposition. The target worth 50 points is only slightly larger than the 100-point circle, and a miss here usually nets only 10 points. The 40- and 30-point targets are also larger, and a ball that misses these targets often falls into the 20-point compartment.

Observe your friends or even yourself as this game is played. Those with high need achievement like to take moderate risks when there is a realistic chance of success. People with low need achievement like to select goals that are either very easy or nearly impossible. How would this translate into a playing strategy for skee ball? Low need achievers would either shoot at the very difficult 50-point target every time or go for the easier, lower point targets where the probability of some success is almost assured. If they do not score on the risky difficult shots, they do not feel bad because it was a nearly impossible task anyway. In addition, if they aim for and score on the easier, lower point targets, they are happy because that is all they set out to do. Those individuals high in need achievement most likely would aim for the 40-point target where there is a moderate risk and a chance for the ball to fall into the 30-point target if the initial target is missed.

✦ FIGURE 6.3 ✦

Skee ball is a popular arcade game that illustrates how differently people with low and high levels of need achievement perform. In skee ball, you roll a wooden ball along a slightly inclined wooden alley whose far end is curved upward so as to project the ball up into one of several concentric circular scoring troughs whose score values increase as the circles decrease in size. Individuals low in need achievement will aim at either the most difficult and risky targets or the very easy, low-risk targets. Individuals with high need achievement will more frequently aim at the moderately risky targets.

Perhaps not surprisingly, high need achievers get better grades in both high school and college and tend to be successful in their chosen profession. Furthermore, they attribute their success to their own efforts and abilities. When they fail, they blame themselves for not working hard enough. Low need achievers, on the other hand, tend to blame their success or failure on luck or on factors outside of their personal control.

Fear of Failure

An important factor in evaluating achievement is **fear of failure.** The combination of this fear and the need for achievement or success often determines what risk an individual is willing to take. For example, if individuals have a high need for success *and* a high fear of failure, they probably will set lower goals for themselves and choose *easy* tasks. Individuals who have a high need for success and a low fear of failure will select *moderately difficult* tasks where they know that they have a realistic chance of succeeding. People with a high fear of failure often select either impossibly difficult tasks or very easy tasks. In the former case, they have an excuse for failing while, in the latter case, they successfully avoid failure.

Fear of Success

Sometimes people fear success as much as or more than failure. Certainly there are times in your life when you have acted in a way that guaranteed you would not be successful. Perhaps you let someone win at a game or sporting event when you knew that you could have won.

Some people are so fearful of success that the fear has a deleterious effect on their lives. For instance, a person might turn down a job advancement he knows he could perform for fear of the responsibilities that accompany it. One leading researcher on this topic has proposed three reasons why people fear success: (1) the extra demands that accompany success, (2) the attention and perhaps rejection that success brings, and (3) the stressful changes in self-concept that accompany being successful (Tresemer, 1977). These reasons are illustrated by a faculty member that I once knew who was offered an administrative position at a higher salary. She declined the position because she believed that becoming an administrator would alienate her from the teaching faculty, the job's excessive responsibilities might interfere with her home life, and she had never envisioned herself as an "administrator." Contrary to what you might guess, research suggests that both women and men are equally susceptible to the fear of success (Kearney, 1984).

Origins of Achievement Motivation

You have probably noticed big differences among your friends in their need to achieve. Some people are driven to succeed while others seem content with more modest accomplishments. What accounts for this variability?

Psychologists believe that child-rearing practices are probably most important. Parents of children with high need achievement are more likely to foster *independence* in their children at an early age. They expect their children to accomplish tasks such as dressing and feeding themselves at an earlier age than do parents of lesser motivated children. These parents are also more likely to praise their children when the desired behaviors are mastered. As a result, children quickly learn to associate their achievements with parental praise and approval.

Another factor that is apparently important is the birth order of a child. Numerous studies have documented that first-born and only children have higher intelligence test scores and perform better in school. As a consequence, these children are more likely to gain entry into prestigious universities and to enjoy greater success in their lives. An often cited example of first borns' achievements is the fact that all seven of the original *Mercury* astronauts were first-born children. In addition, many U.S. presidents were first-born or only children. One study documented that first-born children are much more likely to be Rhodes scholars, National Merit scholars, or listed in *Who's Who* than are later-born children (Altus, 1966).

Psychologists have speculated about why birth order seems to be so important. Part of the reason might be that these children tend to come from higher socioeconomic families than do those of larger families with more later-born children. It is also undeniable that first-born children receive more attention than do the later born. As a parent of two children I found that, like many parents, I had many more pictures of my first-born son's early years than of his younger sister. Of course, a first born also enjoys the privilege of being an only child who receives all the parental attention until the later-born siblings come along.

Later-born children should not despair, however. They tend to be more popular and relaxed than the first born. They also are more likely to develop superior social skills that can be very important in achieving success.

APPLICATIONS: Setting Goals

The process of setting goals and then rewarding yourself when the goal is achieved is called **self-regulation.** Setting appropriate and realistic goals is an extremely important part of our lives. If you set goals that are clearly impossible to attain, you will likely suffer frustration, dissatisfaction, and unhappiness. Conversely, if you set very low goals for yourself, you will not feel satisfaction with your achievements and not develop your full potential. Albert Bandura (1982), a highly respected child psychologist, has suggested rules for appropriate goal setting:

1. Establish short-term, specific goals. It is better to establish short-term, very explicit goals than long-term, more general goals. A goal to become a world-famous scientist is commendable. However, getting a good grade on your upcoming calculus test is a better short-term goal that will also advance you toward your longer-term goal. Like many writers, I set a personal goal to complete a specific number of pages daily in the drafting of this book rather than to complete the entire book by a certain date. I have found that the daily goal is far more manageable and realistic than aiming at a future date.
2. Use concrete rewards. Establish a concrete reward when you attain your short-term goal. If you get an A on your calculus test, reward yourself with that new CD that you have been wanting or see the movie that you missed because you were studying. It is better to use specific, concrete rewards for attaining goals rather than vague, poorly defined rewards such as allowing yourself to relax more. When I complete my quota of daily writing, I try to reward myself by engaging in one of several hobbies that I particularly enjoy.
3. Establish your own standards for success. Your friends or your parents may have a different definition of "success" than you do. Let your own standards guide your behavior. Bandura suggests that using both feedback from others and comparing your achievements with those of others may help establish appropriate standards of success.
4. Be realistic about your abilities. If you are not gifted in the sciences, you are not going to attain a medical degree from Harvard regardless of how much you might want to do so. Adopt a realistic appraisal of where your abilities lie and work toward goals that complement those abilities. If you are not certain where your abilities lie, ask your college counseling or testing center to administer tests that will objectively measure your strengths and weaknesses.

Need for Power

The **need for power** is commonly defined as the desire to control the behavior of other people and to assert one's own authority. People who have a need for power like to tell others what to do and frequently use rewards and/or punishments to bring about such control. There is an important distinction between the need for power and the *need for influence,* defined as the desire to persuade and affect others (Bennett, 1988).

The need for power ". . . is the common denominator which, more than anything else, explains all of man's activities.

FRIEDRICH WILHELM NIETZSCHE, 1844–1900

David Winter (1973) has written extensively on the need for power. He notes that people with a high need for power often are drawn to careers or positions where they can both direct and control the behavior of others (Winter & Stewart, 1978). College students with a high need for power report that they would like to be teachers, psychologists, and clergymen (Winter, 1973). Winter's research has also shown that these people often establish friendships with people who are less well known and relatively unrecognized by other students in order to dominate them in the relationship.

A high power need in men has been shown to be a predictor of several impulsive behaviors, such as drinking, gambling, aggression, and sexual exploitation. This often leads to marital conflict and divorce. Research has shown that both men and women with a high need for power, who also have younger siblings or children, do not engage in such impulsive behaviors (Winter, 1988). These conditions may cause *responsibility training* that tends to moderate the impulsive behaviors (Winter, 1988). A sense of responsibility consists of legal and/or moral standards, feelings of obligation, concern about others, concern about the consequences of one's behavior, and self-judgment (Winter & Barenbaum, 1985). Interestingly, one study found that women who had been sexually abused as children had a higher need for power, accompanied by a greater fear of power, as compared to nonabused women (Liem, O'Toole, & James, 1992).

People with a need for power often manifest this need in a variety of interesting ways. They tend to fight and argue more, enjoy gambling, and are prone to substance abuse (Winter & Stewart, 1978). College students with a high need for power like to make themselves conspicuous. This need manifests itself in ways such as putting their name on their dormitory room door, writing letters to the college newspaper, and turning in term papers encased in fancy bindings. They also prefer to participate in directly competitive sports that involve competition between individuals or teams as opposed to sports that involve competition against oneself or the clock (Winter, 1973).

Interestingly, there are no gender differences between college men and women on the need for power. However, men's power needs are often met by participating in sports, being physically strong, and having highly prestigious material possessions (Lips, 1985), whereas women's power needs are often met by putting a greater emphasis on social responsibility, such as volunteering to help a charity (Winter & Barenbaum, 1985).

APPLICATIONS

Do you think you have a high need for power over others or a greater interest in influencing others? You can take the self-tests in Tables 6.4 and 6.5 and see how you compare on these characteristics with other college students.

In selecting a mate, remember that people who display a high need for power possess several characteristics that often make them less than the ideal partner, including tendencies toward alcohol and drug abuse, gambling, aggressiveness, and sexual exploitation.

✦ TABLE 6.4 ✦ The Need for Power

This questionnaire will measure how strongly you need power. Rate each of the statements below according to how true or descriptive they are of you. Rate each statement according to the following 5-point scale:

0	1	2	3	4	5
Not at all like me					Very characteristic of me

_____ 1. I think I would enjoy having authority over others.
_____ 2. I like telling others what to do.
_____ 3. I am interested in obtaining a position of power and influence.
_____ 4. I like having power over others.
_____ 5. Power for its own sake interests me.
_____ 6. I would enjoy being a powerful executive or politician.
_____ 7. I have the personal characteristics that could make me a powerful leader.
_____ 8. I am pretty confident that I could make a good executive or politician.
_____ 9. It is important to me whether or not I am a leader.
_____ 10. I believe enough in my own abilities to try for a powerful or chief executive position.
_____ 11. I want to be the one who makes the decisions.
_____ 12. I expect to have a good deal of power someday.
_____ 13. I enjoy planning things and deciding what tasks each person should do.

Scoring
Add up the total points from your ratings and compare your score to the values below.

Need for Power

Total Score:	11	16	21	26	31	36	41	46	51
	Very low		Low		Average		High		Very high

Adapted with permission from Academic Press. Bennett, J. B. (1988). Power and influence as distinct personality traits: Development and validation of a psychometric measure. *Journal of Research in Personality, 22,* 361–394.

Resolving Motivational Conflict

Oftentimes we find ourselves in situations where we must choose between two or more different wants, needs, wishes, or external demands that are incompatible or contradictory. When different motives are pulling at us in different directions, we are in a **conflict situation.** Psychologists have identified four basic forms of conflicts, as illustrated in Figure 6.4 (Lewin, 1935).

1. Approach-Approach conflict. This is the simplest and the most pleasant conflict situation in which to find yourself. In this situation, we are forced to choose between two things, both of which are desirable. You have probably faced this conflict at a restaurant where you find two entrees that seem equally appetizing to

✦ TABLE 6.5 ✦ The Need for Influence

This questionnaire will measure how strongly you need to influence others. Rate each of the statements below according to how true or descriptive they are of you. Rate each statement according to the following 5-point scale:

0	1	2	3	4	5
Not at all like me					Very characteristic of me

_____ 1. I would like to be able to influence the actions of others.
_____ 2. I like to feel that others are affected by what I have to say.
_____ 3. I really enjoy it when others agree with me or see things my way.
_____ 4. I feel drawn to a career that would allow me to have an important impact on other people or groups.
_____ 5. It pleases me when people follow through with my suggestions.
_____ 6. I am really glad when my ideas and opinions have an impact on other people.
_____ 7. I prefer to work in those situations where I have some degree of influence over the decisions that are made.
_____ 8. I would like feeling that I have had an impact on people's lives.
_____ 9. I would like it if my ideas or actions make a difference in this world, even if I am not given credit for it.

Scoring
Add up the total points from your ratings and compare your score to the values below.

	Need for Influence				
Total Score:	18	23	28	33	38
	Very low	Low	Average	High	Very high

Adapted with permission from Academic Press. Bennett, J. B. (1988). Power and influence as distinct personality traits: Development and validation of a psychometric measure. *Journal of Research in Personality, 22,* 361–394.

you. This conflict is usually easily resolved, after a period of vacillation, when you decide that one of the positive things is slightly more desirable than the other.

2. Avoidance-Avoidance conflict. This is the antithesis of the approach-approach conflict because we now find ourselves in a situation where we must choose between two undesirable alternatives. Going to the dentist is undesirable, but so are tooth decay and gum disease. Another dilemma might be going to a boring job every day or going hungry. In the English language there are several colloquial expressions that we use to describe this conflict, including "being between a rock and a hard place," "being caught between the devil and the deep blue sea," or more commonly being "damned if we do, and damned if we don't." In other words, the consequences are undesirable regardless of what we do. Dennis Coon gives the example of a person who is trapped in a hotel fire 20 stories above the ground (1992, p. 361). Jumping out of the window is one alternative, but the human body cannot survive a fall from 20 stories up. Trying to run through the smoke and flames to safety is equally perilous. A person in

✦ FIGURE 6.4 ✦

We are in a conflict situation whenever we are in a position where we are required to choose between contradictory or incompatible wants, needs, or external demands. This illustrates the four major kinds of conflict situations, where the (+) reflects the positive aspects that attract the individual and the (–) reflects the negative aspects that repel the individual in the conflict situation.

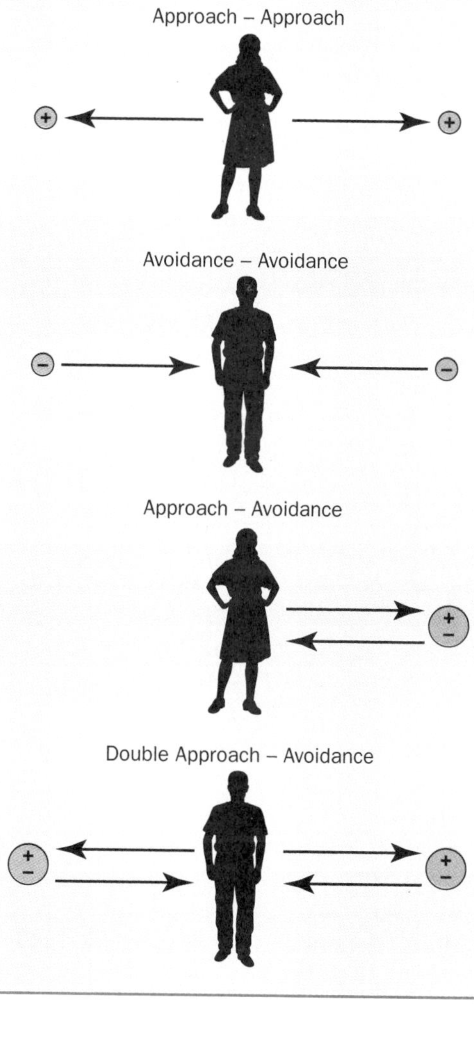

this situation may vacillate between the two choices. Opening the door and seeing the smoke and flames forces the individual to go to the window to jump. But seeing the height and hard pavement below, the individual rushes back to the door again. People are sometimes unable to force themselves to take either alternative and instead "freeze," doing nothing. It is not uncommon for fire-fighters to discover individuals dead in their rooms as a consequence.

Usually the avoidance-avoidance conflict is not as life-threatening as a hotel fire. I once knew a student who needed financial aid and was required to take a heavy course load to qualify. Because of other family obligations, he could not earn passing grades when taking so many courses. The conflict he faced was either taking fewer courses and losing his financial aid or taking a full load of courses and failing academically. Sometimes a conflicted person will "bail out" or leave the conflict situation altogether, a response called "leaving the field" (Lewin, 1935). In the case of my student, he dropped out of college to work full time.

Avoidance-avoidance conflicts are more difficult to resolve than approach-approach conflicts. Usually, they are resolved more slowly and only after considerable agonizing and indecision.

3. Approach-Avoidance conflict. A common conflict situation is one in which there is both a tendency to approach and avoid a situation simultaneously. You love desserts but notice your expanding waistline. A job offer comes with a high salary, but it is in a line of work that you intensely dislike. You covet a new car but undertaking a high monthly payment will be burdensome. We face this kind of conflict situation almost on a daily basis. How do we resolve the conflict?

   We often make a *partial approach* in this conflict situation (Miller, 1944). For example, we find a low-calorie dessert to enjoy or purchase a used car without such a daunting payment.

4. Double Approach-Avoidance conflicts. Most of the conflicts that we face in life are more complex than the three that I have already described. More typically, we find ourselves in situations where the options contain multiple positive and negative factors. In searching for a new home, a person narrows the possibilities down to two choices. Each has both positive and negative aspects. One house is cheaper, closer to work, and has a nice yard (positive aspects) but needs repairs, is located in a deteriorating neighborhood, and adjoins a busy, noisy commercial area (negative aspects). The other house is larger, more modern, and has several desirable features, but it is also very expensive, near poor quality schools, and a long commute from work.

   As with the avoidance-avoidance conflict, individuals tend to vacillate between the options. As any experienced real estate agent can attest, one house will seem more attractive to the buyer but, upon viewing it again, the negative aspects appear more salient so the buyer decides on the other house. However, upon approaching the other house, similar "mixed feelings" begin to surface. The major decisions that we must make in our lives involve this type of conflict. Choosing which college to go to, selecting a major, or deciding upon one of several job offers are all examples of situations where resolving the conflict can often be very stressful. Studies have shown that animals develop ulcers when they are repeatedly subjected to these kinds of conflict situations.

APPLICATIONS: Motivating Others

An appropriate conclusion to a chapter on motivation would seem to be a section on how to motivate others effectively. Unfortunately, this is an extremely complicated problem with no easy, all-inclusive answers. The same behavior can be driven by a variety of motivations. Take the example of motivating the eating response. Eating can be in response to a biological drive, but it can also be a response to a social drive. Furthermore, eating can be under the control of a number of different social motives. A person might be eating because of a need to affiliate with others or as a part of a need to exert influence over another individual. Most behaviors in which we engage are driven by more than one motivation.

To further complicate matters, what motivates one individual might not motivate another. Also, what successfully motivates an individual in one situation might not in a different situation. Time is a critical factor as well. Food or sex may be a powerful motivator in one time period but be totally ineffectual in another, such as directly following a large meal or immediately after a sexual act.

For all these reasons, psychologists have come to appreciate that there is no simple set of rules on how to motivate the behavior of others consistently. Psychologists have developed some rules for motivating certain behaviors in specific situations. One important topic within industrial/organizational psychology, for example, covers what kind of leadership styles most motivate workers in specific work situations. Educators are similarly interested in what manipulations will work to motivate young children to learn more and perform better. Client motivation is a very important factor in clinical psychology for the successful treatment of most disorders. Almost every subfield of psychology is interested in the topic of motivation for one reason or another. However, the manipulations that might motivate a depressed patient receiving clinical treatment are not likely to be applicable to an industrial worker on an assembly line.

Given these important caveats, there are nevertheless some general principles for motivating others that will work in most situations.

1. Reward behavior *after* it is performed, not before. In order for a reward to be optimally motivating, it needs to come after the behavior is performed. In Chapter 3 and earlier in this chapter, I discussed that you should not use rewards to bribe future behavior. Ideally, rewards should be used to provide effective feedback on achievement.
2. Reward achievement, not mediocrity. Rewards are more motivating for the recipient if they are given only when there is exceptional performance, not merely for engaging in a behavior. You are not fooling (or motivating) anyone when you reward mediocrity; even young children can see through this ploy. Rewarding superior achievement will also help increase intrinsic motivation for a task.
3. Use the smallest extrinsic reward possible. Giving an excessively large reward, especially for mediocre achievement, only strengthens the perception that the behavior did not justify the reward. You may wish to review the *overjustification effect* that was described in Chapter 3. Overly large rewards can sap intrinsic motivation for future performance.
4. Intrinsic motivation is generally better than extrinsic. Whenever possible, encourage intrinsic motivation to perform a task. This is particularly important where individuals work independently of others. If individuals find a task challenging and interesting, they will often develop an intrinsic motivation to do it well. A child who feels challenged to play a musical instrument well will be

more motivated than one who is being paid an allowance only to practice a certain amount every day. Occasionally, you may need to use external rewards until the behavior becomes established, but once the behavior is perceived as being enjoyable, the external rewards should be discontinued.

5. Do not be overcontrolling. Foster independence and creativity, assign challenging (but do-able) tasks, and encourage self-directed achievements. Resist the temptation to "help" someone by doing the task for him or her. Being an encouraging and supportive person is better than being overly controlling and will result in more intrinsic motivation to perform well.
6. Establish appropriate goals. Numerous studies have shown that people are more motivated and achieve more when a challenging goal is established. Setting a specific goal that is just beyond a person's grasp is an excellent way to encourage intrinsic motivation. Get the individual to commit to the goal and provide feedback as they make progress. Many companies use these techniques to motivate and encourage their salespeople.

Finally, you should be aware that others are trying to motivate your behavior—sometimes in ways that do not serve your best interests. Advertising is essentially an attempt to motivate you to "need" something that you might not have considered buying. Several companies have been formed to study the shopping habits of Americans and to find ways to motivate us to buy more. A recent book entitled *Why We Buy,* by Paco Underhill (1999) details some interesting findings from this research. Illumination levels, colors, sounds, placement of items, and even smells—all have been shown to influence our motivation to buy. Researchers have found that most shoppers veer to the right when they enter a store. (Coincidentally, over 80% of rats veer to the right in a T-maze as well.) Upon entering a store there is a transition zone where shoppers adjust to the lighting, sounds, smells, and temperature of the store (Underhill, 1999). Items offered for sale in this transition zone are rarely purchased. Other research shows that shoppers who talk to a salesperson and try things on are twice as likely to buy as shoppers who do neither. You may think that you are making purchasing decisions of your own volition, but in reality, marketing experts are hard at work altering your motivations and your subsequent buying decisions.

SUMMARY

- Motivation initiates, sustains, and directs human behavior, and is comprised of needs, drives, goals, and responses.
- Homeostasis is a result of the human body regulating an optimal level of biological conditions. A set point is the optimal level that the body innately attempts to maintain.
- Varying levels of physiological arousal accompany motivation from a drive. Similar to homeostasis, humans innately seek optimal levels of arousal.
- High sensation seekers are individuals who thrive on high levels of arousal, and thus seek out more dangerous or risky activities than low sensation seekers.
- Certain activities are useful in maintaining an optimal level of arousal, and, consequently, maximum test performance.
- Circadian rhythms are physiological changes that occur in 24-hour cycles, which can affect task performance. Changes in sleep cycles, work shift cycles, and jet lag are all activities that may throw your regular circadian rhythm off balance.
- Biorhythms are believed to represent altering physical, emotional, and intellectual cycles that individuals

maintain. However, the theory of biorhythms has yet to be proven, despite extensive research.

- ✦ Intrinsic motivation is attributed to the reinforcement from a behavior itself, whereas extrinsic motivation is attributed to the rewards and punishments that are a result of the behavior.
- ✦ Actions that are taken to benefit others without self-benefit are called altruistic behaviors.
- ✦ Rewarding individuals for an activity they already enjoy doing without reward decreases the incentive value for that particular activity.
- ✦ Eating, drinking, and sexual behavior are biologically based motivations, but are also attributed to other motivating factors. The desire to eat is influenced by physiological factors as well as boredom, anxiety-reduction, and social needs. The feeling of fullness that you experience after eating a large meal is called satiety.
- ✦ Our biological set point is the weight that our bodies attempt to maintain. Set point is influenced by many factors, including genetics, age, hormonal disruptions, climate conditions, tobacco consumption, and physical illness.
- ✦ Social interactions, culture, and learning influence our eating habits. Psychological states such as boredom, anxiety, and depression have also been shown to affect the desire to eat. In addition, taste, smell, and texture influence our eating desires.
- ✦ Externality theory contends that the eating response in obese individuals is triggered by external cues such as the sight, smells, or sounds of foods while internal, physiological cues govern the response in those of normal weight.
- ✦ Nearly all diet programs demonstrate moderate success in short-term weight loss, and virtually no evidence exists that significant weight loss can be maintained over the long term by the vast majority of people. "Yo-yo dieting" may cause accumulations of body fat, increased cardiovascular risks, depression, anxiety, irritability, anger, and mood swings. Suggestions for safe weight loss include increasing exercise, normalizing food intake, and modifying one's negative body image.
- ✦ The sexual act is influenced by many factors other than biologically based motivations. Biological factors include the activation of the sexual hormones estrogen and testosterone. Sexual motivation is also influenced by external factors such as physical contact, pheromones, erotic material, and new sexual partners. Cultural factors, learning, and sexual orientation are also important motivating influences.
- ✦ Human needs are socially motivated as well as biologically motivated. Our desire to affiliate with others reflects our need to establish and maintain social relationships.
- ✦ People demonstrate a need for achievement when they exhibit a strong desire to do well in a situation in which they are being evaluated.
- ✦ Self-regulation involves setting goals and rewarding yourself when the goal is achieved. Suggestions for setting realistic goals include establishing short-term specific goals, using concrete rewards, establishing individual standards for success, and being realistic about your abilities.
- ✦ Humans often display a need for power, which is the desire to control the behavior of others and to assert one's own authority.
- ✦ Conflict situations arise when individuals are pulled in the conflicting directions of different motives. The four basic forms of conflict situations are approach-approach conflict, avoidance-avoidance conflict, approach-avoidance conflict, and double approach-avoidance conflict.
- ✦ Although motivation is complex, there are several general principles that can be effective in motivating others. These include rewarding behavior after it is performed, rewarding achievement, using small rewards, relying on intrinsic motivation, avoiding being overcontrolling, and establishing appropriate goals.

KEY TERMS

altruistic behavior: an intrinsically motivated behavior that is aimed at doing something to help others without any benefit to oneself.

arousal: a physiological reaction to a motivational drive.

asexuals: individuals who have no sexual interest in either sex.

bestiality: an act in which humans have sexual intercourse with animals.

bisexuals: individuals who seek out and engage in sexual relations with members of both sexes.

celibacy: the act of voluntarily abstaining from sex.

circadian rhythms: stable physiological changes that bodies undergo that affect the level of arousal.

Coolidge effect: the tendency for animals to engage in sex with a new partner, even if they showed no further interest in sexual behavior with an original partner.

conflict situation: situation in which different motives are pulling an individual in different directions.

drive: a state that impels and activates a behavior that satisfies a need.

estrogen: sex hormone for females.

externality theory: the belief that the eating response in obese individuals is triggered by external cues, rather than internal cues.

extrinsic motivation: motivation that occurs because individuals are acting on rewards and/or punishments of a behavior.

fear of failure: the fear of not succeeding at achieving a goal.

goal: the objective of behavior directed toward satisfying an existing need.

heterosexuals: individuals who seek out and engage in sexual relations with members of the opposite sex.

homeostasis: the innate drive to maintain biological conditions at an optimal and stable level.

homosexuals: individuals who seek out and engage in sexual relations with members of the same sex.

hypothalamus: a small structure located in the base of the brain that, among other things, monitors glucose levels in the blood to regulate feelings of hunger.

intrinsic motivation: motivation that occurs because individuals find a behavior to be pleasurable and/or reinforcing.

motivation: the process that initiates, sustains, and directs behavior.

need: a condition that exists when we are deprived of something that we want or require.

need for achievement: the desire for accomplishment, even in the absence of external rewards.

need for power: desire to control the behavior of others and to assert one's own authority.

pheromones: an olfactory animal sexual arousal cue.

response: behavior that attains a goal to satisfy a need.

satiety: a sensation of feeling full and not hungry.

self-regulation: the process of setting goals and then self-rewarding when a goal is achieved.

sensation seekers: individuals who consistently seek out high levels of arousal.

set point: an optimal value that the body attempts to maintain.

state: temporary condition that exists due to a specific situation.

testosterone: sex hormone for males.

trait: a relatively stable characteristic or disposition that humans possess as part of their personality.

7

Understanding and Controlling Emotions

Emotions are what make our everyday lives interesting. Joy, fear, anger, love, excitement, surprise, sorrow, disgust, and other emotional states add spice to our lives. Indeed, it is hard to imagine what life would be like without the usual roller coaster of emotional states that we routinely experience. **Emotions** are usually brief feelings, and occur in response to some event in our lives. However, emotions can also be invoked by memories of past events in our lives. For example, I'm certain there are embarrassing things that have happened to you that still elicit strong emotional reactions whenever you think about them. Emotions are always accompanied by some physiological reaction, which I will discuss in detail in the next section.

Psychologists draw a distinction between emotions and **moods.** Moods are usually longer lasting, less specific, and less intense than emotions. We might report that we are experiencing the emotion of sadness because of a sad story we just read, but we report we are in a depressed mood when a more vague feeling overcomes us. Often we are unable to identify what specifically elicits a mood and it takes us longer to recover from it than a temporary emotional state. Mood also affects how we react to situations. If you are in a "bad" mood, an event that might otherwise cause only slight annoyance may instead elicit an intensely angry response. Moods often fluctuate in regular cycles. In one study with college students, students reported being in the worst mood on Mondays and Tuesdays, with the best mood state reported on Friday or Saturday (Larsen & Kasimatis, 1990). The old belief in "Blue Monday" is therefore supported by empirical evidence.

Psychologists are in disagreement about how many basic emotions there are. One view is that there are only three emotions—fear, anger, and pleasure—and all other emotional states are believed to be mixtures of these three elements (Millenson, 1967). Another view maintains there are nine basic emotions, including three that are positive—excitement, joy, and surprise—and six that are negative—anguish, fear, shame, contempt, disgust, and anger (Tomkins, 1982). Still other researchers have proposed other numbers of basic emotions. It is unlikely that any widespread agreement will be reached on what this number should be, or even if there is such a thing as a specific number of basic emotions. Whatever the number, we know that emotions play an important role in our lives. They even affect the way we perceive things. Have you noticed how you perceive the world very differently when you are feeling depressed? Like moods, emotions also affect how we respond to events. The very same stimulus event often elicits very different responses, depending on the emotional state we are in.

Sometimes, emotions are learned. In chapter 3 I discussed how classical conditioning often plays a role in emotions. Stimuli that start out as neutral to us may acquire an emotional component by being paired with an emotion-producing stimulus, such as pain. Although learning plays a role in emotions, the basic emotions of anger, joy, and fear appear to be unlearned. Most theorists agree that only the emotion of excitement is present at birth, but by the age of 2 all the primary emotions are well established. Distress, delight, anger, disgust, fear, elation, and affection for adults all appear before age 1, followed by jealousy, affection for children, and joy, which appear before age 2 (Bridges, 1932).

Physiology of Emotional Arousal

Emotional arousal is always accompanied by physiological arousal. One night I was awakened at 3:00 A.M. from a deep sleep by the incessant wailing of my home security alarm system. After a few moments of disorientation, I jumped out of bed and turned off the alarm. I then proceeded to go downstairs to investigate what had set off the alarm. As I ventured cautiously down the darkened stairs, I noted that my heart was racing and my breathing was very rapid. Not knowing what caused the alarm to go off, I was emotionally aroused and had physiological arousal to accompany it. When emotionally aroused, our body prepares us for what psychologists call "fight or flight." A part of our nervous system called the **sympathetic nervous system** invokes a complicated set of physiological reactions, which gives us a burst of energy and prepares us to either attack or flee, depending upon the perceived circumstances. As I proceeded down the stairs, I had an image of a large, well-armed burglar waiting for me below. Had I been able to measure my physiological reaction to this emotional arousal more completely, I would have discovered the following changes in my body:

1. Pupil dilation. The pupils open wide to allow in the maximum amount of light.
2. Salivary gland secretions. Decreases in secretion result in the commonly perceived "cotton mouth" that occurs with extreme emotional arousal.
3. Heart rate. Increase in heart rate and blood pressure to rush blood to the brain and other parts of the body to prepare it for action.
4. Stomach secretions/intestines. Temporary decrease in stomach secretions and food digestion so that resources can be diverted elsewhere.
5. Increase in sweat secretions to cool the body. This is why we say that someone who is angry or otherwise emotionally aroused is "hot under the collar" and needs to "cool off."
6. Stimulation of the hair follicles causes the hairs to rise, hence the origin of the expression of having a "hair-raising experience." Raising the hairs allows the body to cool more efficiently.
7. Lung function. The small tubes in our lungs, called bronchi, open wide to allow for maximum absorption of oxygen.
8. Blood chemistry changes. The chemical composition of the blood changes to allow for faster clotting, in the event of an open wound. Blood flow to the skin is also reduced to restrict bleeding.
9. Adrenal gland activity. The adrenal glands, located on top of the kidneys, release hormones that cause heart rate, blood pressure, and blood sugar levels to increase. All of these prepare the body for immediate action.

This is only a partial list of the very complicated and adaptive physiological reactions that accompany emotional arousal. Any stimulus that triggers the sympathetic nervous system will cause all of these reactions to occur. Furthermore, all of these reactions occur automatically, without any conscious effort on your part.

Going back to my security alarm, upon investigating the cause, I discovered a Miller moth fluttering in front of one of the motion detectors in my living room. I quickly dispensed with the "intruder" using a fly swatter and went back to bed. The sympathetic nervous system requires 20 to 30 minutes to return the physiological functions to normal levels, which is why we notice that we continue to be aroused even after the emergency has passed. In my case, I was unable to get back to sleep for nearly an hour.

In addition to the sympathetic nervous system, we have a complementary system called the **parasympathetic nervous system,** which supports the body in nonemergency situations. It often, but not always, causes the opposite physiological reactions to occur. When not emotionally aroused, for example, our heart rate and breathing slow down, pupils constrict, and digestion is promoted. These two systems work independently but cooperatively with one another to manage appropriate physiological responses, depending upon the arousal state we are in. After emotional arousal, the parasympathetic system goes to work to restore the physiological functions to normal ranges. It functions more slowly than the sympathetic system, which is why arousal remains high for a period of time after the stimulus that elicited it is no longer present.

Can our emotional state affect our physical health as well as our mental state? There is increasingly convincing evidence that this is the case. While the physiological reactions that occur with emotional arousal are adaptive in the short term, preparing us for "fight or flight," they are damaging to our health if they are maintained over long periods of time. I will be discussing this in much greater detail in the next chapter. It is also possible for a sudden emotional state to be fatal. Recently it was reported that a man died of a heart attack shortly after the police informed him of the death of his wife in a traffic accident. There have been numerous documented cases of people being "scared to death," particularly in wartime situations. Voodoo is a primitive religion based on a belief in sorcery. In Voodoo, a hex is placed on individuals in the belief that it will cause them to die. People who are aware that they have been "cursed" often do, in fact, die. Because of their belief in the power of the hex, their emotional response is identical to that of someone facing imminent death. The hex becomes a self-fulfilling prophecy.

Reading Emotions in Others

An important part of social interaction with others is the ability to appropriately read the feedback others give about their emotional state. Even young children are quite aware when they are in the presence of another child who lacks this ability, and they tend to shun such children. In adulthood, women are often better than men at monitoring the emotional states of others (Hall, 1987). Adults are particularly sensitive to signs of emotional distress in children. You've probably noticed how exceedingly difficult it is to ignore the sounds of a crying baby in a restaurant or a store, as such sounds make us annoyed and irritated. Some scientists believe that we are innately sensitive to these sights and sounds of distress, which has obvious biological adaptive value as it encourages adult attention to a young infant's needs and increases survivability in the young. Even very young infants display signs of distress when they hear another infant crying. Interestingly, female infants are much more likely to cry in sympathy than are male infants.

There are several ways that we monitor the emotional state of others, including facial gestures, eye gaze, body movements, and posture.

Facial Gestures

What is the best way to gauge another person's emotional state? Usually just a brief glance at another's face will give you a quick appraisal of his or her mood and how he or she is feeling. Often we can do this even when the other person is attempting

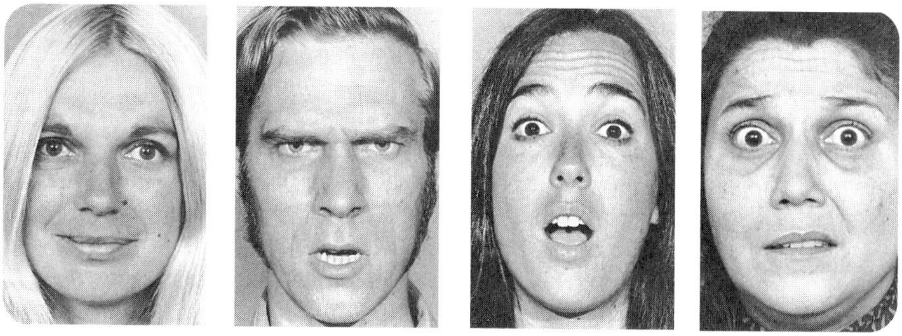

Figure 7.1

These photographs of facial expressions were shown to individuals in the United States, Brazil, Chile, Argentina, and Japan. People were asked to match the facial gesture with the appropriate emotion being displayed. These facial gestures were accurately recognized by a large proportion of people in each of the five cultures.

to hide how he or she is feeling. I'm always surprised at how quickly others who know me well (particularly my wife) can judge my mood state with a mere glance, despite my best efforts to camouflage my feelings.

Charles Darwin was one of the first scientists to discuss in detail how animals and humans share many similar facial expressions. If you have ever had a pet dog, you know that their faces can register emotions of happiness or sadness in ways very similar to humans.

There appear to be certain facial expressions that are almost universally recognized across most cultures. Look at the facial expressions for happiness, disgust, surprise, sadness, anger, and fear illustrated by the photographs in Figure 7.1. Paul Ekman and his colleagues (Ekman, Sorenson, & Friesen, 1969; Ekman, 1972) showed these photographs to individuals living in the United States, Brazil, Chile, Argentina, and Japan and asked them to match the emotions being displayed.

The face is the image of the soul.

MARCUS TULLIUS CICERO, ROMAN STATESMAN AND ORATOR, 106–143 B.C.

People were able to appropriately match the emotions shown in the majority of the cases for each of the divergent cultures. Across the five cultures, happiness was the emotion recognized most accurately. Subjects accurately matched the photo showing happiness 97% of the time, followed closely by the emotions of surprise (94%), and disgust (92%). Anger was recognized 86% of the time, while sadness was correctly matched 79% of the time. The most difficult facial gesture to recognize was fear, with 66% accuracy. When it comes to communicating emotional states, facial gestures appear to be almost a universal language. Children who are born deaf and blind have no opportunities to learn about facial gestures from others. Yet, even these children use the same facial gestures as everyone else to register happiness, sadness, disgust, and other basic emotions (Knapp, 1978).

APPLICATIONS

There is a saying "laugh and the world laughs with you, cry and you cry alone." This may sound like simple-minded advice but there is some truth in it. The fact of the matter is, sometimes we just don't *feel* like being in a jovial mood. If you are like me, advice from well-meaning friends to "smile, things aren't that bad!" seems more an irritant than helpful advice. However, research suggests that just the act of forcing yourself to smile may indeed make you happier. In one experiment, college students were asked to either intentionally frown or smile. The students who were smiling reported feeling happier and found cartoons more humorous than the frowning students did (Laird, 1974). In another experiment, students who mimicked emotional reactions were shown to experience the same physiological reactions as people experiencing true emotional responses (Ekman, Levenson, & Friesen, 1983).

You may find it difficult to walk around with a forced smile on your face all day. You can demonstrate the effects of activation of the facial muscles involved in smiling by holding a pen or pencil in your teeth. Conversely, frowning muscles are activated when you hold a pen in your mouth with just your lips. Studies have indicated that cartoons will seem funnier when the pen is in your teeth, activating the smiling muscles. You might want to try this when you are studying sometime. I developed a habit years ago of often working at my computer while holding a pen in my teeth, so that I can readily jot down things as I type. I've noticed this trick works for me, and you might want to give it a try, as well.

Eyes

Many poets have described how eyes are the "windows to the soul." We often attempt to "read" other people by looking carefully into their eyes. We often question the honesty of people who won't "look us in the eye" when speaking to us. And of course, lovers look longingly into each other's eyes, at least during the courtship phase of the romance.

People often report feeling uncomfortable when speaking with someone wearing dark sunglasses, because they are deprived of an important source of information about the emotional state of the other person. Recently, a professional golfer has been highly criticized in the press for wearing dark wraparound sunglasses that hide his emotional reactions during televised golf events. Personally, I find mirrored sunglasses the most disconcerting, as the only thing you see when you gaze into the eyes of a person wearing these is an image of yourself!

People who avoid eye contact are often perceived as unfriendly or shy. There is nothing quite as unsettling as trying to carry on a conversation with someone who refuses to make eye contact. We interpret eye contact as a sign of interest in us and in what we are saying. However, there is a fine boundary between intermittent eye contact and prolonged staring, which is usually interpreted as a sign of anger or hostility. Interestingly, in the animal kingdom staring is almost universally considered an act of hostility. This is true not only within species, but between species as well. The next time you come face to face with a hostile dog, resist the urge to stare him down. The dog will interpret your steady gaze as an overt act of hostility, and will react accordingly.

What is it exactly that we look for when gazing into another's eyes? According to Eckhard Hess (1975), we are judging the size of another's pupils. The size of the pupils are controlled by the sympathetic nervous system, and enlarge when we are emotionally aroused, interested in something, or carefully attending to something. Hess demonstrated the power of pupil size by showing men pictures of identical women with pupils either enlarged or nearly closed. The men consistently judged

Which of these faces seems most attractive to you? The photographs are identical, except that the face on the right has larger pupils. Using pictures of women's faces, psychologists have found that men judge the faces with enlarged pupils as friendlier and more attractive.

the pictures of women with the enlarged pupils as friendlier and more attractive. Other studies have shown that people interpret pupil dilation as an indication of sexual arousal in members of the opposite sex. Turkish rug dealers used pupil dilation centuries ago to judge how interested a prospective customer was in purchasing one of their rugs. If the rug salesman saw the pupils of the customer highly dilated while viewing one of his offerings, he would hold out for a higher price.

Body Language

We also effectively communicate our emotional state with our body posture, how we move our body, and the gestures we use, which collectively define our **body language.** Have you ever observed the body language of people who were emotionally aroused? Typically they make numerous body movements, particularly ones that involve touching, scratching, or rubbing their own body. They also make repetitive body motions such as tapping or shaking their foot, tapping their fingers, and so forth. We often describe such people as being "nervous," but actually they are just emotionally (and physiologically) aroused.

Our body language often communicates more than we would like it to. We tend to turn and face people we like or find attractive, and also lean slightly forward toward them. In addition, we stand closer to them and literally "greet them with open arms," whereas we tend to fold our arms and maintain a greater distance from those we dislike or find unattractive or uninteresting. The distance we stand from people is also quite revealing. We each have invisible boundaries around us and we feel uncomfortable if the area contained within, called our **personal space,** is invaded. You can demonstrate this quite simply by sitting close to strangers on a park bench and watching their reaction. They will typically show multiple signs of distress and most likely will get up and leave the bench. How close we are willing to allow people to approach us depends upon how well we know them and how attracted we are to them. As a general rule, people we have an intimate relationship with can come within 18 inches. For friends, our personal space extends out from 18 inches to

Everyone has a personal space that extends around him or her. People allow others to come into their personal space at varying distances, depending upon how they feel about them. Strangers are kept at "arm's length" while someone we are intimate with can come within 18 inches.

4 feet, while with strangers and casual acquaintances we maintain a distance from 4 to 12 feet. At this distance we are literally keeping strangers at "arm's length." These rules apply to the North American culture only. The Middle Eastern cultures often converse with their faces only inches apart, even with individuals who are not close friends.

Posture is also a good giveaway about an individual's emotional state. People who are fearful are erect and in a posture ready to take immediate action. Sadness or dejection is accompanied by a slumping posture.

Finally, gestures also reveal our emotional state. Each culture has developed a repertoire of gestures that they use to reflect how they feel. These gestures are often culture specific, which can result in some interesting "culture clashes" as you are traveling in foreign countries. Gestures intended to represent a friendly communication in our culture can often be highly insulting in another culture. For example, the "A-Okay" sign is considered an obscene gesture in some southern European countries. Businesses that have international dealings now frequently train their workers in these delicate matters.

APPLICATIONS: Detecting Lies

One application we make in reading the emotions of others is to determine whether or not they are being truthful. Many people think they are very good at detecting lies, but in fact, they are not. In one study, observers who were shown videotapes and asked to judge who was lying did little better than chance (Ekman & O'Sullivan, 1991). This includes people in the criminal justice system, such as FBI agents, local police, and judges. Psychologists and psychiatrists are also inept at lie detecting. Interestingly, the only individuals who consistently score above chance in detecting lies are secret service agents.

None of us could live with a habitual truth teller; but, thank goodness, none of us has to.

MARK TWAIN

Answer the following question about yourself: Do you regularly tell lies? If you answered no, you are most likely being less than candid. A poll of Americans in 1991 showed that 90% of people asked admitted that they were deceitful. The other 10% were probably kidding themselves. The most frequent reasons cited for deceit included lying about one's true feelings, income, accomplishments, sex life, and age. Despite the prevalence of lying, honesty in a friend is something that 94% of people polled thought was an extremely important quality, more important than any other attribute. Furthermore, Americans believe that people are more dishonest now than a decade ago. Americans are becoming increasingly skeptical about the truthfulness of politicians, leading to the popular joke:

QUESTION: How can you tell when a politician is lying?

ANSWER: When his lips are moving.

In one study concerning the prevalence of dishonesty in our everyday lives, 60% of women report they had been lied to for the purpose of obtaining sex (Ford, 1996). Fully 92% of college students admitted anonymously that they had lied to a current or potential sexual partner. One-third of people admit to lying when seeking employment. Studies indicate that lying on employment applications has doubled since 1975. In another survey, 70% of physicians indicated they would deceive an insurance company so that a patient might receive payment for a necessary test.

Scientists often lie to promote their own theoretical viewpoints. Even well-known and highly respected scientists such as Isaac Newton, Gregor Mendel, Charles Darwin, Louis Pasteur, and Cyril Burt have been found to have "fudged" their data on occasion or otherwise engaged in deceitful actions. Perhaps the most pervasive use of deceit is in advertising, including blatant misrepresentation, exaggeration, subtle (but false) implications, and bait-and-switch techniques (Ford, 1996).

A recent book claims that women are better liars than men (O'Connell, 1999), although other studies have not shown any differences. People with charisma and power are also more likely to get away with lying. President John F. Kennedy is cited as an example of a nice-looking man who was very charming and charismatic who "got away with a lot" (O'Connell, 1999). Many of the studies on lying have concluded that people lie differently to attractive people than they do to unattractive people (DePaulo, 1994). Interestingly, their lies are much more transparent and easier to detect when they are lying to the "beautiful people." We are better at detecting lies from someone in our own culture, as compared to someone from another culture (DePaulo, 1994). One researcher claims the most flagrant liars are college students, who lie twice as often as anyone else (O'Connell, 1999).

Lying begins early. Children begin telling fibs at age 2 and become accomplished at it by the age of 5. Given that all this lying is going on around us much of the time, how can we increase our ability to detect when others are lying to us?

Paul Ekman (1985) has conducted the seminal research in this area. Importantly, he notes that there is no certain sign of lying; no single gesture, facial expression, or muscle twitch that *by itself* is a giveaway that a person is being deceitful. Rather, there are only clues that a person is poorly prepared to tell a lie, and clues of emotions that don't match what the person is saying. The commonly believed indicators of lying such as shifty eyes and squirming are not reliable indicators. Posture is also no indication of truthfulness. People are not very good at detecting lies because they attend most carefully to those very factors that are the poorest predictors of lying—namely, words and facial expression. These are the factors that a good liar can most easily disguise. Better cues are given by carefully observing an individual's speech and vocal patterns, body movements, and autonomic nervous system cues.

I never had sex with that woman—Miss Lewinsky.

PRESIDENT BILL CLINTON

Let's examine each of these clues to lying (Ekman, 1985):

1. Speech and vocal patterns. Deception clues include increased numbers of "slips of the tongue," emotional outpouring or tirades, excessively convoluted or sophisticated answers, indirect or evasive answers, and providing more information than was requested. These are not perfect indicators as some people normally speak in these ways. Review of the literature suggests that liars give shorter responses that are more negative or irrelevant (DePaulo, 1994). In addition, false statements are often internally discrepant and characterized by hesitations that are too long or too frequent, and contain repetitions and grammatical errors. Liars also hesitate sometimes before beginning a sentence. Other clues include using nonwords such as "ah" and "uh," and repetitions similar to stuttering, such as "I, I, I think that I. . . ." Less-reliable indicators include a raised pitch, increased loudness, and a lack of emotion in the voice.
2. Body movements. There is an increased frequency of meaningful gestures, called **emblems,** when lying. These emblems are often specific to a culture but are generally well understood by all in the culture. Individuals from the United

States use about 60 different emblems, including gestures such as head-nod yes, head-shake no, wave hello/goodbye, A-Okay sign, thumb up/down, and of course the ubiquitous "middle finger." These emblems are particularly significant when they slip out unintentionally.

Other types of body movement are those that illustrate speech as it is spoken, movements called **illustrators.** They usually involve the hands, although the brow and upper eyelid or even the upper trunk or entire body can be involved. Using the hands or fingers to illustrate a point or describe something is an example of an illustrator. A clue to deceit is a *decrease* in the normal number of illustrators used. During lying, there is an increase in self-manipulating gestures, such as rubbing or scratching oneself, except when people are highly motivated to escape detection, in which case they use fewer of these behaviors (DePaulo, 1994).

3. Autonomic nervous system clues. I described earlier the sympathetic and parasympathetic nervous systems, which together constitute the autonomic nervous system. Lying usually involves emotional arousal, and the autonomic nervous system signals that arousal in a variety of noticeable ways. Breathing becomes more rapid and irregular (often with a heaving chest), perspiration increases, there is blushing or blanching in the face, pupils dilate, and the frequency of swallowing and blinking increases. These changes occur involuntarily, are extremely hard to inhibit, and for that reason can be very reliable clues that a person is lying. However, these cues merely signal that the person is emotionally aroused, and do not indicate what specific emotion is being aroused. An innocent person being accused of deceit could show emotions of anger, fear, or excitement that could also show up as autonomic system activation. No single cue should ever be used as an indicator of lying. Rather, the lie catcher must use cues from voice, words, face, and body to confirm suspicions of deceit. One reason most people do so badly in judging deceit is that they rely too much upon what people say and ignore the discrepancies between the expressive behaviors and what is said (Ekman, 1997). With training, a person can accurately identify when someone is lying 85% of the time (Ekman, O'Sullivan, Friesen, & Scherer, 1991).

Polygraph

> Any fool can tell the truth, but it requires a man of some sense to know how to lie well.
>
> **SAMUEL BUTLER**
> *Note-books*

The **polygraph** or "lie detector" is a device frequently used by police in criminal investigations. It measures several physiological responses that accompany emotional arousal, including changes in breathing, pulse rate, blood pressure, and perspiration. Polygraphs are being increasingly used by corporations to screen employees for honesty and to uncover employee theft.

It is important to remember that the polygraph does not detect lies. It only measures physiological responses associated with emotional arousal. It is not able to distinguish between different emotions such as anxiety, guilt, or annoyance. Each of these emotions causes the same physiological arousal. As a result, an innocent person who is being tested may, because he or she is emotionally aroused by being tested, be deemed a liar. Polygraph tests are inaccurate about one-third of the time. Unfortunately, they label the innocent as guilty much more frequently than they label the guilty as innocent. Some studies have shown up to 90% of the innocent are judged to be guilty (Kleinmuntz & Szucko, 1984; Lykken, 1984). Most state courts do not allow polygraph testimony in criminal or civil trials. Furthermore, the Congressional Office of Technology Assessment has cautioned against its use for personnel security screening (U.S. Congress, 1983, p. 4), and the American Psychological Association (1986) has also cautioned against its use. The polygraph is ineffectual with pathological liars, or even with practiced liars. Several factors have been shown to invalidate test results, including deliberate changes in breathing patterns, biting the tongue, and tightening the anal sphincter, all of which cause physiological arousal to every question. Laboratory research has also shown that the use of tranquilizers or alcohol by the individual being tested can mislead the polygraph examiner. Results have also been shown to be affected by the testee's ethnicity, and whether or not testees are depressed (Waid & Orne, 1982). One study even found a birth-order effect, with later-born children being more effective liars who were better able to elude detection (Waid & Orne, 1982).

My advice to you is that if you are one of the many Americans who are tested annually with a polygraph, *refuse to take the test if you are innocent.* On the other hand, if you are guilty and others believe you are guilty, you should take the test as it may support your false claims of innocence. Research has shown about 20% of guilty people are misclassified as innocent (Lykken, 1984).

Recent research at the Salk Institute in La Jolla, California, suggests that modern computer technology may eventually aid in lie detection. Researchers have programmed a computer to recognize very brief facial expressions that Paul Ekman has shown often precede the telling of a lie (Bartlett, Hager, Ekman, & Sejnowski, 1999). These facial expressions range from a slight crow's-feet crinkling around the eyes that often occurs with a smile, to the contraction of forehead muscles associated with a scowl. These are involuntary muscle movements that are very difficult to fake. The computer has consistently outperformed human nonexperts and has performed as well as highly trained experts. This approach offers hope that a better lie detector will be developed—one that is more accurate and less intrusive than the existing polygraph technology.

Increasingly common are relatively inexpensive electronic devices offered to the public that purport to be able to indicate when someone is lying. Many of these machines use only the voice to judge whether a lie is being told. At best these machines might measure stress in the voice but this is not necessarily indicative that someone is telling a lie. Accusing someone of lying is serious, and you would be well-advised to avoid any of the commercial products, all of which lack any scientific validation. The collective research on lying consistently reveals how difficult it is to detect a lie, especially when people are highly motivated to get away with their lies (DePaulo, 1994). By the way, you may think you can better detect lies in someone that you know very well, but all the research suggests otherwise. In fact, we are more trusting of those we know well, especially our spouses, and believe (incorrectly) that we can easily and accurately gauge how truthful they are being.

Gender Differences in Emotionality

In our culture, women are generally considered to be more "emotional" than men. Several research studies lend credence to this belief. I mentioned previously that women are better than men at reading the emotional signals of others. Women also use more facial expressions to show emotion than do males. Interestingly, however, when measuring physiological aspects of emotional reactivity, women have been shown to react less strongly than men to the same emotionally arousing stimulus. Thus, if a man and a woman were to witness another person in distress, the woman would show the distress more through overt means such as facial gestures and body movements, whereas men would react more covertly, through physiological changes. This may be specific to our culture, where most boys are taught early on to hide overt signs of emotionality.

APPLICATIONS: Controlling Emotions

There are two components to an emotional response. There is the *cognitive appraisal* of the situation causing the emotional response, and there is the *physiological response* that occurs after that appraisal is made. You can control the intensity of your emotional response by trying to work on both of these factors. Let's examine the physiological response first. I spoke briefly about controlling arousal in the previous chapter when I discussed how it affects task performance. I recommended some breathing exercises to reduce arousal. Similar techniques will work in highly emotional situations. Take large deep breaths and concentrate on exhaling slowly through your nose. Most people find these breathing techniques cause them to relax, and the physiological correlates that go with emotional arousal are minimized.

Equally important is the cognitive appraisal of the emotionally charged situation. The way we think about or appraise a situation often influences how we respond to it. If someone pulls out in front of you in traffic, you can think to yourself what an idiot the person is and how stupid the driver acted. You might further appraise the act as an intentionally aggressive act directed specifically toward you. If this is your cognitive appraisal, then you will likely get very angry and may engage in acts of retribution. However, you may alternatively appraise the driver's act as unintentional, perhaps thinking about times you yourself have committed similar egregious driving faux pas. You might also think that possibly the driver had some good, but not obvious, reason for the blunder, such as being in a hurry because of a family emergency. If you cognitively appraise the situation in these terms, you are much more likely to control your emotional responses. I will discuss driving anger in greater detail, later in this chapter.

For help in controlling your emotions, you might wish to try a technique used by those who practice meditation and yoga; repeat a saying or sound (called a mantra) over and over to yourself to prevent yourself from thinking about the situation in inappropriate ways. Remember that strong emotional arousal can be very debilitating to task performance, particularly when the task is very difficult. For me, hitting a golf ball well is a very difficult task. Like most golfers, I sometimes find myself thinking negative thoughts as I line up to hit the ball. These negative thoughts ("I know I'm going to mess up this shot!") lead to an emotional response and tend to become self-fulfilling prophecies. One of the best pieces of golf advice I ever received was to say to yourself over and over the word "back" as you take the club back to swing. As the club starts going forward, you say the word "hit." It may sound simplistic, but it is very hard to have negative thoughts as you are concentrating on saying "back, back, back, back, hit!" This is just one example of how a mantra can be used to avoid inappropriate cognitive appraisals.

Perhaps one of the most emotionally arousing situations for college students is the anxiety accompanying tests. In the previous chapter on motivation I described several techniques for controlling this kind of arousal.

Emotion and Aging

Our early years can be characterized as a turbulent emotional roller coaster. I am certain you have frequently witnessed how infants and young children can go from a state of jubilant laughter to being extremely distraught, often in a matter of minutes or even seconds. Childhood and adolescence can also be filled with angst, as we sort through our changing relationships with parents and friends.

Recently, researchers have focused on what happens to us emotionally during the second half of our lives. The **socioemotional selectivity theory** maintains that as people age, they increasingly become aware that they have a limited amount of time left to live (Carstensen, 1995). As a result, older people shift more of their attention toward satisfying emotional goals and relationships. Long-term relationships with family and friends come to assume an increasingly high importance. Furthermore, as they approach the end of their lives, the emotional component of relationships becomes more important.

Are emotional feelings less intense in old age? One might expect so, since we experience declines in our ability to experience many other sensory sensations as we age. However, research shows that emotions are experienced with the same subjective intensity in old age as they are in our youth. However, the amount of physiological arousal associated with emotions does decline as we get older. The good news for older people is that they experience fewer negative emotions and equivalent or greater levels of positive emotions as compared to younger people. Levels of reported happiness and joy in older people are the same as in younger people. One advantage of aging is that older adults have greater control over their emotions, including greater stability of mood states. When negative emotions are experienced, they last for a shorter duration as compared to younger adults.

As compared to middle-aged married couples, there is less emotional turmoil in older couples' interpersonal relationships, including less anger, disgust, belligerence, and whining in their discussions. Older adults are more effective at managing their negative emotions while enjoying the same frequency and duration of positive emotions as younger people (Carstensen and Charles, 1998). Overall, this paints a positive picture of what we can expect in our emotional life as we approach the end of our lives.

Although there are many emotions that we experience each day, I will concentrate here on three that are particularly important to us: anger and its associated aggression, love, and happiness.

Anger and Aggression

Anger is one of our most basic emotions, and it sometimes leads to aggressive behaviors. Anger can vary in intensity from very mild annoyance to such an intense feeling that we may temporarily lose control of our behavior. Because of the strong link between anger and aggression, psychologists often talk about the two as similar entities.

Causes of Anger

What makes you angry? There are considerable differences between individuals. Most people have certain things that make them very angry or "push their buttons." For instance, I have known people who are otherwise very calm and collected who become extremely angry and aggressive when they get behind the wheel of their car. This "Jekyll and Hyde" metamorphosis is always as fascinating to observe as it is difficult to understand.

James Averill (1983) asked a large number of people to keep a diary about what made them angry for one week. Most people reported they get at least mildly angry at least several times a week. Misconduct by friends or loved ones was particularly likely to induce anger, particularly if the other person's act was perceived as intentional, unjustified, and avoidable. This anger toward friends or family accounted for over half of the reported anger incidents. Subjects reported that they usually dealt with this anger by speaking directly with the offending persons about their behavior, as opposed to attacking them or allowing the angry feelings to fester inside (Averill, 1983). As the poet William Blake phrased it:

> I was angry with my friend:
> I told my wrath, my wrath did end.
> I was angry with my foe:
> I told it not, my wrath did grow.

Sometimes anger is more impersonal, such as when it is directed at objects, bad smells or tastes, uncomfortable temperatures, and so forth. Personally, I become incensed by what I have termed "the obstinance of inanimate objects." By this, I mean the anger that is felt when some inanimate object like a shoestring or button breaks at the most inopportune moment, or when an object that you drop rolls to the most inaccessible location possible.

Frustration

The **frustration-aggression hypothesis** was an early theory about the causes of anger and aggression (Dollard, Miller, Doob, Mowrer, & Sears, 1939). According to this view, the primary cause of anger and aggression is a feeling of frustration. You may recall from the previous chapter that frustration occurs when a person is blocked from reaching an expected goal. If you are rushing to campus to take an important college examination, you may feel frustrated and angry when your car won't start, or when other drivers on the road impede your progress. Although most psychologists agree that frustration is an important factor in anger, most feel that other factors are equally important. All unpleasant events, including those that do not cause frustration, can give rise to feelings of anger (Berkowitz, 1983). When experiencing something unpleasant, we feel the impulse to both fight and flee. Which course of action we pursue depends on the circumstances we find ourselves in. For example, if someone has said something to you that has angered you, your response will vary depending upon whether it was from a good friend, your spouse, your boss, or a 350-pound football player with a chip on his shoulder. Your responses could vary from striking out verbally or physically to doing nothing. The fight or flight response depends upon a variety of factors, including our past experiences in dealing with anger (Berkowitz, 1983).

Innate Tendencies

Sigmund Freud, who believed that all humans are born with a drive to be aggressive, formulated another early viewpoint on aggression. He believed that this drive, along with the sexual drive, was important in the formation of one's personality. A famous Austrian animal ethologist named Konrad Lorenz also believed that aggression was innate, and that it was adaptive in man, as in animals, because it allowed the most fit to survive and reproduce. Lorenz felt that the suppression of these aggressive instincts caused the anger to build up, sometimes to the point where a violent explosive act resulted. He believed in the necessity of venting anger to control it. Do you feel better after kicking the tire of your car that went flat at a particularly bad time? The emotional release that results from acting out of anger is called a **catharsis.** Psychologists agree that this may indeed temporarily diffuse anger under certain circumstances, but under other circumstances expressing anger can bring about more anger. Studies have suggested that making angry gestures, like flipping off that driver who cut in front of you, can actually lead to higher levels of anger and may lead to further acts of escalation and retribution.

Genetics

Do genetics play a role in aggression? In the 1970s it was found that men who were born with an extra Y chromosome were much more likely to display episodes of aggressive behavior than were men who did not have this extra chromosome. For example, prisoners who had been convicted of a violent crime were found to more frequently possess this extra chromosome. Nevertheless, many psychologists feel that the evidence for a genetic basis for aggression is still inconclusive. If genetics are a factor, they are likely not one of the major causes.

Hormones

There is some evidence that the level of sex hormones promotes aggression in males. Drugs that block the effects of these hormones have been shown to reduce aggression in males. One research study showed a correlation between testosterone levels in both male and female prison inmates and the violence level of the crime for which they were convicted. Since this was only a correlational study, it is not certain whether the testosterone caused the violence or whether the prison environment was responsible. The available evidence is suggestive that hormones play a role in stimulating aggression, but further research will be needed for a final determination.

Learning

Although biological factors likely play some role in aggression, most psychologists believe that learning is one of the most important factors. Aggressive behaviors are often encouraged and reinforced, particularly in the American culture. Many parents teach their children to stand up for their rights, and to fight if they have to. As I discussed in the chapter on learning, most parents in the United States believe in, and use, corporal punishment in rearing their children. Children who were reared in a physically abusive environment often raise their own children the same way. Abusive parents were often victims of abuse themselves as children.

One of the biggest sources of learned aggression is through **imitation.** Children who see their parents being rewarded for being aggressive will frequently imitate this behavior. The mass media are also a rich resource for children to view the effects of aggression. In the movies and on television, aggression is frequently shown as an effective way to solve problems. The number of movies where the hero solves problems through peaceful means, as in the movie *Gandhi,* is far outnumbered by those in which violent aggression is used. The violence that is depicted is often antiseptic, with no suggestion of the unfortunate consequences for the victim or the perpetrator.

There is a continuing debate about whether viewing violence causes aggression. Several studies are suggestive that long-term viewing of violence causes children, especially boys, to be more violent. One study found that boys who prefer violent television programs at age 8 are more aggressive, both at that age and 10 years later (Lefkowitz, Eron, Walder, & Huesmann, 1977). There is also evidence that children who are very aggressive *seek out* violent television programs, so the direction of the causality is not clear (Huesmann & Eron, 1986). What is known is that when television is introduced to cultures that have not previously experienced it, the homicide rate increases dramatically (Centerwall, 1989). In addition to media portrayals of violence, video games with violence as the central theme are becoming increasingly popular with children. The long-term effects of these games remain to be determined.

Pornography

Some politicians and religious leaders have blamed the increasing availability of pornography for violence and aggression, both in children and in adults. Pornography is readily available to everyone who has access to the Internet. Several studies have shown that overall there are no major adverse effects from viewing pornography. However, in recent years there has been an increase in pornography that depicts violence and threats, often involving women in subservient roles. A favorite theme is that of women forced into sexual activities against their will, but who come to eventually find the experience pleasurable. One survey of the research in this area concluded that watching violent pornography increases aggressive behavior in those who view it (Malamuth & Donnerstein, 1982). The survey further concluded, however, that it was the violence more than the sexual content that was most damaging.

Predicting Aggressive and Violent Behavior

The emotion of anger can lead to aggressive behavior, and that aggression can sometimes become violent. Psychologists and psychiatrists are often called upon to make professional judgments about whether a person's behavior is likely to be a danger to self or others. This frequently occurs in the judicial system where parole boards make decisions concerning the release of a prisoner based on such judgments. Psychologists and psychiatrists are also frequently called upon by the courts to testify as "expert witnesses" about the likelihood of a person becoming dangerous. Do these professionals, based on their education, training, and experience, have an extraordinary ability to make predictions such as these? Unfortunately, they do not.

Numerous studies have shown that mental health professionals, even those with extensive training and experience, are little better than laypeople in predicting which individuals will become violent. Several studies indicate that in almost two out of three cases, professionals in psychology incorrectly predicted which violent criminals would repeat their offenses. Two recent books, Margaret Hagen's *Whores of the Court* (1997) and Robyn Dawes's seminal *House of Cards: Psychology and Psychotherapy Built on Myth* (1994), reviewed hundreds of research studies on this topic. These studies confirmed that the extent of psychological training, the type of training, and the years of clinical experience all were irrelevant factors affecting the accuracy of such clinical judgments.

There is a better alternative, however. The accuracy can be considerably improved by making **actuarial judgments,** which involves applying empirically derived rules that will examine the relevant factors. This is exactly what automobile insurance companies do when they compile accident rates on the basis of age, gender, marital status, and past-driving record. Similarly, there are known characteristics that can be used to predict the potential violent behavior of prisoners. One study in Pennsylvania showed that predictions based only on (1) the type of offense that led to imprisonment, (2) the number of past convictions, and (3) the number of violations of prison rules were consistently more predictive of criminal behavior of released prisoners than were psychologists' or psychiatrists' "expert" clinical judgments. Furthermore, actuarial judgments can be made quickly and cheaply by the use of a simple computer program. Other factors that have been found to be associated with a tendency toward violent behavior include

- a history of physical abuse as a child
- witnessing violence in the home as a child
- genetic factors; having a close relative with a history of mental illness
- exposure to a large amount of violence on television
- lack of remorse after hurting someone
- brain damage
- history of acting violently as a child
- a history of attempting suicide
- a history of torturing animals during childhood.

Perhaps not surprisingly, most mental health professionals resist the actuarial approach. They consider such a mathematical approach "dehumanizing" and claim it ignores the uniqueness inherent in each individual. They find it difficult to believe that their diagnostic skills, often honed over many years of training and practice, can be bettered by a formulaic strategy operated by a computer program.

APPLICATIONS: Preventing and Controlling Aggression

Do psychologists have effective ways to prevent or control aggression? Several approaches have been tried, with mixed results. Recall Freud's thinking that aggression is a biological drive that builds up like steam in a pressure cooker, and without periodic release an explosion is likely. Based on this view, many therapists recommended that people relieve their aggressive tendencies or "let off steam" through vigorous exercise, watching or participating in sports, or even hitting a punching

> When angry, count ten before you speak; if very angry, a hundred.
>
> **THOMAS JEFFERSON**
> *A Decalogue of Canons for Observation in Practical Life*

bag. A verbal catharsis was also recommended. As we saw earlier, engaging in aggression merely begets more aggression. Merely witnessing violence can make people more aggressive, as is witnessed by the increased incidence of spouse abuse that immediately follows Monday night football or the Super Bowl. A Denver policeman once told me he dreaded the times right after the end of a Bronco's football game, particularly when the home team was defeated, as the number of domestic abuse calls skyrocketed. Hence, the catharsis approach is no longer believed to be an effective method to head off aggression.

A more effective approach has been to teach people conflict resolution skills. Several such programs have been developed for relationship conflict, job conflict, and other situations. The legal profession also offers mediation services to help resolve conflicts in an objective and impersonal manner.

Finally, society must take certain actions to control aggression. Families who are in stressful situations often resort to aggression. This stress often comes about because of poverty, overcrowding, or personal distress. Many psychologists believe that society needs to improve its efforts toward helping people deal with these stressful circumstances or, more ideally, to help reduce or eliminate the factors causing the stress.

Road Rage

Probably the most likely situation for you to encounter someone else's anger and aggression is while driving. The American Automobile Association claims that the incidence of aggressive driving, commonly referred to as **road rage,** has been increasing by 7% per year since 1990. There were 1,800 reported incidents of road rage behavior that led to violence in 1996.

Jerry Deffenbacher has been one of the leading researchers in road rage for the past 10 years. His research has suggested that driving-related anger is a personality trait that is related to the more general personality trait of anger but is narrower and more situation- or context-related than the general trait of anger (Deffenbacher, Oetting, & Lynch, 1994). By surveying over 1,500 college drivers, six distinct situations were found to trigger the driving anger response: (1) *hostile gestures,* where another driver signals his or her anger or displeasure at the driver; (2) *illegal driving,* where another driver violates common traffic laws; (3) *police presence,* in which police are present in a driving situation; (4) *slow driving,* in which another driver or pedestrian slows traffic flow; (5) *discourtesy,* where other drivers engage in discourteous, as opposed to illegal, behavior; and (6) *traffic obstructions,* where events such as traffic jams or road construction frustrate or impede the driver. Deffenbacher and his colleagues have created a driving anger scale that measures drivers' anger in these six situations.

Do you ever get extremely angry with other drivers? You can take the test in Table 7.1, which will compare you with other college students. People who score high on this test are three times more likely to be provoked while driving, and are three times more likely to have angry, irrational reactions while driving than people who score low. High-anger drivers view common encounters on the road as personal affronts and can act violently and become self-righteous about even minor traffic inconveniences. These people often appear calm in other situations but

✦ TABLE 7.1 ✦ Driving Anger

This test describes common situations that occur during driving that may make you angry. Imagine that each of the situations described is actually happening to you while driving. Then, rate the amount of anger that would be provoked in each situation, using the following rating scale:

1 Not at all
2 A little
3 Some
4 Much
5 Very much

_____ 1. Someone makes an obscene gesture toward you about your driving.
_____ 2. You pass a radar speed trap.
_____ 3. Someone runs a red light or stop sign.
_____ 4. Someone honks at you about your driving.
_____ 5. Someone is weaving in and out of traffic.
_____ 6. A police officer pulls you over.
_____ 7. You are driving behind a large truck and cannot see around it.
_____ 8. A bicyclist is riding in the middle of the lane and slowing traffic.
_____ 9. Someone is slow in parking and holding up traffic.
_____ 10. A truck kicks up sand or gravel on the car you are riding in.
_____ 11. Someone speeds up when you try to pass them.
_____ 12. A slow vehicle on a mountain road will not pull over and let people by.
_____ 13. Someone backs right out in front of you without looking.
_____ 14. You are stuck in a traffic jam.

Scoring:
Add up all the scores listed below. The higher the score, the more likely it is that you are easily provoked and angered while driving. You may compare your driving anger with that of other college students by using the chart below.

Score	Percentile	Score	Percentile
21	0	47	50
26	1	49	60
30	3	50	64
32	5	52	72
35	10	54	79
38	17	56	86
40	22	57	89
41	25	59	93
42	28	60	95
43	32	64+	99
45	40		

Interpretation: The percentile tells the percentage of people who score at or below your score. For instance, a score of 40 falls at the 22nd percentile, which means that 22% of drivers have a driving anger score at or lower than yours and 78% have a higher score.

SOURCE: Reproduced with permission of authors and publisher from: Deffenbacher, J. L., Oetting, E. R., & Lynch, R. S. Development of a driving anger scale. *Psychological Reports,* 74, 1994, 83–91. © Psychological Reports 1994.

quickly turn hostile when sitting in the driver's seat. As you drive, you have probably noticed that some individuals become extremely angry at what are seemingly minor infractions by another driver, such as someone cutting in front of them unexpectedly. Others have a very high threshold for anger, and respond with only mild annoyance to such incidents (Deffenbacher, Oetting, & Lynch, 1994).

Deffenbacher and his colleagues have found interesting gender differences in driving anger. Women get angry about things that interfere with their driving, such as traffic obstructions, road repairs, and illegal driving (speeding, running stop signs, etc.) by other drivers. Men get angry with police presence and with slow drivers. Overall, however, men and women are about equally angry while driving.

APPLICATIONS

If you are a person who frequently becomes extremely angry while driving, you might want to consider counseling. As few as 8 short counseling sessions can be effective in getting angry drivers to rethink their attitudes (Deffenbacher, Oetting, & Lynch, 1994). Angry drivers are counseled to realize that everyone makes inappropriate driving mistakes on occasion. Remembering and accepting this fact helps make people more patient when they encounter a difficult situation. High-anger drivers should also learn relaxation techniques. One recommendation is that they play their favorite music or audio-book tapes as a way to lower their anger.

Finally, what should you do when you encounter an angry driver? Experts on traffic safety make the following recommendations:

- Avoid eye contact with an aggressive driver.
- Don't make or return obscene gestures. Also avoid making faces and yelling, as things can quickly escalate out of control if you do.
- Don't tailgate or engage in any "tit for tat" behaviors.
- Disengage from the situation by slowing down or allowing the angry driver to pass.

A soft answer turneth away wrath.

PROVERBS 15:1

LOVE

Love: the most enticing and yet elusive emotion of them all. Some people feel that this is a topic that should be "left to the heart," and not studied scientifically. However, psychologists disagree. There has been a considerable amount of research done on this emotion and some of the findings may surprise you.

Psychologists draw a distinction between liking and loving. **Liking** includes feelings of respect and admiration for another individual. On the other hand, **loving** involves deeper feelings of needing someone, caring deeply for and trusting him or her, and showing tolerance. Liking and loving are not completely independent, and many psychologists feel that true love cannot occur unless we also like an individual. You can like an individual without loving him or her, but loving someone in the absence of liking the person seldom, if ever, occurs.

Mysterious love, uncertain treasure,
Hath thou more of pain or pleasure!
Endless torments dwell about thee:
Yet who would live, and live without thee!

ADDISON
Rosamond

Kinds of Love

One of the leading researchers on love proposes that love has three basic components: (1) **intimacy,** which involves feelings of being close and connected to another individual, and includes feelings that you can talk to and closely confide in another without risk; (2) **passion,** the intense sexual attraction you feel toward another; and (3) **commitment,** a decision that you wish to continue the relationship for an extended period of time (Sternberg, 1986). These three dimensions are, to a certain extent, independent. You may be passionately in love with someone for the evening but have little interest in sharing feelings of intimacy with the person or in making a commitment beyond the short run. There are seven different kinds of love, depending on which combination of these three components exist (Sternberg, 1986):

1. Infatuation. Passion exists, but not intimacy or commitment.
2. Liking or friendship. Intimacy is present, but not passion or commitment.
3. Empty love. Commitment, but no passion or intimacy.
4. Romantic love. Both passion and intimacy exist, but not commitment.
5. Companionate love. Feelings of intimacy and commitment, but lacking in passion.
6. Fatuous love. Feelings of both passion and commitment, but no intimacy.
7. When *all three* components exist, Sternberg claims there exists the ideal and highest form of love, which he calls **consummate love.**

If all three factors of passion, intimacy, and commitment are missing then love is absent.

Styles of Love

Clyde Hendrick, a former classmate of mine from my undergraduate days, and his wife, Susan, have conducted research on differing styles of love (Hendrick & Hendrick, 1986). Their research has extended the seminal work of John Lee (1973) who proposed three primary and three secondary love styles, which I will briefly describe here. These styles of love are learned rather than innate, and individuals can have more than one preference of love style during their lifetime. We sometimes have preferences for two different styles at the same time, each preference being satisfied by a different partner (Lee, 1973).

As you read the following descriptions, see if you can identify your own preference or preferences in love style. You will also, no doubt, recognize lovers you have had (or currently have) as you read these descriptions. The rather unusual names for these love styles come from ancient Greek and Latin.

Primary Love Styles

1. **Eros.** This style of love is always based on a powerful physical attraction. These lovers know exactly what physical attributes they are looking for in a lover and become very excited when they encounter a person who fits their ideal. They often experience "love at first sight." You have probably known this type of person who sees someone he or she finds particularly attractive and instantly claims "I think I'm in love!" Erotic lovers seek to get to know their beloved

quickly, intensely, and in a sexual manner. They are very expressive both verbally and in touching the object of their desire. They consider finding and living with their ideal partner the most important thing in their lives.

2. **Storge.** In this style, love develops slowly and not at a fever pitch. There is no love at first sight, as in the erotic style. Feelings start with affection and progressively grow stronger as the relationship matures. They perceive love as a special friendship where individuals share time and interests. They have no preference for a particular body type. There is no constant preoccupation with their beloved, and they refrain from being excessively demonstrative about their feelings. They take time to get to know their partner before engaging in sexual relations. This is the love that starts out slowly as a friendship, and slowly but surely transforms into a deeply felt love. As the French writer Molière put it, "Love is often a fruit of marriage."
3. **Ludus.** This style is characterized by individuals who go through a succession of lovers. They find it difficult to devote their entire life to one person, taking the philosophy that there are plenty of "fish in the sea." Their love is playful and noncommittal. They are never jealous and avoid partners who are. Lovers of this style are often candid with their beloved about their interests in others. They are reluctant to settle down or get too involved with just one person, and find many different physical types attractive. Furthermore, they don't feel extreme excitement when meeting someone new and never experience love at first sight. They enjoy having several partners at the same time, and can love them all equally. Sex is seen as something that is fun, and is not a sign of commitment.

Secondary Love Styles

John Lee (1988) believed that several other secondary love styles arise from various combinations of the above three primary styles. He likens love to the rainbow of colors that are possible from various combinations of the three primary colors of red, blue, and yellow. He describes three familiar secondary love styles that frequently appear in American society.

4. **Mania.** This secondary style is a mixture of eros and ludus. Love strikes like a lightning bolt out of the sky. The person is obsessed with the beloved, very jealous, and extremely possessive. Such people demand constant reassurance and commitment from their beloved, while at the same time hold back their own feelings for fear of being hurt. They demand that their partner show more affection to them, yet they rarely find sex with their chosen either satisfying or reassuring. Strangely, the manic lover doesn't even *like* the beloved, and would not choose him or her as a lasting friend. They enjoy a type of "love-hate" relationship with their beloved, being attracted and repelled simultaneously. Lee uses the analogy of an addict's relationship to heroin. This is the love style of many young people who become suddenly captivated with another person. With maturity, most abandon this style and move on to other more satisfying styles, although middle-aged individuals sometimes resort to this style, after a more sedate storgic marriage has grown dull. The partner is the one who ends the relationship, and the manic lover doesn't get over it for a long time (Lee, 1988).

5. Pragma. This style is a combination of ludus and storge. Called pragmatic lovers, these individuals see finding a suitable mate as a practical problem, which can be solved by prudent efforts and the application of good common sense. They have what is described as a "shopping list" of qualities they seek in their partner, although physical qualities are usually unimportant (Lee, 1988). Compatibility in religious and political views and in social class background are deemed important. They often find their beloved in a social setting where they can get to know the person before making any commitment. Computer-dating agencies can prove helpful in the search, but the pragmatic lover also seeks out a partner by joining a club, a church, a charity group, or a political party in the hope of finding someone compatible. They refrain from excessive displays of emotion, but like to receive signals of affection and commitment from their chosen. Being the practical type, they don't believe in a special "chemistry" between lovers.
6. Agape. This is a combination of the eros and storge styles and, according to Lee, is the style of love encouraged by the Christian religion. He also believes that it is the style practiced most infrequently in adult relationships. This style is a selfless, giving, altruistic love, whose practitioners consider love a duty, even if no strong emotional feelings are present. Their actions reflect a gentle, patient, dutiful, and caring love that lacks any self-interest. The agapic lover feels an intense sense of duty to care for the beloved with affection.

Research has confirmed that these six love styles are conceptually distinct (Hendrick & Hendrick, 1986). The questionnaire illustrated in Table 7.2 will help you determine which love style fits your own personality (Hendrick, Hendrick, & Dicke, 1998).

What difference does it make what love style you and your partner prefer? The more similar the love styles, the more likely it is that two lovers will enjoy a satisfying relationship (Lee, 1988). Lee illustrates his styles with a circle and triangle diagram, which is shown in Figure 7.2. You can compare your love style with that of your beloved and see how closely they match. Some love styles are more compatible than others. For example, a storgic and a pragmatic lover will make a good match (note their proximity in Figure 7.2). In contrast, a manic and storgic lover will often be in conflict. We will learn in a later chapter more about how similarities are important in lasting interpersonal relationships.

Stages of Love

As most anyone who has been in love can attest, romantic relationships often go through predictable stages, including a beginning, middle, and (unfortunately and sometimes painfully) an end. Relationships progress through up to five stages (Levinger, 1980).

1. Initial attraction. This is the rush of emotional excitement that accompanies the beginning of the relationship. We typically, but not always, are attracted to people who are similar to us, as I will discuss further in chapter 11.
2. Buildup stage. In this stage, partners learn more about each other, often sharing intimate information about themselves. The emotional excitement continues in

✦ TABLE 7.2 ✦ The Love Attitudes Scale

This questionnaire measures the six love styles originally conceptualized by Lee (1973).

Instructions:
Listed below are several statements that reflect different attitudes about love. For each statement indicate how much you agree or disagree with that statement. The items refer to a specific love relationship. Whenever possible, answer the questions with your current partner in mind. If you are not currently dating anyone, answer the questions with your most recent partner in mind. If you have never been in love, answer in terms of what you think your responses would most likely be.

For each statement:

1 = Strongly agree with the statement
2 = Moderately agree with the statement
3 = Neutral—neither agree nor disagree
4 = Moderately disagree with the statement
5 = Strongly disagree with the statement

_____ 1. My partner and I have the right physical "chemistry" between us.
_____ 2. I feel that my partner and I were meant for each other.
_____ 3. My partner and I really understand each other.
_____ 4. My partner fits my ideal standards of physical beauty/handsomeness.
_____ 5. I believe that what my partner doesn't know about me won't hurt him/her.
_____ 6. I have sometimes had to keep my partner from finding out about other lovers.
_____ 7. My partner would be upset if he/she knew of some of the things I've done with other people.
_____ 8. I enjoy playing the "game of love" with my partner and a number of other partners.
_____ 9. Our love is the best kind because it grew out of a long friendship.
_____ 10. Our friendship merged gradually into love over time.
_____ 11. Our love is really a deep friendship, not a mysterious, mystical emotion.
_____ 12. Our love relationship is the most satisfying because it developed from a good friendship.

(continued)

this stage, but the relationship is still tenuous. One study using college students revealed that nearly half the romantic relationships in this stage had broken up by the end of the academic year (Berscheid, Snyder, & Omoto, 1989).

3. Continuation stage. In this stage, the relationship becomes relatively stable. Much of the initial emotional excitement has dissipated and the relationship has "settled in." The partners enjoy each other's company and continue to share intimacies with each other. They find communication to be easy and

✦ TABLE 7.2 ✦ Continued

_____ 13. A main consideration in choosing my partner was how he/she would reflect on my family.
_____ 14. An important factor in choosing my partner was whether or not he/she would be a good parent.
_____ 15. One consideration in choosing my partner was how he/she would reflect on my career.
_____ 16. Before getting very involved with my partner, I tried to figure out how compatible his/her hereditary background would be with mine in case we ever had children.
_____ 17. When my partner doesn't pay attention to me, I feel sick all over.
_____ 18. Since I've been in love with my partner I've had trouble concentrating on anything else.
_____ 19. I cannot relax if I suspect that my partner is with someone else.
_____ 20. If my partner ignores me for awhile, I sometimes do stupid things to try to get his/her attention back.
_____ 21. I would rather suffer myself than let my partner suffer.
_____ 22. I cannot be happy unless I place my partner's happiness before my own.
_____ 23. I am usually willing to sacrifice my own wishes to let my partner achieve his/hers.
_____ 24. I would endure all things for the sake of my partner.

Scoring:
Add up your total score for the questions indicated below to determine your own love style(s). The *lower* the total score for each love style, the more this love style fits you.

Love Style

Eros	**Ludus**	**Storge**	**Pragma**	**Mania**	**Agape**
Questions					
1–4	5–8	9–12	13–16	17–20	21–24
Total score					
_____	_____	_____	_____	_____	_____

SOURCE: Reprinted by permission of Sage Publications, Ltd. from Hendrick, C., Hendrick, S. S., & Dicke, A., *Journal of Social and Personal Relationships.* © Sage Publications 1998.

enjoyable. Successful, long-term marriages remain in this stage, with partners listening to each other and validating each other's opinions.

4. Deterioration. The beginning of the end. In this stage communication breaks down, and one or both partners feel they are not getting their fair share from the relationship. This frequently occurs in a relationship when one of the partners changes and the other does not. Oftentimes the deterioration occurs slowly, but it can also happen very rapidly.

✦ FIGURE 7.2 ✦ A Circle and Triangle Illustration of Lee's Love Styles

The three primary styles are at the apexes of the triangle. Each pair of primaries are combined in two ways—along the triangle or around the circle. For example, Eros and Storge combine to form one of two possible combinations: Agape or Storgic Eros. Lee maintains that the closer in proximity the two love styles are on this chart, the more likely it is that two lovers' styles will match and a satisfying relationship will result.

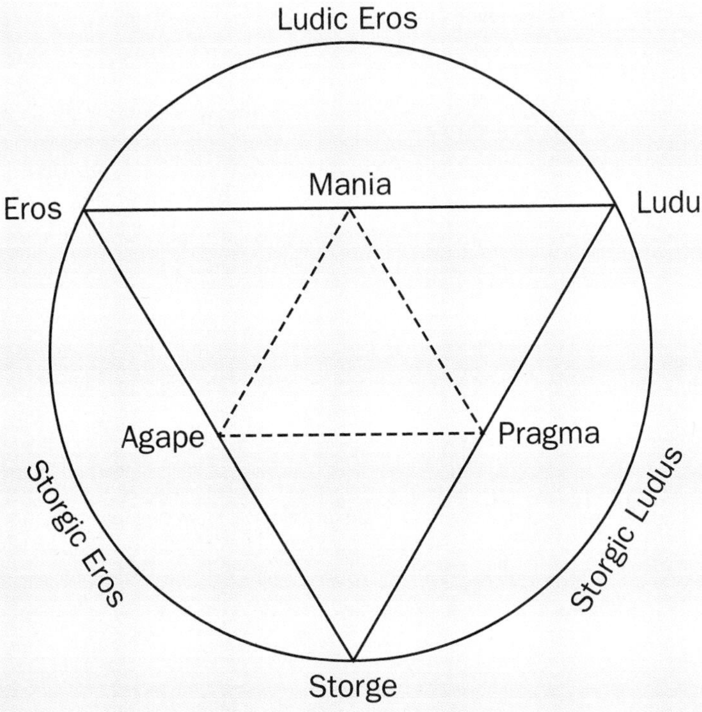

SOURCE: Taken from Lee, J. A. In R. J. Sternberg & M. L. Barnes (Eds.), *The psychology of love*, Yale University Press, Copyright 1988. Reprinted with permission.

5. Ending. Usually one partner decides to end the relationship. Only rarely do both partners reach this decision simultaneously. Interestingly, women initiate the breakup more frequently than men, who are more often clueless about problems in the relationship and therefore don't foresee this stage coming. Contrary to what many believe, men are also more upset than women about the relationship ending (Levinger, 1980).

In love, the one first cured is the one most completely cured.

LA ROCHEFOUCAULD
Maxims

The Ability to Love

Is everyone capable of experiencing the emotion of love? Sadly, the answer is no. A large amount of research has shown conclusively that the ability to love and form loving relationships is shaped by our past experiences. Harry Harlow (1971) con-

Figure 7.3

Research by Harry Harlow (1971) on learning to love used young monkeys who had been separated from their mothers at birth. The monkeys were raised with surrogate mothers, consisting of either a wire frame or a cloth-covered wire frame, as illustrated here. The monkeys were well cared for in terms of their physical needs, but did not receive any traditional maternal nurturing.

ducted some of the earliest research in this area using rhesus monkeys. Infant monkeys were removed from their mothers shortly after birth, and were raised with wire and cloth surrogate mothers (see Figure 7.3). The infant monkeys were well-fed and received good physical care, but were raised in isolation from their mothers and thus deprived of all maternal love. These monkeys were later introduced to other monkeys their own age. These emotionally deprived monkeys were incapable of forming friendships with, or even playing with, the other young monkeys. Upon maturing, they were not receptive to sexual advances from other monkeys. Harlow artificially impregnated the female monkeys and observed their parenting skills with their offspring. The monkeys deprived of love failed to feed or care for their young (Harlow, 1971). In fact, the mothers treated their offspring so badly that Harlow had to remove them from their mothers to prevent them from being killed.

Sadly, young human infants often experience similar conditions early in their life. In the United States in the early 1900s many orphanages raised infants in conditions similar to Harlow's infant monkeys. During this time it was commonly believed that too much human interaction would "spoil" an infant. Therefore, infants in some orphanages (then called foundling homes) were well fed and cared for physically, but did not receive the emotional stimulation they required, including the normal cuddling and emotional interaction typically received by infants. They were often left in their cribs for extended periods of time, with little or no contact from their caretakers. René Spitz (1945) examined the outcomes for these infants and found that between 30 and 100% died within 1 year. Those who did survive were retarded in both their physical and intellectual development. Furthermore, they were socially incompetent and unresponsive to their environment.

Psychologists have coined the term **attachment disorder** to describe children who have experienced this kind of emotional deprivation. This disorder is associated with severely pathological parental care, characterized by (1) persistent disregard for the child's emotional needs for comfort, attention, stimulation, and affection; (2) disregard for the child's physical needs; and/or (3) repeated changes in caretakers (Gardner, 1997). The longer these conditions exist, especially during the first 2 years, the more damaging the effect on a child's later ability to form loving relationships.

Children with attachment disorders display several kinds of pathology, including an inability to give or receive love, manipulative and superficial interactions with others, lying and stealing, self-destructive behaviors, and aggression and cruelty to others, including pets (Gardner, 1997). They have an undeveloped conscience, show an inability to form or sustain friendships, and often have a preoccupation with fire, blood, and gore.

The prognosis for such children is poor, especially if they have been exposed to emotional deprivation for an extended period of time early in their lives. The damage is usually done by age 3 or 4, and interventions after that are usually ineffective.

Well-meaning and unsuspecting people have adopted young children from foreign orphanages, sometimes only to discover that they were raised in these very kinds of emotionally deprived conditions. Adoptive parents often believe that if they just love these children enough, they will overcome their inability to love. Sadly, these adoptive parents almost invariably find out otherwise.

HAPPINESS

Human happiness is so important, it transcends all other worldly considerations.

ARISTOTLE

For most people, the most important emotion for our daily lives is that of happiness. Most would agree that if happiness is absent, just about everything else is unimportant.

Psychologists refer to happiness by the term **subjective well being** and believe that it contains two components: (1) a *cognitive* component, which reflects your judgment about how satisfied you are with your life, and (2) an *affective* component, which reflects your pleasant or unpleasant emotional reactions to events in your life.

How happy are most people? Several surveys have asked this question of large numbers of Americans and about 90% report that they are either "very happy" or "pretty happy" with the remaining 10% saying they are "not too happy" (Diener & Diener, 1996). Furthermore, the level of happiness of Americans has been stable over time, at least from 1946 to 1989 (Veenhoven, 1993). The level of happiness that is reported in America has been relatively unaffected by wars, downturns in the economy, changes in weather patterns, or other socially destabilizing influences.

There are interesting differences in levels of happiness between countries. In a comparison of 24 countries, Portugal and Greece were found to be the most unhappy while Denmark and Sweden were the happiest (Inglehart, 1990). A positive correlation was found between the economic wealth of the nations and their reported level of happiness, as is illustrated in Figure 7.4, reflecting that wealthier nations report higher feelings of well being. In another survey of 43 nations, only the impoverished countries of India and the Dominican Republic reported they were more unhappy than happy (Veenhoven, 1993).

Measurement of Happiness

How happy are you? Psychologists have used a variety of techniques to assess happiness in individuals. One frequently used approach is shown in Table 7.3 (Fordyce, 1988). This quick little test will allow you to compare your level of happiness to other college students in the United States.

✦ FIGURE 7.4 ✦ National wealth and reports of happiness in 24 nations.

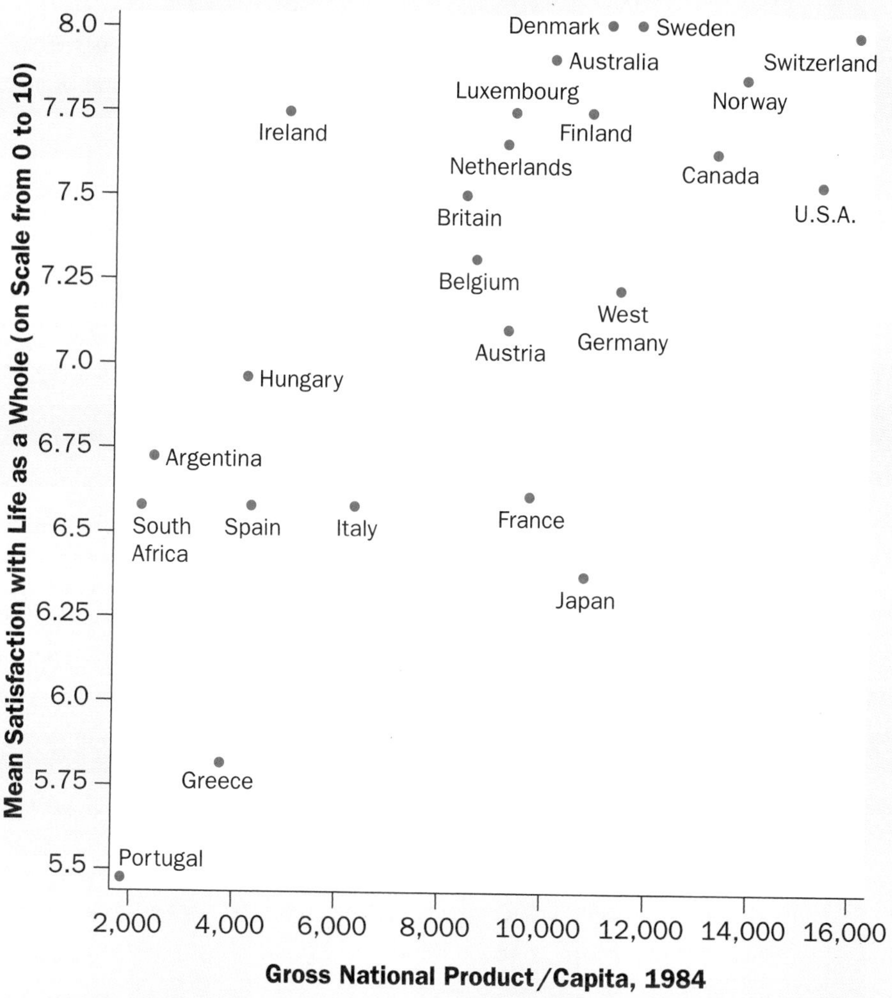

SOURCE: Inglehart, R., Culture shift in advanced industrial society. Copyright 1990 by Princeton University Press.

What exactly is this sometimes-elusive thing we call happiness? It includes the presence of positive emotions, the absence of negative emotions, and a general satisfaction with one's life (Myers & Diener, 1995). The research on happiness suggests that positive and negative emotional states are *not* the opposite of one another, but rather are largely independent. This means that the amount of positive emotions you are experiencing is unrelated to the amount of negative emotions you might also be experiencing. Some people experience a lot of both negative and positive emotions—and some experience more of one type than the other. To be truly happy,

✦ TABLE 7.3 ✦ Happiness Questionnaire

Part I. Directions:
Use the list below to answer the following question: IN GENERAL, HOW HAPPY OR UNHAPPY DO YOU USUALLY FEEL? Check the *one* statement that best describes *your average happiness.*

_____ 10 Extremely happy (feeling ecstatic, joyous, fantastic!)
_____ 9 Very happy (feeling really good, elated!)
_____ 8 Pretty happy (spirits high, feeling good.)
_____ 7 Mildly happy (feeling fairly good and somewhat cheerful.)
_____ 6 Slightly happy (just a bit below neutral.)
_____ 5 Neutral (not particularly happy or unhappy.)
_____ 4 Slightly unhappy (just a bit below neutral.)
_____ 3 Mildly unhappy (just a little low.)
_____ 2 Pretty unhappy (somewhat "blue," spirits down.)
_____ 1 Very unhappy (depressed, spirits very low.)
_____ 0 Extremely unhappy (utterly depressed, completely down.)

Part II. Directions:
Consider your emotions a moment further. *On the average,* what percent of the time do you feel happy? What percent of the time do you feel unhappy? What percent of the time do you feel neutral (neither happy nor unhappy)? Write down your best estimates, as well as you can, in the spaces below. Make sure the three figures add up to equal 100%.

ON THE AVERAGE:

The percent of time I feel happy	______%
The percent of time I feel unhappy	______%
The percent of time I feel neutral	______%
TOTAL:	100%

Scoring:
To find your combination happiness score do the following: Multiply your score from Part I times 10 and add the percentage of time you report that you are "happy." Divide

(continued)

however, you have to experience lots of positive emotions and relatively few negative emotions.

Factors That Do Not Affect Happiness

There have been some interesting studies on variables that do and do not affect happiness. The surprising findings are that most things that you probably think would affect long-term happiness have little or no effect, and are appropriately labeled the "myths of happiness" (Myers & Diener, 1995). For example, you might think that you will be a lot happier after you complete your college education, but research has showed that this has only a negligible effect on level of happiness (Lykken &

✦ TABLE 7.3 ✦ Continued

the resulting number by two [Combination score = (intensity scale score × 10 + happy %) / 2]. For example, a person who checked a score of 7 (mildly happy) in Part I and reported he or she was happy 60% of the time would have a combination happiness score of 65: [(7 × 10 + 60)/2 = 65].

You can then compare your score with data that Fordyce (1988) collected on 3,050 college students using the table below:

Combination Happiness Score	% of People Who Fall At or Below This Level of Happiness
97	70
78	60
62	50
43	40
7	30
7	20
0	15

Interpretation of Your Score:
If your combination score was 78, you fall at the 60th percentile, which means that you are as happy as or happier than 60% of the college students that were sampled. In other words, you are as happy as or happier than 3/5 of the college students previously measured.

Fordyce (1988) found that people who score high on this test have a low level of fear, hostility, tension, anxiety, guilt, confusion, anger, and other negative emotions. High scorers also have a high level of self-esteem, are emotionally stable, have a strong social orientation, and are outgoing, spontaneous, extroverted individuals. They have relatively few health concerns or personal problems, and are engaged in warm and satisfying love and social relationships. Fordyce (1988) further describes these people as optimistic, worry free, present oriented, and well directed (p. 370).

SOURCE: Adapted from *Social indicators research,* Volume 20, Fordyce, M. W., A review of research on the happiness measures: A sixty-second index of happiness and mental health. Copyright 1988, with permission from Kluwer Academic Publishers.

Tellegen, 1996). Individuals with Ph.D.s are not significantly happier, on average, than high school dropouts. How about those people in the upper socioeconomic class, with all their money and privilege? As with education, socioeconomic status and income both had insignificant effects on levels of happiness, although people in the lower classes were slightly more prone to negative emotional states. Age has also been shown to be unrelated to happiness, suggesting that there is no one time in life that is significantly happier or unhappier than others. Gender is also unimportant; males and females are about equally happy. You might think this is only true in America, where women have freedoms equivalent to men, but over 100 studies with 16 different countries all show no large gender differences for happiness. Perhaps surprisingly, race also has little to do with happiness. African Americans are just as happy as whites, and are even slightly less vulnerable to depression. How physically attractive an individual is has also been shown to be unrelated to level of happiness. Those who are unattractive may suffer other disadvantages (see chapter 11), but a feeling of unhappiness is not one of them.

What if you won the lottery and were suddenly a multimillionaire? People fantasize about this, and their fantasies usually include how happy they would be with their new cars, huge mansion, vacations in the Caribbean, and other extravagances. Despite the old saying "money can't buy happiness," many people devote a lot of time and effort trying to find out if this is so. I indicated earlier that wealthier nations are happier than poorer nations (see Figure 7.4). Is the same true of individuals? For the most part, no. The only time more money makes you significantly happier is if you are so poor that you cannot afford life's basic necessities, such as food, clothing, and shelter. Once you are able to afford these, additional affluence matters very little. In Colorado a few years ago, the state lottery had an idea to promote ticket sales. They held a reunion of all the past winners of at least a million dollars at a luxury hotel. Their idea was to film interviews with these people, to be used in future television commercials promoting lottery sales. The winners would be asked to testify as to how much happier they were after suddenly becoming millionaires. A problem arose when the winners consistently reported they were no more happy (or unhappy) than before they had won the money. Needless to say, these interviews were not aired in future lottery commercials. The lottery winners did report that the sudden affluence made them *temporarily* happier, but it was surprisingly short lived. These findings have been substantiated in studies with other lottery winners (Argyle, 1986; Bickman, Coates, & Janoff-Bulman, 1978). Still, wealth holds a certain allure. I had an assistant once tell me she didn't believe that money brought happiness, but that given a choice she would rather be unhappy and rich as opposed to unhappy and poor.

Many people believe that the state of their physical health is a big determinant in how happy they are. How happy could one be, they surmise, if one were suddenly to become blind or paralyzed? Health is like wealth; without it you can be miserable, but having it is no guarantee of happiness (Myers & Diener, 1995). People who suddenly develop a severe physical disability (such as a spinal cord injury) are temporarily very unhappy, but they quickly adapt and subsequently report a near-normal level of happiness within several weeks (Diener & Diener, 1996). Notably, of individuals with extreme quadriplegia (total paralysis from the neck down), 93% report they are glad to be alive, and 84% consider their life to be average or above average (Hellmich, 1995). One study looked at individuals with severe, multiple handicaps (Wacker, Harper, Powell, & Healy, 1983). Most of these people were unmarried, uneducated, and unemployed. Despite these circumstances, 96% reported they were satisfied with their living arrangements, and 82% with their social lives. People with severe mental problems have similar reports of subjective well being.

Personality Traits of Happy People

Research on happiness indicates that four inner traits consistently mark happy people: self-esteem, a sense of personal control, optimism, and extraversion (Myers & Diener, 1995). Let's examine each of these traits.

1. Self-esteem. Happy people like themselves. They believe that they get along better with others than the average person. They also believe they are more intelligent, more ethical, and healthier than the average person. However, the linkage between self-esteem and happiness is stronger in Western cultures, where governments exist for the individual, than in collectivist cultures, where groups take priority over individuals (Diener, Diener, & Diener, 1995).
2. Personal control. Happy people feel that they are in personal control of their lives. They generally believe that they control their life circumstances, rather than the other way around. This is probably related to the finding reported above that people living in an individualistic Western culture are happier, as people trapped in a collectivist or totalitarian regime often lose their sense of personal empowerment. Severe poverty also reduces the options for controlling one's life, which is why extremely impoverished people report higher levels of unhappiness.
3. Optimism. Happy people take the most hopeful view of matters, and believe that good will ultimately triumph over evil. Optimists usually look on the bright side of things, and avoid cynicism. Optimists are generally more successful, healthier, and happier than are pessimists.
4. Extraversion. Extraverts are people who are more sociable, fun loving, talkative, and affectionate than introverted people. They are also more comfortable reaching out to others. They are happy when they are alone as well as when they are with other people.

One difficulty in identifying traits associated with happiness is that while they are correlated with happiness, they may or may not *cause* happiness. That is, good self-esteem may cause happiness, but it is equally plausible that happiness causes people to have high self-esteem. Since it is well known that personality traits are genetically influenced (see chapter 1), there has been recent speculation about the role of heredity on happiness. I will discuss this topic further in the next section of this chapter.

Other characteristics have been found in happy people. One important factor is having a meaningful job that brings with it a sense of satisfaction and accomplishment. Meaningful work is challenging but not overwhelming. The rewards of work for happy people extend well beyond the paycheck (Myers & Diener, 1995).

People who are religious also report higher levels of happiness than those who are not. Studies show that happiness increases both with strength of religious affiliation and frequency of church attendance (Myers & Diener, 1995). A Gallup poll taken in 1984 indicated that highly spiritual people were twice as likely to report they were "very happy" than were those low in spiritual commitment (Gallup, 1984). As with the previous studies on personality traits and happiness, it is not clear that having religious convictions *causes* you to be happy. It may be that happy people seek out situations where they can socialize with people with views similar to their own, and church activities are merely one avenue for doing so. In any event, the research belies the famous statement by Karl Marx that "the first requisite for the happiness of the people is the abolition of religion."

Heritability of Happiness

Since certain personality traits are correlated with happiness, and since we know that personality traits are at least partially inherited, is it plausible that there may be

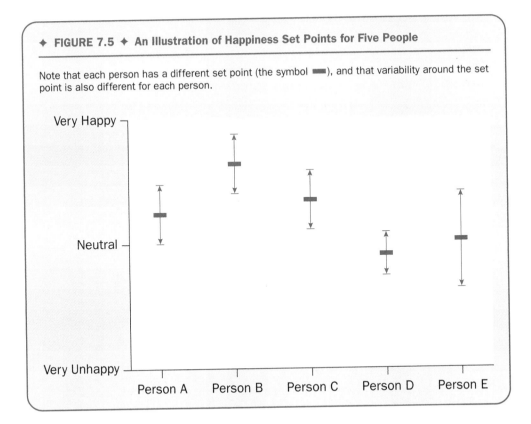

✦ FIGURE 7.5 ✦ An Illustration of Happiness Set Points for Five People

Note that each person has a different set point (the symbol ▬), and that variability around the set point is also different for each person.

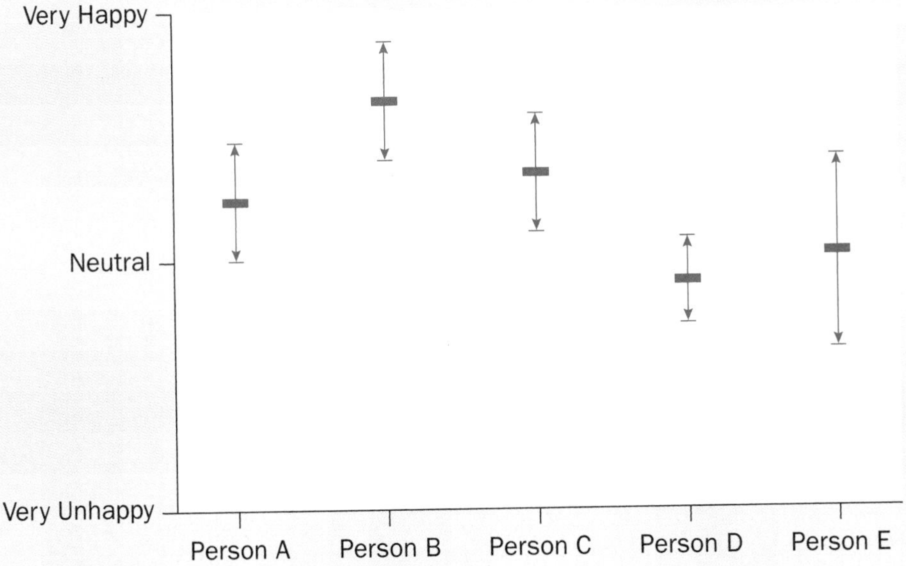

some genetic basis for happiness? David Lykken and Auke Tellegen (1996) believe so, and report some interesting research findings to buttress their position.

In order to understand their arguments, we need to distinguish the differences in happiness between different individuals and the variations in happiness of an individual over time. If you were to measure the happiness level of 10 individuals, you would likely get 10 different results. There are considerable differences in happiness between individuals. Similarly, if you were to accurately monitor an *individual's* happiness on 10 separate occasions, you would likely get 10 different readings. Thus happiness varies between different individuals, as well as within individuals over time.

An individual's happiness revolves around a fixed point, called a *set point.* You may recall in chapter 6, I described how an individual's weight is governed around a relatively fixed set point. A set point for happiness is similar. This is how happy an individual feels *on average.* There may be situational factors that make the person feel more or less happy than this set point at any given point in time. Figure 7.5 illustrates the happiness set points for five different people. The vertical bars reflect how much variability in happiness the person experiences around the set point. You will notice that not only are the set points different *between individuals,* but so is the amount of variability *around* the set point for each person. Some individuals experience a wide range of feelings of happiness, as illustrated by Person E. Others have feelings of happiness that move in a relatively narrow range, as illustrated by Person D.

Lykken and Tellegen (1996) have examined the role of heritability in happiness by studying middle-aged twins born in Minnesota from 1936 to 1955. They administered a questionnaire to 2,310 twins asking them how happy and contented they were. Some of the twins were retested after intervals of 4.5 and 10 years. If there is a genetic basis to happiness, then one would expect a stronger correlation between identical twins as compared to fraternal (i.e., dizygotic) twins. Also, environmental factors can be assessed by looking at twins who were reared in the same environment (i.e., family) as compared to those who had been separated at, or shortly after, birth and were reared in different family environments.

Lykken and Tellegen found that the stable component of happiness—the happiness set point—was largely determined genetically. Their data indicate that 80% of the differences in people's happiness set point is genetically determined and thus is primarily established at birth. They also determined that about one-half of the variability in happiness *around* an individual person's set point is also due to genetic factors, with the other half due to the effects of experiences unique to each individual. They state that ". . . we are led to conclude that individual differences in human happiness—how one feels at the moment and also how happy one feels on average over time—are primarily a matter of chance" (p. 189). The "chance" factor they refer to is the genetics a person is born with, which of course an individual has no control over. Like previous researchers, they found no significant effect on happiness from socioeconomic status, educational attainment, or family income. In contrast to some earlier studies, they found no large effect from religious commitment.

As I noted in chapter 1, breakthroughs in the understanding of the role of genetics in various aspects of our behavior have been particularly striking in the last 20 to 30 years. It now appears that even how happy we are may have a very strong genetic basis.

Biological Basis for Happiness

Unquestionably, being happy has a biological significance beyond just making us feel good. As you have probably noticed, happiness is energizing. When we are feeling upbeat we are more likely to be interested in doing things. This was important in our evolutionary history, as happiness led to behaviors that obtained food and shelter, and encouraged social interactions and sexual behavior, all important for the survival of the species. It was primarily happy people who came up with new inventions, explored new lands, and engaged in creative endeavors. Furthermore, when we are feeling happy we are much more likely to help others, what psychologists call the "feel good–do good" phenomenon.

> Happiness depends, as Nature shows, less on exterior things than most suppose.
>
> **WILLIAM COWPER**

APPLICATIONS: Fourteen Fundamentals for Being Happy

Perhaps you were not fortunate enough to inherit a happy disposition. Is there anything you can do to be happier? Michael Fordyce (1977, 1983) developed a program to help people live happier lives. He outlines 14 basic principles for increasing happiness, even if you weren't born happy. The following is an extremely abbreviated description of his 14 fundamentals for a happier life:

1. Be active and keep busy. Avoid getting bogged down with the boring, monotonous, and routine. Engage in activities you enjoy, be it sports, hobbies, or whatever.
2. Socialize more. People who deprive themselves of socializing with others are much more likely to be depressed. Spend as much time as possible with friends and family. Become acquainted with as many different people as possible by joining a club, attending social events, taking a class, or participating in other group activities.
3. Engage in meaningful and productive work. Choosing a career is vitally important to your happiness. Don't choose a career just because it will bring you wealth. Many people choose professions such as law, engineering, or computer science only to discover that it brings them little happiness or satisfaction. It is important to find work that you will personally find meaningful, and that you perceive to be productive.
4. Get organized. Happy people tend to be very organized. Develop a list of accomplishments you hope to complete each day and stick with it. Avoid doing things impulsively.
5. Stop worrying. Worrying is the "arch enemy" of personal happiness. Remember, you have little control over most of the things that cause you worry. Furthermore, research indicates that 90% of the things you worry about will never happen.
6. Lower your expectations and aspirations. As a general rule, high expectations lead to disappointment while low expectations lead to pleasant surprises. Unhappy people often set such unrealistic expectations for themselves that they are doomed to failure and the subsequent unhappiness that accompanies it. Avoid the tendency to think that you will be happy when you finish school, get married, have children, win the lottery, and so on. Happiness lies in the present, not in the uncertain future.

I have learned to seek my happiness by limiting my desires, rather than in attempting to satisfy them.

JOHN STUART MILL

7. Be positive and optimistic. Think about positive, pleasant things. Don't dwell on the negative. Happy people tend to look on the bright side of things, regardless of how bad their personal situation.
8. Concentrate on the present. Put the past, and any negative things that may have happened in it, behind you. Don't worry excessively about tomorrow; your future will take care of itself. If you are unhappy in the present, you will likely be unhappy in the future, as well.
9. Develop a healthy personality. Fordyce emphasizes that people with a healthy personality have four personal qualities: (a) they like themselves; (b) they accept themselves; (c) they know themselves; and (d) they help themselves.
10. Become an outgoing, social individual. Work on becoming more outgoing and extraverted by joining a club or organization that shares your interests. Smile more. Remember the research I cited earlier that shows that your mood will improve when the facial muscles used in smiling are activated. Other people are attracted to smiling, friendly individuals.
11. Be yourself. Say what you think, and behave the way you want to. Be spontaneous. Don't worry about what other people think.

12. Abolish negative feelings. According to Fordyce, the tendency to "bottle things up" inside is one of the most significant causes of psychological distress. He maintains you will be happier if you talk about the things that are bothering you. Seek help from others, including professionals, if you have problems that you can't handle by yourself.
13. Develop close, loving relationships. According to Fordyce, this is the *most important* thing you can do to increase your happiness. Spend time and effort on developing and maintaining your close relationships.
14. Prioritize happiness. Make being happy the most important priority in your life. Become sensitive to the importance it plays in your life and actively pursue ways to increase your happiness. After all, what is there in your life that is more important?

The Secret to Perpetual Happiness

Many people have sought the answer to a life of uninterrupted happiness. If you are like most people, you have said at one time or another, "My life would be *so* much happier if. . . ." Usually this sentence is completed by things like winning the lottery, finishing college, being better looking, or other tangible changes. We have already seen that none of these things makes us *permanently* happier. Why not?

The answer lies in a concept called **adaptation level** (Helson, 1964). For all stimuli, we have a level of stimulation against which we judge the intensity of new stimuli. I discussed in chapter 2 how we quickly adapt to sudden changes in illumination. Our eyes can adapt quite well to a dimly lit room in a matter of minutes. Similarly, the ocean may feel excruciatingly cold when you first get in the water but after a few minutes you adapt to the new temperature, which then feels normal. Adaptation happens in all of our senses. Smells that initially seem unbearable come to be unnoticed after a short while. That first bite of Mexican food is so spicy you think you can't stand it, but a few bites later it seems very tolerable. Furthermore, this adaptation to a new level occurs unconsciously and without any effort on your part. We also have little control over how quickly we adapt to the changes. Our bodies are physiologically programmed to notice changes, but once the changed environment remains constant, we quickly adapt to it and pay the changes little notice.

What has this got to do with happiness? Quite a lot. I discussed earlier how people who suddenly come into a large amount of money report they are *temporarily* happier but quickly revert back to the level of happiness that existed before the windfall. A similar phenomenon occurs with most good (or bad) fortune: a temporary change in our level of happiness followed by a reversion back to our original set point of happiness. Just as with smells, tastes, temperatures, or any other sensation, we notice the change but then quickly adapt to it. If your income were to suddenly triple, you would certainly notice the difference. Your bills would be paid more quickly, you might drive a better car or live in a better apartment or house. But the adaptation level corresponding with your new income would quickly shift and suddenly the new, higher income level would be the comparison against which your wealth-related happiness would be considered. In order to derive additional happiness from income, it would have to double or triple *again,* but even this would only result in another temporary shift in your adaptation level of happiness. Similarly, a sudden drop in income would only bring a short period of displeasure, until the adaptation level shifted and one became accustomed to the new situation.

Happiness depends upon change, and disappears when continuously present. Perpetual happiness would require that good things happen to us continuously and repeatedly, and happen with a regularity and intensity that did not allow us time to adapt to the previous level. If you think about it, you quickly realize that even under the most Utopian circumstances, this is not ever going to happen. Perpetual happiness? Forget about it!

Pleasure is very seldom found where it is sought.

SAMUEL JOHNSON
The Idler

SUMMARY

- Emotions constitute an important part of our everyday lives. Moods are longer lasting, less specific, and less intense than emotions. Psychologists disagree about the number of basic emotions that exist.
- Physiological arousal that accompanies emotional arousal includes pupil dilation, salivary gland secretions, increased heart rate, decreased stomach secretions, increased sweating, hair follicle activation, increased lung efficacy, blood chemistry changes, and adrenal gland activity.
- The sympathetic nervous system prepares us to fight or flee in emergency situations while the parasympathetic nervous system supports bodily functions in nonemergency situations.
- We monitor the emotional states of others by observing their facial gestures, gazing into their eyes, and monitoring their body language.
- Lying is a frequent part of our everyday behavior. Lies are difficult to detect in others. Clues that may indicate lying include certain speech and vocal patterns, specific body movements, and autonomic nervous system clues such as rapid breathing, sweating, blushing, pupil dilation, blinking, and swallowing.
- The polygraph is not accurate in detecting lying. Advanced computer programs have been devised that measure lying behaviors more accurately.
- Women differ from men in the way they display emotionality.
- Emotional responses consist of both a cognitive appraisal of the situation causing the emotional response and a physiological response after the appraisal is made.
- Emotional reactions can be controlled through breathing exercises, thinking appropriately about what caused the emotional arousal, and using techniques taught in meditation and yoga.
- Emotionality changes as we get older. Older people put a greater emphasis on satisfying emotional goals and having satisfying emotional relationships. As we age, emotions are experienced with the same intensity although there is less emotional turmoil related to interpersonal relationships.
- Anger is a frequently experienced emotion. Anger often occurs as a consequence of interpersonal dealings with friends or family. Anger is also elicited when we become frustrated. There is evidence that anger may be an innate behavior that has, to some degree, a genetic basis.
- Hormones and learning play an important role in anger and aggression. In addition, humans often imitate the angry or aggressive behaviors of others.
- Using actuarial data is the best way to predict aggressive and violent behavior in others. Several factors, including physical abuse, childhood exposure to violence, brain damage, and suicide attempts, among others, have been shown to be associated with a tendency toward violent behavior.
- We sometimes experience the anger of others when in driving situations. This anger is referred to as road rage. Psychologists have distinguished certain behaviors that trigger road rage, such as hostile gestures, driving slowly, and discourteous behavior. Counseling has been shown to be effective for people engaging in road rage. When experiencing road rage from others you should avoid eye contact, ignore gestures, not engage in retaliatory behaviors, and disengage from the situation.
- Love is one of the most powerful emotions. Psychologists distinguish between loving and liking. One widely accepted theory posits that love includes the components of intimacy, passion, and commitment. Other theorists have hypothesized the existence of different kinds or styles of love. One popular theory identifies the existence of three primary love styles, including eros, storge, and ludus as well as the secondary love styles of mania, pragma, and agape, which are combinations of primary love styles.

- Romantic relationships go through several stages, including initial attraction, buildup, continuation, and ending.
- Not everyone has the ability to love. Infants who have experienced emotional deprivation early in their lives often suffer from an attachment disorder that prevents the establishment of emotional bonds.
- Happiness, or subjective well being, consists of a cognitive and an affective component. Most people report they are happy. Different levels of happiness are reported between countries.
- Happiness includes the presence of positive emotions and the absence of negative emotions.
- Factors that do not affect long-term happiness include education, socioeconomic status, level of income, aging, gender, race, physical attractiveness, physical health, and wealth.
- Personality traits of happy individuals include high self-esteem, a sense of control, optimism, and extraversion.
- An individual's level of happiness revolves around a fixed point called a set point, which may be largely genetically determined.
- Suggestions for living a happier life include being active, socializing, being productive, getting organized, avoiding worry, lowering one's expectations and aspirations, and being optimistic. Further suggestions include concentrating on the present, being outgoing, being yourself, abolishing negative feelings, and developing close relationships. It is also important to make being happy an important priority in your life.
- It is impossible to attain perpetual happiness. We quickly adapt to circumstances that make us temporarily happy.

KEY TERMS

actuarial judgments: applying empirically derived rules to predict behavioral outcomes.
adaptation level: the level of stimulation that is used to judge the intensity of new stimuli.
agape: a love style that is selfless, giving, and altruistic.
attachment disorder: a psychological disorder caused from childhood emotional deprivation.
body language: a way of communicating that includes the way we move our hands, arms, or legs, as well as the position, posture, and movement of our bodies.
catharsis: the emotional release that results from acting out anger or frustration.
commitment: a decision to continue a relationship for an extended period of time.
consummate love: the ideal and highest form of love; when passion, intimacy, and commitment are all present.
emblems: meaningful gestures exhibited when an individual is lying.
emotions: usually brief feelings that occur in response to some event in our lives; always accompanied by some physiological reaction.
eros: a style of love that is based on a powerful physical attraction.
frustration-aggression hypothesis: a theory that stipulates that the primary cause of anger and aggression is a feeling of frustration.
illustrators: body movements that illustrate speech as it is spoken.
imitation: the act of simulating the behavior of another individual.
intimacy: feelings of being close and connected to another individual; feelings of being able to confide closely in another individual without risk.
liking: feelings of respect and admiration for another individual.
loving: deep feelings of need, caring, trust, and tolerance for another individual.
ludus: a style of love that includes experiencing numerous lovers; includes a reluctance to settle down or to get too involved with one person, and a tendency not to experience love at first sight.
mania: a secondary style of love that is a mixture of eros and ludus.
mood: a psychological state that reflects how an individual is feeling.
parasympathetic nervous system: the part of the nervous system that supports the body in nonemergency situations.
passion: intense sexual attraction for another individual.
personal space: an invisible boundary signifying a comfortable distance from others.
polygraph: aka lie detector; a device that measures physiological responses that accompany emotional arousal.
pragma: a love style in which individuals see finding a mate as a practical problem.
road rage: aggressive driving that originates from driving-related anger.
socioemotional selectivity theory: as people age, they become increasingly aware that they have a limited amount of time left to live, and the emotional component of relationships becomes more important.

storge: a love style where love develops slowly, and feelings start with affection and progressively grow stronger as the relationship matures.

subjective well being: a state of emotion that reflects your judgment about life satisfaction and emotional reactions to events in your life; synonymous with happiness.

sympathetic nervous system: the part of the nervous system that elicits physiological arousal to provide energy to respond to a threatening situation.

8

THE PSYCHOLOGY OF STAYING HEALTHY

He who has health, has hope; and he who has hope, has everything.

ARABIAN PROVERB

Many years ago I worked with a university colleague who seemed to be the picture of health. He maintained a normal weight, exercised regularly, only smoked occasionally, and drank alcohol in moderation. He enjoyed both a prestigious, rewarding career as a university administrator and a happy family life as a husband and father. However, over a period of a few years, several personal catastrophes befell him. First, the university removed him from his highly coveted administrative position and forced him to return to the teaching faculty. Shortly thereafter, his adolescent daughter began to behave in a bizarre fashion, displaying many symptoms of schizophrenia, and his son began to experience serious social and academic problems. Finally, his by then crumbling marriage ended in divorce after his wife became romantically involved with another woman.

During this time, I observed that my colleague increased his consumption of alcohol and tobacco significantly, stopped exercising regularly, experienced a noticeable weight gain, reported recurring sleep difficulties, and appeared to be seriously depressed. Before long, he developed a case of chronic bronchitis, from which he never fully recovered. His physical condition continued to spiral downward and, in a matter of a few months, he died of congestive heart failure. I believe that it was more than just coincidental that his personal difficulties and his untimely death were linked so closely in time. Subsequent research on the relationship between a person's emotional state and his or her physical health has borne out my beliefs.

How the Mind and Body Are Linked

The idea that the workings of the mind might be interlinked with a person's health has been around since ancient Greece. Sigmund Freud formalized this idea in the early 20th century when he noted that some of his patients showed symptoms of physical illness in the absence of any organic disorder. Freud believed that these physical illnesses were the result of unconscious emotional conflicts.

The field of *psychosomatic medicine* also developed early in the 20th century. The word **psychosomatic** alludes to the interaction of the mind and the body. Psychosomatic disorders are not, as popularly believed, "all in the mind." Instead, these disorders reflect occurrences where the mind is affecting the body *and* the body is affecting the mind. A psychosomatic illness is a physical disorder that is *affected by* emotional and psychological factors but is not necessarily *caused* by them. They are not imaginary illnesses; they are as real (and discomforting) as any other illness.

The Field of Health Psychology

In the late 1970s a subspecialty of psychology known as **health psychology** was formed. The goals of this specialty are to promote and maintain good health, to prevent and treat illness, to study the physiological and psychological factors that cause illness, and to improve the practices and policies of the health care system. The field of health psychology recognizes that both health and illness result from the critical interactions of psychological, biological, and social forces. Health psychologists are particularly interested in studying certain maladaptive behaviors, such as smoking, alcohol consumption, drug abuse, unprotected sex, and reckless driving, which can negatively impact our health. They are also interested in how our personalities and thinking processes can work either to maintain good health or to cause illness.

✦ **TABLE 8.1** ✦ **Self-Assessment of Your Lifestyle**

Answer "yes" or "no" to the following questions regarding your lifestyle.

____ 1. I usually sleep 7 or 8 hours a night.
____ 2. I am at or near my appropriate weight.
____ 3. I rarely drink alcohol or do so in moderation.
____ 4. I eat breakfast almost every day.
____ 5. I never smoke cigarettes.
____ 6. I engage in regular and vigorous physical exercise.
____ 7. I hardly ever eat between meals.

Count the number of "yes" responses to the above questions. If you answered "yes" to 6 or 7 questions, you have a very healthy lifestyle. Research has shown that the more of these lifestyle behaviors you adopt, the better your health will be, particularly in the later years of your life.

In the past few decades, most physicians have developed a greater appreciation of the role the mind plays in the determination of health. They have become increasingly aware of instances where patients' thoughts were directly related to their health and, at times, to their very survival.

Lifestyles and Health

Research has shown that our lifestyles are critically important to our health. Lifestyles are the general patterns of behavior people engage in as part of their everyday lives. Before proceeding further, read the questions in the self-assessment test in Table 8.1 and answer them truthfully as they apply to your personal lifestyle. Table 8.1 refers to what psychologists consider to be the seven most important lifestyle behaviors for maintaining good health and promoting longevity.

The unhealthy lifestyles that many Americans adopt are very familiar to us. They include lack of exercise, too little sleep, alcohol or drug abuse, unhealthy diet, overeating, and smoking. How important are behavioral lifestyles for health compared to other factors? At least half of all premature deaths in the United States, defined as those occurring before age 65, are directly attributable to unhealthy behaviors (Powell, Spain, Christenson, & Mollenkamp, 1986).

In fact, the lifestyles we choose to adopt may become a life-or-death decision for each of us. A U.S. Surgeon General's report (1979) stated that approximately half of the mortality in the United States may be due to unhealthy behavior or lifestyle. The report further suggested that 7 of the 10 leading causes of death in the United States could be reduced significantly by changing only six habits: poor diet, smoking, lack of exercise, alcohol abuse, maladaptive responses to tension and stress, and increased use of medications to lower blood pressure.

One study asked several thousand adults, ranging in age from 20 to 75, questions about their lifestyles (Belloc & Breslow, 1972). At all ages, the health of individuals was better as the number of healthy lifestyle behaviors increased. Surprisingly, individuals who followed all 7 healthy lifestyle behaviors reported that their health was about the same as those individuals 30 years younger who practiced few or none of these behaviors. In a follow-up study, the percentage of people who died during the ensuing 9 years declined significantly with increased adoption of healthy lifestyles. Older people experienced a greater impact from this change in behavior than younger individuals. In addition, the effect of lifestyle was found to be more critical for the health of men as compared to women (Breslow, 1983).

APPLICATIONS: Changing Behaviors That Cause Illness

The unfortunate thing about this world is that the good habits are much easier to give up than the bad ones.

W. SOMERSET MAUGHAM

Let's examine some of the unhealthy lifestyle behaviors that contribute to poor health and/or premature death and see how you can change them.

Smoking

The latest data from the U.S. Centers for Disease Control and Prevention (CDC) show that 24.1% of all adults are smokers. The rate has dropped only .6% since 1997, despite all the publicity about the negative health effects of smoking. Surprisingly, recent surveys indicate there is an *increasing* rate of smoking among college students. Smoking is most common among persons aged 18 to 44 years (27.7%) and least common among persons aged 65 years or older (10.9%). Sadly, the low percentage of elderly smokers may be accounted for by the fact that many of them have already died from smoking-related illnesses. Each day, 3,000 more teenagers become regular smokers (Novello, 1990). Smoking is directly related to nearly a half million deaths annually in the United States (Raloff, 1994). Smoking incidence is inversely related to education level and socioeconomic status, with people living below poverty level being much more likely to smoke. Only 11.3% of people with a college education are smokers.

One must wonder why people continue to smoke when the deleterious health effects are widely known. One reason, which is now widely accepted even by tobacco companies, is that smoking is addictive. Nicotine has been found to be as addictive as both cocaine and heroin. It should not be too surprising that people are positively reinforced for smoking. Nicotine causes certain pleasant effects. For instance, it increases the release of certain neurotransmitter substances in the brain that improve mental alertness, sharpen memory, and reduce tension and anxiety (Pomerleau & Pomerleau, 1989). People also use smoking as a coping mechanism to regulate moods (Parrott, 1993). Some people use it to increase arousal while others smoke to reduce stress and anxiety. An overwhelming majority of schizophrenics and alcoholics are smokers (Glassman, 1993). There are specific nicotine receptors in the brain and, with respect to schizophrenics, smoking helps quiet their disturbed thought processes. Individuals with some severe mental disorders are literally self-medicating themselves when they smoke.

I can personally attest that quitting smoking is difficult. Although I have not smoked in over 30 years, having quit while a student, I still feel the occasional urge to light up. Quitting is difficult but not impossible. The average smoker tries to quit 5 or 6 times before attaining success (Sherman, 1994). Nevertheless, 90% of exsmokers successfully quit smoking on their own (Novello, 1990).

If you are not presently smoking, do not begin. The majority of people who smoke state that they wish they could quit. If you are a smoker, first try to quit "cold turkey," particularly since this approach is often very successful. Aids such as nicotine gum and the nicotine patch can also be of some help. A review of 17 studies with over 5,000 participants indicated that 22% of people using the nicotine patch were able to quit compared to only 9% of people using a placebo. Furthermore, the nicotine patch combined with antismoking counseling increased the success rate to 27% (Fiore, cited in Sherman, 1994). The antidepressant Welbutrin has also been found to help people stop smoking. After 1 year, the rate of abstention from smoking was 30.3% for individuals who received only the antidepressant and 35.5% for individuals who received the antidepressant in combination with a nicotine patch (Jorenby, et al., 1999).

If you have been unsuccessful in quitting smoking on your own, you should avail yourself of these kinds of smoking cessation aids. As a general rule, a combination of these chemical aids and antismoking counseling is the most effective approach. Other approaches, such as hypnosis or listening to subliminal taped messages (see chapter 2), have proven to be ineffectual.

Eating Healthy

"You are what you eat," fact, fiction, or some of both? Evidence suggests that eating food high in carbohydrates (bread, potatoes, and pasta) increases substances in the brain that make us feel relaxed, sleepy, and less sensitive to pain (Spring, 1988). On the other hand, a diet low in carbohydrates improves concentration and alertness. Prolonged malnourishment, especially among young children, can cause permanent cognitive deficits. The effects of cholesterol on health are still being debated although evidence suggests that men who reduce their cholesterol levels are less likely to suffer heart disease (Roberts, 1987). Excessive consumption of salt has been implicated in high blood pressure in several studies.

To cease smoking is the easiest thing I ever did. I ought to know because I've done it a thousand times.

MARK TWAIN

And now, some bad news for you fast-food fans. Diets that are high in fat and low in fiber contain biochemicals that promote the growth of cancer cells (Cohen, 1987). Diets that include high-fiber vegetables, such as broccoli, cabbage, and cauliflower, inhibit such cancerous growths. However, there is good news for every person with a sweet tooth. The widely held belief that the consumption of sugar causes people, especially children, to become hyperactive has been disproved (Spring, Chiodo, & Bowen, 1987).

If you want to live a long and healthy life, you might want to try and emulate the healthy eating habits of Seventh Day Adventists. They eat well-balanced, low-fat diets and avoid smoking and drinking. Research has indicated they have much longer life expectancies than average and lower rates of all forms of cancer (Ilola, 1990). However, if you find it difficult to live the abstinent lifestyle of the Seventh Day Adventist, you can still do one simple thing that will increase longevity and help prevent illness. Eat breakfast every day, even if you are not hungry in the morning. Skipping breakfast deprives your body, especially the brain, of the nutrients needed to function most efficiently. Eating breakfast will help you think more clearly during the day.

Exercising

It is well known that regular and vigorous exercise is essential to good health and longevity. Exercise is particularly important in the prevention of coronary heart disease and it can improve your mental health as well. People who exercise consistently feel better about themselves, suffer less anxiety, and have lower levels of depression (Dubbert, 1992). Despite the known benefits of exercise, less than 20% of Americans exercise regularly or intensely enough to accrue health benefits. Even a moderate amount and intensity of exercise is beneficial. Walking just 4 hours per week, for instance, has been shown to have demonstrable health benefits (Tucker, Aldana, & Friedman, 1990).

If you are like the 80% of Americans who do not exercise regularly, the following suggestions from research findings regarding how to begin and maintain an effective exercise program might help you:

1. Get a medical checkup. Starting a sudden and vigorous exercise program can be dangerous to your health. If you are out of shape or have not exercised regularly, you should check with your physician before beginning any exercise program.
2. Make exercise fun. You need to find exercises that are at least somewhat enjoyable. If you do not enjoy running, try swimming or bicycling. To prevent boredom, rotate between exercises. Exercise should never be physically painful.
3. Make a commitment. Lack of commitment is one of the primary reasons that people stop exercising or fail to do so regularly. Promising someone important in your life that you are going to exercise regularly may help you stick to it. Two years ago, I joined an athletic club. The fact that I am paying a monthly fee helps keep me going regularly, just to get my money's worth.
4. Use social influences. Enlist the support of your family and friends. Their praise and encouragement will keep you going. My wife is very good about giving me verbal praise almost every time I exercise. Most of the commercial gyms schedule social events that combine exercise with socializing. These events range from group bicycle rides to volleyball games to hiking. This provides an excellent way to get in shape and to socialize with new friends at the same time. If possible, get a friend to exercise with you. My wife recently joined my athletic club, and I find I go more frequently now that we can exercise together.
5. Keep a record of your progress. Keeping a written record of your progress will serve as a powerful motivator. I mentioned earlier that I had kept a record of how many miles I had jogged. As I saw how many hundreds of miles I had accomplished, it served as an incentive to do even more. When starting an exercise regime, write down, for example, how many push-ups you can do, how far you can jog, or how much weight you can lift. Periodically update the numbers so that you can see the progress you are making. Simultaneously, keep a written record of your weight.
6. Set goals. Most people will stick to an exercise program if they are working toward some concrete goal. When I started exercising, I set a goal of being able to jog for three miles. By slowly increasing the distance I ran in incremental steps, I was eventually able to achieve the goal. Set goals that are realistic and measurable (i.e., 100 sit-ups rather than "getting in better shape") so that you will have concrete evidence of your progress.
7. All things in moderation. It is not necessary to exercise vigorously every day. Several studies have shown that even moderate exercise three or four times a week will have tremendous health benefits. In fact, there are diminishing returns for exercising beyond this level. Further, if you become a slave to a rigid exercise schedule, you will be less likely to stick with it.

8. Take advantage of opportunities to exercise. You can accomplish a lot of exercising in the course of your daily life. Take the stairs rather than the elevator or escalator. Walk or bicycle instead of driving. Combine exercise with activities you find pleasurable, such as dancing, gardening, or recreational activities whenever possible.

Alcohol and Substance Abuse

Misuse of alcohol is a factor in more than 10% of all deaths in the United States (U.S. Surgeon General, 1979). Alcohol has been implicated as a direct risk factor for cancer of the larynx, oral cavity, liver, and esophagus. It also is a frequent factor in accidents, suicides, and homicides. Alcohol abuse often leads to domestic violence, marital separation and divorce, and frequently interferes with social and professional performance.

It is estimated that 90% of college students and 68% of adult Americans consume alcohol on occasion. Approximately 12% of Americans are estimated to be heavy drinkers, defined as those who either consume alcohol daily or consume large quantities intermittently. Regular consumption of three or more alcoholic drinks daily is typically considered problematic and is frequently accompanied by health problems. The best estimates indicate that there are 12 million alcoholics in the United States (U.S. Surgeon General, 1979).

What is the best way to control excessive alcohol consumption? The most popular treatment approach is Alcoholics Anonymous (AA), a nationally recognized self-help organization. Approximately 10% of alcoholics in the United States are members. AA maintains that alcoholism is a disease, and it encourages members to confess their weaknesses and to surrender themselves to a higher power. It also encourages members to associate with other people suffering the same problem. Members are urged to abstain completely from alcohol.

Are these types of self-help programs effective? Only 10% of alcoholics treated in abstinence-based programs such as AA have quit drinking completely after 18 months or longer and another 26% reported only moderate drinking (Armor, Polich, & Stanbul, 1976).

Alcoholism, like other addictive behaviors, is resistant to change. Only about 1 in 5 will recover completely, while nearly half will either die prematurely or remain dependent on alcohol (Seligman, 1993). As with smoking, quitting on your own is a very effective strategy. In one large survey of people who had succeeded in stopping substance abuse, only 3% report that they were helped by doctors and only 1% were helped by psychologists, psychiatrists, or self-help groups. The majority of respondents reported that they had help from friends and family, especially spouses. The most successful individuals were those who quit drinking alcohol on their own. In fact, patients who received printed self-help materials were just as successful as those who received both counseling and Antabuse, a drug that causes nausea and vomiting when combined with alcohol. One prominent clinician who has reviewed the effectiveness of different treatments for alcoholism has concluded, "Sadly, formal treatments work only marginally better than the natural rate of recovery" (Seligman, 1993, p. 213).

Treatment approaches that emphasize the philosophy that alcoholism and other substance abuse are behavioral problems rather than "diseases" appear to be most effective. This approach emphasizes the belief that patients are not helpless victims of a disease but are capable of changing their own behavior. Alcoholism or any other substance abuse is not something that just "happens" to us; it is a learned behavior. There is no conclusive evidence that some people have an "addictive personality." Many of the personality traits seen in addiction, such as emotional insecurity, depression, dependency, and criminality, appear to be the result of addictive behaviors, not the cause (Sobel & Ornstein, 1996). Another fallacy is that there is a gene for addiction that dooms us to alcoholism. Over 80% of people with two alcoholic parents do *not* become alcoholics.

Finally, it is important to dispel the notion that a single exposure to an addictive substance will doom a person to a life of addiction. Less than 1% of people who have used cocaine are now regular users (Sobel & Ornstein, 1996). Only 36% of people who begin smoking cigarettes become addicted. Almost no one who takes a single drink, smokes a single cigarette, or sniffs cocaine once will become addicted. We are in control of our behavior; we make conscious choices every time we choose to smoke, drink, or inhale a drug. We are as capable of unlearning addictive behaviors as we are of learning them, and it is not always helpful or necessary to receive professional assistance to accomplish this goal. With respect to alcohol abuse, my best advice is to attempt to deal with the behavior yourself and turn to professional help only if your best efforts prove ineffectual.

LIFE EXPECTANCY

Each of us has a certain life expectancy or period of time that we can reasonably expect to live. The life expectancy of babies born in the United States in 1900 was 48 years compared to approximately 76 years today. This dramatic increase has been due primarily to rapid advances in controlling disease, particularly infectious disease. Nevertheless, there are many factors besides disease that account for a person's expected life span. Earlier I noted that lifestyles play an important role in life expectancy. For instance, males born in Russia today have only a life expectancy of 58 years, primarily due to the rampant alcoholism present in that society. Interestingly, the life expectancy of physicians in the United States is considerably shorter than that of nonphysicians. This difference could be due to any number of factors, including physicians' stressful work conditions, their increased tendencies toward alcohol and drug abuse, and other unidentified factors associated with their profession. However, lifestyle data provide only part of the information on an individual's expected life span. Scientific studies have determined that our genetic makeup plays an important role in our life expectancy and that old age does tend to "run in families."

Millions long for immortality who do not know what to do with themselves on a rainy Sunday afternoon.

SUSAN ERTZ

Is it possible to predict one's life expectancy? If you are interested in the best estimation of your own life expectancy, answer the questions contained in the self-assessment test in Table 8.2. As you can see from the questions contained in this test, there are diverse, and sometimes surprising, factors that affect life expectancy. Remember, life expectancy tests such as this one only predict the average life expectancy of respondents. There are hundreds of factors that affect life expectancy, of which only a few are shown in Table 8.2. Your individual expectancy may vary, depending on circumstances and factors not measured by this test.

✦ **TABLE 8.2** ✦ **Life Expectancy**

This test will tell your approximate life expectancy and will help delineate some of those factors in your life that contribute to or subtract from your longevity.

Find your life expectancy in years according to the chart below.

Life Expectancy in Years

Present Age	Male	Female
17	60.8	67.2
18	59.9	66.2
19	58.9	65.2
20	57.9	64.2
21	56.9	63.2
22	56.0	62.2
23	55.0	61.2
24	54.0	60.2
25	53.0	59.3
26	52.0	58.3
27	51.1	57.3
28	50.1	56.3
29	49.1	55.3
30	48.2	54.3
31	47.2	53.4
32	46.2	52.4
33	45.2	51.4
34	44.3	50.4
35	43.3	49.4
36–38	41.4	47.5
39–41	38.5	44.6
42–44	35.7	41.7
45–47	32.9	38.8
48–50	30.1	35.9

Life expectancy (from above table) = __________ years

To the above total, add or subtract years according to the following factors. Skip those statements that do not apply to you.

_____ If your mother or father has lived past 70, add 1 year for every 5-year period per individual.

_____ If a parent, grandparent, brother, or sister died of atherosclerosis (heart attack, angina, or stroke) before the age of 50, subtract 4 years; before the age of 60, subtract 2 years.

_____ If you or one of your parents or grandparents has had diabetes, thyroid disorders, breast cancer (if you are a woman), cancer of the digestive system, or a strong allergic tendency (asthma, chronic bronchitis, emphysema), subtract 3 years for each incidence.

(continued)

✦ **TABLE 8.2** ✦ **Continued**

_____ For each 10 pounds that you are overweight, subtract 1 year.

_____ If you are a light or moderate drinker (no more than 2 drinks per day), add 2 years.

_____ If you are a heavy drinker (more than 2 drinks per day), subtract 8 years.

_____ If you completely abstain from alcohol, subtract 1 year.

_____ If you smoke 2 or more packs of cigarettes a day, subtract 8 years; 1 to 2 packs, subtract 4 years; one-half to 1 pack, subtract 2 years; nonsmokers, add 2 years.

_____ If you have lived most of your life in the West-North-Central United States (North or South Dakota, Nebraska, Kansas, Minnesota, Iowa, Missouri), add 1 year. If you have lived mostly in the mid-Atlantic states (New York, New Jersey, Pennsylvania), subtract 1 year.

_____ If you exercise moderately at least 2 or 3 times a week (long walks, jogging, bike riding, swimming, etc.), add 3 years.

_____ If you sleep more than 9 hours a night, subtract 4 years; more than 10 hours, subtract 6 years.

_____ Add 3 years if you are married. Subtract 1 year for every decade (10 years) that you have remained unmarried after age 25.

_____ Is your personality reasoned and pragmatic? Add 1 to 3 years, depending on how reasoned and pragmatic you feel you are. If you are aggressive, intense, and competitive, subtract 1 to 5 years, based on your evaluation of the degree or severity. Subtract slightly more if you are male, slightly less if female.

_____ If you consistently use seat belts and drive at the speed limit, add 1 year. If you own a snowmobile, subtract 1 year.

(continued)

Illness and the Immune System

Although you are unaware of it, the biological equivalent of World War II is constantly taking place inside your body. Your **immune system** constitutes the defensive system that fights off a variety of different "invaders" that threaten your health. Although scientists still do not understand many things about how the immune system works, recent breakthroughs in medical research have provided us with a greater understanding of how its functions intertwine with the workings of the mind.

Your body is constantly on the lookout for foreign invaders, called **antigens.** It quickly recognizes an antigen that enters the body and mobilizes to attack it. The most common "invaders" are bacteria, viruses, fungi, and protozoa. Because these substances permeate our environment, it is impossible for us to completely avoid them. In fact, most play a very useful role in nature and only a few threaten our health. Bacteria, for example, serve the useful purpose of breaking down organic matter into simpler units. However, a select few do cause tuberculosis, scarlet fever, and food poisoning.

Viruses, which are the smallest antigens, are particularly insidious. Once inside your body, the virus first attaches to a cell, then enters the cell, and subsequently

✦ TABLE 8.2 ✦ Continued

_____ If you have less than a high-school education, subtract 2 years. If you have 4 years of education beyond high school, add 1 year; 5 or more years, add 3 years.

_____ If your job is sedentary (e.g., clerk, secretary, desk job, etc.), subtract 3 years. If it is active (e.g., mail carrier, construction worker, dancer, etc.), add 3 years.

_____ Do you regularly fly long distances? Subtract 1 year.

_____ If you are wealthy (annual income of at least $75,000 or more), subtract 2 years.

_____ If you are over age 60 and still working, add 2 years; over age 65, add 3 years.

_____ Are you basically a happy person? Add 1 to 2 years, according to degree. Dissatisfied? Subtract 1 to 3 years, again according to degree.

_____ Have you had psychoanalysis? Add 1 year.

_____ Women over age 30 who have had annual pap smears and breast examinations, add 2 years. If you check your breasts at least once a month, add 2 more years.

_____ If you are over age 40 and have a proctoscopic exam every 2 years, add 2 years.

_____ If you keep the thermostat in your home at 69 °F, or sleep in a cold room, add 2 years.

Add the plus and minus figures above and total below:

Total pluses and minuses = __________

Now, add or subtract this number to or from the life expectancy data in the beginning of this table and you will have your total life expectancy below.

Your total life expectancy = __________ years.

SOURCE: Adapted from Gardner (1980).

takes over the cell's functions by issuing its own instructions to reproduce. Eventually, a virus reproduces enough to rupture the cell, spread, and infect other healthy cells. Viruses are responsible for the illnesses you suffer most frequently, including colds and the flu.

People who suffer from *allergies* have an overactive immune system that attacks even harmless substances, such as tree pollen, animal dander, tree molds, or particular foods. In these individuals, the immune system is incapable of distinguishing between these harmless invaders and more lethal antigens. Our bodies offer a battle plan to defend against these invaders. The "soldiers" that our body uses to attack the invading antigens are **lymphocytes,** a specialized type of white blood cell. These originate in bone marrow and travel to other organs where they mature into fully functioning units that are ready to fight. Our bodies establish several lines of defense against invaders: (1) The first line of defense is our skin and the mucous membranes that line our respiratory and digestive tracts. While the skin serves as a physical barrier against the invaders, the mucous membranes contain antibodies that actually attack them. Even though this is an effective defense, inevitably some antigens break through and enter the body. (2) The second line of defense consists of specialized white blood cells in our blood and tissues that attack and consume invading substances. When antigens manage to penetrate this second defense and invade cells in our body, they encounter another protective barrier. (3) This third line of defense, called **killer T-cells,** recognizes body cells that have been invaded and destroys them. Furthermore, these killer T-cells "remember" an invader they have dealt with previously and destroy it more efficiently at subsequent encounters. Unfortunately, however, some invaders are more difficult to deal with than others.

Our immune system functions more efficiently at certain times during our life span. We have almost no immune defense system when we are born. During early infancy and childhood, the immune system develops more completely, especially with the help of childhood immunizations. During adolescence and most of adulthood, the immune system functions at a very high level, but with the onset of old age, its effectiveness steadily declines. Factors within our control that cause our immune system to function with less efficiency, regardless of age, include poor nutrition and fatigue.

Stress and the Immune Response

Have you ever noticed that you are more likely to get sick during periods of high stress? Scientists have confirmed that the incidence of respiratory infections greatly increases during periods of high stress (Jemmot & Locke, 1984) and we now know that high levels of stress function to suppress the immune response and leave the body more prone to infection. Stress decreases the amount of killer T-cell activity (Kiecolt-Glaser, Dura, Speicher, Trask, & Glaser, 1991). Killer T-cell activity is lower in lonely people and in individuals in unhappy marriages (Kiecolt-Glaser, et al., 1987). Furthermore, weak immune functions are present in individuals whose spouses recently died (Jemmot & Locke, 1984). There is a growing body of evidence of an association between stress and the ability of the immune system to ward off illness. Because stress is such a critical factor in the efficient functioning of our immune system, it has received a great deal of attention from psychologists.

Definition of Stress

We all experience stressful events on a daily, if not hourly, basis. Stress consists of both psychological responses (anger, fear, excitement, etc.) and physiological responses (rapid breathing, increased heart rates, etc.). *We experience stress whenever we face events that we perceive to be threatening to either our physical or psychological well-being.* Furthermore, stress occurs when a person's interaction with the environment results in the perception, whether real or imagined, that there are greater demands on the individual than resources available to deal with those demands. When the demands and the resources are mismatched, a discrepancy exists.

For example, an upcoming test in organic chemistry may place demands on several of your resources, including your *physical, psychological,* and *social* resources. You may find that the many hours of required studying tax you physically and cause you to become extremely fatigued. Psychological resources may be depleted as you worry about the exam or become depressed about the possibility of failure. And finally, the time preparing for the exam may place a heavy demand on your social resources by limiting the amount of time you can spend socializing or by affecting your relationships with close friends or family.

Individuals make their own assessments of impending demands, their personal resources, and the discrepancies that exist between them. For instance, if you determine that your chemistry test requires 20 hours for adequate study but only 12 hours remain until the exam, then you have realistically perceived a discrepancy that will likely cause you stress. Sometimes, however, we perceive a discrepancy where none exists. For example, you may have studied adequately but still feel stress because you perceive that the demands of the exam exceed the resources that you were able to devote in preparation for the test. Stress results from the perception or *cognitive appraisal* of a discrepancy, regardless of whether it actually exists.

Sources of Stress

Events that we perceive as harmful or threatening are known as **stressors.** Stressors can range in form from catastrophic events, such as an automobile accident or house fire, to the minor annoyances and frustrations in everyday life. Moreover, stressors can be persistent and recurring or of short duration. Let's examine some of the most common kinds of stressors that most of us face.

Life Events

Psychiatrists Thomas Holmes and Richard Rahe interviewed a large number of men and women from varying backgrounds and identified 43 life events that most people rated as stressful. They subsequently developed the Social Readjustment Rating Scale that lists these life events and rates them according to how much social adjustment each event requires (Holmes & Rahe, 1967). For example, the death of a spouse was rated the most stressful event because it requires the greatest amount of social adjustment. Going on vacation, on the other hand, exemplified a life event that requires only minor adjustments. Table 8.3 illustrates these 43 life events with their corresponding readjustment values, which have been updated (Miller & Rahe, 1997). You may measure your own personal life-change score by checking off those events that have occurred in your life over the past 24 months. Research generally has found that the greater the number of stressful life events, the more likely a person is to become ill (Holmes & Masuda, 1974; Johnson, 1986; Rahe, 1974, 1987). However, these findings do not denote an extremely strong relationship, probably because people get sick and have accidents for several reasons besides stress (Sarafino, 1994). Nevertheless, there is a consistent relationship between life events and illness, particularly for those who experience a large number of life events.

Daily Hassles

As you undoubtedly recognize, a lot of the stress that we experience on a daily basis comes not from major life events but from lesser events. Finding that your car has a flat tire just when you are about to leave to take an important examination is very stressful but not catastrophic. Misplacing things, loud noises, and making necessary home repairs are other examples of what psychologists have referred to as **hassles.** The most frequent hassles reported by subjects included concerns about weight, health of a family member, the rising prices of consumer goods, home maintenance,

> The misfortunes hardest to bear are these which never came.
>
> JAMES RUSSELL LOWELL

✦ TABLE 8.3 ✦ Social Readjustment Rating Scale

The life events below are ranked according to the amount of life readjustment required. Add up the scores for all of these events that have occurred in your life in the past 24 months. Remember to take into account multiple occurrences of the same event.

Life Event	Readjustment Value
Death of a spouse	119
Divorce	98
Death of close family member	92
Marital separation	79
Fired from work	79
Major personal injury or illness	77
Jail term	75
Death of close friend	70
Pregnancy	66
Major business readjustment	62
Foreclosure of mortgage or loan	61
Marital reconciliation	57
Gain of new family member	57
Change in health or behavior of family member	56
Change in financial state	56
Retirement	54
Change to different line of work	51
Change in number of arguments with spouse	51
Marriage	50
Spouse begins or ends work	46
Sexual difficulties	45
Mortgage or loan greater than $10,000	44
Child leaving home	44
Change in responsibilities at work	43

(continued)

and losing or misplacing things (Kanner, Coyne, Schaefer, & Lazarus, 1981). As with life events, our health is related to the frequency of our exposure to these daily hassles.

Uplifts

Stress can also be created by those desirable experiences that bring joy or pleasure to our lives. Winning the lottery or getting a promotion at work are examples of desirable experiences that have been termed **uplifts** (Kanner, et al., 1981). Winning a million dollars in a contest would probably introduce unimaginable stress into your life when you suddenly must deal with, among other things, tax consequences, legal complications, and the requests and expectations from friends and relatives. Does

✦ TABLE 8.3 ✦ Continued

Change in living conditions	42
Change in residence	41
Trouble with in-laws	38
Begin or end school	38
Outstanding personal achievement	37
Change in work hours or conditions	36
Change in schools	35
Christmas	30
Trouble with boss	29
Change in recreation	29
Mortgage or loan less than $10,000	28
Change in personal habits	27
Change in social activities	27
Change in eating habits	27
Change in sleeping habits	26
Change in number of family get-togethers	26
Vacation	25
Change in church activities	22
Minor violations of the law	22

Scoring:
Total score for events that occurred to you in the past 24 months = ________

Based on previous findings, approximately 80% of people with more than 430 life-change points will become ill within the near future. For comparison, approximately 50% of individuals with 285–430 points and 33% of those with 215–285 points will experience illness. No significant health problems will be reported in people with less than 215 points.

SOURCE: Reprinted from *Journal of Psychosomatic Research,* Volume 43, Miller & Rahe, Life changes scaling across 30 years, Page 282, Copyright 1997, with permission from Elsevier Science.

the stress from these desirable consequences also have a deleterious effect on our health? Most research studies suggest little or no relationship between health status and the number of uplifts experienced. Apparently our bodies are better able to tolerate the stress from desirable rather than undesirable events.

Frustration and Conflict

In chapter 6 I discussed how **frustration** occurs whenever we are blocked or thwarted from achieving a goal. The more motivated we are to achieve a goal, the greater the frustration when our efforts are hindered. Frustration results in a negative emotional state and becomes one of the major causes of stress in our lives. Conflicts are another major source of stress. As discussed in chapter 6, various kinds of

✦ TABLE 8.4 ✦ Ten Most Common Hassles

Daily hassles are the frustrating and irritating demands that we face on a daily basis. Kanner and others (1981) developed a scale of these minor stressors and asked middle-aged adults to check those that they commonly experienced. Below are the 10 most commonly reported hassles.

Hassle	Percentage of Times Checked
1. Concerns about weight	52.4
2. Health of a family member	48.1
3. Rising prices of common goods	43.7
4. Home maintenance	42.8
5. Too many things to do	38.6
6. Misplacing or losing things	38.1
7. Yard work or outside home maintenance	38.1
8. Property, investment, or taxes	37.6
9. Crime	37.1
10. Physical appearance	35.9

Research has suggested that the relationship between hassles and health is even stronger than it is between life events and health, even though neither factor by itself is a powerful predictor of one's health status (Weinberger, Hiner, & Tierney, 1987; Zarski, 1984).

SOURCE: Reprinted from *Psychological Science,* Volume 1, Kanner, A. D., Coyne, J. C., Schaefer, C., & Lazarus, R. S. Comparison of two modes of stress management: Daily hassles and uplifts versus major life events. Copyright 1981, with permission from Kluwer Academic Publishers.

conflicts arise when a person must choose between two or more incompatible alternatives (e.g., going to the dentist or suffering from a toothache). Conflicts that last a long time and involve difficult decisions may result in additional stress.

Environmental Stressors

Many aspects of our environment seem to conspire to introduce stress into our lives. Natural disasters such as earthquakes, hurricanes, or floods can introduce very high levels of stress. The fact that they are unpredictable events creates an even higher stress level. Research has shown that numerous psychological problems follow these types of large-scale disasters. Symptoms include nightmares, irritability, difficulty concentrating, and a general unresponsiveness (Lindy, Green, & Grace, 1987). Fortunately, these symptoms are usually short-lived and subside soon after the environmental disaster ends (Bravo, Rubio-Stipec, Canino, Woodbury, & Ribera, 1990).

Compared to natural disasters, the human-made environmental disasters or problems with which we contend on a daily basis are more problematic psychologically. These include factors such as air pollution, crowding, traffic congestion, and noise pollution. Human-caused disasters such as the nuclear reactor accident at Three-Mile Island in Pennsylvania or accidents with toxic chemicals can trigger

Hassles consist of everyday annoyances that occur in our lives. Experiencing a flat tire at a particularly inopportune moment would constitute such a hassle. The frequency of hassles has been found to be a good predictor of a person's health status.

high levels of stress that persist for many years (Baum & Fleming, 1993). Human-caused disasters affect us more than natural disasters because we reasonably expect that adequate precautions have been taken to prevent them from happening. We are more understanding of, and less stressed by, the machinations of nature.

Predictability and Familiarity of Stressors

Is an event less stressful if you can predict that it is going to occur? Even though you know that your taxes are payable annually on April 15, does this knowledge make it any less aversive or stressful? Individuals generally prefer predictable stressors over those that are unpredictable (Lanzetta & Driscoll, 1966; Perkins, Seyman, Levis, & Spence, 1966). However, predictability does *not* necessarily reduce the aversive consequences of a stressor (Furedy & Chan, 1971; Furedy & Doob, 1972).

Does familiarity with a stressor reduce its impact? For instance, if your dentist says you need a root canal, will the stressful impact be greater because you are personally familiar or unfamiliar with the procedures involved? Unfamiliar stressors have only slightly more serious health consequences (Johnson & Sarason, 1979; Gardner, Ostrowski, Pino, Morrell, & Kochevar, 1992).

✦ TABLE 8.5 ✦ The Perceived-Stress Scale

You can measure how much stress you perceive in your life by answering the following questions:

1. In the last month, how often have you felt:
   a. unable to control the important things in your life?
      0. Never
      1. Almost never
      2. Sometimes
      3. Fairly often
      4. Very often
   b. confident about your ability to handle your personal problems?
      0. Very often
      1. Fairly often
      2. Sometimes
      3. Almost never
      4. Never
   c. that things were going your way?
      0. Very often
      1. Fairly often
      2. Sometimes
      3. Almost never
      4. Never
   d. that difficulties were piling up so high that you could not overcome them?
      0. Never
      1. Almost never
      2. Sometimes
      3. Fairly often
      4. Very often

Scoring:
Add up the scores indicated by the answers you have selected. In Cohen and Williamson's (1988) national study, women scored an average of 4.7 points while men averaged 4.2 points.

SOURCE: Reprinted with permission by Sheldon Cohen. Taken from Cohen, S., & Williamson, G. M. (1988). Perceived stress in a probability sample of the United States. In S. Spacapan & S. Oskamp (Eds), *The social psychology of health.* Newbury Park, CA: Sage.

APPLICATIONS: Measuring Your Level of Stress

Do you experience a great deal of stress in your personal life? Sheldon Cohen and Gail Williamson (1988) worked in conjunction with pollster Louis Harris to ask a large group of Americans the questions shown in Table 8.5. You can answer these questions and compare your perceived stress level to a national sample. Individuals with low perceived-stress scores are more likely to report that they experience good health and practice good health habits such as exercising, not smoking, and eating healthy meals (Cohen & Williamson, 1988).

Responses to Stress

In chapter 7, I discussed the physiological responses that occur when we are emotionally aroused. Exposure to a stressor elicits several of these physiological responses, including increased heart rate and breathing, sweating, and even trembling in the arms and legs, if the stressor is a powerful one. These reactions explain why "stressed-out" individuals are often described as "sweating it out" and "shaking in their boots."

Walter Cannon (1929) coined the term **fight or flight** to describe the physiological responses to a stressor that is interpreted as a danger to ourselves. These complicated physiological responses prepare our body to take an action to either fight or flee depending on the circumstances. Cannon also noted that these responses can have either helpful or harmful results. In the short term, the responses are helpful because they prepare our body for action. However, *prolonged* arousal can be very harmful to our physical health.

Hans Selye (1956) described what happens to the body when stress is prolonged. He called the series of physiological reactions made by the body the **general adaptation syndrome,** which characterizes the body's reaction as occurring in three stages:

1. Alarm reaction. The stress hormones that are released mobilize the body for immediate action. The body, unable to maintain this intense arousal state for very long, must instead move to the second stage. As stated earlier in the chapter on emotions, the sudden and intense arousal of this stage can sometimes be severe enough to cause death.
2. Resistance stage. In this stage the body attempts to adapt to the stressor. Physiological arousal declines slightly but remains higher than normal. The continuous physiological arousal associated with this stage makes the body vulnerable to a variety of health problems, including high blood pressure, asthma, and illnesses associated with an impaired immune system.
3. Stage of exhaustion. If the stressor is severe and repeated or prolonged, the body enters the exhaustion stage. The body can tolerate heightened arousal for only so long before the body's ability to resist the stressor becomes depleted. When this stage occurs, the immune system's ability to defend against illness becomes severely compromised, resulting in the increased probability of serious illness or even death.

Stress, Personality, and Illness

The five leading causes of death in the United States are heart disease, cancer, stroke, accidents, and influenza/pneumonia. These five causes alone account for the vast majority of deaths that occur each year. Stress and personality play a significant role in each of these illnesses.

Coronary Heart Disease and Strokes

Cardiovascular disease accounts for more than 40% of deaths in the United States. Genetic components as well as several behavioral factors account for this disease. Individuals who experience major life stressors, such as those illustrated by the Social Readjustment Rating Scale (Table 8.3), are more likely to suffer from heart disease and heart attacks (Garrity & Marx, 1979). Individuals who have heavy work loads or job responsibilities and who are dissatisfied with their jobs also have a much higher incidence of heart disease (Cottington & House, 1987). Prolonged stressors cause hormones to be released into the bloodstream, which can damage arteries and the heart. These hormones contribute to the hardening of the arteries, high blood pressure, and ultimately, heart attacks or strokes. In addition, stress can cause the heart to beat irregularly, resulting in sudden death.

Individuals under high stress conditions often adopt behaviors that can directly contribute to heart disease. Cigarette smoking, high levels of alcohol consumption, inadequate physical activity, and overeating have all been implicated in heart disease and strokes (Epstein & Jennings, 1986).

Type-A and Type-B Personality

Certain personality types are much more prone to heart disease. Interestingly, this fact was first observed by an upholsterer who was recovering chairs for a physician who specialized in the treatment of patients with heart disease. The upholsterer noticed that the front sections of each chair seat in the waiting room were particularly worn. In other words, the patients with heart disease were literally "on the edge of their seats" awaiting their doctor's appointment. This observation led psychologists to describe a type of personality, characterized as the **Type-A personality,** which is associated with heart disease. The Type-A behavior pattern consists of three characteristics (Chesney, Frautschi, & Rosenman, 1985):

1. Competitive achievement orientation. Type-A individuals are very self-critical and strive hard to reach goals without taking any joy in their efforts or accomplishments.
2. Time urgency. Type-A individuals are time driven and fight a constant battle with the clock. They are impatient with delays, take on too many commitments, and often try to accomplish several things at one time.
3. Anger/hostility. Type-A individuals quickly become hostile or angry even though they may or may not express their anger overtly.

Type-A individuals also react differently to stress. Type-A individuals respond more quickly and more forcefully to stressors, particularly if they perceive the stressors as threats to their personal self-control (Carver, Diamond, & Humphries, 1985). Curiously, Type-A individuals often create stress in their own lives not only by seeking out situations where they will be placed in competitive, demanding situations, but also by setting artificial deadlines for themselves (Byrne & Rosenman, 1986).

Are some components of Type-A behavior more important for health than others? The anger/hostility component is by far the most deadly. One study examined the

✦ TABLE 8.6 ✦ Test of Anger or Hostility

Are you a hostile, angry, or aggressive individual? This test will measure your tendencies on these characteristics. Read each statement and circle the number that indicates how angry this event would make you feel. Be honest in how you rate yourself.

	Not at all Angry	Slightly Angry	Moderately Angry	Very Angry
Someone falsely accuses you of lying	1	2	3	4
You get blamed for a mistake someone else made	1	2	3	4
You receive very poor service at a restaurant	1	2	3	4
Your computer crashes at a very inopportune time	1	2	3	4
You ruin your favorite article of clothing due to carelessness	1	2	3	4
Someone doesn't return your phone call	1	2	3	4
A person makes an obscene gesture at you for a minor driving incident	1	2	3	4
Someone spreads a rumor about you that is not true	1	2	3	4
A friend borrows an article of clothing and returns it ruined by a stain	1	2	3	4
A salesperson accidentally charges you too much for an item	1	2	3	4

Scoring:
Add up the total points from the numbers you have circled. An average score is about 15 to 18. The higher your score, the greater your tendency to anger and hostility.

mortality rate of 255 male physicians over a 25-year period. These men had taken a psychological test that measured hostility while they were in medical school 25 years earlier. Those physicians who had high scores on the hostility scale also had mortality rates several times higher than the men who had low hostility scores (Barefoot, Dahlstrom, & Williams, 1983). Health psychologists have labeled hostility as "the most deadly emotion." Anger and hostility are particularly harmful when feelings are repressed rather than expressed, or when feelings are self-directed. In addition, hostility characterized by suspiciousness, resentment, antagonism toward others, and frequent outbursts of anger seems to be particularly dangerous to one's health (Dembroski & Costa, 1988; Smith, 1992).

Do you consider yourself a hostile person? Most people don't perceive themselves this way even if others do. The short test in Table 8.6 will allow you to assess your personal level of hostility.

APPLICATIONS

Reducing Your Hostility Level

Several strategies have proven helpful in teaching people to become less hostile. The following are a few of these strategies (Williams, 1989):

1. Become self-aware. Work toward becoming increasingly aware of angry, hostile, or cynical thoughts. Keep a log of these hostile thoughts in a notebook, including what happened, what thoughts you had, what feelings you experienced, and what actions you took. Merely noting these feelings and reviewing them weekly can help you become more aware of the hostile, angry feelings and can reduce their frequency of occurrence.
2. Interrupt your thoughts. As soon as you have a hostile or cynical thought, try to interrupt it. A simple and effective technique that you can use is to place a large, flat rubber band around your wrist. Each time you catch yourself engaging in hostile or cynical thoughts, pull the rubber band away from your wrist and snap it. Don't make this horribly painful. Snap it just hard enough to draw your attention to the negative thoughts you are trying to avoid. The mild pain will help interrupt the flow of the thoughts and direct them in a more positive direction.
3. Develop empathy. When angry at someone, mentally try to place yourself in his or her shoes. For example, if the harried restaurant employee appears to be ignoring you, try and imagine how difficult it would be for you to meet all the demands of that job.
4. Laugh at yourself. One characteristic of angry, hostile people is that they seldom laugh at themselves or use humor to defuse their anger. Try and see the humor in your own behavior and learn to laugh at yourself. We all enjoy being around others who can laugh at life's difficult situations and diffuse tense situations with humor.

> If I had no sense of humor, I would long ago have committed suicide.
>
> **MAHATMA GANDHI**

5. Learn to relax. Later in this chapter I will describe several techniques you can use to help in relaxation.
6. Become a better listener. Try to spend less time talking and more time listening to others. Make an effort to listen carefully and to understand what others are saying. Hostility and cynicism often result from misunderstanding about what others are saying.
7. Become assertive. As an alternative to becoming aggressive, learn to be assertive by developing skills that will allow you to stand up for your rights. Practice assertiveness skills such as saying "no" when you do not want to do something, speaking up when you feel you are right, and otherwise expressing your feelings and desires in an honest, straightforward manner while respecting the rights of others.
8. Practice trusting others. Cynical people often question the motives and actions of others. Practice learning to trust others more. Start by trusting others in situations where little or no harm will come to you if the other person betrays your trust. As you become reinforced for these behaviors, you will find yourself more and more willing to trust others.

✦ TABLE 8.7 ✦ Measuring the Type-A Personality

Check all the items that apply to you. Answer as honestly and truthfully as you can.
Do you:

_____ Have a habit of explosively accentuating various key words in ordinary speech even when there is no need for such accentuation?
_____ Finish other persons' sentences for them?
_____ Always move, walk, and eat rapidly?
_____ Quickly skim-read material and prefer summaries or condensations of books?
_____ Become easily angered by slow-moving lines or traffic?
_____ Feel impatience with the rate at which most events take place?
_____ Tend to be unaware of the details or beauty of your surroundings?
_____ Frequently strive to think of, or do, 2 or more things simultaneously?
_____ Almost always feel vaguely guilty when you relax, vacation, or do absolutely nothing for several days?
_____ Tend to evaluate your worth in quantitative terms (number of A's earned, amount of income, number of games won, and so forth)?
_____ Have nervous gestures or muscle twitches, such as grinding your teeth, clenching your fists, or drumming your fingers?
_____ Attempt to schedule more and more activities into less time and, in so doing, make fewer allowances for unforeseen problems?
_____ Frequently think about other things while talking to someone?
_____ Repeatedly take on more responsibilities than you can comfortably handle?

Scoring:
If all or most of these items are checked, you have behaviors consistent with a Type-A personality. If only a few of these items apply, you are more likely a Type-B personality.

9. Practice forgiveness. We all make mistakes and need the forgiveness of others. Practice forgiveness as an alternative to anger when someone mistreats you.

Measuring Your Personality Type

In contrast to the Type-A personality, the **Type-B personality** is characterized by low levels of competitiveness, little or no time urgency, and low levels of anger and hostility. These individuals are considerably more "laid back" and deal with life's challenges in more adaptive and healthy ways.

Always forgive your enemies—nothing annoys them so much.

OSCAR WILDE

Are you more of a Type-A or a Type-B individual? You can take the test in Table 8.7 and measure your own tendencies relative to these two personality types.

Cancer

Cancer is the number-two killer of individuals in the United States. One out of 4 people will have cancer in his or her lifetime. The incidence of many cancers has steadily risen over the past 20 years. The greatest increase has occurred with lung cancer, a direct result of tobacco use. As with coronary heart disease, both behavioral factors and personality traits have been associated with the occurrence of cancer. Other factors implicated in the increased likelihood of cancer include using alcohol, sunbathing, engaging in first sexual intercourse at an early age, having a large number of different sexual partners, and maintaining certain dietary habits (Snyder, 1989). In addition, an individual's exposure to environmental pollutants, such as pesticides and herbicides, and to occupational carcinogens, such as asbestos or polyvinyl chloride (PVC), is also implicated in causing cancer. Adjusting one's lifestyle can greatly reduce or eliminate most of these behavioral factors associated with the occurrence of cancer.

The degree to which stress influences a person's susceptibility to cancer is not clearly understood (Fox, 1978; Morrison & Paffenbarger, 1981). Even though stress does alter immune functioning, changes in stress may be associated with either increased susceptibility or increased resistance to cancer, depending on the circumstances. The effect of stress varies from individual to individual as well as from cancer to cancer (Snyder, 1989).

Personality can also play a role in the incidence of cancer. One study followed the health status of women with breast cancer for a period of 2 years (Jensen, 1987). The cancer's spread was greater among women who had repressed personalities, characterized by a failure to express their negative emotions. A similar study followed breast cancer patients for 10 years and found that patients who felt helpless, hopeless, and stoic had a greater recurrence of the cancer and a lower survival rate (Pettingale, 1984). These findings have led health psychologist Lydia Temoshok and others to describe a Type-C, or cancer-prone, personality (Temoshok & Fox, 1984). The **Type-C personality** is described as repressed, apathetic, and hopeless. However, there is still no clear evidence that emotional factors relevant to cancer are any different from those implicated in other diseases. It is conceivable that Type-C personalities are prone to many different kinds of illnesses rather than cancer specifically.

Influenza and Pneumonia

Respiratory problems such as influenza and pneumonia are a major cause of death in the United States, particularly among older individuals. Stress is believed to be related to the occurrence of these illnesses due to the diminished capability of the immune system under high stress conditions. Stress also leads many individuals to begin or continue smoking, which is a behavior shown to be a direct causal factor for these illnesses.

Accidents

Accidents are a leading cause of death in the United States. Automobile accidents kill nearly 50,000 people and injure about another one-half million each year. Almost 300,000 people suffer brain damage each year as a result of automobile-related accidents. The greatest health threats to young people, by far, are injuries sustained in automobile accidents.

As with the other leading causes of death, accidents are related to both personality and behavioral factors. Imagine that you are speeding toward an intersection when you see the traffic light turning from yellow to red. The amount of stress that you are under likely will influence your decision to stop or run the light. If you are late for an important job interview, for instance, your decision might be directed toward the more risky behavior and significant health consequences. Large numbers of traffic injuries and deaths are caused by this particular behavior every year. Cer-

Regular, vigorous exercise has been found to reduce stress, increase feelings of happiness, and extend one's life expectancy.

tain personality characteristics also influence individuals to adopt the riskier behaviors that lead to higher accident rates. As discussed earlier, high sensation seekers enjoy engaging in risky behaviors such as motorcycle riding, sky diving, mountain climbing, and other activities that increase their likelihood of injuries or even death.

APPLICATIONS: Techniques for Reducing Stress

Many people adopt maladaptive behaviors to reduce stress. These include cigarette smoking and the excessive use of alcohol, illegal drugs, and prescribed medications. While these behaviors may offer short-term stress reduction, the long-term effects create far more problems than they solve. Consequences include physical, emotional, and even economic problems. The following are alternative solutions that are easy to learn and effective.

Exercise

Vigorous physical exercise, such as running, is one way to cope effectively with stress (U.S. Surgeon General, 1979). Simply going outside to run serves to remove you from the stimuli that commonly cause your stress, such as your school or work environment, family pressures, and other tensions. Furthermore, the act of making vigorous, repetitive movements causes you to focus on your body's functioning, including breathing and visceral sensations, and results in stress reduction. Finally, there is evidence that vigorous exercise produces the chemical secretions in your brain which create a state of euphoria, commonly known as the "runner's high" experienced by long-distance runners. However, the stress-reducing capabilities of exercise are short-lived, usually lasting about 60 to 90 minutes. Longer-term stress reduction needs additional techniques.

Meditation has proven to be a very effective way to reduce blood pressure, lower arousal, promote relaxation, and counteract other effects of stress.

Muscle Relaxation

You have to stay in shape. My grandmother, she started walking five miles a day when she was 60. She's 97 today and we don't know where the hell she is.

ELLEN DEGENERES

People often advise other individuals to "just relax." Unfortunately, this well-intentioned advice is rarely helpful. Telling yourself to calm down is usually equally ineffective. To reduce stress, you must *learn* to relax. One technique called **muscle relaxation** has been proven very effective. Locate a quiet environment where you will not be disturbed. Lie down or sit in a comfortable chair. Begin by tensing the muscles in your right arm until they begin to tremble. Hold the muscles tightly for about 5 seconds before letting go. Now allow your hand and arm to go limp and become completely relaxed. Repeat this procedure 2 or 3 times, alternately tensing and relaxing the muscles. Repeat the tension-release procedure with your left arm until it feels very relaxed. Apply the procedure to your right leg, your left leg, your abdomen, your chest, and your shoulders. Similarly, clench and release the muscles in your neck, jaw, and throat. Generate tension in your forehead and scalp by wrinkling the skin on your forehead, and then concentrate on relaxing these same muscles. Alternately tighten and release the muscles around your mouth. Finally, alternately curl your toes and relax them. Continue practicing these progressive tensing-releasing exercises until you can achieve complete relaxation throughout your body. After becoming experienced in these techniques, you should be able to achieve complete body relaxation in 5 to 10 minutes.

Meditation and Relaxation

People in the Far East have used meditation techniques to achieve stress reduction for many years. These techniques can significantly reduce your blood pressure, breathing

✦ TABLE 8.8 ✦ Measuring Test Anxiety

Read the following statements and rate how they apply to you, using the following scale:

0 = Never
1 = Sometimes
2 = Often
3 = Always

_____ 1. I do not feel that I study properly for tests.
_____ 2. I typically begin to feel nervous several days before a test.
_____ 3. My nervousness increases on the day of the test.
_____ 4. I feel that I will do poorly on tests.
_____ 5. If I do not know an answer, I begin to panic.
_____ 6. I get confused while taking tests.
_____ 7. Even if I have prepared adequately, I feel unsure of my answers.
_____ 8. I forget information that I have studied.
_____ 9. While I'm taking a test, I tell myself that I do not know the answers.

Scoring:
Add up the total points for all of the questions. If you have a score of 12 or higher, you may suffer from test anxiety. The higher your score beyond 12, the more debilitating the test anxiety will be. If all or even most of these statements frequently apply, you should consider seeking assistance in dealing with your test anxiety.

rate, and other physiological signs of arousal (Benson, 1975). The techniques are simple and easily learned. Find a quiet environment and sit in a comfortable position. Close your eyes and deeply relax all your muscles, beginning with your feet and progressing up to your face. Allow the muscles to remain deeply relaxed. Begin breathing through your nose and concentrate only on your breathing. As you breathe out, say a word or make a sound to yourself that you repeat silently or in quiet, gentle tones. Benson suggests using the syllable *one* because of its neutrality and simplicity. Breathe in. As you breathe out, repeat the sound or syllable to yourself again. Then breathe in. Repeat this procedure for 20 minutes. During this time, disregard any thought that enters your mind. Studies have indicated that the employment of these techniques is effective in the treatment of alcoholism, drug abuse, and cigarette smoking (Wills, 1986).

Reducing Test Anxiety

Do you get excessively anxious before taking a test? Some anxiety before an exam is good because it keeps you mentally active and alert. However, as you learned in chapter 6, too much anxiety can have deleterious effects on your performance, particularly on a difficult examination. I have witnessed many students who have failed examinations for which they were well prepared merely because of test anxiety. Are you excessively anxious when you take an examination? The brief self-test in Table 8.8 can help tell you whether your level of test anxiety may be causing you to perform poorly on exams.

The following techniques have proven effective in helping control test anxiety:

Deep Breathing

Changing the way you breathe when anxious can help you stay calm. Take a slow, deep breath through your nose. Breathe in as much air as possible, hold it for two seconds, and then exhale slowly. Repeat this procedure up to 10 times. This is often effective not only in test situations but also in any anxiety-producing situation.

Muscle Relaxation

Practice the muscle relaxation procedures I described earlier.

Creative Visualization

Prior to the exam, lie on the floor on your back with your arms and legs stretched out. Position yourself so that you are feeling comfortable. Close your eyes and visualize the most wonderful, relaxing place that you have ever visited or would like to visit. This could be a lake in the mountains, a serene ocean beach, a beautiful forest, or any other place that is special to you. Imagine your surroundings clearly and in detail. Smell the air; feel the breezes; listen to the sounds of your surroundings. Imagine walking through this special place and carefully examining whatever you see. When you are feeling relaxed and at peace, count to 3 slowly and open your eyes. Practice this procedure for a few weeks whenever you recognize you are feeling anxious. If you feel yourself becoming anxious during a test, close your eyes, do the deep breathing exercises, and visualize your special place. You should quickly feel yourself begin to relax.

Controlling Negative Thinking

A major factor in test anxiety is self-doubt and negative thinking. Students who suffer from test anxiety often engage in negative thoughts before and during an examination. Avoid thoughts like "I know I'm going to fail this exam," "I'm going to be embarrassed in front of my friends when I fail," or "I never do well on exams." Thinking about failure can prove to be a self-fulfilling prophecy. Instead, send yourself positive thoughts, such as "I am well prepared for this test," "I know I can do well on this exam," and "I've been successful on harder exams than this." Replace negative thoughts such as "This is a long test!" with "I have plenty of time to complete the exam."

Visualizing Success

Many professional athletes enhance their performance by visualizing the correct moves before attempting them. Professional golfers and football field-goal kickers have used visualization with great success. You can do the same on an exam. Visualize yourself performing well in a test situation. Visualize remaining calm, carefully reading the questions, and calmly answering them. The mind can have difficulty distinguishing between what has actually taken place and what has been mentally visualized, so positive visualizations add to your self-confidence and help you relax during an examination. Rehearse these visualizations both prior to and during the examination.

Finally, do not use test anxiety as an excuse. Some students blame test anxiety for their failures when actually they have not studied carefully or thoroughly. If you are unprepared for an exam, you have good reason to be anxious.

These are only a few of the methods for controlling test anxiety. Your college's counseling center likely has people trained to assist you further if the described techniques do not prove effective.

Moderators of Stress

All of us experience stress in our lives. In fact, it would be a rather boring existence if our lives were completely devoid of any stress. Furthermore, psychologists know that *some* stress is good for you. As discussed in the chapter on motivation, a moderate level of stress helps us perform better, particularly on more difficult tasks. Researchers in health psychology also have found that moderate levels of stress help activate the immune system.

Severe and persistent stress has the most serious health consequences. And yet some individuals constantly function under very severe levels of stress and suffer few or no health consequences while others similarly situated become ill. Health psychologists have studied these individuals who remain healthy in order to determine what seems to "immunize" them against the health consequences of stress. They have discovered that there are several factors, called **moderators of stress,** that help protect us from the consequences of life's stress or strain.

Psychological Hardiness

There are 3 personality characteristics, representing psychological **hardiness,** that differentiate between people who do, and do not, get sick under the influence of stress (Kobasa, 1986; Kobasa & Maddi, 1977). Think of these 3 personality characteristics as *the 3 C's:*

1. Control. Psychologically hardy people believe that they can influence events in their lives. They feel that they are in control of their destiny. People who believe that fate or chance determines how their future is going to play out usually believe that they are not in control of their lives.
2. Commitment. Hardy people have a strong sense of purpose or involvement in the events, activities, and people in their lives. They frequently turn to others for support in times of stress. They persevere in life and resist giving up in times of stress. They are strongly committed to their friends, spouses, chosen occupations, and other important aspects of their lives.
3. Challenge. Hardy individuals enjoy challenges. They view changes in their lives as opportunities for growth rather than threats to their security. A safe and stable life does not particularly appeal to them. They seek out opportunities that will constantly challenge their abilities.

Of these 3 characteristics, *commitment* and *control* are the 2 most important in serving as buffers to the effects of stress.

Self-Efficacy and Control

Self-efficacy refers to an individual's own judgments of his or her ability to cope with stressful situations. How you react to stressful situations and the amount of stress that you experience are directly related to your beliefs about how effective your actions will be. When people have self-confidence in their abilities, they are more likely to exercise control over their environment. Individuals who are low in self-efficacy often do not attempt to control their fate, even when such control is readily available. In the chapter on learning I described a phenomenon called learned helplessness in which dogs that had been subjected to repeated and unavoidable shocks subsequently developed an inability to learn to avoid future shocks. This occurred even when avoiding shocks involved only the simple task of jumping over a barrier. People with low self-efficacy share a similar perception that they have little ability to deal with unpleasant events in their lives.

Sense of Control

Have confidence that if you have done a little thing well, you can do a bigger thing well too.

STOREY

Individuals are far more likely to feel a great deal of stress when they view events as uncontrollable and beyond their ability to change. When the same stressful events are perceived as within our control, they are perceived as much less stressful. Undoubtedly, you have experienced this type of situation many times in your own life. If you are at a restaurant and a baby nearby is crying, you will find it much more stressful than when it is your own child who is crying. In the former situation, you have little control over the crying, whereas in the latter situation you do.

People who believe that they are in control of stressful events are much more resistant to the negative health consequences of stress. How do you rate on perceptions of self-control? You can take the short test contained in Table 8.9 to measure your own sense of control.

Social Support

Social support refers to the existence of a network of people that you feel you can rely upon, especially in times of crisis. It may consist of family and friends, church, social clubs, professional organizations, or even your employer. There is a strong relationship between social relationships and health. Individuals who are socially isolated or who are not well-integrated socially are less healthy and more likely to die prematurely (House, Landis, & Umberson, 1988). Social isolates, including some unmarried individuals, experience higher rates of suicide, accidents, debilitating mental illness, and, in general, deaths from all causes when compared with people who maintain strong social support (House, et al., 1988).

The person who tries to live alone will not succeed as a human being. His heart withers if it does not answer another heart. His mind shrinks away if he hears only the echoes of his own thoughts and finds no other inspiration.

PEARL S. BUCK

One study of several thousand adults found that people who had low social support were twice as likely to die in the next 9 years as those with strong social support (Berkman & Syne, 1979). It appears that social support is a more critical factor for health in men than in women. Men lacking in social relationships are 2 to 3 times more likely to die in the following 10 to 12 years (House, et al., 1988). The effect is not as strong in women, whose mortality is increased 1 to 2 times. The risk of death from lack of social support is even stronger than the risk for mortality from cigarette smoking (House, et al., 1988).

Social support is also important in our ability to survive potentially fatal illnesses. One study looked at women with breast cancers that had spread to other parts of their bodies (Spiegel, 1991). One group received routine medical care while another group attended a weekly support group. In the support group they discussed their fear of death, visited other members when they were hospitalized, attended the

✦ TABLE 8.9 ✦ Testing Your Sense of Control

What is your sense of control? Answer each of the following questions using the following rating scale:

A. Almost never B. Seldom C. Often D. Almost always

_____ 1. How often do you find yourself feeling helpless or hopeless?
_____ 2. How often do you find yourself in a situation that seems out of your control?
_____ 3. How often do you find yourself needing to have your life well planned and organized?
_____ 4. How often do you find yourself feeling sad or depressed?
_____ 5. How often do you find yourself fearful of losing control over your life?
_____ 6. How often do you find yourself feeling insecure?
_____ 7. How often do you find yourself needing to control the people around you?
_____ 8. How often do you find yourself needing to control your environment?
_____ 9. How often do you feel the need to have your daily activities highly structured?
_____ 10. How often do you feel secure?

Scoring:
For items 1 to 9, (A) = 1 point; (B) = 2 points; (C) = 3 points; (D) = 4 points.
For item 10, (A) = 4 points; (B) = 3 points; (C) = 2 points; (D) = 1 point.
If your total score is greater than 24, you likely feel that you lack control.

SOURCE: From Daniel A. Girdano et al., *Controlling stress and tension.* © 1990 by Allyn & Bacon. Adapted by permission.

funerals of members who died, and worked together on projects of mutual interest. After 2 years, virtually all of the patients receiving routine medical care had died while one-third of the cancer patients in the support group were still alive. Other studies have reported similar findings with other illnesses, including heart disease and leukemia.

APPLICATIONS: Increasing Your Social Support

What can you do to strengthen your social network and thereby help fend off illness or reduce the effects in stress in your life? The following suggestions will help you accomplish this:

1. Strengthen relationships with family and friends. Maintain close contacts by keeping in touch, and by joining with them in activities. Use the telephone or e-mail to maintain contact if you live far apart.
2. Be a joiner. Join clubs or organizations that interest you. Doing so will widen your social network. If you are religious, become actively involved in church programs.

At work, participate with fellow employees at social functions—join sports leagues or other groups that will foster relationships with fellow employees.

3. Confide in someone. Talking with someone you trust about your concerns can be therapeutic and helpful in protecting you from illness. The confidant can be a friend, family member, or professional counselor. One study indicated that confiding in a professional, such as a psychologist or a lawyer, was more beneficial than a family member or friend (Lindenthal & Myers, 1979).
4. Keep a diary. Writing down your feelings about personal difficulties can be very helpful. People who regularly kept a diary had fewer health problems during the ensuing 4 to 6 months (Pennebaker, 1990).
5. Get a pet. You might not think of your pets as part of your social support network. However, several recent studies have indicated the value of having a close attachment to a pet, particularly for older individuals. Over the course of a year, those elderly individuals with pets (particularly dogs) reported they felt better and made fewer visits to their physicians (Siegel, 1990). The more attached we are to our pets, the better our health (Garrity, Stallones, Marx, & Johnson, 1989). Dogs are a particularly good source of unconditional love. Unfortunately, unconditional love is something that is sometimes in short supply in our dealings with fellow humans.
6. Seek out those with a caring attitude. It is not just the quantity of our social relationships but the *quality* as well. Establish relationships with people who show a caring attitude. Foster those relationships in which you receive positive feedback.
7. Consider marriage. Married people are generally healthier and happier. As I discussed earlier, they have lower suicide rates and lower incidences of serious mental disorders. Being in a supportive marital relationship is one of the best things that you can do to ensure continued good health. Of course, single people can also enjoy these same benefits by ensuring that they have a strong network of social support.

Coping with Stress

When exposed to uncomfortably high levels of stress, everyone attempts to find relief. The strategies and behaviors that people adopt are called **coping mechanisms.** As discussed earlier, sometimes these strategies involve maladaptive behaviors such as smoking, drinking alcohol, or taking tranquilizers, or more healthy coping strategies, such as vigorous exercise, muscle relaxation, and meditation. In this section we will discover more ways to find relief from the tensions caused by stress.

Coping Styles

Before reading further, take the self-assessment test in Table 8.10. Coping mechanisms serve two main functions (Lazarus & Folkman, 1984; Lazarus & Launier, 1978). They can alter the problem that is causing the stress or they can reduce the emotional response to the problem. People who adopt the former strategy are using

✦ TABLE 8.10 ✦ Coping Styles

Remember back over the last year and try to think of a very stressful personal crisis or life event that you have experienced. The more recent and stressful the event, the better. Think about how you handled the stressful situation. Read the statements below and check off those that described how you tried to deal with the situation. Check off all those that apply.

_____ 1. Attempted to look at the positive aspects of the situation.
_____ 2. Evaluated the situation by trying to step back and look at it objectively.
_____ 3. Used prayer for guidance and strength.
_____ 4. Took out my feelings on other people when I became angry or depressed.
_____ 5. Tried to keep my mind off the situation by busying myself with other things.
_____ 6. Adopted the philosophy that everything would work itself out and decided not to worry about it.
_____ 7. Tried to take things one step at a time.
_____ 8. Looked at several different alternative ways that the problem could be solved.
_____ 9. Looked at how I had handled similar situations previously and used that experience to help solve the problem.
_____ 10. Sought a solution by talking to friends and relatives.
_____ 11. Sought help about the problem from a professional person such as a doctor, clergyman, lawyer, teacher, or counselor.
_____ 12. Tried to solve the problem by taking action.

Scoring:
Your text describes 2 major types of coping: problem-focused coping and emotion-focused coping. Count how many of the first 6 statements you checked. These are examples of emotion-focused coping styles. Count how many of the last 6 statements you checked. These are problem-focused styles. See the text for a description of these 2 different styles.

SOURCE: Adapted from *Journal of Behavioral Medicine,* Volume 4, Billings & Moos, The role of coping responses and social resources in attenuating the stress of life events. Copyright 1981, with permission from Kluwer Academic Publishers.

problem-focused coping styles while those who adopt the latter strategy are using *emotion-focused* coping styles.

Imagine a situation in which one of your math professors suggests that you drop his class because you lack an adequate math background to learn the material. You need this course in order to graduate, and his pronouncement causes you a great deal of stress. How might you try and cope with this stress? Individuals adopting a problem-focused style would try to *reduce the demands of the stressful situation* or would try to *expand the resources* they have to deal with it. This involves taking direct action to deal with the stressor. It also involves seeking information or knowledge about the stressful situation that can be used to develop a strategy for its solution. Finally, individuals adopting this coping style often turn to others for social support, help, or reassurance. In the example cited, you might drop the class and take it later after you have taken additional math courses, or seek out either a tutor or student study group to assist you in mastering the material.

Individuals adopting an emotion-focused coping style would attempt to *control the emotional responses* occurring with the stressful situation. They might engage in behaviors to reduce the emotional response, such as using alcohol or drugs. Alternatively, they might employ behaviors to divert their attention away from the problem, such as participating in sports or vigorous exercise, watching television, or going to the movies. In addition, emotion-focused behaviors often include specific emotional responses such as crying, screaming, or using jokes to reduce the strain. In situations where the stressor cannot be changed, such as with the loss of a limb or development of certain medical problems, the individual may come to terms with the situation by simply accepting its permanency. By looking at your answers to the test in Table 8.10, you can determine which of these two coping styles you tend to favor. Problem-focused and emotion-focused coping styles are not mutually exclusive and often are used together.

One study looked at how married couples used these two strategies. They found that both husbands and wives used more problem-focused styles than emotion-focused styles. However, wives used more emotion-focused styles when compared to husbands. Individuals with higher levels of education and income are more likely to use problem-focused coping styles (Billings & Moos, 1981).

Explanatory Styles

Our **explanatory style,** which is the way we habitually explain the causes of good and bad events in our lives, may have important implications, including susceptibility to illness. Three primary explanatory style dimensions have been identified (Kamen & Seligman, 1989):

1. Internal–External. People using an internal explanatory style believe that an event is caused by them personally whereas individuals with an external style believe that an event is caused by its situation. Imagine that a student is trying to explain why she cheated on a test. Using an internal explanatory style, she would explain that, in a moment of weakness, she gave in to temptation and looked at another student's answers. Using an external explanatory style, on the other hand, she would explain that another student made the test answers so visible to her that it was impossible to ignore them.
2. Stable–Unstable. Stable explanations occur when an explainer believes situations are relatively permanent, whereas unstable explanations are transient or fleeting in nature. For example, imagine that you just failed a test. A stable explanation might be that you believe yourself to be stupid and therefore will never do well on tests. An unstable explanation would be that you were just having a bad day and will do much better the next time.
3. Specific–Global. A specific explanatory style explains events in terms of very specific, defined circumstances. For instance, an automobile accident might be explained by the poor road conditions combined with a dark, moonless night. A global explanatory style explains events as being caused by all-encompassing, nonspecific events. In this instance, an automobile accident might be explained by the statement that "I've always been a lousy driver."

Optimism and Pessimism

Two major orientations toward explaining events in our lives emerge, grounded in the explanatory style we use. An **optimist** attributes negative events in life as being due to forces that are: (1) *external* to the individual, (2) *unstable* (i.e., temporary in nature), and (3) *specific* to the events. Failure to pass a driving test would be explained by stating, "The examiner didn't like me. I'll pass it next time. I'm usually good at passing tests." On the other hand, a **pessimist** assumes that stressful events occur because of *internal* character flaws ("I'm a lousy driver") that are a *permanent* part of the individual ("I'll never be a good driver") and will show up at every opportunity ("I'll never pass the driving test, no matter how many times I try").

Whether you possess an optimistic or pessimistic orientation has been found to be a powerful factor for many health-related issues. As you might guess, it is healthier to have an optimistic orientation. Pessimistic explanations tend to promote stress, depression, feelings of ill health, facilitation of physical diseases, and premature death (Miley, 1999). The optimistic–pessimistic orientations also reliably predict how healthy a person will be in the future and how quickly he or she will recover from a serious illness (Scheier & Carver, 1993). However, it is not clear whether it is the pessimistic explanatory style that causes health problems or whether a person's health difficulties cause the pessimism.

APPLICATIONS: Becoming More Optimistic

If you think of yourself as typically being a pessimist, you might want to consider the possible health ramifications of such an outlook. Try the following adaptive techniques used by optimists when confronted with a stressful situation:

> The optimist proclaims that we live in the best of all possible worlds; and the pessimist fears this is true.
>
> **JAMES BRANCH CABELL**

1. Take direct action to solve the problem. Determine exactly what the stressor is and try to decide how you can deal with it. Do not avoid or put off dealing with stressors.
2. Develop a plan. When facing adversity, develop *specific* plans to deal with it. Focus your efforts on managing the problem.
3. Accept the reality of the situation. Optimists are more likely to accept the fact that some situations are stressful and need to be handled. Pessimists are more likely to avoid dealing with problems.
4. Try to grow personally from adversity. Optimists try to make the best of a bad situation. They realize that personal growth can result from dealing with adversity. Pessimists, on the other hand, see no benefit from adversity and tend to quit trying when difficulties arise.

SUMMARY

- Psychosomatic medicine studies the interaction between the workings of the mind and the body. Health psychology, in particular, examines these interactions and the health problems that result from lifestyle behaviors such as inadequate exercise, insufficient sleep, alcohol or drug abuse, deficient nutrition, overeating, and smoking. These behaviors account for a majority of health problems and shortened life expectancy.

- The immune system is the defensive system that wards off disease. Our bodies are constantly invaded by various foreign substances, known as antigens, and must fight off their assaults. The line of defense is the skin that acts as a barrier to entry. In addition, lymphocytes and killer T-cells attack and destroy the antigens.
- Even though the immune system functions best during adolescence and adulthood, extreme or prolonged stress reduces its effectiveness at all ages. Stress consists of both the emotional and physiological reactions that occur when we believe that certain events threaten our physical and/or psychological well-being. When the demands of a certain situation exceed our resources to meet those demands, we experience stress.
- Stressors are events that we perceive to be potentially harmful. They can result from major life events that require life adjustments or from annoying daily hassles. An excessive number of either life events or hassles can have negative health consequences.
- Other sources of stress include the frustrations that result from blocked goals, conflicts, and environmental events. The stressors that are unpredictable and unfamiliar to us are the most stressful. Uplifts, on the other hand, are positive experiences in our lives that, although stressful, do not cause health problems.
- Exposure to a stressor causes a flight-or-fight response. When stress is prolonged, a series of physiological reactions, known as the general adaptation syndrome, occurs. This response consists of three stages: (1) an alarm reaction when the body mobilizes for immediate action, (2) a resistance stage when the body attempts to adapt to the stressor, and (3) an exhaustion stage when the body no longer resists the stressor and its immune system becomes less able to defend against illness.
- Stress and personality are significant factors in the major causes of death in the United States, namely, cardiovascular disease, cancer, respiratory illness, and accidents. The incidence of coronary heart disease and stroke is particularly related to the individual's personality characteristics and the amount of stress experienced.
- Individuals with Type-A personalities are more prone to heart disease, in part because they tend to be competitive, self-critical, time driven, angry, and hostile. Recurrent anger and hostility are especially dangerous to health.
- Techniques to reduce hostility include, among other things, increasing self-awareness, interrupting hostile thoughts, developing empathy, developing assertiveness skills, learning to trust others, and practicing forgiveness.
- The Type-B personality is the opposite of the Type-A and is characterized by low levels of competition, time urgency, and anger or hostility.
- Both lifestyle behaviors and certain personality factors have been implicated as a possible cause of cancer. The Type-C or cancer-prone personality depicts an emotionally repressed individual who feels hopelessness and apathy.
- Other major health problems, specifically influenza, pneumonia, and accidents, increase in frequency when stress is present. Several techniques that exist for reducing stress in general include vigorous physical exercise, muscle relaxation, and meditation.
- Certain personality characteristics, called moderators of stress, serve to "inoculate" us from the effects of stress. These moderators include psychological hardiness, self-efficacy and control, and social support.
- Psychological hardiness occurs in individuals who believe that they have control over their lives, commit to people and activities, and feel challenged by new opportunities. People who are confident in their abilities to cope with stressful situations possess self-efficacy and are more resistant to the negative effects of stressors. Individuals with a strong network of social support, whether from friends, family, or shared activities with others, suffer fewer illnesses that result from stress and recover from illnesses more quickly.
- Individuals who can use coping mechanisms to deal with stress will either alter the problem that is causing the stress or reduce their emotional response to the stressor. They will use an explanatory style to interpret the causes of good and bad events that occur in their lives. These explanatory styles differentiate among individuals who are optimistic or pessimistic.
- Pessimists are less resistant to stressors and suffer more health consequences because they attribute negative events to internal character flaws. However, they can combat their pessimistic outlook by developing and implementing specific plans to address the problem, by accepting the reality of their situation, and by recognizing that they gain personal growth from adversity.
- Certain lifestyle behaviors contribute disproportionately to illness and premature death. These include smoking, poor eating habits, lack of exercise, and alcohol and substance abuse. Suggestions for reducing or eliminating these behaviors are as follows: (1) Smokers can quit "cold turkey" or assist the process with counseling, nicotine patches, or antidepressants; (2) healthy eating habits can be enhanced by eating low-fat, high-fiber foods and by eating breakfast daily; (3) healthy exercise regimes can be made a part of your lifestyle, such as increasing physical exercise, finding enjoyable exercises, mak-

ing a commitment to exercise, exercising with family and friends, keeping a record of your progress, setting concrete goals, and taking advantage of opportunities to exercise; and (4) substance abusers can address their alcohol or drug problems through abstinence and the acknowledgment that their abusing behaviors are within their personal control.

✦ All health-threatening behaviors are potentially responsive to change without professional assistance or self-help support groups. However, under circumstances where someone's best efforts have been ineffectual, professional assistance may be helpful.

KEY TERMS

antigens: foreign bodily "invaders" (such as bacteria, viruses, fungi, and protozoa) that enter and attack the body.

coping mechanisms: strategies and behaviors that offer relief during periods of stress.

explanatory style: the way an individual habitually explains the causes of good and bad events that occur in his or her life.

fight or flight: a term that describes the physiological responses that prepare our body to take an action to either fight or flee from a situation depending on the circumstances.

frustration: a negative emotion that occurs whenever we are blocked or thwarted from achieving a goal.

general adaptation syndrome: a series of physiological reactions that characterizes the body's reaction to stress as occurring in three stages: alarm reaction, resistance stage, and stage of exhaustion.

hardiness: personality characteristics that differentiate between people who do and do not get sick under the influence of stress.

hassles: minor frustrating and irritating demands that we are faced with on a daily basis.

health psychology: a subspecialty of psychology that focuses on maintenance of good health, prevention and treatment of illness, the study of physiological and psychological factors that cause illness, and improvement of the practices and policies of the health care system.

immune system: the body's defense system that fights off a variety of different "invaders" that threaten health.

killer T-cells: cells in the body that recognize and destroy antigens that have invaded the body.

lymphocyte: a specialized type of white blood cell that the human body uses to attack invading agents.

moderators of stress: factors that reduce the consequences of stress.

muscle relaxation: an effective stress-reduction technique.

optimist: an individual who attributes negative events in life as being due to forces that are external to the individual, temporary in nature, and specific to events.

pessimist: an individual who believes that stressful life events occur because of internal character flaws that are a permanent part of the individual.

psychosomatic: referring to the interaction of the mind and the body.

self-efficacy: an individual's own judgments of his or her ability to cope with stressful situations.

social support: the existence of a network of people that individuals feel they can rely upon.

stressors: events that are perceived as harmful or threatening.

Type-A personality: a type of personality that is characterized by competitive achievement orientation, time urgency, anger, and hostility.

Type-B personality: a type of personality that is characterized by low levels of competitiveness, little or no time urgency, and low levels of anger and hostility.

Type-C personality: a type of personality that is characterized as repressed, apathetic, and hopeless.

uplifts: desirable experiences that bring joy or pleasure to our lives.

9

Identifying Problem Behavior

In our interactions with others, we often identify behaviors that we consider strange or unusual. In fact, throughout history people have been fascinated and yet perplexed by the strange behaviors displayed by other individuals. The distinction between behavior that should be considered merely quirky and harmless and behavior that is genuinely problematic is often difficult to make.

Sometimes people who are extremely creative, highly educated, intelligent, or very wealthy are excused for conduct that most of us would consider very peculiar. Such individuals are repeatedly referred to as **eccentrics** because of their odd or whimsical behavior. Michael Jackson, the singer and entertainer, exemplifies the eccentric with his unusual manner of dressing, odd mannerisms, fantasyland lifestyle, and irrational fear of germs. Other famous eccentrics include Benjamin Franklin, who took "air baths" for his health by sitting naked in front of an open window; Alexander Graham Bell, who covered the windows of his house to keep out the rays of the full moon; and James Joyce, who always carried a tiny pair of women's bloomers to wave in the air to show his approval (Weeks & James, 1995).

A study of 1,000 eccentrics over a 10-year period pinpointed 15 characteristics common to eccentrics (Weeks & James, 1995). These characteristics are shown in Table 9.1. Eccentrics are rare with only 1 in 5,000 persons who can be classified as a classic, full-time eccentric. Men and women are equally represented as eccentrics. The self-assessment test in Table 9.1 can tell whether you, or perhaps someone you know, qualify as a true eccentric.

Psychologists do not believe that eccentrics suffer from a mental disorder. Eccentrics choose their odd behavior freely and derive pleasure from it. They usually know that they are different and are glad of it. In fact, most eccentrics are happy, well-adjusted, and joyful people (Weeks & James, 1995).

Americans have a huge vocabulary of terms used to describe people displaying abnormal behavior. This vocabulary includes terms such as "crazy," "nuts," "weird," "insane," "demented," "deranged," "goofy," "strange," "unbalanced," "mad," "maniacal," "loony," "bizarre," or "batty." We also use a number of colorful colloquial expressions, such as: "He doesn't have both oars in the water," "He has a few screws loose," and "Crazier than a mad hatter." Just as Eskimos have dozens of words to describe snow, Americans have a vast array of terms and expressions to describe abnormal behavior.

Defining Abnormality

> Too much sanity may be madness. And maddest of all, to see life as it is and not as it should be!
>
> **MIGUEL DE CERVANTES**

Generally, we are tolerant of other people's behavior no matter how strange or unusual that behavior appears to us. At what point do we describe someone's behavior as being **abnormal?** There is a great deal of debate, even among psychologists, about what constitutes abnormal behavior. For almost every definition of abnormality, there are exceptions where people met the criteria but were, in fact, acting quite normally. In general, abnormal behavior constitutes *those patterns of thought, emotion, or behavior that are maladaptive, disruptive, or harmful to either oneself or to others.* Abnormal behavior can cause an individual personal distress, such as unhappiness, anxiety, depression, or other emotional upset. Conversely, personal distress and emotions can also cause abnormal behavior. Impaired functioning or an in-

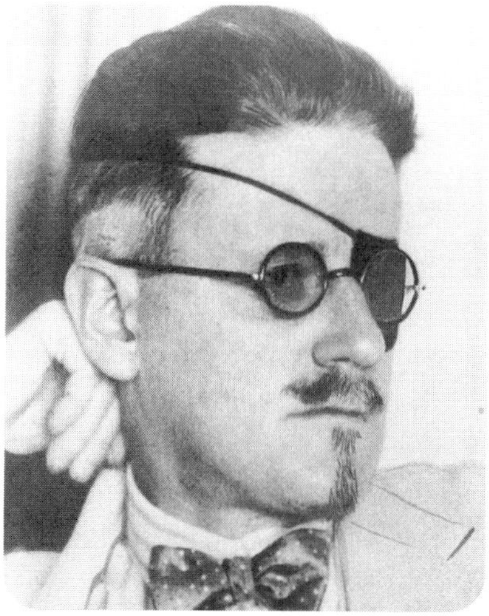

Some famous American eccentrics include Michael Jackson, Benjamin Franklin, Alexander Graham Bell, and James Joyce. Although each of them displayed odd behaviors, psychologists distinguish between eccentric and truly abnormal behaviors.

creased risk of death, pain, disability, or loss of freedom often characterizes abnormal behavior (American Psychiatric Association, 1994).

Some psychologists prefer to avoid using the term "abnormal" when describing behavior because any reference to what is "normal" becomes problematic. Another term that frequently describes disturbed behavior is **psychopathology.** In this chapter I will use these terms interchangeably.

We need more understanding of human nature, because the only real danger that exists is man himself. . . . We know nothing of man, far too little. His psyche should be studied because we are the origin of all coming evil.

C. G. JUNG
Face to Face *interview with John Freeman, BBC TV*

Cultural Specificity

One difficulty that we encounter in determining what behavior is abnormal comes from the different perspectives on behavior that various cultures hold. What is abnormal in the American culture is often considered normal in other cultures. In fact,

✦ TABLE 9.1 ✦ Self-Assessment Test for Eccentric Behavior

Do you qualify as an eccentric? Check those of the following 15 descriptions that apply to you.

_____ I am a nonconformist.
_____ I am a very creative person.
_____ I am very idealistic. I want to make the world better, and make people happier.
_____ I find I am happily obsessed with one or more hobbies.
_____ It seems to me that from early childhood on I was different from other people.
_____ I feel I am very intelligent.
_____ I am very opinionated and outspoken. I am often convinced that I am right and others are wrong.
_____ I am not a very competitive person.
_____ Many people think I have unusual eating or living habits.
_____ I am not very interested in the opinions or company of others.
_____ I consider myself to be mischievous with a good sense of humor.
_____ I am not married.
_____ I am an only child or the eldest child.
_____ I am a bad speller.

David Weeks found these characteristics present in eccentrics. The importance of the characteristics is shown in descending order, with the first 5 being the most definitive. If you possess most or all of the first 5 characteristics *or* any 10 of the 15, you may qualify as an eccentric.

SOURCE: Adapted from Weeks & James (1995).

you would have a difficult time finding almost any behavior that is universally considered abnormal in all cultures. Most cultures consider murder a deviant behavior, but at least one African culture considers the killing of an infant twin perfectly normal. In the past, Chinese peasants commonly killed infant daughters because many preferred male children. Even behavior such as sex with children is sanctioned in some cultures. People who experience hallucinations are often considered psychotic in the United States. On the other hand, Australian aborigines commonly have hallucinatory episodes. Furthermore, behavior that is considered abnormal by a culture in certain situations may be sanctioned in other circumstances, such as killing and cannibalism. However, many cultural anthropologists do claim that two behaviors appear to be universally considered abnormal in any culture: (1) *a failure to communicate with others* and (2) *a consistent unpredictability in one's actions.*

APPLICATIONS: Interpreting the Behavior of Others

Making judgments about other people's behavior is frequently fraught with hazard. Each of us has a definition of what behavior is "normal" but such perspectives are not always shared with others, particularly with those of different cultural or religious backgrounds. For example, deliberately inflicting pain on yourself would be considered "abnormal" by most of us, but it is a common practice in Middle Eastern countries as part of their religious rites. Even within the United States, there is tremendous variation in acceptable behaviors, depending on cultural differences. We each view the behavior of others through our own cultural "lens" or perspective.

Problems can arise when we find ourselves in a situation where others' values are significantly different from our own. This can be particularly problematic when traveling or living in a foreign country. Americans' propensity for imposing their own personal values on those of foreign cultures they were visiting led directly to the coining of the term "Ugly American" to describe their inappropriate attitudes and behaviors. We each need to be sensitive to how our personal values influence our judgments of others' behavior.

Legal Definition

Insanity is a legal term that can be used to explain and excuse criminal behavior. Note that insanity is a legal term, rather than a psychiatric term. Under the Model Penal Code, a person is not responsible for criminal conduct if, at the time of the conduct and as the result of a mental disease or defect, the individual lacks substantial capacity (1) to appreciate the "criminality" or "wrongfulness" of the conduct, or (2) to control the behavior.

The insanity defense has been used successfully to exempt individuals from crimes because of an abnormal mental condition that existed at the time of the crime.

defense is used only in about 2 of every
hose rare cases where it is used, both the
85% of the time that the person was in-
n.

of an insanity plea occurred in 1982 when
g of President Reagan and his press secre-
red the prosecution to prove that Hinckley
le to do so, Hinckley was sent to a mental
has caused a lengthy debate both inside
4, the law has required that the burden of
. The defense now must show that defen-
of their acts. By 1987 several states also
ly ill. This verdict recognizes that defen-
holds them responsible for their behavior.
sorder before the completion of their sen-
nainder of their term (Rosenfeld, 1987).

OLOGICAL DISORDERS

> Insanity is the exception in individuals. In groups, parties, peoples, and times it is the rule.
>
> **FRIEDRICH (WILHELM) NIETZSCHE**
> *Beyond Good and Evil*

iatric interviews with a large and diverse sample of Americans to determine the incidence of various psychological disorders (Kessler, 1994; Regier, et al., 1998). Almost half (48%) of the people interviewed had a diagnosable psychological disorder at some time during their lives. In addition, nearly one-third (30%) had experienced a diagnosable disorder during the previous

12 months. Throughout their lifetimes, nearly 20% of the individuals surveyed had experienced mood disorders such as depression, nearly 25% had suffered from anxiety disorders, and almost 30% had dealt with substance abuse disorders.

Demographic factors affect the incidence of disorders. The most common age for a disorder to appear is the 25-to-32-year age range. As people age, the incidence drops. Women suffer more from depression and anxiety while men struggle more with alcohol and substance abuse problems. Researchers found no significant differences between people living in urban versus rural communities. However, people from lower socioeconomic levels suffered from psychological disorders more frequently than more affluent Americans. Similarly, people with higher levels of education reported fewer disorders. With respect to geographic regions, people in the South suffered from the fewest disorders whereas people in the East experienced the most disabilities. Blacks suffered from slightly more psychological disorders than either whites or Hispanics. Those who were married and never divorced had the fewest disorders, whereas those who were single, separated, or divorced experienced increasingly more disorders respectively (Robins & Regier, 1991). Throughout this textbook I have noted the advantages of being married. A lowered incidence of mental disorders, at least among those married individuals who have never been divorced, can be added to this list of positives.

Myths of Mental Illness

Common Misconceptions

Americans hold several misconceptions about people who are mentally ill. This is probably due, in part, to the distorted information often presented in the news media and in the movies. Some of the most common misconceptions about mental illness include the following (Sue, Sue, & Sue, 1997):

1. *It is easy to spot mentally disturbed people because of their abnormal behavior.* People with mental illness typically do not behave consistently in ways that distinguish them from other individuals. If you were to visit a mental hospital, you would find it difficult to distinguish the patients from the staff based on their behavior alone.
2. *Mental illness is inherited.* It is sometimes believed that if one person in a family has it, other family members will probably suffer a similar fate. Except for a few exceptions, such as certain types of schizophrenia, depression, and mental retardation, heredity does not appear to play a major role in mental illness. As noted in the first chapter, heredity may *predispose* an individual to certain disorders, but the environment is the critical factor in triggering the behavior.
3. *Mental illness can never be fully cured.* Many people believe that once individuals become mentally ill, they can never fully recover. Nearly 75% of those patients who are hospitalized with severe disorders go on to lead full and productive lives with no major recurrence of the disorder.
4. *An inherent emotional weakness is responsible for mental disturbance.* There is a belief that people can avoid mental illness or cure themselves of it if they try hard enough. Many psychological problems are triggered by events over which

the individual has little or no control. For example, the death of a child or a spouse will often trigger depression, and no amount of willpower can reverse it.

5. *Persistent mental illness prevents a person from contributing to society.* There are numerous instances of people who suffered ongoing mental illness but still made significant contributions to society. This list includes the author Ernest Hemingway, artists Vincent van Gogh and Pablo Picasso, and writer Edgar Allan Poe. Many people who suffer from psychological problems are able to lead productive and worthwhile lives.
6. *Mentally ill people are dangerous.* This view may be influenced by television and movies where such characterizations are commonly portrayed. Certainly, some mentally disturbed individuals do commit crimes but then so do many who are not similarly afflicted. Research supports the conclusion that mental patients are not, for the most part, seriously dangerous (Rabkin, 1979).

APPLICATIONS: Avoiding Stigmatization

Given the high incidence of psychological disorders, it is probable that you will have many interactions throughout your lifetime with people who have suffered or are currently suffering from such a disorder. If you are enrolled in a large class, the odds are good that several fellow students share this distinction. Similarly, your workplace probably also includes a number of such individuals.

There is a strong tendency in the United States to stigmatize such individuals. Many of these stigmas are rooted in the common misconceptions that I described in the previous section. As a result of this stigmatization, many individuals who have suffered from a psychological disorder are reluctant to reveal the fact to others. Their reluctance is often based on their perception that such disclosure could negatively affect their relationships with others or even their employment opportunities. Regrettably, these suspicions are often well founded. In 1972, the Democrats nominated George McGovern for president and Senator Thomas F. Eagleton of Missouri for vice president. Twelve days after Eagleton's nomination, he revealed that he had been hospitalized three times in the 1960s for treatment of emotional exhaustion and depression. Eagleton's qualifications for the vice presidency became the subject of a nationwide debate, and he subsequently resigned from the ticket at McGovern's request. The brouhaha attending this revelation clearly illustrated the American people's intolerance for those who have been successfully treated for an emotional problem.

You can help inoculate yourself from stigmatizing those who have suffered emotional problems by familiarizing yourself with the commonly held misconceptions about mental illness that I listed. It might help to remember that nearly half of all people will suffer a diagnosable psychological disorder sometime during their lifetime. There is a very good chance that you might eventually be the victim of such inappropriate stigmas.

The Views of Thomas Szasz

Psychiatrist Thomas Szasz published a very controversial viewpoint on mental illness in 1961 (Szasz, 1961). He maintained that abnormal behavior reflects a failure by society rather than a failure of the individual. Szasz believed that *the concept of mental illness itself is a myth* and that it is merely a label that society uses to stigmatize and subjugate people who deviate from what society declares is "normal." According to this view, the establishment views those individuals who refuse to conform to society's norms as threats. Society labels them as "sick" in order to deny the validity of their problems and in order to justify confining them to mental institutions. Szasz further argued that labeling and treating people as mentally ill denies individuals' responsibility for their own behavior and choices. He believed that such individuals need encouragement to take responsibility for managing and solving their emotional problems.

These views agree with those of many mental health professionals who believe that the primary causes of abnormal behavior rest in society's ills, including poverty, racial and gender discrimination, and social decay. Other mental health professionals, however, believe that these views go too far by blaming society for all mental illness. Regardless of the opinion held, most would agree that Szasz's views have been instrumental in bringing about a closer examination of society's role in defining and treating abnormal behavior.

Assessing Psychopathology

How do mental health professionals determine when behavior constitutes psychopathology? The diagnosis of psychopathology is accomplished principally through the use of four tools that professionals systematically use to record the observations, behaviors, or self-reports of individuals (Sue, Sue, & Sue, 1997).

1. Observations. **Observations** of overt behavior constitute the most basic method of assessing when behavior is abnormal. These observations can occur in a variety of places, including a clinic or laboratory, or in a natural setting such as a schoolroom, a home, or a workplace.

> You can observe a lot just by watching.
>
> YOGI BERRA, ATTRIBUTED

2. Interviews. The **clinical interview** allows a clinician to observe and gather data through a series of questions. The clinician is interested not only in an individual's answers to the questions but also in the nonverbal behaviors such as hesitations, nervousness, and anger. Clinicians are highly trained in how to conduct interviews, a process that is considerably more complicated than merely sitting down and chatting with a client.
3. Psychological tests. The large number of **psychological tests** that clinicians use measure many different aspects of behavior, including personality, maladaptive behavior, social skills, intelligence, vocational interests and skills, and various mental impairments. Tests may be administered individually or in groups. Even though some tests are administered orally, most tests require the client to provide written responses. In most cases, an individual's score on a psychological test is compared to **norms** or scores that have been developed by giving the test to a large, representative sample of individuals. This procedure allows the clinician to compare the frequency of a given test response to the response of individuals who suffer from certain mental disorders. Test responses also allow for a comparison with typical behavior. For instance, in testing for memory impairment, the clinician should know the normal rates of forgetting to

correctly diagnose whether an individual's forgetting is significantly atypical. One form of testing, called a **self-report** inventory, requires an individual to answer specific written questions or to select specific answers from a list of alternatives. A common method of self-report measurement requires individuals to mark whether or not they agree with a list of statements and to indicate the degree of agreement. I have included numerous such self-report tests in this text to give you insight to your own behavior. I have warned you previously to interpret such self-report tests with caution. Human behavior is extremely complex, and while brief self-report tests can be enlightening, they can also be misleading. If you have concerns about any aspect of your behavior, you should rely on the assessment of a mental health professional trained in such matters.

4. Neurological tests. In some cases, a brain dysfunction, often referred to as a neurological impairment, causes abnormal behavior. **Neurological tests** are designed to diagnose and measure the extent of these impairments. These tests typically involve medical procedures, including X rays or computerized brain scans. Brain scans include a technique called *computerized axial tomography,* more popularly referred to as **CAT scans.** In this procedure, beams of X rays scan the different areas of the brain to produce a three-dimensional image of the structure of the brain. These images are extremely useful in diagnosing brain damage or deterioration.

    In recent years, a technique called *positron emission tomography* or **PET scan** has been developed, which allows for the examination of physiological and biochemical processes of the brain as they occur. After injecting a radioactive substance into the bloodstream, the PET scan detects this substance as it is assimilated by the brain. This process allows for an examination of brain functioning as the patient undertakes certain cognitive tasks, such as learning or remembering. One of the most widely used neurological techniques involves electroencephalography in which electrodes are attached to the skull and electrical activity, referred to as brain waves or EEGs, is recorded. Such recordings can be useful in the diagnosis of brain tumors or other brain damage.

    Finally, a technique called *magnetic resonance imaging* or **MRI** recently has been developed. The MRI creates a magnetic field around a patient and uses radio waves to detect abnormalities. The resulting visual images permit technicians to view "slices" of the brain at different levels in the brain structure. In recent years, MRIs have begun to replace CAT scans as the most popular neurological diagnostic tool.

APPLICATIONS: The Dangers of Assessment

The amateur assessment of psychopathology in others can be a hazardous venture. In my sophomore year as an undergraduate, I had the temerity to diagnose one of my aunts as suffering from a certain mental disorder that I had just learned about in a course in abnormal psychology. I mistakenly shared my views with another relative. Unfortunately, word of my amateur diagnosis got back to my aunt, who was understandably very upset with me. This happened nearly 40 years ago, and my aunt has never forgotten or forgiven me for my inexcusable behavior. As with most things, a little knowledge about clinical psychology can be a dangerous thing.

Resist the urge to engage in amateur assessment. Nothing will alienate you from your friends (and relatives!) more quickly or more permanently.

There is also a tendency among those who begin studying psychology to try to diagnose themselves. Students in medical school often see symptoms of every disease they study—in themselves. Similarly, beginning students of psychology often begin to question their own emotional state after perceiving similarities between their own behavior and that which is listed as abnormal. In studying psychology, it is best to remember that everyone displays occasional symptoms or behaviors that might be included as part of a diagnosed illness. However, this does not mean that you are crazy. Resist the urge to see yourself in every category of mental illness. Any serious concerns you might have about your mental health should be addressed by a trained professional, and not by self-examination.

CLASSIFYING PSYCHOPATHOLOGY

DSM-IV

Since the early 20th century, several different schemes for classifying psychological symptoms have been used. One of the earliest systems, devised in 1899, listed 16 major categories of mental disorders. Today, most mental health professionals use a classification system known as the *Diagnostic and Statistical Manual of Mental Disorders* or the DSM. The DSM system was originally devised by the American Psychiatric Association in 1952 and is currently in its fourth edition, known as *the DSM-IV* (American Psychiatric Association, 1994).

The American Psychiatric Association designed the DSM to assist professionals in classifying a particular disorder and not to determine the *causes* of a particular disorder. The system is based on a set of relatively unambiguous criteria that clearly and precisely *describe* a particular disorder and the life circumstances that are related to it. For the purpose of diagnosis, the DSM-IV categorizes the person along five axes or dimensions:

- Axis I. Clinical disorders that are the primary diagnosis of the problem. This axis consists of clinical disorders such as mood disorders, anxiety disorders, psychotic disorders, and eating disorders.
- Axis II. Relatively permanent aspects of the individual's personality that affect the individual's behavior and capability for treatment. Typically, these characteristics or behaviors began in early childhood or adolescence and have persisted into adulthood. For example, personality disorders and mental retardation would fall in Axis II.
- Axis III. Medical conditions. These conditions include physical disorders or illnesses relevant to the understanding and treatment of the individual. As examples, instances of paralysis, malnutrition, kidney failure, or acute pain that could contribute to a disorder would be listed under Axis III.
- Axis IV. Psychosocial and environmental problems. This dimension includes anything in the person's environment that might contribute to the onset or severity of a disorder, such as poverty, social isolation, homelessness, inadequate health services, divorce, or death of a family member.

✦ TABLE 9.2 ✦ DSM-IV Diagnostic Criteria for the Eating Disorder Bulimia Nervosa

A. Recurrent episodes of binge eating, characterized by *both* of the following:
   1. In a given period of time, eating an amount of food that is definitely larger than most people would eat in a similar period of time and circumstances.
   2. A feeling that one cannot stop eating or control what or how much one is eating.

B. Recurrent inappropriate compensatory behavior in order to prevent weight gain, such as self-induced vomiting; misuse of laxatives, diuretics, enemas, or other medications; fasting; or excessive exercise.

C. The binge eating and compensatory behaviors occur, on average, at least twice a week for 3 months.

D. Self-evaluation is unduly influenced by body shape and weight.

E. The disturbance does not occur exclusively during episodes of anorexia nervosa.

SOURCE: Reprinted with permission from the *Diagnostic and Statistical Manual of Mental Disorders,* 4th Ed. Copyright 1994 American Psychiatric Association.

✦ Axis V. Global assessment of level of functioning. On this axis, the clinician makes an overall assessment of how well the individual currently functions and the quality of his or her social relationships and occupational activities. Clinicians use a 100-point scale where the lowest number (1) reflects severe impairment of functioning and the highest number (100) reflects superior functioning with no symptoms.

As noted earlier, one advantage of the DSM-IV categorization system is that it lists specific criteria that must be present in order for a disorder to be diagnosed. For instance, most of us engage in binge eating on occasion. An individual who does this on a regular basis may be suffering from an eating disorder called bulimia nervosa. How would a professional determine at what point a patient had crossed over the line between normal eating habits and pathological eating? Table 9.2 illustrates the specific criteria listed by the DSM-IV that must be present for a diagnosis of bulimia nervosa. Notice that *all* conduct must be present for the diagnosis to be made and that all behaviors must meet a certain frequency and duration. This allows for an objective approach in the assessment and diagnosis of all disorders. Therefore, you can continue to "pig out" once in a while and not worry that you have suddenly become bulimic. Remember that it is common to see aspects of your behavior in numerous psychological disorders. It is important to remember that there is a difference between having certain traits that resemble a disorder, and actually meeting the full criteria for a disorder.

The Danger of Labels

I have discussed how listing specific criteria for the diagnosis of psychopathology has certain advantages. On the other hand, several disadvantages occur when we begin to label certain behaviors as "abnormal."

- Self-fulfilling prophecies. When a person has been labeled in a certain way, his or her behavior will often conform to the diagnosis. For example, a person who is labeled as depressed might begin to show depressive symptoms that would not otherwise occur.
- Interpretation of behavior by others. If you knew that an acquaintance of yours once had been given a diagnosis of schizophrenia, you might have a tendency to examine that individual's every behavior closely for indications of these tendencies even if the disorder was no longer present. Everyone acts a little "crazy" at times, but the presence of a diagnostic label can make us interpret behavior differently.
- Over diagnosis. Once a set of behaviors has been classified as abnormal and given a label, mental health professionals tend to overuse the diagnosis. For example, multiple personality disorders occur very rarely. Prior to 1980, fewer than 200 such cases had been identified in the United States. Since 1980, when the third edition of the DSM manual included new criteria for this diagnosis, more than 30,000 cases have been reported (Nathan, 1994). While it is possible that the criteria allow for a better identification of the disorder, it is also likely that overdiagnosis occurs because mental health professionals are watching for it (Holmes, 1994).
- Differential diagnosis. Many individuals exhibit behaviors and symptoms that overlap with several disorders. Therefore, it is sometimes difficult to determine which diagnosis is correct. Moreover, different professionals may give different diagnoses based on their past experiences and training. Since human behavior is extremely complex, determining a correct diagnosis is never foolproof.
- Making normal behavior "abnormal." Some critics believe that lumping normal behaviors with true mental disorders implies that everyday problems constitute psychopathology. For example, it would be normal to experience profound and prolonged grief following the death of a spouse or a child. A person who is "depressed" in these circumstances has good reason to be. The latest revision of the DSM describes conditions called "mathematics disorder" and "caffeine-induced sleep disorder" (Wade & Tavris, 1996). The fact that you were up several nights drinking coffee while studying for a mathematics test and did poorly on the test does not justify a label of psychopathology!

On Being Sane in Insane Places

Imagine that you were committed to a psychiatric hospital by accident. Do you think that mental health professionals would quickly notice your "normalcy"? David Rosenhan of Stanford University investigated how accurately psychiatric hospitals distinguish between people who are psychotic and those who are perfectly healthy. Rosenhan and several of his colleagues went to a mental hospital and complained that they had been hearing voices that said, "empty," "hollow," and "thud" (Rosenhan, 1973). Reporting only this single fake symptom, the mental hospital staff admitted 11 out of 12 researchers, nearly all with the diagnosis of "schizophrenia."

Once admitted, they dropped all pretense of being mentally ill. Despite the fact that the researchers now acted completely normal, the hospital staff never recognized any of them as impostors. Interestingly, other psychiatric patients *did* recognize that there was nothing wrong with these pretenders. The real patients made comments to the researchers such as "You're not crazy; you're checking up on the hospital" or "I bet you are a journalist." Furthermore, these pseudo patients discovered that the hospital staff diagnosed their normal behaviors as symptoms of schizophrenia. For example, the researchers frequently took notes to record their observations. The staff interpreted this behavior as "excessive note-taking" and labeled it as a symptom of the pseudo patient's schizophrenia.

The researchers found that they were largely ignored during their hospital stay. Daily contact with psychiatrists, psychologists, or physicians averaged about 7 minutes. However, the doctors did dispense over 2,000 pills for them to swallow, which they instead pocketed or flushed down the toilet. Hospitalization ranged from 7 to 52 days before the researchers were discharged. At the time of release, the hospital discharge summaries stated that these patients' symptoms were "in remission" rather than that the patients were cured.

Rosenhan concluded from this research that it is nearly impossible to distinguish between normal and disturbed behaviors in mental hospital patients. Once the patients had been labeled, their behaviors were all interpreted to fit with the diagnosis. Rosenhan used his findings to argue that labeling patients' behavior frequently is not useful and, in fact, is often counterproductive. He also argued that mental hospitals constitute an environment that frequently maintains maladaptive behaviors rather than treating them. His study has generated a great deal of controversy within the mental health field and has served to force mental health professionals to reexamine many of their assessment procedures and hospitalization practices.

Expert Clinical Judgments versus Actuarial Data

Mental health professionals are often called upon to make diagnoses and predictions about an individual's future behavior. These clinical judgments are very important because they often determine whether or not a person will be committed to a mental institution, will receive parole or a prison term, or will be judged competent to stand trial for a crime. Mental health professionals make these judgments on the basis of the information they collect through observations, interviews, and psychological and neurological tests, as I discussed earlier in this chapter. After the evidence is gathered, it is interpreted in one of two ways, either the *clinical method* or the *actuarial method.* In the **clinical method,** clinical experts base their judgments on their memories of and experiences with similar cases and on their knowledge of symptoms that are known to predict particular outcomes. In the **actuarial method** professionals make their judgments by applying rules that have been empirically derived from the correlation of particular factors such as symptoms, age, gender, test scores, medical history, and so forth to particular behavioral outcomes. For example, in the determination of whether a patient has Alzheimer's disease, clinicians who use the clinical method might interview the patient, administer a series of tests, observe the patient's behavior, and then render a clinical judgment based on similar findings from patients they have dealt with previously. In the actuarial method, on the other hand, the diagnosis would be made strictly from test scores of intellectual abilities. How do the two methods compare in accuracy? Experts who used the actuarial method correctly diagnosed Alzheimer's disease 83% of the time while those who used the clinical method made a correct diagnosis only 58% of the time (Leli & Filskov, 1984).

A review of over 100 studies that compared the actuarial and clinical methods found that almost every study showed the actuarial method to be superior (Dawes, Faust, & Meehl, 1989). In chapter 7, which covered emotions, I discussed how actuarial data have proven superior to experienced clinical judgments in predicting which individuals would engage in violent or aggressive behaviors. The preponderance of data now reveal that the actuarial method is consistently superior in diagnosing and predicting a wide range of human behaviors, particularly those involving mental disorders. Despite this fact, many mental health professionals continue to cling tenaciously to a belief that their expert clinical judgments, based on many years of training and experience, are superior to the actuarial data.

Psychological Well-Being

With all the emphasis on abnormal behavior, you may wonder what it is that would constitute the opposite behavior. Too often we tend to think of people as mentally healthy if they are not suffering from depression or other forms of psychopathology. Carol Ryff has argued that this prevailing view never gets to the heart of what she terms **psychological well-being.** She emphasizes that we must define mental health as the *presence* of the positive rather than the absence of the negative (Ryff, 1995).

There are six dimensions of personality that she believes encompass the breadth of psychological well-being (Ryff, 1989).

1. Self-acceptance. The acceptance and satisfaction with oneself and one's past life. It includes maintaining positive attitudes about oneself by accepting both the good and bad qualities.
2. Positive relations with other people. An ability to enjoy warm, satisfying, and trusting relationships with others. It includes showing concern about the welfare of others and a capacity for strong empathy, affection, and intimacy.
3. Autonomy. An ability to act independently and to resist social pressure to conform to certain beliefs and conduct. Autonomous individuals evaluate themselves with respect to personal standards rather than the standards established by others.
4. Environmental mastery. An ability to manipulate and control complex environments. It includes making effective use of surrounding opportunities and an ability to choose or create conditions that meet personal needs and values.
5. Purpose in life. Beliefs that (a) past and present life has a purpose and meaning, and (b) a person has aims and objectives for living. A psychologically healthy individual sets goals in life and feels a sense of directedness.
6. Personal growth. Beliefs that a person (a) grows and expands, (b) opens oneself to new experiences, (c) senses a realization of one's own potential, (d) sees improved behavior in oneself, and (c) realizes that one's changes reflect a greater self-knowledge and effectiveness.

In sum, Ryff believes that ". . . these six dimensions encompass a breadth of wellness that includes positive evaluations of one's self and one's life, a sense of continued growth and development as a person, the belief that life is purposeful and meaningful, the possession of good relationships with other people, the capacity to

✦ TABLE 9.3 ✦ A Test for Psychological Well-Being

Rate each of the following statements according to whether or not it applies to you. Use the following rating scale:

6 = Strongly agree
5 = Moderately agree
4 = Somewhat agree
3 = Somewhat disagree
2 = Moderately disagree
1 = Strongly disagree

_____ 1. I maintain a positive attitude about myself.
_____ 2. I realize and accept that I have both good and bad qualities.
_____ 3. I feel positive about the way my past life has gone.
_____ 4. I enjoy warm, satisfying, and trusting relationships with others.
_____ 5. I am often concerned about the welfare of others.
_____ 6. I am capable of strong feelings about others, including feelings of empathy, affection, and intimacy.
_____ 7. I am able to resist social pressures and, as a result, think and act independently.
_____ 8. I evaluate myself according to my own personal standards, not the standards of other people.
_____ 9. I am not concerned about what others think or expect of me.
_____ 10. I feel confident in my ability to effectively manage my everyday affairs.
_____ 11. I am aware of opportunities that exist and take advantage of them.
_____ 12. I feel that I am in control of my environment.
_____ 13. I feel that there is a sense of purpose to my life.
_____ 14. I believe there is a meaning to both my past and present life.
_____ 15. I believe my life is headed in a certain direction.
_____ 16. I see my life as an opportunity to grow and expand.
_____ 17. I have seen an improvement in myself over time.
_____ 18. As I have grown older, I have learned a lot more about myself.

Scoring:
Individuals with a well-developed sense of psychological well-being tend to agree with the above statements. The higher you score on this test, the greater your psychological well-being. If you disagree with many of these statements, your psychological well-being is probably low.

SOURCE: Based on Ryff (1995).

manage one's life and the surrounding world effectively, and a sense of self-determination" (Ryff, 1995, p. 99).

APPLICATIONS: Measuring Your Own Well-Being

How do you measure up on these six dimensions of well-being? You can answer the questions about yourself in Table 9.3 and see how you fare.

Causes of Abnormal Behavior

Humankind has long wondered about the causes of abnormal behavior. You might believe that psychopathology is a result of the stress and strain of modern life, but there is evidence that mental illness existed long before modern civilization came along. As far back as the Stone Age, it was widely believed that evil spirits inhabited the body and caused people to act in bizarre ways. Evidence indicates that ancient civilizations attempted to cure individuals so afflicted by drilling holes in their skulls to allow the evil spirits to escape (Maher & Maher, 1985). Later civilizations blamed psychological disorders on supernatural forces, gods, goddesses, or demons. This is probably the origin of the question, "What the devil got into you to make you act like that?" As late as the 17th century, Americans executed people suspected of being witches. More recently, however, natural causes have been examined as the source of abnormal behavior. Modern psychologists believe that three factors play a major role in the development of abnormal behavior:

1. Biological factors. These include the following: (a) all aspects of brain function, particularly biochemical factors; (b) genetic predisposition; (c) microorganisms that produce disease; and (d) the interaction of the physical and chemical aspects of the environment on behavior.
2. Psychological factors. These include the behavioral influences of early life experiences, cognitive factors such as learning and perception, and how genetic predisposition and the environment interact to influence all types of behavior.
3. Sociocultural factors. Even though some mental disorders appear in all cultures, others vary greatly across cultures. We now recognize that cultural beliefs and values as well as social roles and expectations all play an important role in determining what behaviors are deemed abnormal.

The importance of all three of these factors can be seen in the psychological disorder of depression. Today, mental health professionals recognize that both biochemical and genetic factors play an important role in this disorder. However, cognitive factors are also important. Research has shown, for instance, that depressed individuals process information about the world differently than nondepressed individuals. Depressed people are more likely to notice negative information (Segal & Bouchard, 1988) and to perceive themselves and others less favorably (Gara, et al., 1993). Also, cultural factors are important in the interpretation of what constitutes depressed behavior. The residents of Finland, for example, commonly behave in a melancholy fashion that many Americans would consider depressed, but the Finnish people consider such behavior typical and normal according to their cultural beliefs. Therefore, any interpretation of abnormal behavior must include the potential role of the biological, psychological, and cultural influences.

In the remainder of this chapter, I will present a brief description of the major kinds of mental disorders. Because the latest revision of the DSM-IV lists over 300 different mental disorders (APA, 1994), even a cursory description of each of these disorders would be beyond the scope of this textbook. Instead, I will focus on the major categories of mental disorders, with additional emphasis on disorders that are more prevalent in college-age students.

Psychotic Disorders

Schizophrenia, one of the most serious mental disorders, is characterized by severe distortion in thought processes, language, perceptions, and emotions. In general, it reflects a loss of contact with reality. Schizophrenia affects approximately 1% of the world's population.

The disturbed mental processes of a person with schizophrenia often consist of a mixture of thoughts and language that seemingly make no sense. Some psychologists have referred to their jumbled language and speech organization as "word salad." Individuals with schizophrenia have a great deal of difficulty in the organization and arrangement of their thoughts. Their conversations often jump from topic to topic, with seemingly no logical connections. Individuals with schizophrenia often also suffer from delusions and/or hallucinations. **Delusions** are *beliefs* that are held without any factual basis. For instance, **delusions of persecution** consist of beliefs that others are plotting or conspiring against you. In **delusions of grandeur,** individuals hold false beliefs about their power and importance. In **delusions of control,** on the other hand, they believe someone else is controlling their thoughts and behavior. For instance, individuals with schizophrenia may believe that someone has implanted a radio receiver in their brain, which controls their thoughts and actions.

Hallucinations, in contrast to delusions, are *perceptions* of stimuli that do not exist. These can take many forms, such as hearing voices, smelling or tasting imaginary substances, and feeling objects on, or even under, the skin. In addition to these symptoms, individuals suffering from schizophrenia often have blunted emotions, display a flat affect, sustain an inability to experience pleasure, and suffer from social withdrawal. Overall, it is one of the most debilitating mental disorders.

Causes

Some research evidence suggests that schizophrenia begins to manifest itself early in childhood. In one study, psychologists viewed home movies of young children who later developed schizophrenia as adults. Even as young children, they showed poor eye contact with others, poor motor coordination, a lack of responsiveness to others, and a lack of positive emotions (Walker & Lewine, 1990). In the 1960s, many psychologists believed that schizophrenia was caused by bad parenting techniques. However, this belief has now been totally discredited.

Heritability

Considerable evidence indicates that a tendency or predisposition toward schizophrenia can be inherited. For example, both identical twins are more likely to suffer this disorder than are both fraternal twins, who share less genetic similarity. If one identical twin has schizophrenia, there is a 44.3% chance the other one will be similarly afflicted, whereas only 12.1% of fraternal twins will both become schizophrenic. If both parents have schizophrenia, there is about a 30% chance that their child will develop the disorder (Davison & Neale, 1990). It is important to note that even though we may inherit a *predisposition* for schizophrenia, there are certain environmental factors that will be necessary to trigger the disorder. In other words, you could carry a genetic predisposition for schizophrenia and never manifest the disorder if the environmental conditions in which you live foster normal development. As I noted earlier in chapter 1, when it comes to behavior, genes usually suggest but they rarely compel.

Brain Chemistry Imbalance

Individuals with schizophrenia have been found to have an excess amount of brain receptors for the neurotransmitter known as dopamine. Medications that block these dopamine receptors are a common and sometimes effective treatment for schizophrenia. Substances that increase dopamine levels, including cocaine and amphetamines, can exaggerate schizophrenic symptoms. Many scientists believe that the excess of dopamine makes those with schizophrenia overly sensitive to irrelevant external and internal stimuli.

Psychological Factors

Certain psychological factors may trigger schizophrenia in those individuals with a genetic predisposition, but clearly psychological factors alone will not do so. Researchers have tried unsuccessfully to identify precisely what the psychological triggers are. Some evidence suggests that stress may serve as a trigger, but this theory is not conclusive. Precise identification of the relevant psychological factors is complicated because different factors appear with the different types of schizophrenia and with the different rates of onset, such as slow developing versus sudden-onset schizophrenia.

Personality Disorders

Among some of the more interesting abnormal behaviors are those in the category of personality disorders. These include the paranoid and antisocial individuals so often vividly portrayed on television and in the movies. Personality disorders are characterized by the following:

- longstanding and inflexible maladaptive personality traits that impair social functioning *or* cause an individual subjective distress
- difficulty controlling one's temper
- lack of flexibility in dealing with life's problems
- inappropriate perception of self and others

This disorder is a permanent way of behaving and is not due to depression, stress, drug reaction, or any situation that temporarily affects behavior. Rather, it is an ingrained part of an individual's character.

Personality disorders create problems for society because people with this disorder often function independently and need no assistance from others. Therefore, they rarely want or seek help from mental health professionals. For this reason, it is also difficult to determine the exact frequency with which this disorder occurs. The best estimate is that 10% to 13% of individuals will suffer from some type of personality disorder during their lifetime (Weissman, 1993). Mental health professionals usually agree that personality disorders are one of the most difficult disorders to treat.

Major Types

There are many different personality disorders. The DSM-IV combines these into several major categories, some of which are described as follows:

Antisocial Personality Disorder

Serial killer Ted Bundy was believed to have an antisocial personality disorder.

Have you ever known someone who consistently shows a total disregard for the rights and well-being of others? If so, you may have experienced someone with an **antisocial personality disorder.** Such individuals lack both a conscience and a sense of responsibility. Their behavior is often characterized by impulsivity, aggression, and easy irritability. They are often fearless in the face of danger and would just as soon lie as tell the truth. Their antisocial behavior takes many forms and often results in criminal conduct. Delinquency, drug abuse, theft, and even murders are committed without remorse. Oftentimes these crimes go unsolved because these individuals are intelligent enough to avoid detection. Individuals with personality disorders live among us with ease and, in fact, can be charming and manipulative at the same time. Serial murderer Ted Bundy, a previous undergraduate psychology major at the University of Washington, was believed to possess an antisocial personality disorder.

CAUSES. How do people become antisocial? Research suggests that there may be several factors responsible:

- Some individuals learn early in childhood that impulsive, aggressive behaviors are appropriate and even rewarded responses as a result of observing and modeling certain adult behaviors.
- Individuals may possess physiological abnormalities such as abnormal brainwave (EEG) activity. For example, their EEGs often have a preponderance of the slow-wave activity typical of infants or young children.
- Individuals have decreased emotional reactions to negative stimuli, especially those that are related to punishment. The threat of pain or imminent danger elicits a reduced emotional reaction in these individuals, and overall, they experience lower levels of emotional arousal than do other people in similar threatening situations.

Typically, individuals with antisocial personality disorder do not respond well to clinical treatments.

Borderline Personality Disorder

Borderline personality disorder is characterized by extreme fluctuations in mood, self-image, and interpersonal relationships (Sue, Sue, & Sue, 1997). These wide fluctuations result in an inconsistent personality that may be friendly one day and hostile the next. These individuals tend to act unpredictably and impulsively and, as a result, have unstable interpersonal relationships. They have a high rate of suicide and suicide attempts, often the consequence of their recurrent feelings of emptiness and worthlessness.

This disorder occurs in approximately 2% of the population. Interestingly, females are three times more likely to be diagnosed with this disorder. It is the most commonly diagnosed personality disorder, and its prevalence has increased in recent years (Trull, 1995). Many of the factors suspected of causing the antisocial personality disorder are also believed to be responsible for this disorder.

Narcissistic Personality Disorder

The **narcissistic personality disorder** is seen in individuals who have an exaggerated sense of self-importance and strong tendencies to exaggerate their achievements and talents. They have a constant need to be recognized as superior without the corresponding achievements to merit such recognition. Their need for admiration from others is insatiable. They spend a lot of their time with fantasies of being successful, powerful, brilliant, or beautiful. Narcissistic individuals have an irritating sense of entitlement, believing that they deserve special or favorable treatment. They will readily exploit others if it serves their own needs. They lack empathetic feelings for others, often refuse to recognize the feelings and needs of others, and harbor suspicions that others are highly envious of them. They frequently display an arrogant, "holier than thou" attitude toward others that seriously interferes with their interpersonal relationships. The best estimates are that less than 1% of the population suffers from this disorder.

Narcissistic traits are common in adolescents and slightly more likely to occur in males than females. However, presence of narcissistic traits does not imply that a teenager has the disorder or will develop the disorder as an adult.

Anxiety Disorders

He that falls in love with himself will have no rivals.

BENJAMIN FRANKLIN
Poor Richard's Almanac

Most college students are very familiar with feelings of anxiety. Indeed, everyone occasionally experiences feelings of increased arousal that are usually accompanied by fear or apprehension. When experienced with enough intensity, these feelings become debilitating and constitute the clinical category of **anxiety disorders.** The DSM-IV lists many different kinds of anxiety disorders, but I will concentrate on the categories that college-age individuals are most likely to experience personally or to recognize in others.

Panic Disorder

The natural role of twentieth-century man is anxiety.

NORMAN MAILER

Have you ever begun to take an examination and suddenly experienced a very high level of physical arousal accompanied by a fear that you were losing control? Such feelings are little reason for concern because most of us have experienced them on occasion. However, people who suffer from a condition known as **panic disorder** have these feelings regularly, often in the absence of any identifiable event that might trigger such an attack. The symptoms that accompany a panic attack typically include some combination of an accelerated heartbeat, sweating, trembling or shaking, chest pain or discomfort, shortness of breath, nausea, feeling of dizziness or lightheadedness, a feeling of unreality or detachment from oneself, a fear of losing control, numbness or a tingling sensation, and chills or hot flushes. The DSM-IV states that four or more of these physiological sensations must be present and reach a peak within 10 minutes of the onset to qualify as a panic attack.

It should be emphasized that panic attacks are sometimes the normal, expected reaction in certain threatening situations. It is only when these panic attacks occur frequently, without warning, and have no identifiable cause that professional treatment is justified. Sometimes individuals develop a fear of leaving their home because experiencing panic attacks in a public place is intensely uncomfortable.

Phobic Behaviors

A **phobia** is defined as a strong, persistent, and unjustified fear of some specific object or situation. Note the inclusion of the word *unjustified* in this definition. If you are walking along a narrow ledge, high on a mountain, and find yourself fearful of falling, the fear may be completely justified and thus would not constitute a phobia. Note also that phobias can be to a *specific object,* such as spiders, or to a *situation,* such as being in an enclosed space. Recently I attended a professional meeting in San Diego with one of my student research assistants. When I suggested that we visit Sea World and showed her its colorful brochure, she recoiled in horror when she saw a picture of a whale. She later talked about her phobia of whales, a somewhat unusual disorder for a landlocked Coloradan, especially since she had never seen a live whale. She had no clue as to the origin of her fears. Phobias about specific objects are twice as prevalent in women as in men. Common specific phobias involve insects, snakes, heights, the dark, various animals, and lightning. In the chapter on learning, I discussed how classical conditioning can result in the creation of phobias.

We experience moments absolutely free from worry. These brief respites are called panic.

CULLEN HIGHTOWER

Most phobias to specific objects are not debilitating because the person can often successfully avoid such objects. However, there are other phobias that can greatly affect one's normal living.

Agoraphobia

People who have an intense fear of being in places or situations from which escape might be difficult have a condition called **agoraphobia.** These people also fear situations where help might not be available in the event of a panic attack. Agoraphobia sometimes involves fears of fainting or of losing control of bodily functions in public. Some individuals suffering from agoraphobia have a fear of leaving their own home and, as documented in case studies, have lived for years without venturing outside their residence. The phobia sometimes generalizes to a fear of being in crowds, standing in line, or traveling in a public conveyance such as a bus, train, or plane.

Agoraphobia will occur sometime during the lifetime of 3.5% of males and 7% of females. It is one of the most common phobias for which patients seek treatment.

Social Phobia

Individuals who experience intense fears of being scrutinized by other people in social or performance situations and of being evaluated negatively have what is classified as a **social phobia.** Situations that require them to socialize or perform in front of others are either avoided or endured with dread. Even accomplished performers such as Barbra Streisand and the renowned actor Sir Laurence Olivier have admitted to profound "stage fright." Those with social phobia are afraid that their behavior will cause them embarrassment and humiliation, and they literally become "sick with fear." This includes public speaking where others could notice their anxiety, their trembling hands, or cracking voice. Fear of public speaking, one of the most common phobias, occurs in about 20% of the population. However, only about 2% of the population fear public speaking to the extent that it constitutes a social phobia.

Speaking in front of a large group produces extreme anxiety for many people. This form of social phobia is one of the most common for which treatment is sought.

Those with a social phobia often experience severe physiological reactions in a social situation, including a racing heart, sweating, tremors, stomach discomfort, diarrhea, blushing, or mental confusion. These phobic reactions typically materialize during the mid-teen years and may be preceded by social inhibition or shyness in childhood. In some cases, however, the phobia is brought on by a single stressful or embarrassing experience. To some extent, the condition appears to have a genetic basis because it runs in families. Social phobias often last a lifetime and can be very disruptive under some circumstances. For example, a job that requires numerous presentations to groups or socializing with clients would cause extreme discomfort for individuals with this condition.

It is important to note that there is a distinction between social phobia and shyness. Shyness entails uncomfortable feelings in a social situation whereas a social phobia, which is far more pervasive and distressing, interferes with normal functioning. Over 10 million Americans suffer from social phobia, which makes it the most common type of anxiety disorder. In fact, it is the third most common psychiatric disorder after depression and alcoholism. Unfortunately, only 5% of people with this disorder ever receive any kind of treatment. Recent studies have shown that the drug paroxetine HCl ("Paxil") effectively treats this disorder.

Mood Disorders

Mood disorders involve disorders of emotion. They are *disabling* disturbances of moods and feelings, and are frequently accompanied by changes in physical functioning. The two principal forms of mood disorders are major depressive disorder and bipolar disorder.

Major Depressive Disorder

People who are extremely depressed usually experience feelings of intense sadness and self-directed guilt. The five essential symptoms of depression include (Beck, 1967):

1. Sad and apathetic mood
2. Feelings of worthlessness and hopelessness
3. A desire to withdraw from other people
4. Sleeplessness and loss of appetite and sexual desire
5. Change in activity level, to either lethargy or agitation.

Depression is more than mere grief, such as that caused by the death of a loved one. Grieving and major depression differ from each other in that depression involves fear of losing one's mind or thoughts of harming oneself. However, depression that accompanies grief can be an appropriate response to an extremely sad event. Major depression occurs when the symptoms last 2 weeks or more in the absence of any notable cause.

Martin Seligman (1975) has noted that depression is so prevalent that it is "the common cold of mental illness." Estimates of its incidence vary, but as many as 15% of Americans may be suffering depressive symptoms and between 5% and 10% have major depression. Women suffer from this disorder twice as frequently as men. Even though major depression can occur at any age, it is more prevalent during adolescence and old age. Major depression also is associated with greatly increased incidences of pain and physical illness. It is also an equal opportunity disorder in that it is unrelated to ethnicity, education, income, or marital status. Unfortunately, suicide is a frequent consequence of major depression. It is estimated that 15% of people with major depression will kill themselves (Guze & Robins, 1970).

Do you or does someone you know suffer from depression? The self-assessment test in Table 9.4 will give you a good idea whether or not your depression level justifies intervention by mental health professionals. Because major depression is so closely linked with suicide, professional intervention is crucial. If you or someone you know is suffering the symptoms listed above, seek professional help. There are several effective treatments for depression that I will discuss in the next chapter.

Bipolar Disorder

Individuals suffering from a **bipolar disorder** alternate in wide swings between feelings of elation and euphoria, known as the **manic stage,** and feelings of depression. While in the manic stage, these individuals are like a videotape running on fast forward. Typically, they are overly talkative and overly active, and show fewer sexual inhibitions. When talking, their speech is loud, pressured, tangential, and continuous. It is difficult to interrupt them. During the manic stage, self-esteem skyrockets and unbridled optimism abounds. Other manic symptoms include feelings of grandiosity, and decreases in self-control, sleep, and appetite. For instance, individuals having a manic episode are more likely to go on a spending spree, commit an illegal act, drive recklessly, act more assertively, or take on many tasks that they would not under normal circumstances. Interestingly, many famous artists, poets, and musicians have suffered from bipolar disorder and yet remained very creative

✦ TABLE 9.4 ✦ Self-Assessment for Depression

Answer the following true-false questions as they apply to you.

T	F	1. My daily life is not interesting.
T	F	2. It is hard to get started on my daily chores and activities.
T	F	3. I have been more unhappy than usual for at least a month.
T	F	4. I have been sleeping poorly for at least the last month.
T	F	5. I gain little pleasure from anything.
T	F	6. I feel listless, tired, or fatigued a lot of the time.
T	F	7. I have felt sad, down in the dumps, or blue much of the time during the last month.
T	F	8. My memory or thinking is not as good as usual.
T	F	9. I have been more easily irritated or frustrated lately.
T	F	10. I feel worse in the morning than in the afternoon.
T	F	11. I have cried or felt like crying more than twice during the last month.
T	F	12. I am definitely slowed down compared to my usual way of feeling.
T	F	13. The things that used to make me happy don't do so anymore.
T	F	14. My appetite or digestion of food is worse than usual.
T	F	15. I frequently feel like I don't care about anything anymore.
T	F	16. Life is really not worth living most of the time.
T	F	17. My outlook is more gloomy than usual.
T	F	18. I have stopped several of my usual activities.
T	F	19. I cry or feel saddened more easily than a few months ago.
T	F	20. I feel pretty hopeless about improving my life.
T	F	21. I seem to have lost the ability to have fun.
T	F	22. I have regrets about the past that I think about often.

Scoring:
Count up the total number of answers you marked "true." Scores totaling 0 to 4 indicate normal responses to everyday life. Scores from 5 to 10 indicate a moderate degree of depression that can potentially affect your health functioning and outlook. Scores higher than 10 indicate a possible major problem with depression and one that could severely affect both functioning and health.

If you score above 6, and definitely if you score above 10, you should visit with your physician, a psychologist, or a psychiatrist to discuss the problem. They will administer tests to make certain you are not suffering from a medical problem that might mimic depression.

SOURCE: Reprinted with permission. Kemp, B.J., Adams, B.A. The older adult health and mood questionnaire: A measure of geriatric depressive disorder. *Journal of Geriatric Psychiatry and Neurology,* 1995; 8: 164.

and productive during a manic state. For example, the musician Handel composed his famous 4-hour-long *Messiah* during the 3 weeks of a manic episode.

After the manic stage ends, the bipolar individual spirals down to either a normal mood state or into a period of depression. The word "bipolar" reflects this alternation between the two mood states. Bipolar is less common than major depression and occurs in about 1% of Americans. Bipolar disorder affects men and women with equal frequency.

Actress Patty Duke has written and spoken extensively about the ups and downs of living with bipolar disorder. She has described how, prior to treatment, her mood states swung widely between feelings of elation and suicidal depression.

Seasonal Affective Disorder

One of the more interesting forms of a mood disorder occurs when an individual's mood is tied to seasonal or weather conditions. Do you find that your mood fluctuates based on whether it is a sunny or gloomy day? Many individuals are more depressed on dark, gloomy days or in the winter when the days are shorter. Because mood fluctuations are often related to the seasons, the condition is referred to as **seasonal affective disorder,** often shortened to the very appropriate acronym **SAD.** Although the precise causes of this disorder are not known, it is suspected that the seasonal light/dark fluctuations affect hormonal changes, that in turn somehow alter depression levels. One therapeutic technique used with individuals suffering from SAD is exposure to bright light for periods lasting several hours per day.

Causes of Mood Disorders

Genetics

Mood disorders appear to have a genetic component. Individuals who have a first-degree relative with a serious mood disorder are 10 times more likely to develop one themselves. Bipolar disorders have a larger genetic component than major depressive disorder.

Biochemical Factors

A large body of research data suggests that mood disorders have a physiological component. For instance, depressed people have lower levels of the neurotransmitters serotonin and norepinephrine than do nondepressed individuals. Drugs that increase these substances in the brain have been used successfully in the treatment of major depression.

Faulty Thinking Processes

Depressive symptoms reflect faulty cognitive processes in depressed individuals. Depressed individuals often see and interpret their world through a lens of negativity (Beck, 1967). For example, a depressed individual might interpret a friend's joking comment as a sign of being unworthy of anyone's friendship, or construe a failure to accomplish something creative as a reflection of an unsuccessful life. Therapeutic interventions, however, have been developed to assist depressed individuals in correcting their inappropriate methods of thinking and interpreting events.

Dissociative Disorders

Perhaps some of the most intriguing mental disorders are those that are classified as dissociative disorders. With a **dissociative disorder,** an individual experiences major changes in memory without any physical precursor, such as a blow to the head. The word *dissociative* is used to describe this disorder because under extreme stress the person's memories become *dissociated* (i.e., separated) from each other. These disorders have been popularized by books and movies, the most well known being *The Three Faces of Eve* and *Sybil*. In both of these actual case histories, the women claimed to have multiple and completely separate personalities.

The DSM-IV lists several kinds of dissociative disorders. In this chapter, I will describe only the most commonly popularized disorder, dissociative identity disorder, which is more commonly known as multiple personality disorder.

Dissociative Identity Disorder

In dissociative identity disorder, individuals indicate that they have two or more distinct and separate personalities. These personalities are often very different and nonoverlapping. For instance, one personality might be shy, quiet, and retiring; another could be very outgoing and boisterous; another might be very businesslike and proper. Typically, each personality has its own voice and set of mannerisms that are specific to the personality being displayed. Often the personalities deny that they are aware that any other personalities exist. The personalities often differ in vital statistics, such as age and occupation, and in terms of abilities, interests, and preferences. At any given time, one of the personalities "takes over" and guides the individual's interactions with others. Nevertheless, one of the distinct personalities usually emerges as the primary one and appears with the most frequency.

According to the DSM-IV, switching between personalities can take place very rapidly, much like switching channels on a television. This switching of personalities is usually caused by some stressful event.

Typically, the disorder begins in early childhood but is not diagnosed until late adolescence or early adulthood. Some psychologists believe that early and severe instances of childhood abuse, typically before age 5, cause the disorder (Ross et al., 1991; Sachs, 1986). Several studies have indicated that nearly 97% of patients diagnosed with this disorder were physically or sexually abused during early childhood (Ross et al., 1991; Dell & Eisenhower, 1990). The DSM-IV reports that women are three times more likely to suffer this disorder than men.

As I mentioned earlier in this chapter, the incidence of multiple personality disorder has increased dramatically since 1980 when the DSM first described it. Many clinicians believe that this disorder is extremely rare, and some question whether it exists at all. Diagnosis of this disorder usually relies on hypnosis. Researchers have found that persons diagnosed with the disorder are very susceptible to hypnosis and suggestion. Several explanations for the development of multiple personality disorder include the theories that (1) self-hypnosis may be the primary cause of the disorder (Rosenhan & Seligman, 1984); (2) therapists unwittingly produce the disorder by suggesting its existence to clients during therapy; and (3) clinicians who believe in the disorder may deliberately look for and reinforce the symptoms in clients. Typically, the disorder is diagnosed only after a person is being treated for a less serious disorder, thus supporting this argument (Allison, 1978). Most mental health professionals will never see a true case of multiple personality disorder in a lifetime of clinical practice.

The legal community has seriously questioned the existence of multiple personality disorder. Defense attorneys have found it extremely difficult to establish an insanity defense on the basis of this disorder (Bartol & Bartol, 1994). A well-publicized criminal case a few years ago involved a man who killed both of his parents. His enterprising legal defense team successfully argued that he suffered from multiple personality disorder and the judge, concurring, ordered that he receive treatment at the state mental hospital before being tried for the crime. However, the mental health professionals at the state hospital could find no indication of multiple personality disorder and refused to treat him for the disorder. When the judge angrily ordered the treatment anyway, a stalemate ensued while the defendant remained in hospital custody. The matter resolved itself only when the patient contracted leukemia and died.

Sexual Disorders

Sexual behavior is an important part of our everyday life. Satisfaction of our sexual urges meets one of our basic needs and is closely tied to how we feel about ourselves. There are two major kinds of sexual disorders: sexual dysfunctions and paraphilias. *Sexual dysfunction* characterizes disorders in which normal sexual functioning is impossible. *Paraphilias* are disorders in which repeated and intense sexual urges or fantasies occur to situations or objects considered inappropriate by society. Let's examine each of the major categories and describe some of the kinds of behavior that occur within each one.

Sexual Dysfunctions

Sexual dysfunctions occur when some part of the normal sexual response cycle cannot be performed. The normal human sexual response cycle consists of four phases: *sexual desire, excitement, orgasm,* and *resolution.* Sexual dysfunction can occur at any of these four phases but most commonly occurs during the first three.

Lack of Sexual Desire

In the sexual desire phase, individuals normally experience an urge to have sex, have frequent sexual fantasies, and are sexually attracted to others. In some instances, individuals have a lack of interest in sex and, consequently, have a very low level of sexual activity. This condition is known as **hypoactive sexual desire** and is present in about 15% of men and in 20% to 35% of women (LoPiccolo, 1995). Most married couples report that they desire sex at least once a week, and the desire for sex at a frequency less than twice a week is typically classified as hypoactive (LoPiccolo & Friedman, 1988). Some individuals suffer from more than a mere lack of sexual desire; they have an *aversion* to sexual activity. Typically, these people find sex unpleasant or even repulsive. Sexual advances of any kind, including kissing or even touching, can be very unpleasant. Sexual aversion is very rare in men and occurs more frequently with women.

Excitement Phase Disorders

When humans are sexually aroused, a complicated set of physiological changes normally takes place. There is an increase in heart rate, blood pressure, and breathing rate. Blood gathers in the pelvic region, leading to penile erection in men, and swelling of the clitoris and labia in women, in addition to the lubrication of the vagina. Disorders in sexual excitement result in an inability for women to reach orgasm and for men to have an erection. Estimates of the frequency of these disorders vary, but most agree that it is at least 10% for women and about 10% for men.

Orgasm Phase Disorders

During orgasm, the sexual response peaks and sexual tension is released. Several kinds of dysfunctions can take place in the orgasm phase. For men, **premature ejaculation** can occur when orgasm is reached with very little sexual stimulation, usually before or shortly after sexual penetration. It happens most frequently in young or sexually inexperienced men and, on occasion, to men with no sexual dysfunction. The opposite situation exists with **male orgasmic disorder,** in which orgasm is delayed or never occurs after normal sexual excitement. For women, **female orgasmic disorder** occurs when orgasm is never experienced or is very delayed. There is considerable debate about whether a failure to reach orgasm represents a sexual dysfunction for females. Most mental health professionals now agree that orgasm during intercourse is *not* critical to normal sexual functioning in women. Many women can instead experience orgasm through direct stimulation of the clitoris (LoPiccolo, 1995).

Paraphilias

According to the DSM-IV, **paraphilias** are disorders where there are recurring and intense sexually arousing fantasies, sexual urges, or behaviors that involve either nonhuman objects, children, or other nonconsenting persons, and/or the suffering or humiliation of oneself or one's partner. To be classified as a disorder, the behaviors must occur over a period of 6 months or longer. All of these disorders are far more common in men. Most paraphilias are very persistent and typically last for many years unless treated. The disorders can take many interesting and varied forms. I will discuss those that occur most commonly.

Fetishism

Fetishism occurs when an individual *must* use some nonliving object in order to achieve sexual arousal. Among the objects most commonly used are women's underwear, shoes, and boots (APA, 1994). Often the person masturbates while the object is touched, smelled, worn, or used in some other way. In some instances, an individual may ask the partner to wear the object during sexual intercourse. As discussed in chapter 3, some psychologists believe that fetishes are acquired through classical conditioning.

Exhibitionism

In **exhibitionism** individuals have repeated urges to expose their genitals to another person, usually a person of the opposite sex. Sometimes the exhibitionist has only fantasies of doing so, and in other cases will actually carry out the act. The goal of the behavior seems to be the effect of surprise or shock on the recipient. It is very rare for the exhibitionist to actually attempt to engage in sexual activity with the victim. The disorder is most prevalent in men and often develops before age 18 (APA, 1994).

Exhibitionism is symptomatic of individuals who are immature in their approaches to the opposite sex and who often have difficulty in their interpersonal relationships with them. Over half of exhibitionists are married although sexual relationships with their spouses are usually unsatisfactory. Many male exhibitionists have doubts or fears about their masculinity, and some reportedly have a strong bond to a possessive mother (Comer, 1999).

Voyeurs derive sexual excitement from observing unsuspecting individuals, typically strangers, who are naked, in the process of undressing, or engaging in sexual activity. They are often referred to as "Peeping Toms."

Voyeurism

Voyeurism entails the act of observing unsuspecting individuals, typically strangers, who are naked, in the process of undressing, or engaging in sexual activity (APA, 1994). These people are popularly called "Peeping Toms." Voyeurs achieve intense sexual excitement from such observations but, as with exhibitionists, they seek no sexual activity with the victim. The voyeurs may masturbate either during or after the activity. Often, the risk of being discovered adds to the sexual excitement (Comer, 1999). In some cases, voyeurism is the only sexual activity these individuals engage in. The behavior usually emerges before age 15, and typically occurs repeatedly over an extended number of years (APA, 1994).

Pedophilia

In the disorder **pedophilia,** a person receives sexual gratification by watching, touching, or engaging in sexual acts with prepubescent children, generally ages 13 years or younger (Comer, 1999). To be classified as a pedophile, a person must be 16 years of age or older and at least 5 years older than the child victim (APA, 1994). In some instances, pedophiles are sexually attracted to children only, while in other cases they are also attracted to adults. Young girls are most frequently the victims of individuals with this disorder. Pedophilia typically manifests itself during adolescence, frequently in people who were sexually abused as children. As with exhibitionism, the disorder is usually found in people who have immature social and sexual skills.

People with this disorder often are content to merely view child pornography although, in some cases, the pedophile acts out his fantasies. The popularity of Internet youth chat rooms has greatly increased the opportunities for pedophiles to interact and arrange meetings with preteen children, usually under false pretenses. Pedophiles are often attentive to a child's needs in order to gain the child's trust, affection, and loyalty (APA, 1994). Pedophiles will go to nearly any length to obtain access to young children. They often favor occupations that involve working with young children. Some pedophiles have been known to marry a woman with an attractive young child merely to gain access to the victim (APA, 1994). As with many other paraphilias, the condition is often persistent and long lasting.

Sexual Masochism

In **sexual masochism,** the individual is sexually aroused by the act or thought of being humiliated, beaten, bound, or made to suffer in some other way. However, many people with no disorder also have fantasies of being forced into sexual acts against their will. A disorder exists only when such fantasies impair the ability to function or cause an individual great emotional upset. In some instances, masochists will act on their fantasies by hurting themselves, or by enlisting a partner to hurt them. The self-inflicted pain is delivered in a variety of ways, including sticking themselves with pins, shocking themselves, or even self-mutilation. When enlisting a partner's help, the masochistic acts can include spanking, whipping, beating, electrical shock, and various forms of humiliation (APA, 1994). This disorder often first appears in early adulthood. The masochistic acts are often elicited by stressful situations and, in some cases, increase in severity with resulting injury or even death (APA, 1994). The behaviors typically persist for long periods of the masochist's life.

Sexual Sadism

In **sexual sadism** an individual is sexually aroused by the thought or act of inflicting suffering on others. The suffering can be inflicted in a number of ways, including restraining, blindfolding, cutting, strangling, mutilating, or even killing the victim. Sexual sadists also derive arousal by dominating others. When fantasizing about sexual sadism, these individuals typically imagine that they have total sexual control over another person. In some cases, a sexual sadist will link up with a sexual masochist, who is a willing partner to the sexual sadist's fantasies. In other cases, sexual sadists force their behavior on nonconsenting victims. Rapists, for example, sometimes engage in sexually sadistic acts. The disorder frequently manifests itself in early adulthood although the fantasies themselves may have occurred during childhood (APA, 1994). As with masochism, the acts may stay at the same level of intensity or may become more severe. In the latter case, the disorder poses a genuine threat to others who may be victims. Again, the condition is typically long term, as is the case with most other paraphilias.

SUICIDE

Suicide has been termed by some "a permanent solution to a temporary problem." Indeed, that is often (but not always) the case. The incidence of suicide among Americans has been increasing dramatically over past the 4 decades.This is particularly evident among younger people ages 15 to 24, where the incidence has risen more than 300%—while the incidence for all ages has increased by about 20% (NCHS, 1990).

> There is but one truly serious philosophical problem, and that is suicide. Judging whether life is or is not worth living amounts to answering the fundamental question of philosophy.
>
> **ALBERT CAMUS**
> *The Myth of Sisyphus*

Has your life been directly or indirectly affected by a person's suicide? When I ask this question in my college lectures, typically one-third to one-half of the students raise their hand in the affirmative. I have personally known several individuals who have committed suicide, including several college professors. Several years ago I played bridge with a university administrator who seemed very upbeat and happy with his life. Two days later he jumped from the top floor of the university library, killing himself instantly. A colleague, in another department, whom I had known for many years shot himself in the head with a shotgun after being arrested

UNFORSEEN SUICIDE SHOCKS COMMUNITY

A recent newspaper article reported the suicide of a high school student in a small town in Alabama. The suicide occurred one day after the student had encouraged his classmates at a National Honor Society banquet to believe in themselves and accomplish their goals. The student shot himself with a pistol on the soccer field of his high school. Friends and classmates were shocked because he was a very popular and intelligent young man from a loving family who was a finalist to be the class valedictorian. The city's police chief reported there didn't appear to be any major contributing factors other than the student's inability to cope with life itself.

for drunk driving. Once, while at a Girl Scout meeting with my daughter, her best friend's father told me that he had just started a new job and he felt that it signaled a bright future for him and his family. His usually taciturn demeanor was the most upbeat I had seen in a long time. A few days later he committed suicide by carbon-monoxide poisoning. And closest to home, a faculty member who I had hired to teach part-time in our department committed suicide in the middle of the semester. He had stopped in my office the night before to wish me a happy holiday season. He spoke about a book he was completing and discussed his future plans. I detected no sign of unhappiness or depression, and his suicide came as a great shock not only to me, but also to his other colleagues, his students, and his wife. He had given no indication to anyone of his plans and left no suicide note behind.

Incidence of Suicide

The suicide rate in the United States is between 12 and 13 persons annually per 100,000 population. This results in more than 25,000 suicides in the United States each year. This rate is higher than countries such as Egypt, Mexico, Greece, and Spain where the rate is less than 5 per 100,000 annually. Conversely, it is lower than Austria, Germany, Denmark, Hungary, and Japan where the annual rate averages about 20 suicides per 100,000 population (NCHS, 1994; WHO, 1992). Edwin Shneidman, a very influential writer on the topic of suicide, believes that religious affiliation and beliefs may account for these differences between nations (Shneidman, 1993). He has noted that countries that are largely Catholic, Jewish, or Muslim have lower suicide rates when compared to largely Protestant countries. Other research has suggested that the more *devout* the religious beliefs, the lower the suicide rate (Holmes, 1985).

Patterns of Suicide

There are interesting demographic differences in the rate of suicide. Women are three times more likely to *attempt* suicide while men are nearly four times more *successful* in completing the act (Stillion & McDowell, 1996). Men prefer violent means of suicide, such as guns, knives, or hanging whereas women prefer the less violent method of drug overdose. Married people are less likely to commit suicide than are single or widowed individuals and divorced individuals have the highest rate of all (Canetto & Lester, 1995).

There are interesting racial differences in suicide, as well. White Americans commit suicide at twice the rate of African Americans and other racial and ethnic minorities (Stillion & McDowell, 1996). Exceptions are Native Americans, who have suicide rates twice that of the national average.

The suicide rate steadily increases as males become older whereas females maintain a fairly stable and much lower rate at all ages, particularly African-American women. The highest rate of suicide is for Americans 85 years of age and older, especially when debilitating illness is a factor.

Causes of Suicide

There are several major factors that cause individuals to take their own lives, including stressful events, mood and thought changes, alcohol and drug use, mental disorders, and modeling (Comer, 1999).

Stressful Events

Stressful events can frequently trigger a suicide attempt. For instance, earlier I mentioned a colleague of mine who committed suicide a few days after being arrested for drunk driving. One particularly powerful stressor that results in many suicides is the loss of a loved one through death or divorce. Stress that results from natural disasters, serious illness, or occupational events is also frequently a precursor to suicide.

Mood and Thought Changes

Significant changes in mood or ways of thinking often precede a suicide. Increases in a wide variety of feelings, including sadness, anger, frustration, anxiety, tension, or shame can serve as a trigger. Individuals who are in severe psychological discomfort from such feelings often seek relief through suicide.

Suicidal individuals frequently develop 1 of 2 specific patterns of thinking. One involves feelings of **hopelessness,** which is a persistent belief that things will never get better despite what the individual does or how the individual's circumstances may change. Sudden and long-term feelings of hopelessness are the best single indicator that an individual may be suicidal. Suicidal individuals sometimes adopt what has been called **dichotomous thinking** wherein they view their problems in very fixed terms with a limited number of solutions. They lose perspective and see solutions to their problems in an "either/or" dichotomy. In these circumstances, suicide becomes one of the limited alternatives they see available as a solution.

Alcohol and Drug Use

Well over half the individuals who attempt suicide do so while under the influence of alcohol, and nearly one-fourth are legally drunk. The use of illicit drugs often plays a role in suicide attempts in both teenagers and young adults.

Psychological Disorders

Several specific psychological disorders are often implicated in suicides. Mood disorders, substance abuse disorders, and schizophrenia are among the most common disorders that trigger suicides. One particularly lethal combination of disorders appears to be depression and alcohol dependence (Cornelius et al., 1995). It is ironic that people who are depressed often turn to alcohol, a chemical depressant, for relief.

Interestingly, researchers have noted that with depressed individuals the risk of suicide actually increases as their depression and mood improve. This accounts for the common observation that an individual who committed suicide was in a particularly happy frame of mind immediately before the act. While some people have expressed a belief that such individuals were upbeat because they had made up their mind as to what they were going to do, many psychologists instead believe that the change in moods energizes these individuals to carry out their suicidal intentions. In any event, a sudden and inexplicable change in mood from severe depression has been found to be a reliable predictor of suicidal intentions.

Modeling

One of the more curious facts about suicide is the tendency for individuals to imitate or *model* the behavior after either observing or reading about someone else who has done so. Particularly powerful are suicides by celebrities, highly publicized suicides, or suicides by close friends or colleagues (Comer, 1999). As an example of this, Phillips (1974) found the national suicide rate increased by 12% in the week following the suicide of Marilyn Monroe. Any highly publicized suicide, particularly if it has bizarre or unusual aspects, can lead to imitations of the act. This is particularly true among impressionable young people, as evidenced by the numerous suicide attempts following the suicide of rock singer Kurt Cobain.

Suicide among College Students

Perhaps surprisingly, college students are a high-risk group for suicide. About 20% of college students report that they have entertained suicidal thoughts at some point during their college careers (Carson & Johnson, 1985). A 10-year study of college suicide found that suicide was the second leading cause of student deaths after accidents (Seiden, 1966, 1984). These studies revealed that college students who committed suicide were

- older than the average student by about 4 years.
- often graduate students.
- more likely to be men (college women's rate of suicide was lower than college men but higher than among the general population).
- more likely to be foreign students.
- most commonly enrolled in language and literature courses of study.
- above average academically as undergraduates but below average as graduate students.
- dissatisfied with their academic performance and questioned their ability to be successful.
- highly motivated to achieve and had unrealistically high expectations for themselves.
- in their campus residences when they committed suicide.

You might expect that suicides would occur most frequently around mid-term or final exam time when students are anxious about their ability to succeed. However, more suicides occur in February and October, both of which are times near the beginning of the semesters. Students committed suicides more frequently at larger, more impersonal universities than at smaller community colleges and liberal arts colleges.

APPLICATIONS

Detecting Suicidal Intentions in Others

At some time in your life you will probably have personal contact with an individual who is planning to commit suicide. I related to you earlier several such instances that I have encountered personally among my professional colleagues. I have also dealt with several instances of suicidal planning among my students. Is it possible to detect suicidal intentions in others? No set pattern indicates suicidal intentions and, in each of the cases that I experienced, I was caught off guard by the act. Nevertheless, there are some warning signs that should alert you that someone intends personal harm.

1. Talk of suicidal plans or making vague references such as "After I'm gone. . . ." or "If I wasn't around any more. . . ." It is a common myth that people who are serious about committing suicide never talk about it beforehand. In actuality, the opposite is true. Be alert to suicidal comments from your friends, however vague or incidental. Any direct threats to commit suicide should be taken very seriously.
2. A sudden increase in giving away personal items, especially items that are very meaningful to the individual.
3. Sudden and inexplicable withdrawal from contact with others.
4. Indications of feelings of helplessness or depression.
5. Sudden changes in mood states.
6. Increase in aggression or risk taking.
7. Experiencing a sudden life crisis that results in emotional shock, such as the death of a loved one or a failed interpersonal relationship.
8. Sudden feelings of elation, following a severe depression.

How to Help

If you suspect that someone is contemplating suicide, talk to him or her about it. People who are suicidal often welcome the opportunity to talk. If you feel the threat is serious, give the person the phone number of a suicide hot line, a mental health center, or a hospital. Urge the person to call if he or she is feeling distressed. If a person tells you that he or she has a concrete, workable plan for committing suicide, the person is in extreme danger. In this case, you should accompany the individual to the emergency room of the nearest hospital.

Finally, do not blame yourself if someone you know commits suicide. In many cases, the behavior is unpredictable and often inexplicable. In each of the cases that I experienced, I always asked myself afterwards, "Is there something I didn't see in their behavior that I should have? Is there something I could have said or done that would have prevented the suicide?" While these are legitimate questions, the fact remains that oftentimes the behavior occurs with little or no sign of the individual's intentions. Even trained mental health professionals often miss seeing the signals. In addition, suicide is sometimes simply unpredictable. The following poem illustrates this:

Whenever Richard Cory went down town,
We people on the pavement looked at him:
He was a gentleman from sole to crown,
Clean favored, and imperially slim.
And he was always quietly arrayed.
And he was always human when he talked;
But still he fluttered pulses when he said,
"Good-morning," and he glittered when he walked.

And he was rich—yes, richer than a king—
And admirably schooled in every grace:
In fine, we thought that he was everything
To make us wish that we were in his place.

So on we worked, and waited for the light,
And went without the meat, and cursed the bread;
And Richard Cory, one calm summer night,
Went home and put a bullet through his head.

Edwin Arlington Robinson (1897)

Substance Abuse

Many people use drugs every day to alter perceptions or change their mood. The morning cup of coffee that many people enjoy contains caffeine, which helps jump-start our bodies and keeps us alert during the day. Nicotine is another stimulant regularly used by about one-quarter of the people in the United States. Unfortunately, some individuals turn to illegal substances in order to alter their consciousness.

Psychologists draw a distinction between substance abuse and substance dependence. **Substance abuse** occurs when there is a maladaptive pattern of continuing use that lasts over a period of 12 months or more. The use of the substance leads to physical or psychological impairment, causes the individual distress, and continues even though it jeopardizes the safety of the user or those around him or her. **Substance dependence** is more severe than abuse, in that it reflects an inability of the individual to control personal use of a substance. The dependence can be biological and/or psychological. Often users take increasingly larger amounts of the substance, and spend much of their time engaged in activities necessary to obtain the substance. As a result of the dependence, users often engage in actions that seriously jeopardize their social, recreational, and job-related activities. Abuse and dependence can occur to both legal substances, such as alcohol, caffeine, and nicotine, as well as illegal substances.

Substance abuse and dependence occur most frequently to three categories of substances:

- Depressants or sedatives. These include alcohol, opiates, barbiturates, and tranquilizers. They function to depress the central nervous system, thereby inducing sleep and offering relief from anxiety.
- Stimulants. These include amphetamines, cocaine, caffeine, and nicotine. They have the opposite effect of depressants or sedatives in that they energize the

central nervous system. They are typically used to increase alertness and induce feelings of euphoria.

- Hallucinogens. These include marijuana, LSD, and PCP. They alter sensory awareness, often in unpredictable ways. They are sometimes used to gain heightened awareness or increased insight, but effects frequently include distorted perceptions such as hallucinations.

Almost every society throughout recorded history has sanctioned the use of mind-altering drugs, even though their use has been known to be harmful. Some culture's religious rituals include the use of hallucinogens from mushrooms or other plants. Our culture often encourages the use of alcohol as a social lubricant, despite the known hazards resulting from its abuse. Many prescription drugs and even over-the-counter medications can also lead to substance abuse and/or dependence. Regardless of the reasons for using mind-altering substances, the potential for abuse and dependence always exists. How do you know if you have crossed over the line from substance use to abuse? Warning signs include: (1) an inability to meet your obligations at work, school, or home; (2) any threat to your physical well-being; (3) legal difficulties arising from the substance use; and (4) continued use despite recurring social and interpersonal problems, which are exacerbated by the substance use.

What causes substance abuse? The reasons are extremely complex, and include genetic, biological, and physiological factors as well as psychological factors that include personality, sociocultural influences, and behavioral or cognitive factors. This multitude of causal factors often makes treatment of substance abuse disorders problematical.

Eating Disorders

Eating disorders are becoming increasingly common in the United States, particularly among younger people. Eating disorders were considered very rare only a few decades ago. My wife tells about an incident that happened in her sorority while she was an undergraduate psychology major in the 1960s. The members all lived together in a sorority house on the campus of a small, private, liberal arts college in the western United States. One day, one of the sorority sisters unexpectedly walked in on another member in the bathroom. To her surprise, she discovered her sorority sister kneeling down before the toilet, with an array of snack foods positioned on the toilet lid. The student who made this discovery asked my wife about it, knowing that she was a psychology major. Although my wife had taken several courses in abnormal psychology, she was puzzled by the behavior and could find no reference to it in any of her abnormal psychology textbooks. Today, this pattern of behavior would be instantly recognized as a familiar part of the symptoms of an eating disorder.

Current estimates are that as many as 1 in 12 women try to control their weight through self-induced vomiting and nearly 6% abuse laxatives for the same purpose. There are tremendous societal pressures to be thin, especially for women. Numerous research studies have documented the prejudice and stereotypes that plague overweight women. Many years ago I conducted research studies with obese women. Several of them confessed to me that they would rather be dead than be overweight. Given the current societal pressures, it is little wonder that so many women are dissatisfied with their body weight and that they often develop eating disorders to control their body size and shape. Statistics compiled by the Academy of Eating Disorders, a professional organization of mental health experts in eating disorders, are quite revealing. The Academy reported that the average American woman stands approximately 5'4", weighs 144 pounds, and wears between a size 12 and 14. The changing standards for beauty are revealed in the fact that Marilyn Monroe, who was considered one of the sexiest and most beautiful women of her era, wore a size 12. Twenty years ago, fashion models weighed only 8% less than the average woman while today they weigh 23% less. The Academy also noted that there are 3 billion women in the world who do not look like supermodels and only a very few who do. The current obsession with weight has contributed to the prevalence of two major categories of eating disorders: bulimia and anorexia.

Bulimia Nervosa

Bulimia nervosa is characterized by two major behavioral characteristics: (1) **binge eating** or the rapid consumption of large quantities of food and (2) the inappropriate use of various methods to prevent weight gain. Almost all of us binge-eat once in a while, particularly during holiday periods or on special occasions. It is only when it occurs at least twice a week for 3 months or more that the behavior is considered abnormal. The inappropriate methods used to prevent weight gain typically include intentional vomiting (commonly referred to as **purging**), excessive use of laxatives, and excessive exercise to control weight. People with this disorder, almost all of whom are women, typically induce vomiting immediately after binge eating by sticking their finger down their throat to elicit the gag reflex. There is little question that the young woman in the sorority intended to eat and then immediately purge the contents of her stomach into the toilet.

Bulimic individuals are aware that their eating patterns are not normal, and they often feel frustrated and ashamed by their behavior. Many starve themselves for several hours, or even days, before they lose control and binge-eat huge quantities of food. Preferred binge foods are candy, ice cream, bread, and donuts. One study reported the typical woman with bulimia binged an average of 12 times per week and consumed as much as 11,500 calories during a single eating frenzy (Sue, Sue, & Sue, 1997).

It is estimated that between 2% and 4% of the general population are bulimic (APA, 1994). Another 10% report some symptoms of bulimia, such as occasional binge eating or purging, but do not fully meet the criteria for the disorder. The incidence of the disorder is rapidly increasing, particularly in urban areas.

Some people, including many college-age women, believe that the binge eating and purging cycles in bulimia are harmless. In fact, they are extremely dangerous. These behaviors affect the entire digestive system and can lead to electrolyte and chemical imbalances in the body that affect the heart and other major organs. For example, the purging causes a loss of potassium and sodium in the body that can lead to irregular heartbeats, heart failure, and even death. Inflammation and rupture of the esophagus, peptic ulcers, and pancreatitis also can occur from frequent vomiting. If the binge-eating behavior is carried to the extreme, it can actually cause the stomach to rupture.

The frequent vomiting will release stomach acids into the mouth that cause severe tooth decay and staining of teeth. Dentists are often the first to recognize the symptoms of bulimia because the enamel on the inside of the front teeth is usually eaten away causing many individuals with bulimia to have their front teeth capped. A colleague of mine was a clinical psychologist at a university in the southwestern United States where there is an extremely high incidence of bulimia. He hypothesized that bulimia may be more common at this particular university because women tend to dress more sparingly during warm weather, and consequently are more conscious of their body size. Incredibly, women in the dorms purged so frequently that the voided stomach acid required that the university replace the metal drain fixtures in the dormitory sinks.

Anorexia Nervosa

Anorexia nervosa is an eating disorder characterized by an exaggerated fear of becoming overweight and a refusal to maintain body weight above the minimum norm for one's age and height. Anorexics are very conscious of everything they eat. I once met an anorexic who was reluctant to swallow her saliva, fearing that it would add unnecessary calories.

Individuals with anorexia also have a very distorted view of their body size. They think they are fat and remain dissatisfied with their body size and shape even after they have starved themselves into a skeletal form. In my body image research, I discovered several extremely thin anorexic subjects who told me they see a fat person whenever they look in the mirror. In one study, for instance, anorexic women adjusted the width of life-size video images of themselves to represent the size that they believed themselves to be. I found that these women overestimated their body size by nearly 14% (Gardner & Bokenkamp, 1996). This overestimation of body size was specific to body regions, as well. They overestimated the stomach region by nearly 15%, hips by nearly 18%, and the chest region by 13%. Many clinical psychologists believe that body image distortion represents one of the first symptoms to appear in anorexia, and one of the last to be resolved through clinical treatment.

The overwhelming majority of anorexics are females although the incidence among males is increasing. The increase in male anorexics is particularly evident among those participating in sports such as wrestling, where careful attention is paid to one's weight. As with bulimia, the incidence of anorexia has been increasing in recent decades. The average age of onset is 17 years, with particularly high rates observed at both ages 14 and 18 (APA, 1994). A stressful life event often precipitates the illness. As an example, young women who leave home for college sometimes develop this illness early in their college career.

You can never be too rich or too thin.

THE DUCHESS OF WINDSOR

Very serious health consequences result from anorexia. Individuals with this illness are literally starving themselves to death. They develop an abnormally low heart rate and very low blood pressure that can result in heart failure. The singer Karen Carpenter died at age 32 from cardiac arrest that was believed to be a consequence of her anorexia. Other medical consequences of anorexia are reduced bone density that often leads to brittle bones, severe dehydration that can result in kidney failure, and overall muscle loss that induces weakness and fainting. As body fat disappears, the body grows a downy layer of hair all over the body, including the face, in an effort to keep the body warm. Anorexic women frequently fail to have normal menstrual cycles due to their low body weight. Up to 10% of anorexics eventually die from the disorder (APA, 1994).

The singer Karen Carpenter suffered from anorexia. She was 32 years old when she died of cardiac arrest, which was believed to have been caused by her eating disorder.

APPLICATIONS: Detecting Eating Disorders

Eating disorders among college-age students are common. I noted earlier that many female college students feel that binge eating and purging are harmless behaviors. Others are very secretive about their eating behaviors. Accurate diagnoses can be difficult, even for trained professionals. Nevertheless, if you know someone with symptoms of anorexia or bulimia, it is imperative that you encourage the person to seek professional treatment. Remember that eating disorders often have fatal consequences.

SUMMARY

- In our society, we attempt to identify, label, understand, and treat abnormal behavior. Abnormal behavior is distinguished from eccentric behavior because it meets certain criteria, namely that the behavior is maladaptive, disruptive, or harmful either to oneself or to others.

- It is important to take into account an individual's cultural perspectives, mores, and values when deciding whether or not behavior qualifies as abnormal.
- The manifestation of abnormal behavior does not make a person "insane." Insanity is a legal term that is used to explain and excuse criminal behavior. To meet this legal definition, the individual must be unaware that the behavior is wrong or be unable to control the behavior. The insanity defense is rarely used in criminal cases and, when used, is rarely successful.
- The incidence of psychological disorders among the population is quite high, with nearly 50% of Americans suffering from a disorder at some point in their lifetime. The most common disorders are anxiety disorders, depression, and substance abuse. The frequency of disorders decreases as we get older. Demographic factors such as gender, socioeconomic levels, education, and marital status all affect the incidence of disorders.
- Americans hold several myths about mental illness, including beliefs that mental disorders are (1) easy to distinguish, (2) inherited, (3) never fully cured, (4) reflections of emotional weakness, (5) permanent obstacles to leading productive lives, and (6) correlated with dangerous behavior.
- Psychiatrist Thomas Szasz believed that the whole concept of abnormal behavior is a myth and that such behavior reflects a failure by society to address the individual's problems that result from social ills such as discrimination, poverty, and social decay.
- Psychopathology is determined by observations of overt behavior, clinical interviews, psychological tests, and neurological tests. Neurological tests include CAT scans, PET scans, electroencephalography, and magnetic resonance imaging (MRI).
- Psychopathology is frequently classified by using the *Diagnostic and Statistical Manual of Mental Disorders,* 4th edition (DSM-IV). The DSM-IV categorizes an individual along five axes, including (I) diagnosis of the problem, (II) permanent aspects of the individual's personality, (III) medical condition, (IV) psychosocial and environmental problems, and (V) global assessment of level of functioning.
- Classifications that label behavior can be dangerous for several reasons. Behavior labels can result in self-fulfilling prophesies, lead to inappropriate interpretations by others, result in too frequent diagnoses by professionals, and make normal behaviors appear abnormal. One research project showed that mental health professionals were unable to detect when psychologically healthy people were admitted to a mental institution. This research supported the argument that labeling a mental patient's behavior is not always useful and is often counterproductive.
- Diagnoses and predictions about behavior are frequently made by using either the clinical or actuarial method. In the clinical method, judgments are based on the clinical expert's past experience whereas, in the actuarial method, judgments are made by applying empirically derived rules. The actuarial method has proven to be more successful although it has proven less popular with clinicians.
- Psychological well-being is a term frequently used to define mentally healthy behavior. Such behavior includes personal characteristics such as self-acceptance, positive relations with others, autonomy, mastery of the environment, sensing a purpose in life, and personal growth.
- Psychologists believe that there are three major causes of abnormal behavior: biological, psychological, and sociocultural factors. All three factors must be examined and integrated into the understanding and treatment of mental disorders.
- Affective disorders include schizophrenia, a serious mental disorder characterized by severe distortion in thought processes, language, perception, and emotions. Causes include heritability, brain chemistry imbalance, and psychological factors.
- Personality disorders incorporate maladaptive personality traits that impair social functioning or cause subjective distress. Included in this category are the antisocial personality disorder, borderline personality disorder, and narcissistic personality disorder.
- Anxiety disorders are those in which feelings of arousal, fear, and apprehension have debilitating effects on the individual. Included in this category are the panic attack disorder and phobic disorders. Phobias, such as agoraphobia and social phobias, occur when a strong and unjustified fear exists of an object or situation.
- Mood disorders are disabling disturbances of moods and feelings that are often accompanied by changes in physical functioning. Major depression, bipolar disorder, and seasonal affective disorder are the most common types. Genetics, biochemical factors, and faulty thinking processes all play a causative role in mood disorders.
- In dissociative disorders, individuals suffer major changes in memory with no physical basis. A rare example is dissociative identity disorder or multiple personality disorder where individuals develop two or more distinct personalities.
- Sexual disorders include sexual dysfunction and paraphilias. In sexual dysfunction, normal sexual functioning is impossible. Sexual dysfunctions can include lack of sexual desire, inability to be sexually aroused, or inability to reach orgasm. Paraphilias are disorders in which sexual urges occur to inappropriate objects or situations.

This includes fetishism, exhibitionism, voyeurism, pedophilia, sexual masochism, and sexual sadism.

- Suicide is becoming increasingly frequent in our society. Several factors can be responsible for this act, including stressful events, mood and thought changes, alcohol and drug use, mental disorders, and modeling of the suicidal behavior of others. College students are one particular high-risk group for suicide. Several behavioral indicators can help suggest when an individual is planning to commit suicide and permit timely intervention.
- Eating disorders are also becoming increasingly common. The two major categories are bulimia and anorexia. These disorders are caused partly by the changing standards of beauty in our society and by mass media influences. Anorexia is characterized by a refusal both to eat and to maintain a normal body weight. Bulimia is characterized by binge eating followed by purging. Both disorders have serious health consequences that can result in death. The vast majority of individuals suffering from eating disorders are young females.

KEY TERMS

abnormal behavior: patterns of thought, emotion, or behavior that are maladaptive, disruptive, or harmful either to oneself or to others.

actuarial method: the method by which professionals make their judgments by applying rules that have been empirically derived from the correlation of particular factors such as symptoms, age, gender, test scores, and medical history to particular behavioral outcomes.

agoraphobia: a psychological disorder characterized by an intense fear of being in places or situations where help might not be available or from which escape might be difficult.

anorectic: an individual suffering from the eating disorder anorexia nervosa.

anorexia nervosa: an eating disorder that is characterized by an exaggerated fear of becoming overweight and a refusal to maintain body weight above the minimum norm for one's age and height.

antisocial personality disorder: a psychological disorder characterized by impulsivity, aggression, irritability, fearlessness, dishonesty, and a lack of remorse, conscience, or sense of responsibility.

anxiety disorder: a psychological disorder that is characterized by intense anxiety, fear, and apprehension.

binge eating: the rapid consumption of large quantities of food.

bipolar disorder: a psychological disorder that is characterized by wide mood swings that alternate between feelings of elation and feelings of depression.

borderline personality disorder: a psychological disorder that is characterized by extreme fluctuations in mood, self-image, and interpersonal relationships.

bulimia nervosa: an eating disorder that is characterized by binge eating and the inappropriate use of various methods such as purging and laxatives to prevent weight gain.

CAT scan: computerized axial tomography; a procedure that involves having beams of X rays scan the different areas of the brain to develop a three-dimensional image of the structure of the brain.

clinical interview: verbal inquiry that allows a clinician to observe and gather data through a series of questions.

clinical method: the method by which professionals make their judgments of behavioral outcomes based on their memories of and experiences with similar cases, and on their knowledge of symptoms that are known to predict particular outcomes.

delusions: beliefs that are held without any factual basis.

delusions of control: false beliefs that thoughts and behavior are being controlled by another individual.

delusions of grandeur: false beliefs about one's power and importance.

delusions of persecution: false beliefs that others are plotting or conspiring against you.

dichotomous thinking: a thought process in which individuals view their problems in very fixed terms with a limited number of solutions.

dissociative disorder: a psychological disorder that is characterized by major changes in memory without any physical precursor.

eccentric: an individual who may be extremely creative, highly educated, or intelligent, but exhibits an odd, whimsical, or peculiar behavior.

exhibitionism: a sexual disorder that is characterized by a repeated urge to expose one's genitals to others.

female orgasmic disorder: a sexual dysfunction that is characterized by the inability to reach an orgasm.

fetishism: a sexual disorder that is categorized by the need to use some nonliving object in order to achieve sexual arousal.

hallucinations: perceptions of stimuli that do not exist; can be auditory, olfactory, or tactile.

hopelessness: a persistent belief that things will never get better no matter what an individual does or how an individual's circumstances may change.

hypoactive sexual desire: a sexual dysfunction that is characterized by a lack of interest in sex and a very low level of sexual activity.

insanity: a legal term that is used to explain and excuse criminal behavior; a person is not responsible for criminal conduct if the individual lacks substantial capacity to control the behavior or to appreciate the "criminality" of the conduct at the time of the conduct, or if the result of a mental disease or defect.

male orgasmic disorder: a sexual dysfunction that is characterized by delay in reaching or inability to reach an orgasm.

manic stage: feelings of elation and euphoria often characterized by pressured and loud speech, optimism, increased self-esteem, feelings of grandiosity, and decreased sexual inhibition.

MRI: magnetic resonance imaging; an imaging technique that creates a magnetic field around a patient and uses radio waves to detect abnormalities.

narcissistic personality disorder: a psychological disorder that is characterized by having an exaggerated sense of self-importance and strong tendencies to exaggerate one's achievements and talents.

neurological test: assessment tool that clinicians use to measure and diagnose the extent of brain dysfunction and neurological impairment.

norms: scores that have been developed by giving tests to a large, representative sample of individuals; allows comparison to clinical samples.

observation: the viewing of overt behavior; can take place in a clinic, laboratory, or natural setting.

panic disorder: a psychological disorder that is characterized by unwarranted feelings of fear resulting in numerous physical sensations.

paraphilia: a sexual disorder that is characterized by a repeated and intense sexual urge, fantasy, or behavior to situations, objects, or people considered inappropriate by society.

pedophilia: a sexual disorder that is characterized by receiving sexual gratification by watching, touching, or engaging in sexual acts with prepubescent children.

personality disorder: a psychological disorder characterized by maladaptive personality traits, difficulty controlling one's temper, inflexibility in solving life's problems, and inappropriate perceptions of self and others.

PET scan: positron emission tomography; a neurological test that allows for the examination of physiological and biochemical processes of the brain as they occur; involves injecting a radioactive substance into the bloodstream.

phobia: a strong, persistent, and unjustified fear of some specific object or situation.

premature ejaculation: a sexual dysfunction that is characterized by reaching an orgasm with very little sexual stimulation, usually before or just after sexual penetration.

psychological test: an assessment tool that clinicians use to measure different aspects of behavior, including personality, maladaptive behavior, social skills, intelligence, vocational interests and skills, and various mental impairments.

psychological well-being: the presence of positive mental health symptoms such as self-acceptance, positive relations with other people, autonomy, environmental mastery, a sense of purpose in life, and personal growth.

psychopathology: disturbed behavior that is maladaptive, disruptive, or harmful either to oneself or to others; also known as abnormal behavior.

purging: intentional vomiting as a method of preventing weight gain.

schizophrenia: a psychological disorder that is characterized by severe distortion in thought processes, language, perceptions, and emotions.

seasonal affective disorder (SAD): a psychological disorder that is characterized by mood fluctuations that vary according to seasonal or weather conditions.

self-report: a form of testing that requests an individual to answer specific written questions or to select specific answers from a list of alternatives.

sexual dysfunction: a sexual disorder that is characterized by a disruption in the performance of the normal sexual response cycle (sexual desire, excitement, orgasm, and resolution).

sexual masochism: a sexual disorder that is characterized by the act or thought of being humiliated, beaten, bound, or made to suffer in some other way. Impairs the ability to function or causes great emotional upset.

sexual sadism: a sexual disorder that is characterized by the thought or act of inflicting suffering on others.

social phobia: a psychological disorder characterized by an intense fear of being scrutinized and negatively evaluated by other people in social or performance situations.

substance abuse: persistent use of a substance that results in physical or psychological impairment, causes the individual distress, and jeopardizes the safety of the user or others.

substance dependence: maladaptive use of a substance marked by an inability to control its use despite knowledge of harmful effects. The dependence can be both biological and psychological.

voyeurism: a sexual disorder that is characterized by the act of observing unsuspecting individuals, typically strangers, who are naked, in the process of undressing, or engaging in sexual activity.

10

TREATMENT FOR PROBLEM BEHAVIORS

A man should not strive to eliminate his complexes but to get into accord with them: They are legitimately what directs his conduct in the world.

SIGMUND FREUD

Anybody who is 25 or 30 years old has physical scars from all sorts of things, from tuberculosis to polio. It's the same with the mind.

MOSES R. KAUFMAN

We do not have to visit a madhouse to find disordered minds; our planet is the mental institution of the universe.

GOETHE

A recent report released by David Satcher, U.S. surgeon general, and Donna Shalala, secretary of health and human services, stated that a range of effective, well-documented treatments exist for most mental disorders (1999). Despite the availability of these resources, nearly 50% of all Americans who have a severe mental illness fail to seek treatment. The surgeon general reported that good mental health is fundamental to a person's overall health, indispensable to personal well-being, and instrumental to leading a balanced and productive life. The report explained that a revolution in science and mental health service delivery over the last 2 decades has broadened our understanding of mental illness and improved the way that we provide mental health care. Safe and effective options are available now to treat the mental disorders that affect approximately 1 in 5 Americans each year. About 15% of the U.S. adult population uses some form of mental health service every year.

Contrary to some beliefs, disorders such as depression, schizophrenia, and eating disorders are real illnesses that, if left untreated, can be as disabling as heart disease and cancer in terms of lost productivity and premature death. The report recognized that barriers such as stigma of mental illness and financial limitations deter people from seeking help. As a result, a large gap still exists between what research has shown to be effective treatment and what treatment many people actually receive. The surgeon general concluded, "Few Americans are untouched by mental illness, whether it occurs within one's family or among neighbors, coworkers or members of the community."

According to most estimates, less than one-third of Americans who need psychotherapy actually obtain it. This neglect to obtain needed help is due to financial, class, and cultural reasons. Several factors related to social class can predict whether an individual receives psychotherapy, including age, race, and education (Garfield, 1986). White females who are educated and single (divorced, separated, or never married) are most likely to enter psychotherapy (Vessey & Howard, 1993). Oftentimes those individuals in greatest need of therapy are also the least likely to seek or receive it. Females are far more likely to seek assistance than males. Similarly, whites are more likely to seek and enter psychotherapy than are nonwhites. Furthermore, when minorities are accepted for treatment, they are often relegated to the less expensive state and county facilities rather than private hospitals (Mason & Gibbs, 1992). Not unexpectedly, access to health insurance is a major determining factor in who receives treatment. In the past decade, mental health expenditures, as a percentage of the total amount spent on health care, has dropped in half (Bickman, 1999). Increasing numbers of health plans have placed stricter limits on all types of benefits for mental health care (Hay Group, 1999).

In this chapter, I will review the various types of therapies and their effectiveness in treating problem behaviors.

Types of Mental Health Professionals

Several different kinds of mental health professionals are available for the treatment of mental disorders. The major categories of mental health professionals, including the differences in training, formal degrees held, and specializations, follow.

Psychologist

In the United States, psychologists must be licensed in the state where they practice. Technically, individuals are not allowed to call themselves psychologists without such a license. There are two major categories of psychologists:

Clinical Psychologist

A **clinical psychologist** is someone who completed four years of undergraduate work and proceeded to earn a doctoral degree in psychology, most commonly the Ph.D. (doctor of philosophy degree). Postgraduate training typically consists of 5 to 7 years of intensive training in research and clinical skills. In addition, psychologists complete a 1-year internship in clinical training under the supervision of a licensed psychologist. Clinical psychologists typically work with clients who have the more serious mental disorders, such as depression, schizophrenia, suicide, and drug and substance abuse.

Counseling Psychologist

A **counseling psychologist** completes postgraduate training similar to that of a clinical psychologist and similarly holds the doctoral degree, either the Ph.D. degree or the Psy.D. (doctor of psychology) degree. The Psy.D., which takes between 3 and 4 years to complete, is a degree in psychotherapy and has little or no emphasis on research training. As a result, psychologists with the Psy.D. are specifically trained to provide counseling and psychotherapy, not to conduct research. Their training and expertise focus mainly on the adjustment problems experienced in school and occupational populations rather than the more serious mental disorders. Counseling psychologists typically deal with matters such as student, marriage, or family counseling.

Psychiatrist

A **psychiatrist** is a medical doctor who has specialized in psychiatry after completing an undergraduate degree and 4 years of medical school. Psychiatrists usually complete a 1-year internship and 3 years of residency training after medical school. Because of their medical training, they can prescribe medication, psychoactive drugs, electroshock treatment, and other biologically oriented treatments. In contrast, psychologists are not allowed to prescribe medication or any of the other medically based treatments. On the other hand, psychiatrists are not trained in psychological testing and usually defer to psychologists for this type of evaluation. Most laypeople believe that, with the exception of differing graduate degrees, psychiatrists and psychologists have similar backgrounds. In fact, the training is quite different in that psychiatrists take very few courses in psychology. A psychiatrist's primary background and training are in medicine, not psychology.

Psychoanalyst

A **psychoanalyst** has a graduate degree in psychology, psychiatry, or social work and at least 2 years of extensive, supervised training at a psychoanalytic institute. Psychoanalytic principles will be discussed later in the chapter.

Psychiatric Social Worker

The **psychiatric social worker** typically has an undergraduate degree in psychology and an M.S.W. (master's degree in social work) along with 2 years of additional postgraduate training. The training usually focuses on treatment procedures, with a specific emphasis on the family or the community.

Psychiatric Nurse

A **psychiatric nurse** is an individual with an RN (registered nurse degree) with specialized training for working in a mental hospital or other mental health setting. These nurses often work as part of a therapeutic team with other types of mental health professionals.

Selecting a mental health professional can be very confusing for those not familiar with what various titles signify. For example, psychologists are very different from persons who label themselves psychotherapists. In many states, anyone can use the title "therapist" or "counselor" and charge for services without any licensure requirements or state restrictions. Because many such individuals lack formal training in the field of psychology, it is important that an individual carefully investigate the qualifications of any mental health professional prior to the beginning of treatment.

Other mental health professionals include master's level therapists. These individuals have a 2-year graduate degree in clinical psychology, counseling psychology, or social work, and may or may not be licensed. State licensure usually consists of 2 years of postgraduate supervision and completion of a licensure exam.

Even after having decided to seek the help of a qualified psychiatrist, an individual still needs to know what a selected psychiatrist actually does. Some psychiatrists rely primarily on therapy that uses drugs while others avoid all drug interventions. In addition, some psychiatrists have a Freudian orientation while others engage in "talking" psychotherapy, a very different treatment approach. The prospective client should hold a preliminary meeting with any mental health professional under consideration in order to determine the therapist's background, professional training, and therapeutic approach. To assist you in obtaining this information, some states have instituted mandatory disclosure statutes. For example, Colorado law mandates that every mental health professional must provide specific written information to each client during the initial contact (C.R.S. §12-43-214, 1999). Disclosure includes:

1. A statement that lists any degrees, credentials, and licenses of the psychotherapist.
2. A statement that indicates the department of regulatory agencies that oversees the practice of psychotherapy and that the department's grievance board may be contacted at the address and telephone number provided.
3. Information about the methods of therapy, the techniques used, the anticipated duration of therapy, and, if known, the fee structure.
4. A statement that information provided by the client during therapy is legally confidential.

APPROACHES TO THERAPY

Mental health professionals apply many diverse approaches to treat mental disorders. In this section I will describe the major approaches that have been adopted.

Biological Approaches

Biological approaches are based on a medical model of psychopathology that assumes that psychological problems reflect a medical disability of biological origin. These approaches assume that treating the physical aspects can reduce or even remove the symptoms that are troubling the individual. These approaches include such diverse strategies as drug therapy, electroshock therapy, and surgery. Let's examine some of these approaches in detail.

Drug Therapy

Research in the 1950s resulted in the development of drugs that revolutionized the way psychiatrists treat mental illness. For example, several **antipsychotic drugs** were developed to treat schizophrenia, the most disabling of all mental illnesses. These drugs decreased hallucinations and paranoid symptoms and calmed agitated clients. Prior to the development of these drugs, clients with schizophrenia were confined involuntarily to hospitals, often for the duration of their lifetimes. With the widespread adoption of these drugs in the 1960s and 1970s, such clients became sufficiently stabilized to live in community settings, albeit under supervision. Mental hospitals that housed thousands of clients over the years suddenly emptied when many of their clients were discharged. Unfortunately, antipsychotic medications often produce numerous unpleasant side effects, such as fatigue, dry mouth, and disturbances in muscle control. Consequently, clients who rely on these medications often discontinue their use when they see their psychotic symptoms decrease because they believe they are getting better. This leads to a vicious cycle because discontinuing the medication allows the psychotic symptoms to return. Although highly effective, antipsychotic medications do not "cure" the mental illness, and the client's behavior is not completely normal. Residual deficits in the individual's emotional responses and demeanor generally remain.

The other breakthrough in drug therapy came with development of **antianxiety drugs,** frequently referred to as tranquilizers. These drugs have become extremely popular and today are some of the most widely prescribed medications. Valium and Librium are two of the most common examples. They work by depressing the activity of the central nervous system and, as a consequence, reduce a client's anxiety, fear, and tension. These drugs have been shown to be effective in treating a wide variety of disorders including phobias, obsessive-compulsive disorders, panic disorders, and eating disorders. Unfortunately, they are highly addictive and, in some instances, the symptoms reappear when medication is discontinued. Like antipsychotic medications, tranquilizers can have unpleasant side effects that can cause clients to discontinue their use.

Many mental health professionals believe that mental disorders should not be treated by medications alone. In fact, several studies have revealed that a combination of medication and psychotherapy has better long-term therapeutic effects than either medication or psychotherapy alone. Psychiatrists will often require that patients receiving medication be seen regularly by some type of therapist. This is to help patients discuss their problems, monitor the effectiveness of the medication, and note any adverse side effects from the medications.

Electroconvulsive Therapy

Electroconvulsive therapy (ECT) is commonly referred to as "shock therapy." The therapy causes massive changes in the neural transmission systems and biochemical

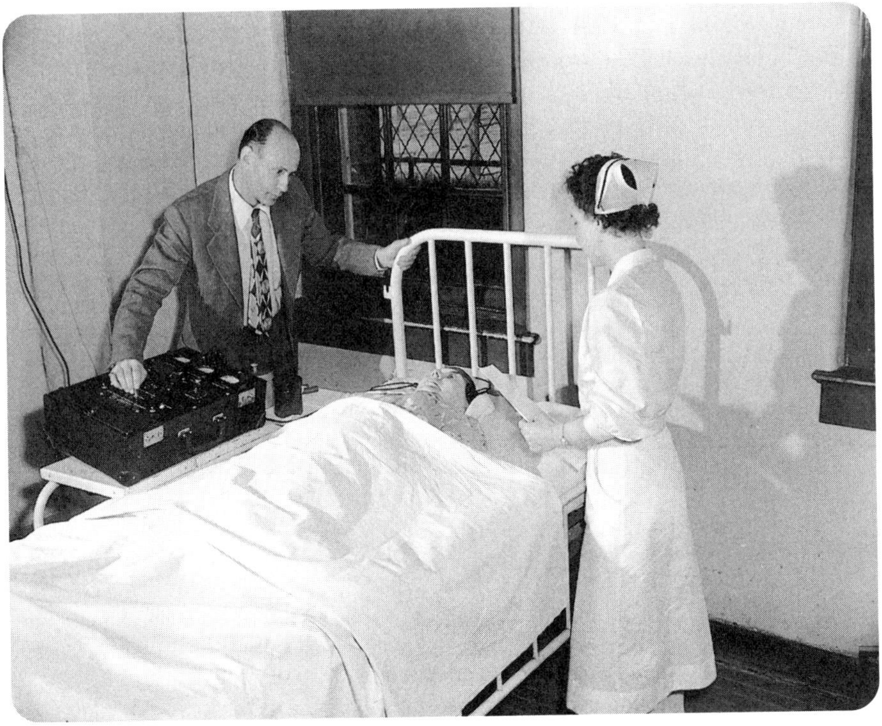

Electroconvulsive therapy (ECT) involves passing an electric current through the brain. The patient is given muscle relaxants prior to receiving the shock. Although very controversial, this treatment has been found to be highly effective in treating severe depression. ECT is usually only used when other methods of treatment have proven ineffectual.

balance of the brain, but no one is certain exactly how these changes reduce depression. An electric current passed through an individual's brain causes convulsions that last for about a minute. The convulsions cause major muscle contractions that are severe enough to break bones. Therefore, muscle relaxants are ingested prior to treatment. The client undergoing ECT often suffers memory loss that can persist for up to an hour following treatment. Recent advances in technology have greatly reduced the risk of long-term memory loss.

Treatments typically consist of 5 to 12 sessions spread out over 2 to 4 weeks. It has been found to be effective in treating severe depression in clients whose symptoms have not otherwise responded to drug therapy or psychotherapy, as well as for some manic disorders. ECT is usually reserved for cases of severe depression in which the risks of nontreatment include an increased probability of suicide or other disabling physical, social, or psychological problems. Interestingly, no one knows exactly how ECT works. Electroshock therapy remains highly controversial and, despite its proven effectiveness, movies and television often portray this type of therapy in a negative light.

Psychosurgery

Unquestionably, the most drastic form of biological therapy is **psychosurgery** where brain surgery is performed to destroy or remove brain tissue. This highly controversial procedure, once performed, cannot be reversed. The most common procedure is the **prefrontal lobotomy** in which the nerve fibers that connect the frontal lobes of the brain to the emotional control centers of the brain are cut. This procedure became popular in the 1940s and 1950s when some 50,000 clients received this treatment. Numerous side effects in many clients, including reduced intellectual abilities and even death, resulted from surgical complications. In the movie *One Flew Over the Cuckoo's Nest,* Jack Nicholson vividly played the role of a mistakenly incarcerated mental client who received a prefrontal lobotomy as punishment for his outlandish behavior. In the movie, the surgery reduced him from a gregarious and powerful personality to a zombie-like cardboard character. The development of modern antipsychotic drugs has made this procedure nearly obsolete, and its use today is only a method of last resort.

My mother grew up during the economic depression in the 1930s. Her roommate and best friend was a woman who suffered emotional problems. They were both very poor and struggled with living, as was common during this time period. My mother noticed that her roommate suddenly began exhibiting odd and unusual behavior. For example, one day my mother returned to their apartment to find her roommate standing stark naked by the side of the road and talking incoherently to the passing people. She was hospitalized, and when other forms of treatment proved ineffective, she received a prefrontal lobotomy. She and my mother remained friends and, knowing her history, I was fascinated whenever she came to visit us while I was growing up. I looked in vain for the surgical scars on her forehead (there are none with this procedure) and examined every nuance of her behavior to see if I could detect anything strange. In her case, the psychosurgery was successful enough to enable her to return to a normal and fully functioning life.

When psychosurgery is performed today, it involves much less extensive damage to the brain than in the past. Even though a proven treatment for some forms of severe depression, psychosurgery is used infrequently because of moral and ethical concerns about the appropriateness of the procedure. For instance, questions arise about the ability of people to give their informed consent for surgery when their condition is severe enough to require it. In addition, the procedure runs the risk of making permanent changes to an individual's personality.

Psychotherapeutic Approaches

Psychotherapeutic approaches emphasize changing behavior by using methods other than biological interventions. While there are numerous approaches, I will describe the techniques and goals of only the major ones.

Psychoanalysis

Therapists who practice **psychoanalysis** subscribe to the beliefs originally formulated by Sigmund Freud, including the theory that emotional problems result from conflicts between the conscious and unconscious aspects of one's personality. Freud believed that clients must become aware or gain **insight** into the unconscious parts of their mind in order to resolve these conflicts. Once insight has been achieved, the client understands the source of the conflict and accepts it on an intellectual level. In addition, clients are required to experience the emotions associated with the original conflict. Freud believed that self-awareness was essential before any resolution of emotional conflicts could be achieved.

The unexamined life is not worth living.

(SOCRATES) IN PLATO'S *APOLOGY*

The unlived life is not worth examining.

ANONYMOUS

Psychoanalysts believe that people who fail to resolve their inner conflicts devote substantial "psychic energy" to repressing urges and impulses that are personally unacceptable. Through repression, individuals keep these feelings at the unconscious level. However, one goal of psychoanalysis is to bring these feelings to a conscious level. Clients naturally resist this goal because their acknowledgment of such thoughts, feelings, urges, or impulses causes them discomfort. Psychoanalysts use several techniques to facilitate this process.

> Psychoanalysis has changed American psychology from a diagnostic to a therapeutic science, not because so many clients are cured by the psychoanalytic technique, but because of the new understanding of psychiatric clients it has given us, and the new and different concept of illness and health.
>
> **KARL A. MENNINGER**

One such technique, called **free association,** instructs the clients to relax and say whatever comes to their mind. They are encouraged to drop their defenses and say anything, no matter how trivial, unimportant, shocking, or bizarre it appears to be. Imagine yourself in a therapist's office trying to submit to this request. Like most people, you would probably find it difficult to express yourself because, to some extent, we are always "on guard" about disclosing our true thoughts and feelings. Psychoanalysts are trained to facilitate this process and to interpret the meaning of any such resistance.

One powerful tool in psychoanalysis is the interpretation of a person's dreams. Freud believed that all dreams have hidden meanings because our psychic defenses are less vigilant when we are asleep, which allows unconscious conflicts or desires to play out in our dreams. Freud emphasized that since the messages in dreams are usually symbolic, we are frequently prevented from obtaining any straightforward interpretation. Freud called some of these symbols **phallic symbols,** which are seemingly innocuous objects, such as a tall building or a railway tunnel, which hold unconscious sexual meanings. For example, if a client had an unconscious desire to have a sexual relationship with someone and the conscious awareness of such feelings was painful, the individual would instead dream of driving a car through a narrow canyon while accompanied by the person he or she desired. In most cases, the symbolism is much more obscure and can only be revealed by probing questions from the therapist.

Another tool in the psychoanalyst's armory is the information that is obtained by examining the relationship that develops between a client and a therapist. Freud believed that clients often developed a therapeutic relationship in which they transferred feelings toward people from their childhood to the therapist. This process, called **transference,** allows the therapist to gain valuable insights about unconscious conflicts that the client might be experiencing. Sometimes clients begin to experience feelings of adoration or even sexual attraction toward the therapist. Psychoanalysts believe the transference is resolved once clients become aware of the unconscious processes that are affecting their behavior.

Today there are many different versions of therapy based on the original psychoanalytic concepts. Although all have the common goal of helping clients understand and resolve unconscious conflicts, the therapeutic techniques differ in many significant ways. Anyone who contemplates undergoing psychoanalytic therapy should discuss all aspects of treatment with the prospective therapist.

A significant disadvantage of psychoanalysis is that it typically involves a lengthy course of treatment and considerable expense. Hour-long sessions often occur several times a week, and therapy can last for months or even years. Since most health insurance plans do not pay for such a course of treatment, psychoanalysis is usually reserved for individuals who can afford extensive treatment.

Humanistic Therapy

The goal of **humanistic therapy** is to promote a client's personal growth and self-fulfillment by assisting the individual in the interpretation of events and experiences in his or her life. Humanistic therapists are nonjudgmental and function as helpers and interpreters of behavior. They believe that the clients' emotional problems result from a lack of self-knowledge, a denial of their feelings, and an inability to fully experience how they are feeling. Therefore, an important part of the therapy is helping clients perceive and accept their feelings. In order to help accomplish this, humanistic therapists function in a very supportive and positive role, giving the client what they term *unconditional positive regard.* Unlike psychoanalysts, humanistic therapists de-emphasize the need to gain insight into repressed memories and stress self-acceptance instead.

This approach is referred to as **client-centered therapy** because it centers on assisting the client in positive ways. Honesty between the client and therapist is encouraged, and the client–therapist relationship is strengthened further by uninhibited communication. The therapist avoids making judgments about the client's feelings or behavior and, instead, emphasizes an empathic and supportive approach. The client-centered therapist's goal is not to direct therapeutic sessions, as might be the case with other types of therapists, but to help clients understand and accept their own feelings. To this end, the therapist resists interpretation of what the clients say but, instead, seeks clarification by restating or echoing the clients' feelings during the course of therapy.

We cannot change anything until we accept it. Condemnation does not liberate, it oppresses.

CARL JUNG
Psychological Reflections

Behavior Therapy

In describing psychoanalysis, I emphasized the importance of clients gaining insight into their problems. Mental health professionals who practice behavior therapies, however, believe that it is unnecessary to develop a deep understanding of what causes the client's problems for treatment to be successful. Alternatively, behavior therapists attempt to deal directly with the problematical thoughts and behaviors. They accomplish this by applying the *principles of learning* that I presented in chapter 3. For example, I discussed how the principles of systematic desensitization are used to help people overcome phobias.

Behavior therapists believe that people behave in a certain way because they have *learned* the behaviors. Subsequently, people who want to stop inappropriate behaviors must either extinguish existing learned behaviors or learn a set of different and more appropriate responses. This is accomplished by using the principles of both classical and operant conditioning. Let's begin by looking at how classical conditioning might be used to change inappropriate behaviors.

AVERSION THERAPY. Recall that classical conditioning occurs when a neutral stimulus, called a conditioned stimulus (CS), is followed immediately by an unconditioned stimulus (UCS), which produces an unlearned response, called an unconditioned response (UCR). After several CS–UCS pairings, the CS alone will elicit a conditioned response (CR), which is very similar to the UCR. For example, the sound of a dentist's drill would be a neutral stimulus (CS) initially, but by pairing the sound with the pain that results from drilling (UCS), the drill alone can acquire the ability to elicit a fear response (CR).

In **aversion therapy,** behavior therapists use this principle to teach clients to associate discomfort with a bad habit. For example, as discussed in chapter 3, alcoholism is treated by using a drug called Antabuse. This drug causes most individuals to become violently ill immediately after they consume alcohol. By pairing the illness with the alcohol, individuals become classically conditioned to feel ill just at the sight or smell of alcohol and, therefore, develop an aversion to it. Individuals develop a comparable aversive response when subjected to treatment that pairs painful, harmless electric shocks with the act of drinking. A similar approach has been applied to smoking. Individuals are forced to smoke continuously by taking a puff every 6 to 8 seconds. Even the most fervent smoker eventually will find this prolonged, rapid smoking to be extremely unpleasant. Even though the smokers will beg their therapist to discontinue the treatment, the therapist insists that they continue until the act of smoking becomes even more noxious. As with the drug Antabuse, clients learn to associate the unpleasant consequences of smoking with the sight, feel, and smell of cigarettes. This form of aversion therapy is an effective treatment for smoking (Tiffany, Martin, & Baker, 1986) and continues to be the most frequently used aversion therapy for smoking cessation (Lichtenstein, 1982). Even though some individuals have applied this quit-smoking program to themselves, they are rarely successful because people tend to stop the rapid smoking before its consequences become sufficiently unpleasant.

Aversion therapy has proven effective in treating a wide variety of undesirable behaviors, such as gambling, stuttering, bed-wetting, nail biting, and compulsive hair pulling. It has even proven effective in treating sexual behaviors such as fetishism and transvestism (Fuastman, 1976). Therapists commonly use aversion therapy in conjunction with supportive counseling because the combined approach is significantly more effective in stopping undesirable behaviors.

USE OF OPERANT CONDITIONING. Behavior therapists also alter maladaptive behaviors by applying the principles of operant conditioning that were discussed in the chapter on learning. The operant principles most frequently used include the following:

- Positive reinforcement. A behavior that is followed by some reward will be strengthened and will occur more frequently. Behavior therapists arrange reward contingencies such that desired behaviors are rewarded.
- Nonreinforcement. Behaviors that are not rewarded are extinguished. Unfortunately, maladaptive behaviors are often inadvertently rewarded. For example, a child may misbehave in order to receive the parent's attention. Therefore, behavior therapists must arrange situations so that no such reward is forthcoming for the undesired conduct. The "time-out" procedure is an example of this approach. When children make an undesired response, they are removed from the situation that is reinforcing the behavior. For example, if they are required to sit in a corner or go to a room for a specified period of time, the undesirable behavior will not be reinforced.
- Punishment. Behaviors that are followed by unpleasant consequences are sometimes suppressed because an individual wants to avoid punishment. This is the same principle behind using Antabuse to treat alcoholics or aversion therapy to stop smoking.

- Shaping. In chapter 3 I discussed how new behaviors could be learned by rewarding closer and closer approximations to the final desired behavior. Behavior therapists often shape new behaviors by using these techniques.

APPLICATIONS: Using Behavior Therapy Principles

Previously, I described how classical and operant conditioning principles could be applied to your own behavior. These are examples of how behavior therapy can be applied to your own life. You should be aware, however, that while these self-applied techniques are effective in treating specific behavioral difficulties, these procedures are not intended for self-treatment for serious personal problems. Instead, a trained therapist should be consulted. Nevertheless, you may find some applications of behavior principles useful for less serious problems.

One particularly effective technique is called **covert sensitization.** The word "covert" refers to the fact that you merely imagine something rather than actually do it. With this technique, you write down a scene that describes some bad habit that you wish to break. The trick is to make the scene so disturbing or disgusting that merely thinking about it makes you uncomfortable enough to discontinue the behavior. Dennis Coon (1992) describes how this technique might be applied to overeating. Using 3" × 5" cards, you should describe scenes related to the consequences of persistent overeating. For example, one scene might be walking on a beach and having other sunbathers stare at your fat and whisper insulting comments. Another scene might involve going into a clothing store and trying on clothes that are too small. This scene might include finding only hideous-looking clothes that will fit. The secret is to visualize the scene that you have described for at least 30 seconds several times a day, while at the same time, visualizing the behavior you wish to control. Find some response that you regularly make during the day and make that behavior contingent on the covert sensitization. For example, if you use your refrigerator several times a day, require yourself to picture one of the above scenarios for 30 seconds *before* you open the refrigerator door. Imagine yourself engaging in the behavior you wish to control (overeating, in this example) and then vividly envision the scene that you have written about. You should carry the cards with the written scenarios during your daily activities. Write as many unpleasant scenarios as you can create and rotate through them so that you are not picturing the same scenes every time. By adhering to this program for a period of time, you will learn to associate the unpleasant scenarios with the undesired behavior, and the frequency of the behavior should decrease.

You can even use this technique directly in situations requiring self-control. Perhaps you have a bad habit of biting your nails. Each time you feel the urge to do so, imagine an unpleasant scene related to the behavior. For example, you might imagine your fingernails painfully chewed down to the bloody quick or jagged, unsightly nails that elicit gasps of disgust from your friends. You may find that such thoughts are surprisingly effective in suppressing the undesired behavior.

Another technique you might find useful involves **covert reinforcement.** In this technique, you covertly visualize yourself being reinforced for certain behaviors. First, select a target behavior that you would like to change. This could be anything from reducing an undesired response, such as eating sweets, to increasing a certain behavior, such as exercise. For example, if you wanted to exercise more regularly, you could visualize yourself putting on your exercise clothes, driving to the gym, and working out on various pieces of equipment. You would then follow up these visualizations by imagining a pleasant, reinforcing scenario such as stepping on a scale and seeing a weight loss, looking in a mirror and seeing a more buff appearance, or having a friend compliment you on how fit you look. To use covert reinforcement effectively, continue to picture the target behavior and follow this visualization with 1 or more of the imagined reinforcements.

Cognitive Therapy

In the **cognitive therapies,** emphasis is placed on how an individual's negative thoughts lead to maladaptive behaviors. Cognitive therapists help individuals to recognize negative thoughts that they are experiencing, biased interpretations they may be making, and errors in logic that characterize their thinking. They help individuals challenge their dysfunctional thoughts, try out new interpretations, and apply new and more effective ways of thinking to their daily lives (Comer, 1999).

Cognitive therapy has proven especially helpful in treating depression. Negative, self-defeating thoughts can cause a person to become depressed (Beck, 1991). Depressed people tend to see themselves, the world, and the future in negative terms. I have witnessed college students who do poorly on an exam engage in this kind of thinking. They see themselves as stupid, believe that nothing good ever happens to them, and think that they will never succeed in their academic pursuits. These kinds of thoughts can lead directly to depression.

There are three kinds of distorted thinking that occur in depressed individuals (Beck, 1985, 1991):

- Selective perception. A tendency to focus on the bad things that happen and to ignore the good things. For example, a person may receive five compliments during the day but will obsess about the 1 insult he or she perceived.
- Overgeneralization. Making inappropriate generalizations from isolated events. You drop a treasured object and think that you are a clumsy person, or fail a single exam and conclude that you are stupid about everything.
- All-or-none thinking. Thinking of each event in your life as completely good or bad, right or wrong, successful or a failure.

Cognitive therapists work with individuals to identify and correct these maladaptive thought processes. Clients are taught to keep track of their thoughts and work in therapy to alter the way in which they interpret and think about events in their lives. By doing so, they can learn to alter their thoughts and thereby improve their moods, relationships with others, and behaviors. The therapist's goal is to help the client acquire tools to be used after the therapy has ended. Cognitive therapy has proven very effective in the treatment of a variety of disorders besides depression, including panic disorders, eating disorders, marital problems, and certain phobias.

Do you ever find yourself engaging in irrational ways of thinking? All of us do at certain times. The self-assessment test in Table 10.1 allows you to measure the extent to which this occurs in your everyday life.

✦ **TABLE 10.1** ✦ **Measurement of Irrational Beliefs**

Read the statements below and place a check mark by those that characterize ways in which you frequently find yourself thinking.

_____ 1. It is important that almost everyone I deal with likes me and approves of what I do.

_____ 2. In order to feel good about myself, it is important that I succeed at everything I do.

_____ 3. I believe that other people should treat me fairly in almost all circumstances.

_____ 4. I get very upset when everything doesn't go exactly like I want or plan it to.

_____ 5. Much of the unhappiness in my life is caused by external things that I cannot control.

_____ 6. I tend to dwell on thoughts about unpleasant things that might happen to me.

_____ 7. I often feel like a failure even when I get positive feedback from others.

_____ 8. If I do one thing wrong, I often feel that my entire life is a failure.

_____ 9. I think that I'm the way I am today because of things that have happened in my past.

_____ 10. I think there is only one way to do things correctly and I am dissatisfied with myself if I can't do things correctly.

Scoring:
Each of these statements reflects an irrational, illogical, and unsound way of thinking. These are the kinds of thought processes that cognitive therapists train their clients to identify and modify. We may all have an occasional thought like these, but if you find that your thinking is frequently like this, it is an indication that it may be irrational and self-defeating.

Variations within Psychotherapeutic Models

In addition to the different psychotherapeutic methods, variations also occur with respect to how therapy is dispensed, such as the number of persons being treated at the same time, the length of treatment, and where treatment occurs. Let's look at each of these variations.

Individual versus Group Therapy

In **individual therapy** an individual meets alone with a therapist, typically for a period of about 50 minutes. In **group therapy** several individuals meet simultaneously with a therapist in a session usually lasting 90 minutes. The psychotherapeutic methods that I have discussed previously lend themselves more easily to individual therapy. For example, it would be very difficult, if not impossible, for a therapist

In group therapy, the therapist meets with several individuals simultaneously. Often the group consists of people who share similar problems. Group therapy has been found to be just as effective as individual therapy for many problems.

practicing psychoanalysis to help several individuals gain insight into their own behavior during the same session.

The clients in group therapy may consist of individuals experiencing similar problems, family members, or even people in the same community. Many psychologists believe that psychological problems emerge in a social setting and are therefore best treated in this setting. Group therapy became popular during World War II when the stresses of combat produced so many psychological problems that the demand for psychotherapists far exceeded the supply. To conserve resources, individual therapists were forced to meet with groups of individuals at the same time. Many therapists were surprised to discover that the group setting seemed just as effective in helping people deal with problems as was individual therapy. What started out as a necessity has now become an increasingly popular alternative way of delivering therapy. A recent survey of a large number of clinicians indicated that about one-third devoted some part of their practice to group therapy (Norcross, Prochaska, & Farber, 1993). Research has shown that group therapy is frequently as effective as individual therapy (Bednar & Kaul, 1994; Vinogradov & Yalom, 1994) and usually offers the advantage of being less expensive. Group therapy is also more cost-effective than individual therapy for community agency settings that lack adequate funding and resources.

Group therapy offers four advantages that are not found with individual therapy (Carlson, 1993):

1. The group setting allows a therapist to observe how individuals interact with others without having to rely on a client's personal interpretations or descriptions, which often prove to be inaccurate.
2. Meeting in a group setting allows several individuals to bring social pressure on another individual to change. This group social pressure can be more effective and more convincing than individual assessments by a therapist.

3. Trying to help other individuals with their problems can be therapeutic and insightful for the individuals participating in the group. People gain insights about themselves from talking with and to others in the group.
4. It is comforting to people to know that they are not alone with their problems. Individuals are often relieved to discover their particular problem is shared with several others.

Long-Term versus Brief Therapy

Several years ago it was common for both clients and therapists to expect that psychotherapy would continue for a long time before good results could be anticipated. This *long-term* approach was characterized by weekly 1-hour meetings that often lasted for many months or even years. Clients who entered into a therapeutic relationship were routinely expected to make a long-term commitment for treatment.

More recently, therapists have come to realize that shorter terms of therapy can be just as effective. One review of 375 studies found that the length of therapy was unrelated to its success (Smith & Glass, 1977). Another review indicated that nearly half of all individuals receiving psychotherapy show significant improvement within 8 sessions, and three-fourths show improvement within 26 sessions (Howard, Kopta, Krause, & Orlinsky, 1986). In *brief therapy* the client and therapist establish the length of therapy and the deadline for its conclusion and decide to focus on a few specific goals. Therapists have found that clients, like most of us, "work to deadlines." In other words, as the deadline to terminate therapy approaches, both the client and the therapist redouble their efforts to bring it to a successful conclusion. Because clients in psychotherapy tend to develop a very comfortable relationship with their therapist, many resist terminating treatment. Brief therapy helps avoid these unnecessary and unproductive long-term relationships. As a general rule, brief therapy lasts between 2 and 6 months (Koss & Butcher, 1986).

Brief therapy is helpful for individuals with *specific problems* that would benefit from solution-focused therapeutic techniques. For instance, a client who wants to strengthen his social skills may benefit more from 12 sessions of social skills training than from 2 years of psychoanalysis where he explores the roots of his social fears. Clients should be aware of the different types of therapy so they can make educated decisions as to which type of therapy would be most helpful to them.

Outpatient versus Hospitalization

In the last several decades there has been a trend to treat more and more mental health clients in an outpatient versus hospitalization setting. I discussed previously how the introduction of certain antipsychotic medications eliminated the need to hospitalize most schizophrenic clients. A similar trend exists with other less serious disorders, as well. The advent of health maintenance organizations (HMOs) has exacerbated this trend because hospitalization is always a very expensive alternative to less restrictive forms of treatment. Unfortunately, the result has been that increasingly more individuals are receiving less hospitalization than they need. In some cases, the symptoms of mental disorders are treated without due consideration of the causes. For example, clients with anorexia who risk starving themselves to death are sometimes hospitalized only long enough to gain enough weight to remove them from immediate danger. The underlying causes of the eating disorder frequently are

A meeting of Alcoholics Anonymous. Such self-help groups are often very effective in helping individuals cope with maladaptive behaviors.

not treated, and the client's "recovery" is short-lived. Also common is treating a depressed suicidal client with an antidepressant medication without treating the underlying causes of the depression. The patient may be hospitalized long enough to be stabilized on medication, but not long enough to address the underlying issues that precipitated the suicidal attempt.

There are some circumstances where individuals who suffer from mental disorders *must* be hospitalized, even if it is against their will. The legal requirements for such *involuntary commitment* vary from state to state, but generally 1 of 3 conditions must be met:

1. The individuals are a danger to themselves (usually suicidal) or to others.
2. The individuals demonstrate bizarre or unusual behavior to the extent that they are out of touch with reality.
3. No acceptable alternative or community resource is readily available to provide assistance to the individual.

Individuals may be committed involuntarily to a mental hospital for a period of 24 to 72 hours. During this time, the hospital staff closely monitors their behavior and prescribes appropriate medications and/or therapy, if warranted.

Mental health centers have emerged in many communities to provide an alternative to hospitalization. They provide a variety of outpatient services, including group and individual therapy, and actively participate in the development of prevention programs. These centers constitute an extremely valuable resource for communities by providing needed mental health services at a fraction of the cost of hospitalization. These agencies rely heavily on state funding, and are constantly vulnerable to decreases in financial support due to ever-changing legislation.

The self-help sections of bookstores are crowded with a variety of offerings to assist people with every imaginable problem. Although some have proven to be an effective form of self-help, the books frequently are written in ways that do little to assist individuals in solving their problems.

Self-Help Groups

Self-help groups provide another increasingly popular and inexpensive alternative to more traditional forms of therapy. Alcoholics Anonymous is an example of this type of self-help therapy, which is peer coordinated and rarely includes a trained therapist. Typically, the participants have experienced similar problems, such as substance abuse, family violence, or eating disorders. All of the members both give to and receive help from others in the group and are usually available to provide support to one another at any hour of the day or night, without charge.

Self-Help Books

A visit to the "self-help" or "personal growth" section of your local bookstore can be quite revealing. There are literally thousands of self-help books available to assist you with any aspect of your life that might be troublesome. I recently logged on to Amazon.com, the popular Web site for purchasing books, and entered the search term "self-help." There were 14,952 titles in this category! Even though I did not browse through all of them, some of the more intriguing titles that I found under the letter "A" included: *Access Your Brain's Joy Center, The Aladdin Factor: How to Ask For and Get Everything You Want, Are You as Happy as Your Dog?* and *Awaken Your Birdbrain—Using Creativity to Get What You Want.* Books with numbers of days in them are always popular, such as: *30 Days to a Happier Marriage,* or, if you desire the opposite result, *31 Days to Ruin Your Relationship.* Apparently, there seems to be a 1-month solution for nearly every problem from *30 Days to a Simpler Life* to *31 Days to Increase Your Stress* (The Miserable Life Series).

Research has found that, in some cases, these self-help books are as effective as the treatment provided by a mental health professional (Christensen & Jacobson, 1994; Scogin, Bynum, Stephens, & Calhoon, 1990). These successful cases usually occur with higher functioning individuals or for problems with less severity. On the other hand, many of the self-help books tender advice that only marginally benefits or actually harms the reader. Unfortunately, professional psychologists have contributed to the problem. In 1981, the American Psychological Association formed the Task Force on Self-Help Therapies to investigate the proliferation and promises of self-help books and tapes. Gerald Rosen, chair of this task force, concluded: "Unfortunately, the involvement of psychologists in the development, assessment, and marketing of do-it-yourself treatment programs has often been less than responsible. Psychologists have published untested material, advanced exaggerated claims, and accepted the use of misleading titles that encourage unrealistic expectations regarding outcome" (Rosen, 1981).

APPLICATIONS: Selecting a Self-Help Book

Psychologists have offered several suggestions for the selection of a good self-help book (Rosen, 1993; Wade & Tavris, 1996):

- Select qualified authors who have conducted research in the area and/or are recognized professionally for their expertise. Do not be taken in just because someone uses the title "Doctor." There is an abundance of phony doctoral degrees available, ranging from honorary titles to mail-order diplomas. Moreover, just because someone has a doctoral degree does not mean that he or she is an expert in *every* psychology topic. Avoid books by authors who are neither researchers nor scholars.
- Personalized testimonials are interesting to read but are of limited value in generalizing the findings to other individuals. The limitations of testimonials were discussed in chapter 1.
- Avoid books based on an author's personal observations, anecdotal experiences, hunches, intuitions, or pseudo-scientific theories. The self-help advice should be based on sound scientific theory and research.
- There should be solid, scientific evidence for the effectiveness of the program. If the only evidence is a series of compelling assertions by the author, the chances are slim that the advice will be helpful. Advice that "sounds good" often isn't.
- Avoid books that promise the impossible. Any book that promises miraculous results in 30 days or suggests "8 simple ways to become wildly successful and happy" is most likely of little value. Any diet book that promises quick and permanent weight loss also falls in this category, as per my discussion on dieting in chapter 6. Wade and Tavris (1996) suggest ruling out any book with the word "instant" in the title. Behavioral change is possible, but it is very rarely "instant." Quick-fix solutions sell books but do not solve problems.
- Avoid books that provide vague advice such as "control your emotions" or "find love in your heart." Self-help advice should consist of systematic, well-defined procedures and not ambiguous exhortations.

Common Features of Psychotherapy

In this chapter I reviewed only a few of the major systems of psychotherapy currently being practiced in the United States. The number of major systems used today has increased from only 36 in 1959 (Harper, 1959) to well over 200. Although the systems vary with respect to the specific techniques employed, all share certain core features (Coon, 1992):

1. Psychotherapy provides for a caring relationship, often referred to as **emotional rapport,** between the client and the therapist. This relationship is characterized by warmth, understanding, acceptance, friendship, and empathy. The client and therapist bond together and enter into a **therapeutic alliance** or relationship of mutual respect and understanding that permits the parties to work toward a common goal of solving the client's problems.
2. Psychotherapy provides a safe setting where clients feel free to address their fears, anxieties, and private thoughts without the apprehension of rejection or loss of confidentiality.
3 All psychotherapeutic systems provide clients with an explanation or rationale for the psychological discomfort they experience and propose a course of treatment to reduce this suffering.
4. Psychotherapy furnishes clients with additional information or insights about themselves and provides them opportunities to change their behaviors in ways that will be beneficial to them.

Because no single therapy is best for all kinds of emotional disorders, many therapists today take an **eclectic approach** in which they adopt whatever technique works best for a particular problem. In addition, many therapists combine techniques by taking the best elements from a variety of psychotherapeutic systems to treat a specific problem. For example, behavior therapy interventions and cognitive therapy techniques are commonly used in combination, and have thus evolved into a cognitive-behavioral approach.

APPLICATIONS: Helping Others

All of us find ourselves in an occasional situation where we need to be a source of comfort to a friend or relative who is having a temporary personal problem or emotional difficulty. For many of the minor, everyday problems that people face, you can be a supportive and effective counselor by using some basic counseling skills. Please note, however, that you should only try to help if the problem is relatively minor. If someone is talking about suicide, threatening to engage in violent behavior, suffering from hallucinations or delusions, or showing any other similarly serious symptoms, you should immediately refer the person to a trained professional.

There are some suggestions regarding basic "counseling" skills that you can employ when working with a friend or relative (Kottler & Brown, 1985; Kottler & Kottler, 1993). The following are skills that are important in *any* counseling relationship:

- Be an active listener. There is an art to being a good listener. Even though most people think they are, many are not. If you have observed young children interact, you may have noticed that they often talk "at" rather than "to" each other. That is, what one child says has little or no influence on how the other child responds. This happens between adults as well when the listener does not respond to what is heard. As Jeffrey and Ellen Kottler (1993) concluded, "If you would simply monitor yourself and others during most interactions, you would notice how rare it is that people are being fully attentive to one another" (pp. 39–40). In counseling it is essential that you show that you really have heard what the other person has said. **Active listening** involves letting others know that you not only heard them but that you *understand* what they said. In active listening, you also communicate your interest in what is being said through head nodding, smiling, eye contact, posture, and tone of voice. Under most circumstances, you should never interrupt a person or be concerned if there are pauses of silence. I will be discussing active listening in far greater detail in the next chapter.

Difficult as it is really to listen to someone in affliction, it is just as difficult for him to know that compassion is listening to him.

SIMONE WEIL
Waiting for God

- Help define and clarify the problem. When talking to people about a problem, it is important to obtain a clear idea of exactly what is wrong. People are much more likely to arrive at a solution to the problem if they understand exactly what the problem is. In counseling, it is important that both you and the person you are trying to help have this understanding. You can check your understanding by asking the person relevant questions to help clarify the problem. For instance, a friend might be very upset because of problems in getting along with parents. "Not getting along" can refer to many different things. It is unlikely that they disagree about everything and, therefore, you should clarify the issues on which they disagree. This alone can substantially help the person discover a solution. There is a saying that a problem well defined is often half solved.
- Do not offer advice. It is always tempting to offer advice to other people on exactly how to solve their problems. Studies have shown that men are much more likely to do this than women, especially when men are speaking to women. This approach is almost invariably a mistake. Trained therapists do not tell clients how to solve their problems. Instead, they talk with clients until their problems become clarified and a solution evolves from the discussion. You have probably noticed how often merely talking about a problem is helpful in discovering a solution. Remain silent and give the person a chance to talk fully and frankly about the difficulty. Do not interrupt to offer unasked-for advice. Most unsolicited advice is ignored.

No one wants advice—only corroboration.

JOHN STEINBECK
The Winter of Our Discontent

- Concentrate on feelings. Good counselors realize that how a person feels is neither right nor wrong. Focus on how the person *feels* but do not pass judgment on those feelings. Perhaps a friend approaches you to discuss feelings of guilt about some act or occurrence. Being judgmental about the behavior, egregious as it might be, will only make the person defensive or hostile. Instead, let the person know that you understand and are making no judgments. If you moralize, the person who has sought your help will not accept your advice, and you will have lost the opportunity to assist a friend in working through an important problem.
- Accept the person's point of view. The person you are trying to help has his or her own point of view, and it might be different from your own. You must try to put yourself in the person's shoes and appreciate that perspective. Counselors

have found that clients are much more open to change when they believe that the person listening to them can see things from their point of view.

- Reflect feelings and thoughts. One of the best tools that you can use is to mirror back the feelings and thoughts the person is expressing. This is especially effective for individuals who have difficulty expressing how they feel. One technique is to simply restate or rephrase the statements made to you in a nonjudgmental manner, which will validate the speaker's feelings, and show that you understand what is being said. For instance, if a friend expresses feelings of sadness, you could reply by saying, "So you have really been feeling down lately?" Clinicians have found this to be a surprisingly effective tool in getting clients to open up about their feelings. Asking open-ended questions, which cannot be answered by a simple yes or no, can also be helpful. In the above example, you might also ask, "What do you think is causing your sadness?"
- Maintain confidentiality. It is very important that the person you are "counseling" knows that you will keep everything in confidence. You will not gain anything by repeating what someone confided in you. Consider how you would feel if someone broke your confidence.
- Be empathetic. The most important aspect in any counseling relationship is **empathy** or a person's ability to share in another's emotions, thoughts, or feelings. This, more than any other single factor, will facilitate the therapeutic process.

I wish to reiterate that the above guidelines are offered to facilitate your efforts to help someone who is having minor, everyday problems. Even professionals know when not to venture into problem areas beyond their expertise. You should never attempt to counsel someone who is having serious problems. The best counseling under these circumstances would be to encourage the person to seek professional help.

EVALUATING PSYCHOTHERAPY

Effectiveness

How effective is psychotherapy? The answer depends on how you ask the question and who makes the judgment. Consumers of psychotherapy are generally satisfied. In 1995, *Consumer Reports* surveyed its 186,000 subscribers about their experiences with psychotherapy (*Consumer Reports,* 1995). Of the 4,000 individuals who reported receiving psychotherapy, 44% who characterized their emotional state as "very poor" prior to treatment reported that they felt good following therapy. An additional 43% who started therapy in a "fairly poor" emotional state also reported significant improvement. The magazine reported that almost everyone who sought help did experience some relief in that therapy helped them feel less troubled and experience more pleasant lives. Not surprisingly, those clients who began therapy with the most severe problems reported the greatest progress. Overall, 62% reported that they were highly satisfied with their mental health provider. By contrast, only about 50% who sought assistance from their family doctor were highly satisfied. Research has shown that family doctors are not very good at diagnosing psychological problems and that they make a correct diagnosis only about 20% to 50% of the time (*Consumer Reports,* 1995). Moreover, family physicians were more likely to prescribe psychiatric medications than were other mental health professionals. Eighty-three percent of the survey respondents reported that their family physicians prescribed psychiatric medications, often without any accompanying form of psychotherapy.

The danger in generalizing from the *Consumer Reports* survey is that its readers tend to have more education and higher incomes than typical Americans. Surveys such as this are useful but do not, by themselves, allow us to conclude that psychotherapy *causes* therapeutic changes. Nor do they take into account lower-functioning individuals who are chronically mentally ill. Fortunately, other studies using more scientifically controlled methodologies have also shown that psychotherapy is effective (Lambert & Bergin, 1994; Lipsey & Wilson, 1993). Studies suggest that individuals who receive psychotherapy are better off than approximately 80% of those who fail to obtain such help (Smith, Glass, & Miller, 1980).

Not all forms of therapy are equally effective for all symptoms. *Consumer Reports* (1995) reviewed the scientific literature on this topic and summarized the best treatment options for the four most commonly reported symptoms. For depression, cognitive therapy brings significant release for about 70% of sufferers. Cognitive therapy typically takes about a month before the client obtains significant relief, and the course of treatment usually requires weekly sessions for a period of several months. Drug therapy is considered equally effective with between 60% and 80% of depressed people reporting marked relief within 3 to 6 weeks. For extremely severe depression, electroconvulsive therapy is effective about 75% of the time.

Serious anxiety is one of the most common disorders for which treatment is sought. This is not your everyday worrying but rather the kind of anxiety that interferes with your daily life. Drug therapy, including tranquilizers, is an effective method to provide fast relief, but the anxiety disorder resumes as soon as medication is halted. The continuous use of medication can result in the client developing a drug tolerance that requires progressively larger dosages for effectiveness and/or a drug dependency that makes it difficult to stop taking the medication. However, drug therapy is effective when severe anxiety results from a life event that causes temporary distress, such as the death of a loved one. These conditions rarely require the prolonged use of the medications. In addition, a combined use of cognitive and behavior therapy similarly provides effective relief and eliminates the potentially negative effects of drug treatment. As I discussed earlier, cognitive therapies emphasize negating irrational thoughts that provoke anxiety.

Panic attacks affect millions of people repeatedly and unexpectedly and can cause extremely uncomfortable symptoms. Antidepressant and antianxiety drugs can prevent panic attacks or, at least, reduce the severity of the symptoms for most people. Cognitive therapy and behavior therapy also provide effective relief to almost all sufferers.

Phobias are strong, irrational fears that can be extremely debilitating under certain circumstances. Behavior therapy has proven most successful in treating phobias, particularly those that focus on specific objects. In chapter 3, I discussed the technique of systematic desensitization, which provides long-lasting relief in a matter of weeks or months. For social phobias, a combination of behavior therapy and antidepressant medications seems to work best.

Finally, research has shown that people who do *not* seek professional help often recover on their own, a phenomenon called **spontaneous remission.** Various studies differ on the percentage of people who accomplish this, but most estimates range between 40% and 70%. It is likely, however, that many of these troubled individuals do seek support from friends, relatives, or the clergy. Given the high rate of cures without therapy, does this mean you should not bother to seek professional help? Not necessarily, since emotional problems depend on factors such as etiology, severity, environment, genetics, and precipitating events. Similarly, psychotherapy effectively reduces the troubling and sometimes debilitating symptoms that accompany a mental health problem. In addition, it helps prevent future occurrences by addressing the underlying causes and speeds up the recovery process.

Misconceptions

Even though psychotherapy is unquestionably helpful in many situations, certain misconceptions have exaggerated its effectiveness. One psychotherapist maintains that therapy promotes three myths that actually *increase* people's level of dissatisfaction (Zilbergeld, 1983):

1. People should always be happy and, if they are not, they should seek psychotherapy to get "fixed." Regrettably, psychotherapy is not the panacea for eternal happiness. It can help us through bad times and give us greater insight into our behaviors, but it is no guarantor of unremitting happiness or a life without problems.
2. Almost any change in behavior is possible. While behavior is subject to modification, it often resists change. Increasingly, evidence shows that many of our personality characteristics are inborn and remain relatively stable throughout our lives. Despite the wishes of some clients, psychotherapy will not transform people into someone they are not.
3. Changing behavior is relatively easy. Maladaptive behaviors that have been learned and reinforced for many years will almost always be very difficult to change. For instance, married couples who have been in long-term destructive relationships often mistakenly believe that a few sessions of marital counseling will alleviate their problems. As I often tell my students, clinical psychologists do not possess a "magic wand" that magically cures problems. Instead, they have powerful and useful tools for treating problems, but not in all cases or under all circumstances.

Psychotherapy does not supplant satisfying work, sustaining relationships, or enjoyable activities (Wade & Tavris, 1996). It can help us, but it cannot serve as a substitute for those things that bring true pleasure and enjoyment to our lives.

When Therapy Helps

Characteristics of a Successful Client

The prognosis for success in psychotherapy depends, in part, on certain characteristics of the client (Gaston, Marmar, Gallagher, & Thompson, 1989; Gaston, Marmar, Thompson, & Gallagher, 1988). Generally, clients who do best in therapy are those who exhibit the following characteristics: (1) fewer serious problems, (2) a strong sense of self, (3) high motivation to improve, (4) appropriate adaptation levels of mental and behavioral functioning, (5) sufficient distress to motivate a change in behavior, (6) commitment to the therapeutic process, (7) expectations of a successful outcome, (8) family support, and (9) a personality style of actively dealing with problems. Finally, the strongest predictors of success are the cooperative attitude of the client toward following through with the behavioral interventions suggested by the therapist and positive feelings during the therapeutic process (Orlinsky & Howard, 1994). Not surprisingly, negative individuals are the least likely to benefit from psychotherapy.

Characteristics of a Successful Therapist

What makes some therapists more successful in treating clients than others? Empathy, warmth, genuineness, expressiveness, and imagination generally have been agreed upon as important characteristics. In addition, those therapists who make clients feel accepted, respected, and understood were more successful in clinical work (Orlinsky & Howard, 1994). Lastly, effective therapists demonstrate a sincere investment in their clients' success.

Unexpected Conclusions Regarding Psychotherapist Training

When we seek professional treatment for a medical disorder, we look for someone who is well trained, knowledgeable, and experienced in treating the specific problem for which we seek care. For instance, when I needed arthroscopic knee surgery, I found a surgeon who had received extensive formal training in this type of surgery and who performed over 500 of these operations per year. These qualifications were very reassuring and indicative of the successful surgery I experienced.

Most people would probably take a similar approach in selecting a mental health professional. Logically one would think that an individual with extensive training and practice in the profession would be the best qualified for providing treatment. Surprisingly, research findings do not support this assumption. There are several myths that clinical psychologists and others hold about what assures high-quality and effective mental health services (Bickman, 1999). Let's examine some of these misconceptions.

Training of Therapist

Virtually hundreds of research studies have been conducted to evaluate the differences in therapist effectiveness that occur among people with various levels of training. These studies compared paraprofessionals who had no graduate training in any mental health field with those individuals who had completed various levels of graduate and postgraduate training. Surprisingly, for the most common psychological disorders, the paraprofessionals were just as effective therapists as were those with more extensive formal training (Dawes, 1994; Bickman, 1999).

In a landmark study, researchers summarized the results of 375 studies that had examined the effectiveness of psychotherapy (Smith & Glass, 1977). Like the researchers before them, they found that psychotherapy was generally effective. Individuals who received therapy had a twice-greater chance of being better off emotionally than someone from a similar group who received none. However, Smith and Glass also found that whether therapists had a graduate degree (M.D., Ph.D., and master's degree) or no advanced degree at all did not affect their effectiveness with treatment. Another study compared the results of 150 research studies in which psychotherapy had been used with children and adolescents (Weisz, Weiss, Han, Granger, & Morton, 1995). The treatment outcomes were equally effective for therapists at the paraprofessional, graduate-student, and graduate–professional levels.

Another extensive review of studies on therapy effectiveness found that professional and paraprofessional therapists were generally equal in effectiveness (Berman & Norton, 1985). However, this study went 1 step further and examined whether the relative effectiveness for professionals and paraprofessionals depended on the different types of problems and treatments. The researchers examined the 4 most commonly occurring categories of client complaint, namely social adjustment, phobia, psychosis, and obesity, and found no reliable differences between professionals and paraprofessionals on effectiveness of treatment.

One can conclude from these and numerous other studies that it is unnecessary to seek out an expensive therapist with a lot of impressive credentials (Dawes, 1994). If verbal therapy is sought, the key variable seems to be how *empathic* the therapist is. To reiterate, empathy is the ability to share in another's emotions, thoughts, or feelings. It is not related to one's academic credentials.

Years of Experience

If the amount of professional training does not matter, how about the number of years that a therapist has been practicing? Surely a therapist who has practiced for many years would be more effective than a novice who is just starting out. After all, what skilled or even semiskilled profession could you name where a person did not become more proficient after years of experience? Surprisingly, a review of research in this area reveals that the amount of experience therapists have is *irrelevant* to their effectiveness in treatment. Perhaps the best-known review of the research in this area was done by Howard Garb (1989). He concluded that once therapists master the basics of psychotherapeutic techniques, they do not increase their effectiveness with additional experience. Garb found this also to be true for clinicians that used a broad variety of psychotherapeutic procedures. This finding is certainly counterintuitive because, as a general rule, we all learn from experience. However, it does fit with the previously discussed findings that the amount of training is irrelevant to psychotherapeutic effectiveness. What is important to note is the finding that experience does not count *once the basic techniques have been learned.* Research evidence indicates that paraprofessionals can quickly master and practice these techniques as effectively as the experienced and highly trained professionals.

Type of Therapy

Earlier I identified the types of treatments that are more effective for specific symptoms. For example, cognitive therapy has been proven to be particularly effective in treating symptoms of depression and panic attacks. In other cases, drug therapy or a combination of drug therapy and psychotherapy is the most productive treatment choice. However, a review of the research findings in this area has shown that, with a few notable exceptions, the type of psychotherapy provided was unrelated to its effectiveness. Other studies have also found that all psychotherapeutic techniques are about equally successful (Omer & London, 1988; Stiles, Shapiro, & Elliot, 1986). However, you should note that not all *therapists* are equally successful. Again, it appears that it is the personal, empathic characteristics of the therapist that are more important than the specific kind of therapy he or she employs.

Length of Therapy

The extensive research literature suggests that length of therapy is often unrelated to its success. For most mental health problems, brief therapy is less expensive and usually just as effective as the longer-term, even multiyear, therapy. Health insurance plans are far more likely to pay for brief therapy.

Licensure

As cited previously, mental health professionals must be licensed by the state in which they practice before they can legally call themselves "psychologist" and offer services for a fee. The primary rationale for the licensure of psychologists is to protect clients from poorly trained or unscrupulous professionals. Moreover, licensure offers further protection because mental health professionals use knowledge and techniques that most clients are ill equipped to understand or evaluate (Dawes, 1994).

Extensive education and additional supervised experience are necessary in order to be licensed. Furthermore, licensed psychologists must pass oral and written examinations. Does the licensure procedure actually help ensure that a psychologist is an effective provider of therapy?

Robyn Dawes, in his book *House of Cards,* argues persuasively that it does not (Dawes, 1994). He believes that instead of assuring the quality of mental health services, it inhibits honesty. Dawes cites an interview with Lee Sechrest, former chair of the psychology department at the University of Arizona and former president of the American Psychological Association's division of clinical psychology (Hayes, 1989). Sechrest has maintained that licensing psychologists reinforces a common human failure, the lack of courage to say that "we do not know how." By granting a license, the state implies that the person *does* know how and has expertise in the area. As Dawes and Sechrest have pointed out, psychologists, in fact, often exceed the boundaries of what they know about effectively changing human behavior. Dawes documents numerous instances where licensed psychologists reached inaccurate conclusions or used therapeutic techniques of questionable value. He concluded that there is no evidence to support the claim that the licensing of psychologists has improved the delivery of mental health services or has benefited the public in any way. Perhaps this should not be such a surprise, after all. Licensure requires advanced graduate training and several years of experience, two factors already shown to be unrelated to a therapist's effectiveness.

Needless to say, many practicing clinicians disagree with these highly controversial views on the value of licensure. Nevertheless, the arguments several prominent psychologists have made about the questionable value of licensure serves to encourage further debate and research about this important issue.

APPLICATIONS: Seeking Professional Help—Finding the Right Therapist

The odds are very high that you or someone close to you will need to seek the services of a mental health professional at some point during your lifetime. I have documented the effectiveness of psychotherapy, and you should not hesitate to seek help when problems arise. Of course, it does not make sense to run to a therapist every time you feel a little "down." However, you should consider seeking help if difficulties cause significant unhappiness and persist for several months or if the problems are significantly interfering with your life. If you believe that the problem is very severe, you should seek assistance immediately. Symptoms such as suicidal thoughts or hallucinations need to be addressed immediately. Any relatively long-term problem that interferes with your ability to lead a happy and fulfilling life should be cause for concern. Remember, you do not have to be "crazy" to seek the help of a mental health professional. He or she can help you with a wide range of problems, ranging from phobias to social anxiety to breaking bad habits such as smoking.

I have prepared the following consumer's guide to assist you in finding help:

- Where to go. For college students, the college counseling center is probably the best place to start. Frequently, psychology departments at larger colleges and universities will operate their own clinic. Many cities have mental health associations that maintain lists of qualified therapists and programs that exist in the community. State psychological associations are also a good resource. Many cities have community mental health centers that can provide services, often using a sliding-fee scale based on your ability to pay. These centers can also refer you to private therapists. Many communities maintain 24-hour crisis hotlines staffed by individuals who are trained to provide information over the phone about a wide variety of mental health problems ranging from suicide to parenting. Telephone numbers are listed in your phone book. From this vast array of resources, you should be able to find help in a format and cost range suitable for you.
- Choosing a therapist. It is critical that your therapist is someone whom you like and trust. Remember that several research studies show that an empathetic and caring attitude is more important than academic credentials or years of experience. Before committing yourself to a course of therapy, hold an initial meeting with the therapist. At this meeting determine whether or not the therapist is someone with whom you feel trust and confidence. Seek a therapist who is a good listener, asks relevant questions about your problems, and can help you develop specific and realistic goals. Ask about fees, and if you have health insurance, determine whether the therapy will be covered. Many health insurance companies will only pay for licensed professionals. If you do not have health insurance, many therapists will adjust their fees based on your ability to pay. Remember that you are the consumer and the therapist is working for you. If you hired a plumber or car mechanic, you would not expect to pay if the individual was incapable of fixing the problem. You should have similar expectations of a therapist. You should also inquire about the length of time that the therapist anticipates that treatment will require.

- Avoid therapists who display authoritative, hostile, blaming, belittling, or aggressive manners. Also, be on the lookout for therapists who try to exploit you. Under no circumstances should you agree to have a sexual relationship with your therapist, regardless of the rationale advanced. Such disreputable individuals should be reported to the proper authorities, including the licensure board. Also avoid therapists who tell you that they know exactly what is best for you and insist that you follow their recommendations. A good therapist will always work *with* you to determine the best course of treatment. In general, be a careful and informed consumer. Do not be afraid to comparison shop until you find a therapist with whom you feel comfortable.
- Choosing a therapy. There is no simple answer to which therapy to choose. I discussed earlier how the kind of therapy is generally less important than the personal characteristics of the therapist. If cost is a big consideration, you should consider self-help groups that are available often for little or no cost. Group therapy is typically less expensive than individual therapy and can be just as effective for most problems. Brief therapy is also less expensive and, as discussed previously, often as effective as long-term therapy. Avoid therapists who encourage a prolonged dependence on them. If your problem has a biological basis, remember that only psychiatrists can legally prescribe medication.
- When to quit. Many personal problems can be persistent and difficult to resolve. On the one hand, you should not expect a miracle cure after only 1 or 2 sessions. Give the therapist a fair chance and stick with the prescribed course of treatment. On the other hand, you are the ultimate judge about when to stop treatment. As a general guideline, if you believe that you are not making progress in a reasonable period of time, find someone else. This is not to say, however, that you should quit therapy when it gets difficult or intense. Many people have a natural reaction or tendency to stop attending therapy when something painful emerges. In this case, stopping would not be in your best interest because it could be a defense to avoid difficult emotional work. Or sometimes feelings of transference will cause you to avoid your therapist. Beware of therapists who encourage you to continue treatment beyond the time necessary or who suddenly find new symptoms that need treatment. Some therapists, intentionally or unintentionally, foster a dependency so that the clients feel incapable of doing anything without first consulting with their therapist. If you find yourself in this kind of therapeutic relationship, you should seriously consider terminating treatment and seeking help elsewhere. Finally, be aware that many health insurance plans limit the number of sessions they will financially cover.

APPLICATIONS: Preventing Psychological Disorders

Our society expends countless time, energy, and money on the prevention of many common health problems. For example, we put fluoride in water to prevent tooth decay, immunize people against contagious diseases, and promote safe sex in order to avoid unwanted pregnancies and sexually transmitted diseases. Interestingly, society takes very little action to prevent psychological disorders. One influential psychologist has noted that research studies show a strong correlation between most mental health problems and one or more of the following: (1) emotionally damaging experiences during infancy and childhood; (2) poverty and other demeaning life experiences; (3) powerlessness and low self-esteem; and (4) loneliness, social isolation, and feelings of being excluded from the mainstream of society (Albee, 1986). As a society, we need to treat the prevention of psychological disorders with the same seriousness that we approach the prevention of physical disorders. How may a society accomplish this?

Some efforts can be directed at *entire* communities. In **primary prevention,** efforts are made to reduce the incidence of behavioral disorders by strengthening or increasing the community resources that promote good mental health and by reducing or eliminating the community characteristics that threaten good mental health (Sue, Sue, & Sue, 1997). Some examples include:

- Educating pregnant women about behaviors that are harmful to their unborn children. Information and counseling on the dangers of alcohol, substance abuse, and smoking during pregnancy could greatly reduce the incidence of brain damage in newborn children. Similarly, so could providing information on the importance of prenatal care. For instance, educating women that certain bacterial and viral infections impair fetal brain development and increase the risk of psychological disorders could prove to be extremely beneficial because prospective mothers may then be more likely to seek prenatal care.
- Providing better day-care facilities for children could greatly increase the psychological well-being of both children and their parents.
- Providing early-childhood enrichment programs, such as Project Head Start, that will serve neglected and deprived preschool children and help them to develop intellectual, social, and emotional skills.
- Implementing programs to help reduce or eliminate racial discrimination toward members of ethnic minorities could help increase community integration.
- Simultaneously providing jobs and reducing poverty levels. People who are employed and live even a modest lifestyle have higher self-esteem and contribute more to the well-being of society.

Surprisingly, sometimes there is considerable resistance against implementing primary prevention techniques (Sue, Sue, & Sue, 1997). Often the benefits are not immediately evident to the taxpayers and legislators who must fund them. Funding for such programs is expensive and takes money away from traditional remedial programs. Many individuals have a tendency to ignore issues that do not directly affect them, and the individuals who are directly affected do not have much power or influence to address the issues. As a consequence, these and other factors introduce considerable inertia into the implementation of effective programs and perpetuate society's more costly response of treating rather than preventing problems.

Secondary prevention involves instituting programs with community resources such as schools, churches, or the police to identify and treat mental health problems in the early stages. An example would be to train people in the community to recognize individuals who are in the early stages of developing alcoholism or drug abuse. Early intervention is less costly and more effective than efforts to treat maladaptive behaviors that have endured for years. In fact, almost any mental health problem responds more effectively to treatment in the early stages of its development. Unfortunately, communities often have few, if any, resources to train community individuals to perform secondary prevention techniques. Instead, many communities have established "walk-in" clinics and crisis intervention facilities to provide these services. Typically, these facilities are so overburdened that clients must wait months before receiving treatment. In addition, the problem is further compounded by the lack of reliable tools for the early diagnosis of problems. Our society often waits until the individual suffers from a fully developed mental health disorder and its corresponding consequences to the community before instituting treatment. We have seemingly forgotten the old maxim that an ounce of prevention is worth a pound of cure.

SUMMARY

- Nearly 50% of Americans who need treatment for mental disorders fail to seek it despite the fact that many safe and effective treatments exist. The barriers that prevent people from seeking treatment include the stigma of mental illness, financial consequences, and discrimination in accessing resources.
- The mental health professionals that provide treatment consist of the following: (1) psychologists who have a doctoral degree in psychology and several years of postgraduate training, (2) psychiatrists who have a medical degree, specialized training in psychiatry, and authority to prescribe medication and implement other biologically oriented treatments, (3) psychoanalysts who have a professional degree and training at a psychoanalytic institute, (4) psychiatric social workers, and (5) psychiatric nurses. Prospective clients are advised to interview the chosen specialist regarding professional background, treatment approach, and length of treatment.
- Biological approaches to therapy assume an underlying physical cause and use drugs, electroconvulsive therapy, and psychosurgical techniques to remedy the disorder.
- Psychotherapeutic approaches, including humanistic and behavioral therapies and psychoanalysis, attempt to change behavior without biological intervention. Humanistic therapy promotes personal growth and self-fulfillment through client-centered therapy and helps clients gain insight into their feelings and perceptions. Behavior therapy emphasizes that most behavior is learned and uses learning principles to change inappropriate behaviors. Individuals can also modify their own behaviors by using covert sensitization, in which they imagine doing something and follow it by unpleasant thoughts, or by using covert reinforcement, in which they visualize self-reinforcement for certain behaviors. Psychoanalysis involves the resolution of conflicts between clients' conscious and unconscious parts of their minds. Psychoanalytic techniques include free association, dream analysis, and evaluation of the transference process.
- Cognitive therapy emphasizes how the thinking process leads to maladaptive behaviors. This therapy focuses on helping clients change their irrational or inappropriate methods of thinking.
- Within each psychotherapeutic model, various techniques exist. Individual therapy involves interactions between a single client and a therapist whereas in group therapy several individuals meet simultaneously with one or two therapists. Group therapy is frequently as effective as individual therapy and offers several other advantages. Long-term therapy involves weekly sessions over an extensive time period while brief therapy lasts between 2 and 6 months. Both are considered about equally effective.
- In recent years, there has been an increasing trend toward outpatient therapy where clients receive treatment without being hospitalized. However, the more serious disorders still require hospitalization for various lengths of time.
- Self-help groups are comprised of individuals who all suffer from the same problems. This form of therapy often provides an inexpensive and yet effective method of treatment. Self-help books also can be effective although many of them offer advice that is of no benefit or is actually harmful. To select such books, one should find qualified authors who present scientific evidence for the effectiveness of the proposed program. Books that are based on testimonials, impossible promises, and vague advice should be avoided.

- All forms of psychotherapy have certain features in common. These include creation of emotional rapport, establishment of a safe setting, and provision of a rationale and explanation for the client's discomfort. These therapies also provide individuals with information or insight, which allows them to change their maladaptive behaviors.
- Individuals can use counseling skills to help others who are having minor difficulties. Skills include being an active listener, helping to define and clarify the problem, concentrating on feelings in a nonjudgmental manner, accepting the person's point of view while reflecting his or her feelings and thoughts, and being empathetic. Avoid giving advice and maintain strict confidentiality. Counseling by untrained individuals should always be confined to the less serious behavior problems.
- Numerous research studies have revealed that psychotherapy is generally very effective with about 80% of the participants being better off after receiving therapy.
- Even though certain types of therapy are better for some specific disorders, there is little overall difference in the effectiveness between different therapeutic approaches.
- About 40% to 70% of people who have mental disorders recover without any treatment.
- Misconceptions about psychotherapy include the beliefs that it can make people constantly happy, change any behavior, and make changes occur without effort.
- Clients who have fewer problems, a strong sense of self, a solid motivation to prevail in therapy, and a commitment to the therapeutic process are more likely to be successful in therapy. Therapists who are empathetic, very expressive, and sincerely invested in their client's success are most successful.
- Several factors have been shown to be unimportant in the effectiveness of a therapist. These include the level of formal training, the number of years or experience practicing therapy and, for most problems, the type of therapy practiced. Licensed therapists are not considered more effective than unlicensed therapists.
- To find a therapist, go to a college counseling center or community mental health center. State psychological associations can also refer qualified therapists. It is important to choose a therapist who you like and respect and who has an empathetic and caring attitude. The personal characteristics of the therapist are more important than the kind of therapy practiced. Clients should terminate therapy when they feel that it has resolved the problems being treated or is no longer effective.
- There is an increasing need to emphasize the prevention of mental health problems. Primary prevention techniques consist of efforts to improve community attitudes and resources to prevent mental disorders. Secondary prevention techniques serve to identify mental disorders in the early stages by training community workers to recognize and refer at-risk individuals before the problem worsens. Unfortunately, a lack of resources as well as other impediments has restricted the effectiveness and implementation of these prevention techniques in the United States.

KEY TERMS

active listening: using communication skills such as head nodding, smiling, eye contact, posture, and tone of voice to let another person know that you heard and understood what he or she said.

antianxiety drugs: also known as tranquilizers; medication that reduces a patient's anxiety, fear, and tension.

antipsychotic drugs: medication that decreases psychotic symptoms such as delusions, hallucinations, paranoia, and distorted thinking.

aversion therapy: a type of psychotherapy that uses classical conditioning to teach clients to associate discomfort with a bad habit.

biological approach: therapeutic approach that is based on a medical model of psychopathology that assumes that psychological problems reflect a medical disability of biological origin.

client-centered therapy: a type of therapy that centers on assisting the client in positive ways.

clinical psychologist: a mental health professional who is licensed with a doctoral degree in psychology; typically works with individuals who have more serious mental disorders.

cognitive therapy: a type of therapy with emphasis on how an individual's negative thoughts lead to maladaptive behaviors.

counseling psychologist: a mental health professional who is licensed with a doctoral degree in psychology; typically works with individuals with less severe problems such as occupational and school problems, and marriage or family counseling.

covert reinforcement: a behavioral therapy technique that involves visualization to associate a pleasant scenario with a desired behavior.

covert sensitization: a behavioral therapy technique that involves visualization to associate an unpleasant scenario with an undesired behavior.

eclectic approach: a therapeutic approach that uses the effective components of various psychotherapeutic approaches.

electroconvulsive therapy (ECT): a medical treatment for depression that involves sending electrical current through an individual's brain, causing changes in the neural transmission systems and biochemical balance of the brain; also known as shock therapy.

emotional rapport: the caring relationship between a therapist and client, characterized by warmth, understanding, acceptance, friendship, and empathy.

empathy: the ability to share in another's emotions, thoughts, or feelings.

free association: a technique used by psychoanalysts that involves the client saying whatever comes to mind; this technique helps the client bring feelings to a conscious level.

group therapy: a form of therapy in which a group of several individuals meets simultaneously with a therapist.

humanistic therapy: type of therapy that attempts to promote a client's personal growth and self-fulfillment by assisting the client in the interpretation of events and experiences in their lives.

individual therapy: a form of therapy in which an individual meets alone with a therapist.

insight: awareness of the unconscious parts of one's mind.

phallic symbols: objects that appear in dreams that hold unconscious sexual meanings; based on Freudian theory.

prefrontal lobotomy: a type of psychosurgery that involves cutting the nerve fibers that connect the frontal lobes of the brain to the emotional control centers of the brain.

primary prevention: efforts that are made to reduce the incidence of behavioral disorders by weakening or decreasing the community characteristics that threaten good mental health.

psychiatric nurse: a mental health professional with a registered nurse degree and specialized training for working in a mental hospital or other mental health setting.

psychiatric social worker: a mental health professional who has a master's degree in social work; typically focuses on treatment procedures, with a specific interest on the community and/or family.

psychiatrist: a medical doctor who has specialized in psychiatry after completing medical school; can prescribe medication, psychoactive drugs, and electroshock treatment.

psychoanalysis: a type of therapy that is based on the theory that emotional problems result from conflicts between the conscious and unconscious aspects of one's personality.

psychoanalyst: a mental health professional who has a professional degree in psychology, psychiatry, or social work, and has at least 2 years of extensive, supervised training at a psychoanalytic institute.

psychosurgery: a biological therapy in which brain surgery is performed to destroy or remove brain tissue.

secondary prevention: efforts that are made that involve instituting programs with community resources such as schools, churches, or the police to identify and treat mental health problems in the early stages.

spontaneous remission: a phenomenon in which an individual recovers from a psychological disorder without any professional treatment.

therapeutic alliance: the relationship between the therapist and client that consists of mutual respect and understanding; permits the parties to work toward a common goal of solving the client's problems.

transference: a psychoanalytic process that occurs when a client transfers feelings toward other individuals to the therapist.

11

INTERACTING WITH OTHERS

Few things are more important in our lives than our relationships and interactions with others. Literally, from the moment that we are born, the nature and extent of our relationships serve to shape our lives in critical ways. In chapter 7 on emotions, I discussed the plight of children who fail to develop close relationships with their parents or caretakers very early in their lives. These children can develop a debilitating syndrome called attachment disorder that often can prevent them from developing close relationships with anyone.

Why are interpersonal relationships so important to us? Reasons change as we get older. When we are very young, parental bonds are very important for meeting our physical and emotional needs. As we get older, parental bonds typically become weaker as we gain independence and our relationships with peers begin to take center stage. With adolescence, our romantic relationships with others become increasingly important as we develop an interest in sexual activity. Relationships often change again from a relationship focusing on sexual attraction to a deeper, more meaningful connection. With the birth of children, relationships between married partners often undergo further complex changes because the needs of the children take precedence. As the children mature, relationships in the family constantly change not only between parents and children but also between spouses. Finally, as our offspring gain their independence, we enter a different phase of our lives where our relationships with our spouse and close friends take on increasing importance.

A careful examination of relationships at all these stages of our lives is well beyond the scope of this book. Instead, I will focus attention on the relationships that develop during late adolescence and early adulthood because that is the most likely target audience of this text. Let's begin by examining the important topic of interpersonal attraction. What are the important factors that lead to one person being attracted to another, and how might we use this information to help us acquire and maintain important interpersonal relationships?

Affiliation versus Attraction

Affiliation

Psychologists draw a distinction between affiliation and attraction. **Affiliation** is a desire or motivation to be with others, regardless of whether we like or dislike those others. I briefly discussed the human need for affiliation in the chapter on motivation. We affiliate with others for a variety of reasons. We often seek affiliation when we are bored or lonely. We also want to be with others when we are fearful or anxious because it makes us feel better. There is truth in the saying that "misery loves company." If you watched television after Princess Diana's death, you probably noticed the strong need that people had to affiliate in groups and share their grief. Affiliation at a time such as this allows people to clarify their feelings and to compare their reaction to the reactions of others (Hill, 1987).

This need to compare ourselves with others led the famous social psychologist Leon Festinger to propose what he called *social comparison theory* (Festinger, 1954). Festinger maintained that people compare themselves to others in order to determine *social reality.* For instance, it is fairly easy to determine the *physical reality* of whether you are relatively tall or short by merely comparing yourself to others around you. However, determining how smart you are is not so easy. To do so we must also compare ourselves with others. Festinger believed that to test social reality we compare ourselves to others who are similar to us. If you are like the typical college student, you engage in this "social comparison" whenever examinations are handed back. Typically, heads swivel as students try to compare the score they earned with those of their friends, or even strangers, sitting around them. A failing score is much less painful when you know that your failure was shared by many others.

Social comparison also allows us to defend ourselves from threatening emotions. Several studies have shown that people like to compare themselves to others who are worse off than they are because it makes them feel better about their own situation. For example, cancer patients often seek out other cancer patients who are more seriously ill than they are, allowing them to feel that they are healthier than the comparison group (Taylor, Falke, Shoptaw, & Lichtman, 1986). Such comparisons help them defend against the anxiety associated with a potentially life-threatening disease. Often patients prefer to affiliate with other patients who are coping well with the disease because the association allows them to feel more optimistic and hopeful about their own future (Taylor & Lobel, 1989). It is for this reason that many cancer patients find cancer support groups so helpful and reassuring.

Oftentimes we will affiliate with others because we need their help in achieving some goal. Because there are goals that individuals alone cannot achieve, affiliation becomes the only means through which mutual interests can be reached. In the 1800s it was common for surrounding neighbors to get together to help a person build a barn. Everyone participated in the "barn raising" in anticipation that they might subsequently benefit themselves from such group cooperation. Working as a part of a political campaign is another example of people who become affiliated in a common goal. After an election, the initial affiliations with other campaign members typically dissipate as each individual gravitates toward other affiliations with different goals. In some situations people may affiliate with others for many years with little or no subsequent interpersonal attraction. Nevertheless, we know that affiliation often serves as a precursor for interpersonal attraction.

Interpersonal Attraction

Attraction refers to a *positive attitude or emotion* that we feel toward others. It is more than just wanting to be with or near someone. Rather, it is the feeling that makes us want to know someone and seek that person's companionship or friendship. Although the word "attraction" is commonly associated with physical attraction, it is not limited to members of the opposite sex. Certainly you have had the experience of meeting someone for whom you almost instantly experienced positive feelings. Often we are unaware of the nature of what exactly makes this person so appealing to us. Social psychologists have conducted numerous studies to determine precisely what variables are responsible for attraction to another person.

Proximity and Exposure. **Proximity** refers to how close things are in space, time, or order. In attraction research, it refers to how physically close you are to others. Close proximity exists if you regularly sit next to someone in class, if your apartment is adjacent to another, or if your cubicle at work is close to a coworker's. The closer the proximity, the more likely you are to come into regular contact with another person.

Proximity and its recurrent contacts play an important role in interpersonal attraction. It is hard to be attracted to someone with whom you seldom or never have contact. We often find ourselves in situations where we have frequent contact with strangers. For instance, if you wait at the bus stop with the same people day after day, chances are that you will begin to recognize each other and interact. At first the interactions are superficial, such as a nod of the head, a smile, or a comment about the weather. Eventually, the interactions become more personal as you learn more about each other.

We experience increasingly more positive responses to something unfamiliar when we have increasingly more contact with it (Moreland & Zajonc, 1982). This is true across a wide variety of dimensions, including art, music, foreign languages, advertisements, and that stranger sitting next to you in class. Humans typically react with mild annoyance to new stimuli, including strangers. With repeated exposure and greater familiarity, the anxiety decreases. In these instances, familiarity often breeds friendship or at least a feeling of liking. This is precisely why advertisers run the same commercial over and over and why during elections politicians expose you to their name and photograph so extensively.

There is one significant caveat to these findings. Repeated exposure does not work if the initial reaction was negative (Swap, 1977). In fact, repeated exposure to a stimulus that was originally disliked can increase the initial negative feelings. If you hated the song on the radio the first time you heard it, you will probably hate it even more the 100th time you hear it. This effect is important in interpersonal attraction because the first impression you make often becomes a lasting one, either good or bad. First impressions will be discussed in much greater detail later in this chapter.

Physical Attractiveness. Sometimes we take an almost instantaneous like or dislike toward other people, even before we get a chance to know them very well. This often occurs because we are making our judgments on the basis of a person's physical attractiveness. **Physical attractiveness** refers to a combination of facial and bodily characteristics that are perceived as aesthetically pleasant or appealing. Social psychologists have found that physical attractiveness is one of the most important reasons why people initially like or dislike each other. This is true despite the fact that people typically say that traits such as honesty and humor most attract them to others (Buss & Barnes, 1986). Men are affected more by female attractiveness than women are by male attractiveness (Feingold, 1990).

Despite the saying that "beauty is in the eye of the beholder," there is considerable agreement among people about who is or is not physically attractive. This is true even when judging beauty across racial and ethnic divisions (Cunningham, et al., 1995). Even though we may know beauty when we see it, it is often difficult for us to identify precisely what makes a person beautiful.

Males rate facial photographs of females as most attractive when those females have what can be described as "childlike" features: large, widely spaced eyes, small nose, and small chin. Males also rate as attractive those women who have "mature" features: prominent cheekbones, narrow cheeks, high eyebrows, large pupils, and a big smile (Cunningham, 1986). Other researchers have taken a different approach for defining what makes an individual attractive. By using a computer program, they were able to average a number of different faces into one composite facial image (Langlois & Roggman, 1990). Interestingly, they found that the larger the

✦ FIGURE 11.1 ✦

Composite faces generated by using a computer to average the features of several different faces. The faces from left to right represent 6 different composite sets of faces. Faces from top to bottom represent composite levels of 4 faces, 8 faces, 16 faces, and 32 faces. Adults judged the attractiveness of the composite faces as more attractive than almost all of the individual faces comprising the composite pictures. The composite faces became more attractive as more faces were entered. Look at the photos in the bottom row, which are generated from 32 different faces, and see if you judge them as more attractive than the top row, which are generated from only 4 faces.

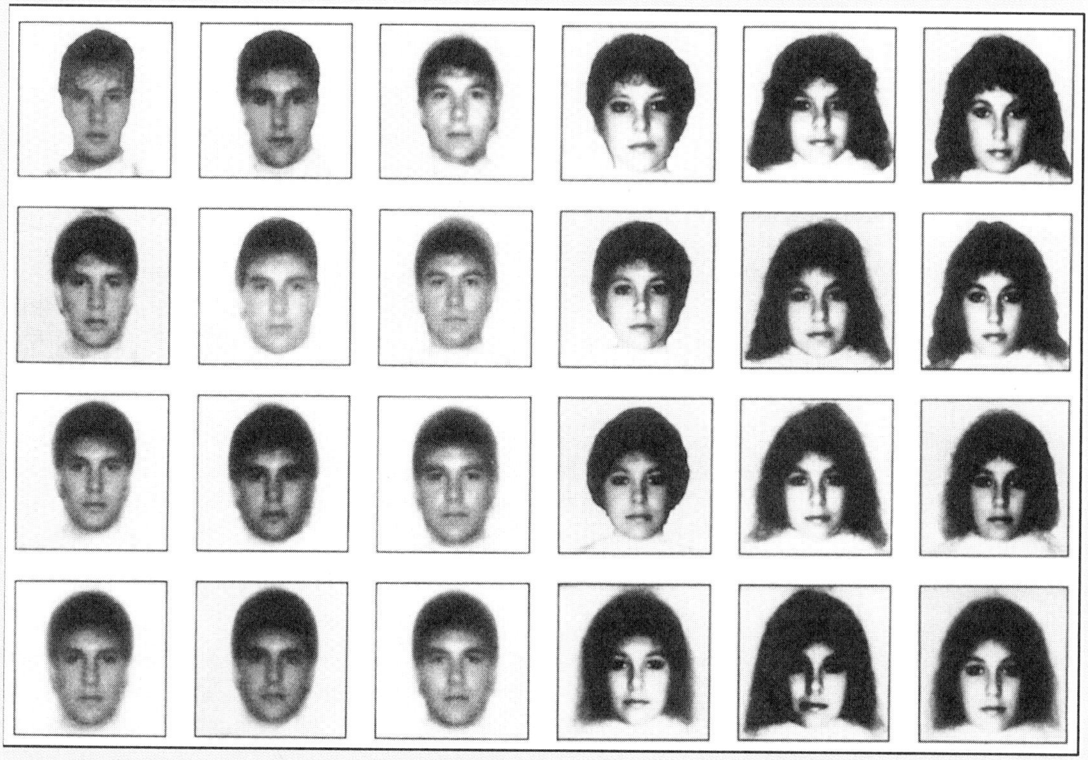

number of faces that were averaged, the more attractive the face was rated (see Figure 11.1). For most people, an attractive face is one whose individual components represent the arithmetic average (Langlois, Roggman, & Mussleman, 1994). Psychologists speculate that the average face is deemed attractive because of our familiarity with these average characteristics.

Physical attractiveness involves more than just a handsome or pretty face, of course. It involves many different physical characteristics, and the relative importance of those characteristics differs among individuals. For example, several studies have shown that the ratio of a woman's waist to her hips is a critical factor for

The Lord prefers common-looking people. That is the reason he makes so many of them.

ABRAHAM LINCOLN

men, with the ratio of smaller waist to larger hips being judged more attractive. A person's own physical characteristics can also affect his or her view of what is attractive in others. For example, a very short man might find very tall women unattractive irrespective of their facial features and a very tall woman might disregard facial attractiveness in short men. However, the encouraging news in all this research is that physical attractiveness becomes less important as relationships evolve. Early in romantic relationships, physical attractiveness is the most important factor, but later in the relationship, factors such as flexibility and compatibility come to be more important (Murstein & Azar, 1986).

It is only shallow people who do not judge by appearances. The true mystery of the world is the visible, not the invisible.

OSCAR WILDE
The Picture of Dorian Gray

Although it seems unfair, attractive people tend to receive numerous advantages in life from the moment they are born through old age (Brehm, 1985). Attractive infants receive more positive attention, not only from strangers but even from their parents. They are also judged to have more positive characteristics, such as sociability and competence, than are unattractive infants (Karraker & Stern, 1990). Teachers give more attention to attractive students and judge them to be more competent. Even our legal system works against the unattractive. Several studies have shown that attractive people receive fewer severe penalties for felonies and misdemeanors.

One study found that physically attractive individuals were judged to be more outgoing, nurturing, sensitive, interesting, poised, sociable, and sexually responsive. They were also thought to have better marriages, attain more social and professional success, and enjoy more fulfillment in life than those less attractive (Dion, Berscheid, & Walster, 1972).

A fair exterior is a silent recommendation.

PUBLIUS SYRUS
Maxims

How about the downside of being attractive? Surely, there must be some disadvantage to being "drop dead good looking." There are a few studies that suggest some downside to being attractive. Beautiful women, for example, are judged to be more vain and materialistic (Cash & Duncan, 1984). Other studies have shown that extremely attractive people are judged less trustworthy, less honest, less sensitive to others, and more likely to engage in extramarital affairs. Taken as a whole, this research suggests practical applications. Given the generally widespread stereotype that beauty is equated with good, we all have compelling reasons to appear as attractive as possible. Although most people are not born beautiful, they can help nature along with the assistance of grooming cosmetics and clothing. The findings that attractiveness benefits us in our professional and personal lives supports the growing popularity of plastic surgery with both men and women to enhance their appearance.

SIMILARITY. Do birds of a feather flock together or do opposites attract? Conventional wisdom seems unclear on this issue. You probably have known two people who, seemingly very different, were attracted to one another and perhaps enjoyed a lasting friendship or romantic relationship. Social psychologists have conducted hundreds of research studies on this topic and the verdict is very clear. The more similar we are to others, the more we are personally attracted to them. Of course there are exceptions, but not as many as you may think. One of my closest and oldest friends is a person who shares very different views than I do, ranging from politics, music, and art through personal pursuits such as hobbies and entertainment. Even though some people might think it strange that we are such close friends, we really share many more similarities than dissimilarities in our interests and pursuits. We both trained in similar areas of psychology, previously taught similar classes at the same university, pursued similar careers in teaching and administration at other universities, still actively participate in psychological research, and have many mutual friends. Frequently the similarities between people are not as obvious as the dissimilarities.

If you're not like me, I hate you.

HOWARD STERN, "RADIO SHOCK JOCK"

Similarity of *attitudes* is particularly important in attraction because attraction increases as the proportion of similar attitudes increases. Most people assume that a stranger holds attitudes similar to their own (Hoyle, 1993; Krueger & Clement, 1994), especially when the stranger is physically attractive (Miyake & Zuckerman, 1993). Psychologists have pondered why similarities of attitudes are so important in interpersonal attraction. Leon Festinger (1954) addressed this issue as part of his social comparison theory that I described earlier. He believed that we turn to other individuals to receive validation that our opinions are correct. According to this view, our interest in the opinions of others occurs only because we want to verify what we already believe rather than because we seek accurate information.

Perhaps surprisingly, similarity in physical attractiveness is also important. Several studies have shown that romantic partners tend to pair off on the basis of similarity of physical attractiveness. This is true both for couples who are dating as well as for married couples (Zajonc, Adelmann, Murphy, & Niedenthal, 1987). You can confirm this yourself by going to a crowded public place like a shopping mall or airport and observe the similarities in attractiveness among couples. Furthermore, people become upset when they perceive couples who are physically mismatched in attractiveness (Forgas, 1993). A good example of this was the marriage of singer Lyle Lovette, who was considered physically unattractive, and the movie actress Julia Roberts, who starred in the movie *Pretty Woman.* A great deal of public comment and displeasure was expressed about their "mismatched" relationship.

There is even a matching of attractiveness in same-sex friendships for both men and women (McKillip & Reidel, 1983). College roommates are more dissatisfied in their relationship when large discrepancies in their attractiveness exist. According to one study, with such dissimilarities, the more attractive of the two is the person who expresses the greatest dissatisfaction (Carli, Ganley, & Pierce-Otay, 1991).

This desire to associate with others similar to us has been called the **matching hypothesis.** It extends well beyond similarities in attitudes and physical attractiveness. Research studies have shown that we are attracted to and "match up" with individuals on numerous other variables, such as (1) sociability, (2) expressing emotions, (3) religious preferences, (4) self-concepts, (5) acceptance of traditional gender roles, (6) attitudes toward smoking, drinking, and engaging in premarital sex, and even (7) whether we are a "morning" versus an "evening" person (Baron & Byrne, 1997). Indeed, we can conclude that birds of a feather do flock together.

RECIPROCAL LIKING. We all like those who like us. Psychologists refer to this mutual liking as **reciprocal liking,** and it plays an important role in interpersonal attraction. Admittedly, it is hard to dislike someone who gives you positive feedback about yourself, even when it is inaccurate or an obvious attempt at flattery. Furthermore, the source of the feedback is relatively inconsequential. A stranger's positive evaluation is almost as important as that of a close friend. Merely a belief that someone likes us is sufficient enough to increase our attraction to that person. Robert Baron and Donn Byrne (1997) succinctly summarize this reciprocal liking phenomenon by stating, "In brief, we like those who like us or who we *believe* like us" (p. 265).

APPLICATIONS: Fostering Relationships

We find ourselves in situations every day where we want to influence how someone regards us. Essentially, we are striving to make ourselves as interpersonally "attractive" to the other person as possible. Remember, in the present context, interpersonal attraction refers to a *positive attitude or emotion* that we feel toward others or that others feel toward us—and not just physical attraction. Based on the important factors that I have previously described, certain applications are possible. In order to increase the odds that someone will develop a positive attitude or emotion toward you, you could do the following:

- Proximity and exposure. Whenever possible, arrange situations so that you will be in close and frequent contact with the other person. For instance, perhaps you are seeking a promotion at work. Try to arrange your work schedule so that you are in close contact with the person making the decision. The more frequent your contacts with that person, the better. Repeated exposure helps, even if the person just sees you passing by. I was once approached by a male student who was interested in meeting a fellow female student. His attempts to strike up a relationship with her had been unsuccessful, and he sought my advice about how to better get to know her. Because I knew that the female student was planning to take my course in perception, I recommended that the prospective suitor also sign up for the class and then sit next to her during every session. I also suggested that he become the student's lab partner during class activities. This approach would regularly place him in close proximity to her and provide him with multiple exposures, just as the research recommended. Although the male student had no interest in the topic of perception, he took my advice. During the semester, the female student's attitude toward the male student slowly evolved from indifference to liking and, eventually, into a romantic attraction. The upshot was that they finished the class together (she received an "A" and he failed), got married, and had two children. The principles of proximity and exposure worked their magic.
- Physical attractiveness. Remember the principle that most people equate beauty with goodness. If you want others to hold you in positive regard, you need to maximize your physical attractiveness to the greatest extent possible. Even if you were not "born beautiful," you can do many things to maximize your appearance, particularly grooming, dress, and posture. Avoid things that distract others from your best possible appearance, such as tattoos, body piercings, unusual jewelry, unconventional hairstyles and color, and so forth. These things may seem "cool" and attractive to you, but others may not share this view. If these types of self-expression are important to you, perhaps you can express yourself in a manner that can be concealed when necessary, such as for important interviews or employment.
- Similarity. Remember the principle that we are more likely to be attracted to people that we believe are similar to ourselves. Therefore, in interpersonal interactions you should stress your similarities rather than your dissimilarities. This approach requires that you learn about the other person's background and interests and emphasize those features that are similar to your own. This does

not mean that you should lie or fabricate information about yourself. Almost any two people will share many commonalities once they get to know each other well.

- Reciprocal liking. Remember the fact that people like people who like them. Invariably, you will improve how positively people regard you by communicating to them that you like them. Oftentimes we hide our positive feelings about others or fail to do a good job communicating our feelings. This does not imply that you must put on false airs or always "kiss up" to someone you do not like. Most people do things that we like as well as things we dislike. Emphasizing the "likes" will help your interpersonal attractiveness immeasurably.

Liking versus Loving

As our relationships with others evolve, we often develop positive feelings about another person and subsequently conclude that we "like" the person. Psychologists draw an important distinction between liking and loving. As discussed in chapter 7, love is a powerful emotion characterized by heightened physiological and emotional arousal. What about liking? Is it just a milder form of love, or is it something fundamentally different? Certainly, liking and loving share things in common. It is hard to imagine being madly in love with someone that you do not like. Some psychologists have speculated that this is possible (Walster & Berscheid, 1971). However, others feel that it foretells a doomed relationship.

I never met a man I didn't like.

WILL ROGERS

Psychologist Zick Rubin (1973) has written extensively about his research on the distinction between liking and loving. He notes that there are several kinds of "liking," and that it can mean different things at different times. We can like our car, our best friend, and our boss and yet feel quite different emotions toward each one. Rubin argues that, despite the different emotions, there are two fundamental dimensions of liking: *affection* and *respect.*

Affection is liking that is based on how one individual personally relates to another individual. It is experienced as an emotional warmth and closeness. This is the nice feeling that you have when someone you like walks into the room. **Respect,** on the other hand, is liking that is based on the characteristics or actions of another person that we admire. Rubin maintains that respect is a cooler, more distant type of liking, such as respect for individuals who voice their beliefs. If you have no feelings of affection or respect for a person, then you probably do not like that person. This does not, however, mean that you necessarily *dislike* the person. In fact, we have neither feelings of particular like nor dislike for most people.

At times, the distinction between liking and loving becomes hazy. If you experience strong emotions toward your dating partner, you may wonder if it is really love or just strong liking. Rubin has developed two separate tests, called loving and liking scales, to measure this distinction. These scales are illustrated in Table 11.1. He asked several hundred dating couples at the University of Michigan to complete each scale. They answered the questions both with respect to a person they were dating and then with respect to a close, same-sex friend. He found that dating couples both liked *and* loved their partners while they mostly just liked their friends.

You may wish to take this test yourself. If there is someone that you think you truly love, you might want to answer the questions on both scales as they apply to

✦ TABLE 11.1 ✦ Love Scale and Liking Scale

Rate each of the following statements from 1 to 9, with respect to how much you agree or disagree relative to the specific person you are rating. Use the following scale for your ratings:

1	2	3	4	5	6	7	8	9
Not at all true; disagree completely				Moderately true; agree to some extent				Definitely agree

Love Scale

____ 1. If __________ were feeling bad, my first duty would be to cheer him/her up.
____ 2. I feel that I can confide in __________ about virtually everything.
____ 3. I find it easy to ignore __________'s faults.
____ 4. I would do almost anything for __________.
____ 5. I feel very possessive toward __________.
____ 6. If I could never be with __________, I would feel miserable.
____ 7. If I were lonely, my first thought would be to seek __________ out.
____ 8. One of my primary concerns is __________'s welfare.
____ 9. I would forgive __________ for practically anything.
____ 10. I feel responsible for __________'s well-being.
____ 11. When I am with __________, I spend a good deal of time just looking at him/her.
____ 12. I would greatly enjoy being confided in by __________.
____ 13. It would be hard for me to get along without __________.

Now rate the person on the following statements, using the same rating scale.

Liking Scale

____ 1. When I am with __________, we almost always are in the same mood.
____ 2. I think that __________ is unusually well adjusted.

(continued)

your feelings about that person. High scores on both scales are an indication of love. This supports the notion that if you love someone, you also like him or her. If the liking score is significantly higher than the love score, it may be more of a "liking" relationship.

Among those whom I like or admire, I can find no common denominator, but among those whom I love, I can: all of them make me laugh.

W. H. AUDEN

Fear, Anxiety, and Attraction

Several interesting studies have been conducted that suggest that fear and anxiety may intensify interpersonal attraction. In one seminal study, an attractive young woman interviewed male college students as they walked across a creaky, scary suspension bridge that spanned a deep gorge. The same woman interviewed other students as they crossed a sturdy bridge that rested only a few feet above the ground.

✦ TABLE 11.1 ✦ Continued

____ 3. I would highly recommend __________ for a responsible job.
____ 4. In my opinion, __________ is an exceptionally mature person.
____ 5. I have great confidence in __________'s good judgment.
____ 6. Most people would react favorably to __________ after a brief acquaintance.
____ 7. I think that __________ and I are quite similar to one another.
____ 8. I would vote for __________ in a class or group election.
____ 9. I think that __________ is one of those people who quickly wins respect.
____ 10. I feel that __________ is an exceptionally intelligent person.
____ 11. __________ is one of the most likable people I know.
____ 12. __________ is the sort of person whom I myself would like to be.
____ 13. It seems to me that it is very easy for __________ to gain admiration.

Scoring:
Add up the total points separately for the liking and loving scale. Rubin (1973) obtained the following average love and liking scores for dating partners and same-sex friends:

	Women	**Men**
Love for partner	90.57	90.44
Liking for partner	89.10	85.30
Love for friend	64.79	54.47
Liking for friend	80.21	78.38

You can compare the score you obtained with the scores above to see whether it corresponds more closely to the average liking or loving score. For example, if you were a male rating a partner you were dating you would compare the score you obtained above to the average scores for a male love for a partner (90.44) versus liking for a partner (85.30).

SOURCE: From Z. Rubin (1973). Reprinted with permission.

The students on the scary bridge subsequently rated the woman as more attractive than those who were crossing the sturdy bridge. The attractive woman gave all the subjects her telephone number in case they later had questions about the experiment. The students on the scary bridge were more likely to telephone the woman (Dutton & Aron, 1974). Hence, the anxiety evoked by the suspension bridge appeared to increase the men's attraction toward the woman.

Several other studies have confirmed that unpleasant arousal and adversity do indeed increase interpersonal attraction between men and women. For example, couples from mixed religious backgrounds report stronger degrees of romantic love than those from similar religious backgrounds. It appears that the conflicts arising from a mixed religious background, including those among other family members, created arousal that strengthened the couple's attraction to one another (Rubin, 1973). This same premise was presented hundreds of years ago when the 1st-century Roman poet Ovid wrote a treatise on romance. In that work, he advised men, among other things, to take their dates to the Colosseum to watch gladiators fight because the arousal from that experience would certainly increase their romantic passion.

These findings have implications for dating couples today. Sharing a scary or arousing experience with your date should increase mutual attraction. How might you arrange such an experience? Going to a horror movie, riding the scariest rides at an amusement park, or even attending an exciting athletic contest that involves a great deal of physical contact may all do the trick.

Choosing a Mate

Over 90% of people in the United States eventually marry. How do almost all of us eventually pair up with someone? From the previous discussion of interpersonal attraction, you would correctly guess that we seek someone who is very similar to ourselves. Numerous studies have shown that married couples are very similar in age, religion, education, race, and ethnic background. There is even a moderate correlation of attitudes and opinions. Married couples tend to have similar heights, weights, IQ's, and even eye color. One study suggested that the more similar the personality characteristics, the more solid the marriage (Kim, Martin, & Martin, 1989).

What characteristics would you look for in a prospective mate? Men and women largely agree on the qualities that are most important (Buss, Abbott, Angleitner, & Asherian, 1990). Table 11.2 ranks the desired characteristics of potential mates for American men and women. Note the differences in order in which men and women rank some of these characteristics. As you might suspect, men rate physical attractiveness higher than women whereas being ambitious is more important to women than to men.

Communicating with Others

The ability to communicate effectively with others is one of the most important skills that we can acquire. It can literally "make or break" your chances for success in the workplace and in your marriage. Success in our personal relationships with friends and acquaintances is also grounded in our ability to communicate effectively.

APPLICATIONS

Good communication involves two components: good talking and good listening.

Being a Good Talker

Almost everyone likes to talk, but only a relative few are really good at it. Do you think that you are a good talker? Most people believe they are even though many of those people are mistaken. Talking and communicating are *not* the same thing. Talking is effective only if the talker clearly conveys and the listener attends to and understands what is being said. There are several essential factors for effective communication when you are talking (Fontana, 1990):

✦ TABLE 11.2 ✦ Ranking of Desired Characteristics of Potential Mates for American Men and Women

A ranking of 1 is most important and 18 is least important.

Characteristic	Rank Males	Rank Females
Mutual attraction–love	1	1
Emotional stability and maturity	2	2
Dependable character	3	3
Pleasing disposition	4	4
Education and intelligence	5	5
Good health	6	9
Good looks	7	13
Sociability	8	8
Desire for home and children	9	7
Refinement, neatness	10	12
Ambition and industriousness	11	6
Similar education	12	10
Good cook & housekeeper	13	16
Favorable social status or rating	14	14
Similar religious background	15	15
Good financial prospect	16	11
Chastity (no prior sexual intercourse)	17	18
Similar political background	18	17

SOURCE: Taken from Buss et al., *Journal of Cross-Cultural Psychology,* Vol. 21, p. 19, Copyright © 1990 by Sage Publications, Inc. Reprinted with permission of Sage Publications, Inc.

- ✦ Use of humor. Someone is more likely to listen to what you are saying if you use humor while talking. This does not necessarily mean telling jokes. Interspersing humorous remarks or short witticisms in your speech can greatly facilitate the communication process. Is there anything more tiresome than listening to a humorless individual? The ability to laugh at ourselves when appropriate can also be helpful. The occasional self-deprecating remark shows others that we do not take ourselves too seriously or place ourselves above others and that we accept our fallibility.
- ✦ Keeping it interesting. Everyone has been on the receiving end of boring conversation, and knows how difficult it is to pay attention and maintain an interest under these circumstances. It is the responsibility of the talker to make certain that what is being said is of relevance and interest to the listener. A good talker is one who is acutely aware of the other person's interests and concerns. Boring talkers are often clueless about the effects they are having on the listener, and are either unaware of or indifferent to the social signals that bored

listeners emit. They may prattle on for hours, seemingly unaware of the deadly and mind-numbing effects on their listener. These signals often include the following: fidgeting, exaggerated sighs, glancing at one's watch or the door, angry looks, sharp intakes and exhalations of breath, casting eyes upwards, restless hand and body movements, nervous clearing of the throat, and repeated but unsuccessful attempts to break into the conversation. Those who are bored often make half-finished statements, such as, "'Well, I really must be . . . ,' 'Okay then, can we talk about that next time we . . . ?' 'It's a pity I haven't time to . . .'." (Fontana, 1990, p. 37). On the other hand, positive social signals that indicate your discussion is interesting to the listener include the following: eye contact, an alert expression, leaning forward, smiles, unforced laughter, nods, and gestures. When you are talking, be alert for both negative and positive signals.

- Don't monopolize the conversation. Effective communication between two or more people includes the opportunity for everyone to have a chance to talk. This sounds simple enough, but frequently it does not happen. The next time that you are in a group engaged in conversation, note how equally the talk time is distributed between each member. Often, one or more individuals will dominate the conversation. These same individuals often display that irritating habit of interrupting someone in mid-sentence or finishing someone's sentence for the speaker. It appears that people who dominate conversations either are unaware of what they are doing or feel the importance of their personal commentary justifies their behavior. Nevertheless, there is no excuse for dominating a conversation that inevitably stifles effective communication.
- Talk purposefully. Effective talkers stay focused on the topic. They avoid rambling and meandering from topic to topic. How often have you asked someone a question only to listen to a 5-minute answer that addressed everything except the question you asked? On the other hand, effective talkers are not so rigid that they refuse to follow new directions in the conversation. They carefully listen to questions and address them directly. Fontana notes that "questions are often an excellent guide to what the other person is really thinking or really interested in or really worried about" (Fontana, 1990, p. 50).
- Avoid annoying mannerisms. Constant repetition of such expressions as "ya' know," "I mean," "right?" and "okay?" is extremely distracting to even the most patient listener. I once had an accountant who frequently called me about tax matters. This highly educated and otherwise extremely articulate person would interject "Ya' know what I mean?" between almost every sentence. As a result, I had great difficulty following her conversation and often wanted to end it as quickly as possible. Equally distracting is the habit of fiddling with eyeglasses, pencils, or other objects while talking. This author is guilty of the latter and can attest to what a hard habit it is to break.
- Speak rapidly. Do you notice how your mind tends to drift when someone is speaking to you ever so s-l-o-w-l-y? A rapid rate of speech is more effective as it implies expertise, intelligence, confidence, and enthusiasm. Studies have shown that advertisements that were speeded up 25% better held the listener's attention and were perceived as more persuasive. A good indicator that you are speaking too slowly occurs when other people finish your sentences for you or when they nod in agreement before you get to the point of your statement.

Mary Mitchell (1998), in her book on making a good first impression, offers the following additional conversational Dos and Don'ts:

- Do not tell any joke that takes more than 30 seconds to complete. If you have ever been trapped listening to a joke that goes on and on before the punch line, you know exactly what I mean. Jokes that are off-color or involve race or ethnicity should always be avoided.
- Avoid certain topics. Your health, politics, and religion should be at the top of this list.
- Stand upright, but not at attention.
- Do not fold your arms while listening.
- Keep your hands away from your face.
- Do not shift your weight from leg to leg. This gives the impression that you are uncomfortable and want to escape as quickly as possible.

No one would talk much in society, if he knew how often he misunderstands others.

GOETHE
Elective Affinities

Making Small Talk

Many of the conversations that we engage in daily fall into the nonsubstantive "small talk" category. Small talk constitutes the little banter or chitchat that individuals regularly use to serve as the conversational grease that can lead into more meaningful conversations. When we meet someone for the first time at a party, we begin interacting in this manner. Individuals who are shy or have a social phobia are very uncomfortable at the prospect of engaging in such verbal banter.

Small talk *is* a big deal. It serves the important purpose of getting individuals to begin interacting with one another. Bernardo Carducci has written a useful book entitled *The Pocket Guide to Making Successful Small Talk* (1999). He notes that every great love story and every major business deal began with small talk during the initial contact. Carducci has worked with many shy individuals to help them learn the art of small talk and has offered the following suggestions:

- Start with a simple declaration. Make the opening remark by stating a simple declaration such as, "It sure is hot today." This shows the other person that you are open to conversation. The opening declaration does not have to be some deep philosophical comment or discourse. In fact, you would probably be put off by a stranger who began a conversation in such a manner.
- Introduce yourself. Be specific. Give the other person some personal information about yourself. Do not say, "I work in industry." Instead say, "I work in robotics and artificial intelligence." This provides the other person with an opportunity to ask for more specifics or to comment on your profession.
- Select a topic others can relate to. A discussion about the properties of subatomic particles or nuclear fission is going to scare off most conversationalists. Talk about a movie that you saw or a great restaurant that you recently discovered. Do not be concerned with making brilliant conversation. Small talk consists of discussions about relatively insignificant matters.
- Associate the topic with other subjects. For example, relate the movie you saw to a play with the same theme. This will keep the conversation moving.
- Pay attention. Do not watch other people moving around the room while the person is speaking to you. It is especially important to pay attention and look

Eye contact is important, especially when first meeting someone. This person is shaking hands, but his gaze tells us that he is interested in things other than the person he is meeting.

Good listening skills are very important in interpersonal interactions.

the person in the eye when first introduced. Avoid what politicians used to call the "Dirksen handshake," behavior named after a Washington politician who was infamous for shaking someone's hand at a party while surveying the room for someone who was more important or more interesting to talk to.

✦ End the conversation gracefully. Have you ever been talking to someone and have that person walk off after an awkward pause? People with poor skills in small talk often do not know how to end a conversation gracefully. A simple statement like "It has been nice talking to you" or "I hope we will meet again" allows you to make a graceful exit.

Being a Good Listener

In the previous chapter I briefly discussed the importance of being a good listener when in a counseling situation. The importance of listening extends well beyond the therapeutic relationship, however. Effective listening is one of the most critical skills that you should acquire in order to improve your everyday interactions.

There is a distinction between hearing and listening. We "hear" a train go by. We "listen" when we actively seek to obtain information. It involves *attending to* and *processing* what is heard. As with so many other aspects of human interaction, many people think they are good at listening but few truly are. How often have you experienced a situation where you are talking and notice that the other individuals can hardly wait for you to finish so that they can talk? Have you noticed how often individuals ask you a question that is merely a thinly disguised excuse for them to begin talking about their own concerns or interests? Unfortunately, we often notice these shortcomings in others while being oblivious to the fact that we do the same thing ourselves.

The following are several important rules for effective listening:

✦ Pay attention. It sounds simple, but it is one of the most commonly violated rules of effective listening. When individuals speak to you, stop what you are doing and give them your full attention. When people enter my office at the university, I immediately try to stop whatever I am working on, turn my chair to face them directly (rather than merely turning my head in their direction), set aside whatever I am working on, and give the visitors my full and undivided attention. Body language, such as leaning toward the other person or maintaining good eye contact, also communicates your interest in what is being said. I will elaborate further on the role of nonverbal communication later in this chapter.

- Do not interrupt. Resist the urge to interrupt someone in the middle of a sentence or thought. Studies indicate that men are much more likely to do this to women than vice versa. Do not anticipate what other people are going to say and attempt to complete their thoughts for them. Allow moments of silence while other persons collect their thoughts and find a way to express them. Sometimes people feel uncomfortable at any momentary lapse in a conversation and cannot resist the urge to fill the gap with their own talking. This impulse can have a deadening effect on conversation.
- Attend to nonverbal cues. Being a good listener includes being a good observer. You can obtain a great deal of information from people's gestures, body posture, facial gestures, amount of eye contact, position of the body, and facial expressions. Are they speaking to you with their arms folded and leaning slightly backward? If so, this posture communicates their feelings and attitudes toward you. Also, be attentive to qualities of voice such as loudness, pitch, rate of speech, hesitations, and silences. They are all instructive of what the person is communicating. Again, I will discuss nonverbal communication in greater detail in a later section.
- Be empathetic. You will recall that empathy is the ability to share in another person's emotions, thoughts, or feelings. In chapter 10 I noted that empathy is the single most important characteristic in a counselor. It is also a significant factor in being a good listener. This is not surprising because a skilled counselor is, in fact, a skilled listener. Put yourself in other people's shoes while you are listening so that you can better understand how they see a situation.
- Keep an open mind. Resist the urge to make hasty judgments about what the person is saying. Avoid being too quick to disagree, criticize, or reject what is being said. Be patient and listen to the entire message before jumping to any conclusions. We have all been hasty in our judgments as listeners, and it can have injurious results. A good rule is, when in doubt, suspend judgment.
- Reflect what is being said. Have you ever talked with someone who listened stone-faced and without any response? Disconcerting, isn't it? Effective listeners can communicate that they understand what the talker has said by verbally reflecting the ideas and feelings being communicated. **Reflecting** involves restating the important parts of a message in your own words. Reflecting entails saying things like "In other words, you are saying that . . . "; "You mean . . . "; or "I understand your feeling that. . . ." This approach also helps to clarify information and correct any misunderstandings that you may have because the speaker will confirm whether or not your reflections are accurate.

Effective listening is an acquired skill. If you want to be good at it, you will have to practice doing it. It is a lot easier to be a talker than a listener, a situation that probably accounts for why we have so many "good" talkers in the world and so few good listeners. I cannot overemphasize how important effective listening skills are in both your personal and professional life. There are not many jobs where being a poor listener is a desired characteristic. One of the greatest compliments I can receive is when a troubled student or colleague confides in me, "You are a really good listener."

"Listen. I've *tried* to communicate with him, but he's like a broken record: 'None of your bee's wax, none of your bee's wax.'"

Reflective listening involves restating the important parts of the message that you are hearing and not just responding in a repetitive fashion.

Information Transmission—Rumors Revisited

Among all the world's races . . . Americans are the most prone to misinformation. This is not a consequence of any special preference for mendacity. . . . It is rather that so much of what they themselves believe is wrong.

JOHN KENNETH GALBRAITH

Imagine that a fellow student comes to you and relays a rumor that one of the female physics professors on campus was being fired by the vice chancellor because the department chair had found out about her having a romantic relationship with a freshman male student who came from a prominent family. Now imagine that you pass this information along to your closest friends, who in turn inform several of their friends. Would the tale be correctly relayed to the others?

One interesting aspect of communication is what occurs when information is transmitted or "passed along" from one individual to another in a repetitive fashion. Some of the earliest research in this area was done during and after World War II (Allport & Postman, 1947). Social psychologists were interested in this communication process because of the distortions that were observed when information was passed sequentially from individual to individual. Perhaps you recall the children's party game, often known as "telephone," where 1 person gives a brief message to another individual, who passes it down the line. Usually after 6 or 7 people repeat the message, the subsequent message bears little resemblance to the original communication.

I once had an eye-opening experience along these lines. Several years ago while I was lecturing to a class on the topic of information transmission and rumors,

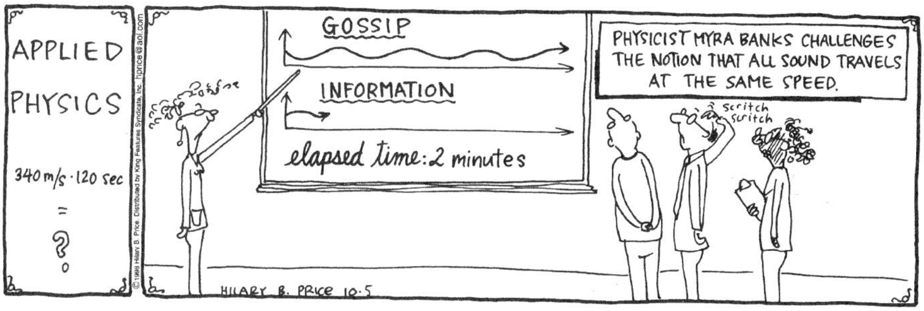

Information gets distorted as it passes from individual to individual. It may also appear that such distorted information travels faster than normal.

I asked the class to be candid and tell me any rumors that they had heard about me recently. I was quite surprised to hear that rumors were circulating that: (a) I was getting divorced from my wife; (b) I was studying at night to become a minister; and (c) I had a compulsive gambling problem. I thought it would be interesting to trace back each of these rumors, see how they got started, and determine how various distortions had entered into the stories as they passed from student to student.

This is precisely what the social psychologists did during their studies of rumor transmissions. Information becomes distorted in certain systematic ways as it is passed from individual to individual. Three general processes occur:

1. Sharpening. As a message is passed along, some parts of it become selectively accentuated in the retelling. That is, certain aspects of the story are very salient and are always part of the retelling. Which aspects are sharpened depends on several factors, including the interests, motives, and emotions of the individual doing the retelling. In the story about the professor who was fired, what aspects of the story do you think might be sharpened and why?
2. Leveling. Certain aspects of messages are also dropped from the original message. There are several reasons why this may occur, including misunderstanding the original facts, information that was not heard or understood, or aspects of the message that were of little interest. In addition, certain aspects of a lengthy message may simply be forgotten in the retelling. Are there some relatively unimportant aspects in the previous story that would likely be dropped in the retelling?
3. Assimilation. Messages become altered in the retelling in order to fit the beliefs and biases of the person telling the story. Stereotypes also can alter the story as can information that does not seem to fit logically. For example, in the above story, the female physics professor might become a male physics professor in the retelling, owing to the prevalent number of male professors in general and the number of male physicists in particular. This gender change would also fit our stereotype that male professors are more likely to initiate a romantic relationship with a student than a female professor, all in contradiction to the actual facts in the original rumor.

All three of these factors are at work in selectively altering a message as it gets retold. Long messages typically become shorter as both the sender and receiver make selective changes in content due to their needs, values, biases, fears, expectations, and prejudices. Be aware that the next rumor you hear and prepare to pass along has likely already been distorted by the factors of sharpening, leveling, and assimilation.

Nonverbal Communication

When we communicate with others, we choose our words carefully because we believe that the verbal component is the most important factor. Nevertheless, the individuals with whom we are communicating are probably directing their attention to factors other than just our words.

We usually find ourselves in situations where we cannot or should not freely verbalize our true feelings. In communicating with others, we often say things that we think they want to hear rather than what we feel. When meeting someone we personally dislike, we try to disguise our dislike by carrying on a conversation that hides our true feelings. Oftentimes, though, our actions speak louder than our words. In fact, the emotional impact of our verbal message may depend very little on the words we speak. One study found that the emotional impact of a communication is influenced only 7% by the actual words spoken. In contrast, 38% of the emotional impact comes from what the researcher calls the vocal message. This vocal message includes tone of voice, vocal inflections, stress on certain words, pronunciation, and the length and frequency of pauses. Another 55% of the emotional effect comes from other nonverbal behavior such as facial expressions, posture, body movements, gestures, eye contact, and so forth (Mehrabian, 1986). What happens when the verbal message and the nonverbal behavior do not match? The nonverbal message is almost invariably the one to which people pay the most attention (Mehrabian, 1986). Furthermore, these nonverbal behaviors are extremely difficult, if not impossible, to control (DePaulo, 1992). Most of us are very astute at picking up on these nonverbal cues, which Baron and Byrne (1997) describe as a "silent but eloquent language" (p. 38). Let's examine in further detail some of the channels through which we communicate nonverbally. As you read this section, you should keep in mind the importance of cultural differences in all nonverbal communication. As I will note, what is perceived as a positive form of nonverbal communication in one culture is often viewed negatively in other cultures.

The face is the image of the soul.

CICERO

- Facial expressions. In the chapter on emotions I described how facial expressions play an important role in communicating how we feel, particularly since many facial expressions are universal across different cultures and nationalities.
- Eye contact. In chapter 2 I discussed the importance of being able to see into another individual's eyes. People who wear dark or mirrored glasses are often perceived as less friendly and less open in their relations with others. As noted previously, we perceive the amount of pupil dilation in another person's eyes as an indication of his or her attraction or interest in us. The amount of eye contact is also an important nonverbal cue. As a general rule, we interpret good eye contact as a sign of liking or friendliness (Kleinke, 1986). On the other hand, people who avoid our gaze are often perceived as unfriendly, shy, or showing a dislike for us. If you have ever attempted to carry on a conversation with someone who refuses to maintain eye contact, you know how disconcerting it is. We gaze into other people's eyes to measure their interest in what we are saying. Too much eye contact, however, can have a negative effect. Staring

unremittingly at another individual is almost always interpreted as a sign of anger or hostility. If you have ever had a stranger stare at you, then you know how extremely uncomfortable this can be. In downtown Denver a few years ago, one motorist shot and killed another motorist who had pulled up beside his car and stared at him. Even animals interpret staring as a sign of anger or hostility. As I mentioned in a previous chapter, one is ill advised to stare at an angry, barking dog because it can elicit increased hostility in the animal. Cultural factors also play an important role in eye contact. For the Japanese it is a sign of disrespect to look a superior in the eye. As a result, when Japanese employees do not look at American managers in the eye, the managers may suspect the subordinates of being evasive.

- ✦ Body movements, gestures, and posture. One way that we communicate with others is through **body language,** which includes the way we move our hands, arms, or legs, as well as the position, posture, and movement of our bodies. Body language frequently offers cues about another person's emotional state. For example, we attribute a high incidence of self-touching, rubbing, or scratching to either nervousness or emotional arousal. We also interpret body language as an indication of how much someone likes or dislikes us. Chris Kleinke (1986) reported that college students have more than 100 nonverbal behaviors categorized in terms of how much liking or disliking the behaviors communicate. Nonverbal behaviors that signal liking include touching or moving closer, smiling, nodding one's head, using expressive hand gestures, opening the eyes or raising the eyebrows, leaning toward another person, and orienting one's body so that it is facing the other person. Behaviors that indicate disliking include frowning, moving away, yawning, sneering, shaking one's head, and grooming one's self (Kleinke, 1986).

One study suggested that even the way we sit communicates feelings of warmth and empathy. College students viewed videotapes of counselors who sat with their arms and legs in different positions. Those who sat with their arms resting on the arms of their chair or with their hands in their lap were judged as the warmest and most empathic. In addition, those who sat with both feet on the floor or with their legs crossed at the knees or ankles were also judged favorably. Conversely, counselors who sat with arms crossed or in an informal, open-leg posture, either with the ankle of one leg resting on the knee of the other or with one foot propped on a chair and the other on the floor, were judged as coldest and least empathic (Smith-Hanen, 1977). Most of us ignore body language in our interactions with others. Nevertheless, its influence on feelings of liking and affection is far reaching. Studies have demonstrated that body language greatly affects social interactions, marital relationships, counseling sessions, and even tipping behavior. This latter phenomenon was demonstrated in a study in which servers would either stand upright or squat down next to customers while taking drink orders (Lynn & Mynier, 1993). It was believed that customers would interpret squatting down as a sign of friendliness because that posture would improve eye contact and bring servers physically closer to their customers. As predicted, the servers who squatted down received larger tips than did those who remained standing. Chris Kleinke (1986) goes so far as to recommend a course on body language as a valuable tool for teaching social skills.

- Touch. We communicate nonverbally with others constantly through touch. The English language is replete with phrases using the word. We are "touched" by a sad movie, or we find a story very "touching." The phone company advises us to "reach out and touch someone," and we describe a person as an "easy touch." Touching is one of the most intimate forms of physical closeness and communicates different meanings depending on who does the touching and under what circumstances it occurs. Touch can signal affection, sexual interest, dominance, caring, or even aggression. The message that touching conveys will depend on how gentle or rough the touch, how brief or prolonged the contact, the context in which the touch takes place, whether it comes from a friend or a stranger, and whether it is given by a member of the same or opposite sex. In circumstances where touching is considered acceptable, it generally has positive results. This effect was illustrated by yet another study with waitresses working in restaurants (Crusco & Wetzel, 1984). Waitresses who touched their customers briefly while giving change received significantly larger tips than those who refrained from touching. Several studies have shown that some fairly complicated rules have evolved about who touches whom. With young couples, males are more likely to touch females whereas the opposite is true among couples in their 40s or older. Touching is also an indicator of status and dominance. A higher status individual feels free to touch a lower status person, but the opposite rarely occurs. Similarly, a person in a position of power is far more likely to touch those with less power than vice versa. A boss can freely touch workers, but workers feel uncomfortable in reciprocating the gesture. Of course, cultural factors also play an important role in touching. One psychologist watched people engaged in conversation in coffee shops at various locations in different countries and counted the number of times that one person touched another during a 1-hour period (Jourard, 1966). He observed the following number of touches: 180 for San Juan, Puerto Rico; 110 for Paris; 2 for Gainesville, Florida; and 0 for London.
- Voice. We often communicate a great deal by the speaking patterns we use and the tone of our voice. These features of the voice, called **paralanguage,** communicate messages above and beyond that of the words themselves. Psychologists describe 4 components of speech that serve as communicators: (1) *voice qualities* that include the resonance of the voice and how we articulate our words, (2) *vocal characterizers* that include sounds like laughing, crying, coughing, or belching, (3) *voice qualifiers* that reflect the intensity of sounds and any accents used, and (4) *vocal segregates* that are the sounds we use between words or sentences, such as "um," "ah," or "uh huh." We can vary these 4 components to communicate a range of feelings or emotions without changing the words we use. Demonstrate this to yourself by reciting the alphabet in a way to denote anger, sadness, or happiness. In normal speech we speak with a high pitch, fast pace, and moderate loudness. When we are sad or depressed, we speak slower and usually in a softer, lower pitch. In chapter 7 I discussed how voice qualities change when a person is lying. You probably have experienced speaking with individuals on the telephone and, from these cues, created an image of their personality and their appearance. If you are like me, you are often surprised to find how "different" these people actually appear when you finally meet. Research has shown that we hold certain stereotypes about people

based on characteristics of their voice (Addington, 1968). For example, men with "breathiness" in their voice are seen as young and artistic whereas women with this voice quality are seen as pretty, feminine, petite, high-strung, and shallow. People with flat voices are seen as masculine, sluggish, and cold. A nasal voice is nearly always perceived as undesirable. Men with tense voices are perceived as older, unyielding, and cantankerous whereas women with a similar voice are seen as young, emotional, high-strung, and less intelligent. Fast-paced speaking results in a perception of animation and extroversion in both men and women. Men with high-pitched voices are seen as dynamic, feminine, and artistic. As you can see from these findings, your voice is going to communicate a great deal about you regardless of the words you choose.

- Personal space. We also communicate with others by the closeness with which we approach them during interactions. Anthropologist E. T. Hall conducted the seminal research in this area (Hall, 1966). He described four distinct "personal distances" that people prefer to have when interacting with others. You might imagine these as imaginary circles around a person during interpersonal interactions. *Intimate distance* extends from 0 to approximately 18 inches. We reserve this space for our parents, children, intimate friends, and lovers. We feel uncomfortable if strangers invade this intimate personal space although we will allow professionals, such as doctors, dentists, and nurses, to come this close. We often tell people that we dislike to "get out of my face," which is a direct reference to someone invading our intimate space. *Personal distance* extends from about 1 to 4 feet around our body. This is usually the zone in which we have personal conversations with close friends. If a stranger invades this space, people typically feel uneasy and will defend this space to the extent that it is possible. Sometimes, in crowded areas such as a bus, elevator, or train, we are forced to sit or stand very close to strangers. Often individuals in these situations will avoid eye contact. *Social distance* extends from 4 to 10 feet beyond our body and is used for impersonal business and casual conversations. We use this space to keep strangers and people with whom we are not close "at arm's length." Experiment by trying to have a personal or intimate conversation with a close friend at this distance and notice how odd it feels. *Public distance* extends out 10 feet and beyond. We use this distance when speaking to a crowd, watching a play, or observing an athletic event. Conducting private or personal business at such a distance is impossible and usually considered very inappropriate. The distance at which we stand from others can be very revealing. One study examined how closely married couples stood to one another. Couples who were in troubled marriages stood significantly farther away from one another during conversations than those who were happy and low in conflict (Crane, Dollahite, Griffin, & Taylor, 1987). The unhappy couples were literally distancing themselves from each other. Interesting ethnic differences are apparent in the amount of personal space that individuals feel comfortable with. Americans, Germans, and English like more distance while Arabs, Greeks, Latin Americans, and French prefer to interact at closer distances. If you have visited France or Latin America, for example, you may have noticed the "dance" that often takes place between a native and an American as they try and find a comfortable distance from which to communicate. Typically, the native is constantly advancing as the American is retreating.

APPLICATIONS: Effective Nonverbal Communication

Recall the findings that the emotional impact of a communication is influenced only 7% by the actual words used in speaking. The remaining 93% comes from the nonverbal aspects of what is said. Let's summarize some things that can be done to utilize our nonverbal communication skills.

- Maintain good eye contact but not "too good." Staring unremittingly into someone's eyes as he or she speaks can be unnerving. Be conscious of ethnic differences. Some cultures believe that it is disrespectful to maintain eye contact while speaking, and others interpret it as a sign of hostility. For example, Koreans avoid eye contact as a gesture of respect. Many Asian cultures avoid eye contact during conversations, and it should not be interpreted as a lack of interest.
- Use body language effectively and positively. When interacting with another, move closer and lean your body toward the person. Smile, nod your head at appropriate times, use expressive hand gestures, and orient your body so that it is directly facing the person you are interacting with.
- Speak fairly rapidly and modulate your voice with a variety of intensities and inflections.
- Use the power of touch, but do so carefully. Be aware that strangers usually do not like uninvited touch. As a general rule, men do not like to be touched by other men. However, it can be an effective way to communicate that you care to someone with whom you are close. Be sensitive to how others react to your touch.
- Respect another's personal space. Do not move closer than about 4 feet unless you are a close personal friend. Be aware of cultural differences in what constitutes acceptable personal space.

First Impressions

Conventional wisdom holds that you never get a second chance to make a first impression. Truer words were never spoken. Numerous studies by social psychologists have shown that we quickly make judgments about others based on impressions that we form in the first few seconds or minutes after we meet them. The seminal research in this area was conducted over 50 years ago (Asch, 1946). One group of subjects was told the following descriptive terms about a person:

> Intelligent, industrious, impulsive, critical, stubborn, and envious

A second group of subjects was told the person was

> Envious, stubborn, critical, impulsive, industrious, and intelligent

Note that the second list of terms is exactly like the first, only in reverse order. People who heard the first order, with the positive traits listed first, formed a far more positive impression of the person being described than did the subjects who heard the second order. Asch concluded that there is a **primacy effect** at work when we evaluate people. We assign much more importance to the things we learn *earlier* as compared to the things we learn later. Another compelling demonstration of this is given by the following two sentences:

(a) Today I saw Keith steal something from a store. Keith is usually very honest.
(b) Keith is usually very honest. Today I saw Keith steal something from a store.

What is your impression of Keith after reading sentence (a)? If you are like most people, it is unfavorable. We first learn that Keith is a thief and then later learn that this is not his usual behavior. It may appear that someone is trying to excuse his criminal behavior. In sentence (b), we initially learn that Keith is honest but then discover he stole something. Most people attempt to reconcile (or make fit) the information they learn later with the information learned earlier. In the second sentence we learn that a usually honest Keith stole something. We may try to reconcile that fact by imagining that he did so out of desperation, or that he had a justifiable reason for doing so. After all, there must be *some* reason that he suddenly became a thief. The primacy effect causes us to pay the most attention to the information learned earliest and to reconcile any subsequent conflicting evidence with that initial impression.

The primacy effect even impacts our judgments of a person's abilities. In one experiment, participants watched two individuals ("testees") take a 30-item test that was supposedly an intelligence test (Jones, Rock, Shaver, Goethals, & Ward, 1968). One testee scored well on the early questions but did poorly on the later ones. The other testee did poorly on the initial questions but finished with mainly correct answers. Both testees answered 15 of the 30 questions correctly. Participants rated the testee who did well early in the exam as much more intelligent than the testee who started out poorly but finished strongly. When asked to estimate how many items each testee had answered correctly, the participants estimated that the one who started out strongly answered 21 correctly while they estimated that the one who started with several incorrect answers answered only 13 correctly. Remember, both actually answered 15 of the 30 items correctly. This finding shows that looking good early makes much more of an impression than looking good later. Psychologists have subsequently discovered that it is far more difficult to correct an initial bad impression than to destroy one that is initially good.

APPLICATIONS: Making a Good First Impression

You can frequently put these findings to use, such as when you prepare a resumé or job application. Perhaps you have both strong and weak points that you will need to include in your resumé. For instance, you may have good previous job experience and possess job skills relevant to the position you seek. However, you also may have several jobs that you left because of differences with the boss or periods of extended unemployment. In your letter or resumé, list the strong points *first,* in order to take advantage of the primacy effect. In that way, a prospective employer will be more likely to reconcile the later weak points with the positive initial impression.

Most psychologists believe that people form strong impressions within the first 5 minutes, and often much sooner than that. Furthermore, such impressions once formed are extremely resistant to change. Is it fair that someone will form a lasting impression of you after only meeting you for a few minutes? Fair or not, it is a fact of life that will greatly affect your relationships with others. In this section I will describe some of the most important factors that go into making a first impression and suggest ways that you can use them to your own benefit.

In this section I will often refer to Mary Mitchell (1998) who has written a very informative book about the impressions that are formed in the first 5 minutes of meeting someone. She stated that the first time you meet someone, you ". . . step into a bright and unforgiving circle of light. Everything about you is intensified and exaggerated—your manner, gestures, voice, and facial expressions" (Mitchell, 1998, p. 1). When you first meet someone, both danger and opportunity for first impressions abound. You could unwittingly be guilty of any of a long list of potential mistakes. These range from minor irritations to major distractions. Your dress, mannerisms, voice, and even your posture send a message. Awareness of these factors allows you to make minor changes that result in a major difference in the first impression you convey. Because a discussion of each of these factors is well beyond the scope of this book, I will concentrate on the most important factors in making a first impression.

- Appearance. Earlier in this chapter I discussed the importance of physical attractiveness. You will recall that people generally regard those who are physically attractive as highly sociable, dominant, sexually responsive, mentally healthy, intelligent, and socially skilled (Feingold, 1992). Unless you are a male or female fashion model, you probably are not among those blessed with extraordinary physical attractiveness. A great deal of physical attractiveness is genetically determined, and there is nothing you can do to change that. However, each of us can maximize our attractiveness, often in relatively simple ways. Nothing sends out a more immediate first-impression message than dress and grooming. Think about what you notice first when you are introduced to someone. Most likely it is his or her physical attractiveness, much of which is determined by dress and grooming. I can think of several people that I have known personally whose careers, I believe, were seriously impeded by this single factor. I recall a close friend and fellow graduate student who was probably the most articulate and intelligent of anyone in our class. He was a farm boy and insisted on wearing bib overalls everywhere he went. He also cut his own hair and generally presented an extremely unkempt appearance. He confessed to me that this had been a substantial issue with his mentor and other professors at another psychology doctoral program in which he had been enrolled and was finally asked to leave. Similar problems arose in our program and eventually he left without completing the doctoral degree. Although his appearance alone did not derail his education, I have wondered how different his professional career might have been had he complied with suggestions about his appearance.

  Fair or not, for some individuals a compromise in personal values, such as their appearance, may be necessary in order to get that first opportunity. I cannot overemphasize the importance of appearance on the first impression that you make and the effect it can have on your professional success. Dress neatly and appropriately. Shine your shoes. Pay attention to grooming, including such details as clean fingernails. If you are a woman, wear makeup applied in a way to maximize your looks, even if you believe such practices are superficial. Do not

First impressions are important, especially in job interviews.

display your tattoos or body piercings. Use the numerous books and magazines available to assist with developing an attractive and appropriate appearance and style. Refer to the visual illusions described in chapter 2 if you want to appear taller or thinner. There are ways to enhance the appearance that nature gave you.

- ✦ Body language. After physical attractiveness, body language is probably next in importance in the formation of first impressions. Body posture is one of the first things people notice. A person who slouches gives an impression of being depressed or, at least, less alert than someone who sits or stands upright. Remember, the earlier research suggested that (1) if you sit, keep both feet on the floor; (2) if you cross your legs, do so only at the knees or ankles; and (3) do not sit or stand with your arms crossed. Review the earlier section on applications of effective nonverbal communication, paying particular attention to eye contact and personal space. Remember that your body language speaks volumes and you want to make certain it is conveying the correct message.
- ✦ Launching an effective conversation is an important part of making a favorable first impression. Review the earlier suggestions for making effective small talk. When first meeting someone, a favorable impression occurs when you (1) use the person's name if you know it, (2) introduce yourself and accompany it with a firm handshake, (3) give the other person your full attention, (4) turn your body and lean slightly toward the person, and (5) use the person's name in conversation as soon as you can. You become a good conversationalist, which translates into being a good listener, when you (1) give an occasional nod and say "Yes," or "I see," at appropriate times, (2) get the other person to talk by asking questions, (3) follow-up on the information you are given by the other person, (4) avoid controversial subjects whenever possible, (5) never discuss your health, (6) do not be argumentative, and (7) do not brag. Remember, it is the rare individual who does not like to talk about himself or herself. A person who asks others questions about themselves is inevitably perceived as a great conversationalist.

All of these suggestions may sound like common sense, but the fact is that most people are either unaware of the importance of these details or do not care what kind of impression they make. Careful attention to these suggestions will help you make the most positive first impression possible. It can pay rich dividends in social and professional success for a very small investment.

Impression Formation

Obviously, we strive to make a more permanent good impression in our subsequent dealings with people. Social psychologists have examined the role of several factors in this type of long-term **impression management.** Even though everyone makes efforts to accomplish this, most people do so in an unsystematic and haphazard fashion. Oftentimes we lack direct and immediate feedback about the kind of impression we are making. Let's look at the various tactics commonly used and examine the research that shows their effectiveness. These tactics fall into two major categories: (1) **self-enhancement** or our efforts to make ourselves look good and (2) **other-enhancement** or our efforts to make another person feel good in our presence.

APPLICATIONS: Basic Tactics in Impression Formation

Self-Enhancement

- The most common self-enhancement strategy involves trying to improve our physical appearance, through dress, personal grooming, and the use of nonverbal cues. The role these play in first impressions has already been discussed. There are numerous studies documenting that this tactic is indeed effective, at least under certain conditions. For example, women who dress professionally are evaluated more favorably for management positions than women who dress more casually (Forsythe, Drake, & Cox, 1985). Even something as seemingly insignificant as eyewear can be important. One study found people are judged to be more intelligent if they wear glasses (Terry & Krantz, 1993). Similarly, long hair for women or beards on men reduce impressions of intelligence (Terry & Krantz, 1993). Perfume or cologne enhances the impression you make but only if used in moderation (Baron, 1989).
- Emphasizing the positive. A song that was popular when I was young stated "You've got to accentuate the positive, eliminate the negative, latch on to the affirmative, and don't mess with mister in-between." Is this good advice? When trying to impress others should you only dwell on your successes and never mention your failures? Being a braggart is a good shortcut to making a bad impression. On the other hand, understating one's accomplishments will often lead others to question your self-confidence. The secret is your ability to strike a balance between the two. One review of the research in this area recommended a two-pronged strategy: (1) be accurate in presenting yourself to people who can verify your claims; but (2) amplify your successes, within reason and de-emphasize your failures for people who have no way of verifying your claims. In this case, modesty holds little advantage, and self-deprecation is defeating (Kleinke, 1986).
- We all have our faults. Should we be candid and advertise them or keep them to ourselves? As a general rule, do not point out your faults. The most important exception to this rule occurs when you are interacting with someone who already knows your faults. In this circumstance, you will probably be suspected of hiding them. Dale Carnegie (1972) in his well-known book *How to Win Friends and*

Influence People, described how admitting one's faults can actually work to your advantage:

> Say about yourself all the derogatory things you know the other person intends to say—and say them before he has the chance to say them—and you take the wind out of his sails. The chances are a hundred to one that he will then take a generous, forgiving attitude and minimize your mistakes (p. 130).

If you watch political debates during an election year, you will often see candidates take this exact approach to disarm a potential attack from their opponents. Attorneys also use this approach when examining their witnesses in the courtroom. The attorney wants to bring out any potentially damaging information that might affect the witness's credibility before the opposing counsel does. This technique allows the attorney to introduce the negative information in the best possible light and to minimize the impact that the information will have on the jury's deliberations.

Should you use this tactic if you are dating someone who you would like to favorably impress? Research suggests that it is advantageous to admit to some fault or offense in the early stages of a relationship *if* it was your mistake *and if* you are certain the other person will eventually find out (Jones & Gordon, 1980). By confessing early, you might win the other person's sympathy and, at the least, show that you have nothing to hide. If, on the other hand, a negative event occurred that was not your fault, such as a car accident that killed someone, it is best withheld until later. An early confession may be suspected as an attempt to arouse sympathy (Kleinke, 1986).

- Name-dropping. A favorite tactic of some people who want to emphasize their own importance is to call attention to an association with a well-known person or respected group of people. Psychologists call this self-presentation tactic **basking in reflected glory** ("Why yes, just the other day I was talking to the president of the university over lunch about this textbook that I'm writing when the governor dropped by our table to say hello . . ."). This strategy can be effective but only if it is communicated subtly. Unfortunately, subtlety is a characteristic that seems lost on most chronic name-droppers. A similar self-presentation tactic that is often used is that of enhancing one's own affiliations while playing down the quality of other people's affiliations ("I graduated from the University of XXX, which everyone knows has a much stronger academic record than XYZ State University").

Other-Enhancement

Other-enhancement tactics occur when individuals expend efforts to make others feel good in their presence. Let's examine some of the most common strategies used to accomplish this:

- On occasion we all attempt to curry favor by paying another person an unwarranted compliment or by giving false praise. Dale Carnegie in his famous book on influencing people alluded to the "gnawing and unfaltering human hunger for appreciation." We all love to get a compliment, and we frequently use this tactic to make a favorable impression on others. Is it an effective strategy? That depends. An important factor is whether the recipient believes that the compliment or praise is false or sincere. Praise and compliments are often perceived as false when the person making the comments has an ulterior motive (Kleinke, 1986). For instance, if you compliment your boss, a person in a position to give you a raise or promotion, he or she may very well question the sincerity of it. In addition, compliments are most likely perceived as sincere when they reflect qualities the recipient actually possesses. Edward Jones and Camille Wortman (1973) analyzed various strategies for giving compliments and make the following suggestions:

1. Play down the dependence you have on the person you are complimenting ("I'm not just saying this because you are my boss, but . . .").
2. Minimize the appearance of having an ulterior motive by arranging the situation so that the compliment is "overheard" by the recipient or is delivered by a disinterested third party.
3. Do not compliment or praise other people in the recipient's presence.
4. Do not exaggerate the compliment to such an extent that it seems untrue.
5. Include a few neutral or mildly negative evaluations along with the praise or compliments in order to make the positive statements more distinct and believable. For example, you might precede a compliment by saying "I don't always agree with everything you say, but . . ."
6. Use negative comments effectively by placing them *first* in the appraisal and by restricting them to a minor fault that the recipient is willing to admit.
7. Compliment an individual privately, rather than in a group.
8. Do not praise small or insignificant accomplishments.
9. Never structure the compliment such that the recipient feels obligated to repeat the act that generated the compliment.
10. Arrange the situation so that the compliment is spontaneous and unexpected by the recipient.
11. Make the compliment *specific* rather than general. For example, compliment a professor on a specific part of her lecture rather than merely saying, "Good lecture today."
12. Focus compliments on accomplishments, such as, "You did great on that test today," rather than attributes, such as, "You are a really smart person."
13. Focus on *feelings* rather than evaluation. For example "I love your sense of humor" will be received more favorably than "That joke you told today was funny."

The science of giving compliments or praise can be very complicated. Nevertheless, it is important because it is usually the single most important other-enhancement tactic that we use in our attempts to make another person feel good.

> I can live for two months on a good compliment.
>
> **MARK TWAIN**

✦ Doing a favor. Another common tactic used in other-enhancement impression formation is to do a favor for someone whom we are trying to impress. On the surface, this may appear to be an innocuous tactic that would rarely fail. In actuality, doing someone a favor is more complicated than it might appear. As with praise and compliments, it is important that the recipient see the favor as being sincerely given and *not* motivated by the desire for personal gain. For example, if you did an unexpected favor for your boss immediately before raises were determined, your sincerity might be seriously suspect. Favors are always most effective when they are attributed to the *generosity* of the person giving them. We discount favors that appear unintentional or accidental and attribute them to chance (Kleinke, 1986). For example, if a friend gives you a gift out of kindness, you will appreciate it more than if you receive a gift because someone drew your name for a Christmas gift exchange. Favors are most effective in impression formation when the person doing the favor is of *equal or higher status* than the recipient. For example, I would appreciate a favor done for me by the university president much more than he would appreciate one done by a lowly department chair. The *appropriateness* of the favor is also important. Years ago, as department chair, I agreed to write a brief letter requesting a residency extension for a foreign student. After the extension was granted, the student insisted on showing his appreciation by taking my wife and me out to dinner and, very surprisingly, showering us with expensive gifts from his native country. This was a very uncomfortable situation, particularly because these favors seemed completely inappropriate in light of the small effort that I had expended on his behalf. In this case, because showing appreciation in this manner was the student's native custom, we accepted the gifts but later donated them to charity. Another important aspect is that the favor should not subject the recipient to *high costs* or to costs that exceed the favor's value. For example, 5 years ago my daughter's college roommates surprised her with a pet rabbit on her birthday. Since that time, she has had to spend hundreds of dollars on cages, food, bedding, veterinarian care, pet sitters, and housing that accepts pets. Favors are also less effective if the recipient feels obligated to reciprocate. Often invitations to dinner or an event, or even just receiving Christmas cards, can make the recipient feel obligated to reciprocate in kind. When electing to do a favor for someone, you need to take each of these factors into account. Sometimes what you intend as a favor for someone, as a means of ingratiating yourself to him or her, is perceived as something very different.

✦ You learned earlier in this chapter that people are attracted to individuals who are similar to them. Does this mean that if you agree with another person's opinions that he or she will be more favorably impressed than if you disagree? As you have probably guessed by now, it depends: As with compliments and favors, the agreement must be expressed in a way that *minimizes the perception of ulterior motives, maximizes credibility,* and *maximizes reinforcement* (Kleinke, 1986). Let's examine techniques to accomplish each goal. To minimize the perception of an ulterior motive, the agreement should be either overheard by the recipient or communicated by a disinterested third party. For instance, hearing that "John totally agrees with you on that very point" is more credible and less suspicious than if John himself tells you that he agrees. You can also preempt the problem by agreeing with other individuals *before* they express their opinion. Do not agree with someone if you feel strong external pressure to do so and do not agree too frequently. Your agreement will have little credibility in these circumstances. Credibility is increased if you agree on the important issues and disagree, at least mildly, on unimportant ones. Strive to arrange it so that your agreement is maximally reinforcing. Several research studies have revealed that people appreciate agreement more if they have recently been confronted with disagreement. In addition, they are more favorably impressed with someone who changes from disagreement to agreement rather than the reverse (Gerard & Greenbaum, 1962; Stapert & Clore, 1969; Jones & Wein, 1972). Agreement is particularly reinforcing when the recipient senses it as a measure of his or her persuasiveness.

✦ Self-disclosure. When interacting with another person, do you reveal a great deal about yourself? Do you readily express your thoughts and feelings without hesitation or are you cautious about revealing information about yourself? **Self-disclosure** is the act of readily exchanging information with another that refers to one's self, including personal states, disposition, events in the past, and plans for the future. Does self-disclosure form a positive impression about you in the eyes of others? Under certain circumstances, it does. Interestingly, highly personal self-disclosure is more acceptable to others when it comes from a woman as opposed to a man (Derlega & Chaikin, 1976). Men are not liked when they do not disclose anything about themselves but are disliked even more when they disclose too much about themselves. Both men and women are liked best when they disclose some information but not too much (Kleinke & Kahn, 1980). Self-disclosure is more acceptable when it comes from a friend rather than a stranger and when it is directed to someone similar in age (Kleinke, 1986). People particularly prefer someone if they feel the other person has disclosed information out of trust and respect. Kleinke (1986) summarized the research in this area with several suggestions: (1) engage in self-disclosure, but not to an excessive extent; (2) remember that people are more open to hearing self-disclosure from women than from men; and (3) self-disclosure is received most warmly by those who themselves engage in disclosure. In sum, Kleinke (1986) states, "Our goal with people we want to know is to disclose enough about ourselves to build intimacy but not so much as to cause discomfort. Over time, the amount of self-disclosure we can comfortably communicate will grow" (p. 158). Upon revealing the positive and negative consequences of self-disclosure, Anita Kelly and Kevin McKillop (1996) recommend that individuals should self-disclose about a bothersome secret only if they are particularly troubled by it. They recommend that individuals considering self-disclosure of this nature should first scrutinize potential recipients for the ability to *maintain confidentiality* and the ability to *offer helpful insights* about the disclosed information. Only if *both* of these conditions are met should self-disclosure take place. Remember that self-disclosure has the potential to help in impression formation but also has downside risks.

✦ Using people's names. One of the simplest tactics that you can use to enhance impression formation is to *remember and use* people's names. In the chapter on memory, I discussed several mnemonic devices to aid in remembering people's names. Obviously, you will not be able to *use* a person's name if you are unable to recall it. Once you have the memory intact, you should use the name—but do so judiciously. Using people's names is one of the 6 cardinal rules that Dale Carnegie (1972) outlined for getting other people to like you. The other 5, by the way, are showing a genuine interest in the person, smiling, being a good listener, talking about the person's interests, and making the person feel important.

From *Build a Better Life by Stealing Office Supplies* © 1991 United Feature Syndicate

Self-disclosure of information can be beneficial in impression formation, but only if done correctly.

The "ulterior motive" problem also arises here, as it did with doing favors, giving compliments, and agreeing with another person. Name use is not reinforcing if someone is repeatedly using our name and we think it is because they might want some sort of favor. For instance, used-car salespeople often do this to a fault. The question also arises whether to address people on a first or last name basis. Again, different circumstances dictate different strategies. Last names are preferable when addressing someone who you do not know well, is significantly older than you, or has an authoritative position over you. The increasingly popular trend of retail clerks, office receptionists, and other "strangers" to address a customer, client, or patient by the person's first name may be considered rude and unprofessional. In impression formation, the best rule is: If in doubt, use the last name. If people are uncomfortable with this formality, they will let you know. Finally, people are more impressed if you use their names in subsequent encounters than if you use it a few minutes after meeting them. Most of us are fairly good at remembering names for a few minutes but much poorer at long-term retention.

Again, the memory aids discussed in chapter 4 should be helpful for this purpose.

As you can see, impression formation is a complicated business. Is it worth all the effort? Several studies have indicated that use of these techniques can enhance the impressions that we make upon others. The beneficial effects are such that it can make a significant difference in how others form judgments of you and in how they behave toward you. However, success requires the skillful and careful use of the techniques that I have suggested. You should have noted how each tactic can backfire and actually harm impression formation if used incorrectly. I urge you to give these stratagems a try.

SUMMARY

- Interpersonal relationships and interactions with others are an important part of our everyday lives. For diverse and changing reasons, their importance occurs because of our need to affiliate with others, our desire to compare ourselves with others, and the necessity to seek help in achieving our goals.
- Interpersonal attraction is a positive attitude or emotion that we feel for others.
- Attraction is fostered by both proximity and frequency of exposure to another person.
- Physical attractiveness draws us to certain individuals. Although it is unclear precisely what factors constitute this physical attractiveness, recent research suggests that the "average" face is considered the most attractive and that aspects such as height and weight are also factors.
- Physically attractive individuals receive numerous advantages throughout their lives because, generally, they are judged to have many more positive characteristics than less attractive individuals.
- Similarity between individuals is also important in attraction. We seek out similar individuals because they tend to validate our own beliefs and views of the world. We seek similarity in others along several dimensions, including physical and psychological characteristics.
- Reciprocal liking also fosters attraction. In general, we like those who like us.
- Psychologists draw a distinction between liking and loving. Liking involves affection and respect while loving involves more powerful emotional states. At times the distinction between the two becomes indistinct.
- People can foster relationships in several different ways, including arranging situations for greater proximity and exposure between themselves and others, enhancing their physical attractiveness, emphasizing similarities, and engaging in reciprocal liking.
- Fear and anxiety can, under certain circumstances, intensify mutual attraction.
- Most Americans will eventually marry someone very similar to themselves in age, religion, education, race, ethnic background, and other characteristics. However, men and women do differ in terms of desired characteristics of potential mates.
- The ability to communicate effectively is very important. Good communication includes both the ability to talk and to listen.
- To talk effectively you should use humor, keep the conversation interesting, not monopolize the conversation, talk purposefully, avoid annoying mannerisms, and speak somewhat rapidly.
- The ability to make small talk successfully includes starting with a simple declaration, introducing yourself, selecting a relevant topic, associating this topic with other subjects, paying attention, and being careful to end the conversation gracefully.
- To listen effectively you should pay attention, not interrupt, attend to nonverbal cues, be empathetic, keep an open mind, and reflect back to the listener what was said.
- When information is passed from person to person, several distortions occur. Some parts become selectively accentuated while other parts are dropped. The transmitted material reflects the beliefs and biases of the person passing on the information.

- ✦ Nonverbal behavior is a significant part of the communication process, which includes facial expressions, eye contact, voice characteristics, and body movements, such as gestures, posture, and touch.
- ✦ When communicating with others, it is important to be aware of how closely we approach the other person. We use various personal-space distances for different types of communications that are influenced by our ethnic and cultural differences.
- ✦ Rules for effective nonverbal communication include maintaining good eye contact, using positive body language effectively, speaking rapidly, using touch appropriately, and respecting the other person's personal space.
- ✦ First impressions are very important. They are formed very quickly, usually within the first few minutes, and are relatively long lasting. The first things we learn about others form the strongest impression, and the later information becomes reconciled with the former.
- ✦ Rules for making a good first impression include paying attention to your appearance, using body language effectively, and engaging in appropriate and interesting conversation.
- ✦ Making a more permanent positive impression involves the use of impression formation techniques. These techniques include both making yourself look good and making the other person look good. In order to make yourself look good, you should present a good physical appearance while emphasizing the positive qualities about yourself and minimizing your faults.
- ✦ To make others look good, you should make effective use of compliments and praise. Doing someone a favor can be effective, but only under certain circumstances. Similarly, agreeing with others can help make a positive impression if there is no perception of ulterior motives and if credibility and reinforcement of the agreement are maximized.
- ✦ Self-disclosure results in positive impression formation if we disclose just enough about ourselves to build intimacy but not so much as to cause discomfort in the other person.
- ✦ Using people's names helps foster a positive impression. However, unless directed otherwise, address people by their last names, especially if they are in an authoritative position, are significantly older than you, or are someone to whom you are not personally close.

KEY TERMS

affection: liking that is based on how one person relates to another person and that is experienced as emotional warmth and closeness.

affiliation: a desire or motivation to be with others, regardless of whether we like or dislike those others.

attraction: a positive attitude or emotion that we feel toward others.

basking in reflected glory: a self-presentation tactic of one who wants to emphasize his or her own importance by calling attention to an association with a well-known person or respected group of people.

body language: a way of communicating that includes the way we move our hands, arms, or legs, as well as the position, posture, and movement of our bodies.

impression management: the attempt to make a permanent good impression in dealings with people.

matching hypothesis: the desire to associate with others similar to ourselves.

other-enhancement: efforts to make another person feel good in our presence.

paralanguage: features in tone of voice that communicate messages above and beyond that of the words themselves.

physical attractiveness: a combination of facial and bodily characteristics that are perceived as aesthetically pleasant or appealing.

primacy effect: the tendency to assign more importance to the things learned earlier as compared to the things learned later.

proximity: how close things are in space, time, or order.

reciprocal liking: a mutual liking that plays an important role in interpersonal attraction.

reflecting: restating the important parts of a message in your own words.

respect: liking that is based on the characteristics or actions of another person that we admire.

self-disclosure: the act of readily exchanging information with another that refers to one's self, including personal states, disposition, events in the past, and plans for the future.

self-enhancement: efforts to make oneself look good to other people.

12

Attitude Change and Persuasion

Do you have an "attitude"? It would be very strange if you did not. **Attitudes** are defined as *relatively stable beliefs and feelings that predispose us to react to objects, people, and events in certain ways.* We all hold many different attitudes about many different things. For example, you probably have certain attitudes toward such controversial topics as religion, gun control, or abortion. You also may hold attitudes about people who, for instance, have a short or fat body build or have a different skin color. These attitudes shape our beliefs and our feelings.

Origin of Attitudes

Attitude is a little thing that makes a big difference.

UNKNOWN

Where do our attitudes come from? Most people believe that attitudes are rationally derived by carefully thinking about a matter. Even though people do sometimes arrive at attitudes in this manner, psychologists also know that attitudes are often acquired in an *illogical manner.* In many cases, we are unaware of the many different and powerful factors that shape our attitudes. For example, the tendency we all have to conform our behavior can shape our attitudes. "Political correctness," for instance, has influenced the types of topics that most professors feel free to discuss in the classroom. Habits can also affect attitudes. If you are in the habit of getting up and going to bed early, you probably believe that such behavior is appropriate and common. Many attitudes are also shaped by economic self-interest. Wealthy people, for the most part, maintain very different attitudes about taxation compared to poor people. Each economic group has a "vested interest" in this issue that shows up in their attitudes.

You have probably noticed that attitudes for your generation differ from those held by members of both younger and older generations. This is known as the **cohort effect.** Psychologists have found that each age group, or cohort, has had distinct experiences and, consequently, has developed certain viewpoints or perspectives on a variety of matters. The ages between 16 and 24 are especially critical in the formation of a generation's attitudes (Inglehart, 1990). The major political events and social changes that occur during this age period form the attitudes that are carried throughout one's life. Later events, even though historically important, have less effect on a generation's attitudes. For example, the seminal event in my life during this age span was the Vietnam War. The debates, mass demonstrations, and widespread news coverage of this conflict shaped many of the attitudes that I continue to hold today. The pivotal event for my mother during that period of her life was the Great Depression of the 1930s. Consequently, my mother held very strong views about banking and personal finance that I did not share. Some of the key events that influenced generational cohorts include World War II (1940s), the rise of the civil rights movement (1950s–1960s), President Kennedy's assassination (1963), the rebirth of the women's rights movement (1970s), and the legalization of abortion (1973) (Schuman & Scott, 1989). For people currently in the 15 to 24 age range, the terrorist attacks on the World Trade Center and Pentagon will likely be such a seminal event. Quite likely, these events will permanently influence the political philosophy, values, and attitudes that you hold about life in general.

There is a small but growing body of evidence to suggest that attitudes may have, to some degree, a *genetic origin.* The findings that support this surprising contention primarily come from studies of identical twins. Several studies have shown that identical twins who were separated at birth and raised in totally separate environments still hold attitudes more similar to each other than do fraternal (nonidentical) twins reared apart or than do unrelated individuals reared together (Waller, Kojetin, Bouchard, Lykken, & Tellegen, 1990). Identical twins raised in different environments share similar attitudes on topics ranging from interest in religious occupations and activities through job satisfaction (Bouchard, Avery, Keller, & Segal, 1992). If you wonder how genetics could possibly influence attitudes, recall my discussion of the genetic components of personality characteristics in chapter 1. These personality characteristics, or dispositions, could influence attitudes. For example, if you have a genetic disposition toward sadness, this could easily influence whether you are in a positive or negative mood much of the time (George, 1990). A person who is in a negative mood could, in turn, be more likely to possess negative attitudes toward his or her job, different cultural groups, or any number of things. Only further research will define the extent of genetic influences on attitudes. Nevertheless, it is safe to say that the major component of attitudes is most likely learned and not inherited.

Components of Attitudes

Psychologists believe that attitudes consist of three components: the *emotional, cognitive,* and *behavioral components.*

- Emotional component. When we hold a strong attitude about something, there is usually an equally strong emotional reaction attached to it. If a person holds strong views against interracial marriages, the sight of an interracial couple will likely elicit a strong emotional response. If you hold a negative attitude toward a certain type of food, the mere sight or smell of it may elicit an emotional reaction. In earlier chapters I described how certain physiological responses often accompany an emotional response and how psychologists believe classical conditioning is often involved in learned or conditioned emotional responses. A person is not born with an attitude toward interracial couples; it is a learned response. The attitude, whether positive or negative, may be learned directly through exposure to such couples or indirectly through vicarious learning. In **vicarious learning,** a person acquires attitudes by observing the reactions of others. For example, a child may note the attitudes and emotional reactions of his or her parents toward interracial couples and may learn to react in a similar manner. Humans are particularly adroit at observing and acquiring the emotional reactions of other individuals. In addition, the emotional component of attitudes is very resistant to change. It may persist even after the cognitive and behavior components have been altered.
- Cognitive component. Cognitive components refer to what you *know or believe.* For example, your attitude toward a political party is based on what you know or believe about that party, probably as a result of the information and opinions that you have heard or read. People are then reinforced for expressing certain views relative to those attitudes, which further strengthens them. When we are young, we are mainly exposed to the attitudes of our parents and often acquire similar attitudes by imitating or modeling their behavior. Parents are a source of positive reinforcement when their children model attitudes similar to their own. Unfortunately, this process works as well for negative attitudes such as racial stereotypes as it does for positive attitudes.
- Behavioral component. The behavioral component reflects the way our behavior is affected by an attitude. Attitudes do not necessarily dictate behavior,

✦ TABLE 12.1 ✦ Negative Attitudes Toward Overweight Individuals

A psychological test to measure negative attitudes toward overweight individuals. Read each of the statements below, and rate each according to the following scale:

1	Strongly disagree
2	Mildly disagree
3	Neutral
4	Mildly agree
5	Strongly agree

1. Fat people are less sexually attractive than thin people.
2. I would never date a fat person.
3. On average, fat people are lazier than thin people.
4. Fat people only have themselves to blame for their weight.
5. It is disgusting when a fat person wears a bathing suit at the beach.

Scoring:
Add up the total score for the five questions. The higher the score, the stronger the antifat attitude.

SOURCE: Taken from Morrison & O'Connor (1999). *Journal of Social Psychology,* Volume 139, Page 441. Reprinted with permission of Helen Dwight Reid Educational Foundation. Published by Heldref Publications, 1319 18th St., NW, Washington, DC, 20036-1802. Copyright © 1999.

however. We may have strong feelings against a racial group, for instance, and yet not display any overt discriminatory behavior toward individuals in that group. In that case, there may be a strong affective and cognitive component present, but the behavioral component may be absent. In addition, behavior does not always reflect one's attitudes accurately. The fact that an individual behaves kindly toward members of a certain racial group does not mean that the individual holds a positive attitude toward the members. Our behavior is often shaped and influenced by external forces such that it does not accurately reflect how we feel. Earlier I noted the resistance to change of the emotional component. This explains why individuals who changed their way of thinking about a racial group and now behave appropriately toward that group may still experience an emotional response in the presence of group members.

As you can see, these three components of attitudes can function somewhat independently. For this reason, attitudes can be very difficult to measure accurately. Psychologists often attempt to measure attitudes by observing the behavioral component but, as we saw above, these observations often can be misleading. People tend to express their attitudes differently depending on their audience.

Measurement

The most common way to measure attitudes is through the use of psychological scales or tests. Respondents are typically asked to rate how strongly they agree or disagree with a series of statements. Table 12.1 illustrates a typical questionnaire.

This particular questionnaire was designed to measure negative attitudes toward overweight individuals (Morrison & O'Connor, 1999). For this scale, the authors found that men held stronger "antifat" attitudes than women and that those individuals who were biased against overweight people tended to be authoritarian and politically conservative. As expected, individuals who were overweight themselves held fewer antifat attitudes than individuals who were thin or of average weight. Scales such as this have been widely used to measure overt aspects of attitudes. Techniques used to measure the implicit or unconscious aspects of attitudes are discussed later in this chapter.

CHANGING ATTITUDES

> We are chameleons, and our partialities and prejudices change place with an easy and blessed facility, and we are soon wonted to the change and happy in it.
>
> **MARK TWAIN**

One of the central issues in social psychology has been attitude change. Thousands of research studies have been conducted to examine the most effective means of persuading people to change their attitudes. While several useful techniques have been discovered, psychologists have found that, in general, attitudes are often resistant to change. Companies spend billions of dollars trying to change your attitude about purchasing their product. Obviously, we are not influenced by most of these attempts or we would purchase everything that we see advertised. Political candidates also use the latest scientific findings on attitude change in their campaigns to influence the way we vote. The classic book *The Selling of the President* by Joe McGinnis (1988) details the way such techniques have been used in a presidential election. To no surprise, the government leads in the attitude change business by trying to influence you on a variety of topics from paying taxes to participating in the census, wearing seat belts, avoiding cigarettes, and practicing safe sex. Closer to home, each of us also attempts to change other people's attitudes, usually several times each day. I often try to change the attitudes of my students when I give class lectures. I hope to accomplish the same by writing this book. Anytime you argue a point with someone or attempt to persuade someone to do something, you are trying to create an attitude change. In this section I will discuss some specific techniques that social psychologists have discovered are effective in producing attitude changes. By using these techniques, you should be more effective in changing other people's minds. However, remember that attitudes are often resistant to change and there are no surefire techniques that guarantee success. If psychology had discovered all the secrets to changing inappropriate attitudes, societies would not suffer from the problems of stereotyping, prejudice, and intolerance that presently plague us.

Attitude Change through Persuasion

Persuasion is one technique that often produces a change in beliefs or attitudes, but is often popularly considered just a communication process. Researchers at Yale University took this approach both during and after World War II. During the war, the United States government took an intense interest in learning more about wartime propaganda and persuasion to use on its own citizens as well as on its enemies. At home, the government used propaganda extensively to persuade Americans to buy war bonds, to conserve resources such as gasoline, metals, and sugar, and for a variety of other purposes. Abroad, airplanes frequently dropped pamphlets to convince enemy soldiers to surrender and to persuade civilians to overthrow their rulers. Attempts to change attitudes were also made by both sides using frequent and forceful radio broadcasts. Because these attempts proved relatively ineffective, the United States government encouraged further psychological research on the topic.

The Yale researchers subsequently identified 4 factors in the communication process that are important in influencing persuasiveness: (1) the *person doing the communicating,* (2) the *nature of the message* itself, (3) the *medium by which the message is delivered,* and (4) the *audience to whom the message is being delivered.* Let's examine each of these 4 variables in some detail.

The Communicator

Numerous research studies have shown that communicators who are perceived as *credible experts* are better at persuasion than are low-credibility sources. People who come across as knowing what they are talking about, regardless of whether they actually have expertise, are much more persuasive. This is the reason why, for instance, television commercials and mass media advertisements use actors posing as doctors, complete with white laboratory coats and stethoscopes, to sell health-related products. Because we may be suspicious of someone who is obviously trying to persuade us, advertisers often employ what appear to be "hidden cameras" to show "real people" spontaneously endorsing a product. Such testimonials are perceived to be coming from credible and trustworthy individuals with no ulterior motive. Of course, these "real people" are actually trained actors and actresses, delivering a highly structured and rehearsed message rather than an extemporaneous one. As I discussed in chapter 1, such personal testimonials have little value, but their proven effectiveness in persuasion leads to their continued use in advertising. The *prestige and status* of the communicator are also important because we are more susceptible to persuasion by someone we perceive as highly prestigious and powerful than we are by someone who is not. Physically attractive people are also perceived as more persuasive and more credible than less attractive ones (Pratkanis & Aronson, 1992). Advertisers often exploit these perceptions with their messengers. Notice the inordinate number of attractive individuals and celebrities that bring you the product messages in magazines and on television. Advertisers have also discovered that people who speak rapidly are more persuasive than those who speak slowly (Miller, Maruayama, Beaber, & Valone, 1976). A few years ago Federal Express exploited this fact in a well-known television commercial featuring a boss who talked a mile a minute. There is a common misconception that we are distrustful of fast-talking politicians or salespeople, but the research evidence suggests just the contrary. People who talk fast are generally perceived as having more expertise. However, more recent evidence suggests that fast talkers are more persuasive *only* when the speaker's views are *different* from those of the target audience (Smith & Shaffer, 1991). In summary, we can conclude that persuasiveness is increased when speakers are perceived to be attractive, credible, expert, trustworthy, powerful, and unbiased. However, other research suggests that these communicator variables are most important when the message is *not very important* to the listener, and the impact of these variables tends to dissipate quickly (Chaiken, 1987). When the message is more significant to the listener, other variables assume additional importance.

Words, so innocent and powerless as they are, as standing in a dictionary, how potent for good and evil they become in the hands of one who knows how to combine them.

NATHANIEL HAWTHORNE

The Message

Several characteristics of the message itself have proven to be powerful determinants of the persuasiveness of a message. One very important factor is simple *repetition.*

Do you ever wonder why advertisers run the same commercial over and over again, until you think you cannot stand to hear it one more time? It is because research has shown that a message that is repeated several times is more likely to be persuasive. You have probably heard the saying, "If you repeat a lie enough times, people will begin to believe it." This is true not only for lies but also for other messages as well. This is precisely why politicians pick a simple slogan and repeat it on television, radio, billboards, placards, and campaign literature. Repetition breeds familiarity, and we tend to like, and be persuaded by, that with which we are familiar. This is why most people continue to purchase the familiar brand names rather than switch to inexpensive generic or store brands of equal quality. Persuasion is also facilitated by messages that arouse *strong emotions*. However, the specific way in which this occurs is very important. For example, even though cigarette packages contain various warnings that smoking is dangerous to your health, no evidence indicates that these messages persuade people to stop smoking. For emotional messages to be effective, three conditions must be present (Leventhal, 1970): (1) the message must arouse a great deal of fear; (2) the recipient must believe that failure to heed the message will result in terrible outcomes such as disease or death; and (3) the recipient must believe that compliance with the message's recommendation will prevent the fearful outcomes. A message that merely frightens, without showing how to reduce the fear, is usually rejected or ignored by the recipient (Jepson & Chaiken, 1986). Studies have suggested that fear-based messages are particularly effective in changing attitudes related to health behaviors, such as those used to persuade people to exercise more, eat less, and stop smoking.

Are messages that present only one side of an argument more or less persuasive than two-sided messages? It depends. If someone who holds a contrary attitude is receiving the message, it is better to use the two-sided approach. By acknowledging both sides of the argument, the message becomes more persuasive and more difficult for the audience to resist. By presenting both the pro and the con arguments, two-sided messages also make people more resistant to later persuasive arguments against the original message (Lumsdaine & Janis, 1953). You can inoculate people against strong persuasive messages by first exposing them to messages that weakly attack their beliefs and attitudes (McGuire, 1964). Politicians often try to disarm their opponents' messages by doing this very thing.

Is the "soft sell" or the "hard sell" more effective in changing attitudes? Research suggests that we are more readily persuaded by messages that do not appear to be designed to blatantly change our attitudes. For example, messages that are accidentally overheard are more persuasive than those that are delivered directly (Walster & Festinger, 1962). We tend to distrust people who appear to deliberately set out to change our minds on something. This is why you rarely see the "hard-sell" approach in advertising anymore.

> All effective propaganda must be limited to a very few points and must harp on these in slogans until the last member of the public understands. . . . As soon as you sacrifice this slogan and try to be many-sided, the effect will piddle away.
>
> **ADOLF HITLER**
> *Mein Kampf*

The Medium

We are bombarded daily by persuasive messages from a variety of media, including newspapers, magazines, radio, television, videos, movies, and even electronic mail. Which medium is most effective? You probably will not be surprised to learn that the answer is, "It depends." In general, face-to-face messages are more persuasive than those presented through the mass media. It is a lot harder to ignore a salesperson at your front door than on a television commercial. We generally pay more attention to personal messages and give more thought to their content. Obviously, though, the mass media offer the advantage of reaching millions of people. Research suggests that messages delivered via the print media, such as newspapers and magazines, are better when the message is difficult to understand (Lippa, 1994). When the message is simple and easy to comprehend, audio or audiovisual messages are most effective (Chaiken & Eagly, 1983). In addition, the previously discussed communicator variables, such as attractiveness, credibility, likableness, and so forth, vary in their importance depending upon the media format. Richard Lippa (1994) concluded ". . . an attractive, likable, and charismatic speaker is often more persuasive in audio or audiovisual messages, whereas a speaker who is not attractive (but who may be logically convincing) is more persuasive in print messages" (pp. 243–244). He illustrates this finding by citing the first televised presidential debate in 1960 between Richard Nixon and John F. Kennedy. Kennedy was widely perceived to have won the debate based on his tanned, relaxed, and charismatic appearance as compared to Nixon's wooden, pale, perspiring, and swarthy appearance. Studies showed that individuals who either read transcripts of the debate or heard only an audiotape found Nixon's arguments to be much more persuasive. In this instance, style won out over substance since Kennedy subsequently won the 1960 election.

Recently, the state of Florida launched an antismoking campaign aimed at middle- and high-school students. According to the U.S. Centers for Disease Control and Prevention (CDC), smoking rates nationwide among American teenagers increased 50% between 1988 and 1996. The number of youths who started smoking daily before the age of 18 increased by 73% over the same period of time. The CDC estimated that if current trends continued, some 5 million youths eventually will die from smoking-related diseases. To combat this trend, Florida initiated an aggressive, youth-oriented ad campaign, dubbed the "truth campaign," that targeted tobacco companies through billboards and eye-catching commercials. Teenagers helped produce the broadcast and print ads that poked fun at the tobacco industry. The ads included a chubby man lounging in a woman's swimsuit, smoking a cigarette, with the caption, "No wonder tobacco executives have to hide behind sexy models." Another features youngsters making prank calls to tobacco executives. Yet another ad portrayed a chic Academy Awards–like event "in downtown Hades" where an award for the most deaths in a single year is up for grabs among Suicide, Illicit Drugs, Tobacco, and Murder. In the audience are infamous killers such as Adolf Hitler and Josef Stalin. When Tobacco, represented by a clean-cut executive type, wins the award, he exclaims: "I want to thank all you smokers out there. This one is for you." In addition to the ads, Florida also began vigorously enforcing the laws related to smoking age limits. How effective was this approach? Florida experienced the largest annual drop in teen-age smoking in nearly 2 decades. Smoking dropped 19% among middle-school students and 8% among high-school students during the 1 year between February 1998 and February 1999. These results show how effective a carefully crafted and executed mass media appeal can be on attitudes toward smoking. Impressively, these attitudes previously had been shown to be very resistant to change.

The Audience

To be effective in persuasion and attitude change, you must be aware of the characteristics of the target audience. For example, you would structure a message differently if you were speaking to a group of high-school dropouts as compared to a group of college graduates. Audience variables such as intelligence, self-esteem, and gender all influence how effectively a message is received. More-intelligent people are better able to understand a persuasive message and to critically evaluate the pros and cons of the arguments, even though they are less likely to change their attitudes. A highly intelligent person is more likely to be persuaded when the message is complex and the argument sound, but less likely to be persuaded when the message is simple and the argument flawed (Eagly & Warren, 1976). Self-esteem functions similarly to intelligence. People with high self-esteem are more attentive to the message, but less likely to be persuaded. In comparison, individuals with low self-esteem are more easily persuaded, but are often withdrawn and less attentive to the message (Wood & Stagner, 1994). Perhaps surprisingly, people with moderate self-esteem are more easily persuaded than individuals with either high or low self-esteem.

APPLICATIONS: Being an Effective Persuader

Do not believe in anything simply because you have heard it. Do not believe in anything simply because it is spoken and rumored by many. Do not believe in anything simply because it is found written in your religious books. Do not believe in anything merely on the authority of your teachers and elders. Do not believe in traditions because they have been handed down for many generations. But after observation and analysis, when you find that anything agrees with reason and is conducive to the good and benefit of one and all, then accept it and live up to it.

BUDDHA

Imagine that you are asked to give a speech to a group of people that you do not know in order to persuade them to exercise more. Using the information that you have just learned, how would you design your speech so that it will have the greatest chance of changing your audience's attitude about exercising?

First, prior to making your presentation, try to obtain an audience profile that includes information such as educational level, employment area, age range, gender, and so forth. Next, as the communicator you must establish your expertise and credibility. This would be easiest if you were in good physical condition and if you dressed and acted in a manner that displayed your fitness. By doing so, you would establish your credibility even further by maximizing your appearance. Then you must convince your audience that you possess expertise on the topic even though you have no vested interest in the subject matter other than promoting their healthy lifestyle. In other words, you do not own a gym and are not selling exercise equipment or soliciting health club memberships. As you proceed with your presentation, speak rapidly and confidently about the merits of exercise. Repeat the key points of your message several times. Emphasize the increased dangers of dying prematurely that are associated with lack of exercise in order to arouse maximum fear in your audience. Convince your listeners that just a few minutes of strenuous exercise a day would prevent such an untimely end. Mention both the pros and cons of exercising but lead them to the conclusion that the benefits far outweigh the risks. Use your audience profile to determine the complexity of the arguments you will present. If they are a highly educated group, you could present more complicated facts to back up your arguments but be sure that your arguments are sound.

If you carefully follow this scenario, your chances of changing attitudes will increase. This does not mean, however, that your audience will immediately change their attitudes about exercise. As I mentioned earlier, certain factors will assist in changing attitudes, but no "secret technique" will ensure success. If there were, we would each be at the mercy of other people who could manipulate our attitudes at will.

Why People Change Their Attitudes: The Cognitive Approach

The research that I just described helped psychologists understand when attitudes are most susceptible to change and *how* to produce such changes. Much of this research was done during World War II or in the following decade. The more modern approach to attitude change, known as the *cognitive perspective,* addresses the question of *why* people change their attitudes. That is, it looks at the actual cognitive processes that are involved when attitudes are changed and people are persuaded. Specifically, it examines (1) what people think about when they are exposed to persuasive messages; and (2) how these thoughts and basic cognitive processes determine whether, and to what extent, people undergo changes in their attitudes (Baron & Byrne, 1997).

The most influential cognitive theory is called the **Elaboration Likelihood Model** or ELM for short (Petty & Cacioppo, 1986; Petty, Cacioppo, Strathman, & Priester, 1994). According to this theory, when people hear a persuasive message, they think about the argument that was made, and also those that were not made. According to ELM, it is these *thought processes,* not the actual message itself, that leads to either attitude change or resistance to change. Note the contrast in this view with the body of research that I reviewed earlier in which the emphasis was placed on the communicator, the message itself, the medium, and the audience.

According to ELM, two different processes occur and each requires different amounts of *cognitive effort* on the part of the recipients of the message. The first is known as the **central route,** which happens when recipients find the message interesting, important, or personally relevant. It also happens when there is nothing that prevents the recipients from paying careful attention to the message, such as distractions or prior knowledge. When processing a message via the central route, the recipients pay careful attention and deliberate thoughtfully about it. They evaluate the soundness of the argument and, if the reactions are favorable, may change their attitude and hence be persuaded.

What happens if the recipients find the message uninteresting or irrelevant to themselves? In this case, they are not motivated to pay careful attention and examine it thoughtfully. In these circumstances, the message is processed through the **peripheral route.** You might think that little attitude change or persuasion would take place when this happens, but actually, just the opposite is true. According to ELM theory, attitude change may occur if the message induces positive feelings in the recipients. For example, automobile makers often attempt to persuade car buyers by showing their product being driven by a very attractive individual or being driven through extraordinarily beautiful scenery. Another approach is to make the source of the message very credible by using individuals with expertise or high prestige and status, such as movie stars, sports figures, celebrities, doctors, pharmacists, or other equally reputable individuals. In these circumstances, attitude change may take place even though the recipient does not carefully analyze the content of the message.

We are frequently bombarded with messages via this peripheral route. People will use this approach to change attitudes when they have a message in which the recipients will not be interested. Politicians and advertisers use the approach frequently. Mr. Candidate is running for office and is aware that you have neither heard of him nor care about his platform. An advertiser for a new over-the-counter medicine has a product most people do not think they need or want. How might the advertiser change attitudes using the peripheral route? By associating the message with attractive people, beautiful scenery, celebrities, credible spokespersons, clever slogans, or catchy tunes (Baron & Byrne, 1997).

Many research studies have shown that the ELM is accurate. The following findings have been obtained:

- When the message is *not* interesting or relevant, the strength of the argument has little effect on persuasion. However, when the message *is* relevant, the strength of the argument is very important in changing attitudes. In the former case, the message is being processed through the peripheral route while in the latter case the message involves the central route.
- If weak arguments are combined with strong arguments, they *weaken* the persuasiveness of an argument. This is particularly true when the message is relevant or important to the recipient.
- Attitudes changed through the central route *last longer* than those changed through the peripheral route. Both routes can bring about attitude change, but those changes via the peripheral route are more transient and tend to fade more quickly.
- Attitude changes via the central route result in attitudes that are more resistant to later attempts to change them. This is important for politicians, for example, who want their message to change your mind *and* want their message to be resistant to change by other politicians' subsequent messages.
- Attitudes changed through the central route are more likely to result in behavior changes than those through the peripheral route. This is important to advertisers, for example, who do not just want to change your attitude about their product. They want you to purchase it.

So which route should you use if you are trying to persuade someone? In general, the central route will more likely result in permanent attitude changes that are resistant to later change or fading with time. The peripheral route is satisfactory when only short-term changes in attitude are desired.

Cognitive Dissonance

The greatest revolution in our generation is that of human beings, who by changing the inner attitudes of their minds, can change the outer aspects of their lives.

MARILYN FERGUSON

As human beings, we like to achieve a state in which our beliefs, attitudes, and behaviors are all in agreement. Imagine that you have a positive attitude toward the Republican party and strongly believe that its platform will best lead the country. During the election, you will be most comfortable voting for Republican candidates. Because your beliefs, attitudes, and behaviors all agree, you are in what psychologists call a state of **cognitive consistency.** Imagine, however, that a candidate who is particularly appealing to you happens to be in the Democratic party. By voting for this individual, your behavior is out of sync with your beliefs and attitudes. This results in a state of **cognitive dissonance** and causes discomfort. The stronger our beliefs are held, the greater the amount of cognitive dissonance that occurs. We are then motivated to do something to reduce the inconsistency between our beliefs and attitudes and, thereby, reduce the cognitive dissonance.

Let's examine some common situations whereby cognitive dissonance might result. After you carefully study the frequency of repair data for various automobiles, you subsequently buy a car based on its looks even though you know it has a terrible repair history. Or your friend purchases a car that you know is unreliable. When you are asked whether it was a prudent choice, you feel compelled to support your friend's decision. Or perhaps a friend of yours is running for an office in student government and asks you to give a campaign speech. Even though you believe your friend makes a poor candidate, you give a supportive speech anyway. Or you firmly believe that you have no racial or ethnic prejudices and yet find yourself crossing the street one night to avoid walking by three teenagers of another race. In each of these instances, your behavior conflicts with, or is dissonant to, your beliefs and attitudes and usually results in a high level of personal discomfort.

Leon Festinger (1957) developed the original theory of cognitive dissonance and did much of the early research on the topic. Festinger believed that we could reduce the unpleasant state resulting from cognitive dissonance in 1 of 3 ways: (1) reducing the importance of either the belief or the behavior that is causing the dissonance, (2) adding additional elements that explain the discrepancy, or (3) changing either the attitude or the behavior.

Professors frequently witness the process of dissonance reduction in their students. For example, I teach a course in introductory statistics that is a notoriously difficult course required for psychology majors. Many times I have observed students who have done well in their other classes struggle in this course. When they receive a low grade on the first exam, a state of dissonance is created because the act of failing the test is dissonant with the belief that they are good students. This dissonance causes discomfort, and they are motivated to reduce it. How do students accomplish this? Precisely in 1 of the 3 ways predicted above by Festinger. In strategy (1), the students reduce the importance of one of the dissonant elements, such as their original belief that the grade on the first test was important or that their knowledge is reflected in the grades they get. In strategy (2), the students add some element to the situation to facilitate consonance. The students now believe they performed poorly for any one of many plausible reasons such as the exam was poorly constructed, the professor did not grade the exam fairly, their work schedule prevented adequate study time, and so forth. All of these "explanations" serve to reduce the cognitive dissonance. In strategy (3), students simply change one of the dissonant components. Either they change their belief that they are in fact good students or they change their behavior by working harder to achieve a better grade the next time. In each of these instances, the behaviors are *reinforcing* because they reduce the aversive state of feeling uncomfortable. Since such behaviors are reinforcing, we learn to repeat them in future situations where dissonance occurs.

Dissonance theory has spawned a tremendous amount of research. Social psychologists have discovered that certain circumstances facilitate a person changing his or her beliefs or attitudes to reconcile cognitive dissonance. Let's look at 3 examples.

Forced Compliance

You can lead a horse to water but you cannot make him drink. Or can you? Like most people, you probably believe that forcing individuals to do something will have little effect on changing their opinions or attitudes. For example, judges sometimes require violent traffic offenders to attend sessions on anger management in lieu of a jail sentence. Typically, these people attend such sessions primarily to avoid jail time rather than to learn how to control their tempers. Under these circumstances, how likely are they to change their opinions or attitudes?

Festinger's research has clearly documented that, under certain circumstances, people who are forced or paid to do something *will* change their attitudes. Dissonance theory predicts that when people's behavior is injurious to their self-esteem, a conflict exists between their belief in their self-worth and the fact that they have engaged in some behavior that contradicts this belief. Individuals will seek somehow to justify their behavior to reduce this dissonance. One way to do this is to change their attitude to come into compliance with their behavior; in other words, they achieve consonance. Using the earlier example of making a campaign speech for someone you felt was unqualified for the elected office, dissonance theory would predict that you would change your attitude about the person in order to achieve consonance between your belief and your behavior. After your speech, you might say to yourself, "The more I think about it, the better I feel about the job my friend will do."

In a classic experiment demonstrating this fact, subjects first completed a series of extremely boring tasks. Following completion of these tasks, the experimenter asked the subjects if they would assist in the research by trying to convince the next subject group that the tasks were fun and enjoyable. The subjects were offered either $1 or $20 for helping out. After assisting the experimenter, the subjects were asked to rate how enjoyable the task was. As dissonance theory would predict, subjects who were paid $1 had a bigger change in attitude about the boring tasks than did those who received $20. Those paid $1 believed that they had been induced to lie to the next subjects for an unjustifiably small sum of money. They resolved this dissonance by changing their mind about how interesting the tasks actually were. On the other hand, subjects paid $20 realized that they lied strictly to obtain the money and believed that their behavior was justified. They had little or no dissonance to resolve and continued to view the tasks as deadly dull (Festinger & Carlsmith, 1959).

"You cannot legislate morality" is the familiar expression often given to explain the futility of laws passed to correct social irresponsibility and injustice such as discrimination. However, laws can change behavior. People might still be bigots but, by law, they are prohibited from committing overt discriminatory acts. In these circumstances, people might be forced to act in a way that is dissonant with their beliefs. Dissonance theory would predict that under these circumstances the discriminatory attitudes would change to agree with the behavior. Therefore, antidiscrimination laws might indeed be successful in changing people's attitudes. Numerous research studies have supported this finding. Because our self-esteem is an important part of who we are, forced behavior that threatens our image of ourselves can result in attitude change.

BRAINWASHING. During the Korean War, the Chinese Communists captured several American soldiers and exposed them to forced thought control procedures that have come to be called **brainwashing.** About 1 in 6 of these American soldiers were eventually coerced into signing false confessions and endorsing anti-American propaganda. After the war, 21 POWs elected to remain with the Communists and numerous others returned home convinced that communism was the best form of government.

How does one go about "brainwashing" another person? Three techniques have been identified that are successful (Schein, Hill, Lubin, & Williams, 1957):

- Isolation. The target person is completely isolated from all other people who might support ideas contrary to those that the captives hope to inculcate.
- Dependence. The target is made completely helpless and dependent on the captors for everything, including satisfaction of basic needs such as food and water. Sleep deprivation combined with isolation, humiliation, and psychological and physical abuse weaken existing attitudes and beliefs.
- Selective reinforcement. The captors place the target in a situation where they can reward any change in behavior or attitude. Recall my discussion of the concept of successive approximations in chapter 3 on learning and how they are used to "shape" a response. This is exactly what the Chinese captors did. They quickly rewarded even the smallest cooperative behavior or change of attitude at first but eventually required more and more cooperation in order for the target to obtain subsequent rewards.

Patty Hearst is the daughter of a wealthy and prominent San Francisco family. She was kidnapped by members of the radical Symbionese Liberation Army and indoctrinated into their way of thinking. In the photograph above, she is participating in a bank robbery organized by members of the radical group. In her subsequent criminal trial, Miss Hearst claimed that she had been brainwashed by members of the radical group.

Although frequently successful in the short term, attitude changes brought about by brainwashing are usually temporary. For example, the Korean War captives usually reverted back to their original beliefs after returning to the United States.

Do you think someone could brainwash you against your will? A famous example occurred in 1974 when 19-year-old newspaper heiress and college student Patricia Hearst was kidnapped in San Francisco by a band of radicals calling themselves the Symbionese Liberation Army (SLA). They claimed that they abducted her to avenge the crimes her parents, wealthy San Francisco socialites, had allegedly committed against the people of America and the world. Ms. Hearst was held captive in a closet for weeks and indoctrinated with radical rhetoric. Two months later she was photographed carrying a gun during an SLA holdup of a San Francisco bank. Her attitudes and belief system had been changed to the extent that she joined the SLA and adopted a new identity, as well as the name Tania. Ms. Hearst was eventually tried, convicted, and sent to prison for 7 years for the bank robbery despite her claim that she was the victim of brainwashing. President Carter commuted her sentence in 1977. Ms. Hearst, now married and living a normal life in Connecticut, has appeared in several movies and television shows as well as authored several novels. At the time this occurred, there was great controversy about whether Ms. Hearst was legitimately brainwashed or a willing participant. However, as you can see, all the necessary conditions were in place for brainwashing to happen.

CULTS. A problem that has occurred with increasing frequency over recent years has been the formation of various political and religious cults. These cults consist of groups of individuals who are bound together by intense, often faddish devotion to a person or some idealized beliefs. These coercive groups serve to interfere with their members' ability to reason and make free choices. The consequence of this coercion is sometimes disastrous. In 1978, 900 members of the Reverend Jim Jones's People's Temple committed mass suicide by ingesting cyanide-laced Kool-Aid at their Jonestown compound in Guyana. In another example, in 1993 David Koresh and over 80 of his Branch Davidian cult members perished in a fire in their compound near Waco, Texas, after an altercation with federal agents.

David Koresh was the charismatic leader of a cult group known as the Branch Davidian sect. Many members of the group perished in a fire during an altercation with federal agents near Waco, Texas.

Psychologists have studied the processes by which individuals are coerced into cult membership (Galanter, 1989; Singer, 1979; Singer, Temerlin, & Langone, 1990; Zimbardo & Leippe, 1991). Individuals are often recruited during a period of their life when they are suffering from psychological distress, mild depression, indecision, or alienation from their parents. Adolescents having difficulty establishing independence from their parents are particularly at risk for cult involvement. The cult frequently offers simplistic explanations and solutions to the recruits' problems. At first glance, the cult offers the recruits massive amounts of unconditional love, acceptance, and attention in order to generate very positive feelings toward the group and its leader. Individuals are required initially to make small commitments and then successively larger and larger commitments. From an initial obligation to merely attend a brief meeting, additional requirements are added until the member is staying for prolonged periods of time, turning over bank accounts, donating all worldly possessions to the cult, and eventually renouncing all contact with family and friends. Frequently a group identity is established by wearing identical clothes, eating special diets, or undergoing harsh initiation rites. Once firmly established in the cult, access to information is strictly controlled. The member becomes increasingly isolated from the outside world, and total conformity to the leader's commands is required.

Many people believe that only weak individuals are drawn into such cults. However, evidence increasingly suggests that these coercive techniques are extremely powerful and almost anyone exposed to them can be drawn in. The best way to inoculate yourself is to understand what the techniques are and how they work. You should notice how similar some of these techniques are to the brainwashing techniques described earlier.

Conflicts and Attitude Change

A cult is a religion with no political power.

TOM WOLFE

The decisions that we make when torn between two choices often have an effect on our attitudes. The more difficult the decision, the more our attitudes should change. Imagine a person or couple trying to decide whether to buy a home in one of two different neighborhoods. One house is much larger, has several nice amenities, and is affordable, but it is located in an older, run-down neighborhood, far from the buyers' workplaces. The other home is smaller, has fewer amenities, and is much too expensive, but it is located in a very nice part of town near where the potential buyers work. In this situation, the individuals have a great deal of difficulty deciding which home to buy. Whichever decision is made, cognitive dissonance will occur because the buyers made a decision (buying the house) that conflicts with their beliefs (bad location or too expensive). If the individuals decide to buy the larger, cheaper home in the run-down neighborhood, their attitudes about the negative aspects of the location will probably change. If they buy the smaller, more expensive home, they will change their attitude about the price and size. In either case, their attitudes change to become consonant with their actions.

Cost and Attitude Change

One interesting prediction from dissonance theory is that we will value something more if it costs us something. If we pay a great deal for something, we change our attitude about its value in order to bring those beliefs into consonance with our behavior. If you pay too much for a car or house that you did not really like that much, your attitude about it will become more favorable to reduce the dissonance. Community mental-health clinics often make every client pay something for treatment, even if it is only a token amount. They have found that, as dissonance theory predicts, free therapy is not valued as much. When therapy is not valued, clients tend to dismiss the benefits as unimportant and often fail to show up for subsequent appointments. Similarly, animal shelters often charge customers for adopting stray animals in the belief that the pet will be valued more highly and subsequently be treated better. Organizations that have strenuous membership requirements are valued more than those that admit just anyone. This explains why fraternities and sororities that require pledges to perform all kinds of distasteful duties and sometimes undergo hazing before gaining membership are actually preferred over those with no such entry requirements.

Self-Perception Theory

One alternative explanation to dissonance theory is called **self-perception theory** (Bem, 1972). While dissonance theory states that people change their attitudes to comply with their behavior, self-perception theory states that *people simply observe their behavior and then infer an attitude* that is consistent with the behavior. Often we do not understand what causes our own behavior or attitudes. Self-perception theory proposes that individuals examine the context in which their behavior occurs and then infer the attitude. If someone asks you whether you are a conservative or a liberal, you might think back to the last several elections in which you voted and conclude that you are one or the other. In other words, you inferred your political attitude based on your behavior.

Please accept my resignation. I don't want to belong to any club that would accept me as a member.

GROUCHO MARX, *from his autobiography,* Groucho and Me *(1959)*

Both dissonance theory and self-perception theory are correct, depending on the circumstances. Dissonance theory accounts best for instances of attitude change where people suffer aversive consequences or discomfort because of their actions and where people believe that they are responsible for those consequences. Self-perception theory best explains those situations where there are no aversive consequences and no physiological arousal.

Prejudice and Discrimination

Prejudice consists of a negative attitude toward another person based on that person's membership in a social group. Social groups may be delineated by immutable characteristics, such as race, ethnicity, and gender, or by culture, activities, beliefs, conduct, and so forth. In the United States, the number of groups suffering from such prejudice is nearly limitless. Almost any group that you can think of will evoke negative attitudes from some individual. This not only includes obvious groups but also includes less obvious groups such as fraternity members, athletes, or union members. Prejudices serve to allow us to generalize information to an entire group of individuals based on insufficient knowledge from some subset of that group. For example, because we observe that some elected government officials, such as senators and congressmen, are self-serving and corrupt, we generalize inappropriately that all government officials are untrustworthy. Our attitude does not take into account the large number of elected officials, most of whom we never hear about, who serve their constituents loyally and honestly.

Common sense is the collection of prejudices acquired by age eighteen.

ALBERT EINSTEIN

Earlier in this chapter I noted that attitudes consist of the emotional, cognitive, and behavioral components. Since prejudice is an attitude, it also contains each of these components. Strong emotional reactions and feelings often accompany prejudices. If you have watched television interviews with white supremacists or antigay activists, you may have witnessed such extreme emotional reactions as hatred, revulsion, or disgust. The cognitive component of prejudice includes the beliefs or **stereotypes** that we hold about minority groups. These are the overgeneralized beliefs that people have about the targets of their prejudice. Stereotypes are formed from our interactions with family and friends and through the mass media. For instance, when people repeatedly see ethnic minorities portraying criminals in movies and on television, they tend to overestimate the number of times these minorities are involved in violent crimes. This is an example of an *illusory correlation*—that is, seeing a relationship between two things (skin color or ethnicity and crime) that does not actually exist. Return to chapter 5 for a more detailed discussion of illusory correlations in the context of problem solving and reasoning.

The final component of prejudice is behavioral. **Discrimination** is the behavioral component and consists of *overt acts* that treat certain groups in an unfair manner. With prejudice, either some or all three components may be at work. For instance, individuals who are prejudiced against African Americans may have strong emotional feelings and hold numerous stereotypes about them, but they do not overtly treat them differently because of social or legal pressures.

Am I prejudiced? Are you? It depends on your definition of prejudice. If you accept the argument that only one of the three components mentioned above is necessary, then most of us are prejudiced.

It required years of labor and billions of dollars to gain the secret of the atom. It will take a still greater investment to gain the secrets of man's irrational nature. It is easier, someone has said, to smash an atom than a prejudice.

GORDON ALLPORT
The Nature of Prejudice (1954)

Some research findings suggest that everyone is prejudiced and that we use stereotypes, all the time, without even realizing it (Banaji & Hardin, 1996). Psychologists have studied what they call this automatic or **implicit stereotyping.** Previous research on stereotyping primarily asked people to record how they felt about minority groups. Psychologists now realize that these conscious reports told only a small part of the story. As Paul (1998) stated, "How progressive a person seems to be on the surface bears little or no relation to how prejudiced he or she is on an unconscious level . . . so that a bleeding-heart liberal might harbor just as many biases as a neo-Nazi skinhead" (p. 52).

To test for these unconscious biases, researchers presented subjects with a series of positive or negative adjectives, each paired with a characteristically "white" or "black" name. The pairs of words flashed on a computer screen and the subject indicated whether the word was good or bad. The computer measured how long each person took to respond to each pair of words. The surprising findings were that *almost everyone* responded faster when a positive word was paired with a white name or a negative word was paired with a black name. This result occurs because we are used to making these kinds of associations and, therefore, process them more rapidly (Banaji & Hardin, 1996). The pairs of words are presented so rapidly that a person's ability to make deliberate choices is greatly reduced, which allows a person's underlying beliefs to show through. This technique has also been used to measure implicit stereotypes about gays, women, and the elderly.

The existence of these implicit stereotypes does not mean that we are necessarily behaving in a discriminatory fashion. Paul (1998) believes that people who are not overtly prejudiced probably consciously check any unacceptable thoughts or actions following the activation of a stereotype. However, it is still possible that our behavior may be influenced in ways that we are not aware of. Many times the behavior is affected in very subtle ways, including changes in body language. Other times the discriminatory behavior is less subtle. Nathan McCall, in his autobiography *Makes Me Wanna Holler; A Young Black Man in America* (1995), stated that when he and his black friends were walking down the street in Portsmouth, Virginia, they would often hear the activation of electric door locks in occupied cars as they approached.

Whether the expression of prejudice is subtle or not, it will be difficult to claim that it has been eradicated as long as these automatic and largely unconscious reactions remain. To be a truly unbiased nation, we will not only need to change the way people behave but also the way they think. Simple exhortation will not be enough. Antidiscrimination laws, education, and political protest all may work on our conscious beliefs but leave the unconscious unaffected. Furthermore, research has shown that attempts to suppress these automatic stereotypes may actually cause them to return later and stronger than they were before (Macrae, Bodenhausen, Milne, & Jetten, 1994).

APPLICATIONS: Reducing Prejudice

Attempting to eradicate prejudice is daunting, and unfortunately, not likely to occur in several generations to come. Nevertheless, we should still try, and there are some techniques that can help. Let's examine techniques that psychologists have found to be most effective.

Intergroup Contact

It has been widely believed by many politicians and the public in general that prejudice between groups could be reduced by increased contact. The driving force behind the concept of integration is that more frequent contact between the racial groups will breed goodwill. Does it work? Sometimes it does, and sometimes it does not. Merely mixing disparate racial groups together is not enough. In fact, if the increased contact is between privileged majority children and underprivileged minority children, increased tensions and strengthening of stereotypes actually occurs. Research by social psychologists, particularly the pioneering work of Gordon Allport (1954), has shown that increased intergroup contact is only effective when the following conditions are met:

> Prejudices, it is well known, are most difficult to eradicate from the heart whose soil has never been loosened or fertilized by education; they grow there, firm as weeds among stones.
>
> **CHARLOTTE BRONTË**
> *Jane Eyre*

- The groups must have roughly *equal* social, economic, or task-related status.
- Contacts between groups are *informal and intimate* as opposed to formal and casual (Amir, 1969). This provides the groups an opportunity to get to know each other in a setting where they have a better opportunity to view each other as individuals.
- Interactions occur in a way that allows individuals to see that the negative stereotypes they have of each other are false.
- A situation exists where the different groups are all cooperating and dependent on one another to achieve a common goal. There was widespread segregation in the armed forces during World War II. On the few occasions in which African American and white soldiers fought together, instances of prejudice were greatly reduced. Similarly, racial differences exist only infrequently on

athletic teams where members are required to work together and rely on each other to win the contest.

- The people interacting with one another must view each other as typical or representative of their groups. For example, increased contact by whites with only highly educated minorities would not reduce levels of prejudice. In this circumstance, the prejudices would be maintained because of the perception that the other group was not typical.
- Intergroup contacts should be pleasant and noncompetitive. Competition between groups serves to increase the tendency to put participants into "us" and "them" categories and accentuate perceived differences (Amir, 1969).
- Whenever possible, contact should occur between groups that already possess positive attitudes toward each other (Amir, 1969). However, increased contact between groups that are initially hostile to one another can also lead to reduced prejudice if the other conditions listed above are met (Cook, 1985; Riordan, 1978).

One can conclude that increasing contact between groups can be effective in fighting prejudice between those groups but only when the conditions outlined above are carefully followed. Merely throwing different groups together is ineffectual, and may cause more harm than good.

Recategorization

Each of us is a member of several different groups. There is a tendency for people in such groups to see members of their group as "us" and members of other groups as "them." That is, we tend to categorize people into distinct *in-groups* or *out-groups.* When this happens, we often view the out-group in negative terms. Sometimes this represents harmless competition, but at other times it holds more serious negative social consequences.

Since I live in Denver, I am a big fan of the Denver Broncos football team, as are many of the people in Colorado. We collectively see ourselves as part of the in-group who roots for this team. All other football teams, especially those playing against the Broncos, are part of the out-group. However, a curious thing happens when the playoffs begin at the end of the year. If the Denver Broncos are not in the playoffs, then the Denver fans root for whichever team in their particular conference, the American Football Conference (AFC) West in this case, has survived to the playoffs. For example, Denver fans usually disparage the Kansas City Chiefs' team and their fans because of their strong rivalry as members in the AFC West. However, if Kansas City represents the AFC West in the playoffs, then Denver fans suddenly shift their allegiance and begin rooting for the Chiefs to win. Denver fans now have shifted their definition of the in-group to include all teams in the AFC West. If the AFC West team loses, they immediately shift their allegiance to whichever team is representing the entire American Football Conference in the Super Bowl. Suddenly, some team that Denver fans were maligning only a few weeks earlier has become "our team" in the Super Bowl.

Social psychologists call the process of changing the boundaries of what a person considers an in-group (us) versus an out-group (them) **recategorization.** This process happens frequently and often leads to hostility and prejudice toward whoever happens to be the out-group. One racial group sees themselves as members of an ethnic group ("us") and perceives some or all other racial groups as an out-group ("them"). By belittling members of the out-group, we attempt to enhance the value of our own in-group and our own self-identity.

Social psychologists have sought ways that would encourage individuals to modify the boundaries so that they view themselves as members of a single social entity. If African Americans and whites, for example, saw themselves as members of a single social entity (an in-group), it is believed that they would view each other more positively and prejudices would be significantly reduced. A reduction in prejudice would encourage greater intergroup contact, as described in the previous section, which would reduce intergroup bias even more. How can we as a society bring this about? One important factor is *working together cooperatively toward shared goals.* Several research studies have documented that when this happens, there is a sharp reduction in feelings of bias or hostility toward members of the former out-group (Brewer, Ho, Lee, & Miller, 1987; Gaertner, Mann, Murrell, & Dovidio, 1989; Gaertner, Mann, Davidio, Murrell, & Pomare, 1990). For example, this could be accomplished in an integrated school setting by having groups of students with diverse ethnic backgrounds assigned a common task or goal that can only be attained if they all work cooperatively together. If given the opportunity, individuals will often choose to form groups with an ethnic makeup similar to their own. In this circumstance, different ethnic groups often end up competing against each other which, in turn, increases ethnic prejudices.

I have always believed that the best thing that could happen to humankind on Earth would be to receive a credible threat to their existence from an intelligent civilization from another planet. I am certain that we humans would quickly forget about all the differences we focus on with respect to our color, religion, nationality, culture, or gender. We would be "earthlings" united in our goal of survival. I cannot imagine any other scenario that would so successfully bring our entire civilization together. Earth calling Mars. . . .

Changing How We Think

Stereotypes play an important role in prejudice and reflect the way people think about others. Therefore, one approach to reducing prejudice is to alter the thinking processes of individuals. Sometimes this approach may involve nothing more than making people aware of their stereotypical views and asking them to monitor how they think. Techniques in which people are encouraged to pay attention to an individual's unique characteristics rather than to group membership have been tried with some success. Research has shown that under these circumstances people tend to be less likely to rely on stereotypes when making social judgments (Devine, 1989). For example, men in the military often make judgments about women soldiers based on their gender and not on their individual ability. For example, a man might conclude that women are better at radio communications because "women naturally have better verbal skills" or that they are not suited for the battlefield because "women just are not aggressive enough." The military could train soldiers to become aware of this type of stereotypical thinking and give them verbal feedback whenever it occurs. Eventually, this approach should lead to altered ways of thinking and a subsequent reduction of stereotyped views.

Are these various techniques the panacea for solving the problems of stereotyping and prejudice? Unfortunately, no. They are helpful procedures that have proven successful when carefully applied. However, the tendency to stereotype others and the prejudice that accompanies such behavior are very strong in humans. As I noted earlier, in some cases we can suppress the cognitive aspects of such behavior only to see them rebound stronger than before. Prejudice is a social scourge in *all* societies in the world. Because it has existed as long as humankind, some psychologists question whether it possibly served some evolutionary value in our past. Even so, this conduct serves no purpose now, and further research is needed to find ways to counteract its insidious and counterproductive effects. Unfortunately, the likelihood of successful eradication seems to be a very distant goal, at best.

Compliance

Opinions founded on prejudice are always sustained with the greatest violence.

HEBREW PROVERB

Compliance is the act of getting a person to agree to the request of another. You will recognize this behavior as a common daily occurrence: you ask your friends for favors, a charity asks you for a donation, or a salesperson tries to persuade you to buy a product. Notice that getting the other person to comply is different from trying to change a person's attitude. Attitude change *may* bring about a change in behavior but does not necessarily do so. In this section, I will discuss techniques to bring about behavioral changes, regardless of whether or not a corresponding attitude change takes place.

Certainly you have occasionally found your own behavior influenced by a person well-schooled in bringing about compliance, particularly family members and salespeople. We are asked to comply with numerous requests every day of our lives. Some we comply with, but many we do not. What are the rules that govern compliance, and how can we prepare ourselves to resist their effects?

The seminal research on compliance was conducted several years ago by a well-known social psychologist at Arizona State University named Robert Cialdini. An admitted pushover for pitches by peddlers, fund-raisers, and salespeople, Cialdini asked himself precisely the following questions: (1) What are the factors that cause one person to say yes to another? (2) Which techniques work most effectively in getting one person to comply with another? (3) Why is a request that is stated in a certain way rejected while the same request stated another way is successful? He attempted to answer these questions in a variety of ways. He decided to concentrate his examination on the professionals out in the real world who use the principles of compliance to earn a living. As he stated in the preface to his book *Influence: Science and Practice* (Cialdini, 1988), compliance professionals ". . . know what works and what doesn't; the law of survival of the fittest assures it. Their business is to make us comply, and their livelihoods depend on it. Those who don't know how to get people to say yes soon fall away; those who do, stay and flourish." For 3 years he immersed himself in the world of compliance professionals, including salespeople, fund-raisers, advertisers, and others. He conducted extensive interviews with these people and examined the written materials that they used. He also answered newspaper ads for sales trainees so that he could be schooled in the professional techniques of compliance. Cialdini worked in advertising, public relations, and fund-raising agencies to examine their strategies and styles. He discovered that although there were thousands of different compliance tactics that were used, the majority fell within the following 6 basic categories.

Reciprocation

We are more likely to comply with the request of someone who has previously done us a favor than with someone who has not. The rule of **reciprocation** states that once someone has made a concession or done us a favor, we feel obligated to return the favor (i.e., *reciprocate).* This rule is so pervasive in the human culture that sociologists report that virtually all human societies subscribe to it (Gouldner, 1960). The rule is extremely powerful and frequently elicits compliance to a request that, except for a feeling of indebtedness, would otherwise be dismissed.

The reciprocation rule is often used in politics where politicians do a favor for a colleague but then later "call in" the favor when they need that colleague's support for a piece of legislation. Politicians who plan to run for statewide or national office often spend years doing favors for individuals whose support they will be seeking at a later date. Campaign donations from either individuals or corporations are usually given to political candidates with the understanding that a return favor will be granted. Politicians who win reelection are usually those who have done many small personal favors for their constituents. Arranging for a pothole to be filled can pay rich dividends later.

Merchandisers frequently employ this rule very effectively by giving out free samples. For example, if you stop to try a free food sample at a grocery store, you may discover how difficult it is to resist a request to purchase the product. Even the tiny free sample makes us feel indebted to purchase. This explains why companies often encourage you to try their product without obligation for 30 days. The merchandisers have learned that most customers will feel strongly indebted to purchase the product after taking advantage of the trial period.

Surprisingly, this technique works even when the gift or favor is not solicited or even wanted. Organizations or charities that seek money in malls or airports often give small gifts to individuals passing by in the hope that they will return the favor with a donation. Often the solicitors will insist on handing the gift to the individuals, even if they try to refuse it. The Hare Krishna Society employed this tactic very successfully in airports in the 1980s by pressing flowers into the hands of passing strangers. Research suggested that the more surprised the individuals feel by receiving the free gift, the more obligated they feel to return the favor (Milgram & Sabini, 1975). If you are like most people, you probably receive unsolicited gifts quite frequently. A week seldom goes by that I am not mailed free address labels, greeting cards, note pads, or some such inconsequential gift from charities seeking a donation. I notice that I always feel guilty whether I use the gift or throw it away and do not respond to their request. Recently, I received a very long questionnaire in the mail from an organization requesting my cooperation along with a $1.00 bill as a way of "thanking me in advance." I fell for this tactic and spent 30 minutes completing the questionnaire, all the time mumbling to myself that this was way too much work for a lousy dollar. This wise organization knew that its cash gift would not be thrown away, therefore almost ensuring the recipient would comply with their request.

The rule for reciprocation can involve several different but highly effective variations. Let's look at 3 that are commonly used.

Here, Calvin tries the door-in-the-face technique to gain his mother's compliance. Unfortunately for Calvin, his mother seems wise to his attempt at social influence.

Door-in-the-Face Technique

In the door-in-the-face technique, the individuals first make a very large request that they know will likely be turned down. After they are refused, they make a *smaller* request that really represents what they hoped for all along. Since a concession has been made, the person now feels obligated to comply. In fact, I used this technique while selling candy bars to raise money for our high-school band. I went door to door and asked people if they would like to buy 6 candy bars for $5.00. Most said no. (This was in the 1960s when a dollar was worth much more than it is today.) I would then follow that up by asking if they would be willing to buy 1 candy bar for $1.00. This technique was very successful. To make this work, the second request does not have to be small, only smaller than the first one. Recently a neighbor called my wife and asked her if she would be willing to spend the weekend canvassing neighborhoods for a charitable organization. My wife refused this initial request but easily agreed to help when asked just to solicit donations in our immediate neighborhood. Is there someone you would like to meet but are afraid to approach for fear of rejection? Try the rejection-then-retreat technique. First, ask the person for a very large favor such as accompanying you to dinner and a movie. After the person says no, ask if he or she would join you for a cup of coffee sometime. You will be surprised how effective it is.

This technique is frequently used by negotiators or salespeople who make an initial offer they know will be rejected and then scale back their position to one much closer to what they originally wanted. Car salespeople are notorious for this. If you have a car that is worth $5,000 in trade, they will initially offer you only $3,000. After you refuse their offer, they generously increase their offer to $4,000. Because they appear to have made a concession, you feel obligated to reciprocate and comply with this second offer.

That's-Not-All Technique

In this technique, initially a request is made and then, before the recipient can say yes or no, a little something extra is offered to sweeten the deal. You have probably seen this approach used by salespeople on television. They first make the pitch for the handy-dandy food slicer/chopper/peeler for only $19.99. This is quickly followed by, ". . . but wait, that's not all. If you order now, we will include for no extra charge this handy. . . ." I used this technique myself recently to sell a boat that I was very anxious to unload. I found a buyer who wanted the boat but was hesitant to make a decision. I agreed to include several inexpensive accessories, such as water skis, ropes, and an extra gas can. Voilà—boat sold! Research has shown that including something extra before the person can say no greatly increases the probability that he or she will say yes (Burger, 1986).

Foot-in-the-Mouth Technique

If you want someone to comply with your request, it is best if you can establish some type of mutual relationship with the target person, even if that relationship is extremely tenuous. By getting the other person to admit to the relationship, the person making the request gains an edge. In some respects, these target individuals are "putting their foot in their mouth" by admitting to this relationship because it will make them feel more obligated to comply with the request. For example, if you are a parent seeking donations for a community adoption agency, your chances of receiving a donation improve if you can first get the target people to admit that, like you, they are parents themselves. One study showed that college students were nearly 3 times more likely to donate to a charitable cause after admitting to the requester that they were fellow students (Aune & Basil, 1994).

Scarcity

One interesting characteristic of humans is that objects or opportunities are perceived as more valuable when they are less available. Cialdini (1988) labeled this the **scarcity principle,** and its effects can be seen daily. Retailers frequently use a ploy of limiting the purchases of an item on sale to a set number. When we see retailers place a limit on purchases, we perceive the item to be more valuable. Similarly, we are more inclined to rush to make a purchase when the advertisement states that "only 25 are available at each store." Often, salespeople attempt to complete a sale by telling a customer that an item is the "last one available." Although I have no proof of this, I have a strong hunch that motel and hotel managers employ this tactic. When inquiring about a room for the night, I have been told countless times, "We have just one room left." Either I have an uncanny penchant for showing up immediately before the no vacancy sign is lit, or the managers are employing the scarcity principle to fill their inns.

Interestingly, things that one might think would make an object less appealing can actually have the opposite effect if the result is scarcity. A blemish in an article of clothing makes it less desirable for purchase. Yet, a blemish in a coin or a stamp that resulted from an error in the manufacturing process makes those items extremely more valuable due to their novelty. Cialdini (1988) noted the irony of this when he observed, "Imperfections that would otherwise make for rubbish make for prized possessions when they bring along an abiding scarcity" (p. 229).

Another effective way to encourage compliance is to place *time limits* on the availability of some item. In advertisements you often see "for 3 days only" or "24-hour sale." Movie theaters encourage attendance by noting an "exclusive showing, limited engagement, ends soon." Successful salespeople often use this ploy by telling customers that the proffered "special price" will not be available if they decide to purchase later. A local gutter-cleaning service frequently distributes flyers announcing that it will be in my neighborhood and available for hire at a "special price" for only 1 day the next month. All of these tactics have the 1 common goal of making us believe that a commodity is rare or scarce in order to cultivate our compliance.

The scarcity principle is so effective for two reasons. First, as we learned previously, goods that are difficult to get are typically believed to be better than those that are easy to attain. This leads us to conclude that "rarer is better" and encourages our compliance. Secondly, as objects or opportunities become less available, we lose the freedom of choice. Whenever our freedom of choice is limited or even threatened, we feel a strong urge to act against whatever is interfering with our ability to choose. Told that we cannot purchase something because of limited availability, we become even more determined to have it. This "reverse psychology" often leads to behavioral compliance.

The scarcity principle also works well in enhancing romantic relationships. This is commonly referred to as "playing hard to get" and is remarkably effective. By intimating that one is in demand from several other suitors, or that it is difficult to win one's affections, a person hopes to embellish his or her perceived attractiveness. Research has demonstrated the potency of such a strategy (Walster, Walster, Piliavin, & Schmidt, 1973). Job applicants often use this strategy to enhance their attractiveness to prospective employers by telling them that they are also considering several other job offers.

In applying this principle to your own life, you merely need to remember that creating the impression of scarcity can be an effective strategy for gaining compliance from others. The principle will serve you well in a variety of endeavors, including selling items at a garage sale, encouraging a romantic relationship, negotiating business deals, or seeking employment. You can almost always count on people to adhere to the principle that what is scarce must be valuable.

The Low-Ball Technique

One very effective way of gaining compliance is the classic **low-ball technique** that is used notoriously by car dealers and in many other situations as well. As with some other social influence tactics, one first obtains a commitment and then seeks compliance. In the case of purchasing something, the customer is typically offered a very favorable price that induces the customer to make a commitment to purchase. After the decision to purchase has been made, the favorable circumstance that led to the commitment to purchase is suddenly removed. You might think that this would cause the customer to back out of the agreement, but salespeople have shrewdly discovered an invaluable rule: Once a commitment has been made, most customers will stick with it even though the terms have changed disadvantageously for the purchaser. Let's see how this procedure works in a new car purchase. The salesperson offers a very good price on a car, one that is well below the competitor's price. The deal is so good, in fact, that the salesperson has no intention of going through with it. The favorable price is offered only to get the purchaser to *commit* to buying the car. Once that decision is made, the dealer engages in activities to strengthen the customer's commitment to purchase the car. This might include filling out numerous purchase forms, arranging financing terms, or even encouraging the purchaser to drive the car for a day or two. Once the salesperson has determined that the buyer is firmly committed to the purchase, something happens to alter the original low price. Different salespeople try different tactics, but the more common tactics include suddenly discovering an "error" in the financing that will add a substantial amount to the purchase cost, telling the customer that the salesperson's boss will not allow the trade-in allowance originally offered, or the salesperson "forgot" to add on the cost of some accessory that the customer had requested.

I was recently on the receiving end of this technique myself. I had promised my son a new car when he graduated from college. After considerable research, he chose the model he wanted and a price was agreed upon. Papers were drawn up, a trade-in allowance was given for his old car, and we thought everything was set. Suddenly, the dealer called my son to report that the original price he quoted had "accidentally" omitted the air conditioning and an additional $600 would be required if he still wanted that option. The dealer knew full well that my son had his heart set on getting this car and he figured, correctly as it turns out, that he would have little trouble getting his dad to cough up the additional $600. I had made the commitment and found myself reluctant to back out of the arrangement. I rationalized to myself that it was still a reasonably good deal and, besides, how could I disappoint my son at this late point in the process? In other words, I complied and fell for one variant of the classic low-ball technique. As Cialdini (1988) noted, "Automobile dealers have come to understand the ability of a personal commitment to build its own support system, a support system of new justifications for the commitment" (p. 95). All my training in psychology failed to help me avoid this low-ball trap.

People frequently use this technique in their interpersonal relationships as well. This often plays itself out after couples break off relationships, particularly in domestic violence situations. For example, a man promises that he will change his ways if only his partner will take him back. He promises to be more attentive, spend more time with her, stop drinking so much, be less argumentative, control his temper, and so forth. He offers his partner a "deal" that she cannot refuse. Once she makes the commitment to take him back, he reneges on most of the promises, counting on her commitment to keep her in compliance with his wishes. Often, the woman will begin telling herself that he really is trying to change, that he is basically a good person, or some other such rationalization to justify her decision. As Cialdini (1988) noted, "The impressive thing about the low-ball tactic is its ability to make a person feel pleased with a poor choice" (p. 95).

Modeling Others' Behavior

In chapter 3 I discussed how we often model our behavior on our observations of how others behave. This was termed "observational learning." In situations where we are uncertain about how to behave, the modeling of others takes on particular importance (Tesser, Campbell, & Mickler, 1983). Cialdini (1988) refers to what he calls the *principle of social proof,* which states that we determine what behavior is appropriate and correct for ourselves by finding out what other people think is correct. He recognized that doing so usually serves us well. You generally make fewer mistakes by doing what others are doing rather than by acting in a different fashion. Nevertheless, our strong tendency to model the behavior of others can make us more vulnerable to people who will try to manipulate our behavior to comply with their own wishes. What follows are a few examples that illustrate common use of modeling behavior.

Television situation comedies almost always used canned laughter. Research studies have indicated that canned laughter actually causes audiences to laugh more frequently during shows and to rate the shows as more humorous (Fuller & Sheehy-Skeffington, 1974; Smyth & Fuller, 1972). Almost everyone complains about canned laughter, but television producers continue to use it because it effectively gets audiences to model their behavior after the canned laugh track. In other cases, advertisers often use celebrities and noncelebrities to testify about the advantages of their product in the hope that consumers will model their behavior accordingly. Musicians, bartenders, and others who rely on tips for part of their wages often put out a tip jar, salt it with a few dollars, and hope that others will model their behavior after the fictitious customers who appeared to leave tips. Similarly, church ushers often salt collection baskets for the same reasons. Imagine you are sitting in church, and the collection basket is passed to you and all you see lying in it are 5, 10, and 20 dollar bills. Would you be less likely to drop in your usual 1-dollar bill in these circumstances? Modeling is also used effectively by salespeople describing a product or service to an audience. They often prearrange for people to step forward and buy the product, endorse the service, or in some manner ratify what the salesperson has said in the hope that others will follow. This same technique has been the hallmark of preachers at revival meetings for years. They too prearrange for people to step forward and endorse the preacher's words by declaring their faith. To get others to comply, we often need only to open the floodgates a crack. Our strong tendency to model others' behavior will do the rest.

I have already discussed how modeling is most powerful when people are uncertain about how they should behave. Another condition that maximizes the power of modeling is when we are observing the behavior of people who are *just like us.* This is why advertisers often use seemingly "ordinary" people, who are really professional actors, to give testimonials in their commercials. Consider a television commercial for a new automobile. You would more likely be influenced by the effusive testimonials of Bob and Jane Everybody than by a group of civil engineers testifying to the structural integrity of the unibody construction. A significant downside to our tendency to model behavior is the potential to imitate undesirable behaviors, as well. While discussing problem behavior in chapter 9, I noted how a highly publicized suicide often leads to greatly increased rates of additional suicides in the days and weeks that follow. Research by sociologist David Phillips described the power of this effect when he demonstrated that within 2 months after a front-page suicide story, the rate of suicide in the surrounding geographical area increased by an average of 58 more people than usual (Phillips, 1974). He found that the more highly publicized the suicide, the greater the number of subsequent additional suicides. Similarly, the Columbine High School shootings that occurred in April of 1999 elicited a spate of copycat incidents in other schools.

In summary, the tendency to model the behavior of others can often be used, for better or worse, to stimulate a person's compliance with a request by sending the message that many others are behaving in the same way. The tendency to mimic the behavior of others, particularly those we perceive as similar to ourselves, is almost irresistible.

Authority

> To punish me for my contempt for authority, fate made me an authority myself.
>
> **ALBERT EINSTEIN**

We have all been raised to respect authority and, therefore, we are more predisposed to comply with requests from a perceived authority figure. When I discussed problem solving and reasoning in chapter 5, I explained how this tendency sometimes leads us to inappropriate decisions. It also can result in our compliance with a request that we would otherwise dismiss out of hand.

Compliance with authority is critical for an organized and civilized society. Without it, we would ignore rules and laws, and social anarchy would result. We comply with requests from authorities because we naturally assume that they would not be in such a position of power without legitimate justification and because we want to avoid the sanctions of not obeying. Furthermore, we are often rewarded for such obedience.

Unfortunately, this tendency often leads to blind obedience with disastrous consequences. Cialdini (1988) cited the medical establishment as a prime example. Physicians are presumed to be the ultimate authority in all matters related to health care and, as a result, their orders are usually followed blindly by both their patients and other health professionals, such as nurses and pharmacists. This "doctor-knows-best" compliance has led to countless medical errors resulting in serious injury and death. In one very disturbing study, researchers had a stranger call 22 separate nurses' stations in various kinds of hospitals and identify himself as a hospital physician. The caller directed the nurses to give 20 milligrams of a drug to a specific patient in the hospital. Despite the fact that the physician's name was unfamiliar to the nurses and that the prescribed dosage was known by the nurses to be excessive and dangerous, 95% of the nurses proceeded to obtain the drug from the medicine cabinet and to head for the patient's room to administer it. At this point, the experimenter stepped in and stopped the nurses, revealing the nature of the experiment (Hofling, Brotzman, Dalrymple, Graves, & Pierce, 1966). Furthermore, studies indicate that other physicians are also reluctant to countermand the order of a fellow physician, even when they know it is in error.

A similar situation exists for commercial airline pilots. As the pilot in command, rarely are the captain's decisions questioned by the copilot. In fact, investigations of the cockpit tape recordings after fatal accidents have revealed that crashes are often the result of a captain's faulty judgment that went unquestioned by the copilot—even when the decision was known to be flawed. Many commercial airlines have now hired industrial/organizational psychologists to investigate ways in which pilots can be trained to avoid this unquestioned, and possibly fatal, obedience to authority.

Given our propensity to obey authority figures, you can guarantee that unscrupulous individuals will exploit this tendency to assure we comply with their wishes. It is important to realize that the authority figure does not have to be a *legitimate* authority. It is only important that the person be perceived as an authority. Previously, I described how television commercials often use actors posing as doctors to promote over-the-counter medicines or various medical treatments. Con artists take advantage of this method mercilessly. If you have watched any late-night infomercials, you have noticed that the people hawking the latest get-rich-quick real estate scheme drape themselves with all the trappings of authority: an expensive automobile, a mansion, elegant clothing, and an appearance of expertise and accomplishment.

Cialdini (1988) described several ways in which the false illusion of authority can be promoted. Perhaps the easiest way is to simply use a title that carries the aura of authority with it. Perhaps no title carries with it more cachet than "Doctor." Recently I observed a refinance mortgage company running television commercials where the spokesman's name is displayed, followed conspicuously by the letters "Ph.D." I can personally attest that introducing yourself or being introduced by another as "Doctor" instantly changes how you are perceived. You need to remember that prestigious-sounding titles can be easily procured through the mail at a minimal cost or otherwise acquired in a quasi-legitimate fashion.

Clothing also can elicit compliance to authority. As described in the previous chapter, we are more favorably impressed by people whose appearance is enhanced by their manner of dress. Since we are attracted to them, we are also more likely to comply with their requests. Research has shown that we are also more likely to model our behavior after those who are well dressed. One research study had an adult male cross the street illegally when the light was red. Half the time he was dressed in regular street clothes and half the time in an expensive and freshly pressed business suit and tie. The researchers counted the number of times pedestrians waiting at the corner would follow the man across the street. They found that pedestrians were 3 times more likely to join the jaywalker when he was attired in the expensive business suit (Lefkowitz, Blake, & Mouton, 1955).

Clothes make the man. Naked people have little or no influence on society.

MARK TWAIN

We often identify authority figures through the specific clothing they wear, such as police officers' uniforms or judges' robes. Uniforms that reflect authority seem to have a special power over us that increases our willingness to comply. One series of experiments examined the role of uniforms in forcing compliance (Bickman, 1974). An experimenter posing as a stranger asked passersby on the street to comply with some unusual request. For example, people were asked to pick up a discarded paper bag or to stand on the other side of a bus-stop sign. In some cases, the request was made by a person dressed in regular street clothes and, in other cases, by a person dressed in a security guard's uniform. As you might expect, people were much more likely to comply with these odd requests when asked by the person in the security guard uniform. Later research found similar results when the request came from someone wearing a firefighter's uniform (Bushman, 1984).

Another way that we perceive authority is from the kinds of cars that people drive. Do you think you would behave differently toward the driver of a new Mercedes as compared to the driver of an economy car? Imagine you are sitting at a red light behind one of these two cars when the light turns green. Would you be just as quick to honk at the Mercedes as at the economy car? Researchers asked 57 male and female college students this very question. The males said that they would honk faster at the expensive car while the females reported that they would honk only slightly faster at the economy car. The researchers then conducted the actual study by observing 82 drivers who were blocked at a green light behind the two types of cars. Both male and female drivers had little patience with the drivers of the economy car and nearly all of them honked. When the car refused to move, they honked again, and two drivers actually rammed the car from behind. It was a very different story for the luxury car, with half the drivers waiting respectfully behind it and never honking (Doob & Gross, 1968). Other research has shown that individuals vacate their parking spot more quickly when a luxury automobile is waiting for it as compared to a less expensive car. We consciously or unconsciously give deference to people who display the trappings of wealth or authority, be it through the uniform they wear, how professionally they dress, or even the expensive jewelry they display. Along with that deference comes an increased willingness to comply with their requests.

Friendship

When it comes to compliance with the wishes of others, we prefer to say yes to people *we know and like.* However, the "liking" component is far more important than the "knowing" since there are numerous ways that complete strangers can get us to comply with their requests. Salespeople, con artists, and others who wish to manipulate our compliance are aware of these strategies and use them to full advantage.

What is the basis for our *liking* someone? Because this was discussed at length in the previous chapter, I will only briefly reiterate the main factors here. Physical attractiveness is probably the most important single factor. We assign all kinds of favorable traits to good-looking people, such as talent, honesty, and intelligence, and, therefore, are more likely to comply with their requests. For this reason, most television commercials are enacted by physically attractive individuals. We also like and, comply with individuals who are most similar to us. This includes similarity in appearance, background, and interests. Good salespeople are aware of this and make a point of emphasizing these similarities when dealing with a potential customer. Compliments are also an effective way of endearing oneself to another, and those who seek compliance use this tactic liberally. Finally, we tend to like that with which we are familiar. Therefore, we are more likely to comply with the request of someone with whom we have had frequent contact. For example, politicians curry our favor and our vote by making their name and face very familiar to us through various mass media venues.

APPLICATIONS: Inoculation against Compliance Techniques

You can rest assured that there are many people who are aware of these social influence techniques and they will have no compunction about using them to get you to comply with their requests or wishes. Cialdini (1988) discussed in detail how automatic our responses tend to be to these techniques. I can personally attest that I have fallen victim many times. Recently, two teenagers showed up at my door selling magazine subscriptions for some charitable cause. They employed several of the tactics that I discussed above. They were very friendly and told me that a neighbor had sent them over because I was such a nice and generous person. One of them told me that he also lived in the neighborhood and that he often saw me jogging by his house. The other asked what my profession was and then proceeded to tell me of her similar interests in psychology. Next they asked me for a small favor—that I sign a petition they were circulating. Then they asked me for the bigger favor—that I subscribe to several magazines to help support their charitable cause. I was vaguely aware that they were exploiting several social influence tactics but felt helpless in refusing to comply with their request.

> No man can be friendly to another whose personal habits differ materially from his own. Even the trivialities of table manners thus become important. The fact probably explains much of race prejudice, and even more of national prejudice.
>
> **HENRY LOUIS MENCKEN**

Let's examine each of the tactics and the defenses that can be mounted to counter their effects. Perhaps the most difficult to counter is the rule of reciprocation that states that once someone has made a concession or done us a favor, we then feel obligated to return the favor. One defense is merely to reject the requester's initial favor or concession so that we can avoid the situation completely. However, this is often easier said than done. Alternatively, you should be alert to the fact that the original concession or favor was merely a trick for a bigger request. If you recognize that this is the case, you should freely refuse the larger request. If an automobile insurance salesperson offers you some free trinkets for your car, accept them. If there are strings attached, such as scheduling a meeting to review your insurance coverage, you should recognize the social influence tactic and decline. You can alleviate your guilt by recognizing that the free trinkets were merely a way to gain your compliance to the larger request. Always feel free to exploit those attempting to exploit you.

To counteract the scarcity tactic, first you must be aware of how the tactic works and the arousal that it may cause in us. Cialdini suggests that you tune yourself to the internal, visceral sweep and rising tide of arousal that occurs when you are posed to rush to purchase "the last one that is available." As with reciprocation, merely recognizing that the tactic might be at work can help defuse its effectiveness. Following that, we should assess the merits of exactly why we want the item. Cialdini noted that ". . . very often we don't want a thing for the pure sake of owning it. We want it, instead, for its utility value; we want to eat it or drink it or touch it or hear it or drive it or otherwise *use* it. In such cases, it is vital to remember that scarce things do not taste nor feel nor sound nor ride nor work any better because of their limited availability" (Cialdini, 1988, p. 253).

How about the commonly used low-ball technique where you are offered goods or services at one price only to find the price increases after you have made a commitment? Usually we are aware when this has been pulled on us, and we have to make certain to fight the tendency to honor the commitment that was made at the original price. Cialdini (1988) suggests you ask yourself, would I have purchased these goods or services at this revised price if it had been presented to me originally? If the answer is no, then refuse to accept the revised price.

The tendency to model the behavior of others is usually appropriate. We only need to be concerned when the behavior being modeled is obviously fabricated. We know the canned laughter on the television sitcom is fake just as we also know that those interviews with "average consumers" in commercials are not genuine. You need to be on the alert to such obvious fakery and deal with it appropriately. In addition, remind yourself that just because others similar to you are doing something is not adequate justification to model their behavior.

Complying with the requests of authority figures can also be problematic. It would make no sense always to disregard what authorities say because often their advice and recommendations are sound. You do, however, need to recognize how easily authority symbols can be falsified. Uniforms, titles, and the trappings of authority are sometimes just that—trappings—and not a genuine reflection of authority. Cialdini (1988) suggests that you ask yourself two questions when confronted with authority directives: (1) Is this authority *truly* an expert? and (2) How truthful can we expect this expert to be? The first question refers to the necessity of distinguishing a genuine authority from someone who is merely pretending while the second question suggests that we need to ask ourselves whether the authority stands to benefit in some way from our compliance. You must be particularly alert when authorities or experts have a vested interest in your doing their bidding.

Finally, how do we control the natural tendency to comply with the wishes and requests of those whom we like? According to Cialdini (1988), our vigilance should be directed ". . . toward the things that may produce undue liking . . . and toward the fact that undue liking has been *produced.* The time to call out the defense is when we feel ourselves liking the [person doing the requesting] more than we should under the circumstances" (p. 194). Anytime that you feel you have been manipulated into liking the person making the request more quickly or more deeply than would be expected, you should be on guard. This is almost invariably a sign that you are being artificially manipulated to gain your compliance.

Keep these defenses in mind the next time you find yourself facing social influence tactics. You will not have to wait very long—people are attempting to influence your behavior for their own gain on a regular and frequent basis.

SUMMARY

- Attitudes are stable beliefs and feelings that influence how we act. They are often formed in an illogical manner, influenced by factors of which we are unaware, and significantly shaped by the political and social events that occur between the ages of 16 and 24 years.
- Attitudes consist primarily of emotional, cognitive, and behavioral components, which can function somewhat independently, and may originate from genetically derived personality dispositions.
- Psychologists measure attitudes through the use of scales or tests on which the respondents rate their agreement or disagreement with a series of statements.
- Attitudes are often resistant to change. One technique for bringing about attitude change is persuasion.
- Four factors in the communication process influence persuasiveness: (1) the person doing the communication, (2) the nature of the message, (3) the medium of the message, and (4) the audience.
- To be an effective persuader, you need to establish your expertise and credibility, show that you are unbiased, speak rapidly, use an emotional appeal, present both sides of any argument, and take into account the relevant characteristics of the audience, particularly their intelligence and self-esteem.
- Attitude change occurs for a variety of reasons. According to one cognitive approach, called the Elaboration Likelihood Model, people think about a persuasive message and contemplate the arguments that were and were not made. It is those thought processes that may actually lead to attitude change. A message that is delivered via the central route is one that the receiver finds interesting, important, or personally relevant. Such messages are carefully attended to and thought about, a process that may lead to attitude change. Messages delivered via the peripheral route are those the receiver finds uninteresting and personally irrelevant. Both routes can be effective in bringing about attitude change, depending on the circumstances. In general, attitudes changed through the central route are more permanent, more resistant to later attempts to change them, and more likely to result in concomitant modifications in behavior.
- Cognitive dissonance occurs when there is a discrepancy between one's beliefs and one's actions. It causes a person discomfort that can be reduced by (1) reducing the importance of one of the elements causing the dissonance, (2) adding additional elements that explain the discrepancy, or (3) changing either one's attitudes or behavior.
- In certain circumstances, forcing individuals to behave in a certain way can result in a change in their attitudes, such as the use of brainwashing. For example, the Chinese Communists used brainwashing on American POWs during the Korean War. Under those circumstances, brainwashing was an effective means of changing attitudes because the individuals were isolated, made dependent on their captives, and selectively reinforced for any change in attitude or behavior.
- Other examples of brainwashing and effective attitude change have occurred with political and religious cults. Cults appeal to vulnerable individuals who are initially showered with attention and unconditional love when they join but later must make successively larger personal sacrifices and commitments to the group until they have no life outside serving the organization.
- According to cognitive dissonance theory, difficult decisions are often accompanied by attitude change. We are more likely to change our attitude about something if there is a cost involved.
- Self-perception theory provides an alternative to cognitive dissonance and states that people observe their own behavior and then infer an attitude consistent with the behavior.
- Prejudice is a negative attitude toward another person based on the person's membership in a social group. Like attitudes, prejudiced beliefs consist of emotional, cognitive, and behavioral components.
- Recent research suggests that prejudice is extremely widespread, even among those who feel that they are completely nonprejudiced. These studies show that prejudice and stereotyping often occur at the unconscious level.
- Several approaches have been taken to reduce prejudice, such as (1) increasing the intergroup contact when certain conditions can be met, (2) attempting to get people to redefine the boundaries of what they consider their in-group in order to include individuals

formerly categorized as belonging to the out-group, and (3) altering the way people think about others. All three approaches can be successful, but the fact remains that prejudices are very resistant to change.

- Compliance is the act of getting another person to agree to a request. Several techniques can effectively bring about compliance. The rule of reciprocation states that once someone has made a concession or done someone else a favor, that individual will then feel obligated to return the favor. Several techniques to bring about compliance are based on this rule.
- The door-in-the-face technique involves making a large request followed by a smaller request. The smaller request is likely to be granted if the initial large request was refused.
- In the that's-not-all technique, a request is made and something extra is offered before the person has a chance to deny the request.
- In the foot-in-the-mouth technique, a mutual relationship is established before a request is made.
- Often our compliance is affected by the scarcity principle. Objects or opportunities are perceived as more valuable when they are less available. Hence, we will comply more readily with a request to avail ourselves of something that is scarce.
- The low-ball technique encourages compliance by offering goods or services at an initially favorable price. The price is then raised once a commitment is made to purchase.
- Compliance also can occur when we model the behavior of others. Often we determine what behavior is appropriate for us by observing what other people think is correct. Such modeling can cause us to change our behavior to make it consistent with others.
- We also frequently adjust our behavior to comply with the demands of a perceived authority. Blindly following the dictates of an authority can result in disastrous consequences. Individuals can misrepresent themselves as an authority in a variety of ways, including the use of titles, dress, and the trappings of wealth.
- We are more likely to comply with the wishes of people we know and like.
- Several techniques for inoculating ourselves from efforts to force compliance of our behavior are described. In general, being aware of and alert to the various techniques when they are being used against us can help protect us from them.

KEY TERMS

attitudes: relatively stable beliefs and feelings that predispose us to react to objects, people, and events in certain ways.

brainwashing: thought control procedures that involve isolation, dependence, and selective reinforcement.

central route: an Elaboration Likelihood Model process that happens when recipients find a message interesting, important, or personally relevant, or when the recipient pays careful attention to the message.

cognitive consistency: when one's beliefs, attitudes, and behaviors are in agreement.

cognitive dissonance: when one's beliefs, attitudes, and behaviors are not consistent.

cohort effect: the tendency for each age group to have distinct experiences and to develop certain viewpoints or perspectives on a variety of matters.

compliance: the act of getting a person to agree to the request of another.

discrimination: the behavioral component of prejudice that consists of overt acts that treat certain groups in an unfair manner.

Elaboration Likelihood Model (ELM): a theory that refers to the process of hearing a persuasive message, and then thinking about what was heard.

implicit stereotyping: an automatic tendency to stereotype individuals.

low-ball technique: an effective way of gaining compliance that involves removing a favorable circumstance after a commitment decision has been made.

peripheral route: an Elaboration Likelihood Model process that happens when a recipient finds a message uninteresting or irrelevant, and consequently is not motivated to pay careful attention or examine the message thoroughly.

prejudice: a negative attitude toward another person based on that person's membership in a social group.

recategorization: the process of changing the boundaries of what a person considers an in-group (us) versus an out-group (them) affiliation.

reciprocation: a rule that states that once someone has made a concession or done us a favor, we feel obligated to return the favor.

scarcity principle: the tendency to consider objects or opportunities as more valuable when they are less available.

self-perception theory: a theory that proposes that people observe their behavior and then infer an attitude that is consistent with that behavior.

stereotypes: beliefs that one holds about minority groups.

vicarious learning: acquisition of attitudes by observing the reactions of others.

13

Working with Others in Groups

Never doubt that a small group of thoughtful committed people can change the world: Indeed it's the only thing that ever has!

MARGARET MEAD

Since human beings are a social species, much of our daily life is spent interacting in groups. The demands of modern society require that we live our lives interdependently with others. Many of the complex tasks that we are required to do involve utilizing the knowledge, skills, or expertise of individuals other than ourselves. It is rare indeed that a single individual possesses all of these characteristics. Consequently, we often find ourselves working together in groups to achieve some common goal. Social psychologists have devoted a great deal of time in the research and analysis of how and why groups do or do not work together effectively. All of us have belonged to groups that worked together productively, as well as to groups that were almost totally ineffectual. In this chapter, we will examine some of the important variables that distinguish between these two group outcomes.

If you think about it, you will realize that you are probably a member of at least a dozen or more different groups. Social psychologists consider a **group** to be any *two or more interacting individuals who share common goals, have a stable relationship, are interdependent on one another, and perceive themselves as part of a group* (Paulus, 1989). Note the key terms in this definition include common goals, stable relationship, interdependence, and the perception of group membership. Being a member of a fraternity or sorority meets the definition of belonging to a group. Sitting on a bus with a group of strangers or attending a sporting event does not. In these latter cases, there is no stable relationship or interdependence on each other, and there may not even be a common goal.

Advantages of Belonging to a Group

Why do individuals join groups? I mentioned earlier that one advantage lies in reaching goals that otherwise could not be attained. Belonging to a group also satisfies several social and psychological needs that we all have. Groups allow us to give and receive attention and give us an important sense of belonging. Many times groups allow us access to knowledge or information that we would not have otherwise. For example, if you joined a coin-collecting club, one of your motives probably would be to learn more about coins. Finally, group membership helps us establish our social identity. For instance, joining a political organization would likely result in those individuals identifying themselves positively in several ways, such as seeing themselves as people who have strong interests in politics and government, who take active roles in the democratic process, and so forth. It is the rare individual who does not join groups to meet many of his or her social and psychological needs, and society generally looks upon such isolated individuals with some disdain.

Group Functioning

Normative Behaviors

Normative behaviors are the rules that are established by groups to regulate the members' behavior. Every group has established norms about how or how not to behave and, generally, groups are quite insistent that members "play by the rules." Sometimes the rules are not written down or even verbally discussed. Nevertheless, members who wish to function in the group are expected to learn what the rules are and abide by them. Even very young children quickly learn the harsh reality of breaking the group's unwritten rules, particularly when such behavior results in the child's exclusion from the group.

Think about the normative behaviors that are expected of you in the classroom. Even though professors typically do not spell out all these rules at the beginning of the course, most class members fully understand the protocols for classroom behavior they are expected to follow. Undoubtedly, you have been in classes where 1 or more students have violated these rules. For example, even though asking questions and taking part in classroom discussions are considered normative behaviors, students who repeatedly ask questions every few minutes or attempt to dominate classroom discussions soon feel the disapproval of their classmates.

Roles We Play in Groups

Roles are the specific ways that individuals in groups are expected to behave. Just as the actors in a play have different roles, so do the various individuals within a group. If, for instance, you are the president of an organization, the roles that you are expected to play are quite different from those for the treasurer or secretary. Frequently, on the other hand, we must play multiple roles, sometimes referred to as "wearing different hats." For example, in any given day I find myself playing the roles of a professor to my students, department chair to members of the psychology department, supervisor to my secretary, husband to my wife, and father to my 2 children. This can get very confusing at times because one needs to switch roles very quickly. Even my role as department chair often varies, depending on whether I am with a group of my faculty, or other department chairs, or interacting with higher administrators. Sometimes the different roles that we have to play require conflicting behaviors that lead to **role conflict.** Such conflicts can cause a great deal of stress as people try to make the necessary adjustments. Furthermore, the roles that individuals are forced to assume in a group can sometimes limit their freedom and subsequently require them to take positions or actions with which they do not agree. Despite these complexities, most people usually learn to assume the appropriate role at the appropriate time.

How Groups Change

Changes in Groups

Groups rarely maintain constancy. Instead, they are continuously changing and developing. The nature of these changes often has a significant impact on members of the group.

Social psychologists have shown that groups go through predictable stages of development. These stages are relatively uniform for groups as diverse as fraternities, religious organizations, political parties, and social movements (Worchel, Coutant-Sassic, & Grossman, 1991). When a group is initially forming, the biggest concern involves establishing the group's identity and building morale. Groups typically insist on conformity and punish any deviant behavior during this early stage of development. Strong leaders emerge early in the process, and the group resists cooperating with other groups. As the group develops further, the focus shifts to identifying group goals and encouraging group performance. There is less demand for conformity and a greater willingness to accept the diverse opinions of its members if the group feels such opinions will help group performance. As the group develops further, emphasis on personal reward and recognition increases (Worchel & Shebilske, 1995). Subsequent research findings on small groups have shown that groups are most productive during the *middle phases* of group development when the greatest emphasis is on group performance (Worchel, Grossman, & Coutant-Sassic, 1994).

Individual Changes

Just as groups go through developmental changes, so do individual members of the groups. As a prospective member, the main emphasis is on learning all you can about the group. When you first join a group, the emphasis is on fitting in or on being accepted by the other members. As you become established in the group, you begin to negotiate precisely what roles you will play within the group. With further tenure, group members begin to assert their independence. Finally, as members phase out of the group, they spend most of their time reminiscing about past activities in which the group engaged. No doubt you have joined and left several groups. Think back and see if you experienced these typical developmental stages.

Performance in Groups

Social Facilitation and Social Inhibition

Think about what happens to your performance when you work in a group rather than individually. Imagine, for instance, that you were trying to run the 50-yard dash as quickly as possible. Would you be more likely to run faster by yourself and without an audience or when you were competing against others, either in the presence or absence of an audience? Many research studies have shown that performance frequently *improves* when it is conducted in the presence of others, a phenomenon psychologists call **social facilitation.** A psychologist first documented this occurrence over 100 years ago when he noticed that bicyclists cycled faster when competing against each other as compared to when they cycled alone against a clock (Triplett, 1898). Although subsequent research has supported this general finding, under some circumstances the presence of others can actually interfere with an individual's performance, a phenomenon labeled **social inhibition.** An example of social inhibition commonly occurs when individuals are required to give a speech in front of an audience. Many people find that the speech they have rehearsed and delivered perfectly when alone is delivered with much less skill when standing in front of a large and attentive audience. The fact that the presence of others can enhance or impair performance has led psychologists to investigate precisely what circumstances are responsible for both of these outcomes.

Robert Zajonc (1965, 1980), the leading theorist and researcher in this area, proposed that the presence of others produces feelings of increased arousal, especially when they are paying careful attention to our performance. This arousal can help or hurt performance depending upon whether the performer's responses are dominant or not. Zajonc defined dominant responses as responses that a person is most likely to make in a given situation. However, these dominant responses can be either correct or incorrect for any particular task. Several subsequent studies have led to the following 3 conclusions:

1. The presence of others *improves* performance when a person's dominant responses are the correct ones for a given situation. For example, individuals generally perform simple, well-learned tasks better in the presence of an audience as compared to alone.
2. The presence of others *impairs* performance when a person's dominant responses are the incorrect ones for a given situation. For example, if someone has a tendency to stutter or stammer while speaking, these tendencies would be increased by the presence of others.
3. The presence of others *improves* performance in situations where individuals are highly skilled in performing the task. For example, a champion ice skater may be energized by the presence of a large audience and actually give a better performance than he or she would when practicing alone.

As you can see, whether the presence of an audience helps or hurts your performance can be complicated and depends on several factors.

Social Loafing

What happens to your level of performance when you are working cooperatively within a group setting? If you are a member of an orchestra, do you try as hard when playing with the group as when you are playing alone? Social psychologists have found that as the size of a group *increases,* the amount of effort by individual members *decreases.* This phenomenon has been termed **social loafing** (Latané, Williams, & Harkins, 1979). As a general rule, when individuals believe that an increasing number of other people are participating in a task, they tend to exert less individual effort. In other words, the larger the number of participants, the less work each individual exerts.

Studies have suggested that social loafing can be largely eliminated under circumstances where all individuals in the group are led to believe that their individual performance is being evaluated solely on its own merits (Harkins, 1987). For instance, if you are working with several other classmates on a lab project, social loafing would be less likely to occur if the instructor informed the students that they would be graded on their individual contributions and not on the overall quality of the resulting group project.

Social loafing is also influenced by cultural factors. It is more prevalent in societies that emphasize individual efforts, such as the United States. In collectivist societies, where the emphasis is on group accomplishments, individuals may actually work harder when they are in a group than when they are working alone. For example, research has shown that social loafing occurs less frequently in socialist and Communist countries (Early, 1989).

Bystander Apathy

A very important event occurred in the mid-1960s that had a significant impact on the field of social psychology. Surprisingly enough, the event was a very brutal crime. At 3:00 A.M. on March 13, 1964, a young woman named Kitty Genovese was stabbed to death by a stranger on a street outside her apartment in downtown

New York City. The man chased and stabbed her repeatedly over a 45-minute period while she pleaded for her life. This particular murder stood out because 38 of the victim's neighbors, who had been roused from their beds by her pleas for help, witnessed the murder and did not help in any way. Even though many of these neighbors peered down on the crime scene from their apartment windows or balconies, no one bothered to telephone the police. Considerable publicity followed this event, and news reporters asked psychologists how so many people could stand by and allow a crime such as this to happen without anyone lifting a finger to aid the victim. This tendency for onlookers to fail to provide assistance to those in need is commonly referred to as **bystander apathy.**

Science may have found a cure for most evils; but it has found no remedy for the worst of them all—the apathy of human beings.

HELEN KELLER
My Religion

Two New York City social psychologists began a systematic study of this phenomenon (Latané & Darley, 1970). They theorized that in the Genovese situation, it was precisely *because* 38 people witnessed the murder that no one offered to help. In this circumstance, a process called **diffusion of responsibility** sets in whereby everyone thinks that someone else will probably assist the victim. As a consequence, no one steps forward or assumes a personal responsibility to help.

A series of experiments was designed to test this theory (Latané & Darley, 1968). One laboratory experiment allowed college students to hear another student in an adjoining cubicle using an intercom system. The students heard the student in the adjacent cubicle experience what sounded like an epileptic seizure. When the test subjects individually believed that they were the only ones hearing the other student, 85% of them went to the student's aid. However, if the test subject student believed that one other student also heard the seizure victim, the rate of assistance dropped to 62%. If four other students were known to be listening in adjoining cubicles, only 31% tried to help. These findings dramatically illustrated the diffusion of responsibility that occurs when even a small number of other bystanders are also available to help. Therefore, is it any wonder that none of the 38 bystanders who witnessed the Genovese murder took personal responsibility for providing assistance?

Have you ever walked by a person lying on a street without offering assistance? If you live in any large city, it is likely that you have. In doing so, you have probably noticed that others around you have also continued to walk calmly by the person, also without offering assistance, a phenomenon called **pluralistic ignorance.** This occurs when each individual in a group decides that no assistance is needed based on his or her observations that no one else seems concerned.

This phenomenon was demonstrated in another experiment with college students in which they were brought into a room and asked to fill out a questionnaire. The researchers then began to pump smoke into the room through a ventilation opening. When the students were alone in the room, 75% of them left the room and reported the smoke. However, when 3 students were in the room, 1 of them reported the smoke only 38% of the time (Latané & Darley, 1968). In a demonstration of the power of pluralistic ignorance, the researchers arranged another situation where 3 students were in the room when the smoke appeared. In this test, 2 of the students were actually confederates of the researchers and had been instructed to continue working on the questionnaire while acting as if the smoke was no cause for alarm. Under these circumstances, only 10% of the student test subjects left the room to report the smoke. In fact, the researchers reported that the test subjects continued dutifully to work on the questionnaire as the room filled completely with smoke. They took no action to report the "emergency," even when the smoke became so thick

Sometimes individuals offer no assistance to another individual because they observe that no one else seems to be concerned. This scene of people calmly walking by a homeless person is a common one in most large cities.

that they began coughing, rubbing their eyes, and waving the smoke away from their faces. Observing that the other two students did not seem alarmed, the test subjects also acted unconcerned. As other research has indicated, assistance in an emergency is more likely to be offered if just 1 onlooker acts alarmed. Apparently, just this feedback from 1 other individual is all that is necessary to break the pluralistic ignorance of the onlookers and the impassivity that results.

A large number of research studies have examined what factors will increase or decrease the likelihood that a bystander will intervene in an emergency. Factors that have been shown to *increase* bystander intervention include:

- Similarities between the bystander and the victim, such as gender, age, race, and so forth
- Some personal relationship existing between the victim and the bystander
- Bystander being an empathic individual
- Bystander knowing how to help the victim, such as first-aid training
- Bystander being in a good mood
- Bystander being an emotional individual

Factors that have been shown to *decrease* bystander intervention include:

- The victim showing evidence of bleeding
- Bystander recognizing the victim as a member of a stigmatized group, such as a homeless person
- Bystander being in a hurry to get somewhere
- Bystander having any negative reaction to some characteristic of the victim, such as his or her being dirty, unshaven, disheveled, and so forth
- The presence of a large number of bystanders

APPLICATIONS: Being a Responsive Bystander

In the course of your daily living, it is likely that you will periodically encounter unexpected situations where your help is badly needed. In each of these situations, you will need to decide whether or not to intervene. In some cases, such as a burning automobile or house, your intervention may put you in personal danger and, therefore, you might wisely decide to defer to trained professionals. In many other cases, however, you can provide assistance with little or no risk to your own safety.

The following suggestions will assist you in making an informed decision about whether or not to intervene (Baron & Byrne, 2000):

- Pay attention to what is happening around you. Often in the rush of our everyday lives, we are not as attentive to our surroundings as we should be. Take the time to observe what is going on around you and monitor whether your assistance might be needed.
- Consider possible alternatives. When you observe something unusual, consider the various alternatives. If you smell smoke, is someone burning trash or is it a dwelling that is burning? If a child is screaming, is it because the child is angry or is it because he or she is being abused? Is that man who is chasing the woman merely fooling around or is the woman in danger? In ambiguous situations such as this, take the time to investigate further and decide what would be an appropriate response.
- Assume responsibility. In an emergency, typically you will observe that others are doing nothing. Do not let the unresponsiveness of others guide you into being nonresponsive. Take responsibility for reacting appropriately to the situation.
- Be willing to act. Sometimes, we are frozen into inaction because we fear that we might be acting foolishly. For instance, that person who appears to be in distress might not really need our assistance and might even resent it if we offer to help. While there is always a chance of this happening, it is better to act needlessly than pass by a true emergency. Better to err on the side of caution.

Deindividuation

> An individual in a crowd descends several rungs in the ladder of civilization.
>
> **GUSTAVE LE BON**
> *The Crowd* (1896)

Have you ever found yourself in a group setting where the presence of the group affected your behavior in ways that differed significantly from how you normally behave when by yourself? People at sporting events such as football games often engage in behaviors that they would never consider doing as individuals. People who participate in riots are often caught up in the group frenzy and commit acts of aggression or crimes of theft and looting that they would otherwise consider morally wrong.

Social psychologists have coined the term **deindividuation** to describe and explain the changes in individuals when they become part of a crowd (Festinger, Pepitone, & Newcomb, 1952). Deindividuation refers to the process by which individuals sometimes *lose their personal identities* when functioning as part of a group. There are several conditions that foster deindividuation in group settings. These include emotional arousal, feelings of anonymity, and diffusion of responsibility. Being in a novel environment that produces a great deal of sensory stimula-

Individuals in group settings sometimes engage in antisocial behaviors that they would ordinarily never consider doing. In this photo, individuals are committing theft during a riot.

tion and being under the influence of mind-altering drugs also make the process of deindividuation more likely to occur (Zimbardo, 1970).

Perhaps the ideal setting for studying deindividuation is the Mardi Gras celebration that takes place in New Orleans each year. All the conditions that would lead to deindividuation are present. There are large crowds in a novel environment that generates great amounts of sensory stimulation from the sights, sounds, and smells of the celebration. Participants are emotionally aroused and often under the influence of alcohol. Feelings of anonymity are increased by the masks and costumes that participants wear. The result? People behave in bizarre ways that they would otherwise consider unthinkable. People kiss and engage in sexual acts with strangers, women display their breasts in order to receive a set of cheap glass beads from passing floats, and so forth. An individual witnessing these behaviors on television, or from afar, would likely wonder how such bizarre behaviors could happen.

Deindividuation reflects an altered subjective state with different causes and consequences (Zimbardo, 1970). The anonymity that individuals feel in a group setting can lead them to engage in antisocial behaviors. Anthropological data from various cultures around the world reveal a strong correlation between the extent that societies disguise their warriors with war paint, masks, or garments and the degree of brutality they engage in during battle (Watson, 1973). Similarly, groups of older children dressed in Halloween costumes are sometimes observed engaging in acts of vandalism that they would otherwise never consider.

Deindividuation often can be seen in institutions, such as prisons and mental hospitals, where both employees and inmates wear uniforms and act in roles that strip the groups of their individuality. During World War II, inmates in concentration camps or prisoner of war camps were typically assigned uniforms and given identification numbers. In many cases, the uniformed guards brutalized these inmates.

In some cases institutions intentionally want to deindividualize group members. For instance, the military wants to train soldiers to follow commands. The soldiers must be trained to perform acts of aggression, including killing, that their inner moral code might otherwise prohibit. To accomplish this, new military recruits are given identical uniforms, have their heads shaved, and are issued serial numbers and "dog tags." During basic training they are totally submerged in a novel environment and often emotionally aroused during training. Therefore, all the conditions for the deindividuation process are present.

If you have ever been caught up in crowd behavior, you know that feelings of self-awareness are regularly altered. People in arousing and overstimulating group settings begin to focus more on the events occurring around them and attend less to their own inner values, standards, and attitudes (Diener, 1980). Individuals' self-awareness lowers in such settings and, as a consequence, they may behave in ways that violate their inner moral code. Deindividuation does not always have negative consequences, however. Individuals are also more likely to engage in charitable acts under these conditions (Spivey & Prentice-Dunn, 1990). Apparently, deindividuation has the capability of lessening our inhibitions for a variety of behaviors that range from good to bad.

Social Contagion

In June 1962, a strange illness swept through a textile plant in North Carolina. In a period of 11 days, a total of 62 textile workers required medical treatment for what they claimed were insect bites. The symptoms included feelings of faintness, nausea, severe pain, and disorientation. The workers who reported having the illness consisted of 59 females and 3 males, all white, who all worked the same shift in the same area of the textile plant. A careful investigation by both medical personnel and factory officials failed to turn up a cause for the illness, which soon disappeared.

A subsequent study of this mass illness revealed that it was a case of **social contagion**—that is, the mass psychogenic illness of a group of individuals caused exclusively by psychological factors (Kerckhoff & Back, 1968). Subsequent investigations revealed some interesting conditions led to the mass illness: (1) the workers were all under high stress levels in their jobs because of pending layoffs; (2) their jobs were extremely boring and many workers expressed a desire to quit; (3) an illness caused by insect bites was plausible since insects are common in textile plants; and (4) the "illness" spread through social networks with close friends of the infected workers most likely to report symptoms.

Subsequent studies have indicated numerous instances of such illness due to social contagion. Oftentimes entire buildings are evacuated while health officials search in vain for the source of the sickness. One review of 23 cases of such "illnesses" in various work settings involved over 1,000 individuals. Certain commonalities were noted in these cases, namely (Colligan & Murphy, 1982):

- Most of those afflicted (89%) were women.
- Those who were afflicted worked in tedious, repetitious, and stressful jobs.
- Tension frequently existed between workers and management.
- The illness initially began with social isolates but eventually spread through social networks, such as close friends.

BOX 13.1
A CALM LOOK AT MASS MADNESS: PHENOMENON LINKED TO ANXIETY

***Denver Post* Article on Social Contagion**

McMinnville, Tennessee—First there were fumes that made a teacher sick. Then some students got sick, and the ambulances came, and 170 people went to the emergency room. The school closed for nearly two weeks while experts tested the air and water.

And more than a year later, the people of Warren County found out what had been wrong with their school building.

Nothing.

On Jan. 13, the *New England Journal of Medicine* reported that the mysterious ailment at Warren County High in November 1998 was a form of mass hysteria, called mass psychogenic illness. The symptoms—headache, dizziness, nausea and breathing difficulty—were real. But they weren't caused by a toxin. They were caused by anxiety.

The episode is not as bizarre as it sounds. Analysts say the phenomenon frequently affects schools, factories, offices and army barracks, where people are under stress and share common space.

"It's much more common than most of us realize," says Timothy Jones, an epidemiologist at the Tennessee Department of Health and the lead author of the journal article. At the time of the outbreak, Jones was an officer at the Centers for Disease Control and Prevention.

"The huge majority (of cases) are not published or widely announced, so they tend to be dealt with locally, and they go away and that's the end of it."

But no one knows how often these cases happen, because they rarely are examined scientifically and reported. Even when health-care officials suspect mass psychogenic illness, they are often reluctant to label it as such because of community pressure to pursue an investigation.

The prolonged quest for answers—coupled with intense media attention—only fuels the anxiety and suspicion of a cover-up, at great cost to the community, the journal article says. In the McMinnville case, along with the missed school days, an estimated $93,000 was spent on emergency medical care.

Mass psychogenic illness has occurred throughout the world since at least the Middle Ages.

Centuries ago, outbreaks usually were triggered by fear of demons and spirits, religious ceremonies or feverish dancing. Today, the catalysts more typically are worries about exposure to toxins and bacteria. The journal article's authors say cases might increase with rising fears of bioterrorism.

In Belgium last summer, 250 people complained of illness after drinking Coca-Cola, prompting the largest recall in Coke's 113-year history—2.5 million bottles. It was attributed in large part to mass hysteria.

SOURCE: Marego Athans, *The Baltimore Sun*. Reprinted with permission.

- Physical symptoms were always vague.
- The "illness" eventually faded away in 1 to 2 weeks.

Social contagion is merely one example of the interesting ways that groups can affect individuals and individuals can affect groups. People who are working in stressful and tedious jobs want to quit their jobs but feel inhibited from doing so. Being in a group setting results in deindividuation, and these inhibitions relax. This can manifest itself in a subsequent "illness" that justifies leaving the unpleasant job. Their behavior spreads to others whose inhibitions also relax, and social contagion is under way.

Cooperation Within and Among Groups

Robber's Cave Experiment

A classic experiment on group cooperation was conducted at the Robber's Cave State Park, Oklahoma, in the summer of 1954 (Sherif, Harvey, White, Hood, &

Sherif, 1961). A group of white, middle-class, 11-year-old boys was divided into two sections. None of the boys knew each other prior to the experiment. All the boys enjoyed the typical camp activities, such as swimming, hiking, and camping, and neither group knew of the other group's existence. Each group selected their own group name that was printed on their T-shirts and caps.

After the first week, each group discovered the existence of the other group of boys. They were told that their group would be competing with the other group in a series of athletic competitions. Once the contests began the groups became confrontational, hostile, and antagonistic to each other. The boys even began to raid and ransack each other's camps. However, as competition between the groups increased, the individual groups themselves became increasingly cohesive.

The experimenters then decided to see whether the two groups could be induced to cooperate by setting a common goal for both groups. To accomplish this task, the experimenters created emergencies that could only be resolved by intergroup cooperation. In a case where a water pipe developed a leak, boys from both groups were assigned the duty of locating the leak. In another fabricated emergency, a truck carrying boys to a campsite became stuck in the mud and could only be removed by both groups cooperating with each other. By the end of the experiment the two groups were getting along fine and playing peacefully together. This experiment demonstrated 3 important aspects of group behaviors that have been observed repeatedly in many other group situations: (1) When groups compete against one another, there is increased unity within each individual group. (2) Hostility between groups is increased when the groups are required to compete against one another. (3) Competition and hostility can be greatly reduced or even eliminated by requiring groups to work cooperatively on a common goal. Notice the similarities between these findings and the results of research dealing with the reduction of prejudice discussed in the previous chapter. In both cases, hostility increased as groups competed against one another but diminished when groups worked cooperatively on a common goal.

GROUP DECISION MAKING

Group Polarization

If you have ever been a part of a group decision-making process, you know that sometimes groups make good decisions and sometimes they make bad decisions. For example, during my academic career I have served on dozens of search and screen committees formed to hire faculty members and administrators. Each search committee varies in size but usually consists of 5 to 10 individuals. The task of the search committee is to select the best-qualified candidate from, oftentimes, hundreds of applications. In one instance, I served on a committee to hire a university vice president from a pool of nearly 1,000 applications submitted by many highly qualified candidates. Ironically, the individual who we finally selected turned out to be a completely ineffectual administrator. Each committee member later wondered how we, as a group, could have arrived at such a poor decision from such a large and highly qualified applicant pool.

Research by social psychologists does give us considerable insight into how groups arrive at decisions. For example, several studies have demonstrated that following a group's discussion of an issue, the group as a whole tends to adopt a more extreme decision than would the average individual in the group. This phenomenon is referred to as **group polarization** (Moscovici & Zavalloni, 1969; Myers & Lamm, 1976). For example, a jury that is deciding on the severity of a crime, say, between first degree murder, second degree murder, manslaughter, or acquittal, oftentimes will arrive at a more extreme position than would individual jurors. This extreme position, however, can go in *either* direction. In the case of a jury, the verdict would lean toward the extremes of first degree murder or toward acquittal. One study found that the best predictor of a jury's ultimate verdict is the view held by the majority of the members at the initial polling (Kerr, 1981). Jurors, like other groups, reach a majority consensus because those with the minority opinion tend to shift their views to agree with the majority. This is particularly true when the group is required to reach a unanimous decision (Kaplan & Miller, 1987).

Perhaps the best illustration of group polarization occurred in January 1986, when NASA decided to launch the space shuttle *Challenger* despite the concerns expressed by several engineers relating to the design and safety of its solid rocket boosters. The solid rocket boosters exploded 73 seconds after launch, killing all the crew aboard. An investigation revealed that the engineers' concerns were overruled by groups of high-level officials working for the company that designed the rocket boosters. They were under pressure from NASA officials to launch the space shuttle in a timely fashion. This faulty group decision to launch not only resulted in a needless loss of life but also set back the U.S. manned flight program for quite some time.

Groupthink

Sometimes, when group members are trying to reach unanimity of opinion, they fail to consider realistic alternative courses of action and decide to take a course of action that later proves to be disastrous. Irving Janis described this kind of group process that he labeled **groupthink** (Janis, 1972). Janis analyzed several foreign-policy decisions that he felt reflected groupthink, including the Cuban Bay of Pigs fiasco, the appeasement of Adolf Hitler by British prime minister Neville Chamberlain, and the failure to anticipate the Pearl Harbor bombing by the Japanese. Infamous group decisions that occurred in the business world and led to financial disaster included the ill-fated attempts to introduce a "new" Coca-Cola and a "smokeless" cigarette. If you have ever worked in a large organization, such as a business, governmental agency, or even a university, then you have probably witnessed the detrimental effects from groupthink.

Several conditions can result in groupthink, such as (1) a group that is strongly cohesive or feels a strong sense of togetherness; (2) a group that is isolated from outside views; (3) group leaders who fail to offer impartial leadership, who express strong opinions, who signal their own preferences, and who discourage any dissenting views; (4) a group whose members have similar backgrounds and views and are empowered to make decisions; and (5) stressful circumstances in which a group decision must be reached (Janis, 1972).

Symptoms of groupthink include:

1. Closed-mindedness. The group is not open to alternative ideas or ways of thinking.
2. Rationalization. The group justifies its decisions by any means necessary, including distorting reality and discounting contradictory evidence.

3. Suppression of dissent. Any dissenting views from inside the group are strongly opposed.
4. Illusion of invulnerability. A feeling by the group that their decision is unquestionably correct, which then leads them to excessive optimism and a tendency to make risky decisions.
5. Feelings of unanimity. A feeling that everyone in the group agrees with the decision, even if this is not the case.
6. Emergence of "mindguards." Mindguards are self-appointed members of the group who serve to "protect" other members of the group from receiving information that is inconsistent with the group belief and who suppress any deviant viewpoints.
7. Moralistic beliefs. The group strongly believe in the morality of their actions and therefore ignore any conflicting moral or ethical considerations.
8. Stereotyping of opponents. Those who express dissenting views are stereotyped as stupid, unenlightened, evil, and so forth.

APPLICATIONS: Avoiding Groupthink

Groupthink can result in catastrophic consequences, especially when engaged in by people in positions of power, such as governmental officials. What can be done to avoid groupthink? Janis (1985) offers several suggestions:

- Make certain that dissenting views are heard.
- Ensure that questions that challenge the prevailing views are asked and discussed.
- The group leader should exhibit impartiality by not expressing strong beliefs or positions at the outset of discussions.
- Seek input from experts outside of the group. Views that challenge the prevailing opinions should be particularly sought and encouraged.
- Schedule a second meeting some time after arriving at a consensus, and encourage group members to express reservations or concerns that they might have. This provides groups with a second chance to avoid groupthink.

Despite the clear evidence of the dangers of groupthink, many organizations continue to function in ways that encourage it. This is particularly evident in the higher echelons of government where powerful people often base decisions on the information and advice provided by a small coterie of close and like-minded associates.

Conformity

There is often considerable pressure on members of groups to conform to the wishes or norms of the group. **Conformity** is behavior that occurs when an individual's behavior or attitudes are influenced because of perceived or actual group pressures. Most people have been involved in group activities where they "went along" with the group even though they had personal reservations about doing so. Oftentimes,

✦ FIGURE 13.1 ✦ The Asch (1951) Experiment on Judging Line Lengths

A group of subjects was asked to state which line on the left matches the length of the line on the right. All of the subjects except one were confederates of the experimenter and had been instructed to answer "line C." Results showed that the individual would conform his or her answer to the incorrect group judgment about one-third of the time.

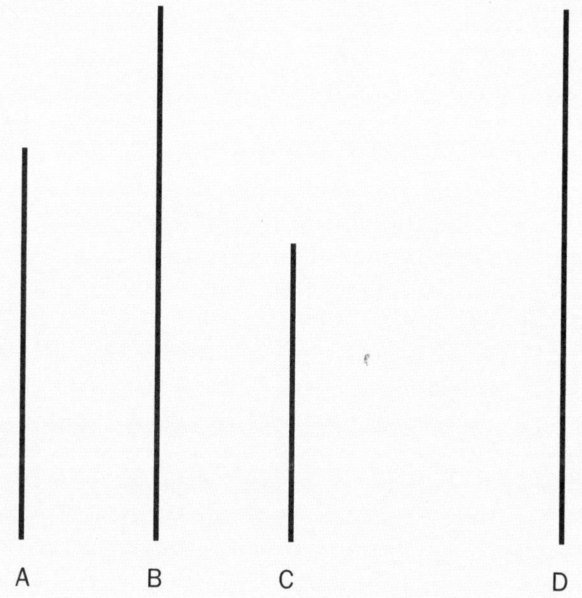

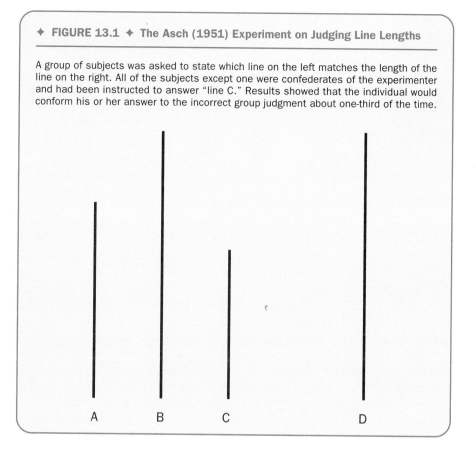

this conformity is helpful or even necessary if a group is to function smoothly. However, this tendency to conform to group pressure can also have disastrous consequences. History is replete with examples of social injustices to others because individuals were conforming to real or perceived group pressures. We are more susceptible to conformity at certain times of our lives. For example, during the teenage years, individuals feel a particularly strong compulsion to conform with what they perceive as group norms. This includes behaviors such as the manner of speaking, dress codes, musical preferences, food choices, and so forth.

Solomon Asch (1951) conducted the classic experiment that demonstrated how powerful the effects of group pressure can be. Several subjects were seated at a table and shown the vertical lines illustrated in Figure 13.1. The subjects were supposed to say which of the three lines on the left, labeled A, B, and C, matched the line labeled D. The obvious answer is that line B matches line D. Unbeknownst to the test subject, who was the last one to render a judgment, all of the other subjects already had been instructed to state that line C was the correct answer. Asch found that under these circumstances about one-third of the test subjects would make their judgment conform to the previous judgments.

Conform and be dull.

JAMES FRANK DOBIE

Several factors have been shown to affect degree of comformity.

- Individual characteristics. Individuals are more likely to conform to group norms when they are strongly attracted to a group, feel that the group does not accept them, anticipate future interactions with group members, lack confidence about their abilities, or suffer from low self-esteem. Both men and women conform more when the topic is one with which they are unfamiliar (Sistrunk & McDavid, 1971). For example, women might conform more when the topic is sports while men might conform more on a discussion of parenting styles.
- Group characteristics. Group conformity increases as group size increases. However, after a group reaches a size of four, little additional conformity occurs with additional members (Tanford & Penrod, 1984). Conformity is also more likely to occur in groups where there is a high degree of cohesiveness. Nevertheless, group conformity decreases greatly if even one member of the group fails to conform (Asch, 1951). The one nonconformist will serve as an effective catalyst to elicit nonconformity in others.
- Task characteristics. With more ambiguity or difficulty in handling the task, the more likely conformity will occur. However, even simple tasks can elicit conformity, as the Asch line-judging experiment demonstrated. For simple tasks such as this, conformity is more likely to occur as the group increases in size. For instance, in a situation where a couple of people are standing on the street looking upward, relatively few passersby will conform and do likewise. On the other hand, few of us can resist the urge to look also when we see a large crowd doing so. For more complicated tasks, group size is less important.
- Social status. Interestingly, research has shown that people with *average* social status are more likely to conform than are those with high or low status (Dittes & Kelley, 1956). People with high social status apparently feel little need to conform to others who they perceive to be beneath them, and individuals with low social status may feel that little would be gained by their conformity.
- Cultural factors. The degree of conformity varies widely among different cultures. In general, those societies that emphasize individual accomplishments foster less conformity than societies that emphasize collectivism, such as socialistic and communistic countries (Smith & Bond, 1994).

Obedience

> Whenever you find yourself on the side of the majority, it's time to pause and reflect.
>
> **MARK TWAIN**

> If you obey all of the rules, you miss all of the fun.
>
> **KATHERINE HEPBURN**

When people are working in groups, they tend to follow the orders of a person who is in a position of authority, a phenomenon that psychologists label **obedience.** Note the distinction between conformity and obedience. In conformity, individuals are frequently not certain what others in the group want or expect. In obedience, an individual is receiving a direct order.

As with conformity, history has shown the horrible consequences that can result from blind obedience. Probably the most egregious example of blind obedience was the Nazi extermination of millions of Jews and other people whom they considered undesirable during World War II. During the subsequent Nuremberg war crime trials, the most common excuse given by those doing the killing was that "I was just following orders."

Most people think that they would be incapable of blindly following orders to hurt another individual, but research in psychology suggests otherwise. A series of very famous studies showed that about two-thirds of ordinary people would severely shock a test subject when requested to do so by the experimenter (Milgram, 1963, 1965). Also recall the experiment discussed in the previous chapter in which nurses blindly obeyed telephone orders from a fictitious doctor to deliver a potentially harmful dose of medication to a patient. Each of us would like to think that we would be different, that we would successfully resist this tendency to obey authority, but in actuality most of us would not. This type of obedience probably occurs because we have long histories of being positively reinforced for doing what authorities tell us and punished when we ignore their mandates.

Psychologists believe that obedience also occurs because people do not feel personally responsible for their actions when responding to the dictates of an authority. Individuals often shift the responsibility and the resulting consequences of their actions to those who gave the orders. The tendency to deny or take responsibility for crimes of obedience is related to several other factors. Both nonreligious individuals and Jewish people are more likely to hold *others personally responsible* for their own actions while Christians are more likely to *deny personal responsibility* (Kelman & Hamilton, 1989). Similarly, religious subjects tend to obey legitimate authorities more so than nonreligious individuals (Bock, 1972). Historically, people have killed millions of individuals in the name of religion, further evidence that religious convictions do not prevent blind obedience. Education and socioeconomic factors also play an important role in assigning responsibility. Less educated individuals and those with lower socioeconomic status are more likely to deny personal responsibility (Kelman & Hamilton, 1989). There are even interesting regional differences in assigning responsibility, with individuals from the Midwest and South being most likely to deny personal responsibility for obedience that results in criminal behavior. Residents of the Northeast and Pacific Coast states have the greatest tendency to assign personal responsibility to themselves.

APPLICATIONS: Resisting Blind Obedience

Are there techniques that we can use to resist the tendency to obey authority in inappropriate situations? Just as history contains many instances where blind obedience led to tragedy, it also includes many instances where individuals and groups appropriately "stood up" to authorities. Social protests during the civil rights movement and the Vietnam War included many such instances that, in all likelihood, brought quicker resolution to injustice and conflict than would have otherwise happened. In more recent history, Boris Yeltsin's willingness to defy authorities, prior to his becoming Russia's president, helped bring about the downfall of communism in that country and many other Eastern European nations.

What specifically can you do to help resist the urge toward blind obedience? You are doing one helpful thing right now, that is, learning about how powerful the effects of obedience are. When people become aware of the research findings on the pervasive effects of obedience, they are more likely to resist it in real-life situations (Sherman, 1980). If you find yourself in a situation where blind and inappropriate obedience is called for, recall the obedience research that I have reviewed. Simply becoming aware of our tendencies to obey can help inoculate you from its deleterious consequences. Other studies have shown that the mere presence of another individual appropriately defying authority can serve as a strong stimulus for others to

Boris Yeltsin stands on a tank protesting against the actions of the Soviet Communist authorities who had attempted to overthrow the presidency of Mikhail Gorbachev in 1990. This example of leadership in the face of adversity led to the eventual downfall of communism in Russia.

follow (Milgram, 1965). In addition, reminding individuals that they, and not the authorities, are personally responsible for harmful actions can reduce the tendency to obey blindly (Hamilton, 1978). You should always question the motives and expertise of authority figures. Remember the research cited earlier about how we often respond inappropriately to mantles of authority, such as uniforms and titles. The power of authorities to command your obedience can always be resisted. Therefore, be conscious of the factors that influence tendencies toward inappropriate obedience and exercise your personal option not to obey.

Leadership

You have no doubt noticed that some groups are more effective at reaching goals than others. The reason is often found in the leadership of the group. **Leadership** is usually defined as *the process by which one member of the group guides and influences other members toward a common goal shared by all members of the group.* How important are leaders? Leaderless groups often wander in scattered directions and are almost always ineffectual in achieving the group's common goal. Indeed, leadership is so critical that anthropologists who have studied organized societies have found that every community had leaders as part of its social organization (Zamarripa & Krueger, 1983).

Leadership has been a topic of great interest to social psychologists with more than 3,000 research studies conducted by academic researchers. Interestingly, Robert House argues that this research literature ". . . has gone largely unnoticed or ignored by policymakers, the press, and practicing managers. In 1988 and again in 1993 *Time* magazine published cover stories addressing the need for leadership in the U.S. political system. Not a single reference was made to any academic studies conducted by leadership scholars" (House, 1995, p. 413). Like so many other topics in psychology, when it comes time to apply the extensive research done on leadership, individuals prefer to "fly by the seat of their pants" and rely on their intuition instead.

Whether a man is burdened by power or enjoys power; whether he is trapped by responsibility or made free by it; whether he is moved by other people and outer forces or moves them—this is of the essence of leadership.

THEODORE H. WHITE
The Making of the President (1960)

The topic of leadership is very complex. For a leader to be effective, several factors come into play. Personal characteristics of the leader are important, such as intelligence, experience, and personality traits. The characteristics of the group to be led are also critical. The leadership needs of an orchestra may differ from the leadership needs of soldiers in combat. In addition, situational factors are also important. Leading a group to survive in the wilderness might require very different skills than those necessary for effectively leading a corporation. The common goals that the group seeks to attain are also important because different goals can require different styles of leadership. In some circumstances, a leader is needed to help a group complete a specific task whereas, in other situations, the leader is needed to foster positive feelings and cohesiveness among the group members. Because of this complexity, no single prescription for effective leadership would apply to all situations. Nevertheless, there are certain commonalities to leadership that broadly apply. Let's begin by examining the kind of person motivated to be a leader.

Who Wants to Lead?

Leadership offers certain advantages but also carries certain disadvantages. People in positions of leadership typically make more money and enjoy higher social status than those whom they lead. In addition, leaders experience a great deal of satisfaction from successfully leading a group of individuals to a common goal.

On the debit side, leadership often requires a huge investment of a leader's time and energy. Those in leadership roles open themselves to criticism from others and often have their motives and their character questioned. As individuals advance higher on the leadership chain, the more scrutiny they receive from those who are being led.

Given these advantages and disadvantages, what kind of person is motivated to lead? Typically, 1 of 2 characteristics typify leaders: (1) *a strong desire to exercise power over others,* or (2) *a strong need to accomplish great things.*

U.S. presidents Harry S Truman and John F. Kennedy are examples of leaders who had a strong need to exercise power. Such leaders tend to lead countries into military conflict. Jimmy Carter and Herbert Hoover, on the other hand, are listed as examples of presidents who wished to accomplish great things. Their leadership was exemplified by the introduction of important new legislation and a willingness to try innovative approaches to leadership (Simonton, 1994).

Of course, many people have a need to exercise power over others and/or wish to accomplish great things and yet never assume a leadership role. Other necessary ingredients are *ambition* and *the ability and willingness to work extremely hard* (Simonton, 1994). A historical perspective of great leaders invariably reveals that they also possessed both of these two very important characteristics.

Leadership Traits

Are some people "natural-born leaders" or do they learn to become effective leaders? Early researchers in leadership formulated the **great person theory** of leadership that proposed highly successful leaders possessed certain traits that distinguished them from others. Moreover, it was believed that they possessed these traits regardless of where or when they lived. Research conducted since 1980 tends to confirm the validity of the great person theory. Successful leaders typically possess 8 traits (Kirkpatrick & Locke, 1991):

- Drive. A strong wish to achieve coupled with ambition, high levels of energy, perseverance, and initiative.
- Honesty and integrity. Ability to engender trust in others, act dependably, and remain open to new ideas.
- Self-confidence. A belief in their own abilities to succeed.
- Creativity. Ability to arrive at innovative and imaginative solutions.
- Expertise. Possession of the necessary knowledge and skills.
- Cognitive ability. Possession of the intelligence to interpret and integrate large bodies of information.
- Leadership motivation. The drive to exercise influence over others in order to achieve shared goals.
- Flexibility. Ability to adapt to the demands of the situation and the needs of the followers.

While all of these traits are important, research suggests that the *single most important trait is flexibility* or the ability to recognize the most appropriate approach or actions to take given the situation. Effective leaders then exercise this flexibility to act appropriately (Zaccaro, Foti, & Kenny, 1991).

The mere possession of these traits does not ensure that someone will be an effective leader, however. In other words, these traits are necessary but not sufficient. Effective leadership may only be understood fully by also taking into account the social situation in which the leadership takes place.

Situational Factors

Earlier in this chapter, I noted that the nature of the situation also dictates the kind of leadership that will be effective. A glance backwards through history reveals that strong leaders often surface during stressful times such as economic crises or war. Adolph Hitler was a corporal during World War I and showed little potential for leadership. However, after losing the war, Germany entered a period of economic crisis and a sense of national humiliation. It was in this climate that Hitler's potential for leadership manifested itself. President Franklin D. Roosevelt also assumed the leadership of the United States during a time of economic depression and imminent entry into World War II. On the other hand, Dwight D. Eisenhower, considered a great military leader, has been perceived as a weak leader by some historians, perhaps because his presidency lasted during a period of relative calm and prosperity in the United States.

Clearly, different situations demand different leadership traits. Leaders need to fulfill different functions in situations with different tasks. What might constitute effective leadership of a football team might be very different from the skills required to captain a ship. Even though the leader must exercise influence, the way that occurs probably would be different in the two situations. Several other important situational elements include the structure of the group, the interpersonal relationships that exist in the group, the outlook and aspirations of group members, and group size (Hollander, 1978). Group size is particularly important because larger groups result in more depersonalized leadership and subsequent lowered levels of member satisfaction and performance. Sam Walton, the founder of Wal-Mart, recognized this problem when his nationwide network of stores grew larger and larger. Consequently, he attempted to visit every store in his vast chain in order to meet and visit with his employees. This leadership tactic resulted in a high level of employee satisfaction and loyalty.

The Charismatic Leader

Have you ever known someone who truly inspired you to do your very best and whose words moved you to accomplish more than you ever thought possible? Individuals who have this capability are often referred to as *transformational* or **charismatic leaders.** The former term seems particularly fitting as these individuals often literally transform the social, political, and economic milieus in which they find themselves, for better or for worse. Commonly cited examples of charismatic leaders include Winston Churchill, Franklin D. Roosevelt, Martin Luther King, Jr., and John F. Kennedy. Several historical as well as contemporary religious leaders can also be characterized as charismatic.

Many psychologists believe that charismatic leadership is born out of crises and stressful situations that the leader's followers must face. Robert House (1995) argues that charismatic leadership comes to the forefront when people experience crises, oppression, discrimination, extremely poor working conditions, or unfair and harsh treatment from sources other than the leader. If you look at the examples of the charismatic leaders that I mentioned, you will see that each one led in tumultuous times. This type of leadership also emerges when situations exist that require exceptional efforts, behaviors, and sacrifices to be made by both the leader and the follower, such as occur with economic depressions or war.

Men make history, and not the other way around. In periods where there is no leadership, society stands still. Progress occurs when courageous, skillful leaders seize the opportunity to change things for the better.

HARRY S TRUMAN

What is it about these leaders that makes them charismatic? One school of thought suggested that they possessed certain traits that I discussed earlier as those that distinguish great leaders. More contemporary theorizing about charisma, however, emphasizes that it is more than just leadership traits. Rather, it is the *special type of relationship* that exists between these leaders and their followers and *the specific actions taken* by these leaders that amplify the effects of their actions on their followers. Specifically, how do these individuals accomplish this?

There are 4 essential components of charismatic leadership (Bass, 1998):

1. Idealized influence. Leaders are admired, respected, and trusted. Followers identify with leaders as their role models and pattern their own behavior after them. Followers believe that their leaders possess extraordinary capabilities, persistence, determination, and very high standards of ethical and moral conduct. These leaders also communicate a "vision" that their followers find compelling. They communicate a dedication to their followers and a willingness to sacrifice their own self-gain for the benefit of their followers. They are particularly effective in appealing to the hopes and desires of their followers.

People buy into the leader before they buy into the vision.

JOHN C. MAXWELL

2. Intellectual stimulation. Charismatic leaders stimulate their followers to be creative and innovative in their thinking. They encourage their followers to approach old problems or situations in new ways by questioning assumptions or reframing problems. These leaders make every effort to include their followers in addressing and solving problems or in devising possible solutions. They refrain from criticizing followers' mistakes or ideas, especially when those ideas are different from their own.
3. Inspirational motivation. Charismatic leaders engage in behaviors that motivate and inspire their followers by providing meaning and challenge to their efforts. These leaders have a unique ability to convince people that they can accomplish more than they ever thought possible. They create a team spirit, display extraordinary enthusiasm and optimism, clearly communicate goals that the followers share, and demonstrate a commitment to accomplishing those joint goals. By their behaviors, they frequently set an example for others to follow.
4. Individualized consideration. Charismatic leaders ". . . pay special attention to each individual follower's needs for achievement and growth by acting as coach or mentor" (Bass, 1998, p. 6). They attend to their followers' needs by (1) recognizing the desires of each individual, (2) accepting that each follower has individualized strengths and weaknesses, (3) encouraging two-way exchanges in communication, (4) using a hands-on managerial style, (5) personalizing their interactions with others by using their names or referring to previous conversations, (6) applying the skills of a good listener, (7) delegating tasks effectively, and (8) discretely and tactfully monitoring their followers' progress. Overall, they display a genuine concern for the well-being of others.

We are tempted to conclude that charismatic leaders are always a positive force in the world. Unfortunately, history does not allow us to reach such a conclusion. There have been numerous instances where charismatic individuals have used their leadership powers for nefarious purposes. Perhaps the most striking example in recent world history was Adolph Hitler. If you have watched films of any of his speeches, you can clearly see how enraptured the German people were with his style. Millions of Germans followed his leadership, resulting in the tragedy of World War II and the loss of over 20 million lives. More recently, there have been incidents of religious leaders who have developed cult followings that eventually led to mass suicides or murders. Examples of charismatic but evil leaders abound in all aspects of our society from business to religion to politics. Awareness of the characteristics of charismatic leaders helps provide insight into their powers and inoculate us from their influence.

Gender Differences

When it comes to leadership, it is still a man's world. In many countries, there is an almost complete absence of women in governmental leadership roles. In the United States, fewer than 5 of the companies making up the Fortune 500 major corporations are headed by women. Furthermore, more than 100 of the Fortune 500 do not have *any* female corporate officers. According to a New York–based research company, in 1996 women represented just 2.4% of those holding corporate titles of chairman, vice chairman, CEO, president, or executive vice president. Furthermore, women had only 1.9%

of the top-paying jobs. There has been, however, an increasing trend of women in leadership positions since World War II that was brought on, in part, by the clear demonstration of women's leadership capabilities during that war. How do women fare in leadership positions? Do they have a different leadership style than do men?

Alice Eagly and her colleagues have explored the question of sex differences in leadership effectiveness (Eagly, Karau, & Makhijani, 1995). She examined the results from 96 studies that compared male and female leadership effectiveness. *Taken as a whole,* these studies revealed no gender differences in leadership effectiveness. However, when she looked at the individual studies, Eagly found some situations where gender differences were important. For example, women were more effective leaders in jobs that are traditionally considered to be feminine and that are oriented toward interpersonal skills. Women are particularly effective leaders in settings where a task requires the leader to attend to individuals' needs and feelings. Leadership roles in education, government, and social service organizations are examples. Men were found to be more effective in jobs that are traditionally viewed as masculine and that are oriented toward task completion and the ability to direct and control people. Military leadership roles are one example. Of course, many tasks require a combination of interpersonal and task orientation, and, in such cases, the most effective leaders are those who can use both "masculine" and "feminine" leadership strategies as the situation requires.

Leadership in the 21st Century

We have seen that the topic of leadership is very complex, indeed. Several important factors must be taken into consideration, including the traits possessed by leaders, the needs of the group being led, and situational factors. Adding to this complexity is the fact that society is changing in ways that will undoubtedly require different leadership styles in this century.

For many individuals, it is leadership in their workplace that most directly affects their lives. No matter what your position in an organization, it is very likely that you are looking to someone for effective leadership. Robert House (1995) is a leading scholar on the topic of leadership in the workplace. He has argued that the 21st century will impose substantial new role demands on leaders. He cites several important changes taking place this century, including increased ethnic diversity in the workplace, a more rapid pace of environmental and technological change, more frequent geopolitical shifts affecting borders, and increased international competition.

House argues that business, government, and military organizations will need to change in ways that will place new demands on future leaders. He cites the ongoing technological changes that result in most routine, repetitive work being done by machines interfaced with computers. In the new century, work will become more intellectual and less physical. He argues that, as a result of these changes, people in the workplace increasingly will work without direct supervision. The role of leaders, he argues, will be to motivate workers to develop individual initiative as well as a willingness to take personal responsibility for doing their job without direct supervision.

These changes unquestionably will alter the way that followers look to their leaders for guidance and will force a reevaluation of what constitutes effective leadership. The topic of leadership promises to continue to be a complex and dynamic area of scholarly interest.

The final test of a leader is that he leaves behind him in other men the conviction and the will to carry on.

WALTER LIPPMANN
New York Herald Tribune

SUMMARY

- An important part of our everyday lives is the activity of working in groups. A group consists of 2 or more individuals who share common goals, have a stable relationship, are interdependent on one another, and see themselves as part of a group.
- Belonging to a group meets our social and psychological needs, gives us a sense of belonging, allows us access to knowledge possessed by the group, and helps us develop a social identity.
- Groups function according to rules that are called normative behaviors. Individuals in groups behave in specific ways called roles. We are frequently required to switch roles in different group situations.
- Both individuals in groups and the groups themselves evolve over time. Groups progress from an initial emphasis on establishing a group identity and building morale to a later emphasis on identifying group goals, enhancing personal rewards, and recognizing members' contributions. Similarly, individual members evolve from their initial emphasis on being accepted by the group to determining what role(s) to play, asserting their independence, and then eventually phasing out of group participation.
- An individual's performance is often higher when conducted in a group setting. However, under some conditions, the presence of others can interfere with an individual's performance.
- Social loafing refers to the phenomenon of reduced individual effort when working in a group. Individuals in a larger group are also less likely to assist those in need because of a diffusion of personal responsibility.
- Pluralistic ignorance occurs when individuals fail to assist others because they observe that other people are also not assisting.
- Research studies have identified several factors that will increase or decrease bystander intervention. Paying careful attention, considering possible alternatives, assuming responsibility, and being willing to act increase a person's likelihood of giving assistance.
- Deindividuation occurs when individuals lose their personal identities and have less self-awareness while functioning in a group setting. In this circumstance, behavior is often very different than it would be if acting as an individual.
- Social contagion refers to the phenomenon in which an imagined illness spreads through some members of a group. Certain conditions have been shown to increase the likelihood of this phenomenon.
- Studies on cooperation within and between groups has shown that competition between groups causes greater unity within each group, that hostility between groups increases as groups compete, and that requiring groups to work toward a common goal reduces competition and hostility.
- When groups make decisions, group polarization will often occur where the group will adopt a more extreme decision than the average individual in the group would have done.
- In groupthink, groups sometimes arrive at very poor decisions. This occurs because of group cohesiveness, homogeneity of members' backgrounds, isolation from outside views, failure of leadership, and stressful circumstances.
- To avoid groupthink, the group should be exposed to dissenting views and questions, impartial group leadership, outside input, and multiple meetings before a decision is made.
- Groups often cause the behavior or attitudes of individual members to change in conformance with the group. Factors known to influence conformity include the social status of its members, cultural factors, and various characteristics of the individual, the group, and the task at hand.
- Individuals working in groups tend to obey the instructions from an authority. In some cases, this can lead to disastrous consequences. Obedience occurs because individuals shift personal responsibility to the person giving the order. Awareness of the factors that cause obedience can help inoculate individuals from its effects.
- Leadership occurs when 1 individual guides and influences other members toward a shared goal. There are both advantages and disadvantages to assuming a leadership role.
- Traits that characterize effective leaders include drive, honesty and integrity, self-confidence, creativity, expertise, cognitive ability, leadership motivation, and flexibility. Of these traits, flexibility is the most important.
- Situational factors are also important in determining which traits are most effective in a particular leadership role.
- Charismatic leaders, also known as transformational leaders, are those who have the ability to motivate and inspire followers in extraordinary ways. Such leaders often emerge during times of crisis or in stressful situations.
- Charismatic leadership includes 4 essential characteristics: (1) idealized influence, (2) intellectual stimulation, (3) inspirational motivation, and (4) individualized consideration. Charismatic leaders can have a positive or negative effect on the social milieu in which they function.

- Research has indicated that no overall difference in leadership abilities occurs between males and females. However, there are certain situations where males or females function most effectively as leaders.
- Societal changes in the 21st century, including technological advances, increasing ethnic diversity, frequent geopolitical shifts, and international competition will impose new role demands and requirements on leaders.

KEY TERMS

bystander apathy: the tendency for onlookers to fail to provide assistance to those in need.

charismatic leaders: individuals who have the ability to inspire others to do their very best, and provide charisma, intellectual stimulation, inspirational motivation, and individualized consideration.

conformity: behavior that occurs when an individual's behavior or attitudes are influenced because of perceived or actual group pressures.

deindividuation: the process by which individuals lose their personal identities when functioning as part of a group.

diffusion of responsibility: a process in which everyone thinks that someone else will probably assist a victim.

great person theory: a theory that proposes that highly successful leaders possess certain traits that distinguish them from others. The traits include drive, honesty and integrity, self-confidence, creativity, expertise, cognitive ability, leadership motivation, and flexibility.

group: any two or more interacting individuals who share common goals, have a stable relationship, are interdependent on one another, and perceive themselves as part of a group.

group polarization: a phenomenon in which a group as a whole tends to adopt a more extreme decision than would the average individual in the group following a group's discussion of an issue.

groupthink: a group process that occurs when group members are trying to reach unanimity of opinion. They fail to consider realistic alternative courses of action and decide to take a course of action that later proves to be disastrous.

leadership: the process by which one member of the group guides and influences other members toward a common goal shared by all members of the group.

normative behaviors: the rules that are established by groups to regulate members' behavior.

obedience: the tendency to follow the orders of a person who is in a position of authority.

pluralistic ignorance: a phenomenon in which individuals in a group fail to provide assistance based on their observation that no one else seems concerned.

role conflict: when the different roles one has to play require conflicting behaviors.

roles: the specific ways that individuals in groups are expected to behave.

social contagion: a mass psychogenic illness of a group of individuals caused exclusively by psychological factors.

social facilitation: the improvement of performance when it is conducted in the presence of others.

social inhibition: the inhibition of performance when it is conducted in the presence of others.

social loafing: as the size of a group increases, the amount of effort by individual members decreases.

14

APPLICATIONS OF PSYCHOLOGY

In the concluding chapter of this text, I will examine some specific ways in which knowledge about psychology is being applied to different professions as diverse as law, sports, education, and business. Of course, the largest application of psychological principles involves the fields of clinical and counseling psychology. Since these topics have been discussed in some detail in both chapter 9, Identifying Problem Behaviors, and chapter 10, Treatment for Problem Behaviors, I will not describe these applications further here.

PSYCHOLOGY AND LAW

My personal interest in the applications of psychology to law was undoubtedly influenced by my wife who, after working many years in the field of psychology, became an attorney. As a law student and as a practicing attorney, she would frequently point out to me the extensive amount of crossover between the two fields.

It is only natural that the professions of psychology and law would share many common interests. Both professions are concerned with predicting, explaining, and controlling behavior. Indeed, law is the primary instrument by which society controls human behavior. The law constitutes a system of rules for the control of human social behavior. Both psychology and law operate under the assumption that behavior has specific causes, and does not occur randomly (Crombag, 1994).

Given these similarities, one would be tempted to think that the two fields operated cooperatively for many years. In fact, this has not been the case. Research in the area of psychology and law was virtually nonexistent until the mid-1970s. Even now, many in the legal profession cast a wary eye at psychological research and its applications to the field of law. The reasons for this are very complex and well beyond the scope of this text. The following are only a few of the major differences in perspectives that the two professions have about human behavior:

- In both civil and criminal law, there is an emphasis on individual responsibility. A person is found liable because it is assumed that each individual is responsible for his or her actions. Psychology, on the other hand, frequently emphasizes unconscious and uncontrollable forces that operate on an individual's behavior.
- American social psychologists believe that human beings are generally "nice persons" while law, especially criminal law, is characterized by a more cynical view of human nature (King, 1986).
- Law necessarily accepts the notion of "free will" in determining the causes of human behavior. Law ". . . operates on the model of man as a free, conscious being who controls his/her actions and is responsible for them" (Kapardis, 1997, p. 7). Psychologists are more inclined to take into account an individual as a thinking, feeling, and believing totality as well as a person who interacts with his or her environment in a dynamic way (Clifford & Bull, 1978). Recall that in chapter 1 I discussed the importance of the deterministic viewpoint in most modern psychologists' thinking about human behavior.
- Psychologists believe that understanding differences between individuals is central to understanding human behavior. Bartol and Bartol (1994) note that ". . . law is often skeptical about psychology and its history of favoring individual differences over equal application of the law."

Despite these differences, psychology has gainfully addressed several questions of interest to law. For example, is decision making by jurors affected by information they are told to disregard? Is eyewitness testimony, which is relied on heavily in criminal cases, accurate regarding the events associated with a crime? Is hypnosis a valid technique to increase the accuracy of eyewitness testimony? Are individuals suffering from severe mental disorders capable of making decisions in their own best interest? Are lie detectors accurate in detecting deception? Let's examine in detail some of the research areas of psychology as they have been applied to law.

Eyewitness Testimony

The eyes are more exact witnesses than the ears.

HERACLITUS

As I mentioned previously in the chapter on memory, eyewitness testimony is very important in criminal cases. Elizabeth Loftus (1979), a leading researcher on eyewitness testimony, examined cases in England and found that a criminal conviction was obtained 74% of the time when eyewitness testimony was used even though only *one* eyewitness was available in half of the cases. However, numerous cases have documented situations in which an innocent person was convicted of a crime solely due to faulty eyewitness testimony.

In chapter 4, I described the fallibility of the human memory and how merely changing the way in which a question was worded can alter eyewitness testimony. For example, asking an eyewitness how fast two cars were going when they "crashed into one another" versus when they "bumped into one another" will result in very different testimony. Furthermore, the credibility of eyewitnesses and their statements is affected by the behavior they display during questioning. Those eyewitnesses who speak firmly, answer questions promptly, and maintain good eye contact with the questioner are perceived as more credible because we associate these behaviors with honesty.

After you've heard two eyewitness accounts of an auto accident, it makes you wonder about history.

BITS & PIECES

One major problem with eyewitness testimony is the propensity of eyewitnesses to falsely identify an innocent person. The most common procedure for eyewitness identification in criminal cases is a lineup. The suspect is commonly placed in a lineup with several other people, and the eyewitness is asked to identify the guilty individual. There are several potential problems with the lineup procedure (Lindsay, 1994). For example, if the eyewitness remembered that the suspect was an African-American male and the lineup contained only three black men, the eyewitness's choices then become significantly restricted. In that case, the eyewitness might select one of the African Americans based on the plausibility of the choice rather than a true identification based on all physical characteristics. In another common procedure, the eyewitness is shown pictures of suspects before the lineup. Then, during the lineup, the suspect may be selected merely because he or she looked the most familiar, regardless of guilt or innocence surrounding the crime. Another complication with lineups occurs because, most commonly, all suspects are presented at the same time. An alternative procedure has the suspects themselves, or photographs of suspects, presented *one at a time* to eyewitnesses whereupon they are asked whether or not the suspect was the individual they witnessed during the crime. This *sequential lineup* results in significantly fewer false identifications than does the typical simultaneous lineup (Lindsay, 1994).

Events that occur after an incident can also interfere with the memories of an eyewitness. Police investigating a crime often make "suggestions" during their ques-

A psychologist who specializes in jury selection assisted the defense attorney in selecting the jurors for the O. J. Simpson murder trial. Many attorneys believe that the most critical part of the trial system is selecting jurors who will be sympathetic to their arguments.

tioning, which then become incorporated into the eyewitnesses' memories. For instance, asking "Did you see the *stop sign* at the intersection?" will greatly increase the probability that an eyewitness will report seeing a stop sign compared to others who were not asked the question (Loftus & Palmer, 1974). Merely suggesting facts can lead to eyewitnesses incorporating those suggestions into their memories and subsequent testimony.

If you witnessed a crime committed by a person of the same race as yourself, would your memories be more accurate than if you witnessed a crime by someone of a different race? A large body of research suggests that an **own-race bias** exists in eyewitness testimony. That is, face recognition is more accurate for faces of one's own race than for other races (Bothwell, Brigham, & Malpass, 1989). This can lead to increased false identifications when the suspect is of a different race than the eyewitness.

Jury Selection

In selecting a jury, both the defense and prosecuting attorneys are allowed to eliminate a certain number of potential jurors either *for cause* (the juror is biased, infirm, hostile to the defendant, and so forth) or *without cause*. The latter are called peremptory challenges and allow the prospective juror to be dismissed without any stated reason.

A jury consists of twelve persons chosen to decide who has the better lawyer.

ROBERT FROST

Lawyers have always used their best common-sense judgments about human nature to assist in selecting jurors. In recent years, attorneys have begun to hire psychologists to assist them in a process that has come to be called **scientific jury selection.** For example, during the O. J. Simpson murder trial, the defense attorneys hired a prominent psychologist to assist them in selecting jury members that would be sympathetic to their defendant. Many attorneys believe that a case is won or lost as soon as the members of the jury have been selected.

How do psychologists assist attorneys in selecting sympathetic jurors? First, they examine demographic data about the prospective jurors, including information such as age, education, occupation, political affiliation, religion, and socioeconomic status. Because attorneys are not allowed to question prospective jurors, this information must be collected from available public records. The demographic information is then used, sometimes in conjunction with elaborate statistical procedures and mathematical probability formulas, to generate an educated guess about whether the juror would be sympathetic to the defendant. The psychologists also assist attorneys in evaluating jurors by carefully observing their nonverbal behavior during jury questioning. As I described in chapter 11 on interacting with others, nonverbal behaviors can be very revealing.

How effective are these jury selection techniques? Research has revealed that scientific jury selection is slightly better than attorneys either randomly selecting jurors or applying the traditional "commonsense" approach (Zeisel & Diamond, 1978). The scientific selection techniques are particularly effective in selecting jurors who are or are not sympathetic to the imposition of the death penalty. However, Bartol and Bartol (1994) summarize the findings by noting that ". . . the persuasiveness and nature of the evidence strongly outweigh any personality or specific characteristics of individual jurors" (p. 178). They also note, "When the evidence is ambiguous or poorly presented, the characteristics of the jurors might carry greater weight in the decision making process, although it appears that group dynamics, rather than individual differences, plays the more significant role" (p. 178).

Jury Behavior

Our legal system assumes that jurors enter a trial free from significant biases. In fact, prospective jurors are frequently asked if they can set aside any negative feelings or biases they might have toward the defendant and make a judgment based strictly on the law. If jurors answer "no" to this question, they are excused for cause. If they answer "yes," they are often allowed to serve, assuming there is no other disqualifying factor.

Despite jurors' claims that they are unbiased, considerable evidence suggests that biases are frequently present. Many jurors hold either a pro-prosecution or a pro-defense bias. In either case, the jurors view the evidence presented through the filter of their own past experiences and beliefs, all of which influence them to conclude that the defendant did or did not commit the crime. Kassin and Wrightsman (1988) devised an attitude test that measured whether jurors were pro-prosecution or pro-defense. The true-false test included statements such as "Any suspect who runs from the police probably committed the crime" and "Too many innocent people are wrongfully imprisoned." They then used mock juries, made up of volunteers, who were given written evidence and arguments before being asked to reach a verdict. Mock jurors holding a pro-prosecution bias found the defendant guilty 81% of the time compared to those holding a pro-defense bias who found the defendant guilty only 52% of the time. In some cases, the personal biases held by jurors are so strong that they override the evidence presented at the trial.

A sampling of the research on juror biases reveals the following findings:

- Attractive defendants are less likely to be found guilty than are unattractive defendants (Perlman & Coxby, 1983). However, if the attractiveness assisted the person in committing the crime, such as an attractive woman on trial for swindling money from an elderly man, then jurors are more likely to find the attractive defendant guilty (Tedeschi, Linskold, & Rosenfeld, 1985).
- Jurors are unable to ignore information that slips out in court despite orders from the judge to disregard such information. Inadmissible evidence such as prior convictions often influences jurors' decisions (Watson, deBortali-Tregerthan, &

Frank, 1984). Attorneys sometimes use this to their advantage by intentionally asking leading questions even though they know the opposing attorney will object to such questions being asked.

- Jurors are instructed not to let the potential severity of the punishment affect their decision of guilt or innocence, but research suggests that it frequently does (Sales & Hafemeister, 1985).
- Jurors are instructed to suspend judgment about guilt or innocence until all the evidence is presented. However, jurors typically arrive at an opinion early in the trial. This opinion then makes it difficult for them to judge fairly the evidence that is subsequently presented.

Interestingly, these factors become less important as the seriousness of the crime increases or as the evidence becomes more clear cut (Tedeschi, Linskold, & Rosenfeld, 1985). Although some bias is inevitable in jurors, the jury system generally works well in the majority of cases.

Environmental Psychology

Environmental psychology studies the relationship of the environment to human behavior. Humans interact with their environment and, in the process, the environment both affects them and is affected *by* them. For instance, environmental psychologists study the effects of noise and overcrowding on behavior. They often work closely with architects in the design of buildings and with city planners in the design of cities, parks, open spaces, zoos, and museums.

The design of gambling casinos provides an interesting example of how the environment of a building affects behavior. A great deal of thought and scientific research goes into the design of these spaces to ensure that they maximize the probability that a customer will enter, stay, and gamble. For example, certain bright colors encourage gambling behavior. Slot machines and gaming tables placed in strategic and scientifically determined locations optimize their allure to the gambler. Casinos have found that gamblers like the noise of coins falling into coin trays of slot machines and the bells or other noises that typically signal when a person hits a jackpot. Therefore, slot machines have been designed specifically to maximize these sounds, resulting in a loud cacophony of noise inside all casinos. The locations of certain areas, such as restaurants, cashiers, elevators, and restrooms, are strategically situated so that the patrons must walk through the gambling areas before reaching their desired destination. Windows and clocks are missing to help ensure that the gambler loses track of time. Some casinos even experimented with the introduction of pleasant odors into the ventilation system after some studies suggested that certain odors increase gambling activity. One casino reportedly tried introducing pure oxygen into the ventilation system to help keep gamblers awake and alert. Casinos offer but one example of how studies on environmental influences have been manipulated in order to influence the behavior of those individuals occupying a space.

Effects of Noise

Our environment is becoming increasingly noisy. In larger cities, the din of traffic, construction, and other environmental noises bombards our senses continually. The seemingly omnipresent music in offices, stores, restaurants, and even gas stations also affects our mood and behavior. In addition, it seems increasingly rare these days to go into a restaurant without televisions blaring some sports event from nearly every wall.

Environmental psychologists have conducted extensive studies on the effects of noise on behavior, and the findings are quite complex. In some cases, noise seems to affect our behavior very little. In other cases, it either measurably impedes or facilitates our performance on tasks, depending on the specific circumstances. In general, people adapt to noise fairly quickly *as long as the source of the noise is predictable* (Glass & Singer, 1972). For example, if you moved into housing adjacent to a busy freeway, you would probably adapt quickly and eventually not even notice the highway noise. On the other hand, if you lived in a quiet neighborhood that suddenly had heavy traffic noise due to a temporary detour, you would probably notice the change immediately and be affected by the noise.

Noise also affects our moods. Noises that are loud or unidentifiable most often cause annoyance or fear. One study of neighborhood noises found that the *normalcy* of the noise determines our reaction to it (Levy-Leboyer & Naturel, 1991). For example, the sound of lawn equipment in the summer usually does not irritate us because such sounds are normal for that time of year. However, a jackhammer operating outside your window at 8 A.M. would not be as well received. Researchers also have found that sounds are more annoying when the person responsible for making them is perceived as *being able to control the noise.* If you lived next to an elementary school, you would probably accept the loud sounds of children playing because it would be unreasonable to expect the school to make the children play quietly. However, you would hold a different attitude about a neighbor who hosts loud parties that keep you awake all night.

Increasingly, evidence suggests that long-term exposure to loud noise harms our physical and mental health. The long-term exposure of schoolchildren to loud levels of noise has been associated with increased blood pressure, inability to concentrate, and less perseverance in problem-solving tasks (Cohen, Evans, Krantz, Stokols, & Kelly, 1981). Furthermore, moving these children to a quieter environment did not reverse the deleterious effects, suggesting that some cases of long-term exposure to noise may have permanent effects.

Overcrowding and Density

Environmental psychologists draw a distinction between crowding and density. **Crowding** refers to the *psychological feelings* that come from either (1) a sense of a loss of privacy or (2) the overstimulation that results from being forced into close proximity to others. **Density** refers to *the amount of living space that is available per person.*

Early animal studies with rats suggested that high-density living conditions might lead to several undesirable consequences. Rats who were forced to live in high-density conditions had increased levels of abortions, infant mortality, and disruptions in mating and maternal behaviors. Even "rat crime" increased as demonstrated by a greater frequency of rats viciously attacking each other (Calhoun, 1962). These findings led some observers to believe that similar effects might occur with humans who live in overcrowded conditions. The high incidence of crime in big cities is often cited as proof of this phenomenon.

Laboratory research has failed to demonstrate any reliable connection between overcrowding and negative effects on humans (Freedman, 1979). The conditions in Tokyo offer supporting evidence for this contention. Tokyo has one of the highest population densities in the world. Their subways are particularly notorious for being overcrowded. Despite these crowded conditions, Tokyo has a very low crime rate compared to less-crowded cities in the United States. Even though the exact effects of crowding on human behavior have yet to be determined, we may conclude that, in general, crowding does result in a high level of stress *when it causes us to lose control over our immediate social environment.*

The long-term effects of overcrowding on human behavior are not clear. Tokyo subways are infamous for being overcrowded, with "pushers" being employed to cram the maximum number of people into each subway car. Despite the overcrowding, the crime rate in Tokyo is much lower than in the United States.

How density affects you psychologically is determined in part by the relationships you have with those with whom you are in close proximity. You may find high density in an elevator or subway unpleasant and yet the same density at a party enjoyable. Measures of density typically include the number of inhabitants per acre, the number of people living in a room, the number of rooms per housing unit, and the number of housing units per structure.

In the chapter on interpersonal interactions, I described the concept of personal space and how, depending on the social circumstances, humans need to have a certain amount of space around them. As density increases, others encroach on our personal space with greater frequency. Urban studies in the United States have shown that an increase in density corresponds with increases in infant mortality, delinquency, inadequate care of young, and mental hospital admissions. In addition, high density levels are associated with poorer physical health, psychological and physical withdrawal, and weakened family relationships (Galle, Gove, & McPherson, 1972; Gove, Hughes, & Galle, 1979).

Architectural Psychology

The field of **architectural psychology** is a growing specialty that blends the professions of psychology and architecture together closely to design buildings that overcome problems associated with overcrowding and density. In many instances, existing space can be remodeled to reduce the feelings of overcrowding without actually increasing the total space available. For example, one study compared students who lived in two different dormitory arrangements. In one dorm, 40 students lived with the traditional long, central corridor with rooms located on each side. In an identical dorm, the researchers redesigned the space by dividing the hallway in half, placing unlocked doors in the corridor, and converting 3 center bedrooms into a lounge area. At the end of the year, the students in the divided dorm reported that they experienced less stress from crowding, developed more friendships, and increased their social contacts with other dorm members. In comparison, students in the traditional dorm reported feeling more crowded and acted less friendly toward other dorm members (Baum & Davis, 1980). Architectural psychology has helped improve living conditions in many businesses, apartment buildings, hospitals, schools, and even prisons by changing the interior designs, including room arrangements.

Industrial/Organizational Psychology

Industrial/organizational psychology, commonly known as I/O psychology, is the study of behavior and the application of behavioral principles to solve the problems and meet the needs of the workplace (Berry, 1998). The general goal of

I/O psychologists is to improve both the performance of workers and the quality of life in the workplace. To accomplish this goal, I/O psychology encompasses several areas of research and application, emphasizing worker motivation, effective leadership techniques, personnel selection, personnel training, job performance evaluation, and job productivity.

As the name implies, I/O psychology consists of two separate subfields. **Industrial psychology** is mainly concerned with personnel selection, job training, and the measurement of work performance. **Organizational psychology** concentrates on the relationships that exist between workers and between workers and their supervisors. In particular, it is concerned with how groups function, what constitutes effective leadership, and what motivates workers to be productive. Because I have covered several of these topics in previous chapters, this chapter will focus on a sampling of other topics within the field of I/O psychology.

Personnel Selection

The Veterans Administration (VA) has a program that helps train former members of the military because many of the tasks for which military people are trained have limited applications in the civilian realm. For example, being trained in armor, such as driving and firing a tank, does not immediately translate to a job in civilian life. The VA recently approached Drs. Kurt Kraiger and Donna Chrobot-Mason who are I/O faculty in my department and asked for assistance in training former military personnel to work as cemetery employees. Apparently, a shortage of people willing to work in cemeteries resulted in this plan to direct former military personnel into this profession. One of the first problems that these psychologists faced was how to select personnel who would find such a job rewarding and fulfilling.

The first step in personnel selection is to conduct a **job analysis** that results in a precise statement of the job requirements. Frequently, I/O psychologists conduct a procedure called **shadowing** during which time they observe workers to see exactly what tasks they perform. In addition, they interview individuals who perform the work and may even perform the job themselves in order to learn the specific requirements firsthand. For cemetery workers, my colleagues identified a series of critical tasks that included setting headstones, carrying and lowering caskets, loading and unloading heavy equipment, using a backpack sprayer, and laying and peeling sod.

The next step in personnel selection is the **recruitment** of qualified and interested individuals. The job analysis, already completed by the I/O psychologists, often determines the appropriate recruitment techniques, including the content and placement of the job announcement. These recruitment options are important because strategies differ depending on the type of job offered. Possible job announcement placements include newspaper ads, radio and TV announcements, public and private employment agencies, college placement offices, and any other resources likely to reach potential applicants. Job announcement content often includes factors such as job requirements, salary and benefits, application procedures, required education and experience, and a description of the company or organization.

In most instances, more than one applicant will apply for a position. Industrial/organizational psychologists assist in conducting **interviews** to help select the most appropriate applicant. Are interviews an effective way to select the best applicant? Even though almost all employers include such an interview, I/O psychologists have actually found interviews to be a very *poor* technique for selecting among candidates (Hunter & Hunter, 1984). Common problems and errors that occur in the interview process include the following (Berry, 1998): (1) Interviews are usually unstructured and free flowing, resulting in different applicants being asked different questions. (2) First impressions, as discussed earlier in chapter 11, play an inordinate role in the final hiring decision. (3) Biases and stereotypes by the interviewer frequently contaminate ratings of applicants. (4) Job applicants and interviewers are all on their best behavior during the interview. In other words, because applicants present themselves in the best possible light and interviewers emphasize the positive aspects of the job, misunderstandings and erroneous conclusions often result.

As an alternative to the traditional interview technique, I/O psychologists have played a major role in improving the interview process through the use of **structured interviews** wherein a predetermined series of questions is used for all applicants. In addition, the interviewer places a greater emphasis on the applicant's knowledge, skills, and abilities as opposed to the applicant's personality, self-described strengths and weaknesses, and past experience. Studies have revealed that structured interviews are twice as valid in selecting the best applicants when compared to unstructured interviews (Weisner & Cronshaw, 1988). Despite this fact, most companies continue to use unstructured interviews, often because interviewers believe that their "gut instincts" are the best predictor of which applicant will be the most suitable.

Another important technique used in personnel selection is **psychological testing.** Industrial/organizational psychologists help develop tests that accurately predict job performance. They ensure that the tests are both reliable (measure consistently) and valid (actually measure those skills that they are designed to measure). The psychologists also ensure that the tests do not discriminate against applicants on the basis of ethnicity, race, or gender. For the cemetery workers, the psychologists developed a physical ability test to measure the applicants' capacity to perform the tasks identified in the job analysis. In particular, the test items included performing tasks such as pushing or pulling a weight across a table, lifting a weight and carrying it sideways for 2 feet, lifting and lowering a mock headstone, and so forth.

In general, psychological tests have proven to be highly effective in selecting appropriate personnel for a vast variety of jobs. Nevertheless, their use remains controversial because of the potential risk of invalid measurements and the possibility of discrimination among various ethnic groups. As I/O psychologists further refine ways to overcome these deficiencies, the use of personnel tests in employee selection will likely increase.

Personnel Training

Almost all jobs require that an employee be trained in order to perform the work tasks correctly and efficiently. Personnel training is thus an important component of I/O psychology. **Training** is defined as ". . . a deliberately planned set of learning experiences designed to modify some feature of a person's behavior" (Berry, 1998, p. 156). It can be designed to increase knowledge, improve a person's skills, and even change attitudes. Training is often needed for new employees but also serves as a refresher for continuing employees.

Before training begins, I/O psychologists conduct a **needs assessment** that addresses the question of whether training is needed and, if so, what the specific nature of the training should be. If employees are performing at a level below reasonable expectations, the I/O psychologist will determine whether the performance problems result from a lack of knowledge and skills or a lack of motivation. Training is used mainly to address problems that are due to deficient abilities and skills. For motivation problems, I/O psychologists often develop an incentive program to boost performance.

If the needs assessment indicates that training is needed, the I/O psychologists then conduct a **training needs assessment** to determine the exact kind and degree of training that are required. Next, they derive a series of explicit **behavioral objectives** based on the previously determined training needs. These behavioral objectives define precisely what changes in knowledge, skills, and abilities should take place so that the effectiveness of training can be maximized.

Finally, **learning tasks** are generated from the behavioral objectives. Learning tasks constitute specific instructions for those individuals doing the training. These objectives specify exactly what behaviors or performance level should be demonstrated at the conclusion of training. Personnel training relies heavily on the information and knowledge that the field of psychology has amassed about learning and memory, as I discussed earlier in chapters 3 and 4.

Job Motivation

The worst job I ever had came during my final high-school years. I had a summer job working for the California Department of Highways. My job was to hoe weeds that lined the high sloping banks of freeways that ran through a city in central California. I worked 5 days a week, 8 hours per day, and received two 20-minute breaks and a 30-minute lunch break. My supervisor would drive me out to the work area, hand me a hoe, tell me what area to hoe, and then drive off, not to be seen again until 5 P.M. when he returned to pick me up. I would gaze out at the acres of weeds and see only the impossibility of ever hoeing enough to make even a dent in the weed population. Daily, I lived for the times when I could go on break or eat lunch and constantly monitored my watch to see how much time remained until the end of the workday.

As I look back on this job, I realize that the work situation was structured in such a way that it guaranteed a low level of motivation to perform well. Let's examine some of the factors that I/O psychologists have identified that are important in motivating workers and see how they applied to my dreary summer job.

- Expectancies. People work hardest when they have three expectations: (1) working extra hard will improve their performance, (2) good performance will be recognized and rewarded appropriately, and (3) the rewards received are perceived as valuable. If *any* one of these three factors is missing, work performance will suffer (Tubbs, Boehne, & Dahl, 1993). In my summer job, I quickly realized the futility of keeping ahead of the weeds regardless of how hard I worked. Furthermore, I also realized that no one cared how hard I worked and that few rewards, verbal or otherwise, would be forthcoming. As a result, my motivation and performance both suffered.
- Goals. Performance improves when people are given *specific goals* to accomplish as opposed to being told to "work hard" or "do the best job you can" (Locke & Latham, 1990). Furthermore, goals that the worker perceives as *challenging* are much better than goals that are easy to reach. However, the

goal must not be so challenging that the worker perceives it as unattainable. In my job, no specific goals were ever set. I was merely told to work hard and chop as many weeds as possible.

- Perceived fairness. Work performance increases when individuals believe that they are being treated fairly by others (Cropanzano & Randall, 1993). Workers typically examine how hard they work relative to the benefits they receive and compare their situation with the work-to-benefit ratio of other individuals. Motivation and performance both suffer when workers perceive that this ratio favors others over themselves. In my case, one of my fellow weed-whackers was the son of a highway department supervisor. Clearly, this worker was being treated deferentially when compared to my fellow weed-whackers and me. For example, we learned that this favored employee was given higher pay and easier jobs to perform. As a consequence, our motivation and subsequent performance suffered. A research study with major league baseball players also confirmed the importance of perceived fairness. Researchers looked at changes in the offensive performance of baseball players, such as hits, walks, stolen bases, and so forth, from 1991 to 1992. Their findings showed that players who believed their salaries were below what they considered to be equitable pay had a reduced level of performance in 1992 whereas those who believed that they were overpaid when compared to their peers made significant improvements in their performance (Werner & Mero, 1999). This study, as well as several others, suggests that being paid *more* than you think you deserve will actually facilitate performance. You may wish to cite this research finding to your employer at the next opportunity.

Increasing Motivation

Industrial/organizational psychologists are interested not only in what factors affect motivation but also in changes that can be made to bring about an *improvement.* Increasing motivation does not guarantee that performance will improve, but it is often a prerequisite. The one exception occurs when the employer expects skills that the worker does not possess. No matter how motivated the worker, a lack of requisite skills will prevent any improved performance.

Several techniques have proven successful in increasing motivation. One technique allows the employees to select the rewards that they will receive for a high level of performance, such as paid vacations, additional leave time, free tickets to sporting or cultural events, and so forth. Performance is enhanced by making the alternatives attractive and allowing the employees to choose the one that appeals most to them individually.

Another approach makes the job itself as interesting as possible. Introducing variety into repetitious tasks or expanding workers' skills and level of responsibility are both important techniques. Many years ago, business executives in Japan discovered that motivation and performance are both greatly increased when you allow workers to have input into how the job should be done.

Job Satisfaction

Workers can be highly motivated, even perform at a high level, and still not be satisfied with their job. Despite literally thousands of research studies conducted on job satisfaction, this topic still remains one with many unanswered questions. Exactly what is it that makes a person satisfied with his or her job?

Find a job you like and you add five days to every week.

H. JACKSON BROWN, JR.

If you ask individuals if they are satisfied with their job, they will probably reply that "it depends." This reflects the fact that there are many aspects to a job and that most people find more satisfaction with some aspects than with others. For instance, they may like the people with whom they work and find the job challenging but believe the pay is below what they deserve. Industrial/organizational psychologists have looked at job satisfaction relative to 3 aspects: (1) the work itself, (2) supervisor relationships, and (3) incentives and rewards of the job. Let's examine each of these briefly.

- ✦ The work itself. One theoretical model identifies 5 basic dimensions of the job that produce satisfaction (Hackman & Oldham, 1976). One is the degree to which the job has a *variety of tasks* that utilize many different skills and abilities. A second is the degree to which a job involves *following something through* from beginning to end. The third is the degree to which a job is *important or meaningful.* Fourth is the degree to which the job allows *freedom and independence.* Last is the degree to which performance of the job results in *feedback* about how effective the worker has been in the job. Based on this model, Berry (1998) concludes that job satisfaction means ". . . the core dimensions of the job are satisfying in that they determine the meaningfulness of the work and/or that the job provides an opportunity for personal growth and development" (p. 283).
- ✦ Supervisor relationships. No matter what job you have, the odds are very good that you have some supervisor to whom you must report. The relationship that workers have with their supervisors is an important part of job satisfaction. Research in I/O psychology suggests that this satisfaction is highly dependent upon the leadership style of the supervisor. These findings suggest that most workers have some preference or expectation about how a supervisor should behave. Job satisfaction is directly related to the discrepancy that exists between the employee's preferences or expectations and the manner in which the supervisor actually behaves. The larger this discrepancy, the lower the job satisfaction.
- ✦ Incentives and rewards. How important is pay in job satisfaction? Probably not as important as you might think. If you have ever been paid well to do an excruciatingly boring or repetitive task, you know why this is true. Research suggests that you can be satisfied with your pay while simultaneously being *dissatisfied* with your job. Furthermore, the incentives and rewards that you receive for working consist of more than just your paycheck. Other possible incentives usually include benefits such as insurance, paid leave, retirement, and opportunities for advancement. As for the pay itself, research suggests that workers have an expectation or understanding about how much money they should be receiving or what a fair wage would be. Dissatisfaction results when the amount they are paid falls below this expectation whereas job satisfaction results when this expectation is met or exceeded (Locke, 1976).

The world more often rewards the appearances of merit than merit itself.

FRANÇOIS DUC DE LA ROCHEFOUCAULD

As you can see, I/O psychology is a very diverse, dynamic, and growing field. It is also a profession that offers many well-paying job opportunities.

✦ FIGURE 14.3 ✦

Modern airplane cockpits contain a seemingly bewildering array of switches and visual displays. Human factors psychologists help design the layout of these visual displays and controls in order to maximize the efficiency of their use.

HUMAN FACTORS PSYCHOLOGY

Our everyday life requires that we interact frequently with machines, tools, displays, and controls. The field of **human factors psychology** deals with how all of these should be designed in order to maximize the efficiency with which they are used. When we drive our car, we are required to look at and very quickly extract the meaningful information from visual displays such as the speedometer, fuel gauge, oil pressure gauge, and other instruments. We are also required to operate the controls such as the radio, CD player, gear shifts, temperature gauges, and windshield wipers—all of which must be designed so that we can use them without being distracted from driving. Human factors psychologists work closely with design engineers to ensure that these devices are compatible with human abilities and limitations. Although these psychologists apply their skills in a variety of areas, the following represent two of the major applications of this specialization.

Visual Displays

A **visual display** is any visual presentation of information. Computer monitors, automobile dashboards, and temperature gauges are all examples of visual displays. Every day we are involved in hundreds of tasks that require us to extract information quickly and accurately from such visual displays. In some cases, our health or even our lives are dependent upon our ability to do so. The accompanying photograph illustrates the extremely complex display in a modern airline cockpit. Pilots must monitor virtually hundreds of dials, gauges, and switch settings while making critical, sometimes instantaneous, decisions about flying the plane. Human factors psychologists work closely with aeronautical engineers to design the most effective and efficient cockpit displays.

A review of studies conducted in the area of visual displays reveals certain basic principles that have evolved from this research. For example,

- A pointer moving against a fixed scale is easier to read than a moving scale against a pointer. This is why the pointer on an automobile speedometer moves against a fixed background rather than the background moving relative to a fixed pointer.
- We most easily interpret movement upwards or clockwise as representing a higher value of whatever is being measured. Thus, increases in temperature are represented by a rising column of mercury and accelerating driving speed by a speedometer dial moving clockwise.
- Colors can help us quickly delineate different categories. For example, many automobile dashboard gauges have color regions included on the displays, such as yellow for caution and red for danger.
- Information presented sequentially at the same location is easier to interpret than information presented simultaneously at several different locations. This is particularly true when large amounts of information need to be interpreted. Many new cars visually display information by pressing buttons on the steering wheel. Menus display sequential information such as the number of miles traveled since the engine was last started, average miles per gallon attained, average speed, number of gallons of fuel remaining in the tank, miles possible on the remaining fuel, and so forth. This information would be considerably more difficult to assimilate if shown separately on individual visual displays.

Controls

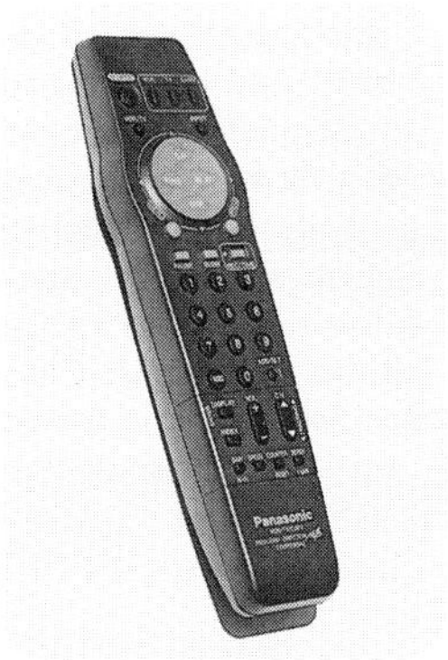

Modern remote devices that control electronic instruments such as TVs, stereos, and VCRs contain a large number of buttons and yet are designed so that individuals can learn to use them quickly and efficiently, even in the dark.

In this era of increasing technology, we are frequently called upon to operate many types of equipment that have complicated controls. Technological improvements are often accompanied by a confusing array of dials and switches. Human factors psychologists have studied how to make these controls operate in a manner compatible with our expectations. For example, we expect a switch that is flipped up to turn something on and a dial that is turned clockwise to increase whatever function it controls. Modern devices are often controlled by buttons. The remote control that accompanies my cable television converter has a total of 44 buttons that control not only my television and cable converter box but also my VCR and stereo. The buttons are carefully organized so that similar functions are found in similar locations. Buttons are also color coded, so that one color controls the TV, another color the VCR, and so forth. The buttons are of various sizes and textures in order to provide kinesthetic feedback even if the remote is operated in total darkness. Rocker switches that control volume and channels are designed so that, as expected, pressing up on the switch increases volume or channel numbers while pressing down reduces these functions. Although these type devices may seem unnecessarily complicated, considerable thought and extensive research goes into their design to make their use as easy as possible.

Another example of human factors research can be seen in the design of hand-operated devices that control the cursor's location on a computer monitor. The computer "mouse" was the first such device developed, but several variations have since been generated, including trackballs and touch pads. I vividly remember my first clumsy and ineffective attempts at controlling the location of the cursor with the mouse and wondered what mad scientist (or human factors psychologist) had conceived such a strange device. However, as millions of us have discovered, the mouse is a marvelously well thought out design that allows the fast and effective control of nearly any computer function with just one hand.

Visual displays and controls are merely two examples of the many areas in which human factors psychologists try to bridge the gap between humans and machines. As technology becomes more sophisticated, the need for applied human factors research will become even more important in our daily lives.

Sports Psychology

The field of **sports psychology** has received increasing attention in recent years. Sports psychologists are specifically interested in improving sports performance and enhancing the benefits of participating in sports.

There has been a growing awareness in recent years that performance in sports is greatly influenced by psychological factors. This applied field of psychology first began to flourish in the 1970s and has played an expanding role in athletics ever since. While this is true at both the amateur and professional levels, it is particularly critical among professional athletes where the participants' physical abilities are far more homogeneous. Similarly, it is critical among highly trained amateur athletes, such as Olympic contenders, where a winning time is often only a few hundredths of a second faster than a nonwinning time. In these instances, psychological factors such as attitude, emotions, and motivation can make the difference between a winning or losing performance.

Sports do not build character. They reveal it.

HAYWOOD HALE BROUN
quoted in James A. Michener's *Sports in America*

The field of sports psychology encompasses many different aspects of psychology, including counseling, personality, attention, arousal, anxiety, motivation, aggression, leadership, and group dynamics. Sports psychologists answer many questions, such as the following: Are there personality differences between high- and low-performing athletes? How can motivation to achieve be increased to ensure maximum performance? How does anxiety affect performance and how may it be controlled? What leadership traits are critical in team sports? What coaching styles maximize performance? How do audiences affect performance? What is the role of team cohesion in performance and how can such cohesion be increased?

The following is a sampling of some of the findings from sports psychology:

- Personality traits. Athletes differ from nonathletes on several personality characteristics. Successful male and female athletes share very similar personality characteristics. Different sports attract individuals with different personality traits. In general, athletes tend to be more independent, more objective, less anxious, more extroverted, and more self-confident than nonathletes are. Personality tests can distinguish between elite world-class athletes and less-gifted athletes about 70% to 80% of the time. However, for athletes of lesser caliber, personality tests are much less accurate.
- Attention. **Attentional focus** refers to an athlete's ability to focus on relevant information during competition while disregarding irrelevant stimuli at the same time. Athletes can be trained to improve their attentional focus and subsequently

their performance. Techniques include **thought stopping,** or the replacement of negative thoughts with success-oriented positive thoughts, and **centering,** which is the technique of focusing attention on relevant task-oriented suggestions. Attention is also affected by arousal; as arousal increases, attentional focus narrows. **Attentional style** refers to an athlete's particular style of attending to stimuli and is highly correlated with performance. Different attentional styles are required for different sports. Skilled athletes attend to and mentally process more relevant information when compared to unskilled athletes.

- Arousal. An optimal level of arousal is necessary for optimal athletic performance. Performance suffers if arousal falls either below or above this optimal level. Sports psychologists, who have developed several techniques to help athletes optimize their level of arousal, often make reference to what they call the dominant response. As mentioned in the previous chapter, a **dominant response** is the response that is most likely to be elicited at any given moment. Increased arousal tends to elicit the dominant response in athletes but, for beginners or nonskilled athletes, it is often the incorrect response. On the other hand, for highly skilled performers, the dominant response is generally the correct response. Similarly, the dominant response is generally the correct response for simple tasks whereas it is frequently the wrong response for complex tasks.
- Anxiety. A major source of anxiety for athletes is the threat to their egos or fear of failure. Sports psychologists distinguish between two kinds of anxiety. **Cognitive state anxiety** is the worry and apprehension aspect of anxiety while **somatic state anxiety** reflects the body's physiological reactions to stress, such as rapid breathing, increased heart rate, muscle tension, and so forth. These two types of anxiety affect sports performance in different ways. As cognitive state anxiety increases, athletic performance decreases. In contrast, as somatic state anxiety increases, performance also increases, but only up to an optimal level. At that point, performance decreases while the somatic state anxiety continues to increase. Sports psychologists have developed several techniques to aid athletes in the effective management of both types of anxiety. These techniques include both physical relaxation procedures and certain cognitive strategies that incorporate the use of hypnosis, imagery skills, and goal-setting tactics.
- Motivation. In the realm of sports psychology, **achievement motivation** refers to athletes' predisposition to either approach or avoid situations in which their performance will be evaluated. Generally, the level of achievement motivation is only a weak predictor of overall athletic performance. While it is a fairly good predictor of long-term athletic success, it is less reliable as a predictor of short-term success. Related to achievement motivation is **self-confidence,** which is the feeling or perception of believing in one's self. In general, female athletes do not have less self-confidence than male athletes do. Self-esteem and confidence increase as a result of successful performance, verbal persuasion, and emotional arousal. Of these, successful performance is most important.
- Aggression. Sports psychologists draw an important distinction between assertiveness and aggression. **Assertiveness** involves the unusual expenditure of effort and energy to achieve some external goal whereas **aggression** is a form of overt behavior that intends to harm or injure another person. Surprisingly, sports psychologists have found little correlation between personality traits of

aggression and actual acts of aggression in sports. Although males have a lower threshold for aggression than females, in general there is no overall difference in aggressiveness between genders. In athletic events, an athlete's perceptions of the opponent's intentions are very important in the determination of whether aggression will occur. More violence occurs when there is a large score differential. Losing also results in more aggression. Acts of aggression sometimes affect athletic performance because of the distraction and high levels of arousal that result. Sports psychologists have found that acts of aggression can be deterred by communicating clearly to athletes that such acts will be severely punished.

- Audience effects. The presence of an audience has a powerful effect on the athlete's performance. Beginning athletes usually suffer a decrement in performance when playing in front of an audience. However, experienced and highly skilled athletes are either unaffected or helped by the audience's presence. Supportive crowds have the effect of raising the arousal level in skilled athletes, often resulting in a significant home-court advantage. The larger, closer, and more intimate the audience is to the athletes, the greater the home-team advantage. For this reason, many modern sports arenas are constructed so that the audience sits very close to the playing field. Teams playing at home tend to be more assertive and aggressive, which also gives them an edge over visiting teams. Teams that play away from home often suffer a decrement in performance because they display increased dysfunctional behaviors such as fouls, turnovers, and so forth. In some situations there may also be a home team *disadvantage.* For example, in both baseball and basketball, teams that are playing critical games where they are expected to win have a tendency to suffer a decrease in performance. Audience effects are about the same for both male and female athletes.
- Team cohesion. **Team cohesion** refers to the tendency of an athletic team to ". . . stick together and remain united in the pursuit of its goals and objectives" (Cox, 1990, p. 369). Teams that have remained together for a long time have more team cohesion and enjoy more success than teams that have a large turnover in personnel. Sports psychologists found that the amount of time it takes for a team to develop an optimal level of cohesion varies for different teams and different sports. Large cultural, ethnic, and socioeconomic differences among team members can reduce team cohesion and have a detrimental effect on team performance. Smaller teams are generally more cohesive than larger teams. Surprisingly, whether teammates like each other has little effect on athletic success. Team cohesion is most important in interactive sports such as football and basketball where members must interact and work together for athletic success. Team cohesion is far less important for sports where there is relatively little team interaction, such as golf or bowling.

Teamwork is the ability to work together toward a common vision. The ability to direct individual accomplishment toward organizational objectives. It is the fuel that allows common people to attain uncommon results.

UNKNOWN

Consumer Psychology

Consumer psychology consists of the scientific study of all aspects of consumers' behavior. We make decisions related to the consumption of some product or service dozens of times a day. We are continually bombarded with advertisements on the

The layout of a modern department store is designed in such a manner as to increase the likelihood of consumers making purchases. Interior design, product placement, and the use of light and color are all carefully controlled to influence shopping behavior.

radio and television, on billboards, and in the print media, all of which are designed to influence our behavior as consumers. When we enter a store, our behavior is being influenced by the careful use of product placement, lighting, and use of color. Product packaging itself is carefully designed to attract our attention and sway our purchase choice. Consumer psychology offers guidance in all these aspects of consumer behavior and more.

Consumer psychologists answer many questions, including these: How can we change the purchasing attitudes of consumers? How can purchase habits become altered? What are the effects of advertising on consumer behavior and how can advertising be enhanced to increase consumption of a product? What marketing strategies, including promotional schemes, are most effective for influencing consumer choices? How can brand recognition be established and brand loyalty increased?

As you have probably recognized in yourself, consumer behavior is not entirely rational. Often we are drawn to a product for reasons other than a legitimate need to purchase it. Even if the need is legitimate, we often are influenced to make purchases based on factors that may be irrelevant to the need for the item.

Nearly 20 years ago, a colleague of mine at another university conducted a study on beer preferences. He found that most college students have strong brand preferences and believe that the flavor of their preferred brand is distinct and superior to that of other brands. My colleague, on the other hand, suspected that these preferences were influenced more by advertising factors and product appearance than by the taste of the beer itself. His informal studies in which subjects were blindfolded and asked to identify their favorite beer from several alternatives revealed that the students could not reliably identify their preferred brand. Subsequent research has shown that under conditions where taste was the only cue available, no noticeable taste differences were identified between assorted brands of beer (Fowler, 1982; Cox & Klinger, 1984). Our strong preferences for one brand or another are influenced by the extensive advertising campaigns and packaging designs devoted to affecting our choices.

Like so many other areas of applied psychology, consumer psychology involves the integration of several subfields within psychology. Mullen and Johnson (1990) have proposed a general model of consumer behavior that integrates specific topics: (1) perception, (2) cognition and memory, (3) learning, (4) emotion, and (5) motivation. Let's examine how these topics are critical to consumer behavior and review some of the general research findings relevant to each.

> No one can deny that much of our modern advertising is essentially dishonest; and it can be maintained that to lie freely and all the time for private profit is not to abuse the right of free speech, whether it is a violation of the law or not. But again the practical question is, how much lying for private profit is to be permitted by law?
>
> **CARL L. BECKER**

1. Perception. Perception is an important key to consumer behavior because it leads to consumer *awareness* (Mullen & Johnson, 1990). For example, it is important that consumers correctly perceive advertisements about a product or service in order to be aware of its existence. It has been estimated that the average consumer is exposed to several thousand radio, television, newspaper, magazine, Internet, and/or billboard advertisements every day. With such a profusion of messages, how do consumer psychologists ensure that the consumer becomes aware of the message about a specific product? Among other tools, they gain the consumer's attention by employing known perceptual principles related to *color, ambiguity, intensity, movement, size,* and *position.* Color advertisements attract more attention than those in black and white. In addition, advertisements often employ ambiguity, where there is an uncertainty, novelty, or lack of clarity present in the advertisement. For example, information is sometimes omitted from advertisements in order that the consumers will fill in the "missing" details by themselves. Various tools are used to make messages more intense, including bright lights or loud sounds. Often, compressed speech techniques are used in which the rate of delivery is greater than normal. Recall my previous discussion about how people tend to pay better attention when listening to rapid speech. Movement is used in many different ways to influence consumers because they tend to better notice objects that are moving. As a general rule, the larger the size of the advertisement, the more effective it will be. For example, you are more likely to notice a full-page magazine ad than you are a smaller advertisement. Even the position of an advertising message or product is critical. Studies have found that advertisements in the upper left corner of a magazine or newspaper receive the most attention. Similarly, certain positions on supermarket shelves, especially those at eye level, receive the most attention. These are but a few of the perceptual variables that consumer psychologists manipulate in an attempt to influence consumers' behavior. The perceptual aspects are critical because if perception is not present, the consumer will neither attend to nor be aware of the product.
2. Cognition and memory. The principles of memory and cognition that I discussed in chapters 3 and 4 have been applied to consumer behavior. Obviously, memory is a key factor because information will not be acted on if the consumer has no memory of it. Cognition refers to the thinking processes that accompany memories. One important consequence of cognition is the establishment of *beliefs* because they reflect how consumers think about products. In chapter 3, I discussed how encoding, storage, and retrieval are key aspects of the memory process. Consumer psychologists have conducted research on the attributes of the stimulus situation that facilitate each of these 3 stages of the memory process. One

> The buyer needs a hundred eyes, the seller not one.
>
> **GEORGE HERBERT**
> *Jacula Prudentum*

The advertising industry is one of our most basic forms of communication and, allegedly, of information. Yet, obviously, much of this ostensible information is not purveyed to inform but to manipulate and to achieve a result, to make somebody think he needs something that very possibly he doesn't need, or to make him think one version of something is better than another version when the ground for such a belief really doesn't exist.

MARVIN E. FRANKEL

important distinction is between recognition and recall memory tasks. Recognition memory involves discriminating between the product to be remembered and other similar products whereas recall requires a reconstruction of the memory about the product. For example, you may not remember the name of a new product (recall), but you would recognize it if you saw it sitting on the shelf among similar items (recognition). Psychologists have found that words that appear frequently are recalled better than words that appear infrequently. However, words that appear infrequently are recognized better than words that appear frequently. This holds implications for consumer behavior. For products where brand choice is guided by recognition at the point of purchase, such as with snack foods, a brand that has been advertised less may be remembered better because it is more easily recognized (Mullen & Johnson, 1990). On the other hand, in the situation where a brand choice is usually made before purchase, such as with automobiles, the more frequently advertised brand will be recalled better. The matter of repetition in presenting a message is a complicated one. Consumer psychologists have found that repetition works best when the consumer is relatively uninvolved in the message, such as listening to the jingles that often accompany product advertisements. When the consumer is very involved in the message, such as researching which brand of computer to buy, the role of repetition is less important. Another key factor is the serial position where the message is presented. Material that is presented at the beginning and at the end is remembered better than information presented in the middle of a message. This has obvious implications for constructing a 30-second television or radio commercial. The next time you watch television, notice how the advertiser tries to get your attention and make key points at both the beginning and the end of the commercial.

I mentioned previously that cognition is intimately tied to the beliefs that consumers have. Consumer psychologists have examined several variables that have an impact upon consumer beliefs. For example, does the price of a product influence consumers' beliefs about product quality? Research has shown that to a limited extent consumers do associate the two together although the relationship is very weak. Surprisingly, there is evidence to suggest that consumers are often unconcerned with price. For instance, only 1 in 8 consumers considered price when selecting a box of cereal and only 1 in 4 when selecting a brand of detergent (Wells & LoSciuto, 1966). When selecting very expensive items, such as a television or an automobile, price does become a more important consideration. Consumer psychologists have also been interested in cognition because of its relationship to persuasion. The importance of variables such as 1-sided versus 2-sided messages, repetition, and source credibility all have been examined. These topics were discussed in chapter 12 and will not be repeated here except to say that they are critical factors in consumers' purchasing decisions.

3. Learning. In chapter 3, you will recall that I described learning as a relatively permanent change in behavior that occurs as a result of practice or experience. This is a topic of obvious interest to consumer psychologists because they want to understand how consumers learn to change their behavior toward certain products. Furthermore, they wish to ensure that any such changes in behavior are rela-

tively permanent and not prone to rapid extinction. One type of learning discussed in that chapter was classical conditioning, sometimes referred to as Pavlovian conditioning. You will recall that an unconditioned stimulus is paired with a conditioned stimulus to elicit an unconditioned response. After repeated pairings, the conditioned stimulus alone comes to elicit the conditioned response. According to Mullen and Johnson (1990) ". . . the classical conditioning model is a very powerful means of describing the effects that commercial advertisements can have on consumers. Classical conditioning can be used to explain the development of emotional responses toward a product, as well as the development of motivational tendencies toward a product" (p. 64). This is precisely why advertisers often pair images of their product with pleasant stimuli such as beautiful music, attractive models, and so forth. As mentioned earlier, consumer psychologists are also interested in preventing extinction once behaviors conducive to brand selection are learned. To accomplish this, companies often "reward" purchasers by including a small gift, such as a toy or gadget, in the purchase. In the 1960s, manufacturers often included a dishtowel or drinking glass in each box of detergent. As a child, I often ate a cereal that I disliked just to get the free toy inside the box. (The secret spy decoder ring was my favorite.) If the cereal makers discontinued the free toy, I quickly extinguished and switched to another brand. Today, manufacturers often include gimmicks such as scratch cards that reveal a certain percentage discount on the next purchase or contests where purchasers have an opportunity to win prizes. Instrumental conditioning, or operant conditioning as it is sometimes called, also includes several known learning principles helpful to consumer psychologists. Manufacturers use "cents off" coupons to shape up the initial purchasing response for a product. Varying schedules of reinforcement, which were discussed in chapter 3, are employed to increase the frequency of buying behaviors and reduce extinction tendencies. Even threats of punishment are used to shape behavior. For example, manufacturers often portray dire consequences that might occur if you do not purchase their brand of tires, medication, or insurance. In the chapter 7 discussion on emotions I described how an automobile tire manufacturer has used such a fear appeal very successfully in its advertising campaign. In general, the widely researched and well-established principles of learning have been found to be very effective in altering the learned purchasing behaviors of consumers.

4. Emotion. Within the context of consumer behavior, a person's emotional state can influence a consumer's *feeling* toward a product. Obviously, consumer psychologists are very interested in whether these feelings toward products are positive or negative and how these feelings develop. One way to develop emotional feelings toward a product is through repeated exposure to the product. This repetition of exposure is frequently done through various advertising media. As a general rule, frequent repetitions lead to more favorable evaluations of a product, which may be independent of any cognitive evaluations of the quality of the product. This is one reason why you find yourself being exposed to the same advertisements over and over. As you may additionally recall from chapter 3, emotions also have a classical conditioning component. Consumer psychologists have found that positive emotions can be conditioned to a product by repeatedly pairing the product with some pleasant stimulus.

Mullen and Johnson (1990) cite an illustration of how this was done with the fabric softener Final Touch (cited by Reed & Coalson, 1977):

> In one frequently repeated commercial, a housewife's use of the product is associated with the effusive love and approval of her husband. Before embracing her in the final scene, the husband addresses their child exclaiming in a tender voice, "Billy, you've got one special Mommy!" . . . In selecting these laundry products these consumers, upon seeing "Final Touch" on the shelf, may be induced to purchase it over a less expensive item, or over no such item, because of the "emotional glow" it evokes (p. 745).

Humor is also used to enhance the effect of a consumer's emotional response to a product. Humor presented in conjunction with a product elicits a positive emotional response that the advertiser hopes will be associated with the product. There is an increasing use of humor in advertising because of the demonstrated effectiveness of this approach. Another approach that elicits emotional responses is an appeal to fear. Several years ago Dial soap used this approach with the slogan "Aren't you glad you use Dial Soap? Don't you wish everybody did?" Advertisements for deodorants and mouthwashes frequently use fear appeals to sell their products.

5. Motivation. In the chapter on motivation, I discussed how motivation serves to direct behavior toward some goal. A need exists and the behavior is directed toward the goal of reducing or meeting that need. Consumer psychologists examine how products can either satisfy an existing need, such as hunger, thirst, sexual gratification, and so forth, or serve to create a need where none may currently exist. Selling soft drinks is an example of the former since we all become thirsty at times, and selling a new product that we do not think we need is an example of the latter. Cellular phones have been in existence for several decades, but their popularity has only skyrocketed in recent years when companies convinced large portions of the population that they needed to be capable of constant telephone communication.

To review, the motivational processes are concerned with how we become aware of a product (perception), develop beliefs about the product (cognition), remember the product (memory), become conditioned to have positive associations regarding the product (learning), develop positive feelings about the product (emotion), and come to desire the product (motivation). None of these processes works independently from each other. Indeed, the interactions between each process can become quite complicated. Nevertheless, consumer psychology has been effective in applying these basic tools of psychology to influence our everyday shopping and buying habits.

EDUCATIONAL PSYCHOLOGY

Educational psychology deals with the topics of teaching and learning. Most often educational psychology focuses on the learning that occurs with school-age children in a classroom setting, but other venues are also relevant. Learning is a lifelong activity for many professions, including law and medicine, where continuing education is mandated. Industry and the military also train individuals on an ongoing basis. There are few, if any, professions that are so static that no additional training or education is required. Since most educational psychologists work with school-age children, this section will concentrate on that aspect of the field.

Listed below are some of the topics addressed by the field of educational psychology:

- Teaching effectiveness. Educational psychologists are concerned with different teaching techniques and their effectiveness with students of different ages and different backgrounds. As children age, significant changes occur in their use of language and in their thinking processes. Teaching strategies must be compatible with these changes in order for effective learning to occur.
- Personal, social, and emotional development. Educational psychologists examine how students develop in terms of personal, social, and emotional development and design effective teaching strategies according to those changes.
- Socialization factors. **Socialization** is the process by which members of society influence the beliefs and behaviors of children, enabling them to participate in and contribute to society. Educational psychologists are interested in how this process affects learning. They are particularly concerned with the relationship of the family to school achievement. For example, what is the effect of preschool or enrichment programs such as Head Start on later learning? What effect does divorce or marital separation have on children's learning? How do single-parent families differ from 2-parent families in terms of the socialization process and what is the impact on learning?
- Learning abilities and problems. Educational psychologists investigate the role of ability and learning styles on individual differences and how they impact the teaching process. They investigate instructional techniques that are best suited for various ability levels, ranging from students with developmental disabilities to the highly gifted. They also design instructional strategies for students with special learning requirements, such as learning disorders, physical and sensory disorders, communication disorders, and emotional or behavioral disorders.
- Cultural factors. Educational psychologists investigate the role that culture plays in learning. Social class differences, as well as ethnic and racial differences, have an impact on the learning process and on teaching strategies used to maximize learning.
- Complex cognitive processes. Educational psychologists study a variety of complex cognitive processes such as creativity, problem solving, and concept learning and devise teaching and learning strategies to assist students in developing these skills.
- Motivation. Educational psychologists are aware of the important role that motivation plays in learning, and they investigate strategies and techniques to maximize motivation in students.
- Testing. Educational psychologists deal with all aspects of measurement and evaluation, particularly with achievement and aptitude testing. They also concern themselves with techniques for assessing learning, such as classroom grading. This type of testing is particularly important for assessing learning disabilities.

The whole art of teaching is only the art of awakening the natural curiosity of young minds for the purpose of satisfying it afterwards.

ANATOLE FRANCE
The Crime of Sylvestre Bonnard

Anita Woolfolk and Lorraine McCune-Nicholich (1980) have observed that people sometimes believe that the findings from educational psychology research are merely "common sense." They give the following examples to refute this notion:

- Classroom management. How can you get young children to stay in their seats and work rather than wander around the classroom? Common sense would suggest that you consistently remind them to remain in their seats every time they get up. If the teacher allows them to break the rule, both the offending child and other students will believe that the teacher is not serious about enforcing the rule. Research on this problem has instead shown that the more a teacher told students to sit down when they were out of their seats, the more often the students got out of their seats without permission (Madsen, Becker, Thomas, Koser, & Plager, 1978). As an alternative, if the teacher ignored the offending students and praised those who were sitting down, the rate of out-of-seat behavior dropped dramatically.
- Skipping grades. Should exceptionally bright children be encouraged to skip 1 or more grades? Common sense often says no because the gifted student will be much younger than his or her classmates and will not have the social skills to appropriately interact with older classmates. It is commonly believed that students who skip several grades are unhappy because they are neither physically nor emotionally ready to deal with older students, especially in the later grades. Research suggests just the opposite. Children who have been accelerated have adjusted as well as or better than children who have not been accelerated (Kirk, Gallagher, & Anastasiow, 1993).

We spend the first twelve months of our children's lives teaching them to walk and talk and the next twelve telling them to sit down and shut up.

PHYLLIS DILLER

- Taking turns. What method should a teacher use in calling on children to participate in a primary-grade reading class? Common sense would suggest that teachers should call on children randomly so that everyone has a chance to participate. In addition, the children will follow along with the lessons and stay alert because they will never know when they are going to be called on to read. Research suggests that sitting young children in a circle and going around the circle and calling on each child in turn leads to better reading achievement than calling on students randomly (Ogden, Brophy, & Everston, 1977).

These research findings in educational psychology confirm a common theme that I have frequently extolled in this book. In psychology, "common sense" often leads one to the incorrect answer.

There are many other areas of applied psychology besides this sampling that I have introduced. The field of psychology is so diverse that it can appeal to individuals with a variety of interests. If you are interested in working with children, then educational psychology might be your calling. If you are oriented toward business and commerce, then industrial/organizational psychology might be your forte. Do you have a strong interest in mathematics and engineering? If so, human factors would be a branch of applied psychology that you might wish to explore.

Hopefully, this chapter, as well as this book in general, has opened your eyes to the many different facets of psychology and the opportunities that exist for the improvement of our everyday lives. As I noted in the first pages of this book, the study of human behavior is endlessly fascinating. It is my hope that the overview of some of the applied aspects of psychology covered in this text will whet your appetite to explore the field in even greater detail.

Summary

- The concepts and tools of psychology have been applied to a large variety of fields, including law, sports, education, business, and counseling.
- Law shares numerous interests and assumptions with psychology. It also disagrees on several key points, such as the role of unconscious and uncontrollable forces on behavior, the existence of free will, and the role of individual differences on behavior.
- Psychologists have conducted extensive research on eyewitness testimony and have demonstrated the potential fallibility of such testimony.
- Psychologists have also examined the processes related to jury selection and how juries behave after they have been selected. This research indicates that several factors affect juries' decisions, including the defendant's attractiveness, the potential severity of the punishment, the inability to comply with judicial instruction to ignore information, and the predetermination of guilt or innocence before all the evidence is presented.
- Environmental psychology examines the relationship of the environment to human behavior. Environmental psychologists often work closely with architects and city planners in designing buildings and recreational spaces.
- Research suggests excessive noise can be harmful under some circumstances but innocuous at other times. Noises that are predictable and controllable are least harmful. Long-term exposure to noise has the potential for relatively permanent harmful effects.
- Crowding and population density also have the potential to be harmful although no reliable connection between overcrowding and negative effects has been found.
- Architectural psychology involves joint efforts by psychologists and architects to design buildings that overcome the problems of density and overcrowding.
- Industrial/organizational (I/O) psychology studies behavior in the workplace. Industrial psychology deals with personnel selection, training, and evaluation while organizational psychology examines interpersonal relationships that exist in the workplace. Personnel selection involves several steps, including job analysis, shadowing, recruitment, structured interviews, and testing.
- Personnel training includes conducting a needs assessment and training needs assessment, determining specific behavioral objectives, and generating relevant learning tasks.
- I/O psychologists are also interested in improving job motivation. Factors that improve motivation include appropriate job expectancies, specific goals, and the perception of fairness.
- Techniques for improving motivation involve using rewards and incentives, making job duties interesting, avoiding needless repetition in job tasks, and expanding workers' skills and level of responsibility.
- Job satisfaction is also an important domain of I/O psychology. Job satisfaction is greatly affected by the nature of the work itself, relationships between workers and supervisors, and the existence of incentives and rewards.
- Human factors psychology deals with how humans interact with machines and equipment. Emphasis includes designing visual displays in ways that permit information to be extracted quickly and accurately and designing controls that can be operated efficiently and accurately.
- Sports psychology deals with improving sports performance and enhancing the benefits of sports participation. For example, sports psychologists examine the role of personality, attention and arousal, anxiety, motivation, aggression, leadership, audience effects, and team cohesion on sports behavior. They also counsel athletes to assist them in improving athletic performance.
- Consumer psychology examines all aspects of consumers' behavior. Of particular interest are the topics related to how we become aware of a product (perception), develop beliefs about the product (cognition), become conditioned to have positive associations regarding the product (learning), develop positive feelings about the products (emotion), and come to desire the product (motivation).
- Educational psychology studies the topics of teaching and learning, particularly with school-age children. Educational psychologists concern themselves with topics such as teaching effectiveness, development, socialization, diverse learning abilities, cultural factors, motivation, and complex cognitive processes such as creativity, problem solving, and concept learning.
- Educational psychologists are also interested in psychological testing of both ability and achievement. The research findings have indicated that many "commonsense" approaches to teaching and education are ineffectual.

Key Terms

achievement motivation: an athlete's predisposition to either approach or avoid situations in which his or her performance will be evaluated.

aggression: a form of overt behavior that intends to harm or injure another person.

architectural psychology: a subfield of psychology wherein psychology and architecture work together closely to design buildings that overcome problems associated with overcrowding and density.

assertiveness: an unusual expenditure of effort and energy to achieve some external goal.

attentional focus: an athlete's ability to focus on relevant information during competition while disregarding irrelevant stimuli.

attentional style: an athlete's particular style of attending to stimuli that is highly correlated with performance.

behavioral objectives: a series of objectives derived by I/O psychologists that define what changes in knowledge, skills, and abilities should take place so that the effectiveness of training can be maximized.

centering: a technique of focusing attention on relevant task-oriented suggestions.

cognitive state anxiety: the worry and apprehension aspects of anxiety.

consumer psychology: a subfield of psychology that consists of the scientific study of all aspects of consumers' behavior.

crowding: the psychological feeling that comes from a sense of a loss of privacy or the overstimulation that results from being forced into close proximity to others.

density: the amount of living space that is available per person.

dominant response: the response in athletics that is most likely to be elicited at any given moment.

educational psychology: a subfield of psychology that deals with the topics of teaching and learning.

environmental psychology: a subfield of psychology that studies the relationship of the environment to human behavior.

human factors psychology: a subfield of psychology that deals with how machines, tools, displays, and controls should be designed in order to maximize the efficiency with which they are used.

industrial psychology: the subfield of I/O psychology that focuses on personnel selection, job training, and the measurement of work performance.

industrial/organizational (I/O) psychology: a subfield of psychology that studies the application of behavioral principles to solve the problems and needs of the workplace.

interview: a meeting between a prospective employee and the employer that is conducted to help select the most qualified applicant.

job analysis: the first step in personnel selection, which constitutes a precise statement of the job requirements.

learning tasks: in I/O psychology, the specific instructions that are generated from the behavioral objectives for individuals conducting job training.

needs assessment: an I/O psychology procedure that addresses the question of whether training is needed and what the specific nature of the training should be.

organizational psychology: the subfield of I/O psychology that focuses on the relationships that exist between workers and between workers and their supervisors.

own-race bias: the tendency to more accurately recognize faces of one's own race.

psychological testing: I/O psychology personnel selection techniques that predict job performance.

recruitment: a step in personnel selection that includes the placement of the job announcement to solicit prospective employees.

scientific jury selection: the process by which defense attorneys hire prominent psychologists to assist them in selecting jury members that will be sympathetic to the defendant.

self-confidence: the extent to which one believes in one's self.

shadowing: a procedure in which I/O psychologists observe workers to see exactly what tasks are being performed.

socialization: the process by which members of society influence the beliefs and behaviors of children, enabling them to participate in and contribute to society.

somatic state anxiety: the body's physiological reactions to stress, including rapid breathing, increased heart rate, and muscle tension.

sports psychology: a subfield of psychology that studies sports performance and how to enhance the benefits from participating in sports.

structured interview: an alternative to the traditional interview in which a predetermined series of questions is used for all applicants.

team cohesion: the tendency of a team to stick together and remain united in the pursuit of its goal and objectives.

thought stopping: techniques that are used to replace negative thoughts with success-oriented positive thoughts.

training: a deliberately planned set of learning experiences designed to modify some feature of a person's behavior.

training needs assessment: an I/O psychology procedure that is used to determine the exact kind and degree of training that is required.

visual display: any visual presentation of information.

Glossary Terms

abnormal behavior: patterns of thought, emotion, or behavior that are maladaptive, disruptive, or harmful to either oneself or to others.

accommodation: changing the shape of the lens, which allows the lens to focus the inverted image on the retina.

achievement motivation: an athlete's predisposition to either approach or avoid situations in which his or her performance will be evaluated.

active listening: using communication skills such as head nodding, smiling, eye contact, posture, and tone of voice to let another person know that you heard and understood what he or she said.

actuarial judgments: applying empirically derived rules to predict behavioral outcomes.

actuarial method: the method by which professionals make their judgments by applying rules that have been empirically derived from the correlation of particular factors (such as symptoms, age, gender, test scores, and medical history) to particular behavioral outcomes.

adaptation level: the level of stimulation that is used to judge the intensity of new stimuli.

affection: liking that is based on how one person relates to another person and that is experienced as emotional warmth and closeness.

affiliation: a desire or motivation to be with others, regardless of whether we like or dislike those others.

aggression: a form of overt behavior that intends to harm or injure another person.

agoraphobia: a psychological disorder characterized by an intense fear of being in places or situations where help might not be available.

algorithm: a problem-solving strategy that involves attempting every possible solution until a solution is reached.

altruistic behavior: an intrinsically motivated behavior that is aimed at doing something to help others without any benefit to the self.

ambiguous figures: visual information that can be interpreted in more than one way.

analytic hierarchy process: a computer program that reaches a solution by weighing the various alternatives and then by making comparisons between all possible alternatives.

anchoring-and-adjustment heuristic: the tendency to reach decisions by making adjustments in information that is already available.

anorexia nervosa: an eating disorder that is characterized by an exaggerated fear of becoming overweight and a refusal to maintain body weight above the minimum norm for one's age and height.

anosmia: a condition in which an individual cannot smell certain odors.

antianxiety drugs: also known as tranquilizers; medication that reduces a patient's anxiety, fear, and tension.

antigens: foreign bodily "invaders" (such as bacteria, viruses, fungi, and protozoa) that enter and attack the body.

antipsychotic drugs: medication that decreases psychotic symptoms such as delusions, hallucinations, paranoia, and distorted thinking.

antisocial personality disorder: a psychological disorder characterized by impulsivity, aggression, irritability, fearlessness, dishonesty, and a lack of remorse, conscience, or sense of responsibility.

anxiety disorder: a psychological disorder that is characterized by intense anxiety, fear, and apprehension.

architectural psychology: a subfield of psychology wherein psychology and architecture work together closely to design buildings that overcome problems associated with overcrowding and density.

aromatherapy: the use of fragrances to treat a wide variety of psychological and physical problems.

arousal: a physiological reaction to a motivational drive.

arrival time: method of sound localization that detects the source of a sound by when it arrives at each ear; most effective for lower pitched sounds.

asexual: individuals who have no sexual interest with either sex.

assertiveness: an unusual expenditure of effort and energy to achieve some external goal.

attachment disorder: a psychological disorder caused from childhood emotional deprivation.

attentional focus: an athlete's ability to focus on relevant information during competition while disregarding irrelevant stimuli.

attentional style: an athlete's particular style of attending to stimuli that is highly correlated with performance.

attitudes: relatively stable beliefs and feelings that predispose us to react to objects, people and events in certain ways.

attraction: a positive attitude or emotion that we feel toward others.

auditory nerve: responsible for transmission of neural impulses to the brain.

autokinetic effect: a perceptual illusion that occurs when a stationary light is viewed against total darkness; the light will appear to be moving in unpredictable ways.

availability heuristic: the tendency to make judgments about an event based on how many memories of an event are immediately available in memory.

aversion therapy: a type of psychotherapy that uses classical conditioning to teach clients to associate discomfort with a bad habit.

base-rate information: the frequency or probability for a given thing to occur.

basilar membrane: a flexible membrane located in the cochlea; flexes when vibrations from the ossicles send waves throughout the fluid in the cochlea.

basking in reflective glory: a self-presentation tactic of one who wants to emphasize his or her own importance by calling attention to an association with a well-known person or respected group of people.

behavioral genetics: a subfield of psychology that examines the role of heredity on human behavior.

behavioral objectives: a series of objectives derived by I/O psychologists that define what changes in knowledge, skills, and abilities should take place so that the effectiveness of training can be maximized.

behavior modification: a process by which reinforcements are used to change inappropriate behaviors, thoughts, and feelings.

bestiality: an act in which humans have sexual intercourse with animals.

binge eating: the rapid consumption of large quantities of food.

biofeedback: a procedure that uses sensors attached to the body, which gives feedback to the individual about various physiological functions.

biological approach: therapeutic approach that is based on a medical model of psychopathology that assumes that psychological problems reflect a medical disability of biological origin.

bipolar disorder: a psychological disorder that is characterized by wide mood swings that alternate between feelings of elation and feelings of depression.

bisexual: individuals who seek out and engage in sexual relations with members of both sexes.

blind spot: the place where the optic nerve exits through the retina and where no visual receptors exist.

body language: a way of communicating that includes the way we move our hands, arms, or legs, as well as the position, posture, and movement of our bodies.

borderline personality disorder: a psychological disorder that is characterized by extreme fluctuations in mood, self-image, and interpersonal relationships.

brainstorming: technique by which groups effectively engage in problem-solving activities.

brainwashing: thought-control procedures that involve isolation, dependence, and selective reinforcement.

brief therapy: Therapy in which the client and therapist agree upon the length of therapy and the deadline for its completion. Therapy usually lasts between 2 and 6 months.

bulimia: an eating disorder that is characterized by binge eating and the inappropriate use of various methods such as purging and laxatives to prevent weight gain.

bystander apathy: the tendency for onlookers to fail to provide assistance to those in need.

cataracts: a visual disorder in which the lens becomes cloudy causing difficulty with seeing fine detail.

CAT scan: computerized axial tomography; a procedure that involves having beams of x rays scan the different areas of the brain to develop a three-dimensional image of the structure of the brain

catharsis: the emotional release that results from acting out anger or frustration.

celibacy: the act of voluntarily abstaining from sex.

centering: a technique of focusing attention on relevant task-oriented suggestions.

central route: an elaboration likelihood model process that happens when recipients find a message interesting, important, or personally relevant, or when the recipient pays careful attention to the message.

charismatic leaders: individuals who have the ability to inspire others to do their very best, and provide charisma, intellectual stimulation, inspirational motivation, and individualized consideration.

chunks: organizing information into separate and meaningful parts to increase the ability to remember.

circadian rhythm: stable physiological changes that bodies undergo that affect the level of arousal.

clairvoyance: the ability to correctly forecast a future event.

classical conditioning: learning that allows us to form associations between events in our environment.

client-centered therapy: a type of therapy that centers on assisting the client in positive ways.

clinical interview: verbal inquiry that allows a clinician to observe and gather data through a series of questions.

clinical method: the method by which professionals make their judgments of behavioral outcomes based on their memories of and experiences with similar cases and on their knowledge of symptoms that are known to predict particular outcomes.

clinical psychologist: a mental health professional who is licensed with a doctoral degree in psychology; typically work with individuals who have more serious mental disorders.

cochlea: a fluid-filled and coiled tube in the inner ear that the ossicles rest against.

cognitive consistency: when one's beliefs, attitudes, and behaviors are in agreement.

cognitive dissonance: when one's beliefs, attitudes, and behaviors are not consistent.

cognitive state anxiety: the worry and apprehension aspects of anxiety.

cognitive therapy: a type of therapy with emphasis on how an individual's negative thoughts lead to maladaptive behaviors.

cohort effect: the tendency for each age group to have distinct experiences and to develop certain viewpoints or perspectives on a variety of matters.

commitment: a decision to continue a relationship for an extended period of time.

compliance: the act of getting a person to agree to the request of another.

conditioned emotional response: the response wherein a previously neutral stimulus has acquired the ability to arouse an emotional response.

conditioned response (CR): a response that has been conditioned to a previously neutral conditioned stimulus.

conditioned stimulus (CS): an originally neutral stimulus that is paired with an unconditioned stimulus, and elicits a conditioned response.

conditioned taste aversion: learning to avoid eating something that has previously been associated with illness.

conduction deafness: caused by blockage of the outer ear canal, or damage to the eardrum or ossicles; can be helped with the use of a hearing aid.

cones: receptors on the retina, mostly located in the center of the brain, which are color sensitive and allow for the perception of finer detail.

confirmation bias: the propensity to seek evidence that verifies our personal beliefs as opposed to evidence that refutes them.

conflict situation: situation in which different motives are pulling an individual in different directions.

conformity: behavior that occurs when an individual's behavior or attitudes are influenced because of perceived or actual group pressures.

consumer psychology: a subfield of psychology that consists of the scientific study of all aspects of consumers' behavior.

consummate love: the ideal and highest form of love; when passion, intimacy and commitment are all present.

continuous reinforcement: when a desired response is reinforced each time it occurs; important when shaping behavior.

convergent thinking: the act of putting together a group of often disparate facts to find a solution to a question or problem.

Coolidge effect: the tendency for animals to engage in sex with a new partner, even if they showed no further interest in sexual behavior with an original partner.

coping mechanisms: strategies and behaviors that offer relief during high levels of stress.

cornea: the part of the eye that images first pass through, which bends the light rays, partially focusing the image.

correlated: the relationship that exists when two things reliably occur together.

counseling psychologist: a mental health professional who is licensed with a doctoral degree in psychology; typically work with individuals with less severe problems such as occupational and school problems, and marriage or family counseling.

covert reinforcement: a behavioral therapy technique that involves visualization to associate a pleasant scenario with a desired behavior.

covert sensitization: a behavioral therapy technique that involves visualization to associate an unpleasant scenario with an undesired behavior.

creativity: the ability to produce innovative and valuable ideas and to solve problems in unique and useful ways.

crowding: the psychological feeling that comes from a sense of a loss of privacy or the overstimulation that results from being forced into close proximity to others.

cultural barriers: obstacles that arise due to cultural constraints that allow problems to be solved in only a certain way.

dark adaptation: the process of switching visual sensitivity from high illumination levels to low illumination levels.

decibels (db): measurement of sound amplitude.

deductive reasoning: drawing conclusions from general statements about what is known to be true to specific and logically consistent conclusions.

deindividuation: the process by which individuals lose their personal identities when functioning as part of a group.

déjà vu: "already seen"; the strong feeling of remembering scenes or events that are actually being experienced for the first time.

delusions: beliefs that are held without any factual basis.

delusions of control: false beliefs that thoughts and behavior are being controlled by another individual.

delusions of grandeur: false beliefs about one's power and importance.

delusions of persecution: false beliefs that others are plotting or conspiring against you.

density: the amount of living space that is available per person.

determinism: an assumption of causality; the belief that everything we do is caused by something.

dichotomous thinking: a thought process in which individuals view their problems in very fixed terms with a limited number of solutions.

diffusion of responsibility: a process in which everyone thinks that someone else will probably assist a victim.

discrimination: the behavioral component of prejudice that consists of overt acts that treat certain groups in an unfair manner; the ability to distinguish between stimuli.

dissociative disorder: a psychological disorder that is characterized by major changes in memory without any physical precursor.

dissociative identity disorder: a psychological disorder that is characterized by having two or more distinct and separate personalities; aka multiple personality disorder.

distributed practice: intervals of studying distributed over a period of time.

divergent thinking: the ability to conceive a variety of different ideas to solve the same problem.

dominant response: the response that is most likely to be elicited at any given moment.

doppler shift: change in sound that occurs when an object approaches and then passes.

drive: a state that impels and activates a behavior that satisfies a need.

DSM: Diagnostic manual for mental disorders published by the American Psychiatric Association. Currently in its fourth edition and referred to as DSM IV.

eardrum: flexible membrane in the ear that vibrates when sound strikes it.

eccentric: an individual who may be extremely creative, highly educated, or intelligent, but exhibits an odd, whimsical, or peculiar behavior.

eclectic approach: a therapeutic approach that uses the effective components of various psychotherapeutic approaches.

educational psychology: a subfield of psychology that deals with the topics of teaching and learning.

elaboration likelihood model (ELM): a theory that refers to the process of hearing a persuasive message, and then thinking about what was heard.

elaborative rehearsal: linking an item to be remembered to other information already contained in long-term memory.

electroconvulsive therapy (ECT): a medical treatment for depression that involves sending electrical current through an individual's brain, causing changes in the neural transmission systems and biochemical balance of the brain; also known as shock therapy.

emblems: meaningful gestures exhibited when an individual is lying.

emotional barriers: inhibitions and fears of appearing foolish in the eyes of others.

emotional rapport: the caring relationship between a therapist and client, characterized by warmth, understanding, acceptance, friendship, and empathy.

empathy: the ability to share in another's emotions, thoughts, or feelings.

encoding: the method by which memories are stored in long-term memory.

environmental psychology: a subfield of psychology that studies the relationship of the environment to human behavior.
episodic memory: memory of personal experiences that represent episodes in our lives.
eros: a style of love that is based on a powerful physical attraction.
estrogen: sex hormone for females.
exhibitionism: a sexual disorder that is characterized by a repeated urge to expose one's genitals to others.
explanatory style: the way an individual habitually explains the causes of good and bad events that occur in his/her life.
externality theory: the belief that the eating response in obese individuals is triggered by external cues, rather than internal cues.
extinction: the weakening of a response due to lack of reinforcement; occurs in both classical and operant conditioning.
extrasensory perception (ESP): the ability to gather information beyond the five primary senses; implies that perceptions can occur in the complete absence of any sensation.
extrinsic motivation: motivation that occurs because individuals are acting on rewards and/or punishments of a behavior.
farsightedness: a condition in which we can clearly see far away, but things up close are blurry.
fear of failure: the fear of not succeeding at achieving a goal.
female orgasmic disorder: a sexual dysfunction that is characterized by the inability to reach an orgasm.
fetish: sexual arousal caused by an object.
fetishism: a sexual disorder that is categorized by the need to use some nonliving object in order to achieve sexual arousal.
fight or flight: a term that describes the physiological responses that prepare our body to take an action to either fight or flee from a situation depending on the circumstances.
fixation: an inability to view a problem from a fresh perspective.
fixed-interval schedule: a reinforcement schedule in which a set amount of time must elapse between successive reinforcements.
fixed-ratio schedule: a reinforcement schedule in which a response is reinforced after a fixed number of responses.
flashbulb memories: long-term memories of unexpected and emotionally arousing events.
flavor: sensation that depends on both odor and taste.
framing: posing a question in a certain way.
free association: a technique used by psychoanalysts that involves the client saying whatever comes to mind; this technique helps clients bring feelings to a conscious level.
free will: the belief that human behavior is not controlled by the environment, by past experiences, or by genetics, and that humans are free to behave as they want.
frustration: a negative emotion that occurs whenever we are blocked or thwarted from achieving a goal.
frustration-aggression hypothesis: a theory that stipulates that the primary cause of anger and aggression is a feeling of frustration.
functional fixedness: a type of fixation in which we become preoccupied with one solution to a problem and fail to see other alternative solutions.
gambler's fallacy: the incorrect belief that one is likely to win because of the outcome of previous events.
general adaptation syndrome: a series of physiological reactions that characterizes the body's reaction to stress as occurring in three stages: alarm reaction, resistance stage, and stage of exhaustion.
goal: the objective of behavior directed toward satisfying an existing need.
great person theory: a theory that proposes that highly successful leaders possess certain traits that distinguish them from others. The traits include drive, honesty and integrity, self-confidence, creativity, expertise, cognitive ability, leadership motivation, and flexibility.
group: any two or more interacting individuals who share common goals, have a stable relationship, are interdependent on one another, and perceive themselves as part of a group.
group polarization: a phenomenon in which a group as a whole tends to adopt a more extreme decision than would the average individual in the group following a group's discussion of an issue.
group therapy: a form of therapy in which a group of several individuals meets simultaneously with a therapist.
groupthink: a group process that occurs when group members are trying to reach unanimity of opinion. They fail to consider realistic alternative courses of action and decide to take a course of action that later proves to be disastrous.
habituation: the process by which repeated presentations of a stimulus does *not* cause a response.
hair cells: located on the basilar membrane; generates neural impulses from sounds which are then collected and transmitted to the brain.
hallucinations: perceptions of stimuli that do not exist; can be auditory, olfactory or tactile.
hardiness: personality characteristics that differentiate between people who do and do not get sick under the influence of stress.
hassles: minor frustrating and irritating demands that we are faced with on a daily basis.
health psychology: a subspecialty of psychology that focuses on maintenance of good health, prevention and treatment of illness, the study of physiological and psychological factors that cause illness, and improvement of the practices and policies of the health care system.
hertz (hz): The number of cycles between high and low air pressure that occur in one second; related to a sound's pitch.
heterosexual: individuals who seek out and engage in sexual relations with members of the opposite sex.
heuristic: a "rule-of-thumb" problem-solving approach that involves using a strategy that previously worked in a similar situation.
hindsight bias: the tendency to believe the results were foreseeable, once the outcome of an event is given; aka the "I-knew-it-all-along" phenomenon.
hippocampus: a brain structure that serves as a filter or gatekeeper and permits a portion of the information in short-term memory to enter into long-term memory.

homeostasis: the innate drive to maintain biological conditions at an optimal and stable level.

homosexual: individuals who seek out and engage in sexual relations with members of the same sex.

hopelessness: a persistent belief that things will never get better no matter what an individual does or how an individual's circumstances may change.

human factors psychology: a subfield of psychology that deals with how machines, tools, displays, and controls should be designed in order to maximize the efficiency with which they are used.

humanistic psychologist: psychologists who emphasize the capacity of people to make conscious decisions about their own lives.

humanistic therapy: type of therapy that attempts to promote a client's personal growth and self-fulfillment by assisting the client in the interpretation of events and experiences in their lives.

hypoactive sexual desire: a sexual dysfunction that is characterized by a lack of interest in sex and a very low level of sexual activity.

hypothalamus: a small structure located in the base of the brain that, among other things, monitors glucose levels in the blood to regulate feelings of hunger.

illusory correlation: false perceptions in which it is thought that a relationship exists between two variables.

illusory movement: a perception of movement where there is none.

illustrators: body movements that illustrate speech as it is spoken.

imitation: the act of simulating the behavior of another individual.

immune system: the body's defensive system that fights off a variety of different "invaders" that threaten health.

implicit stereotyping: an automatic tendency to stereotype individuals.

impression management: the attempt to make a permanent good impression in dealings with people.

incubation effect: the phenomenon in which the answer to a problem appears only after one stops thinking about the problem.

individual therapy: a form of therapy in which an individual meets alone with a therapist.

inductive reasoning: drawing conclusions from specific facts or observations.

industrial/organizational (I/O) psychology: a subfield of psychology that studies the application of behavioral principles to solve the problems and needs of the workplace.

industrial psychology: the subfield of I/O psychology that focuses on personnel selection, job training, and the measurement of work performance.

insanity: a legal term that is used to explain and excuse criminal behavior; a person is not responsible for criminal conduct if the individual lacks substantial capacity to control the behavior or to appreciate the "criminality" of the conduct at the time of the conduct, and if the criminal behavior is the result of a mental disease or defect.

insight: the sudden and unexpected realization of the solution to a problem; aka the "aha!" phenomenon; also awareness of the unconscious parts of one's mind.

interval schedules: a schedule of reinforcement in which a reinforcement occurs after a certain period of time has elapsed.

interview: a meeting between a prospective employee and the employer that is conducted to help select the most qualified applicant.

intimacy: feelings of being close and connected to another individual; feelings of being able to confide closely in another individual without risk.

intrinsic motivation: motivation that occurs because individuals find a behavior to be pleasurable and/or reinforcing.

iris: colored muscles in the eye that expand and contract; controls the amount of light entering the eye.

irradiation: a perceptual illusion in size distortion that occurs when a bright object is surrounded by a dark object.

job analysis: the first step in personnel selection, which constitutes a precise statement of the job requirements.

keyword technique: a mnemonic system that constructs one or more concrete keywords with a visual image.

killer T-cells: cells in the body that recognize and destroy antigens that have invaded the body.

kinesthesis: information from muscles, tendons, and joints that provides information about the position of limbs.

law of effect: a law that states that an organism is more likely to repeat a response that leads to favorable consequences.

leadership: the process by which one member of the group guides and influences other members toward a common goal shared by all members of the group.

leading the witness: a method of questioning to get a desired answer.

learned helplessness: the inability to learn to avoid an aversive stimuli.

learning: a relatively permanent change in mental state or behavior due to experience.

learning tasks: specific instructions that are generated from the behavioral objectives for individuals conducting job training.

lens: a clear membrane that focuses the inverted visual image on the retina.

liking: feelings of respect and admiration for another individual.

lock-and-key theory: a theory maintaining that an electrical impulse is generated when the "key" of an air molecule containing an odor is inserted into the correctly fitting "lock" receptacle in the nose.

long-term memory: the memory system that allows for the relatively permanent storage of information.

long-term therapy: Therapy that includes weekly one hour meeting that takes place over a period of several months or years.

loving: deep feelings of need, caring, trust, and tolerance for another individual.

low-ball technique: an effective way of gaining compliance that involves removing a favorable circumstance after a commitment decision has been made.

ludus: a style of love that includes experiencing numerous lovers; includes a reluctance to settle down or get too involved with one person, and an inability to experience love at first sight.

lymphocyte: a specialized type of white blood cell that the human body uses to attack invading agents.

Machiavellian: a term for individuals who are manipulative and obsessed with acquiring power.

male orgasmic disorder: a sexual dysfunction that is characterized by the delay or inability to reach an orgasm.
mania: a secondary style of love that is a mixture of eros and ludus.
manic stage: feelings of elation and euphoria often characterized by pressured and loud speech, optimism, increased self-esteem, feelings of grandiosity, and decreased sexual inhibition.
masking: the use of one kind of sound to block another sound.
massed practice: studying in one block of time; aka "cramming"
matching hypothesis: the desire to associate with others similar to ourselves.
mental set: a type of mental fixation by which we attempt to solve a problem using only solutions that worked in the past.
mnemonic: any system or technique that aids in memory recall.
modeling: the act of imitating a specific behavior that was observed.
moderators of stress: factors that reduce the consequences of stress.
mood: a psychological state that reflects how an individual is feeling.
motivation: the process that initiates, sustains, and directs behavior.
MRI: magnetic resonance imaging; an imaging technique that creates a magnetic field around a patient and uses radio waves to detect abnormalities.
muscle relaxation: an effective stress-reduction technique.
narcissistic personality disorder: a psychological disorder that is characterized by having an exaggerated sense of self-importance and strong tendencies to exaggerate one's achievements and talents.
nature-nurture issue: the controversy over the relative importance of heredity and environment on human behavior.
nearsightedness: a visual disorder in which individuals can see up close clearly, but things far away are blurry.
need: a condition that exists when we are deprived of something that we want or require.
need for achievement: the desire for accomplishment, even in the absence of external rewards.
need for power: desire to control the behavior of others and to assert one's own authority.
needs assessment: an I/O psychology procedure that addresses the question of whether training is needed and what the specific nature of the training should be.
negative punishment: a behavior that is undesired is weakened by the removal of a rewarding or pleasurable stimulus when the undesired behavior is exhibited.
negative reinforcer: an aversive stimulus that strengthens responses that permit an organism to avoid or escape from them.
nerve deafness: deafness caused by damage to either the auditory nerve or the hair cells on the basilar membrane; cannot be helped by a hearing aid because the auditory messages are blocked from reaching the brain.
neural consolidation: the process by which a memory trace becomes permanently fixed, by repeated activation of neural circuits.
neurological test: assessment tool that clinicians use to measure and diagnose the extent of brain dysfunction and neurological impairment.
neurotransmitters: chemicals in the brain that allow brain cells to communicate with one another.
normative behaviors: the rules that are established by groups to regulate members' behavior.
norms: scores that have been developed by giving tests to a large, representative sample of individuals; allows comparison to clinical samples.
obedience: The tendency to follow the orders of a person who is in a position of authority.
observation: the viewing of overt behavior; can take place in a clinic, laboratory, or natural setting.
observational learning: learning that occurs by observing and imitating the actions of others.
olfactory bulb: the area in the brain where electrical impulses are received to detect smells; located below and toward the front of the brain, directly above the upper nasal passage.
olfactory receptor cells: receptors responsible for detection of smells; approximately 30 million cells in each nostril.
olfactory sense: the sense of smell.
operant chamber (Skinner box): a device used to research operant learning process; allows control of the stimuli and rewards given to an organism.
operant (instrumental) conditioning: learning that allows us to repeat behaviors that bring about positive consequences and to avoid behaviors that result in unpleasant consequences.
operant response: a term used in operant conditioning that indicates a response to be learned.
optic nerve: a bundle of nerve fibers that transmit electrical impulses to the visual cortex of the brain.
optimist: an individual who attributes negative events in life as being due to forces that are external to the individual, temporary in nature, and specific to events.
organizational psychology: the subfield of I/O psychology that focuses on the relationships that exist between workers and between workers and their supervisors.
orienting response: an automatic response to an unexpected stimulus.
ossicles: three tiny bones in the middle ear; transmits and amplifies vibrations from the eardrum.
other-enhancement: efforts to make another person feel good in our presence.
overconfidence: the tendency to overestimate the accuracy of self-predictions of success or behavior.
overestimation of control: the act of overestimating the ability to control chance in situations where chance determines the outcome.
overjustification effect: adding an incentive for a task that an individual already enjoys; may result in a loss of interest in the task.
overlearning: continuing to study information that has already been learned. Aids in retention and recall of information.
own-race bias: the tendency to more accurately recognize faces of one's own race.
panic disorder: a psychological disorder that is characterized by an unwarranted feeling of fear resulting in numerous physical sensations.
paralanguage: features in tone of voice that communicate messages above and beyond that of the words themselves.
paranormal: phenomenon that function outside of the normal sensory channels.
paraphilia: a sexual disorder that is characterized by a repeated and intense

sexual urge, fantasy, or behavior to situations, objects, or people considered inappropriate by society.

parasympathetic nervous system: the part of the nervous system that supports the body in nonemergency situations.

partial (intermittent) reinforcement: reinforcing a desired response periodically, rather than continuously.

partial reinforcement effect: the finding that responses are much more resistant to extinction following partial reinforcement.

passion: intense sexual attraction for another individual.

pedophilia: a sexual disorder that is characterized by receiving sexual gratification by watching, touching, or engaging in sexual acts with prepubescent children.

peg-word system: a mnemonic system to improve memory recall which involves learning a set of peg words such as 1-bun, 2-shoe and then associating items to be memorized to the peg words.

perception: the complicated process whereby our brain interprets sensations and gives them meaning.

performance: a demonstration of a learned behavior.

peripheral route: an elaboration likelihood model process that happens when a recipient finds a message uninteresting or irrelevant, and consequently is not motivated to pay careful attention or examine the message thoroughly.

personal space: an invisible boundary signifying a comfortable distance from others.

pessimist: an individual who believes that stressful life events occur because of internal character flaws that are a permanent part of the individual.

PET scan: positron emission tomography; a neurological test that allows for the examination of physiological and biochemical processes of the brain as they occur; involves injecting a radioactive substance into the bloodstream.

phallic symbols: objects that appear in dreams that hold unconscious sexual meanings; based on Freudian theory.

phantom limb pain: a phenomenon wherein amputees feel intense pain in arms or legs that are missing.

pheromones: an olfactory animal sexual arousal cue.

phi phenomena: a perceptual illusion of movement that occurs when two lights situated next to one another turn on and off in an alternating fashion.

phobia: a strong, persistent, and unjustified fear of some specific object or situation.

physical attractiveness: a combination of facial and bodily characteristics that are perceived as aesthetically pleasant or appealing.

pitch: the highness or lowness of a sound due to vibration of sound waves.

placebo: a fake pill or injection.

placebo effect: the tendency for people to report that any treatment has helped them, regardless of whether it has any actual therapeutic effect.

pluralistic ignorance: a phenomenon in which individuals in a group fail to provide assistance based on their observations that no one else seems concerned.

polygraph: aka lie detector; a device that measures physiological responses that accompany emotional arousal.

positive punishment: involves the application of an aversive stimulus to stop or weaken an ongoing behavior.

positive reinforcement: stimulus events or behavioral consequences that strengthen the responses that immediately precede them.

post-hoc explanation: explanation of the cause of an event after an event has occurred.

post-reinforcement pause: a pause occurring after a reinforcement is obtained; the higher the ratio of responses, the longer the post-reinforcement pause.

precognition: the ability to correctly perceive future events, such as political and historical events, catastrophes, stock market changes, and such.

prefrontal lobotomy: a type of psychosurgery that involves cutting the nerve fibers that connect the frontal lobes of the brain to the emotional control centers of the brain.

prejudice: a negative attitude toward another person based on that person's membership in a social group.

Premack principle: a behavior that has a high probability of occurring can reinforce another behavior that has a lower probability of occurring.

premature ejaculation: a male sexual dysfunction that is characterized by reaching an orgasm with very little sexual stimulation, usually before or just after sexual penetration.

primacy effect: the tendency to assign more importance to the things learned earlier as compared to the things learned later.

primary prevention: efforts that are made to reduce the incidence of behavioral disorders by strengthening or increasing the community characteristics that threaten good mental health.

primary reinforcers: a reinforcer that strengthens behavior because it satisfies a basic biological need.

proactive interference: the disruption of a newer memory caused by an older memory.

procedural memory: memory of how to accomplish certain tasks.

proximity: how close things are in space, time, or order.

psychiatric nurse: a mental health professional with a registered nurse degree with specialized training for working in a mental hospital or other mental health setting.

psychiatric social worker: a mental health professional who has a master's degree in social work; typically focus on treatment procedures, with a specific interest on the community and/or family.

psychiatrist: a medical doctor who has specialized in psychiatry after completing medical school; can prescribe medication, psychoactive drugs, and electroshock treatment.

psychoanalysis: a type of therapy that is based on the theory that emotional problems result from conflicts between the conscious and unconscious aspects of one's personality.

psychoanalyst: a mental health professional who has a professional degree in psychology, psychiatry, or social work, and has at least 2 years of extensive, supervised training at a psychoanalytic institute.

psychokinesis: the act of using the mind to control physical matter. Examples include levitation and bending an object.

psychological test: an assessment tool that clinicians use to measure different aspects of behavior, including personality, maladaptive behavior, social skills, intelligence, vocational interests and skills, and various mental impairments.

psychological testing: I/O psychology personnel selection techniques that predict job performance.

psychological well-being: the presence of positive mental health symptoms such as self-acceptance, positive relations with other people, autonomy, environmental mastery, a sense of purpose in life, and personal growth.

psychopathology: disturbed behavior that is maladaptive, disruptive, or harmful to either oneself or to others; also known as *abnormal behavior.*

psychosomatic: referring to the interaction of the mind and the body.

psychosurgery: a biological therapy in which brain surgery is performed to destroy or remove brain tissue.

punishment: any consequence to a behavior that decreases the probability of the behavior recurring; the application of an aversive stimulus *after* a behavior has occurred.

pupil: the opening in the middle of the iris; regulated by the iris.

purging: intentional vomiting as a method of preventing weight gain.

radial keratotomy: a surgical procedure in which small incisions are made to alter the shape of the eyeball.

random sample: a sample in which every individual in the population has an equal chance of being included.

ratio schedules: a reinforcement schedule in which a reinforcement will occur after a certain number of responses has occurred.

recategorization: the process of changing the boundaries of what a person considers an in-group (us) versus an out-group (them) affiliation.

reciprocal liking: a mutual liking that plays an important role in interpersonal attraction.

reciprocation: a rule that states that once someone has made a concession or done someone a favor, we feel obligated to return the favor.

recruitment: a step in personnel selection that includes the placement of the job announcement to solicit prospective employees.

reflecting: restating the important parts of a message in your own words.

rehearsal: using repetition to maintain information in short-term memory.

reinforcement: an event that increases the probability that the response that preceded it will be repeated in the future.

reinforcer: a term used in conditioning that identifies something that strengthens a behavior that led to it.

relative loudness: method of sound localization whereby the brain detects differences in sound intensity in each ear, and calculates the direction of the source of the sound; most effective when locating the source of high-pitched sounds; the most effective way to localize sound.

representative heuristic: the tendency to assume that something is a member of a category because it is similar to another item in that category.

representative sample: a group of individuals who have the same characteristics as the population from which they are drawn.

repression: forgetting about painful, embarrassing, or threatening memories; aka motivated forgetting.

respect: liking that is based on the characteristics or actions of another person that we admire.

response: behavior that attains a goal to satisfy a need.

Restricted Environmental Stimulation Therapy (REST): a therapeutic technique in which sensory deprivation tanks are used to help change habits such as smoking, dieting, and alcohol consumption.

retina: the surface at the back of the eye where rods and cones are located.

retroactive interference: the disruption of an older memory caused by a newer memory.

road rage: aggressive driving that originates from driving-related anger.

rods: receptors on the retina which that sensitive to black and white, but not to color.

role conflict: when the different roles one has to play requires conflicting behaviors.

roles: the specific ways that individuals in groups are expected to behave.

saccades: small, rapid eye movements.

sample: a subset of individuals used to generalize findings to the population as a whole.

satiety: a sensation of feeling full and not hungry.

savant: an individual who has extraordinary abilities in one highly defined area, but is severely deficient in most other areas.

scarcity principle: the tendency to consider objects or opportunities as more valuable when they are less available.

schedules of reinforcement: patterns of partial reinforcement.

schizophrenia: a psychological disorder that is characterized by severe distortion in thought processes, language, perceptions and emotions.

scientific jury selection: the process by which defense attorneys hire psychologists to assist them in selecting jury members who will be sympathetic to the defendant.

seasonal affective disorder (SAD): a psychological disorder that is characterized by mood fluctuations that vary according to seasonal or weather conditions.

secondary prevention: efforts that are made that involve instituting programs with community resources such as schools, churches, or the police to identify and treat mental health problems in the early stages.

secondary reinforcer: a reinforcer that strengthens behavior because it is paired with a primary reinforcer.

self-confidence: the feeling or perception of belief in one's self.

self-disclosure: the act of readily exchanging information to another that refers to one's self, including personal states, disposition, events in the past, and plans for the future.

self-efficacy: an individual's own judgments of his or her ability to cope with stressful situations.

self-enhancement: efforts to make oneself look good to other people.

self-perception theory: a theory that proposes that people observe their behavior and then infer an attitude that is consistent with that behavior.

self-regulation: the process of setting goals and then self-rewarding when a goal is achieved.

self-report: a form of testing that requests an individual to answer specific written questions or to select specific answers from a list of alternatives.

semantic memory: knowledge of factual information about our world.
semantic priming: the phenomenon in which a word is easier to recognize after a related word has been flashed previously.
semicircular canals: three fluid-filled canals located in the inner ear that provide information about directional changes of the body or head.
sensation: The process of converting physical stimuli into neural impulses that our brain can interpret.
sensation seekers: individuals who seek out high levels of arousal.
sensory deprivation: a state of being with reduced external sensory stimulation.
sensory memory: a short-term buffer that briefly holds information, and allows information to be transferred to the short-term memory system.
set point: an optimal value that the body attempts to maintain.
sexual dysfunction: a sexual disorder that is characterized by a disruption in the performance of the normal sexual response cycle (sexual desire, excitement, orgasm, and resolution).
sexual masochism: a sexual disorder that is characterized by the act or thought of being humiliated, beaten, bound or made to suffer in some other way. Impairs the ability to function or causes great emotional upset.
sexual sadism: a sexual disorder that is characterized by the thought or act of inflicting suffering on others.
shadowing: a procedure in which I/O psychologists observe workers to see exactly what tasks are being performed.
shaping: a small series of steps that teaches an organism to build upon existing behaviors by selectively rewarding some behaviors and not others.
short-term memory: the memory system that holds information for 20 to 30 seconds; limited to 7 items plus or minus 2. Also referred to as working memory.
Skinner box: see *operant chamber.*
social contagion: a mass psychogenic illness of a group of individuals caused exclusively by psychological factors.
social facilitation: the improvement of performance when it is conducted in the presence of others.
social inhibition: the inhibition of performance when it is conducted in the presence of others.
socialization: the process by which members of society influence the beliefs and behaviors of children, enabling them to participate in and contribute to society.
social loafing: as the size of a group increases, the amount of effort by individual members decreases.
social phobia: a psychological disorder characterized by an intense fear of being scrutinized and negatively evaluated by other people in social or performance situations.
social support: the existence of a network of people that individuals feel they can rely upon in times of crisis.
socioemotional selectivity theory: as people age, they become increasingly aware that they have a limited amount of time left to live, and the emotional component of relationships becomes more important.
soft determinism: a less extreme view of determinism; the belief that human behavior is affected by the combined influence of environment, past experiences, and genetics.
somatic state anxiety: the body's physiological reactions to stress, including rapid breathing, increased heart rate, and muscle tension.
spontaneous recovery: the reappearance of a learned response that had previously been extinguished.
spontaneous remission: a phenomenon in which an individual recovers from a psychological disorder without any professional treatment.
sports psychology: a sub-field of psychology that studies sports performance and how to enhance the benefits from participating in sports.
SQ3R method: A study technique which involves surveying the material to be learned, asking questions, reading, reciting, and finally reviewing the material.
state: temporary condition that exists due to a specific situation.
state dependent learning: the phenomenon that recall of material is better when it is done within the same contextual setting as the original learning.
stereotypes: beliefs that one holds about minority groups.
stimulus generalization: the tendency to respond to similar stimuli once a response has been conditioned.
storge: a love style where love develops slowly, and feelings start with affection and progressively grow stronger as the relationship matures.
stressors: events that are perceived as harmful or threatening.
structured interview: an alternative to the traditional interview in which a predetermined series of questions is used for all applicants.
subjective well-being: a state of emotion that reflects your judgment about life satisfaction and emotional reactions to events in your life; synonymous with happiness.
subliminal perception: the phenomenon of a message being presented below the level of awareness or "below threshold."
substance abuse: persistent use of a substance that results in physical or psychological impairment, causes the individual distress, and jeopardizes the safety of the user or others.
substance dependence: maladaptive use of a substance marked by an inability to control its use despite knowledge of harmful effects. The dependence can be both biological and psychological.
successive approximation: small intermediate steps toward the final desired response.
superstitious behavior: the tendency to attribute receiving a reinforcement to an irrelevant behavior.
suppression: the willful intention of putting something out of our mind.
sympathetic nervous system: the part of the nervous system that elicits physiological arousal to provide energy to respond to a threatening situation.
synapses: gaps between brain cells; allows the cells to communicate among themselves.
synaptic plasticity: a process in which synapses in the brain are altered by experiences; alterations occur by creating new synapses or strengthening existing ones.
tabula rasa: the belief that when a human is born, the mind is a "blank slate."
team cohesion: the tendency of a team to stick together and remain united in the pursuit of its goal and objectives.

telepathy: the ability of one person to send thoughts to another person, or for a person to perceive another's thoughts.

testosterone: sex hormone for males.

testwiseness: a set of skills that individuals can use to improve a test score no matter what the content area of the test; aka test sophistication or testmanship.

therapeutic alliance: the relationship between the therapist and client that consists of mutual respect and understanding; permits the parties to work toward a common goal of solving the client's problems.

thought stopping: techniques that are used to replace negative thoughts with success-oriented positive thoughts.

threshold: the point at which sensation awareness begins.

timbre: the quality of a sound.

tinnitus: a ringing sensation that usually indicates that hair cells have suffered damage.

tip-of-the-tongue phenomenon: the sensation of knowing an answer, but not being able to retrieve it.

training: a deliberately planned set of learning experiences designed to modify some feature of a person's behavior.

training needs assessment: an I/O psychology procedure that is used to determine the exact kind and degree of training that is required.

trait: a relatively stable characteristic or disposition that humans possess as part of their personality.

transduction: the conversion of physical stimuli to electrical impulses.

transference: a psychoanalytic process that occurs when a client transfers feelings towards other individuals to the therapist.

trial and error: the problem-solving approach that involves trying a variety of different responses until discovering a solution.

type-A personality: a type of personality that is characterized by competitive achievement orientation, time urgency, anger, and hostility.

type-B personality: a type of personality that is characterized by low levels of competitiveness, little or no time urgency, and low levels of anger and hostility.

type-C personality: a type of personality that is characterized as repressed, apathetic, and hopeless; aka cancer-prone personality.

unconditioned response (UCR): an automatic response to an unconditioned stimulus.

unconditioned stimulus (UCS): a stimulus that causes an automatic response.

uplifts: desirable experiences that bring joy or pleasure to our lives.

variable-interval schedule: a schedule of reinforcement in which a variable amount of time elapses between successive reinforcements; the first response *after* a variable interval of time has elapsed is reinforced; the shorter the interval, the better the rate of responding.

variable-ratio schedule: a schedule of reinforcement in which reinforcement comes after a varying number of responses made; the faster the response rate, the more rapidly will the reinforcement be obtained; these schedules result in very high rates of responding and great resistance to extinction.

vestibular sacs: two fluid-filled structures located in the inner ear that provide information about body position, movement, and acceleration.

vestibular sense: gives information about the position, movement, and acceleration of the body, allowing for a sense of balance.

vicarious learning: acquisition of attitudes by observing the reactions of others.

visual display: any visual presentation of information.

vividness effect: the tendency to use the information that is most accessible or easily retrieved to make decisions or solve problems.

voyeurism: a sexual disorder that is characterized by the act of observing unsuspecting individuals, typically strangers, who are naked, in the process of undressing, or engaging in sexual activity.

white noise: a broad spectrum of sound frequencies or pitches; sounds like the noise of a waterfall or a running fan; one of the most effective methods of masking sound.

References

Aarons, L. (1976). Sleep-assisted instruction. *Psychological Bulletin, 83,* 1–40.

Addington, D.W. (1968). The relationship of selected vocal characteristics to personality perception. *Speech Monographs, 35,* 492–503.

Albee, G.W. (1986). Toward a just society: Lessons from observations on the primary prevention of psychopathology. *American Psychologist, 41,* 891–898.

Allison, R.B. (1978). A rational psychotherapy plan for multiplicity. *Svensk Tidskrift Hypnosis, 3,* 9–16.

Allport, G.W. (1954). *The nature of prejudice.* Cambridge, MA: Addison-Wesley.

Allport, G.W., & Postman, L. (1947). *The psychology of rumor.* New York: Russell & Russell.

Altus, W.D. (1966). Birth order and its sequelae. *Science, 151,* 44–49.

American Medical Association (1986). Council Report: Scientific status of refreshing recollection by the use of hypnosis. *International Journal of Clinical and Experimental Hypnosis, 34,* 1–12.

American Psychiatric Association (1994). *Diagnostic and statistical manual of mental disorders* (4th ed.). Washington, DC: American Psychiatric Association.

American Psychological Association (1986). Council of representatives statement cited by N. Abeles, Proceedings of the American Psychological Association, Incorporated, for the year 1985: Minutes of the annual meeting of the Council of Representatives August 22 and 25, 1985, Los Angeles, California, and January 31–February 2, 1986, Washington, DC. *American Psychologist, 41,* 633–663.

American Psychological Society (1998, February). APS Observer Special Issue: HCI report 6–Basic research in psychological science (Behavioral Genetics, pp. 37–38). Washington, DC: American Psychological Society.

Amir, Y. (1969). Contact hypothesis in ethnic relations. *Psychological Bulletin, 71,* 319–342.

Amoore, J. E. (1970). *Molecular Basis of Odor.* Springfield, Ill: Charles C. Thomas.

Argyle, M. (1986). *The psychology of happiness.* London: Methuen.

Armor, D.J., Polich, J.M., & Stanbul, H.B. (1976). *Alcoholism and treatment* (R–1739–NIAAA). Santa Monica: The Rand Corporation.

Asch, S.E. (1946). Forming impressions of personality. *Journal of Abnormal and Social Psychology, 41,* 258–290.

Asch, S.E. (1951). Effects of group pressure upon the modification and distortion of judgments. In H. Guetzkow (Ed.), *Groups, leadership, and men.* Pittsburgh: Carnegie.

Aune, R. K., & Basil, M. D. (1994). A relational obligations approach to the foot-in-the-mouth effect. *Journal of Applied Social Psychology, 24,* 546–556.

Averill, J.R. (1983). Studies on anger and aggression: Implications for theories of emotion. *American Psychologist, 38,* 1145–1160.

Badenhoop, M.S., & Johansen, M.K. (1980). Do reentry women have special needs? *Psychology of Women Quarterly, 4,* 591–595.

Bahrick, H. (1984). Semantic memory content in permastore: Fifty years of memory for Spanish learned in school. *Journal of Experimental Psychology: General, 113,* 1–24.

Bailey, J.M., & Pillard, R.C. (1991). A genetic study of male sexual orientation. *Archives of General Psychiatry, 48,* 1089–1096.

Baldwin, J. D. & Baldwin, J. I. (1998). *Behavior principles in everyday life* (3rd ed.). Upper Saddle River, NJ: Prentice Hall.

Banaji, M.R., & Hardin, C.D. (1996). Automatic stereotyping. *Psychological Science, 7,* 136–141.

Bandura, A. (1973). *Aggression: A social learning analysis.* Englewood Cliffs, NJ: Prentice Hall.

Bandura, A. (1982). The self and mechanisms of agency. In J. Suls (Ed.), *Psychological Perspective on the Self* (pp. 3–39). Hillside, NJ: Erlbaum.

Barefoot, J.C., Dahlstrom, W.G., & Williams, R.B. (1983). Hostility, CHD incidence and total mortality: A 25-year follow-up study of 255 physicians. *Psychosomatic Medicine, 45,* 559–563.

Baron, R. A. (1983). The "sweet smell of success"? The impact of pleasant artificial scents (perfume or cologne) on evaluations of job applicants. *Journal of Applied psychology, 68,* 709–713.

Baron, R. A. (1986). Self-presentation in job interviews: When there can be "too much of a good thing." *Journal of Applied Social psychology, 16,* 16–28.

Baron, R.A. (1989). Applicant strategies during job interviews. In G.R. Ferris & R.W. Eder (Eds.), *The employment interview: Theory, research, and practice* (pp. 204–216). Newbury Park, CA: Sage.

Baron, R. A. & Byrne, D. (1997). *Social Psychology* (8th ed.). Boston: Allyn and Bacon.

Baron, R.A., & Byrne, D. (2000). *Social Psychology* (9th ed.). Boston: Allyn & Bacon.

Barron, F. (1988). Putting creativity to work. In R.J. Sternberg (Ed.), *The nature of creativity* (pp. 76–98). New York: Cambridge University Press.

Bartlett, M. S., Hager, J.C., Ekman, P., & Sejnowski, T.J. (1999). Measuring facial expressions by computer image analysis. *Psychophysiology, 36,* 253–263.

Bartol, C.R., & Bartol, A.M. (1994). *Psychology and law: Research and application* (2nd ed.). Pacific Grove, CA: Brooks/Cole.

Bass, B.M. (1998). *Transformational leadership: Industrial, Military, and Educational Impact.* Mahwah, NJ: Lawrence Erlbaum Associates.

Bauer, D.H. (1973). Error sources in aptitude and achievement test scores: a review and recommendation. *Measurement and Evaluation in Guidance, 6,* 28–34.

Bauer, R.A., & Greyser, S.A. (1968). *Advertising in America: The consumer view.* Cambridge, MA: Harvard University Press.

Baum, A., & Davis, G.E. (1980). Reducing the stress of high-density living: An architectural intervention. *Journal of Personality & Social Psychology, 38,* 471–481.

Baum, A., & Fleming, I. (1993). Implications of psychological research on stress and technological accidents. *American Psychologist, 48,* 665–672.

Baum, A., & Valins, S. (1979). Architectural mediation of residential density and control: Crowding and the regulation of social contact. *Advances in Experimental and Social Psychology, 12,* 131–175.

Beck, A.T. (1967). *Depression: Clinical, experimental, and theoretical aspects.* New York: Harper & Row.

Beck, A.T. (1985). Cognitive therapy of depression: New perspectives. In P. Clayton (Ed.), *Depression.* New York: Raven.

Beck, A.T. (1991). Cognitive therapy. *American Psychologist, 46,* 368–375.

Bednar, R.I., & Kaul, T.J. (1994). Experiential group research: Can the canon fire? In A.E. Bergin & S.L. Garfiel (Eds.), *Handbook of psychotherapy and behavior change* (4th ed.). New York: Wiley.

Bell, A.P., Weinberg, M.S., and Hammersmith, S.K. (1981). *Sexual preference: Its development in men and women.* Bloomington: Indiana University Press.

Belloc, N.B., & Breslow, L. (1972). Relationship of physical health status and health practices. *Preventive Medicine, 1,* 409–421.

Bem, D. (1972). Self-perception theory. In L. Berkowitz (Ed.), *Advances in experimental social psychology (Vol. 6).* New York: Academic Press.

Benjamin, L.T., Cavell, T.A., & Shallenberger, W.R. (1987). Staying with initial answers on objective tests: Is it a myth? In M.E. Ware and R.J. Millard (Ed.), *Handbook on student development: Advising, career development, and field placement* (pp. 45–52). Hillsdale, NJ: Lawrence Erlbaum Associates.

Bennett, J.B. (1988). Power and influence as distinct personality traits: Development and validation of a psychometric measure. *Journal of Research in Personality, 22,* 361–394.

Bennett, W.I. (1984). Dieting. Ideology versus physiology. *Psychiatric Clinics of North America, 7,* 321–334.

Benson, H. (1975). *The relaxation response.* New York: Morrow.

Berkman, L., & Syne, S.L. (1979). Social networks, host resistance, and mortality: A nine-year follow up of Alameda County residents. *American Journal of Epidemiology, 109,* 186–204.

Berkowitz, L. (1983). Aversively stimulated aggression: Some parallels and differences in research with animals and humans. *American Psychologist, 38,* 1135–1144.

Berman, J.S., & Norton, N.C. (1985). Does professional training make a therapist more effective? *Psychological Bulletin, 98,* 401–407.

Bernstein, M. (1965). *The search for Bridey Murphy.* Garden City, N.Y.: Doubleday.

Berry, L.M. (1998). *Psychology at work: An introduction to industrial and organizational psychology* (2nd ed.). Boston: McGraw Hill.

Berscheid, E., Snyder, M., Omoto, A.M. (1989). The Relationship Closeness Inventory: Assessing the closeness of interpersonal relationships. *Journal of Personality & Social Psychology, 57,* 792–807.

Brickman, L. (1974). The social power of a uniform. *Journal of Applied Social Psychology, 4,* 47–61.

Brickman, L. (1999). Practice makes perfect and other myths about mental health services. *American Psychologist, 54,* 965–978.

Bickman, P., Coates, D., & Janoff-Bulman, R.J. (1978). Lottery winners and accident victims: Is happiness relative? *Journal of Personality and Social Psychology, 36,* 917–927.

Billings, A.G., & Moos, R.H. (1981). The role of coping responses and social resources in attenuating the stress of life events. *Journal of Behavioral Medicine, 4,* 139–157.

Birch, L.L. (1990). The control of food intake by young children: The role of learning. In E.D. Capaldi & T.L. Powley (Eds.), *Taste, experience, and feeding* (pp. 116–135). Washington: Psychological Association.

Birch, L.L., & Marlin, D.W. (1982). I don't like it, I never tried it: Effects of exposure on two-year-old children's food preferences. *Appetite, 3,* 353–360.

Blackmore, S. J. (1984). A postal survey of OBEs and other experiences. *Journal of the Society for Psychical Research, 52,* 225–244.

Blackmore, S. J. (1997). Probability misjudgment and belief in the paranormal: A newspaper survey. *British Journal of Psychology, 88,* 683–689.

Bock, D.C. (1972). Obedience: A response to authority and Christian commitment. *Dissertation Abstracts International, 33,* 3278B–3279B (University Microfilms, No. 72–31, 651).

Bok, S. (1974). The ethics of giving placebos. *Scientific American, 231* (5), 17–23.

Bornstein, R. F. (1989). Subliminal techniques as propaganda tools: Review and critique. *Journal of Mind and Behavior, 10,* 231–262.

Borrie, R. A., & Suedfeld, P. (1980). Restricted environmental stimulation therapy in a weight reduction program. *Journal of Behavioral Medicine, 3,* 147–161.

Bothwell, R.K., Brigham, J.C., & Malpass, R.S. (1989). Cross-racial identification. *Journal of Personality and Social Psychology Bulletin, 15,* 19–25.

Bouchard, T.J., Avery, R.D., Keller, L.M., & Segal, N.L. (1992). Genetic influences on job satisfaction: A reply to Cropanzano and Hames. *Journal of Applied Psychology, 77,* 89–93.

Bourne, L. E. & Russo, N. F. (1998). *Psychology: Behavior in context.* New York: Norton.

Bransford, J.D., & Stein, B.S. (1984). *The IDEAL problem solver: A guide for improving thinking, learning, and creativity.* New York: Freeman.

Bravo, M., Rubio-Stipec, M., Canino, G.J., Woodbury, M.A., & Ribera, J.C. (1990). The psychological sequelae of disaster prospectively and retrospectively evaluated. *American Journal of Community Psychology, 18,* 661–680.

Bray, G.A. (1969). Effect of caloric restriction on energy expenditure in obese patients. *Lancet, ii,* 397–398.

Brehm, S.S. (1985). *Intimate relationships.* New York: Random House.

Breslow, L. (1983). The potential of health promotion. In D. Mechanic (Ed.), *Handbook of health, health care, and the health professions.* New York: Free Press.

Brewer, M.B., Ho, H., Lee, J., & Miller, M. (1987). Social identity and social distance among Hong Kong schoolchildren. *Personality and Social Psychology Bulletin, 13,* 156–165.

Bridges, K.M.B. (1932). Emotional development in early infancy. *Child Development, 3,* 324–334.

Brockhaus, A., & Elger, C. E. (1990). Hypalgesic efficacy of acupuncture on experimental pain in man: Comparison of laser acupuncture and need acupuncture. *Pain, 43,* 181–185.

Brown, R.T. (1989). Creativity: What are we to measure? In J.A. Glover, R.R. Ronning, & C.R. Reynolds (Eds.), *Handbook of creativity* . New York: Plenum.

Browne, B.A., & Cruse, D.F. (1989). The incubation effect: Illusion or illumination? *Human Performance, 1,* 177–185.

Burger, J.M. (1986). Increasing compliance by improving the deal: The that's-not-all technique. *Journal of Personality and Social psychology , 51,* 277–283.

Bushman, B.J. (1984). Perceived symbols of authority and their influence on compliance. *Journal of Applied Social Psychology, 14,* 501–508.

Buss, D.M., & Barnes, M. (1986). Preferences in human mate selection. *Journal of Personality and Social Psychology, 50,* 559–570.

Buss, D. M., Abbott, M., Angleitner, A., Asherian, A., *et al.* (1990). International preferences in selecting mates: A study of 37 cultures. *Journal of Cross-Cultural Psychology, 21*, 5–47.

Byrne, D.G., & Rosenman, R.H. (1986). The Type A behaviour pattern as a precursor to stressful life-events: A confluence of coronary risks. *British Journal of Medical Psychology, 59,* 75–82.

Calhoun, J.B. (1962). Population density and social pathology. *Scientific American, 206,* 139–148.

Canetto, S.S., & Lester, D. (1995). Gender and the primary prevention of suicide mortality [Special issue]. *Suicidal and Life Threatening Behavior, 25,* 58–69.

Cannon, W.B. (1929). *Bodily changes in pain, hunger, fear, and rage.* New York: Appleton-Century-Crofts.

Carducci, B. (1999). *The pocket guide to making successful small talk.* New York: Mass Market Publishing.

Carli, L.L., Ganley, R., & Pierce-Otay, A. (1991). Similarity and satisfaction in roommate relationships. *Personality and Social Psychology Bulletin, 17,* 419–426.

Carlson, N.R. (1993). *Psychology: The science of behavior* (4th ed.). Needam Heights, MA: Allyn and Bacon.

Carnegie, D. (1972). *How to win friends and influence people.* New York: Pocket Books.

Carson, N.D., & Johnson, R.E. (1985). Suicidal thoughts and problem-solving preparation among college students. *Journal of College Student Personnel, 26,* 484–487.

Carstensen, L.L. (1995). Evidence for a life-span theory of socioemotional selectivity. *Current Directions in Psychological Science, 4,* 151–156.

Carstensen, L. L., Charles, S.T. (1998). Emotion in the second half of life. *Current Directions in Psychological Science, 7,* 144–149.

Carver, C.S., Diamond, E.L., & Humphries, C. (1985). Coronary prone behavior. In N. Schneiderman & J.T. Tapp (Eds.), *Behavioral medicine: The biopsychosocial approach.* Hillsdale, NJ: Erlbaum.

Cash, T.F., & Duncan, N.C. (1984). Physical attractiveness stereotyping among Black American college students. *Journal of Social Psychology, 122*, 71–77.

Castillo, M., & Butterworth, G. (1981). Neonatal localization of a sound in visual space. *Perception, 10,* 331–338.

Centerwall, B.S. (1989). Twin concordance for dishonorable discharge from the military: With a review of the genetics of antisocial behavior. *Comprehensive Psychiatry, 30,* 442–446.

Chaiken, S. (1987). The heuristic model of persuasion. In M.P. Zanna, J.M., Olson, & C.P. Herman (Eds.), *Social influence: The Ontario symposium (Vol. 5).* Hillsdale, NJ: Erlbaum.

Chaiken, S., & Eagly, A.H. (1983). Communication modality as a determinant of persuasion: The role of communicator salience. *Journal of Personality and Social Psychology, 45,* 241–256.

Charness, N. (1989). Age and expertise: Responding to Talland's challenge. In L.W. Poon, D.C. Rubin, & B.A. Wilson (Eds.), *Everyday cognition in adulthood and old age.* New York: Cambridge University Press.

Chesney, M.A., Frautschi, N.M., & Rosenman, R.H. (1985). Modifying Type A behavior. In J.C. Rosen & L. J. Solomon (Eds.), *Prevention in health psychology.* Hanover, NH: University Press of New England.

Christensen, A., & Jacobson, N.S. (1994). Who (or what) can do psychotherapy: The status and challenge of nonprofessional therapies. *Psychological Science, 5,* 8–14.

Cialdini, R.B. (1988). *Influence: Science and practice* (2nd ed.). Glenview, IL: Scott, Foresman and Company.

Cialdini, R.B., Green, B.L., & Rusch, A.J. (1992). When tactical pronouncements of change become real change: The case of reciprocal persuasion. *Journal of Personality and Social Psychology, 63,* 30–40.

Clifford, B.R., & Bull, R. (1978). *The psychology of person identification.* London: Routeledge & Kegan Paul.

Cohen, I.B. (1984, March). Florence Nightingale. *Scientific American,* 128–137.

Cohen, L.A. (1987, November). Diet and cancer. *Scientific American*, 42–48.

Cohen, S., Evans, G.W., Krantz, D.S., Stokols, D., & Kelly, S. (1981). Aircraft noise and children: Longitudinal and cross-sectional evidence on adaptation to noise and the effectiveness of noise abatement. *Journal of Personality and Social Psychology, 40,* 331–345.

Cohen, S., & Williamson, G.M. (1988). Perceived stress in a probability sample of the United States. In S. Spacapan & S. Oskamp (Eds.), *The social psychology of health* (p. 516). Newbury Park, CA: Sage.

Colligan, M.J., & Murphy, L.R. (1982). A review of mass psychogenic illness in work settings. In M.J. Colligan, J.W. Pennebaker, & L.R. Murphy (Eds.),

Mass psychogenic illness: A social psychological analysis. Hillsdale, NJ: Erlbaum.

Comer, R.J. (1999). *Fundamentals of abnormal psychology* (2nd ed.). New York: Worth.

Consumer Reports (1995, November). Mental health: Does therapy help?, pp. 734–739.

Cook, S.W. (1985). Experimenting on social issues: The case of school desegregation. *American Psychologist, 40,* 452–460.

Coon, D. (1992). *Introduction to psychology: Exploration and application* (6th ed.). St. Paul: West Publishing.

Cooper, G. D. (1988). Studies in REST: I. Reduced environmental stimulation therapy (REST) and reduced alcohol consumption. *Journal of Substance Abuse Treatment, 5,* 61–68.

Cornelius, J.R., Salloum, I.M., Mezzich, J., Cornelius, M.D., Fabrega, H., Ehler, J.G., Ulrich, R.F., Thase, M.E., & Mann, J.J. (1995). Disproprotionate suicidality in patients with comorbid major depression and alcoholism. *American Journal of Psychiatry, 152,* 358–364.

Cottington, E.M., & House, J.S. (1987). Occupational stress and health: A multivariate relationship. In A. Baum & J.E. Singer (Eds.), *Handbook of psychology and health (Vol.5).* Hillsdale, NJ: Erlbaum.

Council on Scientific Affairs (1986). Scientific status of refreshing recollection by the use of hypnosis. *International Journal of Clinical and Experimental Hypnosis, 34,* 1–11.

Cowley, G. & Underwood, A. (June, 1998). Memory. *Newsweek,* 49–54.

Cox, R.H. (1990). *Sport psychology: Concepts and applications* (2nd ed.). Dubuque, IA: William C. Brown.

Cox, W.M., & Klinger, E. (1984). Discriminability of regular, light, and alcoholic and nonalcoholic near beer. *Journal of Studies on Alcohol, 44,* 494–498.

Craik, F. I. M., & Lockhart, R. S. (1972). Levels of processing: A framework for memory research. *Journal of Verbal Learning and Verbal Behavior, 11,* 671–684.

Crane, D. R., Dollahite, D. C., Griffin, W., & Taylor, V. L. (1987). Diagnosing relationships with spatial distance: An empirical test of a clinical principle. *Journal of Marital & Family Therapy, 13,* 307–310.

Crisp, A.H. (1970). Premorbid factors in adult disorders of weight, with primary reference to primary anorexia nervosa: A literature review. *Journal of Psychosomatic Research, 14,* 1–22.

Crombag, H.F.M. (1994). Law as a branch of applied psychology. *Psychology, Crime and Law, 1,* 1–9.

Cropanzano, R., & Randall, M.L. (1993). Injustice and work behavior: A historical review. In R. Cropanzano (Ed.), *Justice in the workplace* (pp. 3–20). Hillsdale, NJ: Erlbaum.

Crook, T.H. (1998). *The memory cure.* New York: Pocket Books.

Crook, T.H., & West, R.L. (1990). Name recall performance across the adult life-span. *British Journal of Psychology, 81,* 335–340.

Crusco, A.H., & Wetzel, C.G. (1984). The Midas touch: The effects of interpersonal touch on restaurant tipping. *Personality and Social Psychology Bulletin, 10,* 512–517.

Cunningham, M.R. (1986). Measuring the physical in physical attractiveness: Quasi-experiments on the sociobiology of female facial beauty. *Journal of Personality & Social Psychology, 50,* 925–935.

Cunningham, M.R., Roberts, A.R., Wu, C.H., Barbee, A.P. & Druen, P.B. (1995). "Their ideas of beauty are, on the whole, the same as ours:" Consistency and variability in the cross-cultural perception of female physical attractiveness. *Journal of Personality and Social Psychology, 68,* 261–279.

Davison, G.C., & Neale, J.M. (1990). *Abnormal psychology: An experimental clinical approach* (3rd ed.). New York: John Wiley & Sons.

Dawes, R.M. (1994). *House of cards: Psychology and psychotherapy built on myth.* New York: The Free Press.

Dawes, R.M., Faust, D., & and Meehl, P.E. (1989). Clinical versus actuarial judgment. *Science, 243,* 1668–1674.

Deffenbacher, J.L., Oetting, E.R., & Lynch, R.S. (1994). Development of a driving anger scale. *Psychological Reports, 74,* 83–91.

Dell, P.F., & Eisenhower, J.W. (1990). Adolescent multiple personality disorder: A preliminary study of eleven cases. *Journal of the American Academy of Child and Adolescent Psychiatry, 29,* 359–366.

Dembroski, T.M., & Costa, P.T. (1988). Assessment of coronary-prone behavior: A current overview. *Annals of Behavioral Medicine, 10,* 60–63.

DePaulo, B.M. (1992). Nonverbal behavior and self-presentation. *Psychological Bulletin, 111,* 230–243.

DePaulo, B.M. (1994). Spotting lies: Can humans learn to do better? *Current Directions in Psychological Science, 3,* 83–86.

Derlega, V.J., & Chaikin, A.L. (1976). Norms affecting self-disclosure in men and women. *Journal of Consulting and Clinical Psychology, 44,* 376–380.

Devine, P.G. (1989). Stereotypes and prejudice: Their automatic and controlled components. *Journal of Personality and Social Psychology, 56,* 5–18.

Diamond, J.J., & Evans, W.J. (1972). An investigation of the cognitive correlates of test-wiseness. *Journal of Educational Measurement, 9,* 145–150.

Diener, E. (1980). Deindividuation: The absence of self-awareness and self-regulation in group members. In P.B. Paulus (Ed.), *Psychology of group influence.* Hillsdale, NJ: Erlbaum.

Diener, E., & Diener, C. (1996). Most people are happy. *Psychological Science, 7,* 181–185.

Diener, E., Diener, M., & Diener, C. (1995). Factors predicting the subjective well-being of nations. *Journal of Personality & Social Psychology, 69,* 851–864.

Dinsmoor, J. A. (1998). Punishment. In W. O. Donohue (Ed.), *Learning and behavior therapy* (p. 193). Boston: Allyn and Bacon.

Dion, K.K., Berscheid, E., & Walster, E. (1972). What is beautiful is good. *Journal of Personality and Social Psychology, 24,* 285–290.

Dittes, J.E., & Kelley, H.H. (1956). Effects of different conditions of acceptance upon conformity to group norms. *Journal of Abnormal and Social Psychology, 53,* 100–107.

Dollard, J., Miller, N.E., Doob, L.W., Mowrer, O.H., & Sears, R.R. (1939).

Frustration and aggression. New Haven, CT: Yale University Press.
Dolly, J.P., & Williams, K.S. (1986). Using test-taking strategies to maximize multiple-choice test scores. *Educational and Psychological Measurement, 46,* 619–625.
Doob, A.N., & Gross, A.E. (1968). Status of frustrator as an inhibitor of horn-honking response. *Journal of Social Psychology, 76,* 213–218.
Douek, E. (1988). Olfaction and medicine. In S. Van Toller & G. Doll (Eds.), *Perfumery: The psychology and biology of fragrance.* London: Chapman Hall.
Drewnowski, A. (1990). The new fat replacements: A strategy for reducing fat consumption. *Postgraduate Medicine, 87,* 111–121.
Drewnowski, A. (1995). Metabolic determinants of binge eating. *Addictive Behaviors, 20,* 733–745.
Druckman, D., & Bjork, R. A. (1991). *In the Mind's Eye: Enhancing Human Performance.* Washington, D.C.: National Academy Press.
Druckman, D., & Swets, J. A. (Eds.) (1988). *Enhancing human performance: Issues, theories, and techniques.* Washington, DC: National Academy Press.
Dubbert, P.A. (1992). Exercise in behavioral medicine. *Journal of Consulting & Clinical Psychology, 60,* 613–618.
Dulloo, A., & Girardier, L. (1990). Adaptive changes in energy expenditure during refeeding following low-calorie intake: Evidence for a specific metabolic component favoring fat storage. *American Journal of Clinical Nutrition, 52,* 415–420.
Duncker, K. (1945). On problem-solving. *Psychological Monographs, 58,* Whole No. 270.
Dunnette, M.D., Campbell, J., & Jaastad, L. (1963). The effect of group participation on problem-solving. *Journal of Applied Psychology, 47,* 58–70.
Dunning, D.A. (1987). Situational construal and sources of social judgment. *Dissertation Abstracts International, 48(2–B),* 596.
Dutton, D.G., & Aron, A.P. (1974). Some evidence for heightened sexual attraction under conditions of high anxiety. *Journal of Personality and Social Psychology, 30,* 510–517.
Dweck, C. S., Hong, Y., & Chiu, C. (1993). Implicit theories: Individual differences in the likelihood and meaning of dispositional inference. *Personality and Social Psychology Bulletin, 19,* 644–656.
Dwyman, J., & Bowers, K. (1983). The use of hypnosis to enhance recall. *Science, 222,* 184–185.
Eagly, A.H., Karau, S.J., & Makhijani, M.G. (1995). Gender and the effectiveness of leaders: A meta-analysis. *Psychological Bulletin, 117,* 125–145.
Eagly, A.H., & Warren, R. (1976). Intelligence, comprehension, and opinion change. *Journal of Personality, 44,* 226–242.
Early, P.C. (1989). Social loafing and collectivism: A comparison of the United States and the People's republic of China. *Administrative Science Quarterly, 34,* 565–581.
Eich, E. (1995). Searching for mood dependent memory. *Psychological Science, 6,* 67–75.
Ekman, P. (1972). Universals and cultural differences in facial expressions of emotion. In J.K. Cole (Ed.), *Nebraska symposium on motivation.* Lincoln: University of Nebraska Press.
Ekman, P. (1973). Cross-cultural studies of facial expression. In P. Ekman (Ed.), *Darwin and facial expression: A century of research in review.* New York: Academic Press.
Ekman, P. (1985). *Telling lies: Clues to deceit in the marketplace, marriage, and politics.* New York: W.W. Norton.
Ekman, P. (1997). Deception, lying, and demeanor. In D.F. Halpern & A.E. Voiskounsky (Ed.), *States of mind: American and post-Soviet perspectives on contemporary issues in psychology* (pp. 93–105). New York: Oxford University Press.
Ekman, P., Levenson, R.W., & Friesen, W. V. (1983). Autonomic nervous system activity distinguishes among emotions. *Science, 221,* 1208–1210.
Ekman, P., & O'Sullivan, M. (1991). Who can catch a liar? *American Psychologist, 46,* 913–920.
Ekman, P., O'Sullivan, M., Friesen, W.V., & Scherer, K.R. (1991). Face, voice, and body in detecting deception. *Journal of Nonverbal Behavior, 15,* 125–135.
Ekman, P., Sorenson, E.R., & Friesen, W.V. (1969). Pan-cultural elements in facial displays of emotion. *Science, 221,* 1208–1210.
Ellis, H. C., & Ashbrook, P. W. (1989). The "state" of mood and memory research: A selective review. *Journal of Social Behaviour and Personality, 4,* 1–21.
Epstein, L.H., & Jennings, J.R. (1986). Smoking, stress, cardiovascular reactivity, and coronary heart disease. In K.A. Matthews, S.M. Weiss, T. Detre, T.M. Dembroski, B. Falkner, S.B. Manuck, & R.B. Williams (Eds.), *Handbook of stress, reactivity, and cardiovascular disease.* New York: Wiley.
Ernsberger, P. & Haskew, P. (1987). Health implications of obesity: An alternative view. *Journal of Obesity and Weight Regulation, 6,* 58–137.
Falbo, T., & Polit, D. F. (1986). Quantitative review of the only child literature: Research evidence and theory development. *Psychological Bulletin, 100,* 176–189.
Fay, R., Turner, C., Klassen, A., & Gagnon, J. (1989). Prevalance and patterns of same-gender sexual contact among men. *Science, 243,* 338–348.
Feingold, A. (1990). Gender differences in effects of physical attractiveness on romantic attraction: A comparison across five research paradigms. *Journal of Personality and Social Psychology, 59,* 981–993.
Feingold, A. (1992). Good looking people are not what we think. *Psychological Bulletin, 111,* 304–341.
Festinger, L. (1954). A theory of social comparison processes. *Human Relations, 7,* 117–140.
Festinger, L. (1957). *A theory of cognitive dissonance.* Stanford, CA: Stanford University Press.
Festinger, L., & Carlsmith, J.M. (1959). Cognitive consequences of forced compliance. *Journal of Abnormal and Social Psychology,* 203–210.
Festinger, L., Pepitone, A., & Newcomb, T. (1952). Some consequences of deindividuation in a group. *Journal of Abnormal and Social Psychology, 47,* 382–389.

Fix, A.J., & Daughton, D. (1980). *The odds almanac.* Chicago: Follett.

Foderaro, L. W. (1988, February 4). The fragrant house: An expanding market for every mood. *The New York Times,* pp. C1, C10.

Fontana, D. (1990). *Social skills at work.* Leicester, England: British Psychological Society.

Ford, Charles V. (1996). *Lies! Lies!! Lies!!!: The psychology of deceit.* Washington, DC: American Psychiatric Press.

Fordyce, M.W. (1977). Development of a program to increase personal happiness. *Journal of Counseling Psychology, 24,* 511–521.

Fordyce, M.W. (1983). A program to increase happiness; further studies. *Journal of Counseling Psychology, 30,* 483–498.

Fordyce, M.W. (1988). A review of research on the happiness measures: A sixty second index of happiness and mental health. *Social Indicators Research, 20,* 355–381.

Forgas, J.P. (1993). On making sense of odd couples: Mood effects on the perception of mismatched relationships. *Personality & Social Psychology Bulletin, 19,* 59–70.

Forsythe, S., Drake, M.F., & Cox, C.E. (1985). Influence of applicant's dress on interviewer's selection decisions. *Journal of Applied Psychology, 70,* 374–378.

Fowler, R.L. (1982). Detection of differences in beer composition by brand and level of calorie content. *Perceptual and Motor Skills, 55,* 967–970.

Fox, B.H. (1978). Premorbid psychological factors as related to cancer incidence. *Journal of Behavioral Medicine, 1,* 45–133.

Freedman, J.L. (1979). Reconciling apparent differences between the responses of humans and other animals to crowding. *Psychological Review, 86,* 80–88.

Friedman, M., & Rosenman, R.H. (1983). *Type A behavior and your heart.* New York: Knopf.

Fuastman, W.O. (1976). Aversive control of maladaptive sexual behavior: Past developments and future trends. *Psychology, 13,* 53–60.

Fuller, R.G.C., & Sheehy-Skeffington, A. (1974). Effects of group laughter on responses to humourous materials: A replication and extension. *Psychological Reports, 35,* 531–534.

Furedy, J.J., & Chan, R. (1971). Failures of information to reduce rated aversiveness of unmodifiable shock. *Australian Journal of Psychology, 23,* 85–94.

Furedy, J.J., & Doob, A.N. (1972). Signalling unmodifiable shocks: Limits on human informational cognitive control. *Journal of Personality and Social Psychology, 23,* 111–115.

Gadzella, B. M., & Williamson, J. D. (1984). Study skills, self-concept, and academic achievement. *Psychological Reports, 54,* 923–929.

Gaertner, S.L., Mann, J., Murrell, A., & Dovidio, J.F. (1989). Reducing intergroup bias: The benefits of recategorization. *Journal of Personality and Social Psychology, 57,* 239–249.

Gaertner, S.L., Mann, J.A., Dovidio, J.F., Murrell, A.J., & Pomare, M. (1990). How does cooperation reduce intergroup bias? *Journal of Personality and Social Psychology, 59,* 692–704.

Galanter, E. (1962). Contemporary psychophysics. In R. Brown, E. Galanter, E. G. Hess, & G. Mandler (Eds.), *New Directions in Psychology.* New York: Holt, Rinehart, & Winston.

Galanter, M. (1989). *Cults: Faith, healing, and coercion.* New York: Oxford University Press.

Galle, O.R., Gove, W.R., & McPherson, J.M. (1972). Population density and pathology: What are the relationships for man? *Science, 176,* 385–389.

Gallup, G., Jr. (1984, March). *Religion in America. Gallup Report.*

Gallup, G. H., & Newport, F. (1991, Winter). Belief in paranormal phenomena among adult Americans. *Skeptical Inquirer,* 137–146.

Galotti, K.M. (1999). *Cognitive psychology in and out of the laboratory* (2nd ed.). Belmont, CA: Brooks/Cole & Wadsworth.

Gara, M.A., Woolfolk, R.L., Cohen, B.D., Goldston, R.B., Allen, L.A., & Novalany, J. (1993). Perception of self and other in major depression. *Journal of Abnormal Psychology, 102,* 93–100.

Garb, H.N. (1989). Clinical judgment, clinical training, and professional experience. *Psychological Bulletin, 105,* 387–392.

Garcia, J., Rusiniak, K. W., & Brett, L. P. (1977). Conditioning food-illness aversions in wild animals. In H. Davis & H. M. B. Hurwitz (Eds.), *Operant-Pavlovian interactions*, Hillsdale, NJ: Erlbaum.

Gardner, E.A. (1997). Special needs children. In J.W. Gehrke, S.A. Grob, D.M. Johnson, & S.F. Shink (Eds.), *Advocating excellence: Offering hope for the innocents.* Denver: Denver University Press.

Gardner, R.M., & Bokenkamp, E.D. (1996). The role of sensory and nonsensory factors in body size estimations of eating disorder subjects. *Journal of Clinical Psychology, 52,* 3–16.

Gardner, R. A., & Gardner, B. I. (1969). Teaching sign language to a chimpanzee. *Science, 165,* 664–672.

Gardner, R. M., & Dalsing, S. (1986). Misconceptions about psychology among college students. *Teaching of Psychology, 13,* 33–34.

Gardner, R. M., Friedman, B. N., Stark, K., & Jackson, N.A. (1999). Body-size estimations in children six-through fourteen: A longitudinal study. *Perceptual and Motor Skills, 88,* 541–555.

Gardner, R. M., & Morrell, J. (1991). Body size judgments and eye movements of body regions in obese subjects. *Perceptual and Motor Skills, 73,* 675–682.

Gardner, R., Ostrowski, T., Pino, R., Morrell, J., & Kochevar, R. (1992). Familiarity and anticipation of negative life events as moderator variables in predicting illness. *Journal of Clinical Psychology, 48,* 589–595.

Garfield, S.L. (1986). Research on client variables in psychotherapy. In S.L. Garfield & A.E. Bergin (Eds.), *Handbook of psychotherapy and behavior change* (3rd ed., pp. 213–257). New York: Wiley.

Garner, D.M., & Wooley, S.C. (1991). Confronting the failure of behavioral and dietary treatments for obesity. *Clinical Psychology Review, 11,* 729–780.

Garrity, T.F., & Marx, M.B. (1979). Critical life events and coronary disease. In W.D. Gentry & R.B. Williams

(Eds.), *Psychological aspects of myocardial infarction and coronary care* (2nd ed.). St. Louis: Mosby.

Garrity, T.E., Stallones, L., Marx, M.B., & Johnson, T.P. (1989). Pet ownership and attachment as supportive factors in the health of the elderly. *Anthrozoos, 3,* 35–44.

Gaston, L., Marmar, C.R., Gallagher, D., & Thompson, L.W. (1989). Impact of confirming patient expectations of change processes in behavioral, cognitive, and brief dynamic psychotherapy. *Psychotherapy, 26,* 296–302.

Gaston, L., Marmar, C.R., Thompson, L.W., & Gallagher, D. (1988). Relation of patient pretreatment characteristics to the therapeutic alliance in diverse psychotherapies. *Journal of Consulting and Clinical Psychology, 56,* 483–489.

George, J.M. (1990). Personality, affect, and behavior in groups. *Journal of Applied Psychology, 75,* 107–116.

Gerard, H.B., & Greenbaum, C.W. (1962). Attitudes toward an agent of uncertainty reduction. *Journal of Personality, 30,* 485–495.

Gilbert, A. N. & Wysocki, C. J. (1987, October). The smell survey results. *National Geographic,* 514–524.

Girdano, D.A., Everly, G.S., & Dusek, D.E. (1990). *Controlling stress and tension* (3rd ed.). Englewood Cliffs, NJ: Prentice-Hall.

Glass, D. C., & Singer, J. E. (1972). *Urban Stress: Experiments on noise and social stressors.* New York: Academic Press.

Glassman, A.H. (1993). Cigarette smoking: Implications for psychiatric illness. *American Journal of Psychiatry, 150,* 546–553.

Glicksohn, J. (1990). Belief in the paranormal and subjective paranormal experience. *Personality and Individual Differences, 11,* 675–683.

Gouldner, A.W. (1960). The norm of reciprocity: A preliminary statement. *American Sociological Review, 25,* 161–178.

Gove, W.R., Hughes, M., & Galle, O.R. (1979). Overcrowding in the home. *American Sociological Review, 44,* 59–80.

Greeno, C.G., & Wing. R.R. (1994). Stress-induced eating. *Psychological Bulletin, 115,* 444–464.

Gregory, R. L. (1977). *Eye and brain: The psychology of seeing* (3rd ed.). New York: World University Library.

Guilford, J.P. (1967). *The nature of human intelligence.* New York: McGraw Hill.

Guze, S.B., & Robins, E. (1970). Suicide and primary affective disorders. *British Journal of Psychiatry, 117,* 437–438.

Hackman, J.R., & Oldham, G.R. (1976). Motivation through the design of work: Test of a theory. *Organizational Behavior and Human Performance, 16,* 250–279.

Hagen, M.A. (1997). *Whores of the court.* New York: HarperCollins.

Hall, E.T. (1966). *The hidden dimension.* New York: Doubleday.

Hall, J.A. (1987). On explaining gender differences: The case of nonverbal communication. *Review of Personality and Social Psychology, 7,* 177–200.

Hamilton, G.V. (1978). Obedience and responsibility: A jury simulation. *Journal of Personality and Social Psychology, 36,* 126–146.

Hammerton, M. (1965). The guessing correction in vocabulary tests. *British Journal of Education, 35,* 249–251.

Hanson, D. R., & Fearn, R. W. (1975). Hearing acuity in young people exposed to pop music and other noise. *Lancet, 2,* 203–205.

Harkins, S.G. (1987). Social loafing and social facilitation. *Journal of Experimental Social Psychology, 23,* 1–18.

Harlow, H.F. (1971). *Learning to love.* San Francisco: Albion.

Harper, R.A. (1959). *Psychoanalysis and psychotherapy.* Englewood Cliffs, NJ: Prentice-Hall.

Harris, J. R. (1998). *The Nurture Assumption: Why Children Turn Out the Way They Do.* New York: Free Press.

Hay Group. (1999). *Health care plan design and cost trends—1988 through 1998.* Arlington, VA: National Association of Psychiatric Health Systems and Association of Behavioral Group Practices.

Hayes, S.C. (1989). An interview with Lee Sechrest: The courage to say 'we do not know how.' *APS Observer,* vol 2, no. 4, pp. 8–10.

Hebb, D.O. (1949). *The organization of behavior.* New York: Wiley.

Hellmich, N. (1995, June 9). Optimism often survives spinal cord injuries. *USA Today,* p. 4D.

Helson, H. (1964). *Adaptation-level theory.* New York: Harper and Row.

Hendrick, C., & Hendrick, S. (1986). A theory and method of love. *Journal of Personality and Social Psychology, 50,* 392–402.

Hendrick, C., Hendrick, S.S., & Dicke, A. (1998). The love attitudes scale: Short form. *Journal of Social and Personal Relationships, 15,* 147–159.

Hess, Eckhard H. (1975). *The tell-tale eye: How your eyes reveal hidden thoughts and emotions.* New York, NY: Van Nostrand Reinhold.

Higbee, K. L. (1988). *Your memory: How it works and how to improve it* (2nd ed.). New York: Prentice Hall Press.

Hill, C.A. (1987). Affiliation motivation: People who need people. . . but in different ways. *Journal of Personality and Social Psychology, 52,* 1008–1018.

Hinton, H. E. (1973). Natural deception. In R. L. Gregory & E. H. Gombrich (Eds.), *Illusion in nature and art* (pp. 97–159). New York: Charles Scribner's Sons.

Hofling, C.K., Brotzman, E., Dalrymple, S., Graves, N., & Pierce, C.M. (1966). An experimental study of nurse-physician relationships. *Journal of Nervous and Mental Disease, 143,* 171–180.

Holland, M.K. (1985). Using psychology: Principles of behavior and your life (3rd ed.). Boston: Little, Brown & Company Ltd.

Hollander, E.P. (1978). *Leadership dynamics: A practical guide to effective relationships.* New York: The Free Press.

Holmes, C.B. (1985). Comment on "Religiosity and U.S. suicide rates, 1972–1978." *Journal of Clinical Psychology, 41,* 580.

Holmes, D.S. (1974). Investigations of repression: Differential recall of material experimentally or naturally associated with ego threat. *Psychological Bulleting, 81,* 632–653.

Holmes, D.S. (1990). The evidence for repression: An examination of sixty years of research. In J, Singer (Ed.), *Repression and dissociation: Implications for personality theory, psychopathology, and health* (pp. 85–102). Chicago: University of Chicago Press.

Holmes, D.S. (1994). *Abnormal psychology* (2nd ed.). New York: Harper Collins.

Holmes, T.H., & Masuda, M. (1974). Life change and illness susceptibility. In B.S. Dohrenwend & B.P. Dohrenwend (Eds.), *Stressful life events: Their nature and effects.* New York: Wiley.

Holmes, T.H., & Rahe, R.H. (1967). The Social Readjustment Rating Scale. *Journal of Psychosomatic Research, 11,* 213–218.

House, R.J. (1995). Leadership in the twenty-first century: A speculative inquiry. In A. Howard (Ed.), *The changing nature of work* (pp. 411–450). San Francisco: Jossey-Bass.

House, J.S., Landis, K.R., & Umberson, D. (1988). Social relationships and health. *Science, 241,* 540–545.

Howard, K.I., Kopta, S.M., Krause, M.S., & Orlinsky, D.E. (1986). The dose-effect relationship in psychotherapy. *American Psychologist, 41,* 159–164.

Hoyenga, K.B., & Hoyenga, K.T. (1984). *Motivational explanations of behavior.* Monterey, CA: Brooks Cole.

Hoyle, R.J. (1993). Interpersonal attraction in the absence of explicit attitudinal information. *Social Cognition, 11,* 309–320.

Huesmann, L.R. (1986). Psychological processes promoting the relation between exposure to media violence and aggressive behavior by the viewer. *Journal of Social Issues, 42,* 125–139.

Huesmann, L.R., & Eron, L.D. (1986) The development of aggression in American children as a consequence of television violence viewing. In L.R. Huesmann & L.D. Eron (Eds.), *Television and the aggressive child: A cross-national comparison.* Hillsdale, NJ: Erlbaum.

Hultsch, D.F., & Dixon, R.A. (1990). Learning and memory in aging. In J.E. Birren & K.W. Schaie (Eds.), *Handbook of the psychology of aging* (3rd ed., pp. 359–374). San Diego: Academic Press.

Hunter, J.E., & Hunter, R.F. (1984). Validity and utility of attenuation predictions of job performance. *Psychological Bulletin, 96,* 72–98.

Hutchison, M. (1984). *The book of floating.* New York: Quill.

Ilola, L.M. (1990). Culture and health. In R.W. Brislin (Ed.), *Applied cross-cultural psychology.* Newbury Park, CA: Sage.

Inglefinger, F.J. (1944). The late effects of total and subtotal gastrectomy. *New England Journal of Medicine, 231,* 321–327.

Inglehart, R. (1990). *Culture shift in advanced industrial society.* Princeton, NJ: Princeton University Press.

Iwahashi, M. (1992). Scents and science. *Vogue,* 212–214.

Janis, I.L. (1972). *Victims of groupthink.* Boston: Houghton Mifflin.

Janis, I.L. (1985). Sources of error in strategic decision making. In J.M. Pennings (Ed.), *Organizational strategy and change.* San Francisco: Jossey-Bass.

Jemmot, J.B., & Locke, S.E. (1984). Psychosocial factors, immunologic mediation, and human susceptibility to infectious diseases: How much do we know? *Psychological Bulletin, 95,* 78–108.

Jenkins, J.G. & Dallenbach, K.M. (1924). Oblioescence during sleep and waking. *American Journal of Psychology, 35,* 605–612.

Jensen, M.R. (1987). Psychobiological factors predicting the course of breast cancer. *Journal of Personality, 55,* 317–342.

Jepson, C., & Chaiken, S. (1986). *The effect of anxiety on the systematic processing of persuasive communications.* Paper presented at the annual meeting of the American Psychological Association, Washington, DC.

Johnson, J.H. (1986). *Life events as stressors in childhood and adolescence.* Newbury Park, CA: Sage.

Johnson, J.H., & Sarason, I.G. (1979). Recent developments in research on life stress. In V. Hamilton & D.M. Warburton (Eds.), *Human stress and cognition: An information processing approach* (pp. 97–109). London: Wiley.

Jones, E.E., & Gordon, E.M. (1980). Timing of self-disclosure and its effects on personal attraction. *Journal of Personality and Social Psychology, 38,* 120–130.

Jones, E.E., Rock, L., Shaver, K.G., Goethals, G.R., & Ward, L.M. (1968). Pattern of performance and ability attribution: An unexpected primacy effect. *Journal of Personality and Social Psychology, 10,* 317–340.

Jones, E.E., & Wein, G. (1972). Attitude similarity, expectancy, violation, and attraction. *Journal of Experimental Social Psychology, 8,* 225–235.

Jones, E.E., & Wortman, C. (1973). *Ingratiation: An attributional approach.* Morristown, NJ: General Learning Press.

Jorenby, D.E., Leischow, S.J., Nides, M.A., Rennard, S.I., Johnston, J.A., Hughes, A.R., Smith, S.S., Muramoto, M.L., Daughton, D.M., Doan, K., Fiore, M.C., & Baker, T.B. (1999). A controlled trial of sustained-release bupropion, a nicotine patch, or both for smoking cessation. *The New England Journal of Medicine, 340,* 685–691.

Jourard, S.M. (1966). An exploratory study of body-accessibility. *British Journal of Social and Clinical Psychology, 5,* 221–231.

Kahneman, D., & Tversky, A. (1973). On the psychology of prediction. *Psychological Review, 80,* 237–251.

Kalat, J. W. (1993). *Introduction to Psychology* (3rd ed.). Pacific Grove, CA: Brooks/Cole.

Kamen, L.P., & Seligman, M.E.P. (1989). Explanatory style and health. In M. Johnston and T. Marteau (Ed.), *Applications in health psychology* (p. 73–84). New Brunswick, NJ: Transaction Publishers.

Kanner, A.D., Coyne, J.C., Schaefer, C., & Lazarus, R.S. (1981). Comparison of two modes of stress measurement: Daily hassles and uplifts versus major life events. *Journal of Behavioral Medicine, 4,* 1–39.

Kapardis, A. (1997). *Psychology and law: A critical introduction.* Cambridge: Cambridge University Press.

Kaplan, H.S. (1974). *The new sex therapy: Active treatment of sexual dysfunctions.* New York: Brunner/Mazel.

Kaplan, M.F., & Miller, C.E. (1987). Group decision making and normative versus information influence: Effects of type of issue and assigned decision rules. *Journal of Personality and Social Psychology, 53,* 306–313.

Karraker, K.H., & Stern, M. (1990). Infant physical attractiveness and facial expression: Effects on adult perceptions. *Basic and Applied Social Psychology, 11,* 371–385.

Kassin, S.M., & Wrightsman, L.S. (1988). *The American jury on trial: Psychological perspectives.* New York: Hemisphere.

Kearney, M. (1984). A comparison of motivation to avoid success in males and females. *Journal of Clinical Psychology, 40,* 1005–1007.

Kelly, A.E., & McKillop, K.J. (1996). Consequences of revealing personal secrets. *Psychological Bulletin, 120,* 450–465.

Kelman, H., & Hamilton, V.L. (1989). *Crimes of obedience.* New Haven, CT: Yale University Press.

Kemp, B.J. & Adams, B.A. (1995). The older adult health and mood questionnaire: A measure of geriatric depressive disorder. *Journal of Geriatric Psychiatry and Neurology, 8,* 162–168.

Kerckhoff, A.C., & Back, K.W. (1968). *The June bug: A study of hysterical contagion.* New York: Appleton-Century-Crofts.

Kerr, N.L. (1981). Social transition schemes: Charting the group's road to agreement. *Journal of Personality and Social Psychology, 41,* 684–702.

Kessler, R.C. (1994). The National Comorbidity Survey: Preliminary results and future directions. *International Journal of Methods in Psychiatric Research, 4,* 114.1–114.13.

Keys, A., Brozek, J., Henschel, A., Micklson, O., & Taylor, H.L. (1950). *The biology of human starvation.* Minneapolis: University of Minneapolis.

Kiecolt-Glaser, J.K., Fisher, L.D., Ogrocki, P., Stout, J.C., Speicher, C.E., & Glaser, R. (1987). Marital quality, marital disruption, and immune function. *Psychosomatic Medicine, 49,* 13–34.

Kiecolt-Glaser, J.K., Garner, W., Speicher, C., Penn, G.M., Holliday, J., & Glaser, R. (1984). Psychosocial modifiers of immunocompetence in medical students. *Psychosomatic Medicine, 46,* 7–14.

Kiecolt-Glaser, J.K., Dura, J.R., Speicher, C.E., Trask, O.J., & Glaser, R. (1991). Spousal caregivers of dementia victims: Longitudinal changes in immunity and health. *Psychosomatic Medicine, 53,* 345–363.

Kim, A., Martin, D., & Martin, M. (1989). Effects of personality on marital satisfaction. *Family Therapy, 16,* 243–248.

King, M. (1986). *Psychology in and out of court.* Oxford: Pergamon Press.

Kirk, S., Gallagher, J.J., & Anastasiow, N.J. (1993). *Educating exceptional children* (7th ed.). Boston: Houghton Mifflin.

Kirkpatrick, S.A., & Locke, E.A. (1991). Leadership: Do traits matter? *Academy of Management Executive, 5* (2), 48–60.

Kirsch, I. (1997). Specifying nonspecifics: Psychological mechanisms of placebo effects. In Harrington, A. (Ed.), *The placebo effect: An interdisciplinary exploration* (pp. 166–186). Cambridge, MA: Harvard University Press.

Kleinke, C.L. (1986). *Meeting and understanding people.* New York: W.H. Freeman and Company.

Kleinke, C.L., & Kahn, M.L. (1980). Perceptions of self-disclosure: Effects of sex and physical attractiveness. *Journal of Personality, 48,* 190–205.

Kleinmuntz, B., & Szucko, J. J. (1984). Lie detection in ancient and modern times: A call for contemporary scientific study. *American Psychologist. 39,* 766–776.

Knapp, A. (1978). The effect of ability grouping in specific subjects (setting) on changes of students' social and emotional personality traits. *Psychologie in Erziehung und Unterricht, 25,* 306–314.

Kobasa, S.C.O. (1986). How much stress can you survive? In M.G. Walraven & H.E. Fitzgerald (Eds.), *Annual editions: Human development 86/87.* Guilford, CT: Dushkin.

Kobasa, S.C., & Maddi, S.R. (1977). Existential personality theory. In R. Corsini (Ed.), *Current personality theories.* Itasca, IL: Peacock.

Koss, M.P., & Butcher, J.N. (1986). Research on brief psychotherapy. In S.L. Garfield & A.E. Bergin (Eds.), *Handbook of psychotherapy and behavior change* (pp. 627–670). New York: Wiley.

Kottler, J.A., & Brown, R.W. (1985). *Introduction to therapeutic counseling.* Monterey, CA: Brooks/Cole.

Kottler, J.A., & Kottler, E. (1993). *Teacher as counselor: Developing the helping skills you need.* Newbury Park, CA: Corwin Press.

Kraft, C. L., & Elworth, C. L. (1969). *Measurement of aircrew performance: The flight deck workload and its relation to pilot performance* (NTIS70–19779/AD699934–DTIC).

Krauss, R.M. (1998). Why do we gesture when we speak? *Current Directions in Psychological Science, 7,* 54–60.

Krueger, J., & Clement, R.W. (1994). The truly false consensus effect: An ineradicable and egocentric bias in social perception. *Journal of Personality and Social Psychology, 67,* 596–610.

Laird, J.D. (1974). Self-attribution of emotion: The effects of expressive behavior on the quality of emotional experience. *Journal of Personality and Social Psychology, 29,* 475–486.

Lambert, M.J., & Bergin, A.E. (1994). The effectiveness of psychotherapy. In A.E. Bergin & S.L. Garfield (Eds.), *Handbook of psychotherapy and behavior change* (4th ed., pp. 143–189). New York: Wiley.

Langlois, J.H., & Roggman, L.A. (1990). Attractive faces are only average. *Psychological Science, 1,* 115–121.

Langlois, J.H., Roggman, L.A., & Musselman, L. (1994). What is average and what is not average about attractive faces? *Psychological Science, 5,* 214–220.

Langlois, J.H., Roggman, L.A., & Rieser-Danner, L.A. (1990). Differential social responses to attractive and unattractive faces. *Developmental Psychology, 26,* 153–159.

Lanzetta, J.T., & Driscoll, J.M. (1966). Preference for information about an uncertain but unavoidable outcome. *Journal of Personality and Social Psychology, 3,* 96–102.

Larsen, R.J., & Kasimatis, M. (1990). Individual differences in entrainment of mood to the weekly calendar. *Journal of Personality & Social Psychology, 58,* 164–171.

Latané, B., & Darley, J.M. (1968). Group inhibition of bystander intervention in emergencies. *Journal of Personality and Social Psychology, 10,* 215–221.

Latané, B., & Darley, J.M. (1970). *The unresponsive bystander: Why doesn't he help?* New York: Appleton-Century-Croft.

Latané, B., Williams, K., & Harkins, S. (1979). Many hands make light the work: The causes and consequences of social loafing. *Journal of Personality and Social Psychology , 37,* 822–832.

Lawlis, G. F., Achterberg, J., Kenner, L., & Kopetz, K. (1984). Ethnic and sex differences in response to clinical and induced pain in chronic spinal pain patients. *Spine, 9,* 751–754.

Lazarus, R.S., & Folkman, S. (1984). *Stress, appraisal, and coping.* New York: Springer.

Lazarus, R.S., & Launier, R. (1978). Stress-related transactions between person and environment. In L.A. Pervin & M. Lewis (Eds.), *Perspective in interactional psychology.* New York: Plenum.

LeDoux, J. E. (1998, December 11). Nature vs. nurture: The pendulum still swings with plenty of momentum. *Chronicle of Higher Education,* pp. 7–8.

Lee, J.A. (1973). *The colors of love: An exploration of the ways of loving.* Don Mills, Ontario: New Press.

Lee, J.A. (1988). Love-styles. In R.J. Sternberg & M.L. Barnes (Eds.), *The psychology of love.* New Haven, CT: Yale University Press.

Lefkowitz, M.M., Blake, R.R., & Mouton, J.S. (1955). Status factors in pedestrian violation of traffic signals. *Journal of Abnormal and Social Psychology, 51,* 704–706.

Lefkowitz, M.M., Eron, L.D., Walder, L.O., & Huesmann, L. R. (1977). *Growing up to be violent: A longitudinal study of the development of aggression.* New York: Pergamon.

Leli, D.A., & Fiskov, S.B. (1984). Clinical detection of intellectual deterioration associated with brain damage. *Journal of Clinical Psychology, 40,* 1435–1441.

LeVay, S. (1991). A difference in hypothalamic structure between heterosexual and homosexual men. *Science, 253,* 1034–1037.

Leventhal, H. (1970). Findings and theory in the study of fear and communication. In L. Berkowitz (Ed.), *Advances in experimental social psychology (Vol. 5).* New York: Academic Press.

Levin, J. S. (1993). Age differences in mystical experience. *Gerontologist, 33,* 507–513.

Levinger, G. (1980). Toward the analysis of close relationships. *Journal of Experimental Social Psychology, 16,* 510–544.

Levy-Leboyer, C., & Naturel, V. (1991). Neighborhood noise annoyance. *Journal of Environmental Psychology, 11,* 75–86.

Lewin, K. (1935). *A dynamic theory of personality.* New York: McGraw-Hill.

Lichtenstein, E. (1982). The smoking problem: A behavioral perspective. *Journal of Counsulting and Clinical Psychology, 50,* 804–819.

Lichtenstein, S., Fischhoff, B., & Phillips, L.D. (1982) Calibration of probabilities: The state of the art to 1980. In D. Kahneman, P. Slovic, & A. Tversky (Eds.), *Judgment under uncertainty: Heuristics and biases* (pp. 306–334). Cambridge, England: Cambridge University Press.

Lieberman, D. A. (1990). *Learning: Behavior and cognition.* Belmont, CA: Wadsworth.

Liem, J.H., O'Toole, J.G., & James, J.B. (1992). The need for power in women who were sexually abused as children: An exploratory study. *Psychology of Women Quarterly, 16,* 467–480.

Lindenthal, J.J., & Myers, J.K. (1979). The New Haven longitudinal survey. In I.G. Sarason & C.D. Spielberger (Eds.), *Stress and anxiety: Vol. 6. The Series in Clinical and Community Psychology.* Washington, DC: Hemisphere Publishing.

Lindsay, R.C.L. (1994). Biased lineups: Where do they come from? In D.F. Ross, J.D. Read, & M.P. Toglia (Eds.), *Adult eyewitness testimony: Current trends and developments.* Cambridge: Cambridge University Press.

Lindy, J.D., Green, B.L., & Grace, M.C. (1987). Commentary: The stressor criterion and post-traumatic stress disorder. *Journal of Nervous and Mental Disease, 175,* 269–272.

Lippa, R.A. (1994). *Introduction to social psychology* (2nd ed.). Pacific Grove, CA: Brooks/Cole.

Lips, H.M. (1985). Gender and the sense of power: Where are we and where are we going? *International Journal of Women's Studies, 8,* 483–489.

Lipsey, M.W., & Wilson, D.B. (1993). The efficacy of psychological, educational, and behavioral treatment. *American Psychologist, 48,* 1181–1209.

Locke, E.A. (1976). The nature and causes of job satisfaction. In M.D. Dunnette (Ed.), *Handbook of industrial and organizational psychology.* New York: Wiley.

Locke, E.A., & Latham, G.P. (1990). *A theory of goal setting and task performance.* Englewood Cliffs, NJ: Prentice Hall.

Loftus, E.F. (1979). The malleability of human memory. *American Scientist, 38,* 561–572.

Loftus, E.F. (1993). The reality of repressed memories. *American Psychologist, 48,* 518–537.

Loftus, E.F. (1998). The private practice of misleading deflection. *American Psychologist, 53,* 484–485.

Loftus, E.F. & Ketcham, K. (1994). *The myth of repressed memory: False memories and allegations of sexual abuse.* New York: St. Martin's Press.

Loftus, E., & Loftus, G. (1980). On the permanence of stored information in the human brain. *American Psychologist, 35,* 409–420.

Loftus, E.F., & Palmer, J.C. (1974). Reconstruction of automobile destruction: An example of interaction between language and memory. *Journal of Verbal Learning and Verbal Behavior, 13,* 585–589.

Loftus, E.F. & Zanni, G. (1975). Eyewitness testimony: The influyence of the wording of a question. *Bulletin of the Pychonomic Society, 5,* 86–88.

LoPiccolo, J. (1995). Sexual disorders and gender identity disorders. In R.J. Comer, Abnormal psychology (Ed.), *Abnormal psychology* (2nd ed.). New York: W.H. Freeman.

LoPiccolo, J., & Friedman, J.M. (1988). Broad spectrum treatment of low sexual desire: Integration of cognitive, behavioral, and systemic treatment. In S. Leiblum & R. Rosen (Eds.), (pp. 107–144) *Sexual desire disorders.* New York: Guilford.

Luchins, A.S. (1946). Classroom experiments on mental set. *American Journal of Psychology, 59,* 295–298.

Luckiesh, M. (1965). *Visual illusions: Their causes, characteristics, and applications*. New York: Dover Publications, Inc.

Lumsdaine, A.A., & Janis, I.L. (1953). Resistance to "counterpropaganda" produced by one-sided and two-sided "propaganda" presentation. *Public Opinion Quarterly, 17,* 311–318.

Lykken, D.T. (1984), Trial by polygraph. *Behavioral Sciences & the Law, 2,* 75–92.

Lykken, D. T., & Tellegen, A. (1996). Happiness is a stochastic phenomenon. *Psychological Science, 7,* 186–189.

Lynn, M., & Mynier, K. (1993). Effects of server posture on restaurant tipping. *Journal of Applied Social Psychology, 23,* 678–685.

Mackie, D.M., & Worth, L.T. (1989). Cognitive deficits and the mediation of positive affect in persuasion. *Journal of Personality and Social Psychology, 57,* 27–40.

MacKinnon, D.W., & Hall, W.B. (1972). Intelligence and creativity. *Proceedings, XVIIth International Congress of Applied Psychology* (Vol. 2, pp. 1883–1888). Brussels: Editest.

Macrae, C.N., Bodenhausen, G.V., Milne, A.B., & Jetten, J. (1994). Out of mind but back in sight: Stereotypes on the rebound. *Journal of Personality and Social Psychology, 67,* 808–817.

Madsen, C.H., Becker, W., & Thomas, D.R. (1968). Rules, praise, and ignoring: Elements of elementary classroom control. *Journal of Applied Behavior Analysis, 1,* 139–150.

Madsen, C.H., Becker, W.C., & Thomas, D.R., Koser, L., & Plager, E. (1978). An analysis of the reinforcing function of "sit down" commands. In R.K. Parker (Ed.), *Readings in educational psychology.* Boston: Allyn & Bacon.

Maher, B.A. & Maher, W.B. (1985). Psychopathology: II. From the eighteenth century to modern times. In G.A. Kimble & K. Schlesinger (Eds.), *Topics in the history of psychology* (Vol. 2). Hillsdale, NJ: Erlbaum.

Malamuth, N.M., & Donnerstein, E. (1982). The effects of aggressive pornographic mass media stimuli. In L. Berkowitz (Ed.), *Advances in experimental social psychology (Vol. 15)* (pp. 103–136). New York: Academic Press.

Martindale, C. (1989). Personality, situation, and creativity. In J.A. Glover, R.R Ronning & C.R. Reynolds.(Eds.), *Handbook of creativity. Perspectives on individual differences* (pp. 211–232). New York: Plenum Press.

Marzio, P.C. (1973). *Rube Goldberg; his life and work [by] Peter C. Marzio.* New York, Harper & Row.

Masling, J. M., Bornstein, R. F., Poynton, F. G., Reid, S., & Katkin, E. S. (1991). Perception without awareness and electrodermal responding: A strong test of subliminal psychodynamic activation effects. *Journal of Mind and Behavior, 12,* 33–48.

Mason, M.A., & Gibbs, J. T. (1992). Patterns of adolescent psychiatric hospitalization:

Implications for social policy. *American Journal of Orthopsychiatry. 62,* 447–457.

Mauet, T.A. (1992). *Fundamentals of trial techniques* (3rd ed.). Boston: Little, Brown, and Company.

McCall, N. (1995). *Makes me wanna holler; A young black man in America.* New York: Vintage Books.

McClain, L. (1987). Behavior during examinations: A comparison of "A," "C," and "F" students. In M.E. Ware & R.J. Millard (Eds.), *Handbook on student development: Advising, career development, and field placement* (pp. 40–42). Hillsdale, NJ: Lawrence Erlbaum Associates.

McGinnis, J. (1988). *The selling of the president.* New York: Penguin.

McGuire, W.J. (1964). Inducing resistance to persuasion: Some contemporary approaches. In L. Berkowitz (Ed.), *Advances in experimental social psychology (Vol. 1).* New York: Academic Press.

McKillip, J., & Reidel, S.L. (1983). External validity of matching on physical attractiveness for same and opposite sex couples. *Journal of Applied Social Psychology, 13,* 328–337.

Mednick, S.A. (1968). The Remote Associates Test. *Journal of Creative Behavior, 2,* 213–214.

Mehrabian, A. (1986, September). Communication without words. *Psychology Today,* 53–55.

Meltzoff, A. N., & Moore, M. K. (1992). Early imitation within a functional framework: The importance of person identity, movement, and development. *Infant Behavior and Development, 15,* 479–505.

Melzack, R., & Wall, P. D. (1965). Pain mechanisms: A new theory. *Science, 150,* 971–979.

Melzack, R., & Wall, P. D. (1983). *The challenge of pain.* New York: Basic Books.

Miley, W.M. (1999). *The psychology of well being.* Westport, CN: Praeger.

Milgram, S. (1963). Behavioral study of obedience. *Journal of Abnormal and Social Psychology, 67,* 376.

Milgram, S. (1965). Liberating effects of group pressure. *Journal of Personality and Social Psychology, 1,* 127–134.

Milgram, S., & Sabini, J. (1975). *On maintaining norms: A field experiment in the subway.* Unpublished manuscript, City University of New York.

Millenson, J.R. (1967). *Principles of behavioral analysis.* New York: Macmillan.

Miller, M.A., & Rahe, R.H. (1997). Life changes scaling for the 1990s. *Journal of Psychosomatic Research, 43,*279–292.

Miller, N.E. (1944). Experimental studies of conflict. In J. McV. Hunt (Ed.), *Personality and the behavior disorders*, Vol. 1, 431–465. New York: Ronald Press.

Miller, N.E. (1959). Liberalization of basic S-R concepts: Extensions to conflict behavior, motivation, and social learn. In S. Koch (Ed.), *Psychology: A study of science* (pp. 196–292). New York: McGraw-Hill.

Miller, N., Maruayama, G., Beaber, R.J., & Valone, K. (1976). Speed of speech and persuasion. *Journal of Personality and Social Psychology, 34,* 615–624.

Millman, J., & Pauk, W. (1969). *How to take tests.* New York: McGraw-Hill.

Mitchell, M. (1998). *The first five minutes: How to make a great first impression in any business situation.* New York: John Wiley & Sons.

Miyake, K., & Zuckerman, M. (1993). Beyond personality impressions: Effects of physical and vocal attractiveness on false consensus, social comparison, affiliation, and assumed and perceived similarity. *Journal of Personality, 61,* 411–437.

Morehouse, D. (1996). *Psychic warrior: Inside the CIA's Star Gate Program: The true story of a soldier's espionage and awakening.* New York: St. Martin.

Moreland, R.L., & Zajonc, R.B. (1982). Exposure effects in person perception: Familiarity, similarity, and attraction. *Journal of Experimental Social Psychology, 18,* 395–415.

Morrison, T.G., & O'Connor, W.E. (1999). Psychometric properties of a scale measuring negative attitudes toward overweight individuals. *The Journal of Social Psychology, 139,* 436–444.

Morrison, T.R., & Paffenbarger, R.A. (1981). Epidemiological aspects of biobehavior in the etiology of cancer: A critical review. In S.M. Weiss, J.A. Herd, & B.H. Fox (Eds.), *Perspectives on behavioral medicine* (pp. 135–162). New York: Academic Press.

Moscovici, S., & Zavalloni, M. (1969). The group as a polarizer of attitudes. *Journal of Personality and Social Psychology , 12,* 125–135.

Mozel, M. M., Smith, B., Smith, P., Sullivan, R., & Swender, P. (1969). Nasal chemoreception in flavor identification. *Archives of Otolaryngology, 90,* 367–373.

Mullen, B., & Johnson, C. (1990). *The psychology of consumer behavior.* Hillsdale, NJ: Lawrence Erlbaum Associates.

Murphy, C., & Cain, W. S. (1986). Odor identification: The blind are better. *Physiology and Behavior, 371,* 177–180.

Murray, H.A. (1938). *Explorations in personality.* New York: Oxford University Press.

Murstein, B., & Azar, J.A. (1986). The relationship of exchange - orientation to friendship intensity, roommate compatibility, anxiety, and friendship. *Small group behavior, 17,* 3–17.

Myers, D.G., & Diener, E. (1995). Who is happy? *Psychological Science, 6,* 10–17.

Myers, D.G., & Lamm, H. (1976). The group polarization phenomenon. *Psychological Bulletin, 83,* 602–627.

Nash, M. (1987). What, if anything, is regressed about hypnotic age regression? A review of the empirical literature. *Psychological Bulletin, 102,* 42–52.

Nathan, D. (1994). Dividing to conquer? Women, men, and the making of multiple personality disorder. *Social Text, 40,* 77–114.

NCHS (National Center for Health Statistics). (1990). Advance report of final mortality statistics, 1988. *Monthly Vital Statistics Report, 39,* Table 5. Hyattsville, MD: Public Health Service.

NCHS (National Center for Health Statistics). (1994). Advance report of final mortality statistics, 1992. *Monthly vital statistics report, 43.* Hyattsville, MD: Public Health Service

Neisser, U., & Harsch, N. (1993). Phantom flashbulbs: False recollections of hearing the news about Challenger. In E. Winograd, U. Neisser, et al.) (Eds.), Affect and accuracy in recall: Studies of "flashbulb" memories. (pp. 9–31). Emory symposia in cognition. New York, NY: Cambridge University Press.

Nelson, E. (1976). New facts on biorhythms. *Science Digest, May,* 71–75.

Newport, F. (1996). One-fourth of Americans still smoke, but most want to give up the habit. *Gallup Poll Monthly, 369,* 2–6.

Nisbett, R.E. (1972). Eating behavior and obesity in men and animals. *Advances in Psychosomatic Medicine, 7,* 173–193.

Nixon, C. T., & Frost, A. G. (1990). The study habits and attitudes inventory and its implications for students' success. *Psychological Reports, 66,* 1075–1085.

Norcross, J.C., Prochaska, J.O., & Farber, J.A. (1993). Psychologists conducting psychotherapy: New findings and historical comparisons on the psychotherapy division membership. *Psychotherapy, 30,* 692–697.

Novello, A.C. (1990). The Surgeon General's 1990 report on the health benefits of smoking cessation: Executive summary. *Morbidity and Mortality Weekly Report, 39 (No. RR–12).*

O'Brien, R. M., Figlerski, R. W., Howard, S. R., & Caggiano, J. (1981). *The effects of multi-year, guaranteed contracts on the performance of pitchers in major league baseball.* Paper presented at the annual meeting of the American psychological Association, Los Angeles, Aug. 1981.

O'Connell, S. (1999). *Mindreading: An investigation into how we learn to love and lie.* New York: Doubleday.

Ogden, J.E., Brophy, J.E., & Everston, C.M. (1977, April). *An experimental investigation of organization and management techniques in first-grade reading groups.* Paper presented at the annual meeting of the American Educational Research Association, New York.

Oldenburg, D. (April 3, 1990). Hidden messages. *The Washington Post.*

Omer, H., & London, P. (1988). Metamorphosis in psychotherapy: End of the systems era. *Psychotherapy, 25,* 171–180.

Orlinsky, D.E., & Howard, K.I. (1994). Unity and diversity among psychotherapies: A comparative perspective. In B. Bongar & L.E. Beutler (Eds.), *Foundations of psychotherapy: Theory, research, and practice.* New York: Oxford University Press.

Osborn, A.F. (1963). *Applied imagination.* New York: Scribner's.

Ozelci, A., Romsos, D.R., & Leveille, G.A. (1978). Influence of initial food restriction on subsequent body weight gain and body fat accumulation in rats. *Journal of Clinical Nutrition, 108,* 1724–1732.

Paffenbarger, R.S., Hyde, R.T., Wing, A.L., & Hsieh, C.C. (1986). Physical activity, all-cause mortality and longevity of college alumni. *New England Journal of Medicine, 314,* 605–613.

Palmer, B. (1999, May 10). Click here for decisions. *Fortune, 139,* 153–156.

Pan, Z. & Kosicki, G. M. (1996). Assessing news media influences on the formation of whites' racial policy preferences. *Communication Research, 23,* 147–178.

Parrott, A.C. (1993). Cigarette smoking: Effects upon self-rated stress and arousal over the day. *Addictive Behaviors, 18,* 389–395.

Paul, A.M. (1998, May). Where bias begins: The truth about stereotypes. *Psychology Today, 31,* 52–57.

Paulus, P.B. (1989). *Psychology of group influence* (2nd ed.). Hillsdale, NJ: Erlbaum.

Payne, R. (1959). *The History of Islam.* New York: Dorset Press.

Penfield, W. (1957). Brain's record of past: A continuous movie film. *Science News Letter,* April 27, 265.

Penfield, W. (1975). *The mystery of the mind.* Princeton, NJ: Princeton University Press.

Pennebaker, J. (1990). *Opening up: The healing power of confiding in others.* New York: William Morrow.

Perkins, C.C., Seyman, R.G., Levis, D.J., Spence, H. (1966). Factors affecting preference for signal-shock over shock-signal. *Journal of Experimental Psychology, 72,* 190–196.

Perlman, D., & Coxby, P.C. (1983). *Social psychology.* New York: Holt, Rinehart, & Winston.

Peterson, L. R., & Peterson, M. J. (1959). Short-term retention of individual verbal items. *Journal of Experimental Psychology, 58,* 193–198.

Pettingale, K.W. (1984). Coping and cancer prognosis. *Journal of Psychosomatic Research, 28,* 363–364.

Petty, R.E., & Cacioppo, J.T. (1977). Effects of forewarning of persuasive intent and involvement on cognitive responses and persuasion. *Personality and Social Psychology Bulletin, 5,* 173–176.

Petty, R.E., & Cacioppo, J.T. (1986). The elaboration likelihood model of persuasion. In L. Berkowitz (Ed.), *Advances in experimental social psychology (Vol. 19)* (pp. 123–205). New York: Academic Press.

Petty, R.E., Cacioppo, J.T., Strathman, A.J., & Priester, J.R. (1994). To think or not to think: Exploring two routes to persuasion. In S. Shavitt & T.C. Brock (Eds.), *Persuasion* (pp. 113–147). Boston: Allyn & Bacon.

Phelps, M. E., & Mazziotta, J. C. (1985). Positron emission tomography: Human brain function and biochemistry. *Science, 228,* 799–809.

Phillips, D.P. (1974). The influence of suggestion on suicide: Substantive and theoretical implications of the Werther effect. *American Sociological Review, 39,* 340–354.

Plomin, R., Corley, R., DeFries, J. C., & Fulker, D. W. (1990). Individual differences in television viewing in early childhood: Nature as well as nurture. *Psychological Science, 1,* 371–377.

Pomerleau, O.F., & Pomerleau, C.S. (1989). A biobehavioral perspective on smoking. In T. Ney & A. Gale (Eds.), *Smoking and human behavior* (pp. 69–93). New York: Wiley.

Poon, L.W., & Fozard, J.L. (1980). Age and word frequency effects in continuous recognition memory. *Journal of Gerontology, 35,* 77–86.

Powell, K.E., Spain, K.G., Christenson, G.M., & Mollenkamp, M.P. (1986). The status of the 1990 objective for physical fitness and exercise. *Public Health Reports, 101,* 15–21.

Powley, T.L., & Keesey, R.E. (1970). Relationship of body weight to the lateral hypothalamic feeding syndrome. *Journal of Comparative Physiology and Psychology, 70,* 25–36.

Pratkanis, A., & Aronson, E. (1992). *Age of propaganda: The everyday use and abuse of persuasion.* New York: Freeman.

Prentky, R. (1989). Creativity and psychopathology: Gambling at the seat of madness. In J.A. Glover, R.R. Ronning, & C.R. Reynolds (Eds.), *Handbook of creativity.* New York: Plenum.

Price, R.A. (1987). Genetics of human obesity. *Annals of Behavioral Medicine, 9,* 9–14.

Rabkin, J.G. (1979). The epidemiology of forcible rape. *American Journal of Orthopsychiatry, 49,* 634–647.

Rachman, S., & Hodgson, R. J. (1968). Experimentally-induced "sexual fetishism": Replication and development. *Psychological Record, 18,* 25–27.

Rahe, R.H. (1974). The pathway between subjects' recent life changes and their near-future illness reports: Representative results and methodological issues. In B.S. Dohrenwend & B.P. Dohrenwent (Eds.), *Stressful life events: Their nature and effects.* New York: Wiley.

Rahe, R.H. (1987). Recent life changes, emotions, and behaviors in coronary heart disease. In A.Baum & J.E. Singer (Eds.), *Handbook of psychology and health (Vol. 5).* Hillsdale, NJ: Erlbaum.

Raloff, J. (1994). The great nicotine debate: Are cigarette recipes "cooked" to keep smokers hooked? *Science News, 145,* 314–317.

Redd, E.M., & de Castro, J.M. (1992). Social facilitation of eating: Effects of instructions to eat alone or with others. *Physiology and Behavior, 52,* 749–754.

Reed, D.R., Contreras, R.J., Maggio, C., Greenwood, M.R.C., & Rodin, J. (1988). Weight cycling in female rats increases dietary fat selection and adiposity. *Physiology and Behavior, 42,* 389–395.

Reed, O.L., & Coalson, J.L. (1977). Eighteenth-century legal doctrine meets twentieth-century marketing techniques: FTC regulation of emotionally conditioning advertising. *Georgia Law Review, 11,* 733–782.

Regier, D. A., Kaelber, C.T., Rae, D.S.; Farmer, M.E., Knauper, B., Kessler, R.C., & Norquist, G.S. (1998). Limitations of diagnostic criteria and assessment instruments for mental disorders: Implications for research and policy. *Archives of General Psychiatry, 55,* 1998, 109–115.

Reiser, M. (1982). *Police psychology.* Los Angeles: LEHI.

Reiser, M. (1986). Admission of hypnosis-induced recollections into memory. *American Journal of Forensic Psychology , 4,* 19–28.

Revusky, S. H. (1968). Aversion to sucrose produced by contingent X-irradiation: Temporal and dosage parameters. *Journal of Comparative and Physiological Psychology, 65,* 17–22.

Roberts, L. (1987). Study bolsters case against cholesterol. *Science, 237,* 28–29.

Robins, I.N., & Regier, D.A. (Eds.). (1991). *Psychiatric disorders in America: The Epidemiologic Catchment Area study.* New York: Free Press.

Rodin, J., Silberstein, L., & Striegel-Moore, R. (1985). Women and weight: A normative discontent. In T.B. Sonderegger (Ed.), *Nebraska symposium on motivation, 1984: Psychology and gender* (pp. 267–307). Lincoln: University of Nebraska Press.

Roediger, H.L., Capaldi, E.D., Paris, S.G., Polivy, J., & Herman, C.P. (1996). *Psychology* (4th ed.). Minneapolis: West Publishing.

Rohsenow, D.J., & Smith, R.E. (1982). Irrational beliefs as predictors of negative affective states. *Motivation and Emotion, 6,* 299–301.

Riordan, C. (1978). Equal-status interracial contact: A review and revision of the concept. *International Journal of Intercultural Relations, 2,* 161–185.

Rosen, G.M. (1981). Guidelines for the review of do-it-yourself treatment books. *Contemporary Psychology, 26,* 189–191.

Rosen, G.M. (1993). Self-help or hype? Comments on psychology's failure to advance self-care. *Professional Psychology Research and Practice, 24,* 340–345.

Rosenfeld, S.P. (1987). Insanity defense is riskier now and can turn winners to losers. Associated Press release (*Grand Rapids Press*, p. A17)

Rosenhan, D.L. (1973). On being sane in insane places. *Science, 179,* 250–258.

Rosenhan, D.L. (1983). Psychological abnormality and law. In C.J. Scheirer & B.C. Hammonds (Eds.), *The master lecture series: Vol. 2. Psychology and the law.* Washington, DC: American Psychological Association.

Rosenhan, D.L., & Seligman, M.E.P. (1984). *Abnormal psychology.* New York: Norton.

Ross, C.A., Miller, S.D., Bjornson, L., Reagor, P., Fraser, G.A., & Anderson, G. (1991). Abuse histories in 102 cases of multiple personality disorder. *Canadian Journal of Psychiatry, 36,* 97–101.

Rubin, Z. (1973). *Liking and loving: An invitation to social psychology.* New York: Holt.

Ryff, C.D. (1989). Happiness is everything, or is it? Explorations on the meaning of psychological well-being. *Journal of Personality and Social Psychology, 57,* 1069–1081.

Ryff, C.D. (1995). Psychological well-being in adult life. *Current Directions in Psychological Science, 4,* 99–104.

Sachs, R.G. (1986). The adjunctive role of social support systems. In B.G. Braun (Ed.), *The treatment of multiple personality disorder.* Washington, DC: American Psychiatric Press.

Sales, B.D., & Hafemeister, T.L. (1985). Law and psychology. In E.M. Altmeir & M.E. Meyer (Eds.), *Applied specialties in psychology.* New York: Random House.

Samorajski, T., Delaney, C., Durham, L., Ordy, J.M., Johnson, J.A., & Dunlap, W.P. (1985). Effect of exercise on longevity, body weight, locomotor performance, and passive-avoidance memory of C57BL/6J mice. *Neurobiology of Aging, 6,* 17–24.

Sanders, M.S., & McCormick, E.J. (1993). *Human factors in engineering and design.* New York: Mc-Graw Hill.

Sarafino, E.P. (1994). *Health psychology: Biopsychosocial interactions* (2nd ed.). New York: John Wiley.

Sarnacki, R.E. (1979). An examination of testwiseness in the cognitive test domain. *Review of Educational Research, 2,* 252–279.

Schab, F. R. (1991). Odor memory: Taking stock. *Psychological Bulletin, 109,* 242–251.

Schachter, S. (1971). Some extraordinary facts about obese humans and rats. *American Psychologist, 26,* 129–144.

Schachter, S., & Gross, L.P. (1968). Manipulated time and eating behavior. *Journal of Personality and Social Psychology, 10,* 98–106.

Schachter, S., & Rodin, J. (1974). *Obese humans and rats.* New York: Wiley.

Schachter, S., & Singer, J.E. (1962). Cognitive, social, and physiological determinants of emotional state. *Psychological Review, 69,* 379–399.

Schaie, K.W. (1987). Old dogs can learn new tricks: Intellectual decline and its remediation in later adulthood. Address to the Eastern psychological Association convention.

Schaie, K.W. (1989). The hazards of cognitive aging. *Gerontologist, 29,* 484–493.

Scheier, M.F., & Carver, C.S. (1993). On the power of positive thinking: The benefits of being optimistic. *Current Directions in Psychological Science, 2,* 26–30.

Schein, E.H., Hill, W.F., Lubin, A., & Williams, H.L. (1957). Distinguishing characteristics of collaborators and resistors among American prisoners of war. *Journal of Abnormal and Social Psychology, 55,* 197–201.

Schiffman, S.S., Graham, B.G., Sattely-Miller, E.A., & Warwick, Z.S. (1998). Orosensory perception of dietary fat. *Current Directions in Psychological Science, 7,* 137–143.

Schulman, P., Keith, D., & Seligman, M. E. (1993). Is optimism heritable? A study of twins. *Behavior Research and Therapy, 36,* 569–574.

Schuman, H., & Scott, J. (1989). Generations and collective memories. *American Sociological Review, 54,* 359–381.

Schuman, H., Walsh, E., Olson, C., & Etheridge, B. (1985). Effort and reward: the assumption that college grades are affected by quantity of study. *Social Forces, 63,* 944–966.

Schwartz, N., Bless, H., & Bohner, G. (1991). Mood and persuasion: Affective states influence the processing of persuasive communications. In M.P. Zanna (Ed.), *Advances in experimental social psychology (Vol. 24).* San Diego, CA: Academic Press.

Scogin, F., Bynum, J., Stephens, G., & Calhoon, S. (1990). Efficacy of self-administered treatment programs: Meta-analytic review. *Professional Psychology: Research and Practice, 21,* 42–47.

Segal, N.L., & Bouchard, R.J. (1988). Appraisal of the self-schema constrtuct in cognitive models of depression. *Psychological Bulletin, 103,* 147–162.

Seiden, R.H. (1966). Campus tragedy: A study of student suicide. *Journal of Abnormal and Social Psychology, 71,* 389–399.

Seiden, R.H. (1984). Death in the West—A regional analysis of the youthful suicide rate. *Western Journal of Medicine, 140,* 969–973.

Seligman, M. E. P. (1971). Phobias and preparedness. *Behavior Therapy, 2,* 307–320.

Seligman, M. E. P. (1975). *Helplessness: On depression, development and death.* San Francisco: Freeman.

Seligman, M. E. P. (1993). *What you can change. . .and what you can't.* New York: Fawcett Columbine.

Seligman, M. E. P. (1995a). *Learned optimism.* New York: Knopf.

Seligman, M.E.P. (1995b). *What you can change and what you can't.* New York: Ballantine.

Selye, H. (1956). *The stress of life.* New York: McGraw-Hill.

Shafer, D. R. (1996). *Developmental psychology: Childhood and adoles-*

cence (4th ed.). Pacific Grove, CA: Brooks/Cole.

Shafir, E. (1993). Choosing versus rejecting: Why some options are both better and worse than others. *Memory and Cognition, 21,* 546–556.

Sherif, M., Harvey, O., White, B., Hood, W., & Sherif, C. (1961). *Intergroup conflict and cooperation: The robber's Cave experiment.* Norman, OK: Institute of Group Relations, University of Oklahoma.

Sherman, C. (1994, September/October). Kicking butts. *Psychology Today,* 41–45.

Sherman, S.J. (1980). On the self-erasing nature of errors of prediction. *Journal of Personality and Social Psychology, 39,* 211–221.

Shneidman, E.S. (1993). *Suicide as psychache: A clinical approach to self-destructive behaviour.* Northvale, NJ: Jason Aronson.

Siegel, J.M. (1990). Stressful life events and use of physician services among the elderly: The moderating role of pet ownership. *Journal of Personality & Social Psychology, 58,* 1081–1086.

Siegel, S. (1977). Morphine tolerance as an associative process. *Journal of Experimental Psychology: Animal Behavior Processes, 3,* 1–13.

Simonton, D.K. (1975). Age and literary creativity: A cross-cultural and transhistorical survey. *Journal of Cross-Cultural Psychology, 6,* 259–277.

Simonton, D.K. (1994). *Greatness: Who makes history and why.* New York: Guilford.

Singer, M.T. (1979, Jan). Coming out of the cults. *Psychology Today,* 72–82.

Singer, M.T., Temerlin, M.K., & Langone, M.D. (1990). Psychotherapy cults. *Cultic Studies Journal, 7,* 101–125.

Sistrunk, F., & McDavid, J.W. (1971). Sex variables in conforming behavior. *Journal of Personality and Social Psychology, 17,* 200–207.

Skinner, B. F. (1960). Pigeons in a pelican. *American Psychologist, 15,* 28–37.

Smith, M.L., & Glass, G.V. (1977). Meta-analysis of psychotherapy outcome studies. *American Psychologist, 32,* 752–760.

Smith, M.L., Glass, G.V., & Miller, T.I. (1980). *The benefits of psychotherapy.* Blatimore: The John Hopkins University Press.

Smith, P.B., & Bond, M.H. (1994). *Social psychology across cultures: Analysis and perspectives.* Boston: Allyn & Bacon.

Smith, S.M., & Blankenship, S.E. (1989). Incubation effects. *Bulletin of the Psychonomic Society, 27,* 311–314.

Smith, S.M., & Shaffer, D.R. (1991). Celerity and cajolery: Rapid speech may promote or inhibit persuasion through its impact on message elaboration. *Personality and Social Psychology Bulletin, 17,* 663–669.

Smith, T.W. (1992). Hostility and health: Current status of a psychosomatic hypothesis. *Health Psychology, 11,* 139–150.

Smith-Hanen, S.S. (1977). Effects of nonverbal behaviors on judged levels of counselor warmth and empathy. *Journal of Counseling Psychology, 24,* 87–91.

Smyth, M.M., & Fuller, R.G.C. (1972). Effects of group laughter on responses to humourous materials. *Psychological Reports, 30,* 132–134.

Snyder, J.J. (1989). *Health psychology and behavioral medicine.* Englewood Cliffs, NJ: Prentice Hall.

Sobel, D.S., & Ornstein, R. (1996). *The healthy mind healthy body handbook.* New York: Patient Education Media.

Spencer, D. G., Yaden, S., & Lal, H. (1988). Behavioral and physiological detection of classically-conditioned blood pressure reduction. *Psychopharmacology, 95,* 25–28.

Spiegel, D. (1991). Mind matters: Effects of group support on cancer patients. *The Journal of NIH Research, 3,* 61–63.

Spitz, R. (1945). Hospitalism: An inquiry into the genesis of psychiatric conditions in early childhood. *Psychoanalytic Study of the Child, 1,* 53–74.

Spivey, C.B., & Prentice-Dunn, S. (1990). Assessing the directionality of deindividuation: Effects of deindividuation, modeling, and private self-consciousness on aggressive and prosocial responses. *Basic and Applied Social Psychology, 11,* 387–403.

Spring, B. (1988). Foods, brain and behavior: New links. *Harvard Medical School Mental Health Letter, 4(7),* 4–6.

Spring, B., Chiodo, J., & Bowen, D.J. (1987). Carbohydrates, tryptophan, and behavior: A methodlogical review. *Psychological Bulletin, 102,* 234–256.

Staats, C. K., & Staats, A. W. (1957). Meaning established by classical conditioning. *Journal of Experimental Psychology, 54,* 74–80.

Stanovich, K.E. (1996). *How to think straight about psychology.* New York: HarperCollins College Publishers.

Stapert, J.C., & Clore, G.L. (1969). Attraction and disagreement-produced arousal. *Journal of Personality and Social Psychology, 13,* 64–69.

Sternbach, R. A. (1975). Psychophysiology of pain. *International Journal of Psychiatry in Medicine, 6,* 63–73.

Sternberg, R. J. (1986). A triangular theory of love. *Psychological Review, 93,* 119–135.

Sternberg, R.J. (1995). *In search of the human mind.* Fort Worth: Harcourt Brace.

Sternberg, R.J., & Lubart, T.I. (1991a, April). Creating creative minds. *Phi Delta Kappan,* pp. 608–614.

Sternberg, R.J., & Lubart, T.I. (1991b). An investment theory of creativity and its development. *Human Development, 34,* 1–31.

Stiles, W.B., Shapiro, D.A., & Elliot, R. (1986). Are all psychotherapies equivalent? *American Psychologist, 41,* 165–180.

Stillion, J.M., & McDowell, E.E. (1996). *Suicide across the life span: Premature exits* (2nd ed.). Washington, DC: Taylor & Francis.

Strand, B.Z. (1970). Change of context and retroactive inhibition. *Journal of Verbal Learning and Verbal Behavior, 9,* 126–138.

Straus, M. A. (1994). *Beating the devil out of them: Corporal punishment in American families.* New York: Macmillan.

Straus, M. A., Gelles, R. J., & Steinmetz, S. K. (1980). *Behind closed doors: Violence in the American family.* New York: Doubleday/Anchor.

Strentz, H. (1986, January 1). Become a psychic and amaze your friends! *Atlanta Journal,* p. A15.

Sue, D., Sue, D., & Sue. S. (1997). *Understanding abnormal behavior* (5th ed.). Boston: Houghton Mifflin.

Suedfeld, P. (1975). The benefits of boredom: Sensory deprivation reconsidered. *American Scientist, Jan.–Feb.,* 63.

Suedfeld, P. (1980). *Restricted environmental stimulation: Research and clinical applications.* New York: Wiley-Interscience.

Swap, W.C. (1977). Interpersonal attraction and repeated exposure to rewarders and punishers. *Personality & Social Psychology Bulletin, 3,* 248–251.

Swaab, D.F., & Hofmann, M.A. (1990). An enlarged suprachiasmatic nucleus in homosexual men. *Brain Research, 537,* 141–148.

Szasz, T.S. (1961). *The myth of mental illness: Foundations of a theory of personal conduct.* New York: Hoeber-Harper.

Tanford, S., & Penrod, S. (1984). Social influence model: A formal integration of research on majority and minority influence processes. *Psychological Bulletin, 95,* 189–225.

Taylor, S. E., Falke, R. L, Shoptaw, S.J., & Lichtman, R. R. (1986). Social support, support groups, and the cancer patient. *Journal of Consulting & Clinical Psychology, 54,* 608–615.

Taylor, S.E., & Lobel, M. (1989). Social comparison activity under threat: Downward evaluation and upward contacts. *Psychological Review, 96,* 569–575.

Tedeschi, J.T., Linskold, S., & Rosenfeld, P. (1985). *Introduction to social psychology.* St. Paul: West Publishing.

Temoshok, L., & Fox, B.H. (1984). Coping styles and other psychosocial factors related to medical status and to prognosis in patients. In B.H. Fox & B. Newberry (Eds.), *Impact of psychoendocrine systems in cancer and immunity* (pp. 258–287). New York: Hogrefe.

Tesser, A., Campbell, J., & Mickler, S. (1983). The role of social pressure, attention to the stimulus, and self-doubt in conformity. *European Journal of Social Psychology, 13,* 217–233.

Terry, R.L., & Krantz, J.H. (1993). Dimensions of trait attributions associated with eyeglasses, men's facial hair, and women's hair length. *Journal of Applied Social Psychology, 23,* 1757–1769.

Tiffany, S.T., Martin, F.M., & Baker, T.B. (1986). Treatments for cigarette smoking: An evaluation of the contributions of aversion and counseling procedures. *Behavior Research & Therapy, 24,* 437–452.

Tollefson, N., Cox, E., & Barke, C. (1979). Study behavior and academic achievement. Paper presented at the annual meeting of the Association for the Study of Higher Education, Washington, DC.

Tomkins, S.S. (1982). *Affect, imagery, and consciousness. Vol. 3: Cognition and affect.* New York: Springer-Verlag.

Tresemer, D.W. (1977). *Fear of success: An intriguing set of questions.* New York: Plenum.

Triplett, N. (1898). The dynamogenic factors in pace-making and competition. *American Journal of Psychology, 9,* 507–533.

Trull, T.J. (1995). Borderline personality disorder features in non-clinical young adults: 1. Identification and validation. *Psychological Assessment, 7,* 33–41.

Tubbs, M.E., Boehne, D., & Dahl, J.G. (1993). Expectancy, valence, and motivational force functions in goal-setting research: An empirical test. *Journal of Applied Psychology, 78,* 361–373.

Tucker, L.A., Aldana, S.G., & Friedman, G.M. (1990). Cardiovascular fitness and absenteeism in 8,301 employed adults. *American Journal of Health Promotion, 5,* 140–145.

Tversky, A., & Kahneman, D. (1981). The framing of decision and the psychology of choice. *Science, 211,* 453–458.

Tversky, A., & Kahneman, D. (1982). Judgment under uncertainty: Heuristics and biases. In D. Kahneman, P. Slovic, & A. Tversky (Eds.), *Judgment under uncertainty: Heuristics and biases* (pp. 3–22). New York: Cambridge University Press.

Tyler, R.R., & Cook, F.L. (1984). The mass media and judgments of risk: Distinguishing impact on personal and societal level judgments. *Journal of Personality and Social Psychology, 47,* 693–708.

Underhill, P. (1999). *Why we buy.* New York: Simon & Schuster.

U.S. Congress, Office of Technology Assessment. (1983, November). *Scientific validity of polygraph testing: A research review and evaluation—A technical memorandum,* p.4. Washington, DC: US Government Printing Office.

United States Surgeon General. (1979). *Healthy people: The Surgeon General's report on health promotion and disease prevention* (U.S. Department of Health, Education & Welfare (PHS) Publication No. 79-55071).Washington, D.C.: U.S. Government Printing Office.

Vallone, R. P., Griffin, D. W., Lin, S., & Ross, L. (1990). Overconfident prediction of future actions and outcomes by self and others. *Journal of Personality and Social Psychology, 58,* 582–592.

Vance, J., et al. v. Judas Priest et al., No. 86-5844 (2nd Dist. Ct. Nev., 1990)

Vaughan, E. D. (1977). Misconceptions about psychology among introductory psychology students. *Teaching of Psychology, 4,* 138–141.

Veenhoven, R. (1993). *Happiness in nations.* Rotterdam, Netherlands: Risbo.

Vessey, J.T., & Howard, K.I. (1993). Who seeks psychotherapy? *Psychotherapy, 30, 546–553.*

Vinogradov, S., & Yalomi, I.D. (1994). Group therapy. In R.E. Hales, S.C. Yudofsky, & J.A. Talbott (Eds.), *The American Psychiatric Press textbook of psychiatry* (2nd ed.). Washington, DC: American Psychiatric Press.

Vokey, J. R., & Read, J. D. (1985). Subliminal messages: Between the devil and the media. *American Psychologist, 40,* 1231–1239.

Wacker, D.P., Harper, D.C., Powell, W.J., & Healy, A. (1983). Life outcomes and satisfaction ratings. *Developmental Medicine and Child Neurology, 25,* 625–631.

Wadden, T.A., & Stunkard, A.J. (1987). Psychopathology and obesity. *Annals of the New York Academy of Sciences, 499,* 55–65.

Wade, C., & Tavris, C. (1996). *Psychology* (4th ed.). New York: HarperCollins.

Waid, W.M., & Orne, M.T. (1982). The physiological detection of deception. *American Scientist, 70,* 402–409.

Walker, E., & Lewine, R.J. (1990). Prediction of adult-onset schizophrenia from childhood home movies of the patients. *American Journal of Psychiatry, 147,* 1052–1056.

Waller, N. G., Kojetin, B. A., Bouchard, T. J., Lykken, D. T., & Tellegen, A. (1990). Genetic and environmental influences on religious interests, attitudes, and values: A study of twins reared apart and together. *Psychological Science, 1,* 138–142.

Walster, E., & Berscheid, E. (1971, June). Adrenaline makes the heart grow fonder. *Psychology Today,* 47–62.

Walster, E., & Festinger, L. (1962). The effectiveness of "overheard" persuasive communication. *Journal of Abnormal and Social Psychology, 65,* 395–402.

Walster, E., Walster, G., Piliavin, J., & Schmidt, L. (1973). "Playing hard to get": Understanding an elusive phenomenon. *Journal of Personality & Social Psychology. 26,* 113–121.

Warwick, Z.S., & Schiffman, S.S. (1992). Role of dietary fat in calorie intake and weight gain. *Neuroscience & Biobehavioral Reviews, 16,* 585–596.

Watson, D.L., deBortali-Tregerthan, G., & Frank, J. (1984). *Social psychology: Science and application.* Glenview, IL: Scott, Foresman.

Watson, R.I., Jr. (1973). Investigation into deindividuation using a cross-cultural survey technique. *Journal of Personality and Social Psychology, 25,* 342–345.

Weeks, D., & James, J. (1995). *Eccentrics: A study of sanity and strangeness.* New York: Villard.

Weinberger, M., Hiner, S.L., & Tierney, W.M. (1987). In support of hassles as a measure of stress in predicting health outcomes. *Journal of Behavioral Medicine, 10,* 19–31.

Weisner, W.H., & Cronshaw, S.F. (1988). A meta-analytic investigation of the impact of interview format and degree of structure on the validity of the employment interview. *Journal of Occupational Psychology, 61,* 275–290.

Weisner, W., & Williams, R. (1989). *The trusting heart: Great news about Type A behavior.* New York: Random House.

Weissman, M.M. (1993). The epidemiology of personality disorders: A 1990 update. *Journal of Personality Disorders, 1,* 44–62.

Weisz, J.R., Weiss, B., Han, S.S., Granger, D.A., & Morton. T. (1995). Effects of psychotherapy with children and adolescents revisted: A meta-analysis of treatment outcome studies. *Psychological Bulletin, 117,* 450–468.

Wells, W.D., & LoSciuto, L.A. (1966). Direct observation of purchasing behavior. *Journal of Marketing Research, 3,* 227–233.

Werner, S., & Mero, N.P. (1999). Fair or foul?: The effects of external, internal, and employee equity on changes in performance of major League Baseball players. *Human Relations, 52,* 1291–1311.

Widom, C. (1989). Does violence beget violence? A critical examination of the literature. *Psychological Bulletin, 106,* 3–28.

Willett, W.C. (1998). Is dietary fat a major determinant of body fat? *American Journal of Clinical Nutrition, 68,* 1144–1147.

Williams, R. (1989). The trusting heart: Great news about Type A behavior. New York: Random House.

Wills, T.A. (1986). Stress and coping in early adolescence: Relationships to substance use in urban school samples. *Health Psychology, 5,* 503–529.

Wilson, J.P. (1976). Motivation, modeling, and altruism: A person x situation analysis. *Journal of Personality and Social Psychology, 34,* 1078–1086.

Winter, D.G. (1973). *The power motive.* New York: Free Press.

Winter, D.G. (1988). The power motive in women'and men. *Journal of Personality & Social Psychology, 54,* 510–519.

Winter, D.G., & Barenbaum, N.B. (1985). Responsibility and the power motive in women and men. *Journal of Personality, 53,* 335–355.

Winter, D.G., & Stewart, A.J. (1978). Power motivation. In H. London & J. Exner (Eds.), *Dimensions of personality.* New York: Wiley.

Wolpe, J. (1962). The experimental foundations of some new psychotherapeutic methods. In J. Bachrach (Ed.), *Experimental foundations of clinical psychology* . New York: Pergamon.

Wood, W., & Stagner, B. (1994). Why are some people easier to influence than others? In S. Shavitt & T.C. Brock (Eds.), *Persuasion* (pp. 149–193). Boston: Allyn & Bacon.

Woolfolk, A.E., & McCune-Nicholich, L. (1980). *Educational psychology for teachers.* Boston: Allyn and Bacon.

Worchel, S., Coutant-Sassic, D., & Grossman, M. (1991). A developmental approach to group dynlamics: a model and illustrative research. In Worchel, S., Wood, W., et al. (Ed.), *Group process and productivity* (pp. 181–202). Newbury Park, CA: Sage Publications.

Worchel, S., Grossman, & Coutant-Sassic, D. (1994). Minority influence in group context: How group factors affect when the minority will be influential. In A. Mucci-Faina & S. Moscovici (Eds.), *Minority influence.* Chicago: Nelson-Hall.

Worchel, S., & Shebilske, W. (1995). *Principles and Applications of Psychology* (5th ed.). Englewood Cliffs, NJ: Prentice Hall.

WHO (World Health Organization). (1992). *World Health Statistics Annual.* Geneva: Author.

Zaccaro, S.J., Foti, R.J., & Kenny, D.A. (1991). Self-monitoring and trait-based variance in leadership: An investigation of leader flexibility across multiple group situations. *Journal of Applied Psychology, 76,* 308–315.

Zajonc, R.B. (1965). Social facilitation. *Science, 149,* 269–274.

Zajonc, R.B. (1980). Compliance. In P.B. Paulus (Ed.), *Psychology of group influence* (pp. 35–60). Hillsdale, NJ: Erlbaum.

Zajonc, R.B., Adelmann, P.K., Murphy, S.T., & Niedenthal, P.M. (1987). Convergence in the physical appearance of spouses. *Motivation and Emotion, 11,* 335–346.

Zamarripa, P.O., & Krueger, D.L. (1983). Implicit contracts regulating small group leadership. *Small Group Behavior, 14,* 187–210.

Zanot, E. J., Pincus, J. D., & Lamp, E.J. (1983). Public perceptions of subliminal advertising. *Journal of Advertising, 12,* 37–45.

Zarski, J.J. (1984). Hassles and health: A replication. *Health psychology, 3,* 243–251.

Zatzick, D. F., & Dimsdale, J. E. (1990). Cultural variations in response to painful stimuli. *Psychosomatic Medicine, 52,* 544–557.

Zeisel, H., & Diamond, S. (1978). The effect of peremptory challenges on the jury and verdict. *Stanford Law Review, 30,* 491–531.

Zilbergeld, B. (1983). *The shrinking of America: Myths of psychological change.* Boston: Little, Brown.

Zimbardo, P.G. (1970). The human choice: Individuation, reason, and order versus deindividuation, impulse, and chaos. In W.J. Arnold & D. Levine (Eds.), *Nebraska symposium on motivation, 1969.* Lincoln: University of Nebraska Press.

Zimbardo, P.G., & Leippe, M.R. (1991). *The psychology of attitude change and social influence.* New York: McGraw-Hill.

Zuckerman, M. (1979). *Sensation seeking: Beyond the optimal level of arousal.* Hillsdale, NJ: Erlbaum.

Zuckerman, M. (1990). The psychophysiology of sensation seeking. *Journal of Personality, 58,* 313–345.

Zuckerman, M., Eysenck, S., & Eysenck, H.J. (1978). Sensation seeking in England and America: Cross-cultural, age, and sex comparisons. *Journal of Consulting and Clinical Psychology, 46,* 139–149.

Credits

p. 5	Copyright © Sidney Harris.
p. 8	THE FAR SIDE copyright © FARWORKS, INC. All rights reserved.
p. 10	© A. Ramey/PhotoEdit
p. 58 top	© Bachman/PhotoEdit
p. 58 bottom	© J. Nourok/PhotoEdit
p. 90	Reprinted by permission of the Cartoonist, Steve Dickenson and Copley News Service. All rights reserved.
p. 139	Colorado Historical Society
p. 148	Copyright © Rube Goldberg, Inc. Reprinted with permission.
p. 153	© Stanley Fellerman/CORBIS
p. 155	Reprinted by permission of the Cartoonist, Steve Kelly, Copley News Service and The San Diego Union-Tribune. All rights reserved.
p. 174	BIZARRO copyright © Dan Praro. Reprinted with permission of UNIVERSAL PRESS SYNDICATE. All rights reserved.
p. 189	Copyright © Tribune Media Services, Inc. All rights reserved. Reprinted with permission.
p. 195	© Richard Howard
p. 199	BIZARRO copyright © Dan Praro. Reprinted with permission of UNIVERSAL PRESS SYNDICATE. All rights reserved.
p. 200	THE FAR SIDE copyright © FARWORKS, INC. All rights reserved.
p. 205	Reprinted with special permission King Features Syndicate.
p. 212	© Seth Perlman/AP/Wide World Photos
p. 213	© Erica Freudenstein/CORBIS
p. 229	© 1976 Paul Ekman/ Human Interaction Lab
p. 231	© Picture Press/CORBIS
p. 232	© David & Peter Tumley/ CORBIS
p. 251	© Martin Rogers /Stock Boston
p. 281	© Michael Newman/PhotoEdit
p. 289	© CORBIS
p. 290	© Raoul Minsart/CORBIS
p. 305 (a)	© AP/Wide World Photos
p. 305 (b)	© The Corcoran Gallery of Art/CORBIS
p. 305 (c)	© Bettmann/CORBIS
p. 305 (d)	© Bettmann/CORBIS
p. 321	© Bettmann/CORBIS
p. 324	© Mark Richards/PhotoEdit
p. 327	© Bettmann/CORBIS
p. 331	© David Young-Wolff/ PhotoEdit
p. 341	© AP/Wide World Photos
p. 350	© AP/Wide World Photos
p. 358	© Richard T. Nowitz/CORBIS
p. 360	© Mary K. Denny/PhotoEdit
p. 361	© Bill Aron/PhotoEdit
p. 381	Fig. 1 from *Psychological Sciences,* article by Judith H. Langlois and Lori A. Roggman, Vol. 1, No. 2, March, 1990, pp. 117. Reprinted by permission of Blackwell Publishers.
p. 391	© Associated Press/AP/ Wide World Photos.
p. 392	DELBERT reprinted by permission of United Feature Syndicate.
p. 394	THE FAR SIDE copyright © FARWORKS, INC. All rights reserved.
p. 395	Reprinted with special permission King Features Syndicate.
p. 403	Copyright © Tribune Media Services, Inc. All rights reserved. Reprinted with permission.
p. 409	DELBERT reprinted by permission of United Feature Syndicate.
p. 425 (top)	© Bettmann/CORBIS
p. 425 (bottom)	© Reuters/Archive Photos
p. 434	CALVIN AND HOBBES copyright © Watterson. Reprinted with permission of UNIVERSAL PRESS SYNDICATE. All rights reserved.
p. 451	© 1996 Robert Ullman/ Design Conceptions
p. 453	© David & Peter Tumley/ CORBIS
p. 462	© AP/Wide World Photos
p. 473	© Reuters/Sam Mircovich/Archive Photos
p. 477	© AP/Wide World Photos
p. 483	© Jaques M. Chenet/CORBIS
p. 484	© Myrleen Ferguson/ PhotoEdit
p. 488	© Bohemian Nomad Picturemakers/CORBIS

INDEX

Page numbers in boldface refer to definitions of terms.